"I know of no similar theory project in the past, and the realization of it in this new book by Plys and Lemert is very impressive. Suddenly it seems like this book was exactly what we needed. Original, timely, supremely useful."

—**Etienne Balibar**, *Co-author of* Race, Nation, Class

"Plys and Lemert draw upon Marxist, postmodern, and postcolonial perspectives to offer new ways of thinking about capitalism and its future. For anyone interested in decolonizing theories of historical capitalism, this book is essential."

—**Julian Go**, *University of Chicago,*
author of Postcolonial Thought and Social Theory

Capitalism and Its Uncertain Future

For decades, Charles Lemert has been the leading voice in social theory. In *Capitalism and Its Uncertain Future* he teams up with one of the most creative emerging social theorists, Kristin Plys, to examine how social theory imagines capitalism. This engaging and innovative book provides new perspectives on well known theorists from Adam Smith, and Frantz Fanon, to Gilles Deleuze, while also introducing readers to lesser known theorists such as Lucia Sanchez Saornil, Mohammad Ali El Hammi, and many more. The book examines theories of capitalism from four perspectives: macrohistorical theories of the origins of capitalism; postcolonial theories of capitalism that situate capitalism as seen from the Global South; theories of capitalism from the perspective of labor; and prospective theories of capitalism's uncertain future. This provocative and ambitious, yet accessible, perspective on theories of capitalism will be of interest to anyone who wants to explore where we've been and where we're headed.

Kristin Plys' research sits at the intersection of political economy, postcolonial theory, labor and labor movements, historical sociology, and global area studies. The greater part of her intellectual work analyzes the historical trajectory of global capitalism as seen from working class and anti-colonial movements in the Global South. This research program has led her to take a particular interest in Marxist political economy, social protest against authoritarianism in the 1970s Global South, avant-garde visual art as left politics in the Global South, labor history and histories of café culture, and historical method. She works in multiple languages including Hindi, Urdu, French, Spanish, German, Italian, Portuguese, and Punjabi.

Kristin's first book, *Brewing Resistance: Indian Coffee House and the Emergency in Postcolonial India* (2020) uncovered histories of the resistance movement that was launched from New Delhi's café culture during India's brief period of dictatorship (1975–77). Her current research in-progress investigates how visual artists, writers, poets, Communists, and Maoists fomented opposition against Pakistan's 1977 military coup through a "cultural front" that innovated new forms of anti-authoritarian writing, painting, and poetry rooted in Lahore's vibrant café culture.

Kristin is an Assistant Professor of Sociology and History at the University of Toronto and an affiliate of the Centre for South Asian Civilizations and

Culinaria. She completed her PhD in Sociology at Yale University and has held visiting positions at the Lahore University of Management Sciences in Lahore, Pakistan, the Georg-August-Universität-Göttingen in Göttingen, Germany, the Jawaharlal Nehru University in New Delhi, India, and at the Centre for Development Studies in Thiruvanathapuram, India. Before beginning her PhD, she was a Researcher in Development Economics at Princeton University. Her undergraduate degree is in Cross-national Sociology and International Development from the Johns Hopkins University.

Charles Lemert is University Professor and Andrus Professor of Social Theory Emeritus at Wesleyan University. Among his books are *The Structural Lie: Small Clues to Global Things* (2011), *Why Niebuhr Matters* (2011), *Uncertain Worlds: World-Systems Analysis in Changing Times* (2013, with Immanuel Wallerstein and Carlos Aguirre Rojas), *Globalization: Introduction to the End of the Known World* (2015), and the seventh edition of *Social Theory: The Classical, Global, and Multicultural Readings* (2021). He is at work on, among other books, *Uncertainties of Time: The Past and Future TimeSpace* (with Immanuel Wallerstein, posthumously).

Capitalism and Its Uncertain Future

Kristin Plys and Charles Lemert

NEW YORK AND LONDON

First published 2022
by Routledge
605 Third Avenue, New York, NY 10158

and by Routledge
2 Park Square, Milton Park, Abingdon, Oxon, OX14 4RN

Routledge is an imprint of the Taylor & Francis Group, an informa business

© 2022 Taylor & Francis

The right of Charles Lemert and Kristin Plys to be identified as authors of this work has been asserted by them in accordance with sections 77 and 78 of the Copyright, Designs and Patents Act 1988.

All rights reserved. No part of this book may be reprinted or reproduced or utilised in any form or by any electronic, mechanical, or other means, now known or hereafter invented, including photocopying and recording, or in any information storage or retrieval system, without permission in writing from the publishers.

Trademark notice: Product or corporate names may be trademarks or registered trademarks, and are used only for identification and explanation without intent to infringe.

Library of Congress Cataloging-in-Publication Data
Names: Lemert, Charles C., 1937– author. | Plys, Kristin, author.
Title: Capitalism and its uncertain future / Charles Lemert and Kristin Plys.
Description: New York: Routledge, 2021.
Identifiers: LCCN 2021009091 | ISBN 9781032056050 (hardback) |
ISBN 9781032056043 (paperback) | ISBN 9781003198291 (ebook)
Subjects: LCSH: Capitalism. | Economic policy—Forecasting. |
Social policy—Forecasting.
Classification: LCC HB501 .L3136 2021 | DDC 330.12/2—dc23
LC record available at https://lccn.loc.gov/2021009091

ISBN: 978-1-032-05605-0 (hbk)
ISBN: 978-1-032-05604-3 (pbk)
ISBN: 978-1-003-19829-1 (ebk)

DOI: 10.4324/9781003198291

Typeset in Garamond
by codeMantra

Contents

Acknowledgments	xi

PART I
The Confusion of Capitalist Structures

		1
1	Foundations of a Critique of Capitalist Theories KARL MARX, CAPITAL I (1867)	3
2	Capitalism's Deadly Labor Process KARL MARX, ESTRANGED LABOR (1844)	23

PART II
Macro-Historical Theories of Capitalism

		39
3	The Modern World and Capitalism 1500–1991 FRANTZ FANON/IMMANUEL WALLERSTEIN	41
4	The Modern World-System: Europe or Asia? FERNAND BRAUDEL/ANDRE GUNDER FRANK	52
5	Long-Distance Trade and the Transition to Capitalism DAVID RICARDO/JANET ABU-LUGHOD	61
6	Women's Unpaid Labor and Primitive Accumulation FRIEDRICH ENGELS/SILVIA FEDERICI	67
7	The Agrarian Origins of Capitalism ROBERT BRENNER/ELLEN MEIKSINS WOOD	74
8	Finance and Capitalism ANTONIO GRAMSCI/GIOVANNI ARRIGHI	80

viii *Contents*

9 The City and the Foundations of Capitalism 86
HENRI PIRENNE/OLIVER C. COX

10 A Cyclical Theory of Empire 91
NIKOLAI KONDRATIEFF/IBN KHALDUN

PART III
Postcolonial Theories of Capitalism 97

11 Postcolonial Class Analysis 99
BARRINGTON MOORE/CLAUDIA JONES

12 Capitalism's Soft Imperialism and Global Racism 104
C.L.R. JAMES/WALTER RODNEY

13 The Role of Working Class Violence in National Liberation 112
MOHANDAS KARAMCHAND GANDHI/BHAGAT SINGH

14 Workers, Peasants, Anti-Colonialism 119
VLADIMIR LENIN/NESTOR MAKHNO

15 A Situationist Theory of Underdevelopment 125
ALBERT CAMUS/MUSTAPHA KHAYATI

16 Against the Colonization of Consciousness of Political Economy 132
KWAME TURE/W.E.B. DU BOIS/AMÍLCAR CABRAL

17 Existential Unfolding as Revolutionary Praxis 146
MAO ZEDONG/CHARU MAZUMDAR

18 A Critique of Western Imperialism from Within 151
MUHAMMAD ALI/ULRIKE MEINHOF

19 Rethinking the World Revolution of 1968 158
MARTIN LUTHER KING JR./HO CHI MINH

20 Capitalism as Seen from Its Peripheries 165
DIPESH CHAKRABARTY/ERIC WOLF

21 Orientalism, Postmodernity, and the Problem
with Capitalist Culture 169
EDWARD SAID/FREDRICK JAMESON/AIJAZ AHMAD

Contents ix

PART IV
Theories of Labor and Capitalism 179

22 The Labor Process and Work under Capitalism 181
FREDERICK WINSLOW TAYLOR/HARRY BRAVERMAN

23 A Trade Unionist Theory of Patriarchy 185
EDNA BONACICH/LUCÍA SÁNCHEZ SAORNIL

24 Worker Self-Management and Black Working
Class Consciousness 189
MIKHAIL BAKUNIN/JOSEPH EDWARDS

25 Theorizing the Global Division of Labor 194
ADAM SMITH/FOLKER FRÖBEL, OTTO KREYE,
AND JÜRGEN HEINRICHS

26 Radicalization through Difference 201
JACQUES RANCIÈRE/MOHAMMED ALI EL HAMMI

27 Resistance against the Market and Struggles of Newly
Emerging Working Classes 208
KARL POLANYI/BEVERLY SILVER

28 Culture, Labor, and the Global South 211
E.P. THOMPSON/RAJNARAYAN CHANDAVARKAR

PART V
Capitalism's Uncertain Future 215

29 The Disciplinary Empire and the Resisting Multitude 217
MICHEL FOUCAULT/MICHAEL HARDT AND ANTONIO NEGRI

30 Mass Media and Cultural Violence 226
C.L.R. JAMES/HERBERT MARCUSE

31 The Poverty of Development Economics 240
ABHIJIT V. BANERJEE AND ESTHER DUFLO/SAMIR AMIN

32 Neo-Liberalism and the Madness of Economic Reason 248
NANCY FRASER/DAVID HARVEY

x *Contents*

33 The Great Economic Divide and Globalization   262
JOSEPH STIGLITZ/JÜRGEN OSTERHAMMEL

34 The Structural Nature of Capitalism   268
JOSEPH SCHUMPETER/THOMAS PIKETTY

35 Capitalism and the Environmental Crisis   278
HENRY DAVID THOREAU/WILLIAM NORDHAUS

36 Silenced and Wasted Lives in the Capitalism Order   286
GAYATRI CHAKRAVORTY SPIVAK/ZYGMUNT BAUMAN

37 Left Extremes: Authoritarians v. Libertines   296
SLAVOJ ŽIŽEK/NOAM CHOMSKY

38 Assemblage Theory: The New Necessary Analytics
of Capitalism   303
GILLES DELEUZE AND FÉLIX GUATTARI/MANUEL DELANDA

PART VI
Exploitation and Exclusion   321

39 Exploitative Capitalism in the Global South   323
THE DAR ES SALAAM SCHOOL

40 Capitalism's Zones of Exclusion and Necropolitics   343
GIORGIO AGAMBEN AND ACHILLE MBEMBE

Bibliography   355
Index   373

Acknowledgments

I would like to thank, first and foremost, my co-author, Charles Lemert. Writing this book with Charles has never felt like work since the conversations and engagements we have are so generative and exciting. I am extremely grateful for these intellectual engagements and for our close friendship. And thanks to Geri for bearing with our interruptions at her office in between brainstorming and hangout sessions in Madison Square Park, and probably more obnoxiously, after spending time in various wine bars in Chelsea and the Flatiron District. And for her kindness and hospitality at Charles and Geri's home in New Haven.

Thanks to Julia Adams and Nicholas H. Wilson for conversations about this book that helped me to frame my ideas for a wider (i.e. non-Marxist) academic audience. I thank Noaman G. Ali for conversations about anti-imperialist theories of capitalism, his close read of the conclusion chapter and detailed comments that served to improve an early draft of the conclusion. That too, despite his disagreements with some of my thinking about Maoism.

Thanks to Umaima Miraj for her always exceptional research assistance.

Finally, I thank my parents, Carol Magistrelli and Oleh Julian Plys, for their encouragement and support of this project. I'm so lucky to have a mom like Carol who is always up for a conversation on anti-capitalist theory, even in the middle of the night. Carol also consistently pushes me to write for a general audience and make theory resonant with popular struggles in the United States, Italy, and beyond. Her reminders to lean less on theory and more on praxis keep me rooted in the more practical, and if I've been able to make a contribution beyond academic Marxism, it's because of her influence.

Charles and I have decided to jointly dedicate this book to Immanuel Wallerstein. Each of us had very different relationships to Immanuel but he nonetheless made a lasting and profound impact on both of us. Even the title of this book is quintessentially Wallersteinian. I first met Immanuel when I was a prospective graduate student who was incredibly overwhelmed about choosing which PhD program to go to. When I asked him his advice, he told me that all three programs I was admitted to would serve my purposes but that if I came to Yale we could talk. During my first year of grad school, I remember a holiday party at "the Diner" my closest friend in my cohort and xii *Acknowledgments*

I approached Immanuel and recounted the "late night in the office conversations" we had been having about potential synergies between world-systems and Birmingham School cultural studies. Immanuel generously weighed in our first year of grad school musings and then regaled us with stories of the time Stuart Hall visited the Fernand Braudel Center at Binghamton. We thought this was amazing and talked about this conversation for months. I also remember having dinner at Miya's with Immanuel and Jim Scott after one of the Agrarian Studies lectures and as a first year grad student I was so enthralled by the exchange between Jim and Immanuel and learned so much from this conversation about how they approached scholarly engagement in different ways. I still chuckle to myself when I recall how at that dinner, Jim jokingly asked me if having Manny (as Jim called him) as a mentor is like seeking knowledge from "the Lotus on the mountain top"!

In my second year of grad school, I did a directed reading course with Immanuel and it was by far the best course I took as a grad student. I was aware at the time that directed readings were a burden to faculty, but now as a faculty member myself, I am even more appreciative of his generosity in taking time away from his writing to teach and mentor me. Each week I read a different book Immanuel had written and it was incredible to be able to discuss his own books with him as I was formulating my own way of doing world-systems analysis. I remember him saying to me that he wrote the books so he knew what was in them, and for that reason I should keep the conversation interesting for him by coming prepared to talk about some new, original thoughts I had related to each book. He always encouraged me to look to other disciplines, especially the hard sciences given my background in mathematics and econometrics, and to bring in unconventional theorists and approaches to my engagement with texts and to my writing. He encouraged me to submit the term paper I wrote for the directed reading to a journal even though I never had tried to publish before, and when the paper was rejected on my first try he was incredibly supportive and explained to me how important it is to be confident in what one writes regardless of how others might react to unconventional provocations. It's something I have never forgotten and whenever I receive unhelpful critical feedback I think back to this experience.

After I had defended my prospectus and before I left New Haven to travel to New Delhi for the very first time, I met with Immanuel to ask his advice about how I should approach doing research in this context given his early work in various parts of Africa. I remember that the first words out of his mouth were, "Make sure to see the Taj Mahal." I was initially confused, but then he explained that so often when researchers travel to the Global South to do research, they conflate the city where they are based with the entire country or world region. In order to get a full sense of the place and context travelling around the city, country, etc., is critically important. Local travel, he told me, will lead to moments of great insight. Months later, when I decided to travel from Delhi to Hyderabad for a long weekend, I was looking around the city from the ride from the plane to my hotel and had one of those moments that Immanuel told me I would—where in just seeing the architecture and layout of the city, I felt like I now understood much better some of the debates about how the Mughals shaped the historical trajectory of the Subcontinent.

After spending two years in India doing archival and oral history work, I met Immanuel after returning to New Haven briefly. I began by excitedly saying that I felt that I made this great theoretical innovation based on what I had uncovered in my research. He listened and asked questions, but then paused and told me that what I thought was a new take that I had come up with on my own has already been said and done. It was initially devastating as a grad student about to write their thesis to hear this, but he continued, and told me that Frantz Fanon had made basically the same arguments in his theoretical writings. However, he said, they were misunderstood because Fanon's work has been poorly translated into English. But because of my French proficiency, Immanuel told me, I should read everything Fanon ever wrote in the original French and that it would lead to something really productive for me and my thesis. He then proceeded to recount memories of the conversations he had with Fanon. I took Immanuel's advice, and spent several months reading everything Fanon ever wrote. This felt much like the exercise I undertook in my second year where I read everything Immanuel had ever wrote—important, exciting, and a brief period of intense intellectual growth. While I had read *Wretched of the Earth* before, with Immanuel's framing of the text, I read it in such a different way that time, and ever since that conversation, it's become a lifelong intellectual project of mine to bring Fanon back into world-systems analysis.

I will be forever grateful for all I learned from Immanuel. He was incredibly generous and now that I am a faculty member myself, I appreciate even more his kindness to me in helping me find confidence in my unique voice as a non-fiction writer and in encouraging my creativity in developing my own style of doing theory and history.

Kristin Plys

Like Kristin, I too enjoyed very much our work together. Everything she says about our work meetings here and there is no less true for me. Plus which, important to add, she is first among those who will secure the future of sociology, not to mention the several other disciplines to which she contributes.

My few explicit acknowledgments should not be taken as evidence that I am without debt to the many who have shaped my intellectual formation over the years. There are colleagues, too many to list, who have introduced me to the theorists and ideas that today make it possible for me to read and dare to write about some of the more inscrutable thinkers discussed in this book. In many other places, I have acknowledged the importance of Immanuel, Beatrice, and Kathy Wallerstein in my life as friends. Before Immanuel xiv *Acknowledgments*

and I became friends late in our lives, he was, through his writings, my mentor.

I might add, all too personally, that Kristin and I finished this book in 2020—a bad year for all in so many ways. For me, Geri, and Anna that year was made all the worst by the death of Noah, our son and brother. As I write, Joe Biden has just been inaugurated President of the United States. President Biden knows and speaks quite a lot about the loss of his children. He has lost two, as have I. Matthew preceded his brother in death by some 20 years.

I speak of these deaths not to be morbid, but to remind that with terrible loss comes the promise of working through while remembering those who are gone. *Capitalism and Its Uncertain Future* is meant to question its future by remembering much of modern history by which Capitalism gained its grip on the world for better or worse. Remembering, in this historical sense, occasionally leads to a working through of the disappearance of previous versions of the economic system deployed under its name—as when Fordism buried the pre-scientific production methods of early industrial manufacture. Since the days of Adam Smith, Capitalism has changed many times over. It has been in constant flux.

Yet, Kristin and I resist the "ever onward and upward" dogma that pervades both popular and a good bit of scientific thinking about the modern economic world. Today, early in the 2020s, it is hard to say where Capitalism is headed. We take the position that the loss of Capitalism may not be the worst thing in the world, even if, should it happen, no one has any idea what comes after. Here again, a tribute to Immanuel Wallerstein, who was the first, early in the 1990s, to offer a persuasive argument that the half millennium of the Capitalist world-system had split apart to such a degree that it is no longer a system much less one able, as it had for centuries, to dominate the world. The corollary to Immanuel Wallerstein's idea is that its uncertainty entails the real possibility that one day Capitalism will be lost. We shall see. But we won't see it if we don't keep our minds open to this very strange possibility.

Charles Lemert

Part I

The Confusion of Capitalist Structures

1 Foundations of a Critique of Capitalist Theories

Karl Marx, Capital I (1867)

Admittedly, it is a bit misleading to introduce this book by way of Marx, if only because it is not about highlighting the unique contributions of Karl Marx, nor is it primarily about furthering Marxist thought. Instead, it's a continuation of the broader intellectual project initiated by political economists during the 18th century to describe the capitalist world-system, critique it, and speculate about its future trajectory. But Marx's hypothesis of the long-run historical trajectory of the capitalist world economy still resonates today, and whether one supports or critiques his theses, his *oeuvre* remains the key texts with which theorists of capitalism engage. While Marx clearly stands out as among the first in this tradition, equally important are the works of Adam Smith and David Ricardo, who were more critical of the capitalist world-system than they are typically given credit. This legacy of political economy to describe and critique capitalism continues to the present, and given the many challenges—war, fascism, economic decline, mass migration, climate change, social movements, and so on—facing the capitalist world-system in the current conjuncture, accurate description is more important than ever.

When Marx set out to describe and critique the global system of political economy that we would eventually term capitalism, he was not doing so in a vacuum. Marx's project of political economy was both a critique and an extension of Adam Smith's *An Inquiry into the Nature and Causes of the Wealth of Nations* (1776).[1] Smith's work was arguably the first model of capitalist economic development in the modern Western tradition of political economy. Over the course of the five volumes, Adam Smith endeavors to explain why some nations are poor while others thrive. He begins his analysis with an understanding of labor productivity and how the product of labor is distributed within and among societies.[2] Then, he examines how the accumulation of capital through the labor process fosters an interstate system, whereby "opulent cities" serve as a market not only for local goods and local consumption but for goods from elsewhere and consumption abroad.[3] He shows how this process takes form in many places and in previous historical periods, and then shows how different systems of political economy differentially enrich both states and individuals.[4] Finally, he proposes some policy implications for his model, detailing measures states can take in order to increase the wealth of the nation.[5]

Taking up similar concerns in *Principles of Political Economy and Taxation* (1817),[6] David Ricardo challenges Adam Smith's conceptualization of rents,

DOI: 10.4324/9781003198291-2

4 *The Confusion of Capitalist Structures*

claiming that without a clearer understanding of rent one cannot fully understand the way in which profits and wages contribute to increasing wealth. Rent, claims Ricardo, is the portion paid to the landlord for use of the land.[7] Profit, however, is the value of an item less wages and rents.[8] While Ricardo claims that Smith conflates rent and profit, Ricardo seeks to show that both are governed by different logics. The amount of land at a country's disposal affects the cost of rent. This, along with the quality of land, has great implications for the "progress" of that society.[9] These works—Adam Smith's *An Inquiry into the Nature and Causes of the Wealth of Nations* (1776) and David Ricardo's *Principles of Political Economy and Taxation* (1817)—were important forbearers of Karl Marx, not simply as fodder for critique as is commonly thought, but also for their similarities to Marx's description of the capitalist world-system in *Capital* (1867).[10]

Building on Adam Smith's critiques of the labor process and David Ricardo's arguments on the source of profit in the capitalist economy, Marx's concept of capitalist development was first presented in *The German Ideology* (1846).[11] In it, Marx explains how the hierarchy of nation-states was created within the capitalist mode of production. This description of world-historical capitalism is further fleshed out in Marx's subsequent work and culminates in *Capital* (1867), the defining work of Marxist political economy in which Marx elegantly explains where value is derived, thereby delineating the politico-economic laws of the capitalist system, by beginning and ending with the definition of value, akin to a mathematical proof. Marx's systematic analytical approach, perhaps even more so than his politics, is what makes Marx so compelling and what explains his continued resonance.

In *Capital* (1867), Marx describes the nature of the economic system we would eventually term "capitalism" in a way that is worth quoting in detail:

> As soon as this process of transformation has sufficiently decomposed the old society from the top to bottom, as soon as the labourers are turned into proletarians, their means of labor into capital, as soon as the capitalist mode of production stands on its own feet, then the further socialisation of labor and further transformation of the land and other means of production into socially exploited and, therefore, common means of production, as well as further expropriation of private proprietors, takes a new form. That which is now to be expropriated is no longer the labourer working for himself, but the capitalist exploiting many labourers. This expropriation is accomplished by the action of the immanent laws of capitalist production itself, by the centralisation of capital. One capitalist always kills many. Hand in hand with this centralisation, or this expropriation of many capitalists by a few, develop, on an ever-extending scale, the co-operative form of the labor-process, the conscious technical application of science, the methodological cultivation of the soil, the transformation of the instruments of labour into instruments of labor only usable in common, the economising of all means of production by their use as the means of production combined, socialised labor, the entanglement of all peoples in the net of

the world market, and with this, the international character of the capitalistic regime. Along with the constantly diminishing number of the magnates of capital, who usurp and monopolise all advantages of this process of transformation, grows the mass of misery, oppression, slavery, degradation, exploitation; but with this too grows the revolt of the working-class, a class always increasing in numbers, and disciplined, united, organised by the very mechanism of the process of capitalist production itself. The monopoly of capital becomes a fetter upon the mode of production, which has sprung up and flourished along with, and under it. Centralisation of the means of production and socialisation of labor at last reach a point where they become incompatible with their capitalist integument. The integument is burst asunder. The knell of capitalist private property sounds. The expropriators are expropriated.[12]

Capitalism, Marx contends, began by many expropriations. The transformation of laborers into proletarians—i.e. people who meet their basic needs by selling their labor power; and the transformation of the land into means of production, to name a few. These expropriations allow for the further intensification and spread of capitalism as a system, and also centralizes capital into the hands of a few of those capitalists who are best situated to develop businesses of a larger and larger scale, employing more and more labor, and engaging in global markets. As the system matures, this process will create a condition where fewer and fewer capitalists will be engaged in capital accumulation, and therefore will have monopolies. With monopoly, the working classes will be increasingly immiserated, leading to an inevitable revolt against the system. The tendency toward monopoly will become a fetter on capitalism itself, leading to such a high degree of centralization of the means of production and the socialization of labor that the system will be no longer socially sustainable. At such a time, when the working class revolts against an ever declining standard of living, the expropriators, i.e. capital, will be expropriated by the workers.

While Karl Marx is often credited with having developed the first theory of capitalist development, the classical political economists that were his precursors also had concepts of capitalist development even if they did not employ the term "capitalism." While Marx is commonly thought to have developed a theory of capitalism independent of classical political economy, he was, on the contrary, quite conscious of previous theories and formulated his ideas by both critiquing and building on existing concepts.

Theorizing Capitalism

While the first theories of capitalism were first formulated by classical political economists such as Adam Smith, David Ricardo, and Karl Marx, in the 18th and 19th centuries, the academic inquiry into the nature and future trajectory of the capitalist world economy continues to the present. In recent years, there has been a resurgence of scholarly interest in describing and critiquing capitalism, but the word "capitalism" itself has lost much of its

6 The Confusion of Capitalist Structures

original meaning as it has come to hold many different, and at times contradictory, meanings.[13] As a result of these multiple definitions, theorizing capitalism in the 21st century becomes ever more challenging as there is no scholarly consensus regarding the definition of capitalism. In the following section, I'll present some of the existing definitions of capitalism and assess what is at stake in these ways of thinking about capitalism. The following snapshot of intellectual history is not meant to be an exhaustive survey by any means. It is presented to the reader in order to demonstrate the key mainline theories of capitalism that have resonated in academia and beyond since Marx penned *Capital* (1867) just over 150 years ago.

In the early 20th century, theories of imperialism were developed to explain the changes in the capitalist world economy that transformed society of the time. Central to the concept of imperialism is monopoly finance capital which, as these theorists contend, is oversaturated in wealthy countries. As a result of this overaccumulation, capital can only stave off a potential crisis by expanding commodity production outward geographically in order to maintain a sufficient level of profit.[14] That monopoly capitalism necessitates outward expansion was for Rudolf Hilferding the essential fact of the capitalist world economy, and the only way to maintain and potentially increase the rate of profit for capital.[15] However, as Hilferding acknowledged and John Hobson further expanded upon, imperialism benefits certain segments of the capitalist class, but is "bad business for the nation."[16] In order to expand commodity production to markets abroad, the state must act in the interest of private capital in order to exert political control of foreign territories, thereby forcibly opening new markets. Hobson claimed:

> The economic root of imperialism is the desire of strong organized industrial and financial interests to secure and develop at the public expense and by the public force private markets for their surplus goods and surplus capital... The whole struggle of so-called Imperialism upon its economic side is towards a growing parasitism, and the classes engaged in this struggle require Protection as their most serviceable instrument.[17]

Hobson's critique of imperialism as the form of capitalism that took shape during the conjuncture in which he lived was that imperialism, and thereby capitalism, meant private gain through the public cost of Empire and war-making. His focus remains on how imperialism benefits the capitalist class of the colonizer at the expense of the working class of the colonizing country but neglects to analyze the human toll of imperialism from the perspective of the colonized.

Vladimir Lenin, perhaps the best known theorist of imperialism, proposes a working definition of imperialism at the dawn of the 20th century as having:

> ... five essential features: 1) The concentration of production and capital developed to such a high stage that it created monopolies which play

Foundations of a Critique of Capitalist Theories 7

a decisive role in economic life. 2) The merging of bank capital with industrial capital, and the creation, on the basis of this 'finance capital' of a 'financial oligarchy'. 3) The export of capital, which has become extremely important, as distinguished from the export of commodities. 4) The formation of international capitalist monopolies which share the world among themselves. 5) The territorial division of the whole world among the greatest capitalist powers is completed. Imperialism is capitalism in that stage of development in which the dominance of monopolies and finance capitalism has established itself; in which the export of capital has acquired pronounced importance; in which the division of the world among the international trusts has begun; in which the division of all territories of the globe among the great capitalist powers has been completed.[18]

In Lenin's view, monopolies further stratified the capitalist class, which resulted in finance capital being more dominant and powerful compared to industrial capital. Therefore, imperialism was a solution, not to create more markets in which to sell manufactured goods, but to provide outlets for financial investments as not to flood existing capital markets in Europe and North America, thereby driving down the rate of return. Imperialism's ultimate goal, according to Lenin, is to provide outlets for excess Western capital.

The social process of imperialism, claims Rosa Luxemburg, fundamentally altered how capitalism reproduced itself. From a linear trajectory, capitalist economic reproduction became cyclical, albeit with an underlying secular trend. Luxemburg describes this process as:

> a continuous sequence of individual spirals. Each such spiral starts with small loops which become increasingly larger and eventually very large indeed. Then they contract, and a new spiral starts again with small loops, repeating the figure up to the point of interruption. This periodical fluctuation between the largest volume of reproduction and its contraction to partial suspension, this cycle of slump, boom, and crisis, as it has been called, is the most striking peculiarity of capitalist reproduction.[19]

This model of looking at the trajectory of the capitalist economy of the early 20th century was, for Luxemburg, an explicit critique of Adam Smith and Karl Marx, who Luxemburg contended that in their more linear approach to understanding the trajectory of capitalism insufficiently theorized value.[20]

The German Historical School saw Rosa Luxemburg's cyclical approach to understanding the trajectory of capitalism as a better description of how capitalism works over time when compared to the linear approach of Classical Political Economy. In so doing, this group of theorists innovated new ways to think about the cyclical nature of the capitalist system. These political

8   The Confusion of Capitalist Structures

economists looked to broad sweeps of history for political, social, economic, and military patterns, and from this historical research, generated cyclical theories of the capitalist world economy.

In the early 1920s, on the heels of World War I and with many European economies in shambles, Soviet economist Nikolai Dmitrievich Kondratieff endeavored to explain this chaotic period in European politico-economic history through the concept of the Kondratieff cycle—a 60-year cycle of expansion and contraction of the world economy. In the conjuncture, so posits Kondratieff, one observes the expansion and contraction of the capitalist economy, but over time, if one looks at several of these cycles of expansion and contraction, one sees how the capitalist economy passes from one stage to another.[21] The most constitutive element of the world economy, therefore, is crisis. The fundamental contradiction of capitalism (i.e. that overproduction causes the rate of profit to fall leading to periodic crises), Kondratieff argues, is a constant force. In the production process, capital pays little attention to the constraints of the market, and instead relies on the ever changing conditions of the world economy to propel capitalism beyond moments of crisis.[22]

Joseph Schumpeter, working in the late 1930s and 1940s as Europe was once again enveloped in war and economic crisis, furthered Kondratieff's theory of the cyclical development of the capitalist world economy through the concept of creative destruction. Schumpeter agreed with Marx that capitalism would face an inevitable demise, but thought it would be a result of endogenous economic processes and not a product of class struggle. For Schumpeter, creative destruction is "the essential fact about capitalism," a process that "incessantly revolutionizes the economic structure from within, incessantly destroying the old one, incessantly creating a new one."[23] The logic of capitalism is to accumulate capital. A dominant capitalist class can best accumulate capital by engaging in the world's most profitable activities. When this most profitable activity is first discovered, few capitalists engage in it, and therefore profit margins are high. As other capitalists see that this new activity is especially profitable, they shift from less remunerative activities to this more profitable one. As more firms compete in the most profitable activity, competition increases—and this reduces profit margins. Capitalists who are best positioned within the world-system (which are typically those that are located in the core of the world-system) tend to have more economic, political, and social power vis-à-vis peripheral capital. As a result, they look for another, more profitable activity and thereby a new cycle of creative destruction begins. Creative destruction is a process by which innovation in business leads to the creation and eventual destruction of certain sectors of the economy. New, more profitable sectors are created as more businesses shift into these new sectors. Competition in industry then serves to decrease profitability and ultimately leads to the destruction of certain sectors of the economy. This destruction, however, is accompanied by the emergence of new markets, industries, forms of industrial organization, production technologies, and methods of production.

Foundations of a Critique of Capitalist Theories 9

In 1944, Karl Polanyi published *The Great Transformation*,[24] one of the most important works of political economy. In keeping with the traditions of the German Historical School inherited from Kondratieff and Schumpeter, Polanyi looked to a long sweep of history to trace cycles of the world economy. But instead of looking to economic boom and bust along with war and political developments, Polanyi linked civil society to the expansion and contraction of the world economy, creating the concept of "embeddedness." Polanyi claimed that "what appeared primarily as an economic problem was essentially a social one," while the working class is exploited by the very fact of the extraction of surplus value, it may appear that exploited workers are financially better off having been exploited. But their exploitation, while it may or may not be individually beneficial, because the process "was wreaking havoc with his social environment, his neighborhood, his standing in the community, his craft; in a word, with those relationships to nature and man in which his economic existence was formerly embedded."[25] Polanyi viewed the cyclical movement of the capitalist world economy from the perspective of civil society and likened it to a swinging pendulum that at times pushed toward the "free market" and before realizing the goals of a completely liberalized economy, civil society would push for more protection, swinging the pendulum toward protectionism until capital again pushed back toward liberalism. For "the self-protection of society," Polanyi claimed, is "incompatible with the functioning of the economic system itself."[26]

After 1945, with the consolidation of US hegemony, we see a proliferation of theories of capitalism, each explaining the current state and future trajectory of the system in different ways. Among the first theorists to explain capitalism in the burgeoning world hegemon, the United States, were Paul Baran and Paul Sweezy. Writing in the Neo-Marxist tradition, Baran and Sweezy advance the ideas of theorists of imperialism in light of politico-economic developments in the United States after 1945. They contend that monopoly capitalism, a concept borrowed from Lenin, has reached new heights in the postwar United States. Baran and Sweezy claim that capitalism in the mid-20th century has retreated away from the market as a result of the new principle of organizing the economy and society around large corporations. They write:

> The giant corporation withdraws from the sphere of the market large segments of economic activity and subjects them to scientifically designed administration. This change represents a continuous increase in the rationality of the part of the system, but it is not accompanied by any rationalization of the whole. On the contrary, with commodities being priced not according to their costs of production but to yield the maximum possible profit, the principle of quid pro quo turn into the opposite of a promoter of rational economic organization and instead becomes a formula for maintaining scarcity in the midst of potential plenty. Human and material resources remain idle because there is in the market no quid to exchange against the potential quo of their output. And this is true even though the real cost of such output

10   *The Confusion of Capitalist Structures*

would be nil. In the most advanced capitalist country a large part of the population lives in abysmal poverty while in the underdeveloped countries hundreds of millions suffer from disease and starvation because there is no mechanism for effecting an exchange of what they could produce for what they so desperately need. Insistence on the inviolability of equivalent exchange when what is to be exchanged costs nothing, strict economizing of resources when a large proportion of them go to waste—these are obviously the very denial of rationality which the concept of value and the principle of quid pro quo originally expressed.[27]

Just as John Hobson claimed that imperialism largely benefitted private capital at public expense, Baran and Sweezy demonstrate how the corporation, while a rational bureaucracy that yields more profit than previous forms of business organization, creates poverty, because in order to maintain a monopoly, it artificially creates scarcity even when it has the organizational capacity to produce more than the society needs. This process of corporate monopoly capital creates poverty not only in the countries where corporations are headquartered, but also in the Global South, as resources go to waste in order to create scarcity and preserve monopoly.

However, in keeping with their roots in classical Marxism, Neo-Marxists focus their analysis on commodity production, and contend that the labor theory of value and the resulting class conflict is the essential fact of the capitalist world economy. As Paul Sweezy puts it, "the buying and selling of labor power is the differentia specifica of capitalism."[28] David Harvey similarly writes, "Capitalism is founded, in short, on a class relation between capital and labor."[29] Neo-Marxists working in the mid-20th century focused their analyses on the increasing class conflict of what Ernest Mandel and others called Late Capitalism. He describes

Late capitalism... [as] the epoch in history of the development of the capitalist mode of production in which the contradiction between the growth of the forces of production and the survival of the capitalist relations of production assumes an explosive form. This contradiction leads to a spreading crisis in these relations of production.[30]

As the 20th century wore on, Neo-Marxists grew increasingly concerned with the relationship between the labor theory of value and economic crisis, as in the 1970s and again in the late 2000s, crisis reverberated throughout the global economy. David Harvey explains that because capitalism is a growth-oriented system, "crisis is then defined as lack of growth."[31] Growth, according to Harvey, is contingent upon the "exploitation of living labor in production"; in other words, there is a gap between the value generated by labor and the remuneration it receives. Harvey incorporates this understanding of growth as tied to the labor theory of value by building on Schumpeter's theory of creative destruction to show how the dynamics of class struggle contributes to the organizational and technological change that Schumpeter identified. Harvey claims that while competition certainly leads to dynamism, so does the class struggle which leads to innovations in the production process so that capital can increase the exploitation of labor that is fundamental to the realization of profit.[32]

In the Braudelian tradition, theorists of capitalism are similarly influenced by the German Historical School's emphasis on cycles, but place importance on the role of the state and finance as fundamental constituents of the capitalist world economy. Fernand Braudel famously encouraged us to look away from the market when analyzing the structures of the capitalist world economy, a turn away from both liberalism and Marxism. Instead, Braudel saw capitalism as fundamentally anti-market, in that capitalism depends upon the state to regulate the economy, thereby ensuring the institutional preconditions and arrangements that allow for the realization of profit, to help big corporations maintain global monopolies which allows for significant capital accumulation, and to take on the tasks that are necessary for capital accumulation but are the least remunerative. Braudel claimed that "the truth" of capitalism:

> ... is of course that both state and capital- a certain kind of capital at any rate, the monopolies and big corporations- coexist very comfortably, today as in the past... It has, as it always did, burdened the state with the least remunerative and most expensive tasks; providing the infrastructure of roads and communications, the army, the massive costs of education and research. Capital also lets the state take charge of public health and bear most of the cost of social security. Above all, it shamelessly benefits from all the exemptions, incentives, and generous subsidies granted by the state—which acts as a machine collecting the flow of incoming money and redistributing it, spending more than it receives and therefore obliged to borrow. Capital is never far away from this providential source of bounty.[33]

While Baran and Sweezy see the corporation as a stage of capitalist development unique to the mid-20th-century United States, Braudel looks to historical precedents of the 20th-century corporation, and concludes that historically, the corporation owes its success to two factors—its monopoly on the most remunerative forms of production, and the fact that the state ensures its successes and underwrites its losses. Capitalism is completely dependent on state power for its emergence and growth, and therefore is the very antithesis of the market.[34] Building on Braudel's innovative and insightful conceptualization of capitalism, along with insights drawn from the German Historical School, Immanuel Wallerstein conceives of capitalism as a historical social system with the primary objective of expansion and entrenchment.[35] The defining feature of capitalism, according to Wallerstein, is that the endless accumulation of capital is the primary objective or logic of not just individual capitalists but the system itself. In the pursuit of the

12 The Confusion of Capitalist Structures

endless accumulation of capital, so posits Giovanni Arrighi, capitalism as a system is incredibly flexible and eclectic.[36]

In direct contrast to the Braudelian tradition is the Brennerite Marxist position. In the late 1970s, the journal *Past & Present* famously provided a forum for debate of the Brenner hypothesis that capitalism began in England with the British Industrial Revolution. In this debate, Robert Brenner criticized the Braudelian view for being insufficiently Marxist, in that for Braudelians, capitalism is best seen from the big structures of the world economy rather than in the hidden abode of the production process as Marx details in *Capital* (1867). Brenner also took issue with the Braudelian camp's idea of the *longue durée* and of global analysis of capitalism. He claims that capitalism began much later than Braudel contends, and that this macro approach supports a so-called "Third World" Marxism which asserts that primitive accumulation took place outside of England, maybe before the British Industrial Revolution.[37] Brenner alternately argues that the transformation of agrarian class relations in England allowed the English economy to begin a new path of economic development that other countries could not replicate. This new path, Brenner argues, culminated in the British Industrial Revolution.[38]

In furthering the Brennerite Marxist perspective, Vivek Chibber infamously took on subaltern studies in his book *Postcolonial Theory and the Specter of Capital* (2013), in which he takes issue with "the Subalternist insistence on the unique political consciousness of non-Western agents."[39] Instead, he argues

> that the universalizing categories of Enlightenment thought are perfectly capable of capturing the consequences of capital's universalization and the dynamics of political agency—indeed, these categories are essential to their analysis. If these four propositions are true, it means that at least some of the European theories, Marxism in particular, need not be charged with Eurocentrism simply because they originated in the West.[40]

These critiques of subaltern studies are rooted in Chibber's view of capitalism: that Capitalism (and Marxism) originated in England and then spread across the globe like a contagion. The "colonies," as he writes, did not experience a fundamentally different modernity than that of Europe. Just because one might not observe the exact same power relations in two different places does not warrant a different account of how power works because capitalism is heterogenous and adaptable, and "perfectly compatible with a highly diverse set of political and cultural formations."[41] The resistance of the subaltern, Chibber claims, is therefore simply a reaction against capitalism.

While the two main targets of the Brennerite perspective—Braudelians and subalternists—are quite different from each other, they have two main commonalities that render them incompatible with the Brennerite approach. First, they both contend that capitalism articulates itself differently in the Global South as compared to the Global North, and second, these two

Foundations of a Critique of Capitalist Theories   13

approaches challenge the Brennerite claim that capitalist modernity began in England with the British Industrial Revolution.

As the 20th century wore on, global political economy became increasingly chaotic, and for some scholarly observers, events proved that state monopoly capitalism was in fact destined to unravel due to its own contradictions. In the late 1970s, Michel Aglietta wrote A *Theory of Capitalist Regulation* (1976),[42] the classic work of what became known as the Regulation School. The Regulation School focuses its concern on economic crisis in order to make sense of the stagflation crisis of the 1970s. Aglietta saw the periodic crises of capitalism as part of the "laws of its regulation," moments that generally transformed the world economy and thereby allowed capital accumulation to continue once again.[43] However, observed Aglietta, while previous crises generally led to a "new cohesion," state monopoly capitalism prolonged the social crisis in time by delaying the inevitable through "devalorizations into the inflation process."[44] These attempts by the state to use monetary policy to slow the crisis, Aglietta contends, generate more severe overproduction and fail to bring about the necessary deflation that would end the phase of overproduction and bring about new conditions of production that would temporarily solve the crisis. But Aglietta saw not only economic consequences for state interference in the market on the behalf of monopoly capital, but also saw political and social consequences. By universalizing social conflict through the use of monetary policy benefitting corporate interest, the state in the context of monopoly capitalism shows "a strong totalitarian tendency under the ideological cover of liberalism."[45] The socialization of economic risk can be effective only if the dominant class succeeds in imposing tight social control over labor and other subordinate classes.

The Regulation School tended to focus on the political economy of the stagflation crisis of the 1970s as a way to better understand the trajectory of the capitalist world economy, and as such cautioned against creating a general theory of capitalism. "Regimes of accumulation and modes of regulation are outcomes of the history of human struggles," wrote Alain Lipietz; therefore, he claimed, it was futile to look to a standardized, inevitable pattern of capitalist development.[46] Certain outcomes succeed, he posits, because "they ensure some regularity and permanence in social reproduction."[47] While the Regulation School primarily focused on the structural crises of capitalism, they, unlike theorists of capitalism who preceded them, believed that capitalism had a contingent trajectory shaped by the outcomes of social conflict.

Neoliberal theory similarly came out of the historical moment of the 1970s but was much more successful in shaping mainline ways of thinking about capitalism. Neoliberal theorists contend that capitalism is inherently just and rational, and needs minimal state intervention to secure its functioning. Friedrich Von Hayek wrote that capitalism, "requires adequate organization of certain institutions like money, markets, and channels of information—some of which can never be adequately provided by private enterprise—but it depends, above all, on the existence of an appropriate legal system, a legal

14   *The Confusion of Capitalist Structures*

system designed both to preserve competition and to make it operate as beneficially as possible."[48] While the state plays a minimal role in assuring the preconditions for capital accumulation, Neoliberal theorists contend that the less the state interferes in the market the better for capital accumulation. As Hayek put it, "Freedom... is, of course, merely another name for power or wealth."[49]

The theory of neoliberalism has both economic and political dimensions. "In its economic manifestation," writes Francis Fukuyama, "liberalism is the recognition of the right of free economic activity and economic exchange based on private property and markets."[50] Economic freedom, i.e. the ability to accumulate capital unfettered by state intervention in the market, was for Milton Friedman, "an end in itself," but economic freedom, he claimed, was also a means to achieve political freedom.[51] Capitalism as a system, Friedman contended, was the economic system that promoted the most freedom compared to other ways of organizing the world economy because capitalism "separates economic power from political power and in this way enables the one to offset the other."[52] And in fact, the historical developments of the 20th century proved this to be fact. According to Fukuyama, only liberal democracy stood triumphant over the left alternative, socialism, and the right alternative, authoritarianism. Liberal democracy, which Fukuyama defines as "the doctrine of individual freedom and popular sovereignty" proved to be "durable and resurgent" while other political ideologies failed.[53] A state is neoliberal, posits Fukuyama, when "the state takes *in principle* to the legitimacy of private property and enterprise. Those that protect such economic rights we will consider liberal; those that are opposed or base themselves on other principles (such as 'economic justice') will not qualify."[54] In other words, in states that are neoliberal, the protection of private property and enterprise trump all other concerns, including social and economic justice.

New Institutional Economics rose to popularity in the 1990s. Its most famous proponent, Douglass North, built on the work of Neoliberal theorists such as Milton Friedman and Francis Fukuyama by historicizing and modifying their theoretical arguments. New Institutionalism sees "efficient economic organization [a]s the key to growth" and argues that "the development of an efficient economic organization in Western Europe accounts for the rise of the West."[55] New Institutionalists, just like the Braudelians and the Brennerite Marxists, looked to the origins of capitalism as a historic system to better understand its essential features. Just as the Brennerite Marxists argued, so too do the New Institutionalists contend that capitalism began in Europe as a result of Europe's institutional innovations in the Early Modern period. Douglass North and Robert Paul Thomas argue that the establishment of new institutional arrangements along with the advent of property rights created incentives for individuals to engage in activities that increased both private profit along with "the social rate of return."[56] Other world regions failed to grow, claim North and Thomas, because no incentives were created in order to engage in the accumulation of capital.[57]

Joel Mokyr's recent work furthers this argument, claiming that the uniquely brilliant intellectual contributions of the European Enlightenment allowed capitalism to come into being and flourish.[58] Mokyr argues that New Institutionalists should not only look to institutional explanations for Europe's economic superiority, but also to cultural explanations. In so doing, Mokyr contends, capitalist culture preceded capitalism, creating the preconditions that would ensure its future success. This logic is directly contrary to Marxist ways of thinking about culture, including the Birmingham School, which alternately views capitalist culture as a product of capitalism.

In direct opposition to the Neo-Marxists, the Regulation School, and many other previous theorists of capitalism, New Institutionalists generally attribute crisis (which they term "decline") as a result of too much state intervention in the market, including, most notably, monopoly privileges. As a result of this "persistent tendency toward failure in human organization," i.e. that the state fails to secure the preconditions that would lead to capitalist development, in human history, "Economic growth has been the exception; stagnation and decline have been the rule."[59]

By historicizing neoliberal ideas, New Institutionalists not only offer revisions to neoclassical theory, but also can explain why some states are rich and others poor—because some states developed "good institutions" that secure property rights, protect contracts, motivate exchange, foster saving, encourage investment in human and physical capital, and encourage the advancement of "useful" knowledge.[60] By having "good" institutions, these states are able to thrive when others seemingly cannot. Avner Grief, in his correction of neoliberal theory, reminds us that "markets do not necessarily spontaneously emerge in response to opportunities for profitable exchange,"[61] instead, they must be intentionally cultivated by institutions that protect property rights and provide contract enforcement. It is these institutions that determine the success of a given national economy.

The California School of Economic History emerged as a critique of the New Institutional Economics' Eurocentrism. California School economic historians retain the institutional focus of the New Institutionalists, but instead argue that the advent of capitalism as a historic system cannot be explained without putting Europe's rise in the context of Asia's decline. Kenneth Pomerantz argues that by building on the work of historians who show that

> "the new world, the slave trade, and overseas coercion generally were crucial to European capital accumulation," economic historians can "then proceed to what seems to be a stronger link among capitalism, overseas coercion, and industrialization: namely that the politico-economic institutions of European capitalism and violent interstate competition, combined with some very lucky (for Europe) global conjunctures, made European (especially British) relations with the rest of the Atlantic world unique among core-periphery relationships."[62]

16   *The Confusion of Capitalist Structures*

In direct contrast to the New Institutionalists, the California School contends that the rise of capitalism in Europe was not the result of Europe's immanent virtues, but instead, lucky historical accidents that transformed Europe from the world economy's periphery to its core.

Jean-Laurent Rosenthal and R. Bin Wong claim that the divergence between Asia and Europe can, in fact, be explained by differences in political institutions, but not through the mechanism that New Institutionalists would have us think. It was "Europe's persistent poverty before the late eighteenth century" that led to "the rise of capital-intensive methods of production that characterize the modern economy."[63] These institutions, as Rosenthal and Wong demonstrate, were the "unintended consequence of Europe's political anarchy, not a carefully crafted result of government efforts."[64] Asia's, particularly China's, decline, they argue, cannot possibly be attributed to the fact that "its economic system was incapable of development or because it was hobbled by overarching cultural, environmental, or political factors," on the contrary, its state institutions ensured millennium-long prosperity over a vast empire.[65]

In the late 20th century, another important theoretical tradition, Poststructuralism, proposed yet another new way of thinking about capitalism. Just as the German Historical School and Braudelians before them, Poststructuralists reject a linear concept of history, but unlike theorists who focus on the cyclical nature of capitalism, Poststructuralists see capitalism as, "inseparable from the movement of deterritorialization, but this movement is excorcised through factitious and artificial reterritorializations. Capitalism is constructed on the ruins of the territorial and the despotic, the mythic and the tragic representations, but it re-establishes them in its own service and in another form, as images of capital."[66] Gilles Deleuze and Félix Guattari's definition of capitalism emphasizes the system's dynamism, and while it has echoes of Schumpeter's theory of creative destruction by seeing Capitalism as a system is incessantly deconstructed and reconstructed, they view the system as a combination of past, present, and future.

Unlike previous theorists of capitalism, Poststructuralists delve deeper into the multiple registers of the world economy. As Frederic Jameson reminds us, capitalism, "is at one and the same time an ideology and a set of practical institutional problems."[67] So unlike how, for example, Joel Mokyr and other New Institutionalists see capitalist culture as a precondition for capital accumulation, Jameson contends that

> the ideology of the market ... is somehow generated by the thing itself, as its objectively necessary afterimage; somehow both dimensions must be registered together, in their identity as well as in their difference. They are, to use a contemporary but already outmoded language, semiautonomous; which means, if it is to mean anything, that they are not really autonomous or independent from each other, but they are not really at one with each other either.[68]

Culture has a dialectical relationship to the capitalist world economy, again helping to both unravel and reconstruct it. For Giorgio Agamben, the expropriation of productive activity that characterizes the capitalist world economy aimed at "alienation of language itself, of the linguistic and communicative nature of human beings, of that logos in which Heraclitus identifies the Common. The extreme form of the expropriation of the Common is the spectacle, in other words, the politics in which we live. But this also means that what we encounter in the spectacle is our very linguistic nature inverted. For this reason (precisely because what is being expropriated is the possibility itself of a common good), the spectacle's violence is so destructive; but, for the same reason, the spectacle still contains something like a positive possibility—and it is our task to use this possibility against it."[69] Agamben similarly identifies the dual nature of capitalism—that the very "linguistic nature" in the form of politics that does violence to society—can be subverted to undermine those very politics. In capitalism (at all of its registers), its dynamism is also its own unraveling: its deconstruction.

But just as other theorists of capitalism have done in the past, Poststructuralists have similarly endeavored to describe their current conjuncture by updating existing theory. Jacques Derrida, writing in the early 1990s, identifies the ten "plagues" of neoliberalism as: (1) unemployment; (2) exclusion of the homeless; (3) economic war; (4) contradictions of the free market; (5) foreign debt; (6) arms industry and trade; (7) nuclear weapons; (8) interethnic wars; (9) capitalist phantom states; and (10) international law and its institutions.[70] In pointing out how each of these so-called plagues do not disqualify international institutions, but instead set global humanitarian goals, Derrida demonstrates to neoliberal thinkers (namely Francis Fukuyama) that to theorize capitalism, one cannot simply accumulate and present empirical evidence. For Derrida, theorizing capitalism necessitates "double interpretation," in other words, "the concurrent readings that the picture seems to call for and to oblige us to associate."[71] For capitalism is both the embodiment of freedom that Francis Fukuyama claims it is and the social violence that Agamben, for example, claims it to be.

Analyzing Capitalism

This snapshot intellectual history of theories of capitalism is not meant to be an exhaustive list of every existing theory of capitalism. But it does illustrate how mainline theories of capitalism have changed in the centuries since Adam Smith and Karl Marx first set out to describe, theorize, and critique the new economic system they observed. While mapping out the terrain of the many theories of capitalism seems like an esoteric (and perhaps self-defeating) intellectual exercise, it has real consequences for how we understand the global economy as lived experience. The differences among definitions of capitalism lead to important questions and debates about the nature of the system. The outcomes of these debates over the multiple

18   *The Confusion of Capitalist Structures*

definitions of capitalism have consequences for not only how accurately we can describe capitalism as a system, but also about the likely future trajectory of the system and how it can (or can't) be shaped by human action.

One of the most essential questions that arises from this intellectual history is: Do we understand the system by viewing it from the bottom up as Marx and his followers did, emphasizing how labor creates all value and that the engine of history is the class struggle; or from the top down, as Braudel and followers contend, seeing the big structures that make up the system and haute finance as essential to the endless accumulation of capital? Alternately, as Neoliberal theorists or New Institutionalists might argue, perhaps the "free market" is the key feature of global capitalism? Are states essential in setting the preconditions for capital accumulation as Braudelians, New Institutionalists, and Neo-Marxists claim? Is the historical development of capitalism completely contingent, as the California School claims; completely structural as the German Historical School posits; open to change through human action only at certain historical moments as the Braudelians claim; changeable through political action as theorists of imperialism, Neo-Marxists, and Brennerite Marxists might argue; or through linguistic subversion as Poststructuralists argue?

When and where did capitalism begin? In England during the British Industrial Revolution as the Brennerites argue? In the Italian City States in the Early Modern period as the Braudelians contend? Through Europe's attempts to access financial markets in Asia from the Early Modern period through the 19th century as the California School proposes? And, what role does crisis play in the capitalist world-system? Is it the motor that leads to the further expansion and entrenchment of capitalism as the German Historical School and the Regulation School show? What is the role of culture in constituting capitalism? Did capitalist culture precede capitalism as the New Institutionalists argue? Or does culture have a dialectical relationship to global capitalism as Poststructural theorists contend? Are processes of capitalism and colonialism inherently linked as theorists of imperialism, Neo-Marxists, Braudelians, and the California School show? Or are capitalism and colonialism separate processes as the Brennerites and New Institutionalists claim? And finally, what is Eurocentrism and which theories of capitalism are Eurocentrist? Are the Brennerite Marxists correct in their claim that Marxism is Eurocentric, but it's the correct view as Capitalism began in Europe? New Institutionalists would agree with the Brennerites that capitalism started in Europe because Europe's institutions and their supporting culture led to the advent of capitalism, although these two groups of theorists would likely disagree over the timeline, as New Institutionalists claim that Feudalism ended in 1300 and Capitalism didn't begin until the British Industrial Revolution, leaving a 500-year historical gap that Brennerite Marxist narratives cannot explain. The California School, however, would critique both New Institutionalists and many varieties of Marxism as being Eurocentric for focusing solely on Europe's ascent in the

Foundations of a Critique of Capitalist Theories 19

Early Modern period without analyzing how its interactions with Asia led to these historic developments. So did capitalism originate in Europe or was it the result of a global encounter?

Critiquing Capitalism

These questions and many more remain unresolved, though the scholarly debate of these issues continues. In these debates, Marx's ideas are the common launching point for debate, discussion, and the development of new theories. In the few centuries since Marx first penned *Capital*, all those who have endeavored to describe the capitalist world economy have had to contend with his theories, whether they have supported it, critiqued it, or some combination of the two.

In this book, our endeavor is to understand the nature of capitalism and its future trajectory, as many political economists have done in the preceding centuries. In so doing, we take the position that to understand the historical development of capitalism and its future trajectory, one must view it primarily through the perspective of anti-colonial and working-class movements across the globe. Is this endeavor, you might ask, a Marxist endeavor? Marx certainly took a global view when understanding Capitalism's historical development, and his work on power and inequality among rich and poor countries has left an indelible legacy on the way scholars understand what is today called "economic development." But there remains a debate among political economists as to whether Marx truly took a so-called "Third Worldist" approach to global political economy.

One of the few windows into Marx's views on the Global South can be found in the two newspaper articles he wrote on imperialism in India for the *New York Daily Tribune* in 1853. Disappointingly, in his analysis of India's political economy, he departs from a Marxist analysis by beginning from the premise that before colonialism, "Indian society has no history at all, at least no known history."[72] And Marx views British colonizers as "the first conquerors superior, and therefore, inaccessible to Hindoo civilization."[73] This claim is clearly steeped in the same Eurocentrism of colonialism itself. Although Marx decries the violence of colonialism, stating that "There cannot, however, remain any doubt but that the misery inflicted by the British on Hindostan is of an essentially different and infinitely more intensive kind than all Hindostan had to suffer before,"[74] Marx's primary argument about India's economic development is that in bringing modernity to India, along with irrigation, communication networks, and railways; in other words, by incorporating India into the capitalist world-system, Britain is furthering the goals of world socialism. Marx writes:

> England, it is true, in causing a social revolution in Hindostan, was actuated only by the vilest interests, and was stupid in her manner of enforcing them. But that is not the question. The question is, can

20 *The Confusion of Capitalist Structures*

> mankind fulfil its destiny without a fundamental revolution in the state of Asia? If not, whatever may have been the crimes of England she was the unconscious tool of history in bringing about the revolution.[75]

Ultimately, Marx sees colonialism as bringing modernity to the Global South, and thereby furthering the historical development of capitalism that will bring human society closer to the inevitable global socialist revolution.

For our purposes, the key question is, can Marx's analysis of colonialism in India be read toward a theory of capitalism as seen from the Global South? There are certainly insightful elements of his analysis. Imperialism and colonialism are revealed to be the engine of expansion of the capitalist world-system. This revolution in the Third World, therefore, is fundamental to the project of a socialist revolution worldwide. But Marx's historical analysis posits that there was no such thing as Indian history before colonialism, which, besides being patently false, prevents Marx from seeing the reversal of fortune across the globe in the shift of global power from Asia to Europe: that Asia's previous politico-economic power was based in an alternate logic of accumulation which has bearing on how it came to be colonized, and how it was then eventually incorporated into the capitalist world-system as regions dependent upon the Global North. This missing analysis would help us to better understand capitalist development through understanding why and how Europe went from being an underdeveloped region of the world to inventing a new logic for organizing the world economy that would decenter and recenter the global economy for centuries to come. And then, of course, there's the question of whether or not colonialism is justifiable as a tool for furthering the churn of history toward an inevitable socialist revolution as Marx contends it is. Given the violence caused by colonialism, I would contend that in this case, the means do not justify the ends.

Thus what's missing in Marx's analysis and largely missing from the snapshot history of theories of capitalism presented above are different perspectives of global capitalism, capitalism as seen from the Global South. There are more theories of capitalism out there than what the mainline canon suggests, but they are not as well known. By incorporating these lesser known but equally important and scientifically rigorous theories into the existing canon, we benefit from a more accurate description of capitalism.[76] In the following chapters, we will explore in-depth some of these lesser known theorists.

Notes

1 Adam Smith, *Inquiry into the Nature and Causes of the Wealth of Nations* (New York: Alfred A. Knopf, 1776 [1991]).

2 *Ibid.*, 6.

3 *Ibid.*, 300.

4 Adam, Smith, *The Wealth of Nations*, Books IV–V (New York: Penguin, 1776 [1999]), 4.

5 *Ibid.*, 279.

Foundations of a Critique of Capitalist Theories   21

6   David Ricardo, *Principles of Political Economy and Taxation* (Amherst: Prometheus Books, 1817 [1996]).
7   *Ibid.*, 45.
8   *Ibid.*, 42.
9   *Ibid.*, 47.
10 Karl Marx. *Capital Vol. 1* (New York: Penguin, 1867 [1990]).
11 Karl Marx. *The German Ideology* (New York: International Publishers, 1846 [1976]).
12 Marx. *Capital Vol. 1*, 928–929.
13 Wolfgang Streek, *How Will Capitalism End?* (London: Verso, 2016).
14 John A. Hobson, *Imperialism: A Study* (New York: Cosimo Classics, 1902); Lenin VI. (1939). *Imperialism the Highest Stage of Capitalism* (New York: International Publishers), 53, 75; Rosa Luxembourg, *The Accumulation of Capital* (London: Routledge, 1913 [2003]), 399.
15 Rudolf Hilferding, *Finance Capital: A Study of the Latest Phase of Capitalist Development* (London: Routledge, 1910 [2006]), 365.
16 Hobson, *Imperialism*, Pt. 1, Ch. 4.
17 *Ibid.*, 7.
18 Lenin, *Imperialism*, 89.
19 Luxembourg, *The Accumulation of Capital*, 7.
20 *Ibid.*, 8.
21 Nikolaï Dimitrievitch Kondratieff, *Les Grands Cycles de la Conjoncture* (Paris: Economica, 1992), 497.
22 *Ibid.*, 508.
23 Joseph A. Schumpeter, *Capitalism, Socialism and Democracy* (New York: Harper and Row, 1942 [1976]), 83.
24 Karl Polanyi, *The Great Transformation: The Political and Economic Origins of Our Time* (Boston: Beacon Press, 1944 [2001]).
25 *Ibid.*, 134–135.
26 *Ibid.*, 135.
27 Paul A. Baran and Paul M. Sweezy *Monopoly Capital: An Essay on the American Economic and Social Order* (New York: Monthly Review, 1966), 336–338.
28 Paul M. Sweezy, *The Theory of Capitalist Development* (New York: Monthly Review, 1942 [1970]), 56.
29 David Harvey, *The Condition of Postmodernity* (London: Blackwell, 1990), 180.
30 Ernest Mandel, *Late Capitalism* (London: New Left Books, 1972 [1975]), 562.
31 Harvey, *Postmodernity*, 180.
32 *Ibid.*, 180.
33 Fernand Braudel, *Civilization and Capitalism 15th–18th Century, Volume 3, The Perspective of the World* (New York: Harper and Row, 1979 [1984]), 623–624.
34 Giovanni Arrighi, *The Long Twentieth Century* (London: Verso, 1994), 10.
35 Immanuel Wallerstein, *Historical Capitalism with Capitalist Civilization* (London: Verso, 1983 [1996]), 13.
36 Arrighi, *Long Twentieth Century*, 4.
37 Robert Brenner, "The Origins of Capitalist Development: A Critique of Neo-Smithian Marxism," *New Left Review* 104 (July–August 1977): 25–92.
38 Robert Brenner, "The Agrarian Roots of European Capitalism," in *The Brenner Debate: Agrarian Class Structure and Economic Development in Pre-Industrial Europe*, eds. T.H. Aston and C.H.E. Philpin (Cambridge: Cambridge University Press, 1987), 232.
39 Vivek Chibber, *Postcolonial Theory and the Specter of Capital* (New Delhi: Navayana, 2013), 285.
40 *Ibid.*
41 *Ibid.*
42 Michel Aglietta, *A Theory of Capitalist Regulation* (London: New Left Books, 1976 [1979]).

The Confusion of Capitalist Structures

43 *Ibid.*, 384.

44 *Ibid.*, 384–385.

45 *Ibid.*, 386.

46 Alain Lipietz, "New Tendencies in the International Division of Labor: Regimes of Accumulation and Modes of Regulation," in *Production, Work, Territory: The Geographical Anatomy of Industrial Capitalism*, eds. Allen J. Scott and Michael Storper (Boston: Allen & Unwin, 1986), 19.

47 *Ibid.*

48 Friedrich Von Hayek, *The Road to Serfdom* (Chicago: University of Chicago Press, 1944 [1994]), 43.

49 *Ibid.*, 30.

50 Francis Fukuyama, *The End of History and the Last Man* (New York: The Free Press, 1992), 44.

51 Milton Friedman, *Capitalism and Freedom* (Chicago: University of Chicago Press, 1962 [2002]), 8.

52 *Ibid.*, 9.

53 Fukuyama, *End of History*, 42.

54 *Ibid.*, 44.

55 Douglass C. North and Robert Paul Thomas, *The Rise of the Western World: A New Economic History* (Cambridge: Cambridge University Press, 1973), 1.

56 *Ibid.*

57 *Ibid.*, 2.

58 Joel Mokyr, *A Culture of Growth: The Origins of the Modern Economy* (Princeton: Princeton University Press, 2017), 15.

59 Douglass C. North, *Understanding the Process of Economic Change* (Princeton: Princeton University Press, 2005), 135.

60 Avner Grief, *Institutions and the Path to the Modern Economy: Lessons from Medieval Trade* (Cambridge: Cambridge University Press, 2006), 4.

61 *Ibid.*, 56.

62 Kenneth Pomerantz, *The Great Divergence: China, Europe, and the Making of the Modern World Economy* (Princeton: Princeton University Press, 2000), 185.

63 Jean-Laurent Rosenthal and R. Bin Wong, *Before and Beyond Divergence* (Cambridge: Harvard University Press, 2011), 229.

64 *Ibid.*

65 *Ibid.*

66 Gilles Deleuze and Félix Guattari, *Anti-Oedipus* (New York: Penguin Classics, 1972 [2009]), 303.

67 Frederic Jameson, *Postmodernism: Or, the Cultural Logic of Late Capitalism* (Durham: Duke University Press, 1991), 260.

68 *Ibid.*

69 Giorgio Agamben, *Means Without End: Notes on Politics* (Minneapolis: University of Minnesota Press, 1996 [2000]), 81–82.

70 Jaques Derrida, *Specters of Marx: The State of the Debt, the Work of Mourning and the New International* (New York: Routledge, 1993 [1994]), 100–104.

71 *Ibid.*, 100.

72 Kárl Marx, "On Imperialism in India," in *The Marx-Engels Reader*, ed. Robert C. Tucker (New York: WW Norton and Company, 1853 [1978]), 659.

73 *Ibid.*

74 *Ibid.*, 654.

75 *Ibid.*, 658.

76 Jurgen Kocka, *Geschichte des Kapitalismus* (München: Verlag CH Beck oHG, 2014), 20–21.

2 Capitalism's Deadly Labor Process

Karl Marx, Estranged Labor (1844)

Capitalism is the extraordinary idea that
The nastiest of men for the nastiest of motives
Will somehow work together for the benefit of all.
—Arguably attributed to John Maynard Keynes

One wonders why the attribution of this line to the most famous of liberal economists would excite quotation mavens to argue, as they do, over whether or not Keynes might have said such a thing. The answer could well be that among capitalism's deadly and deadening effects is that, as Karl Marx first said in 1844, capitalism destroys the inherent human values associated with human labor. Those thereby who doubt that Keynes could have uttered words homologous to what Marx had to say about capitalism are vexed no doubt that a famously liberal economist could have come to so sober and radical a conclusion.

Still, it would take little more than a few minutes of serious reading of what **John Maynard Keynes** actually wrote to that he could well have said what is arguably attributed to him. For an easy-to-find example, the following:

> The immense accumulations of fixed capital which, to the great benefit of mankind, were built up in the half century before the war, could never have come about in a Society where wealth was divided equitably. The railways of the world, which that age built as a monument to posterity, were, not less than the Pyramids of Egypt, the work of labor which was not free to consume in the immediate enjoyment the full equivalent of its efforts. ... *Thus this remarkable system depended for its growth on a double bluff or deception.*[1]

This from Keynes's very public declamation written upon his decision in 1919 to quit the British delegation to the Versailles Peace Conference, that in the long run did anything but end the Great War of 1914. Keynes would have no part of the Versailles Treaty because he knew very well that nastiness in peacemaking can (as it did after 1920) spawn an ever more deadly nastiness in its consequences.

DOI: 10.4324/9781003198291-3

24 *The Confusion of Capitalist Structures*

The terms imposed on Germany in 1919 were, in fact, so economically crippling and culturally shaming as to serve as fertile political soil for Hitler's rise to power. In 1920, Hitler became the propagandist for the German Workers Party, which then became the National Socialist German Worker's Party for which he designed the swastika as its dastardly symbol. Nazi political culture was born on February 24, 1920, just more than a month after the Versailles Treaty went into effect on January 10, 1920. Twenty years later, on June 22, 1940, Germany, upon occupying France, returned the favor of humiliation by forcing the French to sign the Armistice at Compiègne in the same railroad car in which Germany was forced to accept the terms of its surrender in 1920.

The Thirty Years War with Germany, 1914–1945, ended just shy of 400 years after the early modern war of the same name that ended in the Peace of Westphalia on October 24, 1648. Westphalia made modern Europe possible by establishing the nation-state as a legitimate political entity borne of the right of states to exercise domestic sovereignty in exchange for granting the same to other sovereign nation-states in the making; hence, the irony of Keynes's comments on the failure of Versailles. Instead of making peace, 1919 led to the definitive end in Europe of what Eric Hobsbawm called the long 19th century that began in what came to be known, after 1848, as a liberal interstate world order when, at long last, the agonies of 1789 played themselves out. This new dispensation Hobsbawm identified as the Age of Capital[2] from 1848 to 1875, after which what remained of the liberal nation-state began its long downhill slide toward the Great War of 1914. After 1945, when the dust had settled, the terms of the Peace of Westphalia were qualified at best by the rise of the United States as the only global superpower able and willing to police violations of the world's now metaphorically sovereign nation-states.

Thus it is that Keynes in 1920 was the prophet of the end of liberal market capitalism and the scientist of a formally mixed macroeconomics, in which monetary policy reduced interest rates while fiscal policy investments spurred infrastructural spending at a time when public works led to job growth. Keynes's economic theory won the day after the global market crisis of 1929. Thereafter, the by-then late modern nation-state became the authority of ultimate resort against the classical free market waiting to be reborn as the neoliberal global marketplace. The theory seemed to work perfectly well. The infrastructural spending, especially on armament manufacturing, ended both the Great Depression and the latter-day Thirty Years War. Just after 1945, Europe and Asia were in tatters that only the United States could knit back into a new kind of fiscal capitalism that bore little more than figurative comparison to the classical laissez-faire market. This is Keynes's double bluff with the ante raised. The invisible hand bets against itself.

In 1920, the sad story of the Age of Capital was a tale only a radically liberal economist like Keynes could tell—a tale that turned on the *double entendre* of the word *liberal*—in respect to which the European, mostly

British, idea of the liberal as a proponent of classical, free market economics as against the emergent American notion of the liberal as a vaguely left of center political party willing to use the state as the market regulator of first and last resort. At some point in the etymological history of a *double entendre*, the doubled meanings had to have passed through a moment of semantic overlap. In the case of the popular understanding of *liberal* that moment of overlap occurred on either side of 1848 when the liberalism associated with the classical political economists won out in the long struggle since 1789 between bloodthirsty radicalisms and conservativisms in search of a restoration of the old order of imperial, if not royal, principles.

The 1848 revolutions in Europe were, in fact, a world revolution that Immanuel Wallerstein defines as the conjuncture in which liberal geo-culture emerged to endure until 1914, more or less, in its primordial form as "[liberal states]...based on a concept of citizenship, a range of guarantees against arbitrary authority, and a certain openness in public life."[3] Before 1848, the classical ideal of free markets guided by Adam Smith's phantasy of an invisible hand predominated among the intelligentsia. But the political history from 1789 to 1848 was fraught with turmoil that masked the slow definite rise of an industrial capitalism that, especially then, was cruel in its exploitation of workers who had no place to go for work because the last vestiges of the feudal agrarian order were all but lost to them. One might say at some risk that from 1789 to 1848, the liberal order of free markets worked its way through those tumultuous times in such a manner that a robust, out-in-the-open global capitalism became possible. Better put, what emerged was a capitalism that by its nature must pursue the endless accumulation of capital cannot help but be global, because it cannot help but to exploit those workers who can be pressed to give away cheap labor wherever in the world it can be found.

The qualities of the post-1848 liberal states in the economic world-system that Wallerstein describes were precisely the political qualities that came to prevail as the liberal ideal in America—the liberalism that Richard Hofstadter famously claimed was there from the beginning of the American republic.[4] But the double meaning of *liberal* turns on the fact that while liberal values of citizenship, checks on authority, and openness would seem to honor classical political economy's *laissez-faire* market place, industrial capitalism imposes a marketplace in which the human values of the laborers are, in effect, murdered in order to maximize economic values accruing to the capitalist class.

"Capitalism," said Keynes, "is the extraordinary idea that the nastiest of men for the nastiest of motives will somehow work together for the benefit of all." The line (even if Keynes did not compose it) is discordant liberalism played as fugue to Marx's narrative line.

So then, the question remains: What was Marx's line? Or some might prefer[5]: Which Marx are we talking about? Either way, the issue at hand is that of whether or not Marx—that is, the body of writings he left when he died March 14, 1883—was two different literary bodies.

26   *The Confusion of Capitalist Structures*

For those old enough to remember, this is the question posed not that long ago by Louis Althusser (1918–1990).[6] In a 1961 essay "On the Young Marx: Theoretical Questions,"[7] he took up a question that in the 1950s had been widely discussed by Soviet Marxists. Were the writings of the 1840s—in particular, "The Economic and Philosophical Manuscripts of 1844" and "The German Ideology" of 1845–1846, if not the "Manifesto of the Communist Party" in 1848—still under the influence of Hegel? Hence the classic 19th-century philosophical issue—idealist or materialist? Was (as Althusser put it) the mature Marx of *Capital I* in 1867 a mature materialist who had out grown a young man's idealism?

Althusser's "On the Young Marx" was quite explicitly written for Western theorists, among whom Marx's early writings were just then being read. His two-Marx theory relied on the notion of an epistemological break derived primarily from Gaston Bachelard (1884–1962), the philosopher of science at the *Sorbonne*, and secondarily the historian of science Georges Canguilhem (1994–1995), who was Althusser's teacher and colleague at the *École normale supérieure* (ENS). That Marx might have been two was, thereby, a normal condition of scientific epistemologies in general, but one of poignant theoretical importance for social theorists. "I merely hope," said Althusser:

> ...that I have been able to give some idea of the extraordinary relation between the enslaved thought of the Young Marx by pointing out something which is generally neglected, that is, the *contingent beginnings* (in respect to his birth) that he had to start from and the *gigantic layer of illusions he had to break through before he could even see it.* ...Of course Marx's youth did *lead* to Marxism, but only at the price of a prodigious break with his origins, a heroic struggle against the illusions he had inherited from the Germany in which he was born, and an acute attention to the realities concealed by these illusions.[8]

Althusser's mature Marx was a hero because he was assumed to have escaped the idealist illusions of his early bourgeois life in Germany. For Althusser, the maturity was in Marx's ultimate ability to describe a scientific, materialist theory of capitalism. Still, a question is left unanswered: Can any intellectual—whether Marxist or other; whether philosopher or scientist— ever escape some degree of bourgeois acculturation?

It would seem obvious, more generally, that any scientific study of capitalism is caught on the horns of a dilemma. It is hard to imagine a thoroughly scientific theory of capitalism without some theory of Marxism. At the same time, many of those with an interest in capitalism cannot imagine how Marx is relevant to their innocent brand of capitalism. This they think because—being capitalisms themselves—in all likelihood they don't realize that capitalism is as much a way of life as an economic system. Thus in their naïveté they suppose that capitalism is simply a normal and natural aspect of life for which no theory (least of all a scientific one) is required. This latter horn, any good theorist will tell you, poses a false dilemma insofar as the daily practice of so global a culture as capitalism surely requires a practical, if not a scientific, theory of how that culture measures success or failure. *Savoir faire*, if not *connaissance*.

Just the same, when it comes to theories of Marx and capitalism, the issue is not whether Marx himself grew out of his youthful ways of thinking, but whether Marxism itself drew on different parts of its founding corpus such that it is better to think of two Marxisms. And no one has more carefully teased out these two strains than Alvin W. Gouldner (1920–1980).

In *The Two Marxisms: Contradictions and Anomalies in the Development of a Theory* (1980),[9] Gouldner jogs memory of Marx's eleventh thesis on Feuerbach: "Philosophers have hitherto only interpreted the world in various ways; the point is to change it." Gouldner, writing nearly a century after the posthumous publication in 1888 of Marx's *Theses on Feuerbach*, meant to breathe new life into a critical and political Marx:

> Marx did not think of his theory simply as social science (the view of "clubby" academicians who want to "normalize" Marxism into something familiar). It was also a doctrine of violent revolution. Marxism is not attempting simply to understand society, it does not only predict the rise of a revolutionary proletariat that will overturn capitalism, but also actively mobilizes persons to do this.[10]

Gouldner wrote in the late 1970s against the sad bourgeoisification of the American academic left which, in the 1960s, had been striving to be true to a kind of critical Marxism by means of an active, occasionally violent, revolutionary praxis.

In the 1960s, students in particular were inspired to action by Students for a Democratic Society (SDS) after 1962; the American Civil Rights Movement of the early 1960s; then by a more radical turn in keeping with Malcolm X's black nationalism; then too by a furious rush of new social movements from third-wave feminism to queer nation politics. The *bouleversements* in the United States were part of a global story. The world revolution of 1968 engulfed various national movements in, among other places, Mexico City, Paris, London, São Paulo, Berlin that were no less radical than the American movements. Worldwide, the young engaged in assaults on an aging and tiresomely regressive liberal order that begrudgingly supported civil rights for many while engaging in a disastrously racist war in Vietnam. Their elders did some good in maintaining and creating social welfare programs for the elderly and the poor. But the good done was drowned out by the rebellious who were mostly middle class, thereby enjoying the assurance of finishing university educations.

The events in and around 1968 were background to Gouldner's theoretical work in the 1970s. Through *Theory and Society*, his then leftist journal,

28   *The Confusion of Capitalist Structures*

Gouldner did his best to make a place in the academy for veterans of the radical 1960s. After his death, his magazine (as he called it) survived but gradually drifted toward the "clubby" academic science he loathed. Gouldner died of a broken heart just when *Two Marxisms* was published. Though there were genetic and personal reasons his heart failed him, he also knew in his heart of hearts that he was playing a losing game. Not long after his death in 1980, Washington University, his home institution, closed down its Department of Sociology, thus to smother the last breath of the radical spirit he represented.[11]

Gouldner's story is worth a brief telling for its contrast to Althusser's. He was living in Europe when Althusser was still active. Gouldner's *Two Marxisms* was a criticism of Althusser's theoretical writings in *For Marx* for his attempt to redeem his own scientistic and Stalinist as justified by the scientific Marx of *Capital I*.[12] At the same time, Gouldner's underlying (if critical) appreciation of Althusser is represented by the title of a collection of his own essays *For Sociology: Renewal and Critique in Sociology Today*[13]—a book that followed by three years his influential *The Coming Crisis of Western Sociology* where the first seeds of two Marxisms project were planted.[14]

Gouldner's theory of the two Marxisms grows out of a strict reading of *The Eleventh Thesis* as a complementary not oppositive statement: "Philosophers have hitherto only interpreted the world in various ways; the point is to change it"—Marxism as science and critique.

> The two readings of Marxism briefly outlined here have, in part, grown up around the nuclear tension between volunteerism and determinism, between freedom and necessity. ... Our Two-Marxisms thesis maintains that both are in fact structural differentiations of a single originally undifferentiated Marxism; that over time the "two" emerge in *part* out of an effort to reduce the real international tensions of original Marxism.[15]

Had it not been for Althusser's desire to carve out a scientific if not scientistic, Marx, the Two-Marxisms debate might never have arisen and Marx would have been viewed as any other great author who, over time, writes differently early than later. But Marx was not simply a great writer. He was a literary *provocateur* who, as Gouldner emphasized, meant to make trouble of a revolutionary kind.

Without, for the time being, taking sides between Althusser and Gouldner, there can be little doubt that Marx made serious trouble across the years from the notable, if episodic, texts of the 1840s to the masterwork of 1867 he boldly entitled *Capital*. It was here of course that the long intellectual march arrived at the conclusions for which Marx earned a reputation as the author who corrected without dismissing the classical political economists by describing not just the systematic nature of capitalism, but also the murderous intent and effect of the modern form of economic domination.

Althusser was right in one respect. Like all other writers working over a good quarter century on a single subject, the final outcome is more mature (if the word must be used) than the earlier explorations. At the same time, the genius of Marx's life-work is that it spawned so many different movements willing to claim the name of Marx. In this, Gouldner was right. At issue among that variety of often contradictory movements is not whether Marx was or was not still bourgeois, but how his body of work allowed for different interpretations and, more to the important point, different programs for changing the world.

Notwithstanding Eric Hobsbawm's periodization of the modern era from 1789 to 1991 as the ages of revolution, capital, empire, and extremes,[16] the long 19th and short 20th centuries were a history of capitalism and the movements seeking to overthrow or, at least, soften its deadly effects. In the struggle, capitalism won in the long run, especially in respect to the revolutionary ideal of overthrowing social and economic structures upon which capitalism depends. Even now, as the world is still dealing with vestiges of the failed Soviet and Maoist experiments, the futility of which undermines the very ideal of social revolution. The world revolution of 1968 was fulfilled in 1991 not by changes attributable to Marxism but by the triumph of the capitalistic, "free" world over its Cold War enemies.

After 1991, the triumph of capitalism as originally conceived has been anything but triumphant.[17] In the first years of the short 20th century, Henry Ford's Motor Company deployed Frederick Winslow Taylor's principles of scientific management[18] to revolutionize not just automobile making but manufacturing itself. Thereafter, the capitalism that on the surface seemed to have entered a newer, ever more modern dispensation lurched more and more toward some strange phantasmagoric distortion of its original ideal of free markets guided by a free hand. Fordism became a managerial capitalism in which owners of the means of production owned nothing particular to the manufactured commodity. Then, in turn, there arose a fiscal capitalism in which even the managerial elites were displaced by financial managers. The CFO hedged the authority of the CEO in a system where the capital accumulated was not real capital per se, but fiscal capital, which bore no necessary relation to the commodities produced, much less to the labor power once central to their production. By the 1990s, after the short century had ended, neoliberalism, an ever more strange kind of capitalism, projected a still more fantastic notion of market freedom as an illusion projected on the global order, whereupon the liberal ideal of political and economic freedoms were utterly beyond the imagination of those most in need of human freedom. Then, too, well into the 21st century (which we can only hope will be very short) global politics are so broken that what markets there are, are left to the devises and desires of the most wealthy. This is now the global economy as little more than an engine for the production of global inequalities. The 1% rules the 99% with abandon in the spirit of unembarrassed greed.

30 *The Confusion of Capitalist Structures*

"Capitalism is the extraordinary idea that the nastiest of men for the nastiest of motives will somehow work together for the benefit of all." Few are those of right mind in these times who would doubt that the words are apt, whoever may first have uttered them.

Liberalisms of both kinds were at least joined on the unspoken assumption that capitalism offered a kind of triage for the most, if not the many. Even the conservative line of some liberalisms begrudgingly claim that the free market allows that anyone willing to work hard might (just might) have some chance of getting ahead. Liberal liberals, on the other hand, believe that the state bears a measure of responsibility to encourage and support that ideal or to care for those who fail for any number of good reasons. Sharp though the differences are, either way the triage effect is that those who can be saved ought benefit from their own efforts or the benefits provided. Though political leaders proclaim allegiance to one or both of these two triage theories, there is scant evidence that even the more generous of the two has done very much to slow the drift toward radically structured inequalities.

In the current century, wherever it may be headed, the one unsettling fact of the global order is exclusion, or as Achille Mbembe has called it, *necropolitics*—of which his prime example is Palestine.[19] The politics of death are a perversion of the politics of the liberal geo-culture. However slim may have been the chances of the poor and marginal under liberal capitalisms, today (when even neoliberalism falls by the way) the global triage takes the form of excluding a growing number of the global 99%. According to *The Manchester Guardian* (November 14, 2017), the world's richest 1% owns 50.1% of the world's wealth. It is not just that the 1% don't care (which, with rare exception, they don't) but that they care too much about creating and enforcing policies of violence that exclude too many of the 99%. What necropolitics amount to are the growing number of zones of exclusion[20]—Douala and Lagos, Jakarta and Dakar, San Juan and Atzlán; and other urban assemblages where the poor gather in vain hope; and in small villages in the interior of India or in the deep Amazon rainforests and other remote regions all but abandoned as the poor flee because Monsanto has sold them bad seeds or Walmart has ruined local markets or villainous war lords killed their fathers or husbands; not to mention all aboriginal reservations in Australia, Canada, the United States, and everywhere in the world where native peoples have been forced to survive on barren lands and deserts; and so on and so on.

Returning now to Marx's foundational theory of capitalism, the question is whether or not he foretold necropolitics, when he said in 1844:

> The political economist tells us that everything is bought with labour and that capital is nothing but accumulated labour; but at the same time he tells us that *the worker, far from being able to buy everything, must sell himself and his humanity.*[21]

Sell his humanity? Is this line—from the opening of Marx's 1844 *Manuscripts*—necropolitics? If so, how does an author who opens with such a strong statement then claim, as he does in the most famous section of the same text, owe a debt of sorts to the political economists?

> We have proceeded from the premises of political economy. We have accepted its language and its laws. We presupposed private property, the separation of labor, capital and land, and of wages, profit of capital and rent of land – likewise division of labor, competition, the concept of exchange value, etc. On the basis of political economy itself, in its own words, we have shown that the worker sinks to the level of a commodity and becomes indeed the most wretched of commodities; that the wretchedness of the worker is in inverse proportion to the power and magnitude of his production; that the necessary result of competition is the accumulation of capital in a few hands, and thus the restoration of monopoly in a more terrible form; and that finally the distinction between capitalist and land rentier, like that between the tiller of the soil and the factory worker, disappears and that the whole of society must fall apart into the two classes – property owners and propertyless workers.[22]

Then, too, one must wonder in respect to Althusser's early Marx, what is bourgeois about such thinking?

Intellectual work is almost by definition bourgeois. An intellectual of any particular kind must be educated, usually well educated in schools that by hook or by crook are expensive as to time and hidden costs as well as fees. If formally educated, the intellectual at least must have access to books and libraries, if not today's techno-media. Marx was supremely well educated. That his education included advanced study of German philosophies—not least among them, the idealists of whom none more prominent at Jena than Hegel—should not be presumed to be disqualifying for a budding radical. Whichever habits of the mind Marx had to break in order to come into his own, he could not have become anything like the mature genius of *Capital* in 1867 without Hegel and his German followers much less the French physiocrats or the British political economists. Thinking is as thinking does, and it does nothing serious outside the thinker's embracing culture.

I could go on, but suffice it to say that Althusser, having been drawn not just to the interpretation of the Soviet Marxists with respect to Marx's early writings, was also, and with good reason, deeply and personally faithful to the *École Normale Supérieure* (*ÉNS*)—surely first among equals as a *haute bourgeois* institution. Althusser was not only a student there after the Second War but the *ÉNS* was home (in a way that Jena was not for Marx). There, Althusser was accepted in spite of his long struggle with mental illness, and more importantly, he gave up a Catholic past for membership in the French Communist Party. In the day, that was more or less openly Soviet if

32   *The Confusion of Capitalist Structures*

not Neo-Stalinist. Never mind that student culture at *ÉNS* was then, like student cultures everywhere, raucous. Legend has it that, in the days after Althusser strangled his wife, graffiti artists wrote on the walls the great bourgeois institution a quotation they attributed to him: *"J'ai toujours rêvé de travailler avec mes mains."*[23]

Whatever may have been Althusser's mental and political diagnoses, it is not wholly incorrect to interpret his retreat into a materialist structuralism as an ameliorating self-medication for the confusions besetting bourgeois intellectuals after the War as France. Liberated from Hitler's evil occupying forces, France had to rethink itself. Hence, in due course, Althusser must have found some comfort in ideas, especially in his famous theory of an Ideological State Apparatus that calls out individuals into subjecthood:

> The category of the subject is constitutive of all ideology, but at the same time and immediately I add that the category of the individual is only constitutive of all ideology insofar as ideology has the function (which defines it) of 'constituting concrete individuals as subjects. In the interaction of this double constitution exists the functioning of all ideology, ideology being nothing but its functioning in the material forms of existence of that functioning.[24]

Incontestably, this is a mouthful that allowed subsequent (mostly American) theorists to reject any and all forms of structuralist theory as to what they prejudicially considered postmodern nonsense. But for Althusser, it was all but common sensical interpretation of what Marx himself did not account for—if ideology distorts understanding, how is that distortion imposed on its believers?

It is to Alvin Gouldner's credit, however, that he saw no purpose in denying his own bourgeois life. To the end, Gouldner began his personal biostatement with the line that he had been in his youth "a street tough kid from the Bronx." Still, Gouldner rose over the years to study with (then form a lifelong friendship with) Robert King Merton (1910–2003) of Columbia University, who himself rose from humble origins as Meyer Robert Schkolnick in a neighborhood of Russian Jews in South Philadelphia. After studying at Harvard in the 1930s, Merton went on to invent the sociology of science, and to make himself into one of modern sociology's most important theorists. After the Second War, Merton at Columbia and Talcott Parsons (1902–1979) at Harvard came to be regarded as leaders of the dominant schools of American sociology (much to the irritation of those associated with America's only indigenous sociological program at the University of Chicago). Yet, Merton, who for many was the epitome of mainstream social science, never broke with Gouldner, the street tough kid who would become in the 1970s the epitome of radical sociology. By then, Gouldner was living a very upper middle-class life in a lovely mansion in an affluent suburb of St. Louis. At Washington University, however, he had been exiled

Capitalism's Deadly Labor Process 33

to a pseudo-Gothic office tower of his own, cut off from the dealings of the Department of Sociology he had helped make the best in the land. Several causes of the exile had to do with the fact that Gouldner remained street tough in his dealings with others who crossed him, including one famous fist fight in the architecturally contrived hallowed halls of the University.

Gouldner, by contrast to Althusser's abandonment of Catholicism, did not break with the experiences of his youth in the Bronx. If he had enjoyed an epistemological break of sorts, it was due not to the more conservative demands of Merton, but to the wider cultural envelope of post-War America. Where Althusser's war-torn France in the late 1940s embarked on a cultural reconstruction, Gouldner's (and Merton's) America in the same period retreated into its affluence and global prowess. Althusser was not shamed for his affiliation with the French Communist Party. But Gouldner, by contrast, had to face the effects in the United States of the Cold War after 1946, and the Red Scare after Senator Joseph McCarthy's rise to notoriety in 1950 threatened even the most cautious of liberal thinkers. Gouldner dealt with these times during the 1950s by becoming, in effect, a left-Weberian—a tendency he affirmed to the very end by abiding with the title he chose for his exile professorship at Washington University, Max Weber Research Professor of Social Theory. Plus which, in those last years of his consideration of the two Marxisms, Gouldner also invented a theory of the intellectual in a time of emergent information technologies. His *The Future of Intellectuals and the Rise of the New Class*[25] took with utter seriousness the technical intelligentsia of the then new class of those who, in effect, owned the technological knowledge by which knowledge itself was already, as today it is, an indispensable competence for cultural prominence in the coming social order.

If there is, as I believe, a good reason for this extended comparison of Althusser and Gouldner, it is to suggest just how very different individuals, contemporaries who in different ways died to their life's work in 1980, came to appreciate Marx and Marxism for all of its complexities without sacrificing the core conviction of Marx's theory of capitalism—that capitalism is deadly for human beings. Even so, capitalism is the foundational structure of bourgeois civilization wherever it may be found—Paris, London, St. Louis, or New York; Seoul, Taipei, Hong Kong, or Singapore; Sydney, Perth, or Johannesburg; even in corners of Lagos and Nairobi or what remains of Beirut, certainly Cairo for the time being. Capital of all kinds— whether it profits from widgets, or from trade in fiscal promises, or bitcoins, or anything of the kind; however it may be accumulated—will grow in value on the backs of those whose subjecthood is called out by capitalism's ideological state apparatuses. Then and there people will die social deaths that sooner or later kill not just the soul but the body as well.

Marx, even in his alleged Hegelian immaturity, was the first to say this in terms that could not long be denied. Capitalism, like it or not, was a culture before it became a practical theory of liberal geo-culture that did not mind

34 *The Confusion of Capitalist Structures*

the grinding exploitation of the earliest generations of laborers in the Age of Capital—factory workers in Lowell, Massachusetts,[26] or those in Manchester,[27] or the slaves and field hands subjected to capitalism's global empire of cotton production.[28]

Has nothing good come from modern capitalism? Much has, of course. But in these times when saints and satans no longer hold sway over the popular imagination, it is hard to measure whatever good is done against the evil shadows human enterprise always casts. In the modern era, those shadows are all-too-easily hidden behind the liberal culture of progress. These days, evil is mere failure—the failure of individuals to do better; or of political systems to care for the needy; or of modern cultures to peel away the patina of moral idealism in order to bite into the rotten core underlying political economies of human labor; or of the failure of global systems to refrain from their cynical insistences that accumulated wealth will "somehow work together for the benefit of all." Evil is a strong word, widely considered a nostalgic carryover from ancient times when religious moralities believed their dogmatic ideas and good actions could stand up to devilish forces or satanic beings.

Yet, through the word is strong it serves a purpose still. If there is an Evil that troubles liberal devotion to the Good of human progress, it is Death. When the individual dies, they can no longer make progress; their good intentions are thwarted. Those left behind grieve what might have been. When people are killed by genocidal terrorism, few are left to grieve the loss. When global enterprises rush ahead in their search for more, they kill the land and seas upon which life depends. Capitalism, above all else, is the accumulation of greed. It cannot keep itself from accumulating resources and pressing human labor to the means of production. This is what capitalism does. It cannot help itself. It is a system construed by human political cultures to be a Frankenstein, some sort of post-human thing sewn together out of bits and parts of a dead humanity.

This is what is meant by necropolitics—the politics of death that Achille Mbembe (following Michel Foucault, Giorgio Agamben, even the likes of Carl Schmitt)[29] describes as founded on the historical principle that "the ultimate expression of sovereignty resides, to a large degree, in the power and the capacity to dictate who may live and who may die."[30] Mbembe thus attempts to transcend at least Althusser's (if not Gouldner's) Two Marxisms theory by the remarkable interpretation that Hegel and Marx straddle the dilemma of the estranged human subject. On the Hegelian horn:

> The human being truly becomes a subject—that is, separated from the animal—in the struggle and the work through which he or she confronts death (understood as the violence of negativity). It is through this confrontation with death that he or she is cast into the incessant movement of history.[31]

If such a principle seems so post-human as to be metaphysical as to contradict the modern liberal ideal of history, then Mbembe sees it as embracing even the horn of the so-called mature Marx, who:

> ... conflates labor (the endless cycle of production and consumption required for the maintenance of human life) with work (the creation of lasting artifacts that add to the world of things). Labor is viewed as the vehicle for the historical self-creation of humankind. Labor is viewed as the vehicle for the historical self-creation of humankind. The historical self-creation of humankind is itself a life-and-death conflict, that is, a conflict over what paths should lead to the truth of history: the overcoming of capitalism and the commodity form and the contradiction associated with both.[32]

If the young Marx was, in fact, Hegelian [How could he not have been?], then did he not envision a necropolitics when in *Estranged Labour* (1844) he describes (in admittedly analytic terms) the four elements of the laborer's estrangement: (1) from nature; (2) from "himself, his own active functions, his life activity..."; (3) from his "species-being, both nature and his spiritual being..."; and (4) from human social relations with others of his kind.[33] However cold-blooded, even philosophical, the language may be, is this not the political economy of Death—the death of the worker's life activity, of his spiritual nature, of his relations with others?

Then, in language far more bloody, is this not what Marx also said in "The Buying and Selling of Labour-Power," in *Capital* (1867):

> In order to be able to extract value from the consumption of a commodity, our friend, Moneybags, must be so lucky as to find, within the sphere of circulation, in the market, a commodity, whose use-value possesses the the peculiar property of being a source of value, whose consumption, therefore, is itself an embodiment of labour, and, consequently, a creation of value. The possessor of money does find on the market such a special commodity in capacity for labor or labour-power.[34]

Moneybags, the capitalist, consumes the worker whose human value is use-value in the accumulation of economic value. One could even say that Marx's capitalist eats human beings alive. Or in Mbembe's formulation, the self-creation of history itself is Death for the very subject it creates. Capitalism is thus "the violence of negativity." Life is Death. Necropolitics. The politics that, especially today, by which "weapons are deployed in the interest of maximum destruction of persons and the creation of *death-worlds*, new and unique forms of social existence in which vast populations are subjected to conditions of life conferring on them the status of *living-dead*."[35]

Still, it remains to ask: Is then capitalism no more than the latest, if not ultimate, stage in the necropolitics of the human condition as such? We live;

36   *The Confusion of Capitalist Structures*

we die. We do some good; we participate in the "violence of negativity." We are mortals; we one day cease to be.

If death is the end of our story, which in a certain sense it is, then is not capitalism a story told in order to press human subjects to work hard in the time being on the belief that ultimately they will never die. If people can persuade themselves to believe that they will not die, then they collude in capitalism's false promise that the Good of Greed always conquers the Evil One we fear. If this is even somewhat so, then all good Marxists, such as may remain, must admit that Max Weber in *The Protestant Ethic and the Spirit of Capitalism* (1904–1905) got much of this quite right. Capitalism in the 19th century would not have become what it became, and still is, without the religious revolution in the 17th century that created Protestant Christianity. Weber saw that the ethic Calvin taught was at least necessary, if not sufficient, onto the energizing spirit of capitalist enterprise. The capitalist works hard, as he or she requires those dependent capitalism's false promises to work harder still because human life depends on the satisfaction of an otherworldly god who alone can assure humanity's only hope for satisfaction in a world after the one of the laborer's travail.

It was not so much the political economy of early capitalism's demographic emergence in the Protestant regions of the North Atlantic world economy, as the fact that capitalism from its first moments is a theory of human history that inclines toward some vague, undefinable future beyond the labors of this world. Weber's contribution to Marx's thinking was that without saying so, he healed the breach of Marxist materialism with Hegelian idealism. In effect, Weber's famous iron cage of rationality can well be understood when:

> … Accompanied by Mr. Moneybags and the possessor of labour-power, we therefore take leave for a time of this noisy sphere, where everything takes place on the surface and in the view of all men, and follow them both to the hidden abode of production, on whose threshold there stares us in the face "No admittance except on business." Here we shall see, not only how capital produces, but how capital is produced. We shall at last force the secret of profit making.[36]

Capitalism, among much else, is the story told by René Girard of things hidden since the foundation of the world[37]—a world that against all probability cannot escape a certain kind of religious hope that the Good beyond greed is hidden because it is the pure, if vain, Hope that drives us in our daily labors, such as they are.

Notes

1 John Maynard Keynes, *The Economic Consequences of the Peace* (New York: Harcourt, Brace, and Howe, 1920 [1919]), 18; emphasis added.
2 Eric Hobsbawm, *The Age of Capital* (New York: Random House, 1975).

Capitalism's Deadly Labor Process 37

3 Immanuel Wallerstein, *World-Systems Analysis* (Durham, NC: Duke University Press, 2004), 65.
4 Richard Hofstadter, *The American Political Tradition* (New York: Knopf, 1948).
5 Achille Mbembe, "Necropolitics," *Public Culture* 15, no. 1 (2003): 14. Quote following is on page 19.
6 Things being what they are, as well they should be, one cannot mention Althusser's name without a remark on the fact that in 1980 he strangled his wife Hélène Rytman, a sociologist. Some consider this bare fact sufficient to denounce him as misogynistic and to scrub his writings for the canon. (How this might be done is itself an interesting question.) On the other hand, Althusser suffered bouts of mental illness throughout his life. After the murder, French courts declined to prosecute, instead committing him to a psychiatric hospital for three years. His intellectual career was at an end.
7 Louis Althusser, "On the Young Marx: Theoretical Questions [1961]," *For Marx* (New York: Vintage/Random House, 1970), 49–86.
8 *Ibid.*, 83–84.
9 Alvin W. Gouldner, *The Two Marxisms: Contradictions and Anomalies in the Development of a Theory* (New York: The Seabury Press, 1980).
10 *Ibid.*, 32.
11 Charles Lemert (with Paul Piccone), "Cruelty and Murder in the Academy: Alvin W. Gouldner and Post-Marxist Critical Theory," in *The Structural Lie: Small Clues to Global Things*, ed. Charles Lemert (New York: Routledge/Paradigm, 2011), 49–75.
12 Louis Althusser, *Lenin and Philosophy* (New York: Monthly Review Press, 1971); in particular the brilliant and structuralist "Ideology and Ideological State Apparatus: Notes towards an Investigation."
13 Alvin W. Gouldner, *For Sociology: Renewal and Critique in Sociology Today* (New York: Basic Books, 1973).
14 Alvin W. Gouldner, *The Coming Crisis of Western Sociology* (New York: Basic Books, 1970), 157–159; Chapter 12.
15 Gouldner, *Two Marxisms*, 34.
16 Eric Hobsbawm, *The Age of Extremes: A History of the World, 194–1991* (New York: Random House, 1994).
17 Charles Lemert, "Changing Global Structures in the Short Twentieth Century, 1914–1991," in *Globalization: An Introduction to the End of the Known World* (New York: Routledge/Paradigm, 2015), 93–121.
18 Frederick Winslow Taylor, *The Principles of Scientific Management* (New York: Harper and Brothers, 1911).
19 Mbembe, "Necropolitics," 11–40. Compare Giorgio Abamben, *Homo Sacer: Sovereign Power and Bare Life* (Palo Alto, CA: Stanford University Press, 1998).
20 Abdou Maliq Simone, *For the City Yet to Come: Urban Life in Four African Cities* (Durham, NC: Duke University Press, 2004); and *City Life from Jakarta to Dakar: Movements at the Crossroads* (London and New York: Routledge, 2010); on Atzlán, Gloria Anzaldúa, *Borderlands/La Frontera: The New Mestiza* (San Francisco: Spinsters/Aunt Lute, 1987); on Kinshasa, Adam Hochschild, *King Leopold's Ghost: A Story of Greed, Terror, and Heroism in Colonial Africa* (New York: Mariner/Houghton-Mifflin, 1998).
21 Karl Marx, "Wages of Labour," in *The Economic and Philosophical Manuscripts of 1844* (Moscow: Progress Press, 1959), 26; emphasis added.
22 Karl Marx, "Estranged Labour," *The Economic and Philosophical Manuscripts of 1844* (Moscow: Progress Press, 1959), 61–62.
23 I always dreamed of working with my hands.
24 Louis Althusser, "Ideology and the Ideological State Apparatus," in *Lenin and Philosophy and Other Essays* (Monthly Review Press 1971 [1969]), 171.
25 Alvin W. Gouldner, *The Future of Intellectuals and the Rise of the New Class* (New York: The Seabury Press, 1979). See also Gouldner's *The Dialectic of Ideology and Technology: The Origins, Grammar, and Future of Ideology* (New York: The Seabury Press, 1976).

38   *The Confusion of Capitalist Structures*

26 Harriet H. Robinson, "Early Factory Labor in New England," *Arthur and Elizabeth Schlesinger Library on the History of Women in America, Radcliffe Institute for Advanced Study, Harvard University* (archived MS of original, 1883).

27 Friedrich Engels, *The Conditions of the Working Class in England* (Moscow: Foreign Languages Publishing House, 1962 [1845]).

28 Sven Beckert, *Empire of Cotton: A Global History* (New York: Knopf, 2015).

29 Like Althusser, Schmitt is commonly nominated for exclusion from the canon of political thought. In his case, the sin is more blatant that Althusser's insanity. He was a Nazi, which of course qualified him, for better or worse, as a student of necropolitics.

30 Mbembe, "Necropolitics."

31 *Ibid.*, 14.

32 *Ibid.*, 19–20.

33 Marx, "Estranged Labour," 68–69.

34 Marx, "The Buying and Selling of Labour-Power," in *Capital: A Critique of Political Economy, Volume I* (New York: International Publishers, 1967), 167.

35 Mbembe, "Necropolitics," 40.

36 Marx, *Capital I*, 176.

37 René Girard, *Things Since the Foundation of the World* (Palo Alto, CA: Stanford University Press, 1987).

Part II

Macro-Historical Theories of Capitalism

In order to better describe and theorize capitalism, many theorists have returned to the origins of the system to better understand what makes capitalism unique from previous ways of structuring a global political economy. In investigating the systemic origins of capitalism as a historical system, many debates and cleavages emerge. While the most dogmatic of Brennerite Marxists, for example, see capitalism as a system that emerged in one county of England during the British Industrial Revolution, Wallersteinian World-Systems Analysts alternately see capitalism as emerging in the Dutch Republic as the result of the interaction of several world regions. The California School of Economic History contends that capitalism resulted from European responses to the decline of Asian Empires, while Andre Gunder Frank, perhaps uniquely, contends that the emergence of capitalism was a fully global process involving all world regions—Asia, Africa, Europe, and the Americas.

In this section of the book, we look to macro-historical theories of capitalism that go back to its systemic origins to interrogate what is unique about capitalism as a historical system. We draw on some of the existing schools of thought such as classical political economy of David Ricardo and classical Marxist political economy of Friederich Engels and Nikolai Kondratieff, and World-Systems approaches of Immanuel Wallerstein, Fernand Braudel, Andre Gunder Frank, Giovanni Arrighi, and Janet Abu Lughod, and Brennerite Marxists, Robert Brenner and Ellen Meiskins Wood. We also include theorists who elude strict categorization into existing camps such as Frantz Fanon, Silvia Federici, Antonio Gramsci, Henri Pirenne, Oliver C. Cox, and Ibn Khaldun.

Fanon and Wallerstein both innovated global theories of capitalist political economy while grappling with the unique challenges capitalism poses to the racialized Global South. Braudel and Frank both interrogated just how global, global capitalism was from its origins. Abu Lughod and David Ricardo examined the role of states that serve as middlemen in long-distance trade and its relationship to the transition to capitalism. Engels and Federici center on the way capitalism relies on the oppression and exploitation of women in order to generate "hidden" sources of surplus value. Gramsci and

DOI: 10.4324/9781003198291-4

Arrighi focus on the role of the state in the historical development of capitalism specifically attuned to openings that may allow for a radical shift in power relations. Cox and Pirenne draw our attention to the role of the global city in processes of capital accumulation and the historical development of capitalism. Kondratieff and Khaldun both challenge a linear conception of historical development in their respective theories of historical cycles.

While each of these theorists provides different descriptions of and perspectives on the origins of capitalism as a historic system, this section examines how through a better description of capitalism's origins and long history, we can better theorize just what makes capitalism different from previous systemic logics of organizing capitalist political economy.

3 The Modern World and Capitalism 1500–1991

Frantz Fanon/Immanuel Wallerstein

Frantz Fanon (1925–1961) was born in Fort-de-France, Martinique, when it was a French colony. In Martinique, he went to school at the French *Lycée Schoelcher*, where he was taught by Aimée Césaire, whose *Discourse on Colonialism* (1950) was a manifesto of decolonizing politics. In 1943, at 18 years, Fanon fled the Vichy-controlled Martinique to join the Free French forces in the war against Nazi Germany. After the War, in 1946, France's General Assembly voted to decolonize his native land, making Martinique an overseas Department. Fanon was, in due course, both a West Indian of the Windward Antilles and a French citizen.

After World War II he returned to Martinique where he completed his baccalaureate, and for a while worked for and with Césaire in politics. Then, he returned to France for graduate studies in medicine at the University of Lyon, where he also trained in psychiatry. At Lyon, he also seriously studied literature and philosophy. These studies contributed to a doctoral thesis, which was rejected. The thesis was nonetheless published soon after as *Black Skin, White Masks*. On completing a psychiatry residency in 1951, he practiced for two years in France before accepting a position as chief of psychiatry at the Blida-Joinville Hospital outside Algiers, where he served from 1953 to 1956. There, according to legend, he cared for the white colonizers during the day and colonized patients at night. The psychiatric unit of this hospital is today known as the *Hôpital psychiatrique Frantz-Fanon Bilda*, a tribute to his heroic work between two worlds. Though Fanon lived in two worlds at this time, his primary sense of himself was as a subject of France's colonial empire. Thus it was that Fanon—like other elite colonized subalterns who passed a good portion of their lives in the white European nation of their subjugation—held fast to a strong sense of his identity as the colonized black man.

But just as much, his name on the Bilda hospital conveys the degree to which Fanon was, after 1954, among the leaders of Algeria's liberation movement. In 1956, he became editor of the movement's newspaper *El Moudjahid*, which, not incidentally, was published in Tunisia the year Tunisia had won its independence from France. Algeria would not win its war of liberation from France until 1962, the year after Fanon's death. In 1960, the Provisional Government of Algeria's National Liberation Front had appointed him its

DOI: 10.4324/9781003198291-5

42   *Macro-Historical Theories of Capitalism*

ambassador to Ghana. It was here that he met Immanuel Wallerstein, who may have been the only white friend to visit Fanon in the National Institutes of Health Hospital in Bethesda, Maryland, where he was being treated for the leukemia that killed him on December 6, 1961.

In Fanon's short life of but 36 years, he had become a global figure—as much for his work in Africa's decolonizing movements as for his now classical critical theories of the violence of white colonizing. His psychiatric experience in Algeria shaped his important theory of just how the global politics of domination intruded upon the consciousness of blacks who suffered under colonization. In his lifetime, Fanon's theories were respected by intellectuals of whom none more prominent in the day than Jean-Paul Sartre, who wrote a famous but seldom read preface to *The Wretched of the Earth* (1961). This last book appeared just as Fanon was dying of cancer. But 1961 was also the beginning of revolutionary times as much in the first world as the third (to use the distinctions then common). After 1965, political figures in the colonial world drew upon Fanon's radical ideas, among them Steve Biko in South Africa and Ernesto Che Guevara in Cuba—martyrs to their versions of decolonizing politics. Then, too, in the world of Black Power politics, Stokely Carmichael and the Student Nonviolent Coordinating Committee in the United States abandoned the nonviolent, integrationist principle after 1967. The year before, Bobby Seale and Huey Newton had founded the American Black Panther Party that, along with the Nation of Islam, was aggressive in defending the internally colonized in the first world. Some, like Stokely Carmichael, migrated to Africa where he assumed the name Kwame Ture after the Ghanaian president Kwame Nkrumah. Fanon's influence was at least Pan-African, but also global—as much in the Euro-American core as in the decolonizing nations in the periphery. Then, of course, there was Malcolm X in the United States who, notwithstanding his distinctive path to a radical decolonizing politics, was in effect a first-world martyr due to his deviation from his third-world Islamic culture. At the extreme, one could even mention Muhammad Ali as a gentle voice in the same cultural movement.

Still, keeping in mind his global political importance, Fanon was first and, in a sense, foremost the physician—a psychiatrist who began his first book *Black Skin, White Masks* with a stark diagnosis of the situation of the colonized black:

> There is a zone of nonbeing, an extraordinarily sterile and arid region, an utterly naked declivity where an authentic upheaval can be born. In most cases, the black man lacks the advantage of being able to accomplish this descent into a real hell. ... Man is not merely a possibility of recapture or of negation. If it is true that consciousness is a process of transcendence, we have to see too that this transcendence is haunted by the problems of love and understanding. Man is a yes that vibrates to cosmic harmonies. ...The black is a black man; that is, as the result of a

series of aberrations of affect, he is rooted at the core of a universe from which he must be extricated.

These are among Fanon's first published words shortly after completing his medical studies and just before he began his practice at the hospital in Blida, Algeria, where he cared for the mental health of the white colonizers and the black colonized.

It is often said that Fanon was a psychoanalyst. If he was, he was not a professional psychoanalyst, strictly speaking. Even in his day—a day when Jacques Lacan dominated the field in France—psychoanalytic training required a number of years, of which there were none available to Fanon between his medical training and his hospital work. Even so, in a deeper sense, Fanon was more truly a psychoanalyst than those who limit their therapeutic work to the psychology of individual patients. Fanon was, it is fair to say, an analyst who treated the human psyche as formed by the panoply of social forces—not at all limited to classical psychoanalyst's notorious "family romance" of the immediate childhood family.

Thus the salience of his opening salvo in *Black Skin, White Masks*. The colonized black suffers a "series of aberrations of affect" because his personal experience "is rooted at the core of a universe from which he must be extricated"—the universe of a globally colonized world. In this, Fanon's analysis of the universal circumstance of the colonized black man is a question already answered by the Négritude movement since the 1930s. The movement's best-known figures were Aimé Césaire, Fanon's teacher in Martinique; Léopold Sédar Senghor, the poet and first President of Senegal; and Léon Damas, also a poet, from French Guiana—all of whom with many others (including Langston Hughes and Jean Paul Sartre) figure prominently in *Black Skin, White Masks*. The Négritude leaders and their affines were all poets and all politically engaged, with a healthy degree of Marxist ideas and commitments. Fanon was no exception. His first book is both personal and poetic in his lament on his own blackness:

> I feel in myself a soul as immense as the world, truly a soul as deep as the deepest of rivers, my chest has the power to expand without limit. I am a master and I am advised to adopt the humility of the cripple. Yesterday, awakening to the world, I saw the sky turn upon itself utterly and wholly. I wanted to rise, but the disemboweled silence fell back upon me, its wings paralyzed. Without responsibility, straddling Nothingness and Infinity, I began to weep.[1]

If this sounds all too poetic, one should not be fooled.

In *Black Skin, White Masks* Fanon redirected his trajectory. His ultimate political position was not to be fully formed until well after 1954, when he became active in Algeria's National Liberation Front. In his first book, Fanon was still very much the psychiatrist—a psychiatrist living between

44 Macro-Historical Theories of Capitalism

two worlds, but with primary clinical and analytic attention to the colonized black person who lives with their black skin by unconsciously hiding behind a white mask as though it were all that they could be. This is why the book is mostly a staking out of Fanon's distinctive analytic position against traditional psychoanalysis. Key chapters on such topics as "The Negro and Psychopathology" use the language of clinical psychology to diagnose the psychology of the colonized black as, in effect, inevitably pathological because he lives in a structurally negative culture. "A normal Negro child, having grown up within a normal family, will become abnormal on the slightest contact with the white world."[2] He explains:

> One can hear the glib remark: The Negro makes himself inferior. But the truth is that he is made inferior. The young Antillean is a Frenchman called upon constantly to live with white compatriots. Now, the Antillean family has for all practical purposes no connection with the national—that is, the French, or European—structure. The Antillean has therefore to choose between his family and European society; in other words, the individual who climbs up into society—white and civilized—tends to reject his family—black and savage—on the plane of imagination ...

Psychopathology is itself normal for the black colonial subject. Fanon's stark conclusion is argued in reference to the then current psychoanalytic and philosophical literature in France. But the references, while respectful, turn on his analysis of the colonial situation. It is in this that Fanon's psychoanalysis becomes a social analysis of the world order.

In *Black Skin, White Masks*, one encounters the early expression of Fanon's social and cultural psychoanalysis in a still developing négritude politics:

> In this connection, I should like to say something that I have found in many other writers: Intellectual alienation is a creation of middle-class society. What I call middle-class society is any society that becomes rigidified in predetermined forms, forbidding all evolution, all gains, all progress, all discovery. I call middle-class a closed society in which life has no taste, in which the air is tainted, in which ideas and men are corrupt. And I think that a man who takes a stand against this death is in a sense a revolutionary.[3]

The first book ends thereby with this foreshadowing of a radical politics to come.

The Wretched of the Earth, his last book, was written when Fanon's political life was in full force. Here, the themes evident in his first book are now subsumed to an explicit and theoretically mature social theory of decolonization. The book begins with "On Violence":

> ... Decolonization is always a violent phenomenon. At whatever level we study it—relationships between individuals, new names for sports

The Modern World and Capitalism   45

clubs, the human admixture at cocktail parties, in the police, on the directing boards of national or private banks—decolonization is quite simply the replacing of a certain "species" of men by another "species" of men. Without any period of transition, there is a total, complete, and absolute substitution. ...To tell the truth, the proof of success lies in a whole social structure being changed from the bottom up. The extraordinary importance of this change is that it is willed, called for, demanded.[4]

Here, in the last line, is where Fanon takes a giant step beyond the more poetic négritude politics of others before him. Césaire had held a strong theory of the necessary violence of the colonial world that required violence to break it apart, but he did not come quite so direct to a call for a revolution willed and demanded—hence inclined toward violence. Fanon, however, was outspoken in respect to violence:

When the colonialists, who had tasted the sweets of their victory over these assimilated people, realize that these men whom they considered as saved souls are beginning to fall back into the ways of niggers, the whole system totters. Every native won over, every native who had taken the pledge not only marks a failure for the colonial structure when he decides to lose himself and to go back to his own side, but also stands as a symbol for the uselessness and the shallowness of all the work that has been accomplished. Each native who goes back over the line is a radical condemnation of the methods and of the regime...[5]

This is Fanon in the coda to "On Violence" in which he raises the ante from the violence in and of the colonized world to become globally structured violence at the core of the modern international world. True, he is not calling for violent revolution in so many words. But it is also true that when the violence of the colonial world is reframed as inherent to international politics and culture, the violence at hand becomes, by its global ubiquity, necessary and inherent in the order of things:

We should flatly refuse the situation to which the Western countries wish to condemn us. Colonialism and imperialism have not paid their score when they withdraw their flags and their police forces from our territories. For centuries the capitalists have behaved in the underdeveloped world like nothing more than war criminals. Deportations, massacres, forced labor, and slavery have been the main methods used by capitalism to increase its wealth, its gold or diamond reserves, and to establish its power.[6]

What Fanon wrote must be interpreted in respect to what he did. He was an active revolutionary after 1954 until his death. He put himself at personal risk, enough to live and work in exile in Tunisia. His life's work was not

46 *Macro-Historical Theories of Capitalism*

so much his writings, as enduringly important as they are, as his political work in attacking the colonial world in Algeria and by extension around the world.

Fanon's *A Dying Colonialism* (1959) was his history of the National Liberation Front and its contribution to the decolonizing of Algeria. It began: "Revolution is mankind's way of life today. This is the age of revolution; the 'age of indifference' is gone forever." Though the book is about Algeria, the statement is about the world as such. The world in question is the modern world of capitalism—a world that began not with the steam engine, but with European voyages across the North Atlantic early in the 16th century—that soon enough created the middle passage of slave trading and of the colonial world upon which capitalism depends even now, for cheap labor and extractable resources. In this, Fanon goes where even Marx could not and would not go—a theory of capitalism as violence that invites a violent reaction.

The very title *The Wretched of the Earth* expresses the path Fanon followed in his short life—from physician to political provocateur to theorist of the global structures that relied upon and created the wretched conditions in the colonial world. Yet, as singular as was his contribution to a global theory, it would remain for others to complete that theory as a theory of the capital world-system. Chief among those who would do just that was the sociologist he met in Ghana, when both were young men, Immanuel Wallerstein.

Immanuel Wallerstein (1930–2019) was born and educated in New York City. He received a BA in 1951, an MA in 1954, and a PhD in sociology in 1959, all from Columbia University, at a time when its sociology department was widely considered one of the best in the nation, maybe even in the world. Columbia's department was very much a mainstream sociology program led by figures such as Robert K. Merton and Paul Lazarsfeld. Yet Wallerstein, destined to become every bit their equal, kept his distance from the mainstream. By his own account, he "first became interested in world affairs as a teenager in New York City, and was particularly interested in the anti-colonial movement in India at the time."[7] His family was politically attuned to the events of the day, both those associated with the Nazis and World War II generally and those entangled in the various factions of left-Marxist politics in New York City. He was thus not only interested in world affairs but in global as well as American politics. Unlike Fanon, Wallerstein did not leave the intellectual life for active political work. Still, politics plays a part in nearly everything Wallerstein does. In May 1968, during the student takeover of administration offices in the now famous Columbia Crisis, he was chief among a small band of faculty who interpreted the students demands to the tone-deaf Columbia University administrators.[8] Over the years since, he was engaged in, among other commitments, the World Social Forum since its founding in Porto Alegre in 2002 and had visited Subcomandante Marcos, leader of the Zapatista Army of National Liberation, at this mountain headquarters in Chiapas. Then, too, to this day Wallerstein writes a bimonthly series of commentaries on geopolitical

The Modern World and Capitalism   47

events, each informed by a lifetime of scholarly and intellectual work, but also each an implicit call for critical understanding and political action.[9]

After an initial intellectual interest in India, early in his doctoral studies at Columbia, Wallerstein received a Ford Foundation grant to support research trips to Africa. Over the years, he visited nearly all the nations of that continent. That first visit was surely a key turning point in his thinking on the way to developing his program of World-Systems Analysis—a scrupulously documented four-volume argument that, since it first appeared in 1974, has become the most influential systematic but critical analysis of the history of the capitalist world-system. This thoroughly academic work of scholarship grew up over four decades preoccupied with the global spread of Western capitalism from the Iberian colonizing penetrations of the then virginal new world around 1500 to the time the capitalist world economy's uncertainty after 1990. But like Fanon, Wallerstein's view of modern Euro-American capitalism grew from roots laid in his own early experiences in Africa. "If my intellectual quest led me early on away from the familiar grounds of my own country to that of contemporary Africa, which was still a colonized continent when I first visited it and began to study it, it was because I had the gut feeling in the 1950s that the most important thing that was happening in the twentieth-century world was the struggle to overcome the control by the Western world of the rest of the world."[10]

Thus it was that Wallerstein met Fanon in Accra in the summer of 1960. He was just beginning his long productive life. Fanon was near the end of his short but, in its way, just as productive a life. Fanon was one of the three most indelible influences on Wallerstein's modern world-systems research program. The other two were Fernand Braudel, the French social historian, and Ilya Prigogine, the Nobel Prize-recognized chemist. The three influenced Wallerstein at different but crucial times as he developed his extensive study of the capitalist world-system. Fanon, of course, came first. He was, to be sure, instrumental in Wallerstein seeing Africa (at least initially) as the global periphery exploited by the capitalist core and its allies in the world economy. But also Fanon was an exemplar of the power of political commitment that underlay the world-systems project, not to mention Wallerstein's refusal to call the project a theory:

> Rereading Fanon in the light of revolutionary movements in the twentieth century should lead us *away from* polemics into a closer analysis of the realities of class structures. ... He pushed us to look for who would take what risks and then asked us to build a movement out of such a revolutionary class. Have the history of the years since he wrote disproved this instinct? I fail to see how and where.

This is Wallerstein writing in 1979 well after what he called the world revolution of 1968 and nearly two decades after he met the revolutionary Fanon in Ghana.[11]

48   *Macro-Historical Theories of Capitalism*

The influence of Braudel is apparent as early as 1974 in *The Modern World-System, Vol I: Capitalism Agriculture and the Origins of the European World-Economy in the Sixteenth Century.* "Braudel more than any one else made me conscious of the central importance of the social construction of time and space, and its impact on our analyses."[12] He initially took from Braudel the concepts of a world economy and especially that of *la longue durée*, which was the first hint of the importance of TimeSpace in his thinking. After 1974, Braudel was so impressed by *The Modern World-System, Vol I* that they taught a seminar in Paris. Then began a continuous relationship until Braudel's death in 1985. Since then, with rare exception, Wallerstein visited Paris in the winter months and notably named his research center at the University of Binghamton after Braudel.

It was Ilya Prigogine who provided Wallerstein the theoretical interstices to Braudel's scheme. In *The End of Certainty: Time, Chaos, and the New Laws of Nature* (1996), among other writings, Prigogine provided the idea that led Wallerstein, somewhat later in his thinking, to sharpen his use of Braudel's concepts of time. In particular, Prigogine's general attitude toward the physical sciences entailed the clarifying concept of chaos as the necessary correlate to scientific determination. Wallerstein makes it clear that Prigogine's notion of uncertainty is already present in Braudel's tripartite theory of time in which events and even structures which may appear to the naive observer as fixed in time become chaotic when they are seen as vulnerable to the intervention of conjunctures arising in the systemic space between the long enduring and the particular event.[13]

Then, too, it is important to realize that no analytic system so many years in the making and of such a (literally) global range could derive from as few as three influences. Wallerstein's *World-Systems Analysis: An Introduction* (2004) is the best resource for an appreciation of the several among many connections in Wallerstein's critical method, including the role of Karl Polanyi in relation to Braudel's idea of the world economy, Andre Gunder Frank as the source of world system*s* (plural), and of course of his response to the many Marxist critiques of world-systems analysis.[14] The enormity of the project being granted, its nuances must be taken into account, even in respect to the three pivotal influences that are not easily reconciled by who wish to follow the threat of Wallerstein's critical attitude toward the capitalist world economy. In particular, while the importance of Braudel's *la longue durée* to Wallerstein's analytic attitude toward modern capitalism is easy to see, the necessarily abstract theories of Prigogine may seem far removed from Fanon's revolutionary politics.

Yet, the thread is there to be followed. All too simply put, *Fanon* was basic to what came to be the global periphery from which capitalism extracts its supplies of cheap labor power and natural resources necessary to its productive process by which surplus value is accumulated. Braudel was crucial to Wallerstein's central analytic reference that capitalism works within

The Modern World and Capitalism   49

particular nation-states, including the historical series of core states, beginning with Iberia in the 16th century, but is always and necessarily a world economy. Then, it was Prigogine who provided the principles of uncertainty and chaos as just as important to historical as natural systems. Hence the literary logic of Wallerstein's (to date) four volumes of critical social history of the capitalist world-system: (1) *Capitalist Agriculture and the Origins of the European World-Economy in the Sixteenth Century*; (2) *Mercantilism and the Consolidation of the European World-Economy, 1600–1750*; (3) *The Second Great Expansion of the Capitalism World-Economy, 1730s–1840s*; (4) *Centrist Liberalism Triumphant, 1789–1914*; two additional volumes are projected ("if I can last it out," as he puts it[15]): (5) 1873–1968/1989 on blossoming and bust of the capitalist system; (6) 1945/1968–2050 on the structural crisis of the capitalist world economy. That anyone already in his 80s (already in 2011) would project these last two of six volumes is a tribute both to the genius of the work and to its logic.

Genius is what genius does, but it is the logic that is important. Whether anyone could in a lifetime do all this is one thing. That it could be imagined is another and this is what counts. Though Marx, in a fashion, attempted something similar, only *Capital I* in 1867 was a more-or-less polished book. And what Marx aimed to do was to generate a theory of capitalism. Wallerstein, always dismissive to theory as such, has produced a critical historical description of actual capitalisms from the transition out of agricultural beginnings in the 16th century to the crisis and uncertainty of the capitalist world economy after 1968–1989. In this last mentioned aspect is where Prigogine's influence again comes into play. In 2004, he wrote:

> The modern world-system in which we are living, which is that of a capitalist world-economy, is currently in precisely such a crisis, and has been for quite a while. … One plausible moment at which to start the story of this contemporary systemic crisis is the world revolution of 1968, which unsettled the structures of the world-system considerably. This world revolution marked the end of a long period of liberal supremacy, thereby dislocating the geoculture that had kept the political institutions of the world-system intact.[16]

He is quick to add that 1968 was at best on the beginning of the crisis, a prelude of sorts to the end of the Cold War in 1989 and collapse of the liberal world culture. But which liberalism?

When it comes to liberalism, Wallerstein is not playing with double entendres. He means rather the geo-culture that emerged after the world revolution of 1848 when both radicalism and conservatism (symbolized all-too-neatly by the extremes in France after 1789) were replaced by a global culture in the Euro-American core states. In effect, this was the beginning of formally democratic, vaguely open civil societies, and qualified

50   *Macro-Historical Theories of Capitalism*

assurances of citizenship rights; in other words, the rationally organized modern nation-states that served the purposes of the capitalist world economy. The world revolution of 1968 began the erosion of naive confidence in such a system, an erosion encouraged by the decolonizing movements of the late 1950s (Cuba and Tunisia for example) and early 1960s (Algeria, most of Africa, the Caribbean); in other words, movements inspired by Fanon, among others, in the négritude movement.

Wallerstein has written extensively on the period from 1945 to 1990—from the rise of the American hegemony after World War II to the stagnation in economic growth associated with the end of the Cold War and the ironic decline of American power.[17] These writings, in effect, cover—however episodically—the periods meant to be discussed systematically in the proposed volumes 5 and 6 of *The Modern World-System* series. Historically, the argument on the period between 1945 and 1990 is fourfold.[18] The United States was the core state in world-system, with Japan and Europe as its alliance of semi-peripheral states. The Cold War was a "formal conflict, in which the U.S.S.R acted as a semi-imperialist agent of the United States." The third world seized on the conflict to assert its right to self-determination and national development. But the 1970s and 1980s was "a period of global economic stagnation," during which the United States fell into decline in part because of the third world's disillusionment in the global capitalism's fatuous promises of progress. The crisis after 1990 is where Wallerstein relies, in particular, on Prigogine to describe (and predict) a bifurcation in the world-system, the surfacing of the chaos what lay below the surface all along, and a long crisis in the capitalist system, perhaps extending even to mid-21st century. Whether capitalism as we knew it can or will prevail is far from certain. But Wallerstein does believe that some version of a world-system will reassert itself. Here, we are dealing with social science fiction, but precisely the kind of fiction good social historical thinking ought to provide. Its genius, if that is what it turns out to be, is that it is fiction based on an empirical history of the capitalist world-system since the 16th century.

Thus, the conclusive purpose of Wallerstein's project is to assert the Braudelian fact that capitalism was *a* world-system among others actual and possible. If capitalism is (or even can be conceived as being) historically bound—*a* world economy, not *the* world economy—then we have a macro-scope with which to view present times, and especially those most acute after 2016 or so. The crisis of our times is more than simply the rise of authoritarian politics based on the racist hatred of immigrant populations. It is (or, perhaps we must say, it may be) due to the utter collapse of the liberal democratic culture that was (and may be no more) the culture that sustained at once the illusion of free enterprise capitalism and of democratic freedoms themselves. World-systems are cultures, politics, and economies all at once; hence, the abiding uncertain future of capitalism itself.

Notes

1 Frantz Fanon, *Black Skin, White Masks*, trans. Charles Lam Markmann (New York: Grove Press, 1952 [1967]), 108.
2 *Ibid.*, 111. Quote following, 115.
3 *Ibid.*, 175.
4 Frantz Fanon, *The Wretched of the Earth*, trans. Constance Farrington (New York: Grove Weidenfeld, 1961, [1963]), 34.
5 *Ibid.*, 220–221.
6 *Ibid.*, 101.
7 Immanuel Wallerstein, Accessed November 25, 2020, https://www.iwallerstein.com. But see also, for details, Immanuel Wallerstein, "Introduction," in *The Essential Wallerstein* (The New Press, 2000), xv–xxii.
8 "Faculty Committee Submits Proposals," *Columbia Daily Spectator* (Sunday, April 28, 1968), 1.
9 The Commentaries appear on his website: https://www.iwallerstein.com.
10 Wallerstein, "Introduction," *Essential Wallerstein*, xvi–xvii.
11 Wallerstein, "Fanon and the Revolutionary Class," *Essential Wallerstein,* 31.
12 Wallerstein, "The Development of an Intellectual Position," https://www.iwallerstein.com.
13 Immanuel Wallerstein, "Time and Duration," in *Uncertainties of Knowledge* (Philadelphia: Temple University Press, 2004), 71–82.
14 See especially in Immanuel Wallerstein, "Historical Origins" (Chapter 1) and "Capitalist World-Economy," (Chapter 2) in *World Systems Analysis: An Introduction* (Durham: Duke University Press, 2004).
15 Immanuel Wallerstein, *The Modern World System IV: Centrist Liberalism Triumphant* (Berkeley: University of California Press, 2011), xvii.
16 Wallerstein, *World-Systems Analysis*, 77.
17 Immanuel Wallerstein, *Geopolitics and Geoculture: Essays on the Changing World-system* (Cambridge University Press, 1991); *The End of the World As We Know It: Social Science in the Twenty-first Century*, (University of Minnesota Press, 1999); *The Decline of American Power* (The New Press, 2003).
18 Immanuel Wallerstein, "Cold War and the Third World: The Good Old Days?" in *After Liberalism* (The New Press, 1995), 10–11.

4 The Modern World-System: Europe or Asia?

Fernand Braudel/Andre Gunder Frank

Fernand Braudel (1902–1985) was born in Luméville-en-Ornois, Gondrecourt-le-Château, France, peasant stock of which he remained proud. He often, at various times, dreamt of the landscape of his native Lorraine. Still, Alexander Lee observes, "the countryside of Eastern France was 'full of military recollections', his imagination was fired by battles and wars more than anything else ..." As things turned out, war was to be an important real-life experience in his early adult life.

Braudel's studies in history began at the Sorbonne in 1920, culminating some years later with the prized *agrégé*. He was still quite young, which may partly explain why his early writings were shockingly positivist, even drab. Braudel's historical mind began to change in 1923 when he began his teaching career in Algeria. There he met the Belgian medieval historian Henri Pirenne whose work was both structural and more material than the prevailing positivism in France. Then, too, the alluring landscapes of North Africa on which early modern economic trading and cross-cultural conflict between Ottoman and Christian cultures reinvigorated Braudel's earlier attachment to the French countryside while inducing him toward a broader view of history than the one Pirenne had inspired. Later he would teach at the University of São Paulo. On board ship returning to Paris from Brazil he met Lucien Febvre, a cofounder with Marc Bloch of the *Annales* school of historical research. They became close friends. Braudel would become the leader of the second generation of *Annales* historians. The influences of mentors and of the local histories of Algeria and Brazil fixed Braudel's interest on the Mediterranean region and the early modern Iberian dominance of the Atlantic trade routes and colonial settlements in the Americas. In 1942, back in France, war would again affect Braudel's life. He was arrested by the Nazi occupiers and imprisoned until the War's end in 1945. In those long years, Braudel famously drafted the notes that would become his first and greatest book, *The Mediterranean and the Mediterranean World in the Age of Philip II*,[1] published in 1949. This massive, two-volume book was the groundwork of the historical theories that caused many in his day, as in ours, to consider him the most important historian of the 20th century, perhaps of the modern era.

The Mediterranean is an enduring contribution for at least the following reasons. First, it begins with the role of the environment even before

DOI: 10.4324/9781003198291-6

The Modern World-System: Europe or Asia?   53

describing the region's historical map. Here is Braudel's first deployment of his theory of *la longue durée*—of long enduring historical time rooted in geological and climatic structures against which, in his words, is situated "[t]he Mediterranean as a Human Unit: Communications and Cities." Hence, *The Mediterranean*'s second major contribution is the displacing of *event history* with its disposition toward a positivistic recital of the facts of political and cultural events as the units of a linear history. Instead of a history of battles and thrones, the book turns in Part Two of its first volume to demographical and economic factors. Then follows the third structural feature of the book—its introduction of *conjunctural history*. "There is no single conjuncture: we must visualize a series of overlapping histories developing simultaneously."[2] The three together comprise the decisive displacement of event history in favor of a strong structural idea notion of "overlapping" histories that transpire in long, enduring geographies, whereupon "the rhythms of material life and other diverse fluctuations of human existence" come into conflict with one another to create the setting wherein the events, politics, and people of a given time and space like the Mediterranean come to pass. Then and only then comes the "story" (if the word applies) of *The Mediterranean World in the Age of Philip II* of Spain and Portugal in the middle decades of the 1550s when Iberia became the dominant force in the Atlantic world. Braudel all but apologizes for the final major section of the book. "It is only after much hesitation that I decided to publish this third section, describing events in the Mediterranean during the fifty years of our study." He wants to keep his distance from event history; yet, the events in the Age of Phillip II are necessary to the story—war, secularization, defeat, and decline. Braudel so wanted to avoid dramatizing major events that the reader must look hard even for a mention of the defeat of the Spanish Armada in 1588 that brought Phillip's Age to its end. The collapse of the Iberian hegemony led to the conjuncture of the historical vectors in which North Atlantic capitalism as we know it today came fully into its own.

Among Braudel's other works, *Civilization and Capitalism: 15th–18th Century*[3]—a three-volume series completed at the end of his career—is not as well known. But it should be. Here, his structural approach to history turns primary attention to as the defining global economy of the modern era. Here, too, Braudel ranges comprehensively in his analysis of modernity as a world-ordering structure. The *Civilization and Capitalism: 15th–18th Century* series was, therefore, a systematic study of the world economy as a system comprising three structural vectors: the demographic and economic features of everyday life; the commercial elements of the cities and states of the economic system; and the role of the capitalism that arose in Europe and the history of its domination of the world economy.

The Structures of Everyday Life, the first volume in the *Civilization and Capitalism: 15th–18th Century* trilogy, does not view everyday life as somehow unrelentingly local or as a function of face-to-face interactions. Braudel's *The Structures of Everyday Life* begins with a hearty dose of demographic facts as

54   Macro-Historical Theories of Capitalism

to the shifts in world population, in which the scale of reference is towns, armies, and navies; followed by the 18th century as "a water shed of biological regimes"—which is say famines, epidemics, plagues, diseases. The first chapter in *Structures* ends with a section on "the many against the few" in the decline of barbarian empires and the disappearance of the pre-17th-century nomads, the conquest of spaces, and the emergence of civilizations contesting each other for which he offers the telling statement: "A culture is a civilization that has not achieved maturity, its greatest potential, nor consolidated its growth."[4] The rest of the book covers topics like daily bread, food and drink, houses and clothing, the spread of technology, money, town and cities—all presented in relation to his history of the early modern world. The subtlety of Braudel's scheme is stated in the Conclusion to *Structures*:

> With *economic life*, we shall be moving outside the routine, the unconscious daily round. However, in economic life the regularities will still be with us: an ancient and progressive division of labour led to the necessary separations and encounters which nourished active and conscious everyday economic life with its small profits, its micro-capitalism (whose face was not unacceptable) distinguishable from ordinary work. Higher still, on the top floor, we have placed real capitalism, with its mighty networks, its operations which already seemed diabolical to common mortals. What had this sophisticated level to do with humble lives at the foot of the ladder, the reader might ask. *Everything perhaps for they are drawn into its operations.*[5]

Here, the readers encounter a trace of Marx's top-down structure where the workers suffer from ignorance of the inner workings of capitalism. But in Braudel's formulation, the humble that endure at the bottom of the ladder are well aware of the diabolical nature of capitalism and are critical theorists of their situation because they are drawn consciously into capitalism's operations. Marx's workers were dumb and alienated. Braudel's were alert and engaged.

In *Wheels of Commerce*, the second book in the *Civilization and Capitalism* trilogy, Braudel considers the extent to which capitalism arose out of prior economic and social conditions that made it possible to the end of making capitalism as we know it possible. In his summary of those conditions, he offers: (1) a robust and expanding market economy, (2) a certain kind of society necessary to capitalism even before it came to be, and (3) "the liberating action of world trade."[6] The wheels of trade are presented as a vector that could be said to crosscut the lower and higher aspects of economic life with which he concluded *The Structures of Everyday Life*. In *The Wheels of Commerce* Braudel lends geographical weight to the analysis by pointing out the interconnection between local town markets and what he calls the higher wheels of trade—fairs, warehouses, granaries, stock markets, and crucially, the penetrating effect of global trade markets that began with the Portuguese and

Spanish colonial interests in the age of Phillip II—interests that were, even then, already part of a growing system of global exchange between Europe and the world as a whole. Though Braudel does not press the *wheels* figure of speech, throughout this second volume in the trilogy nearly every major aspect of the new commercial world *the wheels of commerce*—wheels, plural—depict an ever rolling historical process in which local and regional capitalist markets turn more and more toward the global markets that, in turn, roll in a necessarily close relation to the more local markets. The dynamic factor energizing the wheels of economic history is of course *capital*.

For many, especially social theorists, the most interesting and compelling feature of *Wheels* is Chapter 5 in which Braudel defines the otherwise impossible-to-define concept of "society [a] ... 'a set of sets', the sum of all the things that historians encounter in the various branches of our research."[7] This notion serves two important purposes. The first is to propose a way to account for all of the many and different aspects of collective life that cannot be reduced to any aspect so readily observed as the economy. The second, his idea of society serves to locate social hierarchies as a ubiquitous and seemingly necessary structural feature of the mass of collective activities and institutions that gather together around and inside the economy and the polity; hence, his important historical observation: "Societies in our own time, whatever their political system, are hardly any more egalitarian than those in the past."[8] The structural inequalities of modern society are conditions required of the "certain kind of society necessary to capitalism."

The Perspective of the World, volume three in the trilogy, is where Braudel carefully presents the key concept *world-economies* that became central to Immanuel Wallerstein's version of world-systems analysis developed in the years he and Braudel worked together in Paris after 1975–1976. In 1974, Wallerstein for his part had finished the first volume of *The Modern World-System* which Braudel read avidly. Then began a collaboration that lasted until Braudel's death in 1985 and, in a sense, continued well after through the Wallerstein's Fernand Braudel Center at the University of Binghamton. Though the influences between the older and the younger man were robustly mutual, Braudel admits that the general theory in *The Perspective of the World*, presents in "general outline" the 1974 *World-System Theory*.[9] *Perspective* is far more than an outline of Wallerstein's first volume, just as Wallerstein's subsequent histories of the modern world-system, while grounded in Braudel's masterwork *The Mediterranean*, covered history after the Iberian hegemony by means of his own emergent analytic scheme.

Braudel begins his third volume in the *Civilization and Capitalism trilogy* with a statement that, in the hands of Andre Gunder Frank, would spark an abiding controversy, namely the distinction between a *world-economy* and *world-economies*. The former, of course, refers simply to the fact that the world at large is contrived around an economic system of one or another kind, while the latter insists that in a given conjuncture there can be several world economies, of which modern capitalism after Phillip II is one. The book's

56   Macro-Historical Theories of Capitalism

many descriptive chapters deal with both concepts, in the sense that the first four chapters deal with aspects of Europe's world economy, after which the long fifth chapter considers the world's world economies that were "for and against Europe" before ending with the soon to be controversial statement: "the Far East [was] the greatest of all the world-economies." Then, the sixth and final chapter on the industrial revolution and economic growth could be seen as a qualification of this statement by its strong conclusion on the early capitalist industrial conjuncture in which "material and living standards" soar to previously unheard-of heights.

What remains is that China's ancient world economy may have been "greatest" by one measure and Europe's greatest by another. Hence, the breach Andre Gunder Frank entered.

Andre Gunder Frank (1929–2005) was born to a Jewish family in Germany on the eve of Adolf Hitler's rise to power. They fled, first to Switzerland, then to the United States in 1941. Frank studied at Swarthmore and the University of Chicago, where in 1957 he earned his PhD in economics. Yet, even after many years of schooling in America, Gunder Frank said on his website: "I received very little education if any and learned nothing of any use in any of the many schools that I attended here and there." At the least, the schooling, such as it was, was sufficient, as, again, he put it: "My Chicago PhD in Economics, with Milton Friedman, finally did me some good in Brazil where it proved to be my union card for an appointment to teach anthropology... [at the University of Brasilia]." Thereafter, Gunder Frank became an academic migrant stopping along the way at universities and institutes first in Mexico, then Montreal, then Chile where he advised Salvador Allende's administration. He fled Chile after the military coup in 1973 for Europe where he found academic homes in Starnberg, Norwich, East Anglia, before settling at the University of Amsterdam until mandatory retirement in 1994. In the remaining years until his death in 2005, Gunder Frank continued to move about the world for positions of various kinds in the United States, Europe, Canada, and China.

Yet, amid all these, perhaps the single most important stopover was in Brazil early in the 1960s where Gunder Frank came to appreciate the importance of dependency theory, in large part because of the Fernando Henrique Cardoso, then a young sociologist and social democrat and future president of Brazil. At the time, Cardoso was writing influentially in the early tradition of world-systems theory begun in 1949 by Raúl Prebisch. Dependency theory is the radical economic theory that turns on its head the liberal, modernization idea that the problem in the poorer regions of the world-system is that they had *failed* to modernize. Dependency theories and policies insisted on good economic grounds that the so-called modern and developed nations, far from being interested in developing the underdeveloped regions, are in fact the chief beneficiaries of capitalism's historical interest in creating poverty in the global economic. Capital-rich, so-called mature nations necessarily gave birth to economically immature, dependent regions from which they extracted, among much else, cheap labor power and valuable mineral resources.

Gunder Frank's influential contribution to dependency theory first appeared in a now classic 1966 article in *Monthly Review*, "The Development of Underdevelopment,"[10] where he said:

> It is generally held that economic development occurs in a succession of capitalist stages and that today's underdeveloped countries are still in a stage, sometimes depicted as an original stage, of history through which the now developed countries passed long ago. Yet even a modest acquaintance with history shows that underdevelopment is not original or traditional and that neither the past nor the present of the underdeveloped countries resembles in any important respect the past of the now developed countries. The now developed countries were never underdeveloped, though they may have been undeveloped.

In 1967, Gunder Frank published *Capitalism and Underdevelopment in Latin America: Historical Studies of Chile and Brazil* that lent empirical and analytic texture to the 1966 article. These and other of his early writings made Gunder Frank famous as an early contributor to the world-systems analysis movement that took shape in the mid-1970s and after.

Yet, in time Gunder Frank veered away from the theories of modern capitalism associated with Braudel and Wallerstein. Late in life, he became the foremost proponent of the idea that the capitalist world-economy was neither the first world-economy nor one that arose entirely from Europe's notion of itself as the center of the modern world-system. Gunder Frank came to be a particularly aggressive opponent of Immanuel Wallerstein's work, as of Fernand Braudel's history of the modern world-economy. In the conclusion to his *ReORIENT: Global Economy in the Asian Age* (1998), Frank said:

> Contrary to the mistaken allegations of Braudel and Wallerstein among so many others, our study also leads to the inevitable conclusion that early modern history was shaped by a long since operational world economy and not just by the expansion of a European world-system.[11]

Yet, the three of them were and will be forever connected in a literary matrix that defines the historical time and space of capitalism as we supposed we knew it. Without making too much of Gunder Frank's pride that his last contrarian book belongs in the company of Braudel and Wallerstein, there is good enough reason to see him as part of a matrix—if not an equilateral triangle—portraying the historical fluctuations in the history of Western capitalism.

Today there are numerous commentaries on the theme of a new silk road turned back toward the East. East and South Asia are widely considered to be the possible, if not entirely probable, economic successor to the West's

58 *Macro-Historical Theories of Capitalism*

economic hegemony. In such a time, Gunder Frank's 1998 book *ReORIENT: Global Economy in the Asia Age* serves as a goad for current discussions of the past and future of East Asia in the global economic system. Was East Asia always there as the *first* world economic system? Or is the possible turn toward an East Asian pole, if not a core, a falling away of the European world-system? Gunder Frank makes his position clear in the conclusion to *ReORIENT*:

> Contrary to the mistaken allegations of Braudel and Wallerstein among so many others, our study also leads to the inevitable conclusion that early modern history was shaped by a long since operational world economy and not just by the expansion of a European world-system.[12]

"So how did the West rise?"[13] Gunder Frank's answer to his own question is threefold. The first and most important answer is that "Europeans obtained money from the gold and silver mines they found in the Americas." The second is that they "made more money" off the backs of indigenous people in the Americas. The third answer is that "Europeans also used both American silver money and their own profits to buy into the wealth of Asia itself."[14] Hence, his theme is that the Western world-system "climbed up on Asian shoulders." Curiously, he buttresses this part of his argument with substantial references to Adam Smith's 1776 *Wealth of Nations. ReORIENT* as a whole refers broadly to contemporary economic historians. Yet, at all the crucial points, Gunder Frank takes his departure from Braudel often, even more often from Wallerstein and those in his world-systems analysis circle. For example, on the question of the global economy in 1500—the metonymic date that Wallerstein takes as the beginning of modern world-system—Gunder Frank asks: *1500: Continuity or Break?* He thereby begins his insistence that the modern system was continuous with the long preexisting Asiatic modern product. Here, Gunder Frank's earlier association with world-systems analysis reveals itself in their common regard for the Nikolai Kondratieff's wave theory of economic cycles in the global economy to justify his continuity idea:

> Indeed, even Wallerstein ... refers to the widespread agreement that an expansive long [Kondratieff] "A" phase from 1050 to 1250 was followed by a contractive "B" phase from 1250 to 1450 and then after that by still another expansive "A" phase in the "long sixteenth century" from 1450 until 1640. The evidence ..., however, suggests that this long expansive phase had already begun in much of Asia by 1400 and that it lasted there until at least 1750. Wallerstein's European "long sixteenth century" probably was a belated and more temporary expression of this world economic expansion. Indeed, the voyages of Columbus and Vasco da Gama should probably be regarded as expressions of this world economic expansion, to which Europeans wanted to attach themselves in Asia. Therefore, the continuity across 1500 was actually

far more important and is theoretically far more significant than any alleged break or new departure.[15]

Earlier in *ReORIENT* in the section "Is There a Long-Cycle Roller Coaster?" Gunder Frank claims William McNeill, the author of *Pursuit of Power: Technology, Armed Force, and Society since AD 1000* (1983), as the authoritative voice for his conviction that in the long 16th century in Europe, China remained the center of the economic world. Predictably, he concludes, in regard to 1500 as a beginning of the modern:

> ... that the strongest and most dynamic parts of the world economy still remained in China and India. ...I argue therefore that these and other major Asian economies had, and continued to have, a pattern of long cyclical economic growth teaching the upper turning point of its expansive "A" phase, then passing on to a contractive "B" phase. Moreover, these Asian economies were of course all connected to each other. Therefore, it cannot be "coincidental" and should not be surprising that they were experiencing such expansive and contractive phases nearly simultaneously, if that is what was happening. However, these Asian economies were not only related to each other, they were all part and parcel of a single global economy, which presumably had its own long cycle of development.[16]

The foremost reason that Gunder Frank failed to win the day in his debate is that he failed to account for the key difference in the modern economic system after 1500. Capitalism, as it emerged even from the colonization of the Americas, was itself a departure from not only the Asian mode of production but from premodern economic and cultural systems. Capitalism, whatever else it has been, is a formally rational economic system that came to assume that markets obey, to some large extent, a logic of their own. This obviously is a classically modern view associated primarily with Max Weber and Karl Marx, among others. For Gunder Frank to bolster his continuity theory, he was forced to dismiss all those with whom he disagreed[17]: "Marxists, Weberians, Polanyists, world-systematizers, not to mention most 'economic' and other historians, balk at pursuing the evidence and the argument to examine the sacred cow of capitalism and its allegedly peculiarly exceptional or exceptionally peculiar mode of production." His criticism of those with whom he came to disagree would be more persuasive had *ReORIENT*, its brilliance being granted, been more explicitly an empirical study in comparative economic history. In fact, it is a book of economic theory that is satisfied with asserting the Asiatic Mode Production as global in both senses of the word—a global system and historically inclusive of all rival economic systems.

In the end, Gunder Frank ironically succeeds in calling attention to the distinctive—which is to say, discontinuous nature of the capitalist

60   *Macro-Historical Theories of Capitalism*

world-system—system that surely has endured in spite of its own historical ruptures; and one that, well into the 21st century, may well be entered into a new even uncertain phase. To be fair, by calling attention as Gunder Frank has to the long enduring Asian world-economy—toward which to European world economy seems to have decisively turned, perhaps even to a new quasi-core in the region—he has suggested a reason that the future of capitalism may be in Asia. Though the Asian mode of production was not capitalist, it might be thought of as possessing a deep structural disposition by which its late, long ago, regionally centered economy has been able to embrace the truly modern economic world-system that arose around 1500 in Europe.

Notes

1 Fernand Braudel, *The Mediterranean and the Mediterranean World in the Age of Philip II*, 2 volumes (New York: Harper & Row, 1973 [1963]).
2 *Ibid.*, II, 893.
3 Fernand Braudel, *Civilization and Capitalism: 15th–18th Century, Vol 1: Structures of Everyday Life* (New York: Harper & Row, 1981 [1979]); Fernand Braudel, *Civilization and Capitalism: 15th–18th Century, Vol 2: The Wheels of Commerce* (New York: Harper & Row 1982 [1979]).
4 Braudel, *Everyday Life*, 101.
5 *Ibid.*, 562; emphasis at the end added.
6 Braudel, *Wheels of Commerce*, 606–601.
7 *Ibid.*, 459.
8 *Ibid.*, 463.
9 Fernand Braudel, *Civilization and Capitalism: 15th–18th Century, Vol 3: The Perspective of the World* (New York: Harper & Row 1988 [1979]), 69–70.
10 Andre Gunder Frank, "The Development of Underdevelopment," *Monthly Review* 18 (September 1966): 17–31.
11 Andre Gunder Frank, *ReORIENT: Global Economy in the Asian Age* (Berkeley, CA: University of California Press 1998): 328.
12 *Ibid.*, 327.
13 *Ibid.*, 277.
14 *Ibid.*, 281.
15 *Ibid.*, 329.
16 *Ibid.*, 268.
17 *Ibid.*, 330.

5 Long-Distance Trade and the Transition to Capitalism

David Ricardo/Janet Abu-Lughod

David Ricardo (1772–1823) was born in London in 1772. He began his career as a financier, working in his father's office. His father, a Sephardi Jew originally from the Dutch Republic, had made his fortune on the London Stock Exchange. At age 21, Ricardo left the Jewish faith, and as a result, was estranged from his family for the remainder of his life. However, Ricardo soon amassed a fortune of his own through his financial investments, and by age 30 retired in order to dabble in various intellectual pursuits. It was at this point in his life when he first read Adam Smith's *Wealth of Nations* (1776) and became so captivated by the burgeoning academic discipline of political economy that he decided to begin to write his own works of political economy. Eventually, he became close friends with Thomas Malthus and Jeremy Bentham, who were his main intellectual interlocutors.

In Ricardo's magnum opus *Principles of Political Economy and Taxation* (1817), he develops his own labor theory of value, building on Adam Smith's and John Stuart Mill's monetary theories. This work would later become a key influence for Karl Marx. In the *Principles of Political Economy and Taxation* (1817), Ricardo applies the Ricardian theory of trade, which stresses comparative advantage and promotes free trade as beneficial for all parties involved, to the British colonies. He begins his argument on trade and the colonies from the premise that "the advantages of free trade" are well documented, and the "injustice suffered by colonies" is a result of colonizing countries prohibiting colonies from "selling their produce in the dearest market" and "buying their manufactures and stores at the cheapest."[1] Colonized entrepreneurs, in other words, are prohibited by the fact of their colonization from pursuing arrangements that would afford them the greatest returns.

The root cause of the lack of freedom to pursue one's interest in colonial markets, claims Ricardo, is that the colonizing country acts as a middleman, thereby both increasing the costs of colonial products and reducing the amount of profit that colonized capitalists can accrue on their long-distance transactions. By way of example, Ricardo asks us to imagine that Holland and Jamaica want to exchange commodities in which each country has comparative advantage. Because Jamaica is a British colony, it cannot trade directly with Holland, but must instead import its goods to England, where England then could exchange them with Holland. In this scenario, and as a

DOI: 10.4324/9781003198291-7

result of England's role as the middleman, Jamaica effectively loses its comparative advantage in trade, and it is England that profits from this transaction, not Jamaica. The way in which colonialism interferes in long-distance trade, Ricardo argued, "may be greatly hurtful to a colony" and "partially beneficial to the mother country."[2] By serving as middleman, colonizers "enjoy a sort of monopoly in the country which is so indulgent to them."[3] The country that can place itself as a middleman in long-distance trade networks creates a domestic market that is more extensive and advantageous to that country because it absorbs the comparative advantage of the colonies, transforming it into its own.

In the long run, Ricardo was concerned about the impact colonialism would have on the global economy as a whole. He predicted that as a result, "there will be a worse distribution of the general capital and industry, and, therefore, less will be produced."[4] The decrease of production, he hypothesized, would lead to inflation which would negatively impact consumers, but would generate more profit for commodity producers. Eventually, he argued, the monopoly on colonial trade would be transferred from the state to capital, as business will soon observe just how much profit there is to be made by such an arrangement.

Janet Abu-Lughod, (1928–2013) writing nearly 175 years later, wrote the definitive book on long-distance trade between Asia and Europe, showing how the states and Empires that served as middlemen in the several established trade routes between premodern Asia and Europe greatly benefitted from this position. Abu-Lughod was born in Newark, New Jersey, in 1928. She was denied admission to the PhD program in sociology at Yale, because in the 1960s Yale did not admit married women to the Graduate School of Arts & Sciences and would not make an exception for Abu-Lughod. She earned a PhD in Sociology from the University of Massachusetts, Amherst, in 1966. Abu-Lughod began her academic career working in urban sociology and specializing on cities in the Arab-Islamic world, writing her dissertation book on the city of Cairo. Her most famous book *Before European Hegemony: The World-System A.D. 1250–1350* (1989) is a classic work of world-systems analysis that fundamentally challenged world-systems founder Immanuel Wallerstein's Europe-centered perspective on the origins of the modern world-system. This book marks the first research in world-systems analysis that decenters Europe from the narrative of the origins of capitalism.

Abu-Lughod contends that Europe did not invent the capitalist world-system, it merely took it over when Asia fell into decline and then changed the rules in its favor—shifting from a previous system built on long-term and long-distance exchange to a new system characterized by "trade-cum-plunder."[5] She begins her narrative by positing that the so-called "Dark Ages" were only "dark" for Northwestern Europe,[6] while Southern Europe she characterizes as "flickering and for a time dimmed."[7] During the Medieval period, the Islamic world, which stretched from North Africa to Southeast Asia, was instead the region at the core of the contemporary world economy.[8] "There was no inherent historical necessity," she contends, which led to the eventual "Rise of the West," nor was there any structural reason why the East could not have constituted global capitalism.[9] But Europe did eventually come to constitute the capitalist world-economy, and did so as a strategy to access the world's best and most lucrative commodity and financial markets located in Asia.

During the period of world-history that Abu-Lughod examines, Europe was underdeveloped compared to the rest of Afro-Eurasia. Therefore, to access key resources and the most important and powerful world markets, European merchants and financiers needed reliable ingress to one of three established trade routes to Asia. In the 13th century, there existed three trade routes from Europe to Asia: (1) the northern route from Constantinople through Central Asia, (2) the central route from the Mediterranean coast of Syria/Palestine to the Indian Ocean via the Persian Gulf, and (3) the southern route from Cairo to the Indian Ocean via the Red Sea.[10] Non-Europeans controlled all three routes. The northern route was controlled by the Mongols,[11] the middle route was controlled by the Abbasid Empire from 750 to 1258 until it was destroyed in the military conflict between the Crusaders and the Mongols under Hulegu,[12] and the southern route was controlled by the Mamluk state established in Egypt in the mid-13th century.[13] Since the central route was destroyed by war, Europeans effectively had only two routes, and they controlled neither of them. Therefore, whomever controlled these trade routes had the upper hand over Europe.

The Northern Route from Europe to China was controlled by the Mongol Empire. By the 13th century, Mongol emperor Genghis Khan had conquered much of Eurasia, and had been angling to expand its borders to the East, West, and South. But once the Mongol forces had arrived in Hungary, they suddenly changed strategies, realizing that Europe had little resources or riches that could further the Empire's ambitions.[14] At this point, around 1225, the Mongols decided to focus most of their efforts on conquering the much richer region of China. In the second half of the 13th century, Western Europe first made contact with the Far East through Mongol intermediaries who had successfully unified most of Eurasia, reestablishing the ancient silk route that had been previously fragmented and vulnerable to theft and peril.[15] Europeans hoped to form an alliance with the Mongols in order to gain access to the silk road, and sent a series of papal envoys to establish long-term relations with the Mongol Empire, most famously sponsoring the merchant Marco Polo to undertake a trade mission into the depths of the Mongol Empire. But by the 14th century, the center of the Mongol Empire could not hold. Timür Khan (known by Europeans as Tamerlane) overextended the Mongol military in attempts to prevent the Empire from fragmenting. These many military campaigns, far from restoring the Mongol Empire, led to its downfall and to the end of the Northern Route in the late 14th century.

The Middle Route began on the Mediterranean shores of Syria and Palestine, traversing the desert from the Mesopotamian plain to Baghdad. There,

64 *Macro-Historical Theories of Capitalism*

this route diverged over land through Persia to Tabriz and to its final destination of Northern India controlled by the Delhi Sultanate, or over water, following the Tigris River to the Persian Gulf, stopping in the port of Basra and from there to the Indian Ocean and beyond. The Abbasid Empire, with its capital in Baghdad, controlled this route. As a result, Baghdad in the 8th through the 10th centuries was a global city where merchants, scholars, artists, and scientists gathered from all over the world, and the world's greatest library of the era was housed in the city. But in 1258, the city of Baghdad fell to the Mongol Empire, and was besieged and plundered by the troops of Hulegu.[16] The resulting collapse of the Abbasid Empire allowed neighboring Persia to take the entire Iraq region. This political instability temporarily disrupted the Middle Route, but did not completely destroy trade.[17] The final blow to the middle route instead came from the Crusaders who in trying to conquer the Eastern Mediterranean destroyed most of Syria and thereby cut off Europe's access to this trade route eastward.

As the Mongol Empire disintegrated and European access to the Middle Route cut off as a consequence of the Crusades, the Southern Route became Europe's primary channel of access to Asian trade.[18] The Mamluk Sultanate, with its capital in Cairo, was the primary beneficiary of the destruction caused by the Crusaders in the Levant. The Mamluks came to Syria and Palestine's aid and had driven out the Crusaders by 1291. As a result, Mamluk Egypt gained control of the Eastern Mediterranean. Known for their naval strength, the Mamluks soon lent their aid to Baghdad, to aid in their reconstruction in the wake of the Mongol invasions and to consolidate Mamluk control of trade routes. As:

> whoever controlled the sea route to Asia could set the terms of trade for a Europe now in temporary retreat. For the rest of the thirteenth and indeed up to the beginning of the sixteenth century, that power was Egypt.[19]

The Italian city-states were quick to establish strong trade and diplomatic relationships with the Mamluk Sultanate. Italians guaranteed Mamluk access to European ports, even in the context of increasing Christian-Muslim animosity, and supplied the Mamluks with a steady stream of slaves from Eastern Europe to man the world-renowned Mamluk armies and navies. However, this relationship was not without its contradictions, for the Italians supported the very Mamluk state that blocked their access to Asian trade and "exacted so high a price for goods in transit."[20] Through Abu-Lughod's analysis of diplomatic and trade relations between the Italian city-states and the Mamluk Sultanate, we see that the Egyptian Mamluk state acted as other core powers have throughout history, inserting themselves as middlemen in order to exploit less powerful semi-periphery and peripheral powers, and in so doing, furthering the existing social order that is the basis for their relative dominance in the interstate system.

The Transition to Capitalism   65

By the 15th century, Europe began to conquer the pathways and trade routes that were first developed by non-Europeans in the 13th century. Europe did not invent this system, claims Abu-Lughod, but notes that "the takeover of that system was certainly not according to the old rules."[21] Because the system was accustomed to the coexistence of multiple trading partners, she reasons, it was unprepared for European traders that engaged in short-term plunder rather than long-term exchange.

Abu-Lughod's groundbreaking research teaches us important lessons about the transition to capitalism. While both David Ricardo and Janet Abu-Lughod's analyses emphasize the advantage accrued to states who can insert themselves as middlemen in long-distance trade, Ricardo's ahistoric view of colonialism as nothing more than European states placing themselves in long-distance trade networks as middlemen obscures how long-distance trade contributed to the transition to capitalism. For a millennia, Europeans were at the brunt end of a global trade regime in which Central Asian and North African "middleman states" directly profited from Europe's lack of access to South and East Asian markets and lack of globally desirable goods with which to engage in global trade. By the time Ricardo was writing, in the early 19th century Europe had just begun to overtake Asia as the economically dominant world-region, and then began to do what all other states in world history had done in order to profit from their position within global trading networks—insert themselves as middlemen in global trade networks.

More importantly, because of Abu-Lughod's historical analysis, we can now reread Ricardo as fundamentally failing to capture what is historically unique about capitalism and colonialism. What Ricardo attributes to capitalism—the development of colonialism which allows European powers to insert themselves as middlemen in long-distance trade—is much more universal than Ricardo realizes. In other words, there is nothing particularly capitalist nor colonial about the process that Ricardo identifies. Ricardo failed to capture what was historically novel about colonialism in the context of the emerging capitalist world-economy. Instead, his analysis of the trade relationships between colonizer and colonized are much more universal— the dependent relationships formed through long-distance trade which can exist in any economic system. Again, there's nothing particularly capitalist, nor colonial, about the economic process Ricardo identified.

Abu-Lughod, however, shows us how long-distance trade was essential in the transition to capitalism, but not in the way the mainline theories posit. India and China had much more desirable markets than Europe, and Europe wanted to do all it could to access these lucrative markets. Capitalism and colonialism were an important part of Europe's rise, but not because Europe was able to become a middleman in trade. Europe's rise marked a fundamental divergence from the previous status quo. Capitalism and Colonialism were the means by which Europe was able to fundamentally change the rules of the game in its favor.

Notes

1 David Ricardo, *Principles of Political Economy and Taxation* (Amherst: Prometheus Books, 1817 [1996]), 234.
2 *Ibid.*, 235.
3 *Ibid.*
4 *Ibid.*, 239.
5 Janet Abu-Lughod, *Before European Hegemony: The World-System A.D. 1250–1350* (New York: Oxford University Press, 1989), 361.
6 *Ibid.*, 43.
7 *Ibid.*, 45.
8 *Ibid.*, 3.
9 *Ibid.*, 12.
10 *Ibid.*, 137.
11 *Ibid.*, 143.
12 *Ibid.*, 146.
13 *Ibid.*, 147.
14 *Ibid.*, 141.
15 *Ibid.*, 144.
16 *Ibid.*, 146.
17 *Ibid.*
18 *Ibid.*, 147.
19 *Ibid.*, 149.
20 *Ibid.*, 149.
21 *Ibid.*, 361.

6 Women's Unpaid Labor and Primitive Accumulation

Friedrich Engels/Silvia Federici

Friedrich Engels (1820–1895) was born in Germany in 1820. While often seen as *just* the wealthy businessman who financed Karl Marx, Engels was, no doubt, Marx's intellectual equal and close collaborator. Engels's biographers attribute his relative lack of fame to his personality.[1] He was known to be a modest and self-effacing intellectual, who took little credit for his scholarly contributions. Engels was only 24 when he wrote his first book *The Condition of the Working Class in England* (1845).[2] In it, he analyzes two years of ethnographic research (which he conducted from 1842 to 1844) in proletarian Manchester, observing workers both in the cotton mills where they worked and in the neighborhoods where they lived. But Engels is perhaps best known for his last book *The Origin of the Family, Private Property, and the State* (1885), in which he was among the first theorists to show how capitalism relies on systems of patriarchy and among the first to argue that socialist revolution would drastically improve the lives of women (and men) through more egalitarian gender relations.

Engels claims that the logic of the monogamous family is rooted in "victory of private property over… common ownership."[3] Monogamy ensures that a man knows that his progenitors are in fact his own, and therefore the true inheritors of his wealth. The subordination of wife to husband guarantees "the fidelity of the wife, that is, the paternity of the children." Therefore, within the social confines of the family, "the woman is placed in the man's absolute power; if he kills her, he is but exercising his right."[4] The social function of monogamy is to establish paternity for purposes of inheritance. This, Engels points out, only requires the female partner to be monogamous. In other words, "the monogamy of the woman in no way hindered the overt or covert polygamy of the man."[5] Women are denied sexual freedom as a result of monogamy as a way to preserve and protect family wealth.

The invention of the family in early modern Europe was, for Engels, "the world historic defeat of the female sex."[6] Because men assumed the role of head of household, "the woman was degraded, enthralled, the slave of a man's lust, a mere instrument for breeding children."[7] Women were "pushed out of participation in social production" and into the private sphere where "the wife became the first domestic servant."[8] The family structure created a bind for women, in that they were either excluded from selling their labor power, therefore

DOI: 10.4324/9781003198291-8

68   *Macro-Historical Theories of Capitalism*

prevented from being financially independent, or unable to fulfill socially prescribed family duties and as a result, suffer social opprobrium. In assessing this bind, Engels concludes that "the modern individual family is based on the open or disguised domestic enslavement of the woman."[9] To put it in Marxian terminology: as does the capitalist to the worker, so does to the man to his wife. In the household, the man is the bourgeoisie and his wife, the proletariat.

The solution to women's oppression and exploitation, according to Engels, was what he termed sex-love: "reciprocal love on the part of the loved one," the woman on par with the man, and a new moral standard surrounding sexual intercourse outside the confines of marriage. To further this goal, children, whether born in or out of wedlock, Engels believed, should be cared for collectively as a "public matter."[10] In order to realize these goals for heterosexual relationships, Engels wrote that men *and women* must begin to look at each other not by their personal possessions or physical attributes but by their "personal qualities."[11] But of course, full freedom in heterosexual relationships is only possible, says Engels:

> when the abolition of capitalist production, and of the property relations created by it, has removed all those secondary economic considerations which still exert so powerful an influence on the choice of a partner. Then, no other motive remains than mutual affection.[12]

While Engels made great strides in theorizing how the transition to capitalism led to the subordination of women, Silvia Federici's *Caliban and the Witch* (2004), one of the most meticulously researched historical accounts of how and why the genesis of capitalism resulted in the exploitation and oppression of women, gives a far more convincing historical explanation for contemporary gender inequality. **Silvia Federici** (1942–) was born in Parma, Italy, in 1942. She moved to the United States in 1967 to complete a PhD in philosophy at the State University of New York, Buffalo. She taught in Nigeria for several years before returning to the United States. Settling in Brooklyn, she brought the Wages for Housework movement to the United States. Wages for Housework was founded in 1972 in Padua, Italy, to raise awareness of how the capitalist economy exploits women's unpaid domestic work. Influenced by the Northern Italian autonomous workers movement, the founders of Wages for Housework contended that women should demand compensation for the value they create for capital. Currently, Federici lives and works in Brooklyn, New York, and is a Professor Emeritus of Sociology at the State University of New York, Binghamton.

Federici, like Engels, views the social construction of the nuclear family in the early modern period as the source of women's oppression and exploitation within the capitalist mode of production. Federici writes that:

> the discrimination that women have suffered in the waged work-force has been directly rooted in their function as unpaid laborers in the

home. We can thus connect the banning of prostitution and the expulsion of women from the organized workplace with the creation of the housewife and the reconstruction of the family as the locus for the production of labor-power. However, from a theoretical and political viewpoint, the fundamental question is under what conditions such degradation was possible, and what social forces promoted it or were complicitous with it.[13]

To show how degradation of women accompanied the transition to capitalism, Federici provides us with a feminist account of primitive accumulation. She unearths new historical information which shows how the development of a new sexual division of labor subjugated women's labor and women's reproductive function to the reproduction of the workforce. This process led to the construction of a new patriarchal order based on the exclusion of women from waged work that transformed women's bodies into a machine for the production of new workers. Federici's story is an important critique of the Marxian narrative of the transition to capitalism, as Marx neglected to analyze how women's social roles were transformed along with the transformation of peasants to workers.[14] The transformation of the female body into a work machine necessitated the destruction of the social power of women. Primitive accumulation, as Federici demonstrates, not only transformed peasants into workers, but also created hierarchies of gender that were foundational in structuring what would become the capitalist social order.

Federici begins with the Black Death. Because of the resulting population crisis, capital needed a large and reliable supply of cheap labor; but as labor was scarce, wages remained high. To overcome these demographic challenges, early modern European states criminalized migration, vagabondage, and "crimes against property" as a means to retain labor.[15] But laws criminalizing the working class failed to achieve the desired result, as rebellion against primitive accumulation and desertion of work persisted. By the early 17th century, states tried a different tact. If they couldn't force peasants to become workers, they would grow the labor force through other means. States in Europe and the Americas adopted policies that regulated procreation and women's control over reproduction in order to compel women to carry more births to term, thereby increasing the population. Women were forced out of waged labor both by states and by proletarian men, who saw women's unpaid labor in the home as supporting both the fiscal health of the family and the national economy.[16] For proletarian men, women became a substitute for the land they lost during the enclosures, a basic means of reproduction, "a communal good anyone could appropriate at will."[17]

Legislation was soon adopted to compel women to carry more births to term—the decriminalization of rape and criminalization of contraception. States hoped that by decriminalizing the rape of proletarian women, it would turn the aggressive class-based anger of young proletarian men away from the state and capital and instead against proletarian women.[18]

70 Macro-Historical Theories of Capitalism

For victims of rape, prostitution became the only option of remaining part of early modern European society. So much so that by the 14th century, many European municipalities, particularly in France and Italy, opened publicly managed and tax-financed brothels so that proletarian men, who had little economic means to marry, had access to women's bodies.

The legalization of rape was coupled with the criminalization of contraceptives, thereby forcing women to carry pregnancies to term regardless of the conditions under which the pregnancy occurred. European women had long used herbal medicine to prevent or end a pregnancy, but starting in the mid-16th century, across Europe, states began to punish women for using birth control with sentences of death by drowning or beheading.[19] Most people executed in Europe during the 16th and 17th centuries were women charged with infanticide or witchcraft. Women were soon barred from the medical profession, as it was feared that they would aid other women in procuring birth control or abortion.[20] The result of these policies, as Federici shows, is that:

> down to the present—the state has spared no efforts in its attempt to wrench from women's hands the control over reproduction, and to determine which children should be born, where, when, or in what numbers. Consequently, women have often been forced to procreate against their will, and have experienced alienation from their bodies, their "labor," and even their children, deeper than that experienced by any other workers.[21]

But even with these policies in place, women still refused to obey these policies and to adopt the new model of femininity that encouraged women to be "passive, obedient, thrifty, of few words, always busy with work, and chaste."[22] Therefore, European states "unleashed a campaign of terror against women, unmatched by any other persecution": the witch trials.[23] The witch trials, Federici argues, were a counterattack against women's resistance to the new capitalist social relations that forced them into a very limited social role. The death sentence that accompanied accusations of witchcraft was not prescribed by a specific transgression, but applicable to any form of female behavior that was not tolerated in the new social order, and therefore, "had to be made abominable in the eyes of the population."[24] Most women accused of witchcraft were (1) unmarried, barred from entry to the labor market, and had stolen food for survival[25]; (2) women who had used or helped others to use contraception, which left women in the medical profession particularly vulnerable to accusations of witchcraft[26]; or (3) women who engaged in non-procreative sexual activity, especially women who engaged in sexual activity after menopause. "The witch hunt, then," Federici posits:

> was a war against women; it was a coerced attempt to degrade them, demonize them, and destroy their social power. At the same time, it was

in the torture chambers and on the stakes on which the witches perished that the bourgeois ideals of womanhood and domesticity were forged.[27]

"The political lesson we learn from Caliban and the Witch," Federici instructs:

> is that capitalism as a socio-economic system, is necessarily committed to racism and sexism. For capitalism must justify and mystify the contradictions built into its social relations— the promise of freedom vs. the reality of widespread penury — by denigrating the 'nature' of those it exploits: women, colonial subjects, the descendants of African slaves, the immigrants displaced by globalization.[28]

Federici's solution to ameliorate the social conditions of women in the capitalist world-economy is to acknowledge women's unpaid (and coerced) contributions to capital accumulation by demanding wages for housework. In the capitalist world-economy, she contends, "entire spheres of human activity... appear to be outside the wage relation: slaves, colonial subjects, prisoners, housewives, and students."[29] "Capitalism requires unwaged reproductive labor in order to contain the cost of labor power, and ... draining the source of this unpaid labor would break the process of capital accumulation."[30] By demanding wages from the state ("the real 'Man' profiting from [house]work"), Federici and the Wages for Housework Movement believed that they could potentially degender housework. In *Revolution at Point Zero* (2012), Federici explains how Wages for Housework can promote gender equality in a way that women's entry into the labor market cannot:

> Only when thousands of women will be in the streets saying that endless cleaning, always being emotionally available, fucking at command for fear of losing our jobs is hard, hated work that wastes our lives, will they be scared and feel undermined as men. But this is the best thing that can happen to them from their own point of view, because by exposing the way capital has kept us divided (capital has disciplined them through us and us through them— each other, against each other), we— their crutches, their slaves, their chains— open the process of their liberation. In this sense, wages for housework will be much more educational than trying to prove we can work as well as them, that we can do the same jobs. We leave this worthwhile effort to the "career woman," the woman who escapes from her oppression not through the power of unity and struggle, but through the power of the master, the power to oppress— usually other women. And we don't have to prove that we can break "the blue collar barrier." A lot of us have broken that barrier a long time ago and discovered that the overalls did not give us any more power than the apron— quite often less, because now we had to wear both and had even less time and energy to struggle against them. The

72 Macro-Historical Theories of Capitalism

things we have to prove are our capacity to expose what we are already doing as work, what capital is doing to us, and our power to struggle against it.[31]

Just as Engels saw women's unpaid labor in the home as the primary source of gender inequality in the capitalist mode of production, so does Federici. Her research updates Engels for the 21st century by (1) providing a historically rich and accurate narrative of how the current patriarchal order was forged in the transition to capitalism and (2) by showing how the nuclear family remains the key site of women's oppression and exploitation in the capitalist mode of production.

But in building on Engels, Federici shows how while early feminists thought that women's paid work outside the home would promote gender equality, in fact, it does little to lessen or eliminate gender inequality because it leaves the nuclear family intact. Women who perform paid labor outside the home still perform unpaid labor in the home as part of what is expected of them by the capitalist world-economy solely by virtue of their gender. Both Engels and Federici identify the imperatives of capital accumulation as the cause of women's oppression and exploitation in the capitalist mode of production. And unlike Marx, who claims that capitalism, despite its flaws, marks an improvement in social conditions for subordinate classes compared to previous modes of production, Engels and Federici show how women's social roles in the capitalist mode of production are *worse* than in the previous mode of production. Finally, while both Engels and Federici propose ways to lessen gender inequality within the current mode of production, they also both believe that ultimately, a change in the mode of production is necessary to bring about true equality between men and women.

Notes

1 John Green, *A Revolutionary Life: Biography of Frederick Engels* (London: Artery Publications, 2008), 11.
2 Friedrich Engels, *The Condition of the Working Class in England* (Oxford: Oxford University Press, 1845 [2009]).
3 Friedrich Engels, "The Origin of the Family, Private Property, and the State," in *The Marx-Engels Reader*, ed. Robert C. Tucker (New York: WW Norton and Company, 1884 [1978]), 162.
4 *Ibid.*, 737.
5 *Ibid.*, 745.
6 *Ibid.*, 736.
7 *Ibid.*
8 *Ibid.*, 744.
9 *Ibid.*
10 *Ibid.*, 746–747.
11 *Ibid.*, 748.
12 *Ibid.*, 750.
13 Silvia Federici, *Caliban and the Witch: Women, the Body, and Primitive Accumulation* (Brooklyn: Autonomedia, 2004 [2014]), 95.

14 *Ibid.*, 63–64.
15 *Ibid.*, 82–85.
16 *Ibid.*, 96.
17 *Ibid.*, 97.
18 *Ibid.*, 47.
19 *Ibid.*, 88.
20 *Ibid.*, 89.
21 *Ibid.*, 91.
22 *Ibid.*, 103.
23 *Ibid.*, 165.
24 *Ibid.*, 170.
25 *Ibid.*, 171–173.
26 *Ibid.*, 183–184.
27 *Ibid.*, 186.
28 *Ibid.*, 17.
29 Silvia Federici, *Revolution at Point Zero: Housework, Reproduction, and Feminist Struggle* (Oakland: PM Press, 2012), 8.
30 *Ibid.*
31 *Ibid.*, 21–22.

7 The Agrarian Origins of Capitalism

Robert Brenner/Ellen Meiksins Wood

Robert Brenner (1943–) was born in New York City, USA, in 1943. In 1970, he completed his PhD in history at Princeton University. He is well known for his editorial leadership of the *New Left Review* and is currently professor of history at University of California, Los Angeles, and the director of the Center for Social Theory and Comparative History at UCLA. From the 2000s on, Robert Brenner's work focused on historical analyses of finance capital, but in the earlier part of his career, his research agenda centered on the agrarian roots of the British Industrial Revolution.

Brenner's early essay, "Agrarian Class Structure and Economic Development in Pre-Industrial Europe" (1976), caused one of the biggest controversies in recent economic history, culminating in what today is referred to as The Brenner Debate. The central question of this debate—what caused the transition to capitalism in Europe?—remains one of the most important questions for economic historians and those interested in the origins of capitalism.

In this 1976 essay, Brenner argues that the transition to capitalism was caused by "the emergence of a specific set of class or social-property relations in the countryside—that is, capitalist class relations."[1] The development of capitalist class relations, according to Brenner, depended upon two processes: (1) the end of serfdom and (2) the undermining of small peasant property rights in the interests of enclosure and consolidation of land. In Brenner's comparative analysis of the agrarian class structure in early modern France and early modern England, he finds that because peasants had certain rights to land in France, they remained trapped in the "old Malthusian cycle of underdevelopment"[2]; but English landowners, however, were able to consolidate large landholdings by raising rents and evicting small tenants, as serfdom had been abolished by the 15th century. With large farms, English landlords could make capital improvements that increased output, thereby facilitating a historically unprecedented level of economic development.

Brenner's thesis, he claimed, stood out from the more widely accepted narratives of the transition to capitalism because it hinged on an analysis of class structure. Brenner contended that "it is the structure of class relations, of class power, which will determine the manner and degree to which particular demographic and commercial changes will affect long-term trends in

DOI: 10.4324/9781003198291-9

The Agrarian Origins of Capitalism   75

the distribution of income and economic growth."[3] In asserting the supremacy of class structure in understanding moments of economic transition, Brenner's argument was a critique of two alternate ways of analyzing economic history and understanding the historical trajectory of global capitalism, what he called "the demographic model" and "the commercialization model." Brenner thereby structured the subsequent debate into three camps: (1) Marxist (his position); (2) Malthusian; and (3) Smithian.

Most narratives of the transition to capitalism, Brenner contends, focus on demographic fluctuations and the growth of trade and markets to explain modern economic growth. These Malthusian models, Brenner argues, turn the class structure into an abstraction. In so arguing, Brenner's two main targets are Neo-Malthusian economic historians: MM Postan and Emmanuel Le Roy Ladurie. Postan, in a reply to Brenner, claims that Neo-Malthusians have shown that medieval landlords did engage in the acquisition of land and were interested in increasing their holdings, but they did not devote a large share of their resources to investment for the purposes of growth.[4] The technology to do so was not readily available, but more importantly, improvements that were made tended to emphasize more efficient administration, not large productive investments of capital. Power, Postan argues, accrued based on a different logic—political and military might, family alliances, connections to religious authorities, and the size of one's landed estate—all of which prevented medieval landlords from the pursuit of the endless accumulation of capital. Emmanuel Le Roy Ladurie, in his brief and measured reply to Brenner, makes several corrections of Brenner's interpretation of early modern European history. One of the most interesting is Ladurie's assertion that while perhaps Brenner is correct about how capitalism developed in England, "this is surely only one of many possible routes to 'modernization.'"[5] So while Ladurie agrees that "agricultural capitalism… originates on the great seigneurial demesnes," he also contends that "this 'favorable' evolution of seignurialism towards capitalism is not confined to England. It is also to be found in slightly different forms" in other places and times in European history.[6]

While the Neo-Malthusian targets of Brenner's 1976 critique had a distinct theoretical view from his own, in a subsequent essay, Brenner takes on what he calls "neo-Smithian Marxism" in order to root out fellow Marxists who, in Brenner's view, "displace class relations from the centre of their analyses of economic development and underdevelopment."[7] In so doing, this group of theorists strays from their Marxian roots, Brenner believes, and instead has created a leftist interpretation of Adam Smith. In this critique, Brenner's principal targets are André Gunder Frank and Immanuel Wallerstein. Brenner rejects Gunder Frank's theory of the transition to capitalism because it grounds the origins of capitalism in what Brenner terms "a world commercial network" reliant upon the surplus appropriation of the periphery by the core.[8] Wallerstein, Brenner contends, goes even a step further than Frank in claiming that Europe's transition to capitalism could only occur in the context of the decline of world Empires, which thereby changed the "trade-induced world division of labor."[9] The issue, for Brenner, is that neither the expansion of trade, nor the transfer of surplus from core to periphery, nor the advent of new labor controls can generate economic development.[10]

Wallerstein and Frank's definition of capitalism is reversed, Brenner claims. Brenner contends that "Capitalism is a system in which production for a profit via exchange predominates,"[11] but in Wallerstein and Frank's analysis, Brenner argues, "the appearance of widespread production 'for profit in the market' signal[s] the existence of capitalism." This is flawed logic, says Brenner, "because production for exchange is perfectly compatible with a system in which it is either unnecessary or impossible, or both, to reinvest in expanded improved production in order to 'profit.'"[12] Brenner's critique of Frank and Wallerstein hinges on the fact that, in Brenner's view, they overemphasize the importance of global trade while minimizing the importance of the exploitation of surplus labor toward the creation of profit through the production process.

Unlike Robert Brenner, who focuses much of his intellectual efforts on critique of other scholars, including those who share the same theoretical viewpoint, Ellen Meiskins Wood, while similarly critical of world-systems analysis and other related perspectives, tries to find common theoretical ground with the perspectives she critiques. To that end, her work reads as less of a dismissal, and instead as a critical dialogue aimed at coming to a theoretical consensus about what specifically is historically unique about capitalism.

Ellen Meiskins Wood (1942–2016) was born in New York City, USA, in 1942. She completed a PhD in political science at the University of California, Los Angeles, in 1970 and was a professor of political science at York University in Toronto, Canada, for the duration of her academic career. A committed Marxist, she served on the editorial boards of the *New Left Review* and *Monthly Review*. In 1996, she was inducted into the Royal Society of Canada, one of the highest honors for Canadian intellectuals. She is best known for having developed an influential theory of political Marxism.

In *The Origin of Capitalism* (1999), Meiskins Wood takes up the central question of the Brenner debate— what caused the transition to capitalism in Europe? And while she is certainly in the Brenner camp, her analysis more sympathetically engages with critiques levied at the Brennerite approach. More specifically, she directly addresses charges of Eurocentrism and the role that globalization and imperialism played in constituting the transition to capitalism.

In nearly all previous accounts of the transition to capitalism, Meiskins Wood argues, the necessary constituting elements of capitalism are portrayed as intrinsic but vestigial features of the world-economy; in other words, the seeds have always been there, they just needed to be activated. Therefore, most accounts of the transition to capitalism stress the continuities between capitalism and previous modes of production. However, claims Meiskins Wood, such narratives are not helpful in determining the specificities and the unique facets of capitalism as a world-historical system. For example, market exchange has existed for millennia, and therefore by focusing on the market, there's little we can learn about the specificities of capitalism as this dimension of the world-economy stays relatively constant with changes in the mode of production.

Therefore, Meiskins Wood suggests we look outside the urban hubs of trade in order to locate the origins of capitalism. In analyzing the change in property relations in rural England, Meiskins Wood contends we see the fundamental distinction between capitalism and precapitalist modes of production:

> It has nothing to do with whether production is urban or rural, and everything to do with the particular property relations between producers and appropriators, whether in industry or agriculture. Only in capitalism is the dominant mode of appropriation based on the complete disposition of direct producers, who (unlike chattel slaves) are legally free and whose surplus labor is appropriated by purely 'economic' means. Because direct producers in a fully developed capitalism are propertyless, and because their only access to the means of production, to the requirements of their own reproduction, even to the means of their own labor, is the sale of their labor power in exchange for a wage, capitalists can appropriate the workers' surplus labor without direct coercion.[13]

These capitalist social relations, shows Meiskins Wood, are distinct from the social relations that have dominated most of human history. And the first place and time where one could observe these distinct social relations was the 16th-century English countryside.[14] Because the interests of the English landlord class lie in their "economic powers of appropriation"[15] rather than their relative access to the state, for the subordinate classes in England, conflict over property rights and against enclosure were more important than struggles against taxation.

Meiskins Wood's narrative retains many of the elements for which previous scholars have been charged of Eurocentrism. However, she argues that proponents of what she calls "the commericialization model" (which includes Braudelians like Frank and Wallerstein, along with Malthusians such as Postan and Ladurie) are the most Eurocentrist of all.[16] Even though, as she claims, capitalism was developed in Europe, to view the absence of capitalism in a particular geography as a historic failure is counterproductive for those who claim to be critics of capitalism. Her viewpoint "that certain specific historical conditions in Europe, which have nothing to do with European superiority, produced certain specific historical consequences- such as the rise of capitalism"[17] is not racist, nor derives from cultural chauvinism. Racism and cultural chauvinism, Meiskins Wood claims, are the

78 *Macro-Historical Theories of Capitalism*

two metrics of Eurocentrism. The commercialization model is Eurocentrist, because it fails to account for the change in relations of production that occurred during the transition to capitalism. By assuming that primitive accumulation could occur solely through trade, the commercialization model implicitly must argue that all world regions had a similar capacity to develop a strategy for primitive accumulation; but Europe was first to do so because of its immanent virtues. By focusing on relations of production, Meiskins Wood contends, we can devise an anti-Eurocentric narrative of the transition to capitalism.

But, you might ask, what of globalization and imperialism? Was Europe's primitive accumulation the result of colonialism and imperialism? The left version of the commercialization model posits that European imperialism was decisive in primitive accumulation in Europe. Meiskins Wood argues that while, yes, many European powers were engaged in colonial ventures, only England's colonial empire was capitalist,[18] thereby rendering the commonly assumed link between capitalism and colonialism a bit more complex. In Meiskins Wood's perspective:

> much, if not everything, depended on the social property relations at home in the imperial power, the particular conditions of systemic reproduction associated with those property relations, and the particular economic processes set in motion by them. The wealth amassed from colonial exploitation may have contributed substantially to further development, even if it was not a necessary precondition of the origin of capitalism.[19]

Even though imperialism did not, in her account, contribute to the transition to capitalism, capitalism created new motives and justifications for imperialism, namely colonial conquest that involves dispossession of land and the eradication of preexisting property rights to the end of "economic development."[20] In this distinction between imperialism and *capitalist* imperialism, Meiskins Wood provides a convincing revision to the Brennerite perspective that links the Brennerite narrative of the origins of capitalism to today's globalized economy and the imperatives of contemporary US imperialism.

Because while Brenner structured the terms of The Brenner Debate to focus solely on the comparative European context, Meiskins Wood opens up the Brennerite perspective to a global narrative of the origins of capitalism as tied to social relations of production. Through her serious engagement with critics of the Braudelian persuasion, she is able to place The Brenner Debate in a larger world-historical context, while still retaining the essence of its argument: that capitalism has its sole origins in rural 16th-century England.

Notes

1 Brenner in *The Brenner Debate: Agrarian Class Structure and Economic Development in Pre-Industrial Europe*, eds. TH Aston and CHE Philpin (Cambridge: Cambridge University Press, 1987), 30.

2 *Ibid.*, 61.

The Agrarian Origins of Capitalism   79

3 *Ibid.*, 11.
4 Postan and Hatcher "Population and class relations in feudal society," in Aston and Philpin, *Brenner Debate*, 77.
5 Ladurie "A reply to Robert Brenner," in Aston and Philpin, *Brenner Debate*, 105.
6 *Ibid.*, 105–106.
7 Robert Brenner, "The Origins of Capitalist Development: A Critique of Neo-Smithian Marxism," *New Left Review* 104 (1977): 27.
8 *Ibid.*, 29.
9 *Ibid.*, 30.
10 *Ibid.*, 31.
11 *Ibid.*
12 *Ibid.*
13 Ellen Meiskins Wood, *The Origin of Capitalism: A Longer View* (London: Verso, 1999 [2002]), 96.
14 *Ibid.*, 98.
15 *Ibid.*, 117.
16 *Ibid.*, 27.
17 *Ibid.*
18 *Ibid.*, 147.
19 *Ibid.*, 149.
20 *Ibid.*, 156.

8 Finance and Capitalism

Antonio Gramsci/Giovanni Arrighi

Antonio Gramsci (1891–1937) was born in Ales, Sardinia, in 1891. He was afflicted with Pott disease in his youth, and the resulting spinal issues stunted his growth and gave him a hunchback. In 1911, Gramsci won a scholarship to attend the University of Turin where he studied linguistics and first became acquainted with socialism. In 1913, he joined the Italian Socialist Party, and in 1915, quit his studies in order to devote himself to political work. He wrote for socialist newspapers and gave public talks on various topics. In 1919, he along with some friends from university founded the weekly newspaper *L'Ordine Nuovo*. During the *Biennio Rosso*, Gramsci was committed to the workers councils and was one of few socialists who supported the syndicalist movement in Northern Italy. But with the defeat of the workers' councils, Gramsci began to believe that Lenin was right about worker-occupations and that a Leninist Communist Party was needed in Italy. He soon founded and led the *Partito Comunista d'Italia*. But even though he was the leader of a Leninist Communist Party, he nonetheless continued to support more anti-authoritarian leftist politics, including *Arditi del Popolo*, an anti-Fascist group. Because the Comintern opposed anti-authoritarian left politics, Gramsci was one of few Italian socialists of his era who supported the *Arditi del Popolo*, even though he engaged in vociferous debates with anarchists over leftist strategy in the pages of Gramsci's newspaper *L'Ordine Nuovo* and the anarchist newspaper *Umanità Nova*.

In November 1926, Gramsci was jailed after Benito Mussolini ratified a series of Emergency Laws. He was tried in Rome and sentenced to five years on the Island of Ustica, to be followed by 20 years imprisonment in Turi. By the early 1930s, his health began to fail, and he suffered from a combination of arteriosclerosis, tuberculosis, high blood pressure, angina, gout, and gastric disorders. Observers recounted that in prison, his teeth fell out, he became unable to eat solid food, suffered from convulsions, frequently vomited blood, and had severe headaches. Gramsci was granted an early release in April 1937 for convalescence and died six days after his release from a cerebral hemorrhage.

Gramsci's *Prison Notebooks* are one of the most important works of Marxist theory. One of the central concepts in the *Prison Notebooks* is hegemony, which Gramsci defines as class rule. This class rule occupies two social

DOI: 10.4324/9781003198291-10

spaces: (1) political society and (2) civil society. The dominant class exercises its domination over all other classes via the state in one of two ways: (1) direct domination and (2) hegemony. Hegemony in this sense is the ability of the state to provide moral and ideological leadership, and thus coerce all classes into obeying and believing in the authority of the state. The end goal of this class consciousness is hegemony. In the final stage of class consciousness, the dominant class becomes aware of their present and future interests and those interests become the interests of other groups in society. The hegemonic project of a dominant class has the goal of securing state power and maintaining it in such a way that all subordinate classes believe that the dominant class' interest is their interest as well.

The hegemon manifests its supremacy "as 'domination' and as 'intellectual and moral leadership.'"[1] The hegemonic project of a dominant state has the goal of securing power and maintaining it in such a way that all other states in the world-system believe that the interest of the hegemon is their interest as well.[2] While hegemon's interests are paramount, the dominant must also make some sacrifices to show that it is acting in the collective interest. However, these sacrifices should not erode the economic interests of the hegemon, for hegemony's appeal is that it benefits the economic interests of the dominant. Gramsci elucidates how even though hegemony's mechanism is through politics, hegemony is fundamentally an economic concept:

> there is also no doubt that such sacrifices and such a compromise cannot touch the essential; for though hegemony is ethical-political, it must also be economic, must necessarily be based on the decisive function exercised by the leading group in the decisive nucleus of economic activity.[3]

An essential component of achieving and maintaining that hegemony is the construction of a political ideology, which Gramsci defines as "a creation of concrete phantasy which acts on a dispersed and shattered people to arouse and organise its collective will."[4] Political ideology is a project of the dominant state, constructed to convince all other states that it is acting in the collective interest, thereby securing the dominant state's economic interests across the globe.

The Gramscian concept of hegemony has been a central concept in many subsequent schools of left-academic thought; namely postcolonial theory, cultural studies, critical theory, and world-systems analysis. Within world-systems analysis, admittedly the concept of hegemony in the Wallersteinian tradition comes mostly from Marx, but in the Arrighian articulation, hegemony is Gramscian hegemony read globally.

Giovanni Arrighi, (1937–2009) one of the most important and influential world-systems analysts, was born in Milan, Italy, in 1937. He completed a PhD in economics at Università Bocconi, a stronghold of neoclassical economics. In 1963, he was appointed lecturer in economics at the University College of Rhodesia and Nyasaland, and in 1966, he was jailed and then

82   Macro-Historical Theories of Capitalism

deported for political activities related to Rhodesia's movement for national liberation. He then went to Dar-es-Salaam, which in the 1960s was one of the most important incubators for left intellectuals and activists. At the University of Dar-es-Salaam, Arrighi met leaders in the US Black Power movement and critical scholars, including Immanuel Wallerstein and Walter Rodney. At Dar-es-Salaam, Arrighi shifted his research interests to the issue of national liberation movements and the new states that emerged from decolonization.

Arrighi returned to Italy in 1969, where he was offered a lectureship in sociology at the University of Trento. While initially his lectures were poorly attended, after his first book came out in 1969, those involved in the student movement clamored to get a space in his courses. The Boato faction of the student and workers movement, *Lotta Continua*, welcomed his critique of development theories, while the Rostagno faction tried to disrupt his classes. Romano Madera, active in the situationist student and workers movement and one of Arrighi's students, joined forces with Arrighi to develop a Gramscian strategy for the Italian workers and student movement. They, along with Luisa Passerini, founded the *Gruppo Gramsci* and coined the term *autonomia* which is often mistakenly attributed to Antonio Negri.[5] The aim of the *Gruppo Gramsci* was to, as students and intellectuals, help workers' vanguards develop their own *autonomia operaia* through an understanding of global political economy. In so doing, they hoped to create organic intellectuals in the Gramscian frame. In 1973, the *Gruppo Gramsci* disbanded, at which time Antonio Negri "took the CPOs and the Area dell'Autonomia in an adventurous direction that was far from what was originally intended."[6] In 1979, Giovanni Arrighi moved to the United States where he held professorships in sociology first at the State University of New York, Binghamton, and then at the Johns Hopkins University until his death in 2009.

In his master work *The Long Twentieth Century* (1994), Giovanni Arrighi reads Gramsci (and others) globally and historically. Marx's general formula of capital then becomes "a recurrent pattern of historical capitalism as world-system,"[7] which Arrighi terms a systemic cycle of accumulation. These systemic cycles of accumulation consist of two distinct phases of world-historical capital accumulation: M-C phases characterized primarily by productive accumulation and all of its related processes, and C-M' phases comprised of financialization and related processes. Underlying these phases of capitalist accumulation is a secular trend of intensification of the capitalist world-system in terms of both deeper penetration and geographical expansion. These successive transformations of the world-economy have been led by particular government and business agencies, as Arrighi contends, following Fernand Braudel that "capitalism [is] absolutely dependent for its emergence and expansion on state power as constituting the antithesis of the market economy."[8] Each systemic cycle of accumulation is led by a state that achieves world-hegemony: "the power of a state to exercise functions of leadership and governance over a system of states."[9]

Haute finance is central to this way of understanding global political economy. Arrighi identifies a pattern of "depression, revival, and crisis" when it comes to the "stagnation" that accompanies the end phase of a hegemonic cycle of accumulation.[10] In times of overproduction, either the issue of overproduction is resolved or else:

> the rate of profit must fall, with all the dire consequences that such a fall entails in a capitalist economy, from drops in the rate of investment and productivity growth to the decline of real wages and levels of employment.[11]

In other words, a falling rate of profit leads to a decrease in investment rates. This declining rate of profit and investment "strengthens the disposition of capitalist agencies to keep in liquid form a growing proportion of their incoming cash flows."[12]

At such moments, states may attempt to intervene to stave off crisis. During the beginning of the systemic crisis of US hegemony, "the synergy of reduced inflationary pressures, high real interest rates, massive inflows of capital, and a rising dollar was in keeping with the Reagan administration's objective of strengthening US finance capital."[13] The state response to the beginning of the systemic crisis allowed accumulation to continue, but did not fix the underlying causes of the crisis. In fact, some aspects of state intervention caused economic consequences that exacerbated the crisis. "This flood of US bound foreign capital and the associated appreciation of the dollar were essential ingredients in the transformations of the pre-1995 boom in equity prices into the subsequent bubble."[14] Eventually, the US government was able to use tools of policy and its premier position within the global economy to temporarily bring about a resurgence. However, the underlying causes of the crisis were never resolved, and the bubble burst when the expansion in wealth could not be translated to realized profit. Arrighi contends that "the inflation of the paper value of their assets, and the bubble-induced 'wealth effect' on consumer demand, led corporations to invest well above what was warranted by their actually realized profits."[15]

States play an important part in each systemic cycle of accumulation, as financial expansions are tied to the institutional structures under which capital accumulation is possible. While financial expansion signals a coming of a financial crisis, it also signals the rise of a new global hegemon. As Arrighi and Silver posit:

> All phases of financial expansion have indeed been the 'autumn' of major developments of world capitalism. But they have also been periods of hegemonic transition, in the course of which a new leadership emerged

interstitially and over time reorganized the system so as to make its further expansion possible.[16]

Financial expansions of the global economy lead to innovation in the production process and the ability of capital to realize profit. Capital's ability to reallocate "capital to emergent structures that promise greater security or higher returns than the dominant structure,"[17] is essential in facilitating this process. Former most profitable forms of production are then shifted to states that have less power in the world economy, while more powerful states try to support the most profitable activity to be. This is the process through which new hegemonies are forged. The disorganization of the previous system of accumulation limits the "collective power of the system's dominant groups."[18] A new global hegemony can emerge if it can offer a "new complex of governmental and business agencies endowed with greater system-level organizational capabilities than those of the preceding hegemonic complex."[19] The new hegemonic complex that emerges has greater systemic capabilities of the one that came before it, allowing its national capitalist class a new way to actually realize profit. This new cycle, according to Giovanni Arrighi and Beverly Silver:

> differs from the preceding one in two main respects: the greater concentration of organizational capabilities wielded by the hegemonic state in comparison with its predecessor, and the higher volume and dynamic density of the system that is being reorganized by the hegemonic state.[20]

Financial crisis ends by a new hegemony setting new rules for the system, rules that allow capital to once again realize profit.

In addition to a few parallels in their biographies—active in the northern Italian student and workers movement, jailed for their political work—Arrighi's writings further Gramsci's principle objective to:

> deepen his understanding of the society he had been fighting to change, by clarifying his views on the theories of Marx and on the Marxist tradition, by analyzing the complex and frequently hidden mechanisms of power, by reflecting on the character of his own political party, by formulating possible strategies for future action.[21]

Both Gramsci and Arrighi provide us not only with a theory for understanding the relationship between the state and capitalist development, but in describing the way state and economy track together, expose key weaknesses of the capitalist world-system, thereby providing openings for those who seek a more just and equal future.

Notes

1 Antonio Gramsci, *The Prison Notebooks* (New York: International Publishers, 1971), 57.
2 *Ibid.*, 182.
3 *Ibid.*, 161.
4 *Ibid.*, 126.
5 Arrighi, Giovanni and David Harvey, "The Winding Paths of Capital," *New Left Review* 56 (2009): 61–94, 66.
6 *Ibid.*, 67.
7 Giovanni Arrighi, *The Long Twentieth Century* (London: Verso, 1994), 6.
8 *Ibid.*, 10.
9 *Ibid.*, 27.
10 Giovanni Arrighi, *Adam Smith in Beijing* (London: Verso, 2007), 101.
11 *Ibid.*, 106.
12 Giovanni Arrighi and Beverly J. Silver, "Capitalism and World (Dis)order," *Review of International Studies* 27 (2001): 263.
13 Arrighi, *Adam Smith in Beijing*, 109.
14 *Ibid.*, 112.
15 *Ibid.*, 113.
16 Arrighi and Silver, "World (Dis)order," 261.
17 Giovanni Arrighi and Beverly J. Silver, *Chaos and Governance in the Modern World System* (Minneapolis: University of Minnesota Press, 1999), 33.
18 *Ibid.*
19 *Ibid.*, 34.
20 *Ibid.*, 34.
21 Antonio Gramsci, *Prison Notebooks*, 3 Vols. (New York: Columbia University Press, 2007), 17.

9 The City and the Foundations of Capitalism

Henri Pirenne/Oliver C. Cox

Henri Pirenne (1862–1935) was born in 1862 in a village near Liège, Belgium. He was a student of Godefroid Kurth at the University of Liège, and then became professor of history at the University of Ghent in 1886, a position he held for the duration of his career. Pirenne was arrested in 1916 by German occupiers for his involvement in the resistance, although the extent of his involvement remains unknown to biographers. Legend has it that when questioned by German officers, they became frustrated when he insisted in answering in his native French. Pirenne allegedly told them that he had forgotten to speak German as of August 3, 1914, although it was well known that German was among his working languages, as he had held postdoctoral fellowships in Leipzig and Berlin. Pirenne was interned in Jena, Germany, until the end of World War I and spent his time in prison reading Russian-language history texts that had been smuggled in by Russian prisoners. Pirenne credited these works with providing him a new perspective on European history that took his subsequent work in a more global direction.

His intellectual legacy is cemented by the Pirenne Thesis, which has yet to be fully discredited by economic historians despite being nearly a century old. Pirenne proposed a radical new explanation for the decline of the Roman Empire. Opposing the established narrative that Rome was sacked by barbarians thereby triggering its downfall, Pirenne alternately posited that Rome's fall was a result of the rising power of Arab-Islamic empires in North Africa and Western Asia. Pirenne demonstrated by focusing his analysis on long-distance trade routes that the economic life of the 5th, 6th, and 7th centuries was never disrupted. Trade routes linking the Mediterranean to India and China through the Red Sea and Indian Ocean continued to flourish, he showed, but what had changed was that control of these routes began to be contested. Arab-Islamic Empires waged wars against Roman and Greek merchants for control of Mediterranean trade, and as Romans lost these wars, the locus of European economic activity shifted away from the Mediterranean and northward to Britain, Germany, France, and other areas of northern Europe, thus bringing about the so-called "Dark Ages."

However, the bulk of Pirenne's work was not on the rise of Arab-Islamic Empires, nor on the fall of the Roman Empire, but on trade in Medieval Europe. In 1922, Pirenne was invited to Princeton University to give a series

DOI: 10.4324/9781003198291-11

of lectures on trade and Medieval European cities, which were eventually published by Princeton University Press under the title *Medieval Cities: Their Origins and the Revival of Trade* (1925). The city, claimed Pirenne, is the most important unit of analysis for economic history as it is a visible manifestation of the social, political, and the economic. While cities are not necessary for human survival and are fluid and impermanent, he argued, they are the visible social product of long-distance trade. Merchants, Pirenne shows, were the first truly urban class, and they gravitate to cities that offer security, facilitate communication, provide easy access to ports, and a greater degree of personal liberty compared to the countryside.[1] The first modern European city of note, Pirenne claims, is Venice, as it marked Medieval Europe's first major urbanization after the decline of the Roman Empire. Modern Venice's origins are found in the 10th century, when professional merchants were drawn to the region by its ports, markets, and fairs.[2] Venice was well situated to launch long-distance sea voyages, as at the time, the sole means of realizing large returns was through long-distance trade. "The more distant the journey of the merchant," wrote Pirenne, "the more profitable it was for him."[3] To facilitate these voyages, merchants needed goods for exchange, for which they depended upon the city. Agricultural surplus was brought to Venice to support an urban merchant class which survived on wages paid for labor in manufacturing. In other words, the merchant class made itself "the givers of work" which attracted migration from the surrounding countryside.[4]

By the 13th and 14th centuries, urban social conflicts abounded in Venice,[5] as did periodic economic crises,[6] giving rise to the municipality which was created to solve these problems through collective action. Municipal institutions were bureaucratic organizations with a monopoly on violence[7] that set labor laws along with rules of trade and exchange,[8] put in place a legal code, tax code,[9] and penal code in order to secure persons and property.[10] The municipality also furnished the city with an articulating identity, establishing the values and beliefs[11] of the city. While far from the coherent states we know today, Medieval Venice, claims Pirenne, afforded its citizens freedom to own and sell one's property at will.[12] In other words, for the first time after a long lapse, Europe experienced once again "the power of liquid capital."[13] Pirenne claims that, ultimately, the resurgence of the European city led to the transition to capitalism in Europe.

Writing nearly 40 years later, **Oliver Cox** (1901–1974) was similarly committed to demonstrating the importance of the Medieval European city in the transition to capitalism. Born in Port of Spain, Trinidad and Tobago, in 1901, Oliver Cromwell Cox is best described as one of the most underrated historical sociologists of the 20th century. He moved to the United States to pursue his undergraduate studies at Northwestern University, receiving his BS in 1928. He matriculated to the University of Chicago for a graduate degree in economics, and hoped to specialize in economic history. However, he was dissatisfied with mainline economists' explanations for the Great

88   *Macro-Historical Theories of Capitalism*

Depression, and therefore decided to make a switch to sociology, earning his PhD in 1938. As a result of US apartheid, he then spent the bulk of his career at historically black colleges: Wiley College, Tuskegee Institute, and then Lincoln University. From 1970 until his death in 1974, he taught at Wayne State. But his time at Wayne State was rife with conflict. He had been hired assuming he would teach and supervise dissertations on race, but instead insisted on teaching in his area of expertise—the systemic nature of capitalism. Unlike some sociologists who despite being ignored by their contemporaries posthumously garner establishment acclaim, Cox's legacy fails to reflect the level of depth, importance, and innovation of his scholarship.

Cox's commitments to black nationalism and Marxism, along with his strong constructivist position on race, put him far out of the sociological mainstream for the 1940s and 1950s. These tensions between Cox and his contemporaries are exemplified by his vocal criticism of E. Franklin Frazier, who in 1948 became the first black president of the American Sociological Association. Cox charged Frazier of leading what Cox termed the "Black Bourgeoisie School" of sociology of race for failing to see, as Cox believed, that racism was a result of the class dynamics of capitalism along with historical processes of imperialism and colonialism. The mainline tendency of sociology of race in the 1950s, Cox lamented, erroneously sought explanation in ethnocentrism and primordial prejudice. Cox was therefore not accepted by the subfield of sociology of race, even though he remains best known for his dissertation book (and his only book on race) *Caste, Class, and Race* (1948), which was reprinted by *Monthly Review* in 2010.

The majority of Cox's scholarly work was on the political economy of capitalism in macrohistorical perspective. Cox's main influences include Werner Sombart, the German sociologist, and Paul Sweezy, the Marxist economist,[14] who carefully read and offered critical feedback on many of Cox's manuscripts. But few of his contemporaries in historical sociology and Marxist sociology acknowledged the depth of his contributions to these disciplinary subfields. Scholars today who have taken an interest in Cox's work explain his lack of contemporary acclaim as a product of the racism of the subfields of historical sociology and Marxist sociology. As within these two subfields of American sociology, the most acclaimed and renowned scholars have been historically, and to a large extent still tend to be, white men.

Cox's *The Foundations of Capitalism* (1959) is among the most important, yet most underrated, works of historical sociology. In it, he invents a world-systems analysis before world-systems analysis. The launching point of this work, the capitalist city, is a brilliant and prescient move that only in recent years has begun to be replicated by historical sociologists. In the first half of this over 500-page opus, Cox describes in great historical detail Venice as the progenitor of world-capitalism, and Florence (then Genoa) as key innovators of global capitalism. From the Italian city states, Cox then analyzes the city of Amsterdam and how it was essential in the development of Dutch (and global) capitalism. In part two of the book, he then develops

The City and the Foundations of Capitalism   89

a general theory of capitalism based on his historical analysis of these important early modern European cities. Just as Pirenne claimed in 1925, so did Cox contend that "to understand the nature of the capitalist system it is necessary to examine the characteristics and the processes of development of medieval and early modern European cities."[15] It was in the city, Cox argued, that capitalism was born and sustained. And with each new innovation in the capitalist system, showed Cox, a new city was at the center of innovation. "What was said in wonder about Venice in 1450, about Amsterdam in 1650, and London in 1875 is now very nearly repeated in descriptions of New York."[16] Each capitalist world-hegemon had a city that sustained and represented its dominance.

Venice, for Cox, is the primary object of his analysis in *The Foundations of Capitalism* (1959), as it was there, he argued, the convergence of factors led to unique social innovations that then sparked the transition to capitalism. Through his focus on the city as the place where capitalism can be best seen and analyzed, Cox argues that the British Industrial Revolution, while a key innovation in the global history of the capitalist system, was by no means the origin of capitalism.[17] Instead, he argues that Venice laid the foundations for capitalism, mostly because of its invention of the Capitalist state,[18] but also because the Venetian Republic transformed theology in order to make Catholicism more compatible with capitalism.[19] Venice, Cox shows, created the first capitalist culture, which motivated its citizens to fully embrace the "capitalist way of life" as a "cultural ideal."[20] Through his analysis, Cox concludes that:

> the capitalist city …although apparently constituting a self-sufficient unit, can develop and expand only as it expands its economic role in a wider world of sophisticated and backward communities. Furthermore, it tends to decline and decay as opportunity for such expansion recedes or becomes limited.[21]

Cox's view of the role of a city at the heart of capitalist expansion is that it is through the economy, politics, and culture of the particular city that dependent development occurs. A city becomes an industrial hub, exploiting labor both native and migrant, and subjects the surrounding countryside to its yoke,[22] it colonizes other territories in a dependent way,[23] and it is the launching point for global trade.[24] But as its particular strategy of capital accumulation becomes outdated, the city ceases to be the global hub for business and culture.

While Cox's method of looking to a global city to see capitalist development had gone largely unnoticed for decades, recent trends in global history and historical sociology look to cities, just as Cox did, in order to see processes of globalization and capital accumulation.[25] But just as Pirenne contended in the late 19th century and Oliver Cox did in the mid-20th, global cities continue to be an important unit of analysis for understanding the world-historical development of the capitalist system.

Notes

1 Henri Pirenne, *Medieval Cities: Their Origins and the Revival of Trade* (Princeton: Princeton University Press, 1925 [1980]), 135, 171.
2 *Ibid.*, 114.
3 *Ibid.*, 122.
4 *Ibid.*, 153.
5 *Ibid.*, 154.
6 *Ibid.*, 164–165.
7 *Ibid.*, 182.
8 *Ibid.*, 185.
9 *Ibid.*, 202.
10 *Ibid.*, 170.
11 *Ibid.*, 231.
12 *Ibid*, 194–195.
13 *Ibid.*, 221.
14 See Plys Introduction.
15 Oliver C. Cox, *The Foundations of Capitalism* (London: Peter Owen Limited, 1959), 25.
16 *Ibid.*, 14.
17 *Ibid.*, 481.
18 *Ibid.*, 90–107.
19 *Ibid.*, 57–62.
20 *Ibid.*, 63.
21 *Ibid.*, 480.
22 *Ibid.*, 75–78.
23 *Ibid.*, 72–75.
24 *Ibid.*, 67–72.
25 See Marco D'Eramo, "Dock Life" *New Left Review* 96, (2015); Arndt Graf and Chua Beng Huat, *Port Cities in Asia and Europe* (London: Routledge, 2009); Carola Hein, *Port Cities: Dynamic Landscapes and Global Networks* (London: Routledge, 2011); Alice Mah, *Port Cities and Global Legacies* (Palgrave MacMillan, 2014); Sandy Prita Meier, *Swahili Port Cities* (Bloomington: University of Indiana Press, 2016); Patrick O'Flanagan, *Port Cities of Atlantic Iberia, c. 1500–1900* (London: Routledge, 2016); Saskia Sassen, *Cities in a World-Economy* (New York: Sage, 2011); AbdouMaliq Simone, *For the City Yet to Come: Changing African Life in Four Cities* (Durham: Duke University Press, 2004).

10 A Cyclical Theory of Empire

Nikolai Kondratieff/Ibn Khaldun

Nikolai Dimitrievitch Kondratieff (1892–1938) was born in 1892 to a peasant family living just north of Moscow, Russia. He was educated at the University of St. Petersburg in agricultural economics and statistics. After World War I, he became interested in finding an explanation for the confluence of war and economic downturn that had ravaged Europe. In 1920, he founded his own research institute to this end, the Institute of the Conjuncture, in order to better understand economic downturn and the economic dynamics of World War I.

In the autumn of 1930, at age 38, Kondratieff was arrested and deported to Siberia for allegedly heading the Peasant's Labor Party (most likely a fantasy anarchist political organization), committing "agricultural sabotage," introducing bourgeois ideas into his research, and having an erroneous conceptualization of the USSR's socialist vision.[1] In September 1938, after having spent six of his eight years in prison in solitary confinement, he was convicted of being a "kulak-professor" and was executed by firing squad. Although his work was ignored in the Soviet Union, particularly after his arrest and execution, it was translated from Russian into German and French. Kondratieff's work soon grew popular among some of the most reputable economists of the time, including Joseph Schumpeter, Ragnar Frisch, Wesley Mitchell, and Simon Kuznets (one of the few economists who read Kondratieff's work in the original Russian). His books and papers began to be translated to and published in English in November 1935.

Kondratieff first began developing his theory of long cycles in a 1922 book on the economic conditions of the world economy after World War I. Kondratieff's long cycle is a 60-year cycle of expansion and contraction of the world economy. In the conjuncture, so posits Kondratieff, one observes the expansion and contraction of the capitalist economy, but over time, if one looks at several of these cycles of expansion and contraction, one sees how the capitalist economy passes from one stage to another.[2] This structural determinant of capitalism, Kondratieff posits, has as a consequence, periodic wars and revolutions, the assimilation of new territory into the world-economy, fluctuations in gold production, and changes in techniques of production and communication.[3] While all four of these determinants are often thought of as factors affecting economic development, Kondratieff shows that on the

DOI: 10.4324/9781003198291-12

92 Macro-Historical Theories of Capitalism

contrary, these are the consequences of capitalist development as each factor can influence subsequent economic development but cannot change the trajectory of the world-economy.

Kondratieff's theory of long cycles ignited a great deal of controversy and criticism among economists in the Soviet Union and beyond. Therefore, in 1924, in part to clear the air, he wrote a paper that nevertheless provoked even greater criticism, in part because critics had expected a unified theory, which was not forthcoming. At the time, the four major criticisms of Kondratieff's long cycles revolved around: (1) his use of time series analysis; (2) the fact that the statistical significance of some results did not stand up in replications, (3) some critics' (e.g. Leon Trotsky's) denial of the existence of general and periodic cycles as opposed to the evolution of capitalism, and (4) the lack of causal argumentation in his theory.

To counter critiques that the work was fundamentally acausal, Kondratieff began by pointing out the shortcomings of macroeconomic methods. He did not want to provide a theory for the long cycles he had unearthed, however, because he derived his results from time series analysis in spite of having cautioned against the use of time series in inductive research. In response to criticism, Kondratieff looked for theoretical causes and modified Marx's idea that cycles are caused by a periodic reinvestment of fixed capital every decade or so, introducing the idea of a graduation in the production period and the amount of investment in different kinds of goods over time. Kondratieff believed that future research on long cycles should center on their relationship to technological progress and social and political history.

Kondratieff also sought to counter critics who denied the existence of cycles altogether, claiming that his cycles were a result of endogenous forces and that the cycles could not be adequately shown to be exogenous. But the fact of the matter is that Kondratieff leaned much more toward endogenous explanations than exogenous explanations for the structure of the global economy. This proved to be problematic for him and not simply theoretically; this stance contributed to his eventual arrest and execution. Kondratieff claimed that cycles were driven by endogenous contradictions in the capitalist system and determined by capital accumulation over time; but one of Kondratieff's staunchest critics, Leon Trotsky, countered that such dynamics could be changed by political events. For Trotsky, there were high political stakes in the debate between partisans of exogenous and endogenous causes of capitalist development. If Kondratieff were right that the capitalist system was comprised of an endogenous underlying logic, then anti-systemic ruptures such as the Russian Revolution would be ineffective in bringing about the end of capitalism. That was not an analytical result that Trotsky wanted to admit.

While Kondratieff maintained that he was not a Marxist, he prudently noted that he was simply following Marx's understanding of the genetic process of capitalism. In subsequent debates between Trotsky and Nikolai Bukharin, Kondratieff's view of capitalism seemed to endorse Bukharin's concept of capitalism as a moving equilibrium. As a result of his politically unsatisfactory response to Trotsky's criticism, and therefore, in the view of Soviet officials, his alleged similarities to Mikhail Bakunin, Kondratieff was seen as an anarchist heretic.

Similarly renowned for his cyclical explanations for current events, **Abu Zayd 'Abdu r-Rahman bin Muhammad bin Khaldun al-Hadrami,** (1332–1406) known as Ibn Khaldun, was born in Tunis, Tunisia, in 1332. He was born into an elite Andalusian Arab family with Yemeni ancestry. His family held high offices in *Al-Andalus* (Moorish Spain), but fled to Tunis after the *Reconquista* in 1248. Once settled in Tunis, Khaldun's family held office in the Hafsid Dynasty, a Sunni Sultanate that controlled what is now Western Libya, Tunisia, and Eastern Algeria from 1229 to 1574.

Khaldun received a classical Islamic education. He studied Arabic, memorized the Quran, and was certified in the subjects of the Quran, hadith, *sharia* (law), and *fiqh* (jurisprudence). After completing his Islamic education, he studied mathematics, logic, and philosophy under the guidance of the renowned tutor Al-Abili of Tlemcen, who introduced a young Khaldun to the writings of Averroes, Avicenna, Razi, and Tusi. Khaldun's career aspirations were to follow his family into politics, and found work as a court historiographer for several North African Sultans. He lived and worked in Tunis, Fez, Granada, Bejaia, Tlemcen, Tiaret, and then ended his career in Mamluk Egypt, when in 1384 Sultan al-Malik udh-Dhahir Barquq appointed Khaldun professor at the most prestigious Madrasa in Cairo. After 1401, he became involved with an underground political party *Rijal Hawa Rijal*, which called for social reform. He was placed under arrest for his political involvement with the group and died in jail in 1406.

Khaldun's most famous work *The Muqaddimah* (1377) has recently gained some traction in historical sociology, as the subfield has increasingly begun to look to non-European social theory for fresh theoretical perspectives. *The Muqaddimah* (1377) is one of the first global histories, and is widely thought to be the first historical work that addresses the philosophy of history as Khaldun's launching point in the book is to critique existing historical methodology as biased, using unreliable sources, and merely chronicling a sequence of events instead of providing historical explanation.[4] In his critique of the historical methods of his day, Khaldun instead contends that the goal of history should be to devise a scientific theory of human society.[5] For this innovative way of thinking about history, Khaldun is sometimes thought of as among the first sociologists.

One of the most useful theories from *The Muqaddimah* (1377) is Khaldun's theory of cycles of empire. Each empire, claims Khaldun, falls as a result of its internal contradictions. The resulting vacuum of power provides an entrée for peripheral groups to create a stronger empire in the wake of the fallen empire. The mechanism by which this reconstitution occurs is through Khaldun's concept of *asabiyya*, the bond of cohesion among humans in a group forming a community. When a new empire comes to power, the

94　*Macro-Historical Theories of Capitalism*

people are not accustomed to its rule, and therefore need to be convinced of the "strong superiority" of the ruling class in order to willingly submit to its rule.[6] Once established, a ruling family emerge that "are clearly marked as leaders," and therefore it requires less effort from rulers to make subjects "subservient and submissive" to that empire. The best bases, claims Khaldun, for creating social cohesion are through either religious claims or through "truthful propaganda."[7]

In empires in decline, one observes a dissolution of *asabiyya*. If, for example, an empire is overcommitted and conquers more territory than it can reasonably integrate, the empire will crumble as a result of the inability to maintain social cohesion across the entire territory.[8] When empires are overcommitted, *asabiyya* dissolves into factionalism, individualism, and diminishes the political capacity of the empire. The ability of an empire to expand and to endure, posits Khaldun, is dependent upon the strength of social cohesion among the political class.[9] In territory where there are many different tribes or social groups, Khaldun argues, it is difficult, if not impossible, to establish an enduring empire, as creating cohesion across different religious, ethnic, and language groups poses a significant challenge.[10]

But even if an empire is able to create *asabiyya*, over time, it has a tendency to erode. The nature of empire is for the royal authority to claim all the riches and glory for itself. Inequality and apathy for the ruling class then prevent loyalty to the regime, and as a result the empire weakens as economic inequality and social unrest grow.[11] A cycle of empire, from rise to decline, claims Khaldun, takes about 50–120 years to play out, depending upon the success of political leadership.[12] The first 40 years are characterized by "toughness" and "savagery" as a new political order establishes itself and *asabiyya* is strong during this period. The middle 40 years are characterized by a "sedentary culture" as a result of the "luxury and plenty" associated with successful empire-building. But during this middle period, *asabiyya* wanes to some extent as complacency grows. In the last 40 years of the cycle, inequality is rife. While some have "a life of prosperity and ease," others are completely dependent upon the empire for their survival, and if they dissent, are "dominated by force." In this stage, "group feeling disappears completely."[13] New leadership can then capitalize on the collapse of social cohesion by devising a new way to restore and strengthen *asabiyya*. If successful in this endeavor, a new dynasty can establish itself, since "aggressive and defensive strength is obtained only through group feeling which means affection and willingness to fight and die for each other."[14]

Khaldun's theory of the rise and fall of empire has striking similarities to several concepts that historical social scientists use today. Khaldun's concept of *asabiyya* has many similarities to Emile Durkheim's concept of social solidarity.[15] Writing centuries later, Durkheim similarly contends that within a given state, citizens have a collective identity that links them together and to the collective.[16] But while mechanical solidarity in Durkheim's framework is naturally occurring, Khaldun contends that *asabiyya* must be intentionally cultivated by the ruling classes. For that reason, *asabiyya* also has many similarities to Gramscian hegemony,[17] in that an intentionally cultivated cultural cohesion allows the ruling class to convince all within the boundaries of the empire that its rule serves the interest of all, when ultimately, according to Khaldun, the goal of empire is to enrich the emperor and the political class. Perhaps for our purposes, what is most interesting in Khaldun's theory is its cyclical understanding of society. Khaldun's 120-year long cycles are about half the length of Kondratieff's 60-year long cycles.[18]

While cyclical understandings of global capitalism abounded in the 1920s and beyond,[19] Ibn Khaldun had devised a cyclical theory of empire long before economists and other historical social scientists began using cyclical theories to understand capitalist development. Both Kondratieff and Khaldun used their theories of long cycles to understand the most important historical events of their time—for Khaldun the rise and fall of empire and for Kondratieff World War I and economic crisis. And both Khaldun and Kondratieff had a strong scientistic perspective. They innovated new scientific methods for the study of macrohistory, and even when the results of their scientific inquiry became a political liability for them, they stood behind their results even if it meant imprisonment, or in Kondratieff's case, death. While Khaldun's theory was devised long before the origins of capitalism, he innovated a new way of thinking about historical development, and while the mechanics of Khaldun's and Kondratieff's cycles are quite different, both similarly challenge a linear conception of global historical development.

Notes

1 Kristin Plys, "World-Systemic and Kondratieff Cycles," *Yale Journal of Sociology* (Fall 2012): 130–160.
2 N.D. Kondratieff, "Long Waves in Economic Life," *The Review of Economic Statistics* 17, no. 6 (1935): 107.
3 *Ibid.*, 112.
4 Ibn Khaldûn, *The Muqaddimah: An Introduction to History* (Princeton: Princeton University Press, 1377 [2005]), 24.
5 *Ibid.*, 35.
6 *Ibid.*, 124.
7 *Ibid.*, 126–127.
8 *Ibid.*, 128.
9 *Ibid.*, 130.
10 *Ibid.*, 131.
11 *Ibid.*, 134.
12 *Ibid.*, 136.
13 *Ibid.*, 137.
14 *Ibid.*, 123.
15 Emile Durkheim, *The Division of Labor in Society* (New York: The Free Press, 1893 [1997]).
16 *Ibid.*, 60.
17 See Gramsci, *Prison Notebooks*, Part 2, Chapter 7.
18 Kondratieff, "Long Waves," 106.
19 See Introduction.

Part III

Postcolonial Theories of Capitalism

Many would agree that the difference between traditional and modern world-systems is that traditional forms of economic and political expansion were unabashed imperialisms, while modern global economies are formally rational capitalisms. Here, again, is the difference between Immanuel Wallerstein, who is the leading proponent of this distinction, and Andre Gunder Frank, who in effect ignores it by downplaying the differences between the Asiatic Mode of Production that lay behind the Silk Road and the modern capitalist mode of production and capital accumulation. The Silk Road arose from the Han Dynasty (206 BCE to 220 CE) that was controlled by imperial force a vast Asia land mass—from North and East Asia to the South, including the Indochina Peninsula and today's India and West into Central Asia. The Silk Road is a figurative name, because silk was only one of the major products traded between the West and the East along several trade routes that endured until the end of the Mongol and Byzantine Empires in the 13th and 14th centuries. The trade routes were indeed global in a figurative sense, but they required imperial force to clear the way and secure the routes along which products were exchanged.

By contrast, the capitalist world-economy arose around 1500 with the European voyages across the Atlantic in search of fungible metals and other consumable products of value that could be converted into surplus value in Europe, West and East. Though capitalism sponsored its own often sly brands of violence, it did so under formally rational rules governing its mode of production that allowed for the logic of endless capital accumulation. Capitalism gets away with its high-minded avarice under the protection of a culture of human progress that, in turn, legitimized the nation states that articulated the culture while protecting capital interests—by any means necessary. In other words, modern capitalist world-economy entails a world-system that structures not entirely legitimate relations among nationally organized polities and legitimizing cultures. Otherwise put, capitalism necessarily must evolve into a global political economy with its own geo-culture; which is to say a world-system, simply put.

If there is a sub-rosa structural violence to the system, it is modern capitalism's early and continuing reliance on colonizing the resource-rich regions of the world that also were a source of exploitable labor. Walter Rodney is first among those who argued that, as brutal as slavery was, the exchange value of the enslaved on the open market owed to the productive value of their labor

DOI: 10.4324/9781003198291-13

98 *Postcolonial Theories of Capitalism*

power. Racism was (and is) a secondary legitimating justification for the economic exploitation. Walter Rodney is chief among those who have explained this dynamic, notably for Europe's colonization of Africa—that in turn was the foundational source for the North Atlantic Slave Trade Triangle. He and C.L.R. James are coupled in this section, because together they offer a comprehensive introduction to the varieties of postcolonial theories of capitalism.

A fresh glance at the topics and authors examined in this section could well be confusing. They are many and various. In one sense that is the way of the postcolonial world in which the residual effects of colonization produced a world cut into several parts according to capitalism's political economy. The postcolonial theorists and others detailed in this section have contributed to our common understanding of postcolonial thinking, whether of the former colonies or of the nation-cultures of the colonizers.

Some might be unsettled, for example, by the attention given to Vladimir Lenin, Mao Zedong, and Ho Chi Minh who were founders of different versions of communism. But we note that others were, one way or another, in the ambience of these communisms; hence, Nestor Makhno is paired with Lenin and Charu Mazumdar with Mao, and Martin Luther King, Jr., with Ho. King was hardly an advocate for Ho Chi Minh, but later in his life he opposed the War in Vietnam and may have been assassinated for his turn to the political and economic left. That Mahatma Gandhi was one of the sources of King's nonviolent philosophy could also be seen in his willingness to look to the postcolonial world for instruction. From another angle it may seem strange to see Muhammad Ali identified as a postcolonial figure. Yet, after his defeat of Sonny Liston in 1964, he came out as a member of the Nation of Islam, which affiliation influenced his refusal to be drawn into the American War in Vietnam. Ali was not in any way an affine of the Viet Cong, but he did famously assert that they did him no harm so he would not fight them. Albert Camus may, again, seem a strange figure to appear in the company of many of the others on the list. But Camus was born to poverty in Algeria and later studied at the University of Algiers before moving to Paris after the Nazi occupation. Camus's literature, even his fiction, could be seen as deeply affected by his youth in Algiers and repulsion at the extremes of European depravities. Think of his plays *The Stranger* and *The Fall.* And one might wonder what an American intellectual like Frederick Jameson has to do with Aijaz Ahmad, the Indian cultural theorist. Yet, Jameson in his ambivalent attitude toward postmodernism was, in a high-minded way, preoccupied with what might come after the reign of capitalism. The liberation of India from British rule in 1947 was not an obvious marker of an end to the modern, but it was a turning point toward the global decolonizing movement. With no exception, we can think that all those discussed in this section have some or another relation to the decolonizing movement.

In more general terms, this section on Postcolonialism's necessary opposition to global Capitalism examines a tension that down to the present time remains acute and world shaking.

11 Postcolonial Class Analysis

Barrington Moore/Claudia Jones

Barrington Moore, Jr., (1913–2005) was born in Washington, DC, in 1913. He hailed from an elite background. From a young age he was an avid yachtsman and attended a New England boarding school before attending Williams College, where he majored in Latin and took many courses in Ancient Greek and Classical history. As an undergraduate student, Moore's ambition was to become a professor of classics. He graduated with honors in Latin and received Williams' student prizes for Latin and Ancient Greek.

However, Moore took a yearlong introductory political science course at Williams, in which he was introduced to the work of William Graham Sumner, the founder of Yale's Sociology department. This experience led Moore to pursue a PhD in sociology at Yale after graduating from Williams. Moore completed his PhD in sociology at Yale in 1941 focusing on themes of inequality and authoritarianism. After Yale, he worked at the Office of Strategic Services (a precursor to the Central Intelligence Agency) as a strategic analyst before returning to academia. He was a faculty member at the University of Chicago for a few years before moving to Harvard in 1948. However, he was not appointed in the mainline and anti-communist Social Relations Department, but in area studies at the Russian Research Center, where he remained for the duration of his career.

His most famous book *Social Origins of Dictatorship and Democracy: Lord and Peasant in the Making of the Modern World* (1966)[1] remains a classic work of sociology. The book describes and analyzes the transition from agrarian society to modernity in several European and Asian countries, comparing the class-based trajectories of various states to understand why different modern states developed different political forms. Moore contends that when the bourgeoisie leads the charge to modernity the outcome is parliamentary democracy, when peasants lead the modernization drive the outcome is communism, and when landed elites initiate modernization the outcome is fascism. This comparative historical analysis, based on secondary sources, provides important insights into the class power embodied in different forms of the capitalist state, but also provides a framework for a class analysis that can be levied to compare different politico-economic contexts across the globe.

DOI: 10.4324/9781003198291-14

100 *Postcolonial Theories of Capitalism*

Social Origins is a pathbreaking work of sociology that led to the creation of the subfield of Comparative Historical Sociology (CHS), a field that looks to the past in order to build theory and provide insights into the present. Moore's book set many of the templates for the mainline of this subfield, including using multi-case comparisons, a focus on class as an agent of historical change, and a reliance on secondary historiographical sources. Some of these longstanding features of the field have done more harm than good. Particularly problematic is Moore's "England-centrism," which continues to be reproduced by contemporary historical sociologists.[2] By starting from the English case, Moore implicitly sets England as the baseline case to which all other cases are measured. This thinking remains popular in CHS that England's transition to modernity is seen as the reference category, to which other states' or region's trajectories are analyzed based on how they deviate from that alleged norm.

One of the most glaring missteps of Moore's analysis (and of many contemporary Comparative Historical Sociologists) is his failure to include Haiti's transition to modernity. Using the Haitian Revolution as either a case for comparison, or even perhaps as the baseline case, would have enriched not only Moore's analysis in the book, but would have changed how CHS as a subfield thinks of revolution. The Haitian case would have demonstrated that in addition to class conflict, race-based conflict and imperialism/anti-imperialism are similarly important motors of social change.

During the American Sociological Association's Annual Conference in 2016, this issue was raised by Prof. Zophia Edwards in the Q&A of a panel commemorating the 50th anniversary of the publication of the book. Moore's former PhD student Theda Skocpol's reply was that no historian had written a definitive historiography of the Haitian Revolution by 1966, so there was no way that Moore could have been aware of the Haitian case. However, as Edwards and I later lamented over a glass of wine, C.L.R. James' classic historiography of the Haitian Revolution *The Black Jacobins* (1938) was published in 1938 and remains among the most definitive historiographies of the Haitian Revolution. There's no way one can justify Moore's exclusion of the Haitian case because of a dearth of historiography. At one of the receptions after the panel, I remember talking with a graduate student who dismissed Edward's question as "Third World Marxism" that should die out already within CHS. The conversation soon descended into a rehashing of the Brenner Debate, but this contention surrounding *Social Origins* shows not only how deep an impact the book continues to have, but also how it has closed off certain topics and theoretical perspectives within the mainline of CHS. This continued contention surrounding the book begs the question: what if *Social Origins* were a truly global analysis? Certainly, it would have altered the trajectory of CHS. What if, instead of holding onto Barrington Moore as the founder of CHS, we instead looked to one of Moore's contemporaries, Claudia Jones?

Claudia Jones (1915–1964) was born in 1915 in Port-of-Spain, Trinidad. Her family immigrated to New York City when she was eight years old.

Postcolonial Class Analysis 101

She was educated in New York City, and joined the Communist Party and Young Communist League as a high school student. She became Editor in Chief of *Weekly Review* and the Editor of Negro Affairs for the *Daily Worker*. After multiple stints in various federal penitentiaries for her work with Communist Party USA, she was deported from the United States in December 1955. She was the only black female communist incarcerated and then deported from the United States during the McCarthy Era.[3] In an interview, Jones said of her arrest and deportation:

> I was a victim of the McCarthyite hysteria against independent political ideas in the USA... I was deported from the USA because as a Negro woman communist of West Indian descent, I was a thorn in their side in my opposition to Jim Crow racist discrimination against 16 million Negro Americans in the United States in my work for redress of these grievances, for unity of Negro and white workers, for women's rights and my general political activity urging the American people to help their struggles to change the present foreign and domestic policy in the United States.[4]

Jones then moved to London, where she joined the West Indian Forum and Committee on Racism and International Affairs along with various other Caribbean communist and labor organizations. Soon, she founded the *West Indian Gazette* of which she was Editor in Chief for the remainder of her life. Jones died of heart failure in 1964 and her ashes are interred in High Gate Cemetery near the grave of Karl Marx. While she remains little known in academic circles, Carole Boyce Davies contends that Jones "is one of the most important black radical thinkers ... in African diaspora history."[5]

Jones is best known for devising an intersectional class analysis before there was such a term. But Jones was not only concerned with the intersection of race, class, and gender, but also the way in which imperialism affects class analysis. So we could perhaps term Jones' perspective as an intersectional anti-imperialist class analysis. Jones, like Moore, has a theory of transitions to modernity that emerges from her class analysis. She contends that:

> Imperialism is not prepared to permit the independent development of any new capitalist state, is out to stultify it, make it impossible for the native capitalist to carry out the bourgeois democratic revolution. We know, of course, that as its foundations totter, imperialism seeks more flexible methods of governing the colonies and new means to camouflage its rule.[6]

From Jones' anti-colonial perspective, bourgeois democracy becomes more complicated than it ever was in Moore's analysis. Bourgeois democracy from the perspective of Empire is bifurcated, in that there is parliamentary

102 *Postcolonial Theories of Capitalism*

democracy in the centre of Empire, but democracy is denied to the colonies. Jones writes:

> British imperialist 'democracy' in action, besides, has in each previous war made things worse, not better for the colonial peoples. While pretending to be fighting for the rights of small nations and for democracy, the British ruling class denies to its colonies the most elementary democratic rights.[7]

For Jones, the English path to modernity is not a template to which other countries are compared, but part of a larger system in which the center of empire claims certain rights for itself while denying them to its colonies. This view complicates the Comparative Historical Sociological approach in that England's trajectory to modernity, for example, cannot be compared with say Trinidad and Tobago's trajectory to modernity, because as part of a singular empire, their trajectories are intertwined. Jones's class analysis reveals that CHS cannot compare different state's trajectories without taking the legacy of Empire into account.

But similar to Moore, Jones sees class and class struggle as the motor of historical change. She sees decolonization and development as a product of class struggle. "The West Indian people," she writes:

> have not taken lightly the extensive exploitation of their resources and human labour. Record profits have been declared by domestic and foreign capital interests in the sugar, oil and bauxite industries. But there have been many instances of working class resistance.[8]

But for Jones, this class struggle that is the motor of history is also intersectional:

> Our Party was the first to demonstrate to white women and to the working class that the triply-oppressed status of Negro women is a barometer of the status of all women and that the fight for the full economic, political and social equality of the Negro woman is in the vital self-interest of white workers, in the vital interest of the fight to realize equality for all women.[9]

Jones's class analysis is linked to political outcomes just as it is in Moore's analysis. Jones not only analyzes how class structures and class conflict can produce different political outcomes in different contexts, but also shows the intersectional role that gender plays in leading to these different political outcomes. Jones contends:

> Fascism... enslaves women with particular ruthlessness and cynicism, playing on the most painful feelings of the mother, the housewife, the single working woman, uncertain of the morrow. Fascism, posing as a

benefactor, throws the starving family a few beggarly scraps, trying in this way to stifle the bitterness aroused particularly among the toiling women, by the unprecedented slavery which fascism brings them. We must spare no pains to see that the women workers and toilers fight shoulder to shoulder with their class brothers in the ranks of the united working class front and the anti-fascist people's front.[10]

For Jones, the transition to fascism was not purely a matter of class structures and class conflict, but a result of the intersection of class and gender. The gendered aspect of fascist rhetoric, she demonstrates, is just as salient a factor in this political transition.

If we could imagine a rewrite of *Social Origins* based on a Claudia Jones-style analysis, it would similarly be attuned to class and class struggle, but the analysis would be complicated by several factors. First, it would take an intersectional approach to class struggle and class conflict, being attuned to the way that race and gender intersect with class and similarly influence the historical trajectory toward modernity. In so doing, one would also have to view many of Moore's cases as part of Empire and part of global processes of imperialism. England, France, and the United States would have to be seen as colonizing countries, which would then also complicate the ways in which race, class, and gender intersect to produce certain political outcomes. But this would be particularly complex in the treatment of the Indian case, which Moore treats as a discrete case even though it is a part of the British Empire. In setting up a comparative historical analysis of transitions to modernity using Claudia Jones's theoretical approach, we gain a richer, more complex and accurate, and more global approach to class analysis and political sociology.

Notes

1 Barrington Moore, *Social Origins of Dictatorship and Democracy: Lord and Peasant in the Making of the Modern World* (Boston: Beacon Press, 1966).
2 See Brenner.
3 Carole Boyce Davies, *Left of Karl Marx: The Political Life of Black Communist Claudia Jones* (Durham: Duke University Press, 2008), 1.
4 Claudia Jones, *Claudia Jones: Beyond Containment*, ed. Carole Boyce Davies (Banbury: Ayebia Clark Publishing Limited, 2011), 16.
5 Davies, *Left of Karl Marx*, xiii.
6 Jones, *Claudia Jones*, 160.
7 *Ibid.*, 28.
8 *Ibid.*, 159.
9 *Ibid.*, 87.
10 *Ibid.*, 89.

12 Capitalism's Soft Imperialism and Global Racism

C.L.R. James/Walter Rodney

C.L.R. James (1901–1989) was born in Tunapuna, Trinidad, to the name Cyril Lionel Robert James. From a very young age he was a voracious reader and an astute observer of social life. He attended Queens Royal College where he mastered the style and substance of European culture without letting it master him. There also he was an exceptional athlete, notably in cricket, which would later become the subject of *Beyond a Boundary*,[1] the book in which he deployed Marxist theory to the class boundaries set and fixed in cricket clubs and matches. In the 1920s, he taught English and History in Trinidad and published two novels, *La Divinia Pastora* (1927) and *Triumph* (1929). In 1932, James moved to England where he became a public intellectual, writing for the *Manchester Guardian*, and eventually associating with the Bloomsbury Circle, whose publishing house published his *Black Jacobins* (1938), his history of the Haitian revolutionaries. There also he continued his political work to decolonize Trinidad begun while still in the Caribbean.

The year 1938 was a crucial turning point in James's life. He was then invited to the United States by the Trotskyist Socialist Workers Party, whereupon he travelled to Mexico to meet Trotsky whose ideas would govern his intellectual and political work during much of what turned out to be a long stay in the United States. There also he would advance his thinking on the Negro question in global history, which had been the subject of another 1938 book; *The History of the Pan-African Revolt* would be substantially revised in 1969. This book reveals the extent to which, amid all his literary and political labors, James had already developed a mature theory of the Pan-African revolt as an economic crisis at the heart of global capitalism:

> The history of the Negro in his relation to European civilization falls into two divisions, the Negro in Africa and the Negro in America and the West Indies. Up to the 'eighties of the last century, only one-tenth of Africa was in the hands of Europeans. Until that time, therefore, it is the attempt of the Negro in the Western World to free himself from his burdens which has political significance in Western history. In the last quarter of the nineteenth century European civilization turned again to Africa, this time not for slaves to work the plantations of America but

DOI: 10.4324/9781003198291-15

for actual control of territory and population. Today (1938) the position of Africans in Africa is one of the major problems of contemporary politics.[2]

During his years in the United States, James continued to work and write in many directions at once, including an essay on Herman Melville in which Moby Dick served as a parable for the Anti-Communist movement that led to his deportation in 1954.

Also in 1950, toward the end of his sojourn in the United States, James pulled together his essays on American history and culture which years later were published posthumously as *American Civilization* (1993). The book ranges widely from chapters on individuality in America from 1776 to 1876 and American intellectuals in the 19th century to popular arts in modern America and "the struggle for happiness." But in respect to his general social theory of America and the modern world, the most compelling essay is "Negroes, Women, and Intellectuals" where he offers a succinct critical theory of the several ways the American capitalist system excludes the Negro, among them: the Negro sharecroppers and Negro agricultural laborers are at the mercy of the landlords and merchants, and by these intimidations they not only maintain that domination but extend it over whites as well. Negro labor in industry and inevitably white labor as well where the two work together, until the spread of unionism was at the mercy of industry:

- Probably well over a million white-collar and skilled labor jobs, which in an equal society would be held by Negroes, remain the exclusive preserve of whites.
- The political representatives of industrial management in the Nation are dependent on the political oligarchy of the South for holding check and defeating measures of the welfare state which they consider extreme, such as, for example, the repeal of the Taft-Hartley Act.
- The whole mighty apparatus of government which has now governed the United States for nearly 20 years can be completely upset by the freedom of the popular masses in the South.[3]

In this otherwise empirically local essay, one sees the skeletal structure of James's political economy of race that in larger purview is the groundwork of a complete outline of the political economy of labor under capitalism in the United States. In *American Civilization*, in 1950, James is advancing the earlier idea of W.E.B. Du Bois's *Black Reconstruction in America* in 1935 into a still more general theory of the role of the racial wage in capitalist labor.

Few of the decolonizing Pan-African theorists of the day (not even those much younger, including Frantz Fanon) deployed many literary and theoretical resources to the political realities of the day. More than most postcolonial Blacks, James understood the extent to which decolonization owed to a structural crisis in modern civilization itself. Anna Grimshaw, perhaps the

106   *Postcolonial Theories of Capitalism*

foremost editor and interpreter of James, put this perfectly well in a 1991 essay:

> James's distinctive contribution to the understanding of civilization emerged from a world filled with war, division, fear, suppression and unprecedented brutality. He himself had never underestimated the depth of the crisis which faced modern humanity. In James's view, it was fundamental. It was part and parcel of the process of civilization itself, as the need for the free and full development of the human personality within new, expanded conceptions of social life came up against enhanced powers of rule from above, embodied in centralized, bureaucratic structures which confined and fragmented human capacity at every level.[4]

Yet, Grimshaw understands this very well. James's cultural critique of modernity was never far from his own maturing (increasingly post-Trotskyist) Marxist critique of capitalism in *Dialectic Materialism and the Fate of Humanity* in 1947:

> Thus it is that the moment when the world system of capitalism has demonstrated the greatest productive powers in history is exactly the period when barbarism threatens to engulf the whole of society. The anti-dialecticians stand absolutely dumbfounded before the spectacle of the mastery of nature for human advancement and the degradation of human nature by this very mastery. The greater the means of transport, the less men are allowed to travel. The greater the means of communication, the less men freely interchange ideas. The greater the possibilities of living, the more men live in terror of mass annihilation. The bourgeoisie cannot admit this, for to admit it is themselves to sanction the end of the bourgeois civilization.[5]

This was James writing in 1947 when the white American world was flush with postwar affluence and its newfound role as the dominant world power.

James returned to London upon his deportation by the political nonsense then preoccupying the white American world. Except from occasional visits to Trinidad, he remained in London until his death in 1989. There, he continued his literary and political work, including a notable 1968 essay "World Revolution, 1968," in which James anticipated Immanuel Wallerstein's idea of the world revolution of 1968—a revolution that spelt the end of the modern world-system. James believed that the revolution would be led by Marxists, yet he also urged the Marxists of the day "to be quite clear so as to be able to recognize, welcome and intensify the advances that are taking place instinctively and in the world at large." As before, James at this crucial world moment could see beyond even the Marxists to the developments taking place in the world at large. James was a poet of sorts, a social and political theorist, an historian, and above all a visionary as to the structural morbidity of global capitalism.

Walter Rodney (1942–1980) was born in Georgetown, Guyana. He studied at Queen's College, Georgetown, and the University of the West Indies (UWI), where in both cases he was at the top of his class. After graduating UWI in 1963, he moved to England where he earned the PhD at the School of Oriental and African Studies at the University of London in 1966. He was 24 years old. His doctoral thesis, *A History of the Upper Guinea, 1545–1800*, was published by Oxford University Press in 1970. The book was widely praised for its historical acuity—a first public instance of Rodney's disciplined yet public history. In his short life, Rodney published six history books on aspects of the global Black experience.

Among Rodney's publications, two very different books stand out. One is *The Groundings with My Brothers* (1969), a political statement on the distinctive aspects of the Black Power Movement in the West Indies. "West Indian Society is a veritable laboratory of racialism. We virtually invented racialism."[6] In 1969, the Black Power in the United States had already become a global movement. It would seem, in retrospect, that Rodney was claiming a point of historical privilege for West Indian racism and thus for its Black Power Movement. Yet, he makes the compelling distinction that whatever the parallels between the slave system in the West Indies and in the United States, what was different was the manner in which the European colonial system made West Indian racism unique. His point was that, much as in the United States, slavery forced the white master to accept the "fantastic" gap between himself and his slaves as a condition of his natural superiority to Blacks.

This too applies to the American slave system, but Rodney's experience in the West Indies helped him appreciate the singular effects of European colonial system. Europeans inserted themselves into the indigenous Black societies they colonized. Americans imported their Black slaves, which left them having to invent what social norms and institutions they could in their segregated world. As a result, in the European colonies the colonizers remained a presence by creating a more continuous racial order—in part through inbreeding, but more through the imposition of social gradations by which Blacks could aspire to a position of relative privilege in the dominating capitalist societies. Hence, the series of relations in which some colonized Blacks enjoyed a carefully limited degree of authority and power by their service to the colonizers. One of Rodney's apt illustrations was drawn from his educational experience at the prestigious UWI that, in turn, could have led him to higher positions in the lower ranks of government and business that others had pursued. These were, more or less, subaltern positions offered and directed by the white colonizers, who had also built their own schools and universities to educate West Indian Blacks into their ways by training them in the soft culture of European virtue. Rodney's *The Groundings with My Brothers* was a political call to action for Black intellectuals like himself "to attach themselves to activity of the black masses,"[7] thus to stand

108 *Postcolonial Theories of Capitalism*

against the white colonial system that created the many subaltern strata meant to keep them silent.

How then can the colonized engage in revolutionary action? Rodney's reply: "[Among] New World blacks, ... the history nearest to revolutionary action will be the history of Africans in their new American environments."[8] By contrast, American Black Power revolutionaries like Cassius Clay and Stokley Carmichael became Muhammad Ali and Kwame Ture only after they had discovered the global importance of Pan-African culture—indirectly through the Nation of Islam in Ali's case after 1964 and directly in Ture's case when in 1960 he migrated to Guinea. Pan-Africanism had a serious prehistory in the 19th century but came into its own as a global movement in the first globally inclusive Pan-African conference in late July 1900. It would not be far wrong to suggest that, in turn, the prehistory of Black Power as a global movement was Pan-Africanism, a suggestion supported by the fact that W.E.B. Du Bois, himself a Black Power activist before the name, was active in that 1900 conference, only to become over the years a world leader of the movement.

Still, the fact remains that the West Indian movements were significantly different from both the American and what there was in the European metropoles. This is because the West Indies stands out as the one global region that was at once new world and African in a robust historical sense. As a result, the energy of the West Indian movement was generated by the experience of dealing with a more subtly oppressive and politically complicated colonial situation, while also having a greater direct access to the African histories that were part of their European colonizer's global empire, and thus resources for developing an original idea of Black Power.

Rodney's second notable book was his original contribution to a theory of the structures and methods of European colonizing in a capitalism world-system in a 1973 book. *How Europe Underdeveloped Africa* is a book that ought to be high on the list of classics among those studying the modern world economy. It was published the year before Wallerstein's *The Modern World-System I: Capitalist Agriculture and the Origins of the European World-Economy in the Sixteenth Century* in 1974. Rodney's 1973 book, though less nuanced than Wallerstein's 1974 book, tells much the same story from the point of view of the colonized. Of course, Rodney in 1973 could not cite Wallerstein's 1974 book, but he does cite André Gunder Frank's 1967 book *Capitalism and Underdevelopment in Latin America*. Among Rodney's too often ignored contributions are his distinguishing contributions to dependency theory. If anything, his theory of the development of underdevelopment in Africa is a better exemplar of dependency theory than Latin America, which was the theory's original empirical case.

The opening lines of *How Europe Underdeveloped Africa* are a clue to the degree to which Rodney is plowing new ground:

> Development in human is a many-sided process. At the level of the individual, it implies increased skill and capacity, great freedom, self-discipline,

responsibility and material well-being. ... More often than not, the term "development" is used in an exclusive economic sense—the justification being that the type of economy is itself an index of other social features.[9]

Today, these few lines illustrate the prescient sophistication of Rodney's social theory. Few economists, then or now, consider the extent to which development is a moral dimension of the lives of individuals. Conversely, moral theorists and social psychologists are comparably indifferent to the historical and economic aspects of development. What many in either camp fail to do is consider consistently the developmental pathologists. It is precisely here that Rodney introduces the pathologies association with the development of underdevelopment as, in his words,[10] a "particular relationship of exploitation of one country by another."

But here also, Rodney turns astutely to the capitalist world economy's avaricious interest in controlling African politics by the use of "foreign investment [that] ensures that the natural resources and the labour of Africa produce economic value which is lost to the continent."[11] Rodney, well trained in African history, makes it clear that as European capitalism forced itself on Africa, it failed to recognize that while Europe's industrial technology was more advanced, many of Africa's aesthetic and technological achievements were superior:

> The fact that Europe was the first part of the world to move from feudalism towards capitalism gave Europeans a headstart over humanity elsewhere in the scientific understanding of the universe, the making of tools and the efficient organisation of labour. European technical superiority did not apply to all aspects of production, but the advantage which they possessed in a few key areas proved decisive. For example, African canoes on the river Nile and the Senegal coast were of a high standard, but the relevant sphere of operations was the ocean, where European ships could take command. West Africans had developed metal casting to a fine artistic perfection in many parts of Nigeria, but when it came to the meeting with Europe beautiful bronzes were far less relevant than the crudest cannon. African wooden utensils were sometimes works of great beauty, but Europe produced pots and pans that had many practical advantages. Literacy, organistional experience, and the capacity to produce on an ever-expanding scale also counted in the European favour.[12] ... [Yet, he adds:] European manufactures in the early years of trade with Africa were often of poor quality, but they were of new varieties and were found attractive.[13]

In other words, the Europeans were too utilitarian to recognize the value of Africa's exceptional productive values, which is to say they were blinded by capitalism.

110   *Postcolonial Theories of Capitalism*

Rodney was crystal clear as to the theoretical meaning of this blindness. It is, in reality, due to the fact that the Europeans were looking elsewhere—a vision that not only occluded their ability to see Africa as anything more than a peripheral resource for their world economy:

> African economies are integrated into the very structure of the developed capitalist economies; and they are integrated in a manner that is unfavorable to Africa and ensures that Africa is dependent on the big capitalist countries. *Indeed, structural dependence is one of the characteristics of underdevelopment.*[14]

Thereafter, the remainder of Rodney's *How Europe Underdeveloped Africa* provides the empirical details of the history of Africa's vulnerability to underdevelopment; hence, chapters of the following topics:

- Africa's development before the 15th century when the Europeans came
- Africa's contribution in the precolonial era to European capitalism
- The beginnings of Africa's underdevelopment before 1865
- Africa's contribution to capitalism in the colonial era

The book concludes with a reprise of the general theory in Chapter 6, "Colonialism as a System for Underdeveloping Africa." Here, Rodney returns to the strong dependency theory of *The Groundings with My Brothers* in 1969 by offering a nuanced account of the mechanisms capitalism used to exploit Africa:

> In addition to private companies, the colonial state also engaged directly in the economic exploitation and impoverishment of Africa. The equivalent of the colonial office in each colonising country worked hand in hand with their governors in Africa to carry out a number of functions; the principal ones being as follows: (a) To protect national interests against competition from other capitalists. (b) To arbitrate the conflicts between their own capitalists. (c) To guarantee optimum conditions under which private companies could exploit Africans.[15]

Walter Rodney was in many ways the most theoretically *and* empirically brilliant of the early generations of postcolonial writers. His intellectual brilliance was all the more salient because, even in seemingly academic writings, Rodney was explicitly political in ways consistent with his nonacademic Black Power politics. Politics led to his assassination in Georgetown in 1980. He had but 38 years. Imagine what he might have done had he had more time.

Notes

1 C.L.R. James, *Beyond a Boundary* (Durham: Duke University Press, 1993 [1963]).
2 C.L.R. James, *A History of Pan-African Revolt* (Oakland: PM Press, 2012 [1938; revised 1969]), 37.
3 C.L.R. James, *American Civilization*, edited by Anna Grimshaw and Keith Hart (Blackwell Publishers, 1993 [1950]), 203–204.
4 Anna Grimshaw, *C.L.R. James: A Revolutionary Vision for the 20th Century* (New York: The C.L.R. James Institute and Cultural Correspondence, in co-operation with Smyrna Press, April 1991), 9.
5 C.L.R. James, *Dialectic Materialism and the Fate of Humanity* (The C.L.R. James Archive (on-line), 1947).
6 Walter Rodney, *The Groundings with My Brothers* (London: Bogle-L'Ouverture Publications, 1969), 60.
7 *Ibid.*, 63.
8 *Ibid.*, 58.
9 Walter Rodney, *How Europe Underdeveloped Africa* (London: Bogle-L'Ouverture Publications and Dar es Salaam: Tanzanian Publishing House, 1973), 1, 3.
10 *Ibid.*, 19.
11 *Ibid.*, 34.
12 *Ibid.*, 105.
13 *Ibid.*, 121.
14 *Ibid.*, 37–38; emphasis added.
15 *Ibid.*, 289–290.

13 The Role of Working Class Violence in National Liberation

Mohandas Karamchand Gandhi/Bhagat Singh

Mohandas Karamchand Gandhi (1869–1948) was born in October 1869 to a merchant family in coastal Gujarat, India. He travelled to London to pursue a law degree, and then moved to South Africa, where he became involved in struggles for civil rights. He returned to India in 1915, where he continued his political work, famously leading the Salt March in 1930 to protest the British salt tax, and then led the Quit India Movement (1942–1947). Gandhi is best known for advocating nonviolent resistance as social movement strategy. He believed in living simply, in an *ashram*, wearing hand-spun cloth. Gandhi was assassinated on January 30, 1948, by a Hindu nationalist who believed Gandhi was too favorable to Pakistan in negotiating partition. While Gandhi has been accused of casteism, elitism, and of racism by the left, he also has critics on the Hindu right who accuse him of failing to prioritize Hindus and Hinduism over other religions and religious groups in South Asia. His birthday is celebrated in India as a national holiday.

Mohandas Gandhi's two most popular philosophical concepts are *ahimsa*, nonviolence, and *satyagraha* (nonviolent civil resistance). *Ahimsa*, a term that has its origins in Buddhism, Hinduism, and Jainism, is for Gandhi almost a synonym of *satyagraha*. Both concepts for Gandhi have an "active nature" and are distinct from how Western liberal thinkers conceptualize civil disobedience.[1] Gandhi "treats satyagraha as an opening onto another swaraj—another freedom and equality" distinct from the freedoms enshrined in a liberal democracy which Gandhi terms *prajasatta* (popular government). *Satyagraha*, in contrast, is the freedom underlying religion and ethics, as it necessitates a surrendering of the self, a relinquishment of sovereignty.[2] "In Gandhi's writing," claims Ajay Skaria, "satyagraha is the struggle of being to emerge from its obscuring in formal or theological religions, to open instead onto a freedom, equality, and universality organized around what he calls 'pure means.'"[3]

Sovereignty is an important component of *satyagraha* and registers in several different ways. For Gandhi, sovereign power is not just in the state,[4] but also found in the self. Autonomy is a sovereign power institutionalized in liberal democracy, but in the case of the colonized, autonomy is only granted to some "selves" who are purported by the state to possess the ability

DOI: 10.4324/9781003198291-16

to reason. Thereby, liberal democracy dominates those who are excluded. However, domination is also something that beings inflict on themselves, by regulating feelings, thoughts, actions, and so on. Gandhi therefore claims that in surrendering autonomy through *satyagraha*, one exposes both the violence of liberal democracy and of the self. Or, as Skaria writes, "the subaltern can refuse subordination only by participating in domination. What is lost is the possibility of an exit from subalternity that does not participate in domination."[5]

While Gandhi was given the honorific title of *Mahatma* (meaning "great soul," akin to the Christian term "saint") for his role in India's independence, he wasn't the only figure to receive an honorific title for his role in India's independence movement. Bhagat Singh was given the title *Shaheed* (meaning "martyr," derived from the Arabic and Greek word for "witness") for his efforts in India's freedom movement. And like Mohandas Gandhi, Bhagat Singh also wrote extensively on social movement strategy and theories of national liberation.

Bhagat Singh (1907–1931) was born in 1907 in Banga village in what today is Pakistan. He was born into a Sikh Jatt family that was active in both the Indian Army and the Ghadar Party, an organization founded in 1913 by Sikhs in South Asia, Canada, and the United States to fight for independence. Singh's father and uncles were in and out of jail for their involvement in the Ghadar Party, and as a result, Singh was closest to his grandfather when he was a young boy. Bhagat Singh did not attend the local Sikh school because his grandfather disapproved of the school's loyalty to the colonial state. Instead, his grandfather enrolled him in an English medium Hindu high school, where he learned about Gandhi's *satyagraha*. He soon joined the Gandhian nationalist movement, but after the Jallianwala Bagh Massacre, the Gurudwara Nankana Sahib killings, and the Chauri Chaura Incident, Singh became disillusioned with *satyagraha*. The colonial state, Singh thought, in killing unarmed protestors showed no regard for human life in Punjab. In 1923, Singh matriculated from the National College in Lahore, where he joined and then led the *Naujawan Bharat Sabha*, a Communist youth organization.[6]

Naujawan Bharat Sabha was first established by Dr. Satyapal at National College in Lahore to educate students in leftist political philosophy.[7] This reading group attracted students like Singh who were radicalized by the Gandhian movement but disaffected by Gandhi's failure to address British violence in the Punjab, particularly at Jallianwala Bagh.[8] Comprised of mostly college-aged Jatt Sikh men, *Naujawan Bharat Sabha* had a reputation for machismo. The reading group was based on a *gurukul* system in which older students were assigned a younger student to mentor in Marxist theory.[9] Bhagat Singh, though he was only 19 when he joined, was soon chosen to be its leader as he exhibited an exceptional talent for anarchist and Marxist theory.

Under Bhagat Singh's leadership, *Naujawan Bharat Sabha* evolved from a Marxist reading group into a direct action group aimed at national liberation

114   *Postcolonial Theories of Capitalism*

in Punjab.[10] Bhagat Singh was its chief strategist, circulating his own writings on political theory to direct the movement. Through the mentorship of older Punjabi social movement leaders, Bhagat Singh's political theory evolved into a hybrid of Sikh theology, Punjabi folklore, anarchist, and communist thought.[11] Bhagat Singh read Karl Marx and Mikhail Bakunin as analogues to the Sikh Gurus, men who suffered and forsook gainful employment in order to bring happiness to a suffering world.[12]

After one of their members was killed during a public demonstration in 1928, members of *Naujawan Bharat Sabha* assassinated an Assistant Police Superintendent and then bombed the Central Legislative Assembly.[13] The *Naujawan Bharat Sabha* leadership was tried in the Lahore Conspiracy Case of 1929–1930, and Bhagat Singh, Shivaram Hari Rajguru, and Sukhdev Thapar were hanged despite protests from Mohammed Ali Jinnah and Jawaharlal Nehru.[14] Many of the surviving members of the *Naujawan Bharat Sabha* went on to be influential leaders in the Communist Party of India and after partition, in the Communist Party of Pakistan.

While Singh wrote on atheism and against marriage, Singh, like Gandhi, devoted most of his efforts in political theory to understanding the colonial state, democracy, and how to achieve national independence. Singh claimed colonialism was:

> the exploitation of one nation by another... the English people love liberty for themselves. They hate all acts of injustice except those which they themselves commit. They are such liberty-loving people that they interfere in the Congo and cry, 'shame' to the Belgians. But they forget their heels are on the neck of India.[15]

Singh, like Gandhi, also saw in democracy a domination, but unlike Gandhi, Singh's critique of democracy was based in a reading of Vladimir Lenin.[16] Writes Singh:

> Democracy does not secure, 'equal rights and a share in all political rights for everybody to whatever class or party he may belong' (Kautsky). It only allows free political and legal play for the existing economic inequalities. Democracy under capitalism is thus not general, abstract democracy but specific bourgeois democracy, or as Lenin terms it—democracy for the bourgeois.[17]

"The state," Singh contends, "is not really an end in itself and man is not here for the sake of the state, but rather, these exist for man."[18]

As such, Singh believed that revolution was necessary in order to end colonial rule. Wrote Singh, "When and where did the ruling class ever yield power and property on the order of a peaceful vote—and especially such a class as the British bourgeoisie, which has behind it centuries of world rapacity?"[19] He believed that British rule, because it operated within the

The Role of Working Class Violence 115

logic of capitalism and colonialism, would not be overthrown without violent resistance. Furthermore, this resistance would have to take the form of a class struggle, given that the goal of the British colonial state was to further capitalism. Wrote Singh:

> it would seem that once we stand for the annihilation of a privileged class which has no desire but to pass from the scene, we have therein the basic content of the class struggle. But no, [British Prime Minister] MacDonald desires to evoke the consciousness of social solidarity. With whom? The solidarity of the working class is the expression of its internal welding in the struggle with the bourgeoisie. The social solidarity that MacDonald preaches, is the solidarity of the exploited with the exploiters, in other words, it is the maintenance of exploitation.[20]

Singh argued that cooperation with the British colonial state was akin to collaborating with the capitalist class, as the British state was a representative of the interests of capital.

Therefore, claimed Singh, to create a more just and equal Punjab it was not sufficient to achieve political independence from Britain:

> We want a socialist revolution, the indispensable preliminary to which is the political revolution. That is what we want. The political revolution does not mean transfer of state (or more crudely, the power) from the hands of the British to the Indians, but to those Indians who are at one with us as to the final goal, to be more precise, the power to be transferred to the revolutionary party through popular support.[21]

Singh believed that only a socialist revolution in which power was transferred from the bourgeoisie to the masses would transform colonial society.[22] "After that," Singh argued, "to proceed in right earnest is to organise the reconstruction of the whole society on the socialist basis, if you do not mean this revolution, then please have mercy, stop shouting, 'Inquilab Zindabad' [Long Live Revolution]."[23]

Singh's slogan for independence *Inquilab Zindabad* (and his related slogan *Mazdoor Ekta Zindabad* [Long Live the Workers' Struggle]) was critiqued in the press as too idealistic an aim for a national independence movement. In an editorial, he defended this slogan, claiming that *Inquilab* (revolution):

> is the spirit, the longing of change for the better. The people generally get accustomed to the established order of things and begin to tremble at the very idea of a change. It is the lethargical spirit that needs to be replaced by the revolutionary spirit. Otherwise, degeneration gains the upper hand and the whole humanity is led astray by the reactionary forces. Such a state of affairs leads to stagnation and paralysis in human progress. The spirit of revolution should always permeate the soul of

116   *Postcolonial Theories of Capitalism*

humanity, so that the reactionary forces may not accumulate strength to check its eternal onward march. Old order should change, always and ever, yielding place to new, so that one "good" order may not corrupt the world. It is in this sense that we raise the shout *"Inquilab Zindabad"* [Long Live Revolution].[24]

For Singh, revolution is not an event but a mindset, a collective spirit that compels individuals to unite and agitate for social change and preserves the collective memory of previous struggles for future generations.

While Singh's concept of revolution as collective spirit has echoes in Gandhi's applications of *satyagraha* to the self, Singh's concept of revolution derives not from Gandhi's writings, but from his readings of the *Guru Granth Sahib* (the primary scripture of Sikhism). In one of Singh's first essays, written while still in high school at age 17, Singh claimed that people have a moral obligation to fight injustice, even if it means surrendering one's life:

After his sacrifice, suddenly, we sense a warrior spirit in the preaching of Guru Gobind Singhji. When he realised that a mere spiritual devotion could not do anything, he started Chandi worship and turned Sikh community into a community of worshipers and warriors by synthesising spiritualism and fighting. We find in his poems this spirit. He writes, *"Je tohi prem khelan da chav, sir dhar tali gali mori aav | Je it maarag pair dharijai, sir dhar kaan no dijai."*[25] And then: '*Soora so pahchaniye, je lade deen ke het | Purja-purja kat mare, kabhu na chhade khet.*'[26,27]

Young Bhagat Singh's reading of the *Guru Granth Sahib* led him to the view that the struggle for justice and equality should be fought to the death. And while Singh would later become an atheist, in his jail notebooks he expresses a similar thinking, albeit one couched in secular language. "The aim of life," claimed Singh:

"is no more to control the mind, but to develop it harmoniously, not to achieve salvation hereafter, but to make use of it here below, and not to realise truth, beauty and good only in contemplation, but also in the actual experience of daily life; social progress depends not upon the ennoblement of the few but on the enrichment of the many; and spiritual democracy or universal brotherhood can be achieved only when there is an equality of opportunity in the social, political, and industrial life.[28]

In this passage, Singh similarly puts forth a social movement approach that is internal—about creating within the revolutionary a "harmonious mind"—while also external, in that the meaning of life is not to achieve salvation in the afterlife, but in bringing social justice to life on earth.

If Gandhi's intellectual legacy in the Global North can be understood through his influence on the political philosophy of Dr. Martin Luther

The Role of Working Class Violence 117

King, Jr., then perhaps through that same lens Bhagat Singh can be understood as a precursor to Frantz Fanon. Like Fanon, Singh was influenced by Marxism but rethought it for the context of the Global South. And like Fanon, Singh saw the violence that colonial rule inflicted on Punjab, and concluded that nonviolent resistance would be ineffective in the face of indiscriminate killings of unarmed colonial subjects. And both Singh and Fanon were interested in understanding and transforming the psyche of the colonized. But like Gandhi, Singh's theories of national liberation have multiple registers. Singh's *Inquilab*, while aimed at bringing about national liberation in Punjab, was also aimed at evoking the spirit of national liberation within the self and thereby preserving that spirit of revolution for future generations. The importance of Bhagat Singh, shows Irfan Habib, is not that he sacrificed his life for India's independence, but that he "espoused a revolutionary vision to transform independent India into a secular, socialist, and egalitarian society." As a result of his hanging, "we did not lose merely individuals… we lost rather an alternative framework of governance."[29]

Notes

1 Ajay Skaria, *Unconditional Equality: Gandhi's Religion of Resistance* (Minneapolis: University of Minnesota Press, 2016), 4.
2 *Ibid.*, 5.
3 *Ibid.*, 6.
4 *Ibid.*, 8.
5 *Ibid.*, 9.
6 Chris Moffat *India's Revolutionary Inheritance: The Politics and Promise of Bhagat Singh* (Cambridge: Cambridge University Press, 2019), 48.
7 Ajeet Javed, *Left Politics in Punjab, 1935–47* (Delhi: Durga Publications, 1988), 82; Bhagwan Josh, *Communist Movement in Punjab* (Delhi: Anupama Publications, 1979), 82.
8 Shalini Sharma, *Radical Politics in Colonial Punjab* (London: Routledge, 2010), 37.
9 *Ibid.*, 38.
10 Ram Chandra, *History of the Naujawan Bharat Sabha* (Ludhiana: Unistar Books, 2007), 47; Javed, *Left Politics*, 81; Bhagat Singh, *The Jail Notebook and Other Writings*, ed. Chaman Lal (Delhi: Leftword Books, 2007), 46.
11 Chandra, *Naujawan*, 54; Josh, *Communist Movement*, 85–86; Sharma, *Colonial Punjab*, 43.
12 Sharma, *Colonial Punjab*, 43.
13 Bhagat Singh, *On the Path of Liberation*, ed. Shiv Verma (Chennai: Indian Universities Press, 2007), 46.
14 *Ibid.*, 46.
15 Singh, *Jail Notebook*, 33.
16 See Part III, Chapter 4.
17 Singh, *Jail Notebook*, 56–57.
18 *Ibid.*, 84.
19 *Ibid.*, 66.
20 *Ibid.*, 65.
21 *Ibid.*, 161–162.
22 See also: S Irfan Habib, *To Make the Deaf Hear: Ideology and Programme of Bhagat Singh and his Comrades* (New Delhi: Three Essays Collective, 2007).
23 Singh, *Jail Notebook*, 161–162.
24 *Ibid.*, 141.

25 Translation: If you are interested in playing the game of love, put your head on your palm and enter my lane/In case you put your feet on this path don't fall back, even if you have to lose your life.

26 Translation: Only he is brave who fights for the cause of the poor/He may be cut into pieces and may be killed but he should not leave the field.

27 Singh, *Liberation*, 58–59.

28 Singh, *Jail Notebook*, 91.

29 Habib, *Make the Deaf Hear*, xi.

14 Workers, Peasants, Anti-Colonialism

Vladimir Lenin/Nestor Makhno

Vladimir Ilyich Ulyanov (V.I. Lenin) (1870–1924) was born in 1870 in Simbirsk, a city on the Volga River. Lenin's father was the director of Simbirsk's school system in a city where, before his tenure, 80% of residents were illiterate. Lenin's mother Maria Blank was a Lutheran of German descent.[1] Lenin's family, therefore, was atypical for his hometown. Lenin's father died suddenly at the age of 45 and Lenin's eldest brother, a student at the University of St. Petersburg, was hanged after being accused of plotting to assassinate Tsar Alexander III. As a result, Lenin's mother was banished to Kokuchinko.[2] However, Lenin soon joined the University of Kazan and became involved in anti-government student protests. He was expelled and banished to Kokuchinko, but continued to study, acquiring copies of Marx's writing in the original German, in which, because of his mother, he was fluent. While he never formally completed an undergraduate degree, he was admitted for a law degree at the University of St. Petersburg where he graduated first in his class.

After finishing his education, Lenin settled in St. Petersburg and became involved in revolutionary Marxist politics. He was critical of the existing anti-Tsarist groups who were hostile to Marxism and therefore started his own group, The League of Struggle for the Emancipation of the Working Class. In 1895, he was imprisoned and sent to Siberia for his politics, and while banished, met Nadezhda Krupskaya, a fellow revolutionary Marxist also in banishment.[3] They were married in 1898. Lenin returned to St. Petersburg in 1900 and Krupskaya joined him when her banishment ended. They then moved to Europe—Munich, London, Paris, Geneva, Berne, Zurich—and together founded a Russian-language Marxist magazine *Iskra* (*The Spark*). In Europe, Lenin involved himself in intellectual debates and completed several of his most important manuscripts. In 1917, he returned to Russia upon learning of the impending revolution. He soon presented his "April Theses," a political strategy for a more radical revolution. The Bolsheviks adopted Lenin's strategy as party line,[4] and Lenin continued to craft revolutionary strategy for the Bolsheviks through the Revolution and beyond.

Imperialism, one of the most important and innovative concepts in Lenin's writings, is a means of furthering capitalist ends given the limitations on capital accumulation within a national economy. While in the early

DOI: 10.4324/9781003198291-17

120 *Postcolonial Theories of Capitalism*

19th century, there was a dramatic increase in the amount of capital being concentrated in industry in the largest manufacturing centers of the world, there were few opportunities available that ensured a high return on investment.[5] Because of the over-accumulation of capital in wealthy countries as a result of monopoly finance capital, capital must expand geographically in order to maintain a high level of profit. In *Imperialism: The Highest Stage of Capitalism* (1917), Lenin writes that:

> The epoch of modern capitalism shows us that certain relationships are established between capitalist alliances, based on the economic division of the world; while parallel with this fact and in connection with it, certain relations are established between political alliances, between states, on the basis of the territorial division of the world, of the struggle for colonies, of the "struggle for economic territory."[6]

In Lenin's theory of imperialism, banks play an important role:

> The principal and primary function of banks is to serve as an intermediary in the making of payments. In doing so, they transform inactive money capital into active capital, that is, into capital producing a profit; they collect all kinds of money revenues and place them at the disposal of the capitalist class.[7]

Finance capital is not directly tied to the production process; in other words, the profit that is derived from finance is not derived directly from the exploitation of labor. It is used in the production process when it takes the form of a loan to industry, but it nonetheless exists outside of the production process:

> It is characteristic in capitalism in general that the ownership of capital is separated from the application of capital to production, that money capital is separated from industrial or productive capital and the rentier, who lives entirely on income obtained from money capital, is separated from the entrepreneur and from all who are directly concerned in the management of capital. Imperialism, or domination of finance capital, is that highest stage of capitalism in which the separation reaches vast proportions.[8]

In sum, Lenin's theory of imperialism posits that in moments where there are decreasing returns for industrial capital, capitalists who are best suited to do so shift their capital to finance where there are more opportunities for high returns. But because this capital is concentrated in the Global North, over time, this concentration of capital in one geographic region erodes rates of return on investments. Therefore, capital looks to expand to other geographies in order to secure outlets for investment, thereby increasing, once again, the rate of return.

Nestor Makhno, (1888–1934) a contemporary of Lenin, was born in 1888 in Gulayi-Polye on the Gaichur River in Eastern Ukraine. Makhno's father was a serf of the Seigneur Shabelsky and, after serfdom was abolished in 1861, was employed as a stable boy for his former master. Makhno's father died when he was 11 months old, and as a result, his family descended into extreme poverty.[9] Makhno left school at age nine to become an ox handler so that he could support his family. Once his brothers were able to find work as farmhands, Makhno returned to school, where he excelled in reading and oration. He resented having to work throughout the school year for the families of his wealthier classmates. He recounted that the experience of going to school "filthy and in rags, barefoot and stinking of dung," while his classmates were clean and well fed, awakened him to issues of social inequality. At age 13, Makhno witnessed the landlord's sons beating one of the stable boys for their own amusement. He fearfully ran to the head stable boy, who told the young Makhno that "no one here should countenance the disgrace of being beaten and as for you, little Nestor, if one of your masters should ever strike you, pick up the first pitchfork you lay hands on and let him have it." This, Makhno recalled, was a formative moment that led him to take up revolutionary politics.

While he first became involved in politics through the Social Democrats, in 1905, Makhno joined a group of anarchist peasants in his hometown who met weekly to discuss anarchist theory, current events, and other issues.[10] In 1908 Makhno was arrested by Tsarist forces for his involvement in this group, and found that prison was a great place to continue his studies, particularly in Russian literature, history, and political economy.[11] In Moscow's infamous Butyrki Prison, he read Peter Kropokin's *Mutual Aid*, which had a profound and lasting influence on Makhno's thought.[12] But Makhno was frequently insubordinate, and contracted tuberculosis in solitary confinement.[13]

He remained in prison until 1917, when, after the Revolution, he and other political prisoners were released. At the age of 27, he returned to his hometown where he organized a Gulaye-Polye Peasants Union and was appointed Chairman of the group, but refused, as his anarchist politics compelled him to eschew all formal authority. Through the Gulaye-Polye Peasants Union, Makhno called for collectivization of the land, factories, and workshops,[14] which at first he intended to organize through peasants' and workers' strikes, but in the face of landlord opposition, decided to organize a militia to advance the peasant and worker cooperatives.[15] Makhno's cooperatives were founded on the principle of equality among members and advocated that all tasks, including cooking and other household chores, be shared equally among cooperative members regardless of their gender.

At this point, Makhno's biography clashes with Lenin's. For the Austro-German Empire and for the Red Army, Ukraine was a territory for the taking. Austro-Germany tried to conquer Ukraine from the West and the Red Army encroached from the North. Ukrainian elites soon formed their own

122 *Postcolonial Theories of Capitalism*

army as did local leftists like Makhno, and soon, a savage war for national liberation was underway. In 1918, Lenin and Makhno met in Moscow as Lenin wanted to convince Makhno's militia to join the Red Army. Makhno recorded his recollection of the conversation that night in his journal. Lenin had many questions for Makhno, including:

> How did the peasants of your region interpret the slogan, 'All Power to Local Soviets'? ... Did the peasants of your region rise up against the invading counterrevolutionary German and Austrian armies? What was lacking for the peasant revolts to coalesce into a general uprising in concert with red guard detachments which have defended our revolutionary conquests so heroically?[16]

Makhno was at first evasive, and then finally replied:

> The peasants understood this slogan in their own way. According to their interpretation all power, in all areas of life, must be identified with consciousness and will of the toilers themselves. The villages... were perceived as organs of revolutionary organization and the economic self-management of everyday life in the struggle of working people against the bourgeoisie... the right wing socialists, and their coalition government.[17]

Lenin "was astonished at [Makhno's] reply" and said, "In that case the peasants of your region are infected with anarchism!" Said Makhno, "Is that bad?," to which Lenin responded, "this phenomenon in the peasantry is unnatural"; it "won't persist," and Lenin added, "So, according to you, we should encourage these anarchist tendencies in the peasant masses?" And Makhno replied, "Oh, your party will not encourage them?" To which Lenin said, "And why should we encourage them? To divide the revolutionary forces of the proletariat, pave way for the counterrevolution, end up destroying ourselves along with the proletariat?" "At this point," Makhno writes, "I couldn't restrain myself and became quite upset."[18] The conflict between communist and anarchist ideas continued in Ukraine until Lenin's armies successfully conquered and Makhno's peasant commune was destroyed. Defeated by the Red Army, Makhno fled Ukraine to Poland, Berlin, and eventually Paris where he worked as a carpenter for the Paris Opera and edited a monthly journal *Dyelo Truda* (*The Cause of Labor*) in his free time. He died in 1934 of the tuberculosis he had contracted in prison. His ashes are interred at Père Lachaise Cemetery.

As a theorist, Makhno is best known for his work on workers' and peasants' cooperatives. In the cooperative villages he established after the 1917 Revolution, some villagers were employed in agricultural work and others formed combat groups to defend the villages. Tasks were assigned without regard to gender. Members were given a morning task, either domestic or tending to livestock. The villages had a common kitchen and dining hall where food was prepared, but villagers could, if they wished, use the kitchen to prepare their own meals and then take it home for their families. The village schools were based on Francisco Ferrer's model of schooling, in which there was no atmosphere of coercion, competition, or humiliation of students.[19] Makhno himself operated the seeding machine and did other supplementary farm work. Sundays were days off from work, but members could take the day off whenever they wished as long as they could find someone to cover their responsibilities. In this effort to enact village cooperatives, Makhno saw the state as the primary obstacle. "The State will," he wrote, "cling to a few local enclaves and try to place multifarious obstacles in the path of the toilers' new life, slowing the pace of growth and harmonious development of new relationships founded on the complete emancipation of man."[20] The state, Makhno claimed, was not just an obstacle to workers' and peasants' emancipation, but to economic development in Ukraine. Only through the self-management of society directed by the workers and peasants, Makhno theorized, would liberation be possible. "The final and utter liquidation of the State," he wrote:

> can only come to pass when the struggle of the toilers is oriented along the most libertarian lines possible, when the toilers will themselves determine the structures of their social action. These structures should assume the form of organs of social and economic self-direction, the form of free "anti-authoritarian" soviets.[21]

Nestor Makhno's left critique of the Russian Revolution provides an interesting framework with which to view Eastern European states' relationship to Russia in historical perspective. Makhno contrasts the goals of the Russian Revolution with its realities as seen from Ukraine that the 1917 revolution brought with it "prospects of new free relations between peoples hitherto in subjection,"[22] but that for Ukraine one liberation led to a new subjugation, under the "violent yoke of the Russian State."[23] While Makhno shows how the imposition of Soviet Rule in Ukraine after 1917 suppressed Ukrainian language and culture, most important for Makhno is that the Bolsheviks did not bring more freedom and less exploitation to Ukraine's peasants and workers, but instead a new kind of subjugation different from that of the Tsar but equally exploitative of workers and peasants. But Makhno was nonetheless optimistic that:

> Ukrainian life is filled with all sorts of possibilities, especially the potential for a mass revolutionary movement. Anarchists have a great chance of influencing that movement, indeed becoming its mentors, provided only that they appreciate the diversity of real life and espouse a position to wage a single-minded, direct and declared fight against those forces hostile to the toilers which might have ensconced themselves there.[24]

124   *Postcolonial Theories of Capitalism*

Makhno's theories suggest a different conceptualization of the USSR and of contemporary Russia as seen from the post-Soviet states, one that acted less like an instantiation of Marxist communist ideals and instead an Imperial state—both then and today—colonizing its neighboring states. This view was also shared by Walter Rodney, who saw that Soviet "colonial rule hardly differed from that of the Western European powers."[25] In fact, this theory of the Russian Revolution as seen from Ukraine can help us to understand and explain recent political developments in Ukraine—the EU and Russia can be seen as two former imperial rulers of Ukraine competing for neocolonial influence. Juxtaposed with Makhno's left critique of the Soviet Union, Lenin's theory of imperialism looks more like a "how to guide" rather than a critique of capitalism.

Notes

1 Henry M. Christman, ed., *Essential Works of Lenin* (New York: Dover Publications, 1966).
2 *Ibid.*
3 *Ibid.*
4 Robert C. Tucker, ed., *The Lenin Anthology* (New York: WW Norton and Co, 1975).
5 VI Lenin, *Imperialism: The Highest Stage of Capitalism* (New York: International Publishers, 1917 [1979]), 53.
6 *Ibid.*, 75.
7 *Ibid.*, 31.
8 *Ibid.*, 59.
9 Alexandre Skirda, *Nestor Makhno Anarchy's Cossack: The Struggle for Free Soviets in the Ukraine, 1917–1921* (Oakland: AK Press, 2004), 18.
10 *Ibid.*, 20–21.
11 Peter Arshinov, *History of the Makhnovist Movement, 1918–1921* (London: Freedom Press, 2005), 59.
12 Skirda, *Struggle for Free*, 30.
13 Arshinov, *Makhnovist Movement*, 59.
14 Skirda, *Struggle for Free*, 35.
15 *Ibid.*, 36.
16 Nestor Makhno, *Under the Blows of the Counterrevolution* (Edmonton: Black Cat Press, 1936b [2009]), 137.
17 *Ibid.*
18 *Ibid.*, 138.
19 Nestor Makhno, *The Russian Revolution in Ukraine* (Edmonton: Black Cat Press, 1936a [2007]), 184.
20 Nestor Makhno, "The Struggle Against the State," *Dyelo Truda* 17 (1926).
21 *Ibid.*
22 *Ibid.*
23 *Ibid.*
24 Nestor Makhno, "A Few Words on the National Question in Ukraine" *Dyelo Truda* 19 (1928).
25 Walter Rodney, *The Russian Revolution: A View from the Third World* (London: Verso, 2018), 154.

15 A Situationist Theory of Underdevelopment

Albert Camus/Mustapha Khayati

Albert Camus (1913–1960) was born in Algeria to a French *Pieds Noirs* family of working-class means. He kept his "feet in Africa" as a French citizen. That he was born relatively poor in a French colony was an important biographic fact in the deep background of his literary and philosophical life. He was a good student, good enough to gain admission to a prestigious lycée in Algiers. When he had but 14 years, he came down with tuberculosis which required a period of convalescence outside the city. Just the same, in his lycée years he began the study of philosophy, which he continued after 1933 at the University of Algeria. In the same period, the illness notwithstanding, Camus took a keen interest in sport which is said to have nurtured his group morality. In 1935, he joined the Algerian Communist Party, and soon after, he began writing for a leftist newspaper which allowed him to vent his by then strong critical thoughts after French colonialism. In 1940, he moved to Paris to become editor of a similarly left newspaper. But the Germans were marching on Paris, so he moved into the French zone, to Lyons, where, soon enough, he joined the French resistance to Nazi occupation.

In spite of all this, Camus's writing life advanced. Both the novel *The Stranger* and his major nonfiction philosophical work *The Myth of Sisyphus* were published in 1942. The play *Caligula* was written in 1938 but not performed until after the War. A quirk, if that is what it is, of Camus's literary career was that these three works were the first of four cycles—each with a novel, a philosophical work, and a play. The others were, roughly put, from 1943 to 1952 was the Promethean cycle of rebellion that featured *The Plague*; then from 1952 to 1958, a cycle that emphasized the themes of guilt and exile, for which *The Fall* was the principal literary work alongside plays based on Faulkner's *Requiem for a Nun* and Dostoyevsky's *The Possessed*; then an incomplete final cycle after 1958 cut short by his death in 1960, which left what he intended to be denouement of his career, *The First-Man*.

It is fair to say, however, that the first cycle was foundational to his existentialism and is commonly referred to as the Absurdist Cycle for the fact that all three, in their different ways, turn on the question of suicide. Hence, the often quoted line from the beginning of *The Myth of Sisyphus*: "There is only one really serious philosophical question, and that is suicide." Of

DOI: 10.4324/9781003198291-18

126 *Postcolonial Theories of Capitalism*

course, apart from Camus's early life in Algeria, the fall of France to the Germans was background to this first cycle—which is the cycle that best defines his existentialism and, by implication, his politics. For those interested in Camus's philosophical thinking, *The Stranger* and the play *Caligula* can serve as end pieces. They stand on their own, of course, as a novel and drama. Each in its own way draws an aspect of his principle that "the only serious philosophical question...is suicide."

In brief, *The Stranger* tells of Meursault, a *Pied Noir*, deep in grief over the death of his mother. In agony, he sets upon an overdetermined path of emotional engagements and assaults, ending with an obsessive shooting to death of an Arab for which he is arrested. He is convicted and sentenced to death. He tolerates his days in prison, weirdly due to a sense of necessity. Meursault refuses a priest's offer of divine mercy. His mind and soul were set on the end with the notion that a crowd of angry observers will justify his death and create a society of the doomed. *Caligula*, the play, follows much the same line. Caligula, the Roman emperor in the last century before the Christian era, suffers the same sort of terrible grief at the death of his sister, Drucilla. Like the real Caligula, Camus's character turns sadistic madman, killing at random aiming, it seems, to kill his subjects and his regime. He then is killed by those he provokes (as Caligula himself was assassinated by the Roman Praetorian Guard). The novel was published during the War in a small print run of just more than 4,000 copies. The play was produced after the War and enjoyed some popularity. In time, both became classics of a sort. But, in time, the philosophical essay became one of the most important contributions to the post-War existentialist movement.

The Myth of Sisyphus ranges over a long history of philosophical sources from the Greeks to Heidegger, but unsurprisingly, Kierkegaard is the principal source. Camus writes:

> Of all perhaps the most engaging, Kierkegaard, for a part of his existence at least, does more than discover the absurd, he lives it. The man who writes: 'The surest of stubborn silences is not to hold one's tongue but to talk' makes sure in the beginning that no truth is absolute or can render satisfactory an existence that is impossible in itself.

Camus continues with his definition of the absurd:

> Reflection on suicide gives me an opportunity to raise the only problem to interest me: is there a logic to the point of death? I cannot know unless I pursue, without reckless passion, in the sole light of evidence, the reasoning of which I am here suggesting the source. This is what I call an absurd reasoning.

Then, some pages on, Camus turns not to issues of war or colonization, but to ordinary bourgeois life in the world. The pertinent passage reveals his

A Situationist Theory of Underdevelopment   127

literary acuity as well as the definiteness of his philosophical judgment on the world:

> It happens that the stage sets collapse. Rising, streetcar, four hours in the office or the factory, meal, streetcar, four hours of work, meal, sleep, and Monday Tuesday Wednesday Thursday Friday and Saturday according to the same rhythm—this path is easily followed most of the time. But one day the "why" arises and everything begins in that weariness tinged with amazement. "Begins"—this is important. Weariness comes at the end of the acts of a mechanical life, but at the same time it inaugurates the impulse of consciousness. It awakens consciousness and provokes what follows. What follows is the gradual return into the chain or it is the definitive awakening. At the end of the awakening comes, in time, the consequence: suicide or recovery. In itself weariness has something sickening about it. Here, I must conclude that it is good. For everything begins with consciousness and nothing is worth anything except through it. There is nothing original about these remarks. But they are obvious; that is enough for a while, during a sketchy reconnaissance in the origins of the absurd. Mere "anxiety," as Heidegger says, is at the source of everything.

In this long passage, one finds a most striking description of Camus's idea of the ever-present sense of the absurd in ordinary life.

The original ancient myth of Sisyphus is retold at the end of Camus's book. The story is familiar. Sisyphus having committed vile crimes is sentenced to roll that stone up the mountain until it rolls back, and he starts over. Endless repetition stands for the drudgery of life with no compelling meaning. Camus, then: "If one believes Homer, Sisyphus was the wisest and most prudent of mortals. According to another tradition, however, he was disposed to practice the profession of highwayman. I see no contradiction in this."

To be sure, Camus's conclusion is not drawn simply from ordinary life. In the deep background are of course his experience growing up in Algeria close to colonial subjects and obviously his experiences in France during the war. Camus's existentialism is severe, not anything like the more phenomenologically forward-looking versions. Even Sartre's existentialism, such as it is, was not so dim, otherwise his rewriting of Marxist philosophy, much less his most important philosophical work *Being and Nothingness* (1943), would have amounted to nothing. For better or worse, Sartre's existentialism is better known for its contributions to post-War philosophy. Camus was better known for his literary accomplishments, which led to his being the second youngest author to be awarded the Nobel Prize for Literature at 44 years in 1957.

Yet, Camus's philosophical ideas were clearly related to his politics, which he expressed by his early newspaper essays, his commitment to the

128   *Postcolonial Theories of Capitalism*

Resistance Movement, and his highly personal and public sense of his own North African colony. At the end of *The Myth of Sisyphus*, in a section headed "Philosophical Suicide," he makes his political and moral position clear, if not perfectly clear:

> Thus, I draw from the absurd three consequences, which are my revolt, my freedom, and my passion. By the mere activity of consciousness, I transform into a rule of life what was an invitation to death—and I refuse suicide. I know, to be sure, the dull resonance that vibrates throughout these days. Yet I have but a word to say: that it is necessary. When Nietzsche writes: "It clearly seems that the chief thing in heaven and on earth is to *obey* at length and in a single direction: in the long run there results something for which it is worth the trouble of living on this earth as, for example, virtue, art, music, the dance, reason, the mind—something that transfigures, something delicate, mad, or divine," he elucidates the rule of a really distinguished code of ethics. But he also points the way of the absurd man. Obeying the flame is both the easiest and the hardest thing to do. However, it is good for man to judge himself occasionally.

Born in neighboring Tunisia just a few years after Camus, "dans un milieu modeste,"[1] **Mustapha Khayati** first moved to France in 1960 to study philosophy at the Université Strasbourg. There, he took a course with Henri Lefebvre and soon became a part of Lefebvre's intellectual and social circle. While pursuing his undergraduate degree in philosophy at Strasbourg, Khayati was involved in student politics through the *Groupe d'Étude et d'Action Socialistes Tunisien*, a Trotskyist student group committed to left politics in Tunisia. It was because of his involvement in this group that Khayati was first put in touch with Guy Debord. Soon, Debord convinced Khayati to join the Situationist International. Khayati was on the front lines of the May 1968 student uprising in Paris, and as a result, fled to Brussels in July 1968 to avoid arrest. In Brussels, he stayed with Raoul Vaneigem. However, at the Situationist International Conference in Venice in October 1969, Khayati resigned from the Situationist International, claiming that while he had no ideological differences with the Situationists, he wanted to focus his political efforts on fomenting revolution "dans le zone arabe."[2,3] "Je me sens dans l'obligation d'en être,"[4] Khayati told his fellow Situationists.[5] He then left Europe to fight on the front lines for the *Front Démocratique et Populaire de Libération de la Palestine*, returning to Europe in the Summer of 1970 disillusioned by the presence of far-right forces creeping into North Africa and Western Asia.

After his experiences fighting on the front lines in Palestine, he reinvented himself as a more academic intellectual. In 1979, he completed his PhD in history at the Sorbonne (*Université Paris-Sorbonne, Paris IV*). His thesis "l'Histoire des Perses d'ath-Tha'âlibî" ("Ath-Tha'âlibî's History of the

Persians"), an analysis of a 10th-century scientific manuscript, was supervised by Claude Cahen. After completing his PhD, Khayati went on to have an academic career teaching at *l'Institut d'Études politiques d'Aix-en-Provence* and is now the chair of the *Centre d'Études et de Documentation Économiques, Juridiques et Sociales*, a research center affiliated with the CNRS and located in Cairo. His current academic work focuses on the literary and intellectual history of the Arab world.

However, he remains best known for his political writing penned just before and during the student uprisings in Paris during May '68. His most popular piece is still the essay "On the Poverty of Student Life" (1966). Over 10,000 copies of the pamphlet were initially circulated, and to date, it remains a key text of Situationist concepts and tactics. Intellectual historians see this pamphlet as one of the key events that precipitated the student uprisings in May '68. Henri Lefebvre said of the pamphlet, "It's a very good brochure, without a doubt." However, Lefebvre also said of Khayati that he was often absent at Situationist social gatherings even though he was quite the intellectual force, because he never became a dual citizen like other Tunisians in Paris. Khayati held only his Tunisian citizenship and as a result, Lefebvre said, Khayati "had real troubles."[6]

Khayati's political writings focus not just on the events of Paris in May '68 and on Marxist theory more broadly, but unlike other Situationists, he applies Situationism to contexts outside of Europe. More specifically, much of his political writing is devoted to examining class struggle in North Africa toward a theory of underdevelopment from a Situationist perspective. In "Setting Straight Some Popular Misconceptions about Revolutions in the Underdeveloped Countries" (1967), Khayati argues that revolution takes on a distinct character in "underdeveloped" countries, because colonial domination created "general economic backwardness" making the class landscape of the colonies distinct from that of the "advanced capitalist societies."[7] In the class landscape of an underdeveloped country, the poor peasantry comprises the majority instead of the proletariat.

National liberation movements, argues Khayati, are not entirely revolutionary movements. They only fight imperialism, he contends, and as such are incomplete revolutions that allow for oppressive regimes to install themselves in instances where national liberation movements have succeeded. Peasants, Khayati posits, fight for independence only to be politically dominated and economically exploited by a new regime. Postcolonial states, Khayati writes, build "power and prosperity on the superexploitation of peasants: ideology changes nothing in the matter. In China or Cuba, Egypt or Algeria, everywhere it plays the same role and assumes the same functions."[8]

Khayati also laments the role of the USSR in influencing national liberation movements. The Russian Revolution, Khayati observes, soon turned into a counterrevolution, begetting a dictatorship which claims to be Communist. The false consciousness associated with the politics of the USSR is a disadvantage to the anti-colonial struggle, Khayati argues, because colonial

130 *Postcolonial Theories of Capitalism*

and semi-colonial countries have to fight imperialism by themselves if there is any hope for total revolution on a global scale. True socialism, Khayati points out, is not found in states such as the USSR or China that dominate the working class in the name of Communism. Instead, Khayati contends, "socialism exists wherever the workers themselves directly manage the entire society."[9] Therefore, claims Khayati, the choice facing the colonial and postcolonial working class is either "militarized bureaucratic dictatorship" or self-management "extended to all aspects of social life."[10]

Khayati's hope for the Global South lies in the possibilities of self-management "extended to all production and of all aspects of social life."[11] A self-managed state and economy, he believes, would upend all social hierarchies and mark an end to the army and police state, "but it would also mean the end of all aspects of the old society, the abolition of all its spiritual and material enslavements and the abolition of its masters."[12] Khayati further believed in the potential of self-management, especially in the Islamic context, to eliminate gender hierarchies, which he referred to as a "backward reality of Islamic" North Africa.[13] "Self-management must become the sole solution to the mysteries of power" in the postcolonial world, Khayati contended, "and it must *know that it is that solution*."[14]

By radically upending existing social hierarchies through the possibilities of self-management, Khayati exposes the postcolonial state as simply a continuation of the colonial class structure. "The bureaucratic power built on the ruins of precapitalist colonial society is not the abolition of class antagonisms," he wrote, "it merely substitutes new classes, new conditions of oppression and new forms of struggle for the old ones."[15] The essence of underdevelopment for Khayati, therefore, is a state that continues to uphold the very uneven development imposed by colonial rule. As Khayati put it:

> The only people who are really underdeveloped are those who see a positive value in the power of their masters. The rush to catch up with capitalist reification remains the best road to reinforced underdevelopment. The question of economic development is inseparable from the question of who is the real owner of the economy, the real master of labor power.[16]

While Khayati and Camus seemingly lived opposite lives, Camus as a Frenchman who was influenced by his life in North Africa and Khayati as a North African who made an indelible impact on the Paris May '68 uprising, both thought about politics in similar ways. Khayati's main critique of the typical French student was for "his complacency... the more chains authority binds him with the freer he thinks he is."[17] This bourgeois complacency was central to Camus as well, "the everyday man ... still thinks that something in his life can be directed. In truth, he acts as if he were free, even if all the facts make a point of contradicting that liberty."[18] The solution, to this bourgeois complacency was a lifelong engagement with revolt and freedom.

Camus wrote, "revolt gives life its value. Spread out over the whole length of that life, it restores majesty to that life,"[19] and Khayati posited, "Free creativity in the construction of all moments and events of life is the *poetry* it can acknowledge, the poetry made by all, the beginning of the revolutionary festival."[20] In thinking through these insights on how to eschew bourgeois complacency for a rich inner life that attunes the self toward the politics of revolt, both Camus and Khayati at times in their work held North Africa as their reference category, in so doing, these more universal concepts were crafted with attention to the postcolonial experience while also eschewing particularity and ideographic specificity.

Notes

1 Anna *Trespeuch*-Berthelot, « Mustapha Khayati," in *Dictionnaire biographique Mouvement ouvrier, mouvement social de 1940 à mai 1968 t.7*, dir. C. Pennetier (Paris: Les Éditions de l'Atelier/Les Éditions Ouvrières, 2011).
2 Translation: In the Arab world.
3 *Ibid.*
4 Translation: I feel an obligation to be there.
5 *Ibid.*
6 Kristin Ross and Henri Lefebvre "Lefebvre on the Situationists: An Interview," *October* 79 (1997): 74.
7 Mustapha Khayati, "Setting Straight Some Popular Misconceptions about Revolutions in the Underdeveloped Countries," in *Situationist International Anthology*, ed. Ken Knabb (Berkeley: Bureau of Public Secrets, 2006), 282.
8 *Ibid.*, 283.
9 Mustapha Khayati, "Address to the Revolutionaries of Algeria and of All Countries," *Internationale Situationniste* 11 (October 1967).
10 *Ibid.*
11 Mustapha Khayati, "Class Struggles in Algeria," *Internationale Situationniste* 10 (March 1966).
12 *Ibid.*
13 *Ibid.*
14 *Ibid.*
15 Khayati, "Misconceptions about Revolutions," 284–285.
16 *Ibid.*, 285.
17 Situationist International "On the Poverty of Student Life," in *Situationist International Anthology*, ed. Ken Knabb (Berkeley: Bureau of Public Secrets, 2006), 410.
18 Albert Camus *The Myth of Sisyphus* (New York: Vintage Books, 1955), 42.
19 *Ibid.*, 40.
20 Situationist International "On the Poverty of Student Life," 429. Emphasis original.

16 Against the Colonization of Consciousness of Political Economy

Kwame Ture/W.E.B. Du Bois/Amílcar Cabral

Kwame Ture (aka Stokely Carmichael) (1941–1998) was born in Port of Spain, Trinidad and Tobago, to the name Stokely Carmichael. His primary schooling was at Tranquility School in Port of Spain until he migrated to Harlem at 11 years to join his parents who had settled in New York when he had but two years. His secondary schooling was at the highly selective Bronx Science High School. After graduation in 1960 he went to Howard University in Washington, DC, to study philosophy. There Carmichael continued his vocation as an activist begun already in high school where he organized a protest against a hamburger joint in the Bronx that refused to hire Blacks. At Howard he was a prominent participant in the 1961 Freedom Rides organized by the Congress of Racial Equality (CORE), during which he was arrested multiple times and served hard time in Mississippi's Parchman State Prison Farm. Also at Howard, Carmichael joined the campus affiliate of the Student Nonviolence Coordinating Committee (SNCC).

Upon completing university studies in 1964, he became a field worker with SNCC during Freedom Summer in Mississippi where he worked with Bob Moses and Fanny Lou Hammer. After the summer, Carmichael worked throughout the American South in SNCC actions, notably with the Selma, Alabama, movement and the March to Montgomery in 1965, where, among others, he worked with Martin Luther King, Jr. In 1966 he became chairman of SNCC, succeeding John Lewis, a hero of the 1961 Freedom Riders and today a leader in the United States Congress representing Atlanta and Georgia's 5th congressional district.

During Carmichael's tenure, SNCC expanded its program to include opposition to the War in Vietnam and began to emphasize Black Power as the purpose of Black political action. Carmichael soon became a national and global celebrity for his defiant ideas and charismatic manner, which also led to the FBI investigating him. In 1967 he stepped down from the chairmanship, in part because his celebrity detracted from the political work of SNCC. Soon after, he began his association with the Black Panther Party, while also publishing in 1967 the book *Black Power: The Politics of Liberation in America*,[1] coauthored with Charles V. Hamilton. He was by then a figure of global importance.

DOI: 10.4324/9781003198291-19

Against the Colonization of Consciousness   133

In 1968, he married Miriam Makeba. The following year they moved to Guinea, where he changed his name to Kwame Ture out of respect for his African mentors Sékou Touré and Kwame Nkrumah. Ture thereafter devoted his efforts to revolutionary movements in Africa, notably Nkrumah's All-African People's Revolutionary party. In 1996, he learned he had prostate cancer from which he died in Conakry, Guinea, in 1998.

More than all but a few, Kwame Ture's life was devoted to political action that served directly, in the expression of the day, to raise the consciousness of Black people the world over to their political power. The first of Ture's statement of Black Power was a 1966 speech at the University of California, which began with poignant humor: "Thank you very much. It's a privilege and an honor to be in the white intellectual ghetto of the West."[2] In America in 1966, Black Power was both practically and ideologically aimed at white power, but with the emphatic focus on Black consciousness beginning with the virtual exclusion of whites from the more radical post-integrationist civil rights activities. The idea in the speech reflected his background as a philosopher: "The philosophers Camus and Sartre raise the question whether or not a man can condemn himself. The Black existentialist philosopher who is pragmatic, Frantz Fanon, answered the question. He said that man could not." In effect, whites must deal with their own racism. "Now then, before we move on, we ought to develop the white supremacy attitudes that were either conscious or subconscious thought and how they run rampant through the society today." The speech then declaims a bill of particulars that of the issues affecting the American people generally—from poverty and the War in Vietnam to riots and other instances of social and racial violence. Most notably, Ture was perfectly clear about the role of capitalist's resist to movements seeking to change the order of racial things:

> Now we articulate that we therefore have to hook up with black people around the world, and that that hookup is not only psychological, but becomes very real. If South America today were to rebel, and black people were to shoot the hell out of all the white people there—as they should, as they should–then Standard Oil would crumble tomorrow. If South Africa were to go today, Chase Manhattan Bank would crumble tomorrow. If Zimbabwe, which is called Rhodesia by white people, were to go tomorrow, General Electric would cave in on the East Coast. The question is, how do we stop those institutions that are so willing to fight against "Communist aggression" but closes their eyes to racist oppression? That is the question that you raise. Can this country do that?

In the end, Ture's charisma is evident in his call for white people to change their ways:

> The question is, will white people overcome their racism and allow for that to happen in this country? If that does not happen, brothers and

134   *Postcolonial Theories of Capitalism*

sisters, we have no choice but to say very clearly, "Move over, or we goin' to move on over you."

In the 1967 book *Black Power* with Charles Hamilton, the full range of issues sketched out in the 1966 speech are spelled out chapter by chapter. But here the authors make it clear in the preface to the 1992 edition that Black Power is a global issue:

> We are both far more sensitive to the international implications of our struggle. ... We both believe that until Africa is free, no African anywhere in world will be free. To us, this is self-evident. It is also self-evident that the revolutionary struggle for that goal will not be deterred.

W.E.B. Du Bois (1868–1963) was born in Great Barrington, Massachusetts, a town in the day with few Black households. So white was Great Barrington that, it seems, few among them were troubled by their Negro neighbors. In early childhood, Du Bois had little sense that his skin color was at issue until, well along in primary school, a snotty white girl startled him by rejecting his party card. This likely was his first conscious experience of the color line, one that he wrote of later in life. Du Bois was an excellent student at Great Barrington High School, after which he meant to attend Harvard College. Then came a second rejection. Whatever might have been Harvard's official reasons for rejecting his candidacy, his racial difference was among them.[3] Du Bois redeemed the College's initial rejection when Harvard admitted him in 1888 after study at Fisk University without giving him credit for his course work there. He graduated from the College *cum laude* in 1890 with a major in philosophy, after which he began doctoral studies both at the University of Berlin and Harvard. Du Bois completed the PhD at Harvard in 1896 with a thesis on *The Suppression of the African Slave Trade to the United States of America, 1638–1871*.

The earlier Harvard rejection in 1885 turned out to be fortuitous. He chose instead to study at the historically Black Fisk University where, for the first time, Du Bois lived in a robustly Negro community. Even more to the point of his living among Black people were the two summers of 1886 and 1887 when he left Fisk and Nashville to serve as a school teacher in Alexandria—a poor rural community of Black folk in the hills of Eastern Tennessee. There he truly lived among the poorest of marginalized Negroes, an experience that shaped one the most original, if seldom read, chapters in *The Souls of Black Folk* (1903), "On the Meaning of Progress." The more famous chapter in *Souls* is the first, "Of Our Spiritual Strivings," which contains Du Bois's memorable and oft-quoted lines on the double consciousness of the American Negro:

> One ever feels his twoness,—an American, a Negro; two souls, two thoughts, two unreconciled strivings; two warring ideals in one black body, whose dogged strength alone keeps it from being torn asunder.[4]

Yet, as poetically and theoretically important as Du Bois's twoness maxim is, "On the Meaning of Progress" speaks more directly to the intersectionality between race and class, even gender and perhaps sexuality. It was in a sense the meat on the bones of his theory of double consciousness—a consciousness that Du Bois called attention to later by pressuring the white publishing world to capitalize the N in Negro. In his consciousness, the American Negro was a joining of two culturally equal social forces.

During his two summers in the hills of Tennessee, Du Bois grew especially close to the family of a young woman, Josie, who serves as his literary icon for the oppression of economically impoverished rural Negroes in the South one generation after the end of the Civil War. Hence, "On the Meaning of Progress" is without question a defiant criticism of the white world's ideology of progress; hence also, if by implication, of Capitalism's commitment to endless economic growth. It is not, however, an abstract critique. Du Bois deploys, as often he did, literary nonfiction to tell the story, notably in the chapter's sad, nostalgic ending. "On the Meaning of Progress" is the tale of Du Bois's visit ten years after he had left Fisk. What he found was anything but progress. Josie had left the hills to work in Nashville, there to earn what she had hoped would contribute to the economic prospects of her family. But Alexandria was unchanged. Josie was dead. He left sad, perhaps depressed, not just for Josie but for all those cut off by the color line[5]:

> My journey was done, and behind me lay hill and dale, and Life and Death. How shall man measure Progress there where the dark-faced Josie lies? How many heartfuls of sorrow shall balance a bushel of wheat? How hard a thing is life to the lowly, and yet how human and real! And all this life and love and stress and failure,—is it the twilight of nightfall or the flush of some faint-dawning day?
>
> Thus, sadly musing, I rode to Nashville in the Jim Crow car.

Du Bois rode that car to a brilliant academic career, but also to a long life marked as much by political action and cultural leadership as by scholarship.

After the Harvard PhD, Du Bois taught briefly at Wilberforce College in Ohio before spending a year engaged in field work in Philadelphia studying the Negro community in the City's Seventh Ward. The research was supported half-heartedly by the University of Pennsylvania which declined to grant him so much as a title commensurate to his Harvard pedigree. The result of his insulting tenure at Penn was his first important book, *The Philadelphia Negro* (1899), which gave good evidence that the urban Negro community was anything but a slum of socially undisciplined people. The University of Pennsylvania belatedly appointed Du Bois Professor of History Emeritus in 2012, a half-century after he died. In this relation, Penn was always a day late and a dollar short.

When, in July 1900, Du Bois participated prominently in the first Pan-African Congress in London, he threw himself into a global sea of political

136 *Postcolonial Theories of Capitalism*

action and literary work that consumed much of the remaining 63 years of his life. He died on African soil in 1963—after visits to Africa over many years, after having become a leader in the Pan-African movement, after giving meaning to the African roots of the American Negro, after having migrated to Accra, Ghana, at the encouragement of Kwame Nkrumah—there to work on an encyclopedia of the African people while enjoying the last few years of life. Du Bois left America in disgust at its prevailing racism and cruel politics, compounded in the 1950s by a vicious ideology that targeted him and many others as Communists.

There was, however, a certain irony in Du Bois's frankly socialist values and Pan-African politics. He had earned his status as a race-man (to use the expression then in vogue) on the wings of his sophisticated intellectual work. He was not quite an elitist, but he knew that his education allowed him to engage in racial politics in a unique way; hence, he emphasized the power of the educated as leaders of racial uplift. His program—*the talented tenth*—was shaped concretely by his differences with Booker T. Washington, the principal of Tuskegee Institute, whose racial politics were based on the idea that hard manual labor in fields and factories were the only certain route to what racial uplift could be had. In still another chapter in *Souls*, "Of Booker T. Washington and Others," Du Bois presented an opening salvo against the Tuskegee ideal. Washington betrayed himself in his infamous 1895 Atlanta Compromise Speech, of which the irritating line was quite explicitly a compromise with the white South. "In all things that are purely social we can be as separate as the fingers, yet one as the hand in all things essential to mutual progress." Du Bois's outspoken differences with Washington were surely determined dispositionally by his first-hand knowledge that the hard-working Josies of the world were powerless in the face of the harsh racialized economic inequalities.

By the time of *Souls* in 1903, *The Philadelphia Negro* in 1899 had certified his reputation as a social scientist of Negro life in America—a status enhanced after appointment in 1897 as Professor of History and Economics at Atlanta University, where he conducted fine-grained empirical studies of the American Negro for which Atlanta itself served as a laboratory.[6] Du Bois's Atlanta studies were pervasively empirical, even quantoid; but unlike *Souls*, they were not published in a way that would come to the attention of the general reader. Yet, reports of the research were published in scholarly venues and made it clear that Du Bois had a self-conscious method and purpose in mind, as in "The Study of the Negro Problems."[7]

Du Bois's work early in the 20th century changed in 1910 when he was among the founders of the National Association of Colored People (NAACP). He immediately joined the organization's staff in New York City as Director of Publicity and Research, a role he used to establish *The Crisis*—the monthly magazine he edited for 25 years. The underlying crisis that stood behind *The Crisis* was of course the inherent crisis of the American Negro—the crisis in the souls of Black folk whoever feel their twoness: "...

Against the Colonization of Consciousness   137

two souls, two thoughts, two unreconciled strivings; two warring ideals in one black body...." From 1911 to 1934, *The Crisis*, under Du Bois, served as the voice of the African Diaspora. In America, at the height of its influence, the magazine had 100,000 subscribers who, in turn, passed *The Crisis* on to friends and neighbors in their communities. They read because the magazine was their access to news of events that threatened as of movements that lent hope—lynchings, the rights of women, the Pan-African Movement, the Harlem Renaissance in the 1920s, and much else. Then in 1934, he quit his position at the NAACP in a dispute with its leadership that for years had sought to remove him for fear that his aggressive racial politics would cost the organization financial support. Du Bois returned to Atlanta University to write what may well be his best book.

Du Bois's *Black Reconstruction in America, 1860–1880* is the first important major work of structural social history, the first in the United States without doubt and arguably the first in North Atlantic historiography. *Black Reconstruction* was published in 1935, a good five years before Fernand Braudel was scribbling notes for *The Mediterranean and the Mediterranean World in the Age of Philip II* (published 1949) in Hitler's prisons. It is possible to suggest that Marx's *Capital I* (1867) was a prior classic work of the genre—that is, if one takes into account the seldom read historical sections on the Working-Day (in Part III), on Machinery and Modern Industry (Part IV), on the General Law of Capitalist Accumulation (Part VII), and the conclusion on Primitive Accumulation (Part VIII). But Marx is far less explicit in his theory of history than either Braudel or Du Bois.

To compare Du Bois to Braudel is to read *Black Reconstruction* as—in effect, if not in the author's intention—a book based on his own theory of TimeSpace of the American Negro. It is a theoretical book that reverses the order of historical time. It is also Du Bois at his Marxist best—not a literal application of Marx's ideas so much as an articulation of his key structural ideas. For Du Bois, the fate of Reconstruction is determined by the structural actors he introduces in the book's first three chapters: the Planter class (1) set against and amid the differences between the Black Worker (2) and the White Worker (3). Then in the fourth chapter, Du Bois makes the compelling point that the Civil War was a General Strike by the Black Worker; as he puts in his epigraph to the fourth chapter[8]:

> How the Civil War meant emancipation and how the black worker won the war by a general strike which transferred his labor from the Confederate planter to the Northern invader, in whose army lines workers began to be organized into a new labor force.

This is Du Bois the poet introducing a 700+-page book of empirical historical sociology.

But how does TimeSpace figure in *Black Reconstruction?* TimeSpace, the theory, serves to complicate, even reverse, the linear notion of historical time

138   *Postcolonial Theories of Capitalism*

as a progressive series of events. *Black Reconstruction* does just this by making the general point that the promise of labor would remain even after 1877 when Reconstruction was dismantled, thus returning the Black worker to the conditions from which she had been emancipated. Jim Crow was slavery in all but name. Du Bois remarks[9]:

> We must remember the black worker was the ultimate exploited; that he formed the mass of labor which had neither wish nor power to escape from the labor status, in order to directly exploit other laborers, or indirectly, by alliance to share in their exploitation.

He then goes on to say that when Black workers tried to "join white capital," they were "driven back into the mass of racial prejudice before they had time to establish a foothold." But Du Bois holds to the idea of the promise of Black workers.

Here, Du Bois strikes back at the then prevailing liberal theory of Reconstruction's failure was somehow due to the inability of the Black workers as freed men and women to pull their lives and communities together. Nothing could have been farther from the truth. If one takes Lincoln's Emancipation Proclamation of January 1, 1863, as the beginning of Reconstruction and the beginning of the Long Depression from 1873 to 1896 as the beginning of its end, then the irony of Du Bois's theory of Black labor is evident. In the time of Reconstruction, freed men and women made enormous strides in education in schools supported by white philanthropists, in savings and financial development with the help of the federally supported Freedmen's Saving and Trust Company, in the development of mutual aid and religious societies, in the beginning of political participation, and more. Yet all this was taken away, first and foremost, by the economic crisis that endured more than two decades that, second, opened the way for white racists to close down federal support for Reconstruction in 1877. And yet, Jim Crow notwithstanding, Du Bois concludes the opening chapter on the Black worker remarkably with a hopeful and global statement[10]:

> It was thus the black worker, *as founding stone of a new economic system in the nineteenth century and for the modern world*, who brought civil war in America. He was itself underlying cause, in spite of every effort to base strife upon union and national power.
>
> That dark and vast sea of human labor in China and India, the South Seas and all Africa; in the West Indies and Central America and in the United States—that great majority of mankind, on whose bent and broken backs rest today the founding stones of modern industry—shares a common destiny; it is despised and rejected by race and color; paid a wage below the level of decent living; driven, beaten, prisoned and enslaved in all but name; spawning the world's raw material and

Against the Colonization of Consciousness   139

luxury—cotton, wool, coffee tea, cocoa, palm oil, fibers, spices, rubber, silks, lumber, copper, gold, diamonds leather. How shall we end the list and where?

Then, he concludes: "The emancipation of man is the emancipation of labor and the emancipation of labor is the freeing of the basic majority of workers who are yellow, brown and black." Without intellectual arm waving, here Du Bois is locating the American Negro not just among the African Diaspora, but as part of a global movement of people of color whose time would not come for at least another century after 1877—if not then or yet.

The other question concerning TimeSpace is why, upon leaving the NAACP in 1934, Du Bois returns with a vengeance to his research for *Black Reconstruction*? The answer is that his troubles with the NAACP were due, in some large part, to the Depression of 1929. Even at its worst, early in the 1930s, its leadership and especially its executive Walter F. White, who had long wanted to oust Du Bois for his more radical views, were foolishly unwilling to adjust the NAACP goals to the then harsh economic realities. Oddly, the ultimate dispute was over segregation. At issue was racially segregated, publicly funded housing projects. Whites thought of segregation as narrowly as the legally sanctioned segregation of Negroes. Du Bois had the broader view that emphasized the economic needs of Negroes in harsh times and even saw segregation as having some good cultural aspects—perhaps his hint of an early version of Black Power politics. He quit with a strong letter on June 26, 1934, which said, in part:

> Today this organization, which has been effective for near a quarter-century, finds itself in a time of *crisis* and change, without a program, without effective organization, without creative officers who have either the ability or the disposition to guide [it] in the right direction.

The final word of *The Crisis* was the crisis of the very organization that sponsored it for so long.

What came next for Du Bois was the work that put flesh on the bones of his version of TimeSpace—work clearly influenced by the economic crisis after 1929. Simply put, he asserted that Black workers were central to the evolution of modern industrial labor. To explain this seemingly preposterous idea, Du Bois argued that it was necessary to look backward from the economic crisis of the 1930s to that of the 1870s. This is the original, if uncommon, theoretical method of *Black Reconstruction*—to understand the promise of Black labor is to look back to the first industrial crisis of capitalism in the 1870s in order to look forward to the first full-blown industrial crisis in the 1930s.[11] Historical time can run backwards before to moves forward. Of course, the resolution of the Great Depression after World War II was not the defining moment in the global work of people of color. The 1950s were, however, the crucial moment for the

140   *Postcolonial Theories of Capitalism*

global decolonizing movements that broke open capitalism's exploitative hold on the periphery. Du Bois in 1935 could not have known this would come to be two decades later. But the key to good social history is being able to read the present in relation to its past, then to uncover what the historical-next of the present might be.

This he knew, of course, in 1961 when he returned to his African roots—a move he had long considered in a memoir that was not published until after his death:

> Africans awake, put on the beautiful robes of Pan African socialism.
> You have nothing to lose but your chains!
> You have a continent to regain!
> You have human freedom and human dignity to regain![12]

Du Bois is not always thought of as a leader of the global decolonizing movement against capitalism. Yet, relative to others, great as they were, he lived longer, wrote more, did more on many fronts, and formulated a remarkable number of theoretical interventions. With all this, there is so much that one fails to see that of all the decolonizing leaders, none was honored more the world over. The Soviet Union gave him the Lenin Peace Prize. A talk in China he thought was to a smallish group was broadcast nationally. Africa welcomed and adopted him as a son.

Amílcar Cabral (1924–1973) was born in Bafatá, a town in central Guinea-Bissau when it was still under Portuguese colonial rule. In Bafatá, he grew in a land-owning farming family. His high school education was in Cape Verde, his mother's native island, today the Republic of Cabo Verde. His university education was at the prestigious *Instituto Superior de Agronomia* at the University of Lisbon, where he was a leader among African students. He founded student organizations on African nationalism and was instrumental in establishing the Center for African Studies.

Upon completing his studies, Cabral returned to Guinea-Bissau where the colonial government employed him as an agronomist. This position allowed him to travel widely as a land surveyor. He, thereby, came to know and be known by farm workers and others among the colonized citizens of the colony. His personal experience growing up on a family farm not only motivated his education and occupation in agronomy, but inspired his political motivation to improve conditions in the countryside and eventually to lead the national liberation movement as a founder in 1956 of the African Party for the Independence of Guinea and Cape Verde (PAIGC). The decolonizing movement engaged in open warfare with the Portuguese colonizers from whom the people declared independence in 1973. Cabral was assassinated in 1973 near his home in Conarky, the capital of the Republic of Guinea. His murderer is thought to have been a Portuguese double agent who had infiltrated PAIGC. Portugal recognized the Republic of Guinea in 1974.

Amílcar Cabral was an intense revolutionary organizer, who also was a brilliant theorist critical of colonial oppressors and the weapons by which they could be overthrown. A primary example of his strategic genius is his PAIGC program published in 1969 and meant to apply to several revolutionary movements around the world. The program is notable for its nine succinct *and* ascendingly global principles:

1 Immediate and total independence
2 Unity of the nation in Guinea and the Cabo Verde Islands
3 Unity of the people of Guinea and the Cabo Verde Islands
4 African unity
5 Democratic, anti-colonialist, and anti-imperialist government
6 Economic independence, structuring the economy, and developing production
7 Justice and progress for all based on the elimination of poverty, social welfare, economic inequality, education, human rights, and religious freedom
8 Also interestingly, an effective national defense system
9 International policies in the interests of the nation, of Africa, and of the peace and humanity.[13]

Cabral was deeply thoughtful about the first principle and slogan of the movement *Return to the Source*, which is also the title of a book that collects several of his more important speeches critical of colonial oppression. In many ways, Cabral's thinking was similar to Fanon's, with two exceptions. Cabral engaged in direct war against the colonizer, and he had a different—in some ways, more complete—understanding of the workings of imperial oppression on the colonized:

> The ideal for foreign domination, whether imperialist or not, would be to choose;—either, to liquidate practically all the population of the dominated country, thereby eliminating the possibilities for cultural resistance;—or to succeed in imposing itself without damage to the culture of the dominated people—that is, to harmonize economic and political domination of these people with their cultural personality.[14]

Here, we see the subtlety of Cabral's thinking. For one, he distinguishes between foreign domination as such and imperialism in particular. For another, he distinguishes brutal domination from its shrewd alternative—the harmonization of the political economy with the culture of the dominated people. As a result, culture becomes an important aspect of Cabral's political theory:

> A people who free themselves from foreign domination will be free culturally only if without complexes and without underestimating the

142 *Postcolonial Theories of Capitalism*

> importance of position accretions from the oppressor and other cultures, they return to the upward paths of their own culture, which is nourished by the living reality of its, and which negates both harmful influences of any kind of subjection to foreign culture.[15]

Here is the theme of *returning to the source*—a dominated people retain the cultural source of their collective being as the source of their political power. But Cabral is astutely specific in his theory of culture by drawing the line that ties a culture to both collective and individual identities.

> The definition of an identity, individual or collective, is at the same time the affirmation and denial of a certain number of characteristics which define the individuals or groups, through historical (biological and sociological) factors at a moment of their development.[16]

Cabral does not leave it at that. Identities, both collective and individual, are pliable in the face of the multiple relations that comprise cultures at all levels:

> The definition of an identity, individual or collective, is at the same time the affirmation and denial of a certain number of characteristics which define the individuals or groups, through historical (biological and sociological) factors at a moment of their development. In fact, identity is not a constant, precisely because the biological and sociological factors which define it are in constant change. Biologically and sociologically, there are no two beings (individual or collective) completely the same or completely different, for it is always possible to find in them common or distinguishing characteristics. Therefore, the identity of a being is always a relative quality, even circumstantial for defining it demands a selection, more or less rigid and strict, of the biological and sociological characteristics of the being in question. One must point out that in the fundamental binomial in the definition of identity, the sociological factors are more determining than the biological.[17]

In fact, it is the very plasticity of identities that allows for a "source" to which an oppressed people can return:

> A people who free themselves from foreign domination will be free culturally only if without complexes and without underestimating the importance of position accretions from the oppressor and other cultures, they return to the upward paths of their own culture, which is nourished by the living reality of its environment, and which negates both harmful influences of any kind of subjection to foreign culture.[18]

Against the Colonization of Consciousness   143

Elsewhere in *The Weapon of Theory*, a 1966 speech to an international conference of representatives from colonized or postcolonial nations in Cuba, Cabral's theoretical acuity is all the more striking. In fact, he offers a strong theoretical case for the social structural character of both oppression and importantly for the cultural basis for a revolutionary movement:

> This opinion is the result of our own experiences of the struggle and of a critical appreciation of the experiences of others. To those who see in it a theoretical character, we would recall that every practice produces a theory, and that if it is true that a revolution can fail even though it be based on perfectly conceived theories, nobody has yet made a successful revolution without a revolutionary theory.[19]

To be sure, Cabral is not particularly focused on capitalism's role in oppression or for that matter in liberation (as some would claim). But when considered in the context of other postcolonial actors and thinkers, Cabral's analysis does complete the picture of both the causes of domination and relief there from by revolutionary means.

It may have seemed strange to juxtapose three such apparently different thinkers as Ture, Du Bois, and Cabral. They were, after all, far dispersed on the TimeSpace map the world. One (Du Bois) was at least two generations older than the other two. He lived out his days as an adopted son of Africa, adopted, that is, by the radical Ghanaian leader Kwame Nkrumah, who also adopted Ture. The third, Cabral, lived his life for and in Africa, save for his graduate education in Lisbon. He and Ture were student radicals and organizers, while Du Bois spent his youth in learning the truths of his Negro blood while also becoming very highly educated.

Yet, the three had in common life on the hard soil of their ancestors. Du Bois's summers in the mountains of Eastern Tennessee were, of course, unlike Ture's summer in Mississippi, where in 1964 he worked with the rural share croppers in the same state where he had done hard time in Parchman Prison in 1961. There, he learned firsthand of the terrible toil on hard soil of those Du Bois called Negroes (with the capital N) whom Ture baptized Black's with power. Cabral, like Ture, enjoyed a privileged early life, yet both sacrificed those privileges to work hard in order to organize those colonized by the same global colonizing that Du Bois, using different methods, also fought by his intellectual talents.

When it comes to the diaspora of those colonized by capitalism's endemic avarice, there are differences wrought of capitalism's necessary drive to accumulate capital where surplus value can be harvested. And "harvested" is the right word, whether it is industrial worker cut down to the mechanical nature of his and her labor on the factory floor or the slave bought and sold to be whipped unto the morbid labor of cutting cotton or tobacco, or the agrarian farmers in Guinea growing and harvesting food for their Portuguese

144　*Postcolonial Theories of Capitalism*

colonizers in Iberia, or any other of the ways the racialized poor are cut and drawn to serve Capitalism's obsession with growth that ultimately destroys any liberal notion of progress. Capitalism kills even the least part of the natural human hope for fairness, if not equality.

At the center of his perfect storm of modern contradictions lies the racially excluded—women, men, children thrust into the forest and barren lands from which wealth can be extracted. Ture, Du Bois, Cabral represent three of many global vectors along which these differences and exclusions are dispersed. They were different as their subjects allowed several and many effects—all of them moved by the same causal origin. They help us see that race is not one among many politicized identities from which people come to a consciousness of who they are and who they are meant to be. Nor is race simply the first among equal social identifications. Race is one and alone because racial differences were *the* method by which human labor was commodified. Human consciousness is first and foremost racial consciousness. Without the colonized consciousness of racial others, there would have been no capitalist political economy of the kind all of us live in for better or worse.

Notes

1　Stokely Carmichael (Kwame Ture in the 1992 edition) and Charles V. Hamilton *Black Power: The Politics of Liberation in America* (New York: Random House, 1967 [1992]).

2　Stokely Carmichael (1966). *Black Power* (Speech at the University of California Berkeley: October 29, 1966). Downloaded from *Voices of Democracy* @ https://voicesofdemocracy. umd.edu/carmichael-black-power-speech-text/

3　David Levering Lewis, *W.E.B. Du Bois, 1868–1919: Biography of a Race* (New York: Henry Holt, 1994), 54.

4　W.E.B. Du Bois, *The Souls of Black Folk* (New York: Bantam Books, 1903), 3.

5　*Ibid.*, 52.

6　W.E.B. Du Bois *The Negroes of Farmville, Virginia: A Social Study* (Washington: Government Printing Office; Department of Labor, (January 1898b), 14.

7　W.E.B. Du Bois "The Study of the Negro Problems," *The Annals of the American Academy of Political and Social Sciences* 11 (January 1898a): 1–23. [Reprinted in W.E.B. Du Bois, *On Sociology and the Black Community*, eds. Dan S. Green and Edwin D. Driver (Chicago: University of Chicago Press, 1978)] Compare 1898b.

8　W.E.B. Du Bois, *Black Reconstruction in America: 1860–1880* (New York: Harcourt Brace [New York: Free Press], 1935[1992]), 55.

9　*Ibid.*, 15.

10　*Ibid.*, 15–16; emphasis added.

11　Charles Lemert, "The Race of Time: Deconstruction, Du Bois, and Reconstruction, 1935–1873," in *The Race of Time: The Charles Lemert Reader*, eds., Daniel Chaffee and Sam Han (Routledge/Paradigm, 2009), 130.

12　W.E.B. Du Bois, *The Autobiography of W.E.B. DuBois: A Soliloquy on Viewing My Life from the Last Decade of Its First Century* (Posthumously in New York: International Publishers, 1968), 404.

13　Amílcar Cabral, "*The PAIGC Programme* (1969)," in *Revolution in Guinea,* ed. Richard Handyside (London, 1974). Downloaded July 21, 2019 from https://www.marxists.org/ subject/africa/cabral/paigcpgm.htm; some points are paraphrased.

Against the Colonization of Consciousness   145

14 Amílcar Cabral, *Return to the Source: Selected Speeches* (New York: Monthly Review Press with Africa Information Service, 1973), 40.
15 *Ibid.*, 43.
16 *Ibid.*, 64.
17 *Ibid.*, 65.
18 *Ibid.*, 43.
19 Amilcar Cabral, "The Weapon of Theory Havana: Address Delivered to the First Tri-continental Conference of the Peoples of Asia, Africa, and Latin American in Havana in January 1966." Accessed November 21, 2019. https://www.marxists.org/subject/africa/cabral/1966/weapon-theory.htm.

17 Existential Unfolding as Revolutionary Praxis

Mao Zedong/Charu Mazumdar

Mao Zedong (1893–1976) was born in 1893 to one of the wealthiest families in Shaoshan, Hunan, China. Mao travelled to the provincial capital of Changsha to attend secondary school where he, being from a rural background, was one of the poorest students in school.[1] Influenced by the Xinhai Revolution in 1911, Mao began his political radicalization in his late teenage years. During his college years, Mao read widely on Western political philosophy, including Plato, Aristotle, Kant, Hobbes, Spinoza, Nietzsche, and so on.[2] After college, Mao was a library assistant at Beijing University. While on the margins of intellectual life as a result of his low ranking position and southern accent, he attended lectures and participated in student politics[3] and was particularly taken with the writings of Peter Kropotkin and Mikhail Bakunin. Mao soon began to participate in anarchist student groups.[4] In April 1919, Mao returned to his hometown because his mother was ill, and he found a position as a history teacher in a primary school, offering him a higher salary than his job in the library.[5] Mao followed the events of the May Fourth Movement closely, but gravitated to the anarchist elements in the movement.[6][7] But by the summer of 1920, Mao began to consider himself a Marxist. His "conversion to Communism," claims biographer Steven Meisner, was less an embrace of Bolshevism and more a disillusionment with anarchists in the Russian Revolution.[8] He began organizing small communist groups that would eventually evolve into the Chinese Communist Party by 1921. His first task was to organize the Chinese working class in cities across Hunan province. But in 1925, Mao had to flee the cities under threat of execution. It was during this time that he "discovered" the Chinese peasant. He began to focus his intellectual efforts on better understanding how the rural social structure was the "real foundation of imperialism" and began to conclude that without a peasants' revolution, there could be no national revolution in China.[9] In 1927, Mao decided not only to mobilize peasants, but have the Communist Party retreat to rural areas in order to build a military force that could defeat the Guomindang. In 1947, Mao's Red Army was victorious and he founded the People's Republic of China in 1949. One of the cornerstones of Mao's domestic policy was nationwide land reform aimed at improving rural living conditions and creating a more egalitarian China.

DOI: 10.4324/9781003198291-20

Existential Unfolding 147

Mao's theory of peasant revolt is best encapsulated in his 1927 essay entitled "Report on an Investigation of the Peasant Movement in Hunan." The first goal of a revolutionary peasant movement, after enlisting and organizing the peasant into an organization, is to attack the prestige and soft power of the landowning class.[10] To do so, Mao writes, "is a most serious and vital struggle," which provides a foundation for subsequent economic struggles to reduce rent and secure land for peasants. By undermining the prestige of the landowning class, it weakens the authority of the landlords to oppose subsequent political struggle against them. Mao has several ideas for how this might be done in practice. First, he suggests holding the landlord accountable to local laws; "a man who has been fined by the peasants," Mao writes, "completely loses face."[11] Second, through minor protests and major demonstrations, crowds of peasants can raise awareness of the "offences" incurred by the landlord. Third, Mao suggests that peasants crown the landlord and parade him through the village with a sign stating "Local tyrant so-and-so" or "So-and-so of the evil gentry" while beating brass gongs and waving flags in order to raise awareness in the village of the landlord's offences against the peasants. Fourth, Mao suggests locking up the landlords in the county jail for crimes against the peasantry or banishing them from the village altogether. And finally, for "the worst local tyrants and evil gentry" who have indiscriminately "slaughtered peasants without batting an eyelid," Mao recommends execution after trying the landlords with a peasant tribunal.[12]

After the landlord is either absent or sufficiently discredited, Mao claims, then peasants can take up the economic struggle. Once the rents are sufficiently lowered and food is accessible to all, the village can then take on feudalism at the regional level. In China, claims Mao, there are three power structures that need to be defeated: (1) the state; (2) patrimonialism (what Mao calls "clan authority"); and (3) religious authorities.[13] Together, these three hierarchies constitute, for Mao, a "feudal-patriarchal system," "binding the Chinese people, particularly the peasants."[14] While many of these systems, Mao believed, would weaken after the political and economic struggle against local landowners, it was important for peasant organizations to stay vigilant against both counterrevolutionary propaganda and the mindsets of older people who may be more reluctant to give up deeply ingrained systems of religion, patriarchy, and feudalism.

While the role of ideology is central to Mao's theory of peasant's revolt, Mao's revolution is by no means simply an intellectual exercise. He writes:

> a revolution is not a dinner party, or writing an essay, or painting a picture, or doing embroidery; it cannot be so refined, so leisurely and gentle, so temperate, kind, courteous, restrained and magnanimous. A revolution is an insurrection, an act of violence by which one class overthrows another. A rural revolution is a revolution by which the peasantry overthrows the power of the feudal landlord class. Without using the greatest force, the peasants cannot possibly overthrow the

148   *Postcolonial Theories of Capitalism*

deep-rooted authority of the landlords which has lasted for thousands of years. The rural areas need a mighty revolutionary upsurge, for it alone can rouse the people in their millions to become a powerful force.[15]

Across the Chinese border, **Charu Mazumdar (1916–1972)** was born in Siliguri, Bengal, India, in 1916 and, just like Mao, born into a landowning family. Mazumdar spoke out against social inequality as a teenager and joined the All Bengal Students Association before dropping out of Government Edward College, Pabna,[16] in 1938 to work as a labor organizer.[17] Mazumdar joined the Communist Party of India (CPI) in 1940, and soon assumed a leadership role in the Party in North Bengal. While lacking the charisma of "mass leader" or great activist, Mazumdar was known for his intellectual contributions to the movement and for being especially "well read in the Marxist classics."[18] In the 1940s, when the CPI was periodically banned in India, Mazumdar spent a good deal of time in and out of jail and underground when he wasn't organizing workers and peasants. Mazumdar spent several months in jail during India's 1962 border war with China for alleged Maoist sympathies. In jail, he devoted his time to reading and writing about Maoism.[19] In 1964, Mazumdar joined the newly formed CPI (Marxist) and became more open about his Maoist proclivities, publishing several secret pamphlets in the mid-1960s to that effect. In May 1967, Mazumdar and his more charismatic comrades, Kanu Sanyal (who he had first met in Dum Dum Jail in 1959) and Jangal Santhal, declared Naxalbari village and its surrounding area a liberated zone where police and government officials were barred from entry. Village committees took over the administration of the village along with the schools and judicial bodies. The homes of rich landowners were raided and the titles to their property were destroyed. This relatively small-scale uprising then started a peasants movement in Bengal, which then spread westward leading to the birth of Maoism in India.[20] In 1969, the Naxalite Movement became the Communist Party of India (Marxist-Leninist) and Charu Mazumdar became its General Secretary. In 1972, Mazumdar was arrested for his leadership role in the CPI(ML) and was brutally tortured by police in Alipore Central Jail. After ten days in detention, he died of cardiac arrest[21] at the age of 56.

While inspired by Maoism, what makes the Naxalite movement, and specifically Mazumdar's theoretical contributions, unique from other forms of Marxism-Leninism-Maoism is that Mazumdar focused on the revolution's "existential unfolding as praxis."[22] Mazumdar's revolution is not one in which armed peasants struggle against the dominant classes, but instead one in which unarmed peasants turn on armed dominant classes, stealing their weapons and appropriating their land as a way to peasants' liberation. This unleashing of a particular kind of violence, "annihilation" as Mazumdar terms it, literally endeavors to kill landlords with the very weapons they use against the peasants, and thereby the means of struggle and the symbolism of the movement is just as important in achieving liberation as the end goals.[23]

Mazumdar's concept of annihilation was the heart of his theory of peasants' revolt. Annihilation, for Mazumdar, was the "liquidation" of the class power of feudal classes, which could only occur through building the political power of peasants. The goal of annihilation, Mazumdar claimed, was not to kill individuals, but to "liquidate the political, economic and social authority of the class enemy."[24] "That is why," posited Mazumdar, "the annihilation of the class enemy is the higher form of class struggle."[25] In other words, Mazumdar's annihilation was not simply a confrontation between landlords and peasants, nor was it a struggle for concessions or improvements in living conditions. Annihilation is a strategy for completely reversing the power relations in agrarian society. And just as combatting patriarchal, religious, and state ideology was for Mao, for Mazumdar as well ideas played an important role in annihilation. "We must daily and constantly carry on struggle against revisionist ideas," he urged, "We must evolve a new style of work through our struggle against revisionist ideas. Only thus can we fulfil the heavy responsibility that lies on our shoulders today."[26] Just as it was for Mao, economic and social change, Mazumdar thought, was not enough to create a successful peasant's revolt. At its heart, one had to first encourage a new way of thinking about the world that dismantled peasants' internalization of hierarchies of class, caste, gender, and so on.

In Mao and Mazumdar's theory of what a more just and equal agrarian society might look like and how it might be achieved, they refute a key classical Marxist argument about capitalist development. Instead of passing through a series of uniform stages and each stage as a uniform mode of production, Mao and Mazumdar show that capitalist development, on the contrary, occurs in fits and starts. Old labor regimes coexist with newer social relations, and social transformation need not adhere to a singular trajectory in all places and times. In creating a theory that calls for the upending of existing agrarian social relations, Mao and Mazumdar call our attention to one of the fundamental contradictions of modernity—that older social hierarchies can easily serve newer modes of production.

Notes

1 Maurice Meisner, *Mao Zedong: A Political and Intellectual Portrait* (Cambridge: Polity Press, 2007), 3.
2 *Ibid.*, 11.
3 *Ibid.*, 15.
4 *Ibid.*, 16.
5 *Ibid.*, 17.
6 *Ibid.*, 18.
7 For more on anarchist feminist thought during the May Fourth Movement, see the excellent volume edited by Liu, Karl, and Ko (2013).
8 *Ibid.*, 28.
9 *Ibid.*, 43.
10 Mao Zedong, *Selected Works of Mao Tse-Tung*, Vol. 1 (Peking: Foreign Languages Press, 1965), 35.

150   *Postcolonial Theories of Capitalism*

11 *Ibid.*, 36.
12 *Ibid.*, 39.
13 *Ibid.*, 44.
14 *Ibid.*
15 *Ibid.*, 28.
16 Arun Prosad Mukerjee, *Maoist "Spring Thunder": The Naxalite Movement (1967–1972)* (Kolkata: KP Bagchi & Co, 2002), 289.
17 Nadeem Ahmad, "Charu Mazumdar—the Father of Naxalism," *Hindustan Times*, December 15, 2005.
18 Biplab Dasgupta, *The Naxalite Movement* (Bombay: Allied Publishers, 1974), 4.
19 Ahmad, "Charu Mazumdar."
20 Dasgupta, *The Naxalite Movement*, 15.
21 Mukerjee, *"Spring Thunder,"* 289.
22 Rabindra Ray, *The Naxalites and their Ideology* (New Delhi: Oxford University Press, 1988), 184.
23 *Ibid.*, 184–185.
24 Charu Mazumdar, "March Onward by Summing up the Experience of the Peasant Revolutionary Struggle of India," *Liberation* 3, no. 2 (1969).
25 *Ibid.*
26 *Ibid.*

18 A Critique of Western Imperialism from Within

Muhammad Ali/Ulrike Meinhof

Muhammad Ali (1942–2016) was born Cassius Marcellus Clay in Louisville, Kentucky, to a modest family on the city's west end. His birth name came down from his father's line back to the Civil War era Kentucky planter and politician of the same name. The first Cassius Marcellus Clay was a prominent abolitionist as to slavery, which fact brought him into Abraham Lincoln's political orbit.

The young Cassius of recent times was destined for international fame only partly because of his athletic gifts. More important to his long-term reputation were his actions, words, poems, and the way he presented himself in respect to mid-20th-century virtual slavery and the global oppression of people in the Global South as well as in his native country. Clay was not a good student. He would not have graduated Central High School had not the school's principal declared that he would not deny a high school diploma to a future world champion. As a boy of 12 years, Clay took up boxing when an off-duty police officer, Joe Martin, offered to teach him boxing so he could fend off street kids like the one who stole his bike. Clay was so determined that years after, Martin said that he had taught thousands of boys to box, but Cassius "was willing to make sacrifices ... and was easily the hardest working kid I ever taught."

Clay rose quickly through the amateur ranks to the win the Golden Gloves light heavyweight championship in 1959 and an Olympic Gold Medal in the Rome Olympics in 1960, after which Angelo Dundee, among the best trainers ever in the sport, prepared him for professional boxing. In 1964, he upset the fearsome Sonny Liston to win the world heavyweight championship, and came out as Muhammad Ali, a member of the Nation of Islam. Even his uncanny charm could not hold off the racist vitriol cast upon him.

In 1967, Ali refused induction into the Army, claiming conscientious objector status, whereupon he was indicted by a federal grand jury, costing him his boxing license. His opposition to the War in Vietnam was the first of his public political statements, publicized by the false attribution that he said: "No Viet Cong ever called me Nigger." He was always ready with a clever quote, but he was seldom rhetorically incendiary. By contrast, the legal actions against him were, at least partly, prejudicial toward his religious commitment to the Nation of Islam.

DOI: 10.4324/9781003198291-21

152   *Postcolonial Theories of Capitalism*

Ali lost the better part of five years of his boxing career—years when he was in his prime. When, in 1971, the US Supreme Court ordered that all charges against him be dropped, he was close to his 30th birthday, when most boxers are on the downward slope. Yet he returned to the ring, suffered losses to Joe Frazier and Ken Norton, but persevered. In 1974, he defeated Frazier, which set up the famous fight with George Foreman in Kinshasa, Congo. Foreman, today the most genial of men, was at the time not only a more formidable opponent than Sonny Liston had been, but also a man who presented himself in public as ignorant of the ways of African people and all but openly hostile to them, Ali, and everyone about him. When Foreman landed in Congo, he entered Kinshasa with a German Shepherd—the very dog that the Belgium colonizers used to intimidate those they ruthlessly pressed into their service. Meanwhile, Ali himself, fresh from a hajj to Mecca, was all the more settled into his Muslim faith and practice to which he remained true until his death. He had previously visited Africa and arrived for the fight with Foreman with an obvious familiarity with and appreciation of the people. He became an object of respect and admiration among the Congolese, many of whom ran after him during training runs outside the city.

As for the fight, Ali was a decided underdog. He surprised observers by, in his line, "dancing like a butterfly, stinging like a bee." He was exceptionally fast afoot. If anything, his hands were faster still. Yet, after a flurry of the dancing style in the first round, Ali settled into his rope-a-dope routine against Foreman. He allowed his opponent to punch away as he mostly leaned on the ropes. Foreman exhausted himself trying to put Ali away. By the eighth round, Foreman was exhausted. Ali knocked him out. He was again on top of the boxing world. His astonishing victory in this fight and his way with people as well as his obvious devotion to the people of Africa and their descendants back home won him world fame. Some said that, in that moment, he was the most famous person on the planet—at least to those oppressed by Western Imperialism.

It may seem odd for a figure like Muhammad Ali to appear in a book among so many intellectuals. Yet, he deserves such a place because he was, and remains, witness to how true religious belief can dwell deep inside a person who on the surface would seem to be a joker of sorts. He made fun of those about him and indirectly of himself, but the fun was not making light of what he believed. What he believed was exhibited in what he did. He was, to use the better word, a trickster—one who tricked those about him into listening and following him. His line, "dance like a butterfly, sing like a bee," seems all too feminine (or, better, androgynous sexually) in its way. The butterfly is feminine; the bee, one could say, is masculine. In the early years, Ali unashamedly admired and followed the example of Gorgeous George— the theatrical wrestler who came to dominate this sort of wrestling by his charisma, flamboyance, and generally outrageous stagecraft in the ring— with, among it all, a feminine tease. Ali was, by contrast, less outrageous in self-presentation but just as much a trans-tease. Still, the trickster features of his presentation served to call attention to his unwavering convictions—the early protest against war and many subsequent acts of usually playful defiance. Perhaps his best line, if not the best known, began with his draft refusal and remained part of his political arsenal even when the defiance was unspoken: "I don't have to be what you want me to be." Think of such a line among his followers in Africa and at home those who suffered under regimes of various colonizing kinds that wanted them to be who *they* wanted them to be. One supposes that Franz Fanon, had he survived into the Ali years, would have been the first to say, *yes!*

Capitalism, in particular, is so overly serious with itself and its nasty purposes that its cruel, clumsy failures are no laughing matter. As a matter of fact, most serious radical political movement leaders are not exactly light or funny, with the noticeable exception of Kwame Ture. In 1966 (when he was still Stokley Carmichael), he was asked by a feminist among a gathering of men and women who had been active in on-the-ground political actions, "What is the position of Women in SNCC?" His answer was simply "Prone"—a joke on the sexual affairs in the movement. The self-righteous were outraged but the serious feminists in the group got and took the joke.

If there is a single moment that typifies Ali's genius, it was at the end of a lecture to students at Harvard University's Saunders Theatre after delighting the standing-room-only crowd with his stories and observations. At the end of the lecture, students begged for a poem. Without thinking twice, he said "Me/We!" George Plimpton, who commented on the scene for the film *When We Were Kings*, said that it may have been the shortest poem in the language. More than that, even more, it was token of his powerful charm over people through which shone is heartfelt humility and honest openness to all those with whom he came in contact. The world today could use more of such qualities that, when all is said and done, are capable to speaking truth to power so that the powerful will hear.

Ulrike Meinhof (1934–1976) was born in 1934 in Oldenburg, Germany. Her father was an art historian. In 1936 he became the curator of a museum in Jena and a lecturer at the University of Weimar, moving the family to Jena with him. In 1940, Meinhof's father died suddenly of pancreatic cancer. After the war, Meinhof and her family left Jena because it was soon to become part of the socialist *Deutsche Demokratische Republik* (DDR). In 1949, Meinhof's mother died when Meinhof was only 14 years old. She was then cared for by a boarder Renate Riemeck who the family had taken in when Meinhof's father had died. Riemeck was a medieval historian who introduced Meinhof to politics, literature, and philosophy. Riemeck soon became the youngest female professor in Germany, and raised Meinhof with the help of her partner Holde Bischoff, who was a maternal figure for Meinhof.[1]

As a college student, Meinhof was committed to student politics, eventually joining the *Soziabztische Deutche Studentenbund* along with an anti-nuclear weapons working group. At a press conference in 1958, Meinhof met Rainer

154 *Postcolonial Theories of Capitalism*

Röhl, the editor of leftist magazine *konkret*, with whom Meinhof soon had a romantic and working relationship. Meinhof began writing a regular column for *konkret*, and in 1961, became its editor in chief. In 1968, Röhl left Meinhof for another woman and Meinhof moved with their two children to Berlin. There, she continued to write about left politics for *konkret* and became involved in anti-imperialist struggles. In April 1969, she quit writing for *konkret* over ideological differences with Röhl. Meinhof was increasingly radicalized by the youth movement in Berlin, and Röhl was unwilling to go in that direction. After leaving *konkret*, she decided to create a made-for-television movie *Bambule* about the restricted lives of young women in Germany. The film was completed, but not aired until 1994 due to censorship.

Just as the film had finished production, Meinhof began her involvement with the *Rote Armee Fraktion* (Red Army Faction [RAF]). After joining the RAF, she engaged only in collective writing projects in order to reject the "personality cult" of the individual writer who, through the fact of being a sole-authored theorist, becomes a powerless outsider, observing rather than participating in the political action they write about. While many Meinhof scholars contend that RAF communiques were in fact authored solely by Meinhof, she maintained that they were a collective effort that represented the praxis of the group. She did not return to explicitly sole-authored work until she was imprisoned in 1972. In 1972, Meinhof was arrested for her involvement in the RAF and spent her first eight months in prison in isolation. In 1974, she was transferred to Stammheim Prison in Berlin to stand trial and sentenced for eight years for attempted murder. In May 1976, she was found dead in her prison cell. The exact cause of her death remains open to speculation.

While Meinhof is best known as a revolutionary martyr, even before founding the RAF, she was one of the best known public intellectuals of the German Left in the 1960s. The main themes in her work include war, political freedom, social justice, and the exploitation of women in the workplace (specifically the gender wage gap). Finding affinity and inspiration in the Black Panther Party, Weather Underground, Students for a Democratic Society (SDS), the Brigate Rosse, and Tupacamaros, and influenced by Marx, Marcuse, Lenin, Ho Chi Minh, Frantz Fanon, Che Guevara, and Carlos Margiella, Meinhof's aims in her writing were to bridge the gap between intellectuals and the public, targeting her writing to a public that doesn't read theory. However, her hope was that if her readers did later go on to read Marxist theory, they would be already familiar with its key concepts through her writings. One might compare Ulrike Meinhof to a figure like Rosa Luxembourg. Both women lived in Berlin, were radical leftists, wrote extensively about political economy, vocally opposed war, were imprisoned by the German state, and killed by state agents for their oppositional politics and writings. However, while Luxembourg's legacy continues to this day as one of the most important and brilliant theorists in the history of Marxism, Meinhof's genius as a social theorist has been underappreciated, especially in the academic cannon, even though Ulrike Meinhof is "the most important woman in German politics since Rosa Luxembourg."[2]

Through her writings, Ulrike Meinhof crafted a unique perspective on the global political economy of the 1970s, one that saw and critiqued Western imperialism from within its centers of power. Germany's complicity in the United States War in Vietnam was a central theme of Meinhof's writing. She was critical of not only the military and economic interests that Germany had in supporting the War in Vietnam, but also in how Germany's complicity in the war affected student life. On the student anti-war protests, Meinhof wrote:

> Students have been the ones whose anti-Vietnam protest actions over the past few months have broken down the German press' conspiracy of silence, and turned demonstrations into happenings the public must confront... but now there are demands that the Socialist Student Federation be forbidden and certain students be expelled from their universities, on allegations that the border between political radicalism and crime has been crossed. Is it not a criminal act to drop napalm on women, children and old people; protesting against this is a crime. It is not a criminal act to destroy the harvests necessary for the lives and survival of millions; protesting against this is a crime. It is not a criminal act to destroy energy plants, leper colonies, schools, and dikes; protesting against this is a crime. Terror tactics and torture are not criminal acts; protesting against them is. Suppressing the development of free will in South Vietnam, banning newspapers and persecuting Buddhists is not undemocratic, but protesting against this in a 'free' country is. It is considered rude to pelt politicians with pudding and cream cheese but quite acceptable to host politicians who are having entire villages eradicated and cities bombed. It is considered rude to stand on busy street corners and in train stations and discuss the oppression of the Vietnamese people, but quite acceptable to colonize a people in the name of anti-communist policies.[3]

German aid to the American colonial project in Vietnam not only marked a grave injustice in Meinhof's view, but German repression of student protests highlighted for Meinhof the duality of Germany's postcolonialism—in other words, the German state used the same tactics of colonialism against its own people in order to silence opposition against its imperialist endeavors abroad.

And Meinhof saw this social fact not just in Germany's support for the War in Vietnam, but also in its diplomatic and economic relations with the Shah of Iran. On the Shah, Meinhof commented:

> Iran is really one of the most functional developing countries, and the Shah one of the most functional despots in the Third World with Persian oil clasped tightly in his fist and in the fists of the American,

156   *Postcolonial Theories of Capitalism*

English, and French oil companies, and with the Persian opposition safely in dungeons of the secret police. Ever since the fall of Mossadegh there have been no more complaints. ... The Shah was good looking, his wife had just been on a diet; what could be the problem? And then came the unfortunate police-state visit. The facade came crashing down. In Berlin, police used their truncheons like they hadn't in years. ... The police paid Persians to applaud, and then attack German and Persian student protesters. The truth about the Shah's regime of terror spilled out across the world... The realization that West German capital and the Iranian terror regime are closely allied was pounded into the students by the police.[4]

Meinhof's analysis shows that the West is unable to support dictatorship in the "Third World" without bringing fascism home with it. The violence used against student protestors, just like the repression of the student protestors in Vietnam is part and parcel of the postcolonial condition, and both colonized and colonizer are affected by this singular process that ends in repression and terror for all.

In fact, Meinhof perhaps most controversially sees this same logic in Germany's support for Israel. In her view, support for Israel in Germany is:

not because the humanity of the Jews was suddenly recognized, but because of the ruthless way they waged their war; not because of their rights as citizens but because they used napalm; not because we acknowledged our own crimes but because we admired the Israeli blitzkrieg, in solidarity with brutality, with actions that drive citizens from their home and with conquest.[5]

Just as she argues for Iran and Vietnam, the West, with its history of colonization, respects and defends Israel, not out of sympathy for the Holocaust, but out of admiration for the brutality inflicted by the Israeli state on Palestinians. Through the colonization of Palestine, argues Meinhof, Israel became a part of the West and for that reason only, afforded the respect and privileges associated with such a position.

Meinhof saw the struggle against colonialism and imperialism as one that would take a joint effort—that the West and the Third World were similarly afflicted by the postcolonial condition, and liberation therefore would have to come through opposition not just from people residing in the geographies of globe that were colonized, but also from those in the places that colonized. "The opposition here" in Germany, wrote Meinhof, "and the opposition in the Third World countries must work together."[6]

Both Meinhoff and Ali were unconventional theorists who embraced youth culture and theorized through their political performance. But the substance of their theory was particularly compelling in its critique of Western imperialism from within. Their perspectives held a mirror to the contradictions and hypocrisies of Western Imperialism and its historical legacies. In the German context, this was articulated by Meinhoff as rooted in the legacies of the holocaust making it nearly impossible to separate Germany's support for Israel and the Vietnam War as inevitably bringing fascism back home. Muhammad Ali similarly put forth a complex theory of how the legacies of US racial apartheid were reflected in the Vietnam War. Through Meinhoff's attention to gender and imperialism in the metropole and Ali's thought on race and imperialism in the metropole, empire is not seen as unidirectionally shaping the Global South, but revealed, as Aimé Césaire put it, "the colonizer, who in order to ease his conscience gets into the habit of seeing the other man as *an animal*, accustoms himself to treating him like an animal, and tends objectively to transform *himself* into an animal."[7] Both Meinhoff and Ali showed us how imperialism is reflected back on the metropole revealing the ways imperialism remakes "the West."

Notes

1 Ulrike Marie Meinhof, *Everybody Talks about the Weather—We Don't: The Writings of Ulrike Meinhof,* edited by Karin Bauer (New York: Seven Stories Press, 2008), 23.
2 Quoted in David Kramer, "Ulrike Meinhof: An Emancipated Terrorist?" in *European Women on the Left: Socialism, Feminism, and the Problems Faced by Political Women, 1880 to the Present,* eds. Jane Slaughter and Robert Kern (Westport: Greenwood Press, 1981), 195.
3 Meinhof, *Everybody Talks,* 230–231.
4 *Ibid.,* 184.
5 Ibid., 163.
6 *Ibid.,* 184.
7 Aimé Césaire *Discourse on Colonialism* (New York: Monthly Review Press, 2000), 41.

19 Rethinking the World Revolution of 1968

Martin Luther King Jr./Ho Chi Minh

Martin Luther King, Jr. (1927–1968) was born on January 15, 1929, to a settled family in a relatively prosperous black neighborhood of Atlanta. Both his father Martin Luther King, Sr., and his maternal grandfather Adam Daniel Williams were preachers. The Reverend Williams was pastor of the Ebenezer Baptist Church, the neighborhood's most prestigious congregation. Upon his death in 1931, Martin Luther King, Sr., who had pastored only small rural churches, was called to the Baptist pulpit upon the resolution of controversy over his lack of experience. The deadlock was broken when his maternal grandmother insisted that King, Sr., be appointed pastor at Ebenezer. She did not want to lose the status of being the Church's first lady. Martin Luther King, Jr., was therefore born into a first family of the Sweet Auburn community in Atlanta. His father was a successful businessman in real estate and insurance as well as a pastor of Ebenezer. He was among the black elite in the community. Martin Luther King, Jr., was thus born to a degree of privilege and means not well understood by the white world in the day.

Knowledge of his family and community of origin is important to an understanding of King's political achievements, including the fact that, as time went by, he became a critic of the nation's failure to understand the larger structural issues of American and global racism. King's economic advantages allowed him to attend the ultra-prestigious Morehouse College in Atlanta; Crozier Theological Seminary, then a highly regarded seminary near Chester, Pennsylvania; and Boston University where he received his PhD in philosophy and religion and met his wife Coretta Scott. During his doctoral studies, he read seriously the writings of Reinhold Niebuhr—then as still now the most important politically left religious leader in the nation. Niebuhr's thinking drew a sharp line between the moral behavior of individuals and the economic interests of the state. He argued that the most the society at large can attain is a semblance of justice, not morality in the religious sense. This influence is important because of the mistaken impression that King's nonviolent political philosophy was naive in the face of the vicious racism in the nation.

Also at Boston University he was influenced by the writings of Swedish theologian Anders Nygren who, in the day, was famous for his idea that love

DOI: 10.4324/9781003198291-22

Rethinking the World Revolution of 1968   159

is more than personal charity or romance but also an active force in human life. Niebuhr and Nygren thus were influences before King's trip to India in 1959 to study the teachings of Gandhi. In his 1958 book *Stride Toward Freedom*, written in the wake of the successful Montgomery Bus Boycott, King wrote that "nonviolent resistance is not a method for *cowards*; it does resist."[1] In fact, the method, as he and his followers in the early Civil Right Movement knew very well, was meant to bring into the open the violence of those who would injure protestors with fire hoses, dogs, and bullets. Freedom Riders through the South in the summer of 1961 were brutalized; yet this and other movements ultimately broke the back of racial violence in the American South. King's *Letter from the Birmingham Jail* of April 16, 1963, is his best known and contextually most powerful defense of nonviolent resistance, as his finest public moment was his unforgettable *I Have a Dream* speech at the August 28, 1963, March on Washington.

After 1963, the movement had one brilliant moment before decline set in. The final success of the Selma to Montgomery marches in March 1965 and the passage of the Voting Rights Act of 1965 turned out to be at once the crowning achievement of the nonviolent Civil Rights Movement and its figurative end. Still, Selma would not have been without Bloody Sunday and the violence that came down on participants, three of whom were killed. Then, late the same year, in November 1964 in Waveland, Mississippi, veterans of the Student Nonviolent Coordinating Committee (SNCC) gathered to reflect on the Freedom Summer voter registration project. The meeting turned out to be the beginning of the end for SNCC as a nonviolent organization. The relative failure of the voter drive in Mississippi and growing pressure from young blacks to shift toward more aggressive purposes opened the minds of young men and women, black white, to the growing black power movement. About the same time, the Nation of Islam and Malcolm X came to public attention. His slogan "by any means necessary" was a shock to many liberal whites for whom integration was one thing, violence something entirely other.

Whatever the failures of nonviolence as a method, its successes were more politically muscular than many suppose. Then too, King himself changed with the times. He and other Southern Christian Leadership Committee (SCLC) leaders turned more and more to economic justice issues, which were already a secondary theme of the 1963 March on Washington. In March 1964, King dispelled the popular notion that he and Malcolm X were somehow at unreconcilable odds when they had a warm and very public personal meeting of their ways. In 1965 and 1966, SCLC opened a front in the North with an office in Chicago where they started a war on slums movement with a special focus on open housing. Then, too, Martin and Coretta lived in Chicago for a while in 1966 to dramatize the housing crisis. These were not issues that could attract national media attention, still they told of the story of King's growing focus on the social failure of capitalism's open market ideology.

In his acceptance speech for the Nobel Peace Prize on December 10, 1964, King made economic rights a pillar of justice: "I have the audacity to believe

160   *Postcolonial Theories of Capitalism*

that people everywhere can have three meals a day for their bodies, education and culture for their minds, and dignity, equality, and freedom for their spirits." These three principles were developed in his 1967 book *Where Do We Go From Here?: Chaos or Community?*, where he devoted Chapter 5 to the failure of government and the trade unions to assure access to jobs and economic justice. But the emphasis of the chapter was on "where Negroes can exert substantial influence on the broader economy..." Among them, he said, were: as owners of businesses; as employees and consumers "where their strategic disposition endow them with a certain bargaining strength"; and in the "ranks of organized labor where ... they are found in large numbers as workers ... concentrated in key industries." To be sure, today this would not be viewed as a radical economic program, but then it had a radical effect by calling attention to the economic power of blacks in America.

Martin Luther King, Jr., was not a Marxist to be sure, but neither was he a naive integrationist in his politics or his nascent economic policy. He was murdered on April 4, 1968, while leading local action supporting striking sanitation workers in Memphis. Born into a family of privilege, he died while working for the poor and excluded. His assassination occurred while the Poor People's Campaign he organized was encamped, where five years earlier in Washington, DC, he had delivered his *I Have a Dream* speech. Ralph Abernathy, his coleader in SCLC, continued the Campaign after he was gone.

In the end, it is hard to know how what King learned from Reinhold Niebuhr might have worked in concert with his own convictions of transformative love and nonviolence to shape his political tools; and how, if he had had more time, those tools would have developed into a clear attitude toward capitalism. What is indisputable is that King's deepest instincts were to think first of structural wholes (as did Niebuhr). He was not at all persuaded by liberal social gospel programs of an individual's moral righteousness as the path to social justice. At the least, it can be said that King was a critical thinker in the sense of having a well-formulated idea of outcomes in local actions as means to the end of challenging and altering prevailing oppressive societal arrangements. Plus which, King especially well understood the critical importance of the Negro as a resource for change and as part of his vision for the society itself. Consider the title of *Where Do We Go From Here?: Chaos or Community?* Who is the "we" in the title? And which is the community threatened by chaos? Though King never flinched as to his primary identification as a Black American, he never failed to focus on the structural transformation of the national and global order as necessary to the liberation of Black people the world over. In this, he well understood the double consciousness analysis of W.E.B. DuBois in *Souls of Black Folk*. King's theoretical and political affinities are made perfectly clear in the conclusion to *Where Do We Go From Here?*:

> Among the moral imperatives of our time, we are challenged to work *all over the world* with unshakable determination *to wipe out the last vestiges*

of racism. As early as 1906 [*sic*] W.E.B. Du Bois prophesied that "the problem of the twentieth century will be a problem of the color line."

King, imperfect though he was, still would have rejected the idea that he was the race-man of his time. He was, however, determined to eradicate racism which he viewed as a global problem in his day as it is in ours.

King's global theory of racism was the frame by which he formulated his opposition to the war in Vietnam. On April 4, 1967 (exactly one year to the day before his death), in a speech at Riverside Church in New York City, King began an ever more aggressive attack on the murderous, immoral Vietnam War. In a sermon broadcast on the Canadian Broadcasting Corporation in December 1967, he proclaimed: "I cannot speak about the great themes of violence and nonviolence, of social change and hope, without reflecting on the tremendous violence in Vietnam." King's nonviolent philosophy always was focused on the well-structured violence he sought to tear down.

Ho Chi Minh (1890–1969) was born in 1890 in Hoàng Trù, French Indochina. His father was a scholar, teacher, and imperial magistrate who taught Ho Confucianism, Classical Chinese, and Vietnamese from a young age. While Ho's father refused further promotions, as it meant serving the French colonial state, Ho attended the prestigious Quốc Học—Huế High School for the Gifted—but was expelled in 1908 for his political activism. Ho then decided to travel, finding work on a steam ship which took him to Le Havre, Dunkirk, and Marseille. He then travelled to the United States where, in Harlem, he met Marcus Garvey and began attending meetings of the Universal Negro Improvement Association.

After leaving New York in 1913, Ho spent several years in London working as a pastry chef before moving to Paris in 1919. In Paris, he became involved in the Communist Party. Soon, his articles and speeches came to the attentions of Soviet officials who sponsored his trip to the USSR in 1923. In 1924, Ho moved to Guangzhou, China, where he organized youth education classes and gave lectures on anti-colonial communism. After Chiang Kai-shek's anti-communist coup, Ho returned to Moscow and then to Paris. In 1928, he moved to Thailand, and then India, Shanghai, and Hong Kong where, in 1930, he founded the Communist Party of Vietnam. In 1941, Ho returned to Vietnam to participate in its independence movement. After the August Revolution of 1945, Ho became Premier of the Democratic Republic of Vietnam and issued a proclamation of Independence. By 1954, after Dien Bien Phu, the French conceded defeat, and Vietnam was left divided into the North, a communist state led by Ho, and the South, a dictatorship led by Ngo Dinh Diem.

Still well under the sway of its Cold War ideology, the United States would not accept North Vietnam's sovereignty. By 1965, an increasing number of US troops arrived in South Vietnam. In July 1967, Operation Rolling Thunder began as a sustained Air Force bombardment by US forces against the Democratic Republic of North Vietnam. The CIA estimates that

162   *Postcolonial Theories of Capitalism*

Operation Rolling Thunder caused 52,000 deaths in the North, of which 75% were civilians. In January and February 1968, Ho retaliated by launching the Tet Offensive, which dealt a major blow to the already fading confidence of the US Military and the American public over its War in Vietnam. Though American forces turned back the attack on Hué, Tet marked the beginning of the end of US hegemony in the region. In a still larger sense, Tet was a major victory for anti-colonial movements already well in process of determining the forms their newly independent states would take. But Ho did not live to see the outcome of the Vietnam War. He died of heart failure on September 2, 1969, at the age of 79.

Ho Chi Minh's writings provide a nuanced analysis of anti-imperialism. Unlike Martin Luther King, Jr., who advocated nonviolent resistance, Ho wrote, "colonization is in itself an act of violence of the stronger against the weaker."[2] Because colonization is violence, Ho contended that nonviolent resistance is an insufficient tactic against colonial rule. He wrote:

> The Gandhis and the de Valeras would have long since entered heaven had they been born in one of the French colonies. Surrounded by all the refinements of courts martial and special courts, a native militant cannot educate his oppressed and ignorant brothers without the risk of falling into the clutches of his civilizers.[3]

As Ho elucidates, nonviolent resistance has limited efficacy when colonial agents care little for the sanctity of human life.

Many of Ho's writings draw examples from other decolonizing movements against French imperialism. One recurring example he draws on is of the Tunisian trade union movement, in which Frantz Fanon played an important role. In one essay, Ho recounts the story of a French settler in Tunisia who employed two local men. When the men took a bunch of grapes from the Frenchman's property, he beat them, tied their arms behind their backs, and strung them up by their hands. The men lost consciousness and a neighbor brought them to hospital where each had one hand amputated. In his analysis of this example, Ho writes, "There it is, fra-ter-ni-ty!" and continues[4]:

> In the war to uphold the rule of law, to safeguard justice, civilization, etc., 100,000 Tunisian infantrymen were mobilized, 60 per cent of whom did not come back. At that time Tunisians were covered in flowers and showered with affection. Franco-Tunisian brotherhood was chanted with much love and tenderness, "a brotherhood sealed in blood and glory..." Today, this fraternity has changed its form... it is expressed more eloquently by revolver shots or riding whips... The honourable M. Lucien Saint is too busy expelling communists and journalists to think of the lives of his native proteges.

Later in Ho's life, he was able to avenge the assassinations perpetuated by those he sarcastically referred to in his writings as "the civilizers." The War in Vietnam was one of the iconic examples of US Imperialism and military aggression in the second half of the 20th century. That the Vietnamese Revolution was attacked by American imperialists, fought back, and then won is not just a victory for national liberation movements and the states they created to exert sovereignty, but also, as Göran Therborn puts it, "a frontal attack on capitalism as a system."[6] But to be precise, the Vietnam War was not simply a battle between capitalism and Communism, but instead, a fight for a radical opening within the singular capitalist world-system. "The Vietnamese conflict has detonated the contradictions within US capitalism itself, ... [and] the ideologies of imperialism and racism with which the USA is fighting the war in Vietnam have recoiled on it."[7] Through Ho's strategy, the War in Vietnam exposed many hypocrisies of US hegemony—racism v. universalism, imperialism v. decolonization, military aggression and atrocities v. human rights and sovereignty—and with the Vietnamese victory over the United States, the slow decline of US hegemony was set in motion.

In one of Ho Chi Minh's later essays, he wrote of the importance of elders to the revolutionary cause, stating that "we cannot do heavy work, but leaning on our sticks, we will take the lead to encourage them and impart our experiences to them. We are elders, we must sincerely unite first to set an example to our children."[8] Through example and through conversations with the younger generation, Ho envisioned elders playing an important role in revolutionary politics through their support and education of younger generations. Though he is gone, Ho's writings serve a similar role in imparting his experiences in travelling the world, observing and analyzing the relationship between colonized and colonizer, and in waging Guerrilla warfare against the hegemon of the capitalist world-system; Ho's legacy encourages others to take up revolutionary action and offers solidarity to those experiencing the colonial violence common to the Global South.

It would not be wrong to question this juxtaposition of King, a theorist and practitioner of nonviolence, with Ho, a theorist of legitimate violence against imperialism—neither of whom was particularly focused on capitalism as such. The answer is in the times. Theirs was a time of radical social movements the world over, challenging—and for the most part, changing— global imperialism. That one, King, saw the global issue as racism and the other, Ho, the violence of global colonization does not mean that their

164   *Postcolonial Theories of Capitalism*

purposes were at ultimate odds. King understood the ravages of colonizing forces as Ho did of their complicity in racism. Then, too, both understood violence as endemic to all forms of colonial rule. That King chose a nonviolent politics in pursuit of structural change does not mean that he could not have appreciated Ho's deployment of violent means to the end of liberating his people. That capitalism arose equally from the North Atlantic slave trade triangle in the early 1600s does not mean that American slavery was different in historical circumstance from the suffering of the people of Indochina in the 1800s at a later stage of capitalism's global avarice. Both were victims of the Capitalist World-System that itself began in the earlier voyages of discovery on either side of 1500.

Notes

1 Martin Luther King, Jr., *A Testament of Hope: The Essential Writings and Speeches of Martin Luther King, Jr*, ed. James M. Washington (San Francisco: Harper Collins, 1986).
2 Ho Chi Minh, *Down with Colonialism!* ed. Walden Bello (London: Verso, 2007), 10.
3 *Ibid.*, 9.
4 *Ibid.*, 16–17.
5 *Ibid.*, 14.
6 Göran Therborn, "From Petrograd to Saigon," *New Left Review* 48 (1968): 6.
7 *Ibid.*
8 Ho Chi Minh, "Letter to Old People," in *The Selected Works of Ho Chi Minh* (New York: Prism Key Press, 2011), 89.

20 Capitalism as Seen from Its Peripheries

Dipesh Chakrabarty/Eric Wolf

Dipesh Chakrabarty (1948–) was born in Calcutta, India, in 1948. He attended Presidency College at the University of Calcutta where he completed his undergraduate degree in physics. He received an MBA from the Indian Institute of Management, Calcutta, and then moved to Australia where he earned a PhD in history at the Australian National University. He is a founding member of the Subaltern Studies editorial collective.

In *Provincializing Europe* (2000), Chakrabarty provides an analytical framework useful to researchers doing historical analyses outside Europe. In his endeavor to theorize a way of thinking about history of the "Third World," Chakrabarty posits two distinct logics of history. Following Marx,[1] he begins with distinguishing between capital's "Being" and "Becoming." "Being" for Chakrabarty is the structural logic of capital, a moment in time that describes the state when capital has come into its own, while "Becoming" is the historical process through which capital is realized. Becoming is not simply a calendrical or chronological past, but something that is understood in retrospect.[2] History 1 is a past that is posited by capital itself as a precondition; it is comprised of the things that allow for the reproduction of capitalist relationships. History 2, in contrast, is antecedent to capital, but is not comprised of elements that reproduce the logic of capital. That which comprises History 2 are those elements of society that can exist without giving rise to capital, but it is not a dialectical other of History 1. History 2 is the element of uncertainty in history, a category of social phenomena that interrupts History 1.[3] Chakrabarty believes that in distinguishing between these separate logics of history, he can dispel the notion that history works as a waiting room for capitalism, instead showing that there are limits to the "historical" as separate from theory and structure. The idea that a place is not yet capitalist reproduces the idea of capital and defers to the structural logic of capital. The "Third World" is historically the place to which this "not yet" has been consigned, and therefore, Chakrabarty urges that one must see the history of the Third World through the lens of History 2 as something antecedent to capital, but not comprised of elements that reproduce the logic of capital.[4]

While Eric Wolf similarly wanted to decenter the West from his historical research, he took a markedly different approach from Chakrabarty. Wolf was

DOI: 10.4324/9781003198291-23

166 *Postcolonial Theories of Capitalism*

born in Vienna, Austria, in 1923 to a secular Jewish family. Wolf's father was in business and Wolf's mother, originally from Russia, had a medical degree and was a feminist. In 1933, the Wolf family moved to Czechoslovakia. During World War II, his family fled Nazism, moving to England, where in 1940 he was interned in an alien detention camp near Liverpool. In the detention camp, Wolf met Norbert Elias, who exposed the young Wolf to the social sciences. Later that year, Wolf and his family emigrated to the United States, where he enrolled in Queens College, City University of New York. While he began his undergraduate studies intending to major in biochemistry, he took an anthropology course on a whim and was then hooked to the anthropological approach to understanding human experience. After serving in the US Army during World War II, Wolf completed his undergraduate degree in Anthropology in 1946 and then went to Columbia University on the G.I. Bill, completing his PhD in 1951. He held professorships at University of Illinois, University of Virginia, Yale University, University of Chicago, and University of Michigan, before returning to City University of New York in 1971 as a distinguished professor.

Eric Wolf (1923–1999) was known as a critical and politically engaged scholar, and in 1965 organized one of the first teach-ins in the United States against the War in Vietnam. He was critical of what he called "disciplinary imperialism" within the social sciences that dictates how and what are "more prestigious" objects of study. In his field of cultural anthropology, he was critical of the widely accepted fact that the more prestigious research was that which aided the US military in understanding the myths and values of people in the regions where the United States pursued imperialist and neo-imperialist ends. In his best known book *Europe and the People Without History* (1982), one of his goals was to fight against the disciplinary imperialism of anthropology by focusing on the historical process of European expansion into the "Third World."

The issue at the core of *Europe and the People Without History* (1982) is to challenge the idea that Europeans are the only people who made history. To that end, Wolf goes back in time to the early modern period when European expansion coinciding with the rise of capitalism began. In this centuries-long, globe-spanning analysis, there are two main takeaways. The first concerns Wolf's critique of anthropology that issues of class and political economy need to be brought to the fore of anthropological inquiry in order to decolonize the discipline, and that anthropologists should not concede political economy to sociology, economics, and political science. Human societies and cultures cannot be understood, claims Wolf, in isolation. Instead, anthropologists must place their analysis in the context of a world historical politico-economic system.[5]

But *Europe and the People Without History* (1982) is far more than a methodological intervention for anthropology. The empirical substance of the book, while describing how Europe's encounter with the world shaped both Europe

Capitalism as Seen from Its Peripheries 167

and the rest of the world, centers on the question of "what is capitalism as understood historically and globally." And in the text, there are two competing questions: Is capitalism fundamentally about the endless accumulation of capital? Or, is it fundamentally about the extraction of surplus value from labor? While showing much evidence that might support either hypothesis, Wolf weighs in on the side of extraction of surplus value, claiming that the need for a "disposable mass of labourers from diverse ethnic groups"[6] fuelled capitalist expansion from Europe into the rest of the world. What we think of as a culture associated with certain ethnic groups is simply another means by which to categorize people into different groups within a racial-ethnic hierarchy, and thereby divide the global working class by remunerating ethnic groups differently for the same amount of labor hours worked.

Both Chakrabarty and Wolf build on Marxian concepts of history and capitalism to change the way their discipline does and thinks about historical research. In so doing, they both attempt to recover the history of the Global South and to gain insight into the nature of capitalist expansion in the early modern period. Chakrabarty takes a poststructural approach, emphasizing transition and translation,[7] while Wolf takes a classical Marxist approach, showing how the imperatives of the capitalist mode of production rooted in the extraction of surplus value from labor requires a mass of exploitable labor that can be differentially exploited based on the construct of race-ethnicity.[8]

Both these projects were successful in fundamentally changing how their more ideographic disciplines practiced historical research, and were even more successful in bringing further attention to the immensely important project of recovering the history of the Global South. However, both are ultimately misguided in their attempt to restate a definition of capitalism from the perspective of the Global South.

While innovative in questioning Europe as the historical starting point of capitalism, Chakrabarty's definition of capitalism remains too vague for general use:

> Global capitalism exhibits some common characteristics, even though every instance of capitalist development has a unique history. One can, for one, see these differences among histories as invariably overcome by capital in the long run… one can visualize capital itself as producing and proliferating differences. Historicism is present in all these modes of thought. They all share a tendency to think of capital in the image of a unity that arises in one part of the world at a particular period and then develops globally over historical time, encountering and negotiating historical differences in the process. Or even when 'capital' is ascribed as a 'global,' as distinct from a European, beginning, it is still seen in terms of the Hegelian idea of a totalizing unity— howsoever internally differentiated— that undergoes a process of development in historical time.[9]

168 *Postcolonial Theories of Capitalism*

While innovative in questioning the long-standing line of thinking that capitalism began in Europe and spread outward, his definition simply states that capitalism has some common features across time and space, but takes particular forms in certain places and times. This is certainly true, and this vague definition works for Chakrabarty's end of demonstrating how different ways of thinking about history can elucidate that "no historical form of capital, however global its reach, can ever be a universal"[10]; but beyond that, it is not helpful for determining which social, economic, and political processes are tied to the capitalist mode of production and which are not.

Wolf comes closer in this endeavor, by at first considering both the logic that investments of capital facilitate the accumulation of capital (M-M') and commodity production facilitates the accumulation of capital (M-C-M'); but Wolf is misguided in his endeavor to choose one over the other as the penultimate logic of capitalism. While the extraction of surplus value from labor is a way to securing profit, what Wolf misses is that, in the context of global capitalism, the ultimate goal of any capitalist endeavor is to earn as large a profit as possible, since power, in the context of the capitalist world-system, accrues through the successful pursuit of the endless accumulation of capital. In other words, capital is not the means by which to obtain power, capital is the end goal. As such, both logics (M-M' and M-C-M') can and do coexist as means to capital accumulation.

Notes

1 See Introduction.
2 Dipesh Chakrabarty, *Provincializing Europe* (Princeton: Princeton University Press, 2000 [2008]), 62.
3 *Ibid.*, 63–64.
4 *Ibid.*, 65.
5 Eric R. Wolf, *Europe and the People without History* (Berkeley: University of California Press, 1984 [1997]), 18–19.
6 *Ibid.*, 380.
7 Chakrabarty, *Provincializing Europe*, 71.
8 Wolf, *People without History*, 380.
9 Chakrabarty, *Provincializing Europe*, 47.
10 *Ibid.*, 70.

21 Orientalism, Postmodernity, and the Problem with Capitalist Culture

Edward Said/Fredrick Jameson/Aijaz Ahmad

Edward Said (1935–2003) was born in Jerusalem when Palestine was under British governance. His father was a successful businessman who, in 1947, moved the family to Cairo where he attended Victoria College, an elite British school. He was an excellent student. Just the same, he was expelled for behavior the heads of school found troubling. It was not surprising that the troubling behavior included speaking Arabic. Even though none of the students at Victoria were native English speakers, any student caught speaking another language than English was in trouble. Such was the practice of the colonizers under whom Said was brought up and against whom he would, it seems, devote his later life to exposing and opposing. After Edward's expulsion, the family moved to the United States where his father enjoyed citizenship because of his service with the American Army in World War I. Edward Said then embarked on a brilliant school career—first at Northfield Mount Hermon School, then Princeton University for a BA, and Harvard where he earned his PhD in 1964, the year after he started a teaching career at Columbia University as a Professor of English and Comparative Literature.

Said's educational and academic careers were golden. He could have glided over into the colonizer's world. Instead, he considered himself a refugee when Israel became an independent state. This figure of identification was at least an expression of his sensibility of himself as a child of the Middle East who lived mostly in Cairo with annual family sojourns in Beirut. While his father was Palestinian, his mother was Lebanese, and although he obtained American citizenship, Edward never relinquished his identification with the Palestinians. From 1977 to 1991, at the height of his worldwide scholarly reputation, Said served on the Palestinian National Council and wrote extensively on the Palestinian Crisis, notably in *The Politics of Dispossession: The Struggle for Palestinian Self-Determination* (1994).[1] Whatever some might think of Said's self-identification (as if it were their business), he took his refugee status seriously to the end of his life. On this, he was outspoken in his enthralling end-of-life memoir *Out of Place*, of which he wrote:

> *Out of Place* is a record of an essentially lost or forgotten world. Several years ago I received what seemed to be a fatal medical diagnosis, and it

DOI: 10.4324/9781003198291-24

170　*Postcolonial Theories of Capitalism*

therefore struck me as important to leave behind a subjective account of the life I lived in the Arab world, where I was born and spent my formative years, and in the United States where I went to school, college, and university. Many of the people I recall here no longer exist, though I found myself frequently amazed at how much I carried of them inside me in often minute, even startling concrete detail.[2]

At the very least—and however much readers might suppose that they too remember their lives in detail—Said remembered his life as a self-conscious refugee who became a postcolonial intellectual and activist.

Some of the global left are known to have dismissed writers like Said as mere cultural theorists unable to come to terms with the hard political realities of the postcolonial world. But from the start, in his published 1963 Harvard dissertation, *Joseph Conrad and the Fiction of Autobiography* (1966),[3] Said took up the issue of the white world's bewilderment with the colonial world. Conrad's *Heart of Darkness* tells of Marlow who, in turn, is telling shipmates on the Thames the story of his trip up to Congo where he encounters Kurtz, a deranged white man who considers himself a genius of sorts. The frame of the story is, of course, the colonized natives who are thought to be inept but also subject to Kurtz's maniacal madness. Neither Marlow nor Conrad himself is a star of European respect for the colonized. On the contrary, Conrad's *Heart of Darkness* is a kind of cultural autobiography in which the European heroes are at best confused, at worst evil in their white world attitudes toward the colonized Africans. In an important, much later book *Culture and Imperialism* in 1993, Said says that "*Heart of Darkness* works because its politics and aesthetics are, so to speak, imperialist, which in the closing years of the nineteenth century seemed to be at the same time an aesthetic, politics, and even epistemology inevitable and unavoidable."[4] For more than three decades, *Heart of Darkness* was central to Said's literary imagination. This alone suggests just how essential his own journey from the colonized Near East to the epitome of the white world's culture was critical to his personal and intellectual trajectory. Conrad's book was a signpost along the way to the postcolonial world in which Said lived and wrote. Also in *Culture and Imperialism*, he commented that Conrad wrote:

> ...during a period of Europe's largely uncontested imperialist enthusiasm, contemporary novelists and filmmakers who have learned his ironies so well have done their work *after* decolonization, *after* the massive intellectual, moral, and imaginative overhaul and deconstruction of Western representation of the non-Western world, *after* the work of Frantz Fanon, Amílcar Cabral, C.L.R. James, Walter Rodney, *after* the novels and plays of Chinua Achebe, Ngugi wa Thiongo, Wole Soyinka, Salman Rushdie, Gabriel García Márquez, and many others.[5]

Capitalist Culture 171

Cultural and literary theorist though he was, Said trained his eye on the important, early postcolonial theorist and activists no less than later literary personages writing in and of the postcolonial world—a fact that is evident in his best-known book. *Orientalism* begins with a telling definition of orientalism's political culture[6]:

> Taking the late eighteenth century as a very roughly defined starting point, Orientalism can be discussed and analyzed as the corporate institution for dealing with the Orient—dealing with it by making statements about it, authorizing views of it, describing it, by teaching it, settling it, ruling over it: in short, *Orientalism as a Western style for dominating, restructuring, and having authority over the Orient.*

Orientalism, the book, is a well-documented study of how orientalism—originally an academic subfield among Europeans—first arose in the translation and study of Near Eastern languages and literatures written in Arabic and Sanskrit. Said then describes, with evident personal conviction, the historical context in which orientalism came to be:

> *For my purposes here*, the keynote of the relationship was set for the Near East and Europe by the Napoleonic invasion of Egypt in 1798, an invasion which was in many was the very model of a truly scientific appropriation of one culture by another, apparently stronger one.[7]

For Americans, the Orient referred to the Far East (China and Japan, at first), but for most Europeans it had been the Near Orient just off Europe's shores that was the primary reference.[8]

Orientalism as a whole makes up for its initial impression that Said's magnum opus is overdetermined by the ghosts of his personal past in the Near East. The book is organized with discipline according to three chapters (each with precisely four subsections): (1) "The Scope of Orientalism" is introductory, in the sense of defining his basic idea and setting forth its meaning capsulized the poetic phrase "Orientalizing the Oriental"; (2) "Orientalist Structures and Restructures" is the scholarly heart of the book, wherein Said surveys 19th-century European literatures with respect to Europe's attempts to come to terms with its cultural and political relations to the Near Orient; (3) "Orientalism Now" turns to—in his phrase "Orientalism's Worldliness"—the ways European orientalists came to expand their vision to the Far East, most strikingly after World War II (again for obvious historical reasons): "A wide variety of hybrid representations of the Orient now roam the culture. Japan, Indochina, China, India, Pakistan: their representations have had, and continue to have, wide repercussions, and they have been discussed in many places for obvious reasons."[9] Near Eastern Studies in the US grew upon the prior example of academic orientalism in Europe. And,

172   *Postcolonial Theories of Capitalism*

important to note is his political judgment: "The parallel between European and American imperial designs on the Orient (Near and Far) is obvious."[10]

Orientalism is not casual reading. Yet, anyone who makes the effort cannot fail to be impressed by the way Said creates a new category of cultural and social understanding. Orientalism is a category of understanding that grew out of Europe's experiences in the Near Orient—experiences conceived in such a way that orientalism spread well beyond Europe's regional interest to the world. "Orientalism, as a system of knowledge about the Orient, an accepted grid for filtering through the Orient into Western consciousness, just as that same investment multiplied—indeed, made truly productive—the statements proliferating out from Orientalism into the general culture."[11]

Since Marx, if not Hegel, cultural and social theorists have had to come to terms with earlier classical versions of the vulgar Marxian notion that culture is limited in its power by being an epiphenomenon trapped in the world's superstructure. Whether the word "world" is convenient to Marx's theory of social things is doubtful. But it is no longer irrelevant to a consideration of the material structures under which we live (if ever it was). Those who need, for whatever reasons, to cling to a sharp dichotomy between the ideal and the real—between culture and the political economy—would do well to give up this dichotomous ghost. Global structures are undoubtedly political and economic as well as cultural. It is hard to deny this fact of the world as it is now, that is, if one takes seriously the commodifying effects the culture industry has had on mass culture.[12] Just as much, it may well be time to give up Max Weber's idea late in his short life that social science must be value-neutral. It may well be that Said's personal sense of himself as a refugee intruded on his cultural theories, just, more generally, his cultural disposition obviously stood behind his political life as a Palestinian in exile.

Orientalism, among other of Said's writings, offers a way out of the prison house of our working categories. Orientalism, the phenomenon, whether early in Europe or later in the United States, buttressed not only global imperialisms but also played the key role in global capitalism's domination of the world's political economy, as it has come to be in our time.

Fredric Jameson (1934–) was born in Cleveland, Ohio. His early education was at Moorestown Friends School and Haverford College. After graduating from Haverford College in 1954, Jameson travelled in Europe where he began his lifelong engagement with Continental theoretical culture— especially the German and French traditions, both of which were (still are) at odds with the latent positivism in Anglo-American analytic philosophy. His time in Europe was just when the existentialism associated with Jean Paul Sartre, among others, was still in vogue and structuralism for which by Claude Lévi-Strauss was the major figure, and Roland Barthes's classic *Writing Degree Zero* was fresh from the presses, paving the way for what came to be known as poststructuralism. How much Jameson in his youth took in the nuances of these movements is hard to say.

Capitalist Culture 173

What is not hard to say is that in the year after his European journey, Jameson began doctoral studies at Yale in comparative literature. Already in the late 1950s, Yale was becoming the American center for the study of European theoretical cultures like those Jameson encountered in passing during his year abroad. His advisor at Yale was Erich Auerbach, the author of *Mimesis: The Representation of Reality in Western Literature* (1946), the modern classic of literary theory. It was therefore natural that Jameson's doctoral thesis, published in 1961, would be a reading of Jean Paul Sartre's literary theory—*Sartre: The Origin of Style*. Though Marxism played no important role in this book, it does contain the first, if dim, anticipations of postmodernism in Jameson's conclusion where he favorably quotes Roland Barthes's *Writing Degree Zero* (1954):

> We find in the novel the destructive and at the same time resurrectional apparatus which is peculiar to all modern art. What has to be destroyed is the passage of time, the ineffable continuity of existence: order: whether it be the order of the poetic continuum or that of the novelistic signs, is always an intentional murder. But the passage of time reasserts itself over the writer, for it is impossible to develop a negation in time without elaborating a positive an, a new order which must be in turn destroyed.[13]

The radical cultural theory of Roland Barthes would soon be set alongside Jameson's early study of Marxist theory.

Jameson began his teaching career at Harvard, followed by tenures at Yale, UC San Diego, UC Santa Cruz, before moving to Duke, where today he is the Knut Schmidt-Nielsen Professor of Comparative Literature and Romance Studies and director of Duke's Center for Critical Theory. Over Jameson's six decades of intellectual labor, he has produced some 30 books, each with surplus value born of independent, against-the-grain thinking. Of these, two books in particular take up the question of capitalism's role in between Marxist thinking and polity and postmodern literature and history: *Postmodernism, or, the Cultural Logic of Late Capitalism* (1991) and *The Cultural Turn: Selected Writings on Postmodernism, 1983–1998* (1998). Both are collections of essays written over two decades. The most famous of these is one that appeared in the *New Left Review* in 1984, "Postmodernism, or, the Cultural Logic of Late Capitalism," which serves as the lead chapter of the 1991 book.

"Postmodernism, or, the Cultural Logic of Late Capitalism" was originally a 1984 article in *The New Left Review* and Jameson earlier discussion of sources behind the then flourishing postmodernism debate—from films and fictions to architecture and cities to philosophers and social theorists. But in the article's section title "The Apotheosis of Capitalism," he presents a schematic definition of the postmodern era as such:

> …[T]echnology may well serve as adequate shorthand to designate that enormous properly human and anti-natural power of dead human

174 *Postcolonial Theories of Capitalism*

labour stored up in our machinery, an alienated power, what Sartre calls the counter-finality of the practico-inert, which turns back on and against us in unrecognizable forms and seems to constitute the massive dystopian horizon of our collective as well as our individual praxis.[14]

Jameson relies on Ernest Mandel's 1978 book *Late Capitalism*, to justify his choice of technology as a measure of capitalism's history by reminding that the three conjunctural moments of technological change since the industrial revolution itself were engendered by transformatively new technologies: (1) the steam engine in 1848; (2) electric and combustion engines in the 1890s; and (3) the invention of electronic and nuclear technologies in the 1940s.[15] He then adds that the age in which he was writing—the 1980s and 1990s—was, in effect, a fourth technological moment age in which the machine "turns back on and against us in unrecognizable forms and seems to constitute the massive dystopian horizon," as he said earlier.

Here, then, is where the narrative line turns from Marxism to capitalism's mechanical effects on the collective human community sense of itself—that is, its cultural aesthetic which, in its way, imposes upon the individual's "praxis"; or, better put, its practice not just of a specific art or skill but the practice of ordinary life against the tremendous enveloping mechanical cosmos created by capitalism. Even in this vain attempt to restate his idea in plain language, Jameson's theoretical statement of a new cultural dispensation is convoluted and *convoluting* of practical life on the ground. Yet, any way one puts it, capitalism's intrusion on the cultural sphere confounds. "It seems to be easier for us today to imagine the thoroughgoing deterioration of the earth and of nature than the breakdown of late capitalism; perhaps that is due to some weakness in our imaginations."[16]

Complicated interpretations like these, whether historical or theoretical, inspire understandable skepticism on the part of those concerned with what, to them, are straightforwardly practical sufferings of those in the peripheral regions of the world—sufferings normally thought to be better understood by Marxists than by professional postmodernists. Jameson is well aware that his writing on the postmodern exposes his Marxism, such as it is, to the skepticism of others. He is, without question, a person of the first world in the core of the Capitalist World-System. Yet, he is not ignorant of the problems of the Global South:

> The new multinational stage of capital is then characterized by the sweeping away of such enclaves and their utter assimilation into capitalism itself, with its wage-labour and working conditions: at this point, agriculture–culturally distinctive and identified in the superstructure as the Other of Nature–now becomes an industry like any other, and the peasant simple workers whose labour is classically commodified in terms of value equivalencies. This is not to say that commodification is evenly distributed over the entire globe or that all areas have been

Capitalist Culture 175

equally modernized or post modernized; rather, that the tendency toward global commodification is far more visible and imaginable than it was in the modern period, in which tenacious premodern life realities still existed to impede the process.[17]

Jameson thus uses the language of Marxists to explain a world turned inside-out by capitalism. And this fact, arguable to many, goes directly to the way capitalism has transformed the very idea of the modern:

> The modern henceforth exists in Third World societies... with the qualification that... where only the modern exists, 'modern' must now be rebaptized 'postmodern' (since what we call modern is the consequence of incomplete modernization and must necessarily define itself against a nonmodern residuality that no longer obtains in postmodernity. ...[18]

This statement alone justifies Jameson's inclusion in the company of postcolonial theorists who identify with those subjugate to capitalism's arrogant idea of itself as the engine of modernization.

Aijaz Ahmad (1932–) was born in 1932 in Uttar Pradesh, India, just before its colonial independence from Britain. During partition, he and his family moved to Pakistan. He has held academic positions at York University in Toronto, Jamia Millia University in New Delhi, and Jawaharlal Nehru University in New Delhi. He is currently the Chancellor's Professor of Comparative Literature at the University of California, Irvine.

Ahmad's work can best be described as cultural theory meets Marxist political economy. His early work was a sympathetic critique of postcolonial theory, particularly its more Derridean and deconstructionist iterations. In an interview he gave with Ellen Meiskins Wood for *Monthly Review*, he said that his project was to bridge deconstructionism and political economy, stating that "Sweezy and Magdoff ... should be compulsory reading for Derrideans."[19] In describing his theoretical stance, he added, "People can't quite figure out what kind of a Marxist I am; they seem to have some very fixed categories in their head—Stalinist, Trotskyist, Eurocommunist, Maoist, what have you—and I don't fit any of those categories."[20] Ahmad is certainly a difficult intellectual figure to categorize, in that he straddles two seemingly opposed ways of approaching theory.

While deeply concerned with revolutionary politics in what he calls the "Third World," he finds that much of postcolonial theory misses the mark. "I find it quite reprehensible," he explained:

> ....that American leftists who want to do radical work in areas of culture and ideology, and who constantly make large statements about the politics of the modern world, especially the 'Third World' have been so little engaged with ... revolutionary struggles in imperialized countries—Cuba, Vietnam, Guinea-Bissau, Brazil, Colombia, Chile, China,

176 *Postcolonial Theories of Capitalism*

> Egypt and many others—I am firmly convinced that anyone who had seriously attended to the lessons of that documentation could never so easily downgrade the whole question of revolutionary class struggle in favor of "national allegory," "hybridity," "postcoloniality" or whatever else happens to be the fashion of the day.[21]

For Ahmad, the core of his critique of postcolonial theory is its neglect of structural inequalities derived from capitalism and imperialism. What most postcolonial theorists miss, he argues, is that "postcoloniality is also, like most things, a matter of class."[22]

Global capitalism—or as Ahmad terms it, "imperialist capital"—does two things: "it penetrates all available global spaces" and "leads to the greater proliferation of the nation state form."[23] The effect of global capitalism on culture and ideology is, therefore, contradictory. The result is that cultural theory is caught between two polarities: cultural differentialism and hybridity. At best, the politics of differentialism, posits Ahmad, is pure identity politics, and at worst, when taken to its most extreme conclusions, protofascism. Hybridity, Ahmad warns, in its celebration of contingency, creates a hyper-real globalized present, devoid of any explicit or implicit concept of the *longue durée*, thereby leaving cultural theory with an inability to theorize structural persistence. Homi Bhaba's celebration of hybridity, contends Ahmad, fails to:

> foreground the unequal relations of cultural power *today*; rather, intercultural hybridity is presented as a translation of displaced equals which somehow transcends the profound inequalities engendered by colonialism itself. Into whose culture is one to be hybridised and on whose terms? ... This playful 'hybridity' conceals the fact that commodified cultures are equal only to the extent of their commodification.[24]

Without a theory of global capitalism in the *longue durée*, he adds, cultural theory fails to conceptualize enduring inequalities between the Global North and South, and thereby fails in its aim of a radical politics.

Ahmad's best-known book is *In Theory* (1992), where he expands on the idea that postcolonial theory serves as an erasure of Third World history. Here, Ahmad takes on both Frederick Jameson's and Edward Said's idea that "Third World societies are constituted by the experience of colonialism and imperialism."[25] For Ahmad, if the Third World is defined by its colonial experience, then ostensibly the only logical response able to combat colonial oppression is nationalism. However, if the Third World is solely characterized by colonial domination and nationalism, Ahmad argues, the only response available to cultural theorists like Jameson and Said, then the Third World as such ceases to have any meaningful history, much less material relations of production.[26] In other words, the Third World becomes merely an object of history, devoid of its own history separate from its domination by the West. For if there is only one logical response to colonialism, any history of the Third World becomes merely a product of the history of colonialism is nationalism—a history of the West. In this erasure of Third World history, Ahmad shows that for cultural theory, "Colonialism is now held responsible for its own cruelties, but conveniently enough, for ours too."[27]

Taken to its logical conclusion, Ahmad's critique of postcolonial theory shows that without a theory of capitalism and class struggle in the *longue durée*, cultural theory is unable to take up what, in Ahmad's view, is a worthy goal: to do radical work in the field of culture and ideology, work that serves as a counter-narrative to the erasure of Third World history.

Said, Jameson, and Ahmad provide three distinct paths for reinventing literary theory to better intervene in the debate on culture and capitalism. Said's solution is through the concept of Orientalism as a category of understanding that grew out of Europe's experiences in the Near Orient; experiences conceived in such a way that orientalism spread well beyond Europe's regional interest to the world. The key to Said's *Orientalism* is the way Western literature misperceived "the Orient." In contrast, Jameson's proposed way forward is a postmodernism that is unabashedly Marxist and yet well attuned to issues facing the Global South. Ahmad is critical of Said's anti-imperialism, and goes as far as to question whether Said's approach could be characterized as "leftist" because of its anti-Marxism built on a misguided critique of Marx's newspaper articles about India. Ahmad too is critical of Jameson's postmodernism, particularly the tensions present between Jameson's Marxism and his postmodernism when it comes to analyzing the trajectory of the Global South. However, in introducing these distinct ways of doing cultural theory in the conversation, the three theorists reveal the tensions and possibilities among orientalism, postmodernism, and Marxism as a means to confront capitalism.

Notes

1 Edward Said, *The Politics of Dispossession: The Struggle for Palestinian Self-Determination, 1969–1994* (New York: Random House, 1994).
2 Edward Said, *Out of Place* (New York: Random House, 1999), ix.
3 Edward Said, *Joseph Conrad and the Fiction of Autobiography* (Cambridge: Harvard University Press, 1966).
4 Edward Said, *Culture and Imperialism* (New York: Knopf, 1993), 24.
5 *Ibid.*, xx.
6 Edward Said, *Orientalism* (New York: Random House, 1978), 3; emphasis added.
7 *Ibid.*, 42; emphasis added.
8 *Ibid.*, 1.
9 *Ibid.*, 285.
10 *Ibid.*, 295.
11 *Ibid.*, 6.
12 Max Horkheimer and Theodor Adorno, "The Culture Industry as Deception," in *Dialectic of Enlightenment* (Palo Alto: Stanford University Press, 1944), 120–167.
13 Fredric Jameson, *Sartre: The Origins of a Style* (New Haven: Yale University Press, 1961), 201–202.

178 Postcolonial Theories of Capitalism

14 Fredric Jameson, "Postmodernism, or the Cultural Logic of Late Capitalism," *New Left Review* I, no. 146 (July–August 1984): 77.

15 *Ibid.*, 78.

16 Fredric Jameson, *The Cultural Turn: Selected Writings on Postmodernism, 1983–1998* (London: Verso, 1998), 60.

17 *Ibid.*, 67.

18 *Ibid.*, 60–61.

19 Ellen Meiskins Wood, "Issues of Class and Culture: An Interview with Aijaz Ahmad," *Monthly Review* (October 1996): 12.

20 *Ibid.*, 14.

21 *Ibid.*, 13.

22 Aijaz Ahmad, "The Politics of Literary Postcoloniality," *Race & Class* 36, no. 3 (1995): 16.

23 *Ibid.*, 16.

24 *Ibid.*, 17.

25 Aijaz Ahmad, *In Theory: Nations, Classes, Literatures* (London: Verso, 1992), 171.

26 *Ibid.*, 102.

27 *Ibid.*, 196–197.

Part IV

Theories of Labor and Capitalism

In Part II of this book, we explored macro-historical theories of capitalism that help better describe the unique facets of capitalism, and thereby craft better theories of its systemic origins and long history. In Part III, we took up the postcolonial perspective, interrogating how imperialism fundamentally shapes and structures capitalist political economy. In this section, we look to theories of labor and labor movements in both Global North and South that see capitalism from the perspective of the working classes.

This section examines how the exploitation of labor is foundational to the extraction of surplus value and how workers can push back against the exploitation inherent in the extraction of surplus labor. The way in which labor is exploited, and therefore the way workers movements and trade unions are organized, is dependent upon the racialized and gendered exploitation of labor.

While theorists such as F.W. Taylor, Harry Braverman, E.P. Thompson, and Jacques Rancière examine labor processes in the Global North along with possibilities for labor unrest, Karl Polanyi, Beverly Silver, Joseph Schumpeter, David Harvey, Adam Smith, Folker Froebel, Heinrich Kreye, and Otto Heinrichs open up more global analyses of labor and capitalism. Edna Bonacich, Mikhail Bakunin, Joseph Edwards, Mohammad Ali El Hammi, Paulo Freire, and Rajnarayan Chandavarkar describe racialized labor processes and labor movements in the Global South, while Lucia Sanchez Saornil theorizes gendered labor and its relationship to capitalist exploitation and political economy.

Taylor and Braverman, from opposite polemical positions, theorize how capital dominates labor through a dehumanizing control over the labor process. Bonacich and Saornil show how by dividing the working class through ascriptive qualities such as gender or race, capital exploits racialized and/or female labor more intensively, thereby lowering wages and eroding benefits for all labor. Bakunin and Edwards explore how workers' self-management can benefit workers located in the peripheries of the capitalist world-system. Adam Smith and Froebel, Kreye, and Heinrichs show how globalization can create unprecedented wealth that is unevenly distributed, and argue that instead of resisting globalism, the workers' struggle must instead push back against globalization as a united front. Rancière and El Hammi show that

DOI: 10.4324/9781003198291-25

awareness of the exploitation inherent in the labor process is not enough to provoke the worker to revolt against capitalism, but El Hammi demonstrates that in the encounter with the colonial official, the worker is compelled to radical action through their experience of imperial domination and racism. Through nonlinear theories of capitalist political economy, Silver and Polanyi craft more accurate descriptors of historical capitalism that can aid global labor struggles. E.P. Thompson's substantive and methodological break from previous historiography revolutionized labor history, but Chandavarkar's critique of Thompson opens new ways of labor history of the Global South creating openings to truly reject the European working class as the template to which all other working classes must conform.

By describing and theorizing capitalism from the perspective of the global working classes, we see capitalism as a gendered, racialized hierarchical system, especially for those at the bottom of these many systemically engendered and sustained hierarchies. Through this bottom-up approach, we see how different cleavages are differentially experienced in various nodes of the capitalist economy.

22 The Labor Process and Work under Capitalism

Frederick Winslow Taylor/Harry Braverman

Frederick Winslow Taylor (1856–1915) was born in Philadelphia in 1856. He graduated from Phillips Exeter Academy and was admitted to Harvard. Instead of matriculating, he returned to Philadelphia to apprentice as a machinist. While working at the Midvale Steel Works as a laborer and machinist, Taylor observed that his coworkers were not toiling as hard as they could, and this resulted in higher labor costs for the firm. Once Taylor was promoted to foreman, he began to study and analyze worker productivity on the shop floor. Taylor later became the first management consultant and specialized in the systematic observation of workers in order to uncover strategies to increase efficiency and productivity.

This new approach that Taylor took to management was later termed "scientific management" or "Taylorism." Scientific management employs the assembly line along with machines to pace work and replace craftsmanship. This means that each individual worker is involved in partial production, as no individual worker is solely responsible for an entire finished product. Partial production leads to increased productivity through the innovation of the assembly line. The assembly line assures that production moves at a profitable pace to suit the capitalist. The assembly line dictates the pace of work, for if a worker does not perform their task, the following worker cannot perform theirs. Because workers do not produce a complete product but simply parts of the whole, the manager, in coordinating these parts, gains total control of the labor process. The manager decides how to complete a task and at which pace to do so, hence the worker need not think during the entire course of the day. Workers thereby abandon skill but gain efficiency. Over time, the Taylorist factory leads to skill loss, as within years or perhaps generations, labor loses the knowledge and skill to complete a finished product on their own.

Scientific management or Taylorism marked a significant change in workplace control. Before the end of the 19th century, the most prevalent form of labor control was simple control. Simple control was a repressive system where managers assumed the role of tyrants (benevolent or otherwise). These bosses exercised power personally, intervening in the labor process often to exhort workers, bully and threaten them, reward good performance, fire

DOI: 10.4324/9781003198291-26

182 *Theories of Labor and Capitalism*

(and fire on the spot), and/or favor loyal workers.[1] But with the advent of scientific management, structural control began to predominate. The labor process became more impersonal and control over labor was soon exerted abstractly, through the very structure of work rather than in the form of a tyrannical manager. As a result of Taylor's techniques of scientific management, structural control came to be embedded in the physical and social structure of the labor process.

Harry Braverman (1920–1976) was born in New York City in 1920. He attended Brooklyn College for a year, where he joined the Young People's Socialist League, but left school because he could not afford to continue his studies. Instead, he worked as a metalsmith until World War II when he was drafted by the US Army. After the War, he moved to Youngstown, Ohio, and became a steelworker. There, he joined the Socialist Workers Party but was expelled in 1953. He then began writing and coediting the newspaper *The American Socialist* under the pseudonym Harry Frankel. In 1960, Braverman became an editor for Grove Press where he edited *The Autobiography of Malcolm X*. He went back to school while he was an editor, completing his BA at the New School in 1963. He resigned from Grove in 1967 when the press refused to publish a book by Betrand Russell on American war crimes in Vietnam. He then became the director of Monthly Review Press until his death in 1976.

Braverman's only book *Labor and Monopoly Capital* (1974) sparked a new field within labor studies focused on the labor process and on examining the effects of increased managerial control over the 20th century. Braverman contends that structural control of the labor process is best understood through the rise of Taylorism. While the division of labor has always been present in the capitalist labor process in some form, Taylorism was the first widely successful strategy to use the division of labor to control the labor process in a structural, systematic way. The goal of Taylorism, as Braverman puts it, is to extract "a fair day's work" from labor.[2] A fair day's work from the perspective of capital is the physiological maximum that a worker can work. In order to extract this maximum effort, control of the labor process must rest solely in the hands of capital. Capital resolved to control the labor process by taking decision-making out of the hands of workers and instead entrusting the managerial strata with everyday decision-making pertaining to the labor process.

The three main consequences of Taylorism, as Braverman shows, are: (1) the disassociation of the labor process from the skills of workers, (2) the separation of conception from execution, and (3) capital's monopoly on knowledge of the labor process. All three of these consequences lead to a structural condition in which workers are discouraged from thinking during the workday. Management handles all decisions regarding work, relegating labor to only the physical aspect of work. How work is completed is determined by management or machine, but not by the worker. Labor, in the Taylorist schema, truly becomes just another input. The worker does not

Labor Process and Work under Capitalism   183

invent the process by which the work is completed and has no say over how work is completed or structured. Therefore, the worker is reliant upon managers to understand their place in the work process.

Because Taylorism eliminates the need for workers to think about the labor process, it leads to deskilling over time. For Braverman, this is of profound consequence:

> The novelty of this development during the past century lies not in the separate existence of hand and brain, conception and execution, but the rigour with which they are divided from one another, and then increasingly subdivided, so that conception is concentrated, insofar as possible, in ever more limited groups within management or closely associated with it. Thus in the setting of antagonistic social relations, of alienated labour, hand and brain become not just separated, but divided and hostile, and the human unity of hand and brain turns into something opposite, something less than human.[3]

In so far as Taylorism renders hand and brain as divided and hostile, the worker is not just rendered deskilled, but dehumanized. The division of hand and brain lead to greater structural inequality over time because brainpower becomes concentrated among the managerial classes. For workers, not only are skills lost over time, but as managers increasingly do the thinking for the workers, this deskilling result in fewer promotions of workers into management and the increased degradation of the working classes' ability to engage in critical thinking.

In losing the humanity that comes with critical thinking, the worker becomes more complacent with the capitalist labor process. Initially, labor has a "natural revulsion" to Taylorism and other techniques of scientific management,[4] but with time, capital's structural control over the labor process comes to feel natural. Braverman writes:

> the working class is progressively subjected to the capitalist mode of production, and to the successive forms which it takes, *only as the capitalist mode of production conquers and destroys all other forms of the organization of labor and with them, all alternatives for the working population.*[5]

As new, increasingly alienating ways of structuring the production process begin to feel natural to the working classes, it becomes more difficult to envision alternatives. On a larger scale, this increasing alienation and lack of opportunities to think critically lead to mass alienation. Braverman argues that "The effects of an all-powerful marketplace which, governed by capital and its profitable investment, is both chaotic and profoundly hostile to all feelings of community."[6] One of the many human tragedies of Taylorism is that when the worker needs community most to compensate for the increased alienation and mindlessness of work, the community is similarly eroded.

184 *Theories of Labor and Capitalism*

Braverman wasn't the first to show how capitalism makes hostile, alienating, mindless, and dehumanizing working and social conditions seem natural. This has been a common theme of critics of capitalism since Marx's 1844 Manuscripts.[7] But Braverman updates the 1844 Manuscripts for the late 20th century, showing that over time, workers continually adjust to the ever more exploitative conditions of work in a capitalist world economy, but furthermore these conditions are rendered natural because they are a consequence of structural processes. Individuals might feel alienated and dehumanized, but many lack the critical faculties to connect this feeling of alienation or dehumanization to structures of capitalist political economy. What in Marx's time was a new social phenomenon—the social alienation caused by capitalism—is now obscured by generations having bought into the capitalist labor process. Today, this alienation seems natural and pervades social life well beyond the shop floor. Yet, through acknowledgment and resistance against this dehumanizing labor process, the class struggle is not just a way to better economic conditions for the worker, but a struggle for the reassertion of labor's humanity. Capital seeks to dominate labor through dehumanizing control over the labor process, and labor, somehow, in the face of ever increasing obstacles, manages to retain its humanity.

Notes

1 Richard Edwards, *Contested Terrain: The Transformation of the Workplace in the Twentieth Century* (New York: Basic Books, 1979), 19.
2 Harry Braverman, *Labor and Monopoly Capital* (New York: Monthly Review Press, 1998), 66.
3 *Ibid.*, 87.
4 *Ibid.*, 102.
5 *Ibid.*, 103; emphasis original.
6 *Ibid.*, 195.
7 See Lemert Introduction.

23 A Trade Unionist Theory of Patriarchy

Edna Bonacich/Lucía Sánchez Saornil

Edna Bonacich (1940–) was born in 1940 to a Jewish family in New York City. In 1950, she and her family moved to South Africa, where she witnessed apartheid firsthand. In South Africa, she was recruited to join a Zionist youth movement oriented toward kibbutzim. This group was socialist and based on collectivist, feminist, and anti-racist principles. After finishing high school, Bonacich spent a year in Israel where she began to question Zionism after witnessing the "unjust treatment of the Arab population."[1] In college, she became involved in anti-apartheid efforts, and then returned to the United States for her PhD in sociology. Her graduate work was on how racism divides the working class and "how the working class became complicit in racism, even though it was against its long-term interests."[2] After finishing her PhD at Harvard, she became a faculty member at the University of California, Riverside, where she became involved in the labor movement, both on campus and in greater Los Angeles more broadly. In a 2005 autobiographic essay, she wrote, "In general, I have tried to conduct research that can be of value to the labor movement."[3]

Bonacich is best known for her theory of split labor markets. A split labor market is one in which certain groups of workers gain preferential treatment.[4] In much of Bonacich's work, she focuses on how race-ethnicity has been used to create a multitiered labor market in which job security is provided for one group at the cost of a lack of security and low wages for the other group or groups.[5] Because capital tries to keep wages as low as possible, it utilizes a split labor market in order to pay lower wages to the majority of the workforce.[6] By stoking racial and ethnic tension among groups, capital divides and conquers, causing workers to relish their relatively more secure position and higher wage or to resent the group receiving favorable treatment rather than capital which fuels racial hierarchies for its own gain. By way of example, she looks to the mid-20th-century United States to illustrate how Black workers were paid less for the same jobs compared to whites, used as strike breakers, and excluded from trade unions. White workers were marginally advantaged by this arrangement as their jobs were relatively more secure, and the racial exclusion of nonwhites from trade unions helped white workers to pass pro-union legislation as part of the New Deal. White workers had more access to unions and because of their higher wages

DOI: 10.4324/9781003198291-27

186 *Theories of Labor and Capitalism*

were more likely to engage in costly strikes.[7] Part of what made nonwhite labor cheaper in the mid-20th-century United States was that nonwhites had significant barriers to forming or joining trade unions. Over time, the consequences of the split labor market made nonwhite labor cheaper and therefore more attractive. And as more nonunionized Black workers entered the workforce in the United States, wages declined as did union membership.[8] White workers' response was to legislate against Black strikebreakers and protect the advantages of white labor. While the goal of these types of legislation was never entirely realized, in the long run it prevented workers from uniting against capital, who ultimately benefit from ethnic antagonism in the labor market.

In a passing comment, Bonacich claims that gender hierarchies can similarly produce a split labor market that advantages capital.[9] While Bonacich's work focuses more on racial-ethnic hierarchies in split labor markets, **Lucía Sánchez Saornil (1895–1970)** was primarily concerned with better understanding how women's participation in the labor market and labor movement affected the wage structure. Saronil was born in Madrid, Spain, in 1895 to a working-class family.[10] She attended the Royal Academy of Fine Arts of San Fernando where she studied painting. Talented, she soon began selling her paintings in a Madrid gallery.[11] Saornil also began writing poetry under the male pen name, Luciano San-Saor, when she was in art school. By 1919, she had published poems addressing queer themes in several renowned literary journals. She was influenced by cubist, Dadaist, and futurist poetry, specifically, Guillaume Apollinaire, Hugo Ball, and Filippo Tommaso Marinetti.[12] However, she still kept her day job as a telephone operator. In 1931, her trade union, the *Confederación International de Trabajo* (CNT), led a strike against Saornil's employer Telefónica. Her participation in the strike was a turning point for her, one that brought her in to the anarcho-syndicalist movement. By 1933, she had become the writing secretary for the Madrid chapter of the CNT and was editor of their journal. In 1938, she became general secretary of the *Solidaridad Internacional Antifascista* (SIA). Instead of poetry, she began to write social theory, writing mostly about feminism, gender, and work.[13] But Saornil soon grew disillusioned with the rife sexism and chauvinism in the anarchist left. So she, along with Mercedes Comaposada and Amparo Poch y Gascón, formed *Mujeres Libres* in 1936 in order to put anarcha-feminist theories into praxis, fighting a dual struggle for social revolution and women's liberation.[14]

As a theorist, Saornil rejected anarchist and Marxist narratives, positing that gender equality would follow from a classless society. Saornil alternately contended that the same bourgeois patriarchy that the left critiques is reproduced in leftist circles, and therefore if the left were to be successful in creating a classless society, gender equality would not automatically follow. Saornil argues that women face a unique ontological struggle to retain individual autonomy in a society that socially conditions women to be a mother and nothing else, thereby "annihilating the individual."[15] But actively recruiting women into the anarchist movement is not a sufficient solution, according to Saornil. Instead, she contends, male comrades must be taught that women have their own autonomy outside the household and have an intellectual capacity equal to that of men. Saornil urges anarchist men to understand women not as a mother or sex object, but "Woman as an individual, as a rational, thoughtful, autonomous individual."[16]

Saornil employed her theory of patriarchy within the anarchist left to better understand the intersection of class and gender in the context of the labor movement. She argues that some leftist men lament that women's labor force participation has negatively impacted the "proletarian cause."[17] Because women are paid lower wages than men, they thereby lower the floor on wages, and as a result, reduce wages for men. Saornil accepts this general argument, but places the blame for women's lower wages with the working class and trade union organizations that exclude women. She claims that the male-dominated trade unions and male employers "built an illicit competition between the sexes."[18] In other words, working-class men and male employers collaborated in creating unequal conditions for female workers, to the detriment of both male and female workers. Had trade unions organized against the wage gap when women first entered the workplace, Saornil argues, then perhaps women would not have undermined men's wages and the working class would be stronger, not weaker, for having women join the ranks of labor.

Both Bonacich and Saornil show how by dividing the working class by ascriptive qualities such as gender or race, capital benefits by reducing wages and eroding benefits for all labor. While historically the response among male workers and white workers has been to exclude the marginalized from trade unions, both Saornil and Bonacich show that solidarity among all labor is not just beneficial in the long run or in the global context, but by including all workers in trade unions and in advocating for equal wages and benefits regardless of the race or gender of the worker, white workers and male workers are, in effect, protecting their own wages and benefits as well.

Notes

1 Edna Bonacich, "Working With the Labor Movement: A Personal Journey in Organic Public Sociology," *The American Sociologist* 36 (2005): 106.

2 *Ibid.*, 107.

3 *Ibid.*, 107.

4 Edna Bonacich, "A Theory of Ethnic Antagonism: The Split Labor Market," *American Sociological Review* 37, no. 5 (1972): 547–559.

5 *Ibid.*; Edna Bonacich, "Abolition, the Extension of Slavery, and the Position of free Blacks: A Study of Split Labor Markets in the United States, 1830–1863," *American Journal of Sociology* 81, no. 3 (1975); Edna Bonacich, "Advanced Capitalism and Black White Race Relations in the US: a Split Labor Market Interpretation," *American Sociological Review* 41, no. 1 (1976).

6 Bonacich, "Advanced Capitalism," 36.

7 *Ibid.*, 37.

188 *Theories of Labor and Capitalism*

8 *Ibid.*, 44.

9 Bonacich, "Split Labor Market," 558.

10 Guillaume Goutte, *Lucía Sánchez Saornil: Poetesse, Anarchiste, et Feministe* (Paris: Les Editions du Monde Libertaire, 2011), 3.

11 *Ibid.*, 3–4.

12 *Ibid.*, 4.

13 *Ibid.*, 8.

14 Martha A. Ackelsberg, *Free Women of Spain: Anarchism and the Struggle for the Emancipation of Women* (Bloomington: Indiana University Press, 1991), 176.

15 Lucía Sánchez Saornil, "The Question of Feminism," in *Anarchism: A Documentary History of Libertarian Ideas, Vol. 1: From Anarchy to Anarchism, 300 CE-1939*, ed. Robert Graham (Montreal: Black Rose Books, 1935 [2005]).

16 *Ibid.*

17 *Ibid.*

18 *Ibid.*

24 Worker Self-Management and Black Working Class Consciousness

Mikhail Bakunin/Joseph Edwards

Mikhail Bakunin (1814–1876) was born in 1814 in Pryamukhino, Russia. As a young man, he was an avid reader of French and German philosophy. Once he discovered Hegel, he was "bedazzled,"[1] deciding to become a philosopher in the mold of Hegel. He soon moved to Berlin to pursue a PhD in Hegelian philosophy. Bakunin was the first to translate Hegel into Russian. From Berlin, Bakunin moved to Dresden where he founded *Deutsche Jahrbücher* with Arnold Ruge. And by 1847, at risk of deportation back to Russia, Bakunin moved to Paris, where he met Karl Marx and Pierre-Joseph Proudhon. In his writings, Bakunin claims to have learned much from Marx, who "is incomparably more advanced than I."[2]

Having returned to Germany, Bakunin participated in the revolution of 1848. Soon thereafter, he met up once again with Marx and Engels in Cologne to stage an insurrection in Baden. But having differed with Marx over revolutionary strategy, their friendship soured. They would not meet again until the First International in 1864, where Marx and Bakunin famously divided the left into Marxism and anarchism. Bakunin wanted a more libertarian left, and was particularly disturbed by Marx's "dictatorship of the proletariat," believing that authoritarian rule—even communist rule—could never be anything but a dictatorship *over* the proletariat. Following this line of thinking, Bakunin's followers termed Marx's brand of thinking "authoritarian communism" and Bakunin's "anti-authoritarian communism" or "collectivism."[3]

Bakunin lived in Italy from 1863 until his death in 1876. His goal in settling in Italy was "to unite the Slavs and Italians" for the anarchist cause.[4] In Italy, he penned writings on anarchism and promoted them thereby introducing the concept of anarchism to much of Tuscany and Northern Italy. He also made frequent trips to Barcelona to promote anarchism in Spain, after having met with Spanish exiles in Naples. While Marxism perhaps captivated the majority of the European left, Bakunin established anarchist enclaves in Italy and Spain, and then through migration to the Americas, subsequently introduced anarchism to cities where Spanish and Italian immigrants moved in large numbers such as Buenos Aires and New York City.

Bakunin posited that the most just and efficient way of organizing economic production is through workers' cooperatives. Bakunin claimed that

DOI: 10.4324/9781003198291-28

190 *Theories of Labor and Capitalism*

"cooperative workers associations have demonstrated that the workers themselves, choosing administrators from their own ranks, receiving the same pay, can efficiently control and operate industry."[5] The role of management, Bakunin contends, is not to promote efficiency, but on the contrary, to enhance the power and privilege of the capitalist class. In a letter to a friend, Bakunin wrote, "I want society and collective or social property to be organized from the bottom up by way of free association, and not from the top down by any authority whatsoever. In this sense, I am a collectivist."[6] Bakunin's ideal social organization, both in the workplace and beyond, involved cooperation among individuals toward a common goal instead of top-down institutions. But collectivization was especially important to Bakunin when it came to labor. The worker, Bakunin claimed, should "own the instruments of labor, all the rest is of secondary importance."[7] While wage labor creates private wealth, Bakunin contended that socialized labor could create socialized wealth. Therefore, according to Bakunin, the pathway to socialism is not through workers' control of the state, as Marx contended, but through workers' collective ownership of the means of production and self-management.

Theorist and practitioner of workers' self-management, **Joseph Edwards**, also known as Fundi the "Carribean Situationist," was born George Myers in East Kingston, Jamaica, in 1930. Edwards' father, a part of the Marcus Garvey Movement, was a blacksmith who fitted horseshoes and repaired buggies. As a young man, Edwards gravitated to Rastafari as a reaction against colonialism and white supremacy.[8] In 1954, Edwards, a self-educated refrigeration mechanic, joined the Communist Party of Jamaica and through the Party educated himself in Stalinist theory. As he read more, he became at first a Trotskyite, but then grew critical of Trotsky and of Lenin as well, coming to favor a more anti-authoritarian approach to left politics. Marxism, Edwards initially thought, was compatible with Rastafari, as Soviet communism was on its surface similarly against "Babylon." However, Edwards was critical of the political economy of Rastafari, viewing it as reactionary because instead of fighting for better structural conditions for workers in Jamaica, Rastafari instead calls for repatriation to Africa. But Edwards nonetheless believed that Rastafari's consciousness is radical,[9] in that it seeks spiritual liberation from capitalism and imperialism internalized by the Black self. Edwards therefore appropriates the language of Rastafari in some of his central theoretical concepts.

While involved in left politics for nearly two decades, Edwards did not begin writing theory until the Walter Rodney Riots of 1968. Edwards began writing for the *Abeng* newspaper collective, which after the Walter Rodney Riots, shifted its focus to promoting autonomous struggles influenced by Rastafari and Black Power.[10] Edwards's early writing for *Abeng* critiqued both of Jamaica's political parties from an anarchist perspective and promoted self-management for sugar workers.

While in his 20s, Edwards read and rejected Stalin, Trotsky, and Lenin, and in his 30s, was sympathetic but had critical differences with C.L.R.

Black Working Class Consciousness 191

James, and by the 1970s, Edwards found his radical intellectual community in the Situationist International. Edwards formally affiliated with the Situationist International.[11] By the 1970s, Edwards theorizing began to mature, as he further developed his theory of Black workers control in the context of the Global South.

Some of the key concepts that emerge from Edwards's work are *onemenism*, to explain how certain individuals have a disproportionate amount of power within bureaucratic organizations such as political parties, unions, government, business, and religious organizations. A related theoretical concept developed by Edwards is that of "workers versus *menegement*," which is how Edwards conceptualizes class struggle. *Men* is a Rastifari-derived term meaning degenerate human, while *man* in contrast represents the ideal human. So, *menegement*, for Edwards, is the oppressor class and includes any and all the classes that oppose the interests of the working class, but is also a riff on the workplace-centered class struggle of workers versus management. The other key theoretical concept that emerges from Edwards' writing is that of "Black working-class knowledge," which captures the intersectionality of working-class consciousness, Black consciousness, postcolonial consciousness, and anti-capitalist consciousness.

Much of Edwards's theory centers on the role of trade unions in postcolonial society. As a movement, he contends, the goal of postcolonial trade unions is to strategize for the overthrow of capitalism and to strategically employ its organizational capacity to disrupt American imperialism. The goal of community work, in Edwards' view, is to develop the political consciousness of workers not just where they work, but to consolidate working-class consciousness across workplaces, employment status, and regardless of whether a worker is a wage laborer or does unpaid domestic labor. Edwards's conceptualization of the trade union movement is international in orientation, and divides the global trade union movement into two categories: Black trade unions and European trade unions. While the European working class benefits from higher wages and the welfare state, the postcolonial working class, according to Edwards, is subject to imperialist exploitation. British workers have gained over time, Edwards posits, while Caribbean workers are increasingly exploited over time. Labor internationalism, Edwards claims, has historically been for the unity of white workers and has not been inclusive to workers in the imperialist-exploited countries. Because of the racism of labor internationalists from Europe and North America, and because traditional trade unions in the imperialist-exploited countries work only in the interest of capital, Edwards proposes that independent unions be formed that instead foster daily associations among the working class to educate workers, fight exploitation, and engage in cultural rejuvenation and consciousness building. Edwards contends that spontaneity, typified by wildcat strikes, are the essential weapon of the anti-colonial working class because they reinforce the principle of self-organization, and is therefore the tactic that is most compatible with independent unions.

192   *Theories of Labor and Capitalism*

Independent unions are key, for Edwards, as is workers' self-organization of unions. The two most crucial aspects of an ideal trade union for Edwards is (1) one that organizes small breakout groups in which workers can discuss and educate themselves with the guidance of a trade union organizer (who is *not* an "outside organizer"). These education groups should not only focus on issues in the workplace, but can also work toward combatting internalized imperialism and racism within the postcolonial working class. But the most important characteristic of an independent, self-organized trade union is (2) that it be fully democratic, meaning that the general assembly is responsible for decision-making and not an organizing committee or council that meets separately from the workers to make decisions for the trade union. Without incorporating workers in all decision-making, the organizing committee members, in Edwards' view, are simply worker-bureaucrats engaging in *one-menism*, stifling opportunities for workers' education and hindering participation of all union members.

Edwards' utopian vision is for generalized self-management in society, built on the absolute power of workers, and entailing the abolishment of political parties, universities, prisons, trade unions, armies, police, and state. Edwards's goal in this vision is to develop a society in which workers have more control over their daily lives and in which people work collectively to meet their needs for survival. Self-management, for Edwards, is revolution. Edwards's theory bridges culture and structure in that equal weight is given to political economy and Black working-class postcolonial consciousness; these two concepts have a symbiotic relationship. In this merger of the ontological and the political, Edwards makes a macro-micro link. In its nuanced treatment of the intersectionality of race and class in the context of global capitalism and imperialism in the postcolonial world, his theories offer many useful concepts for contemporary analysis.

In so doing, Edwards's theory of workers movements in the Global South updates Bakunin for the 21st century. Bakunin's theoretical and political goals were to introduce anarchism and unite the working class of the capitalist peripheries of his era (Southern and Eastern Europe), thereby fostering workers self-management in some of the most heavily exploited regions of the capitalist world-system. Edwards furthers and expands on Bakunin's project by updating theory of workers self-management for the postcolonial peripheries of the capitalist world-system.

Notes

1 Guillaume in Mikhail Bakunin, *Bakunin on Anarchism*, edited by Sam Dolgoff (Montreal: Black Rose Books, 2002), 23.
2 *Ibid.*, 25.
3 *Ibid.*, 158.
4 T.R. Ravindranathan, *Bakunin and the Italians* (Montreal: McGill University Press, 1988), 15.
5 Bakunin, *Bakunin on Anarchism*, 424.

6 *Ibid.*, 158.
7 *Ibid.*
8 Quest in Joseph Edwards, *Workers' Self-Management in the Caribbean*, edited by Matthew Quest (Atlanta: On Our Own Authority! Publishers, 2014), 12.
9 *Ibid.*, 21.
10 *Ibid.*, 16.
11 Ibid., 42.

25 Theorizing the Global Division of Labor

Adam Smith/Folker Fröbel, Otto Kreye, and Jürgen Heinrichs

Adam Smith (1723–1790) was born in Kirkaldy, County Fife, Scotland, in 1723. His father, a lawyer and judge, died when Smith was two months old. His mother encouraged him to become a scholar and sent him to the Burgh School of Kirkcaldy, one of the most prestigious secondary schools in Scotland. He matriculated at the University of Glasgow at age 14 and studied Moral Philosophy before going to Balliol College, Oxford, for his graduate studies. Smith then became a faculty member at Glasgow University, teaching courses in logic. Smith was infamously tightlipped about his personal life and personal views on politics, believing that if he were to speak about his ideas, it might detract from his book sales.

Over his lifetime, Smith wrote two books, both of which have continued resonance. His third book was a posthumously published collection of essays based on manuscripts that Smith had attempted to destroy before his death. While his *Theory of Moral Sentiments* (1759) is still read in certain academic circles, Smith's most famous work continues to be *The Wealth of Nations* (1776). It is so iconic in fact that mention of the pin factory as an illustration of the division of labor still elicits knowing groans from any contemporary student of political economy. However, what contemporary interpreters of Smith do not tend to emphasize is that far from being the libertarian he is thought of by some, Smith believed that strong trade unions and high-quality, free, public education were essential in ensuring a minimum quality of life for assembly line workers in the context of a capitalist system.

Adam Smith famously begins *The Wealth of Nations* (1776) with a description of a pin factory, in which output increases as a result of employing different workers to assemble different components of the pin rather than having workers make entire pins from start to finish.[1] Smith shows how there exists not only a division of labor within the manufacturing process, but also a global division of labor, in which individual people and individual countries specialize in certain economic activities, thereby increasing global productivity and output.[2] That a global division of labor arose during the conjuncture of the late 18th century, Smith proposed, is a result of three social processes: (1) improvements in the "dexterity" of labor; (2) time saving as a result of specialization; and (3) machines that facilitate and abridge the amount of labor required by humans.[3] While Smith is optimistic about how

DOI: 10.4324/9781003198291-29

the global division of labor might improve levels of well-being across the developed world, he elaborates certain pitfalls that might prevent the global division of labor from benefitting all members of society equally.

In particular, Smith is concerned about the welfare of labor in the context of 18th-century capitalism. He writes that "The workmen desire to get as much, the masters to give as little as possible. The former are disposed to combine in order to raise, the latter in order to lower the wages of labour."[4] The nature of the manufacturing process, according to Smith, is that labor wants to earn as much as possible while capital wants to pay as little as possible, and therefore, both classes combine in order to pursue their economic interests. Smith writes that it's easier for capital to collude to keep wages low, and therefore, "such combinations" must be "resisted by a contrary defensive combination of the workmen; who sometimes too, without any provocation of this kind, combine of their own accord to raise the price of their labour."[5] For Smith, unions are a naturally occurring phenomena used by the working class as a defense against a united capitalist class, colluding to keep wages low. If labor is unable to collectively bargain for higher wages, Smith concludes, "it would be impossible ... to bring up a family, and the race of such workmen could not last beyond the first generation."[6] The goal of trade unions, in Smith's view, is to keep wages high enough to enjoy a basic standard of living. He writes:

> Thus far at least seems certain, that, in order to bring up a family, the labour of the husband and wife together must, even in the lowest species of common labourer, be able to earn something more than what is precisely necessary for their own maintenance.[7]

Another, pitfall of the division of labor, claims Smith, is how the tedium of mechanized work affects the intellectual life of the worker. One of the three most important roles of sovereign state, according to Smith, is therefore to provide free public education. Education, Smith claims, "may be in the highest degree advantageous to a great society" but is "of such a nature that the profit could never repay the expense to any individual... it therefore cannot be expected that any individual or a small number of individuals should erect and maintain."[8] While Smith believes that education—Physics, Metaphysics, and Ontology—is important for creating an educated class to shape policy and continue the ancient legacy of knowledge production,[9] the most important aspect of public education for the global economy is, according to Smith, a way to prevent alienation and anomie that results from the tedium of work under capitalism.[10] Smith writes that:

> In the progress of the division of labor, the employment of the far greater part of those who live by labour, that is of the great body of the people, comes to be confined to a few very simple operations, frequently to one or two. ... The man whose whole life is spent in performing a few

196 *Theories of Labor and Capitalism*

simple operations, of which the effects are perhaps always the same, or very nearly the same, has no occasion to exert his understanding or to exercise his invention in finding out expedients for removing difficulties which never occur. He naturally loses, therefore, the habit of such exertion, and generally becomes as stupid and ignorant as it is possible for a human creature to become. The torpor of his mind renders him not only incapable of relishing or bearing a part in any rational conversation, but of conceiving any generous, noble, or tender sentiment, and consequently forming any judgement concerning many even of the ordinary duties of private life. ... His dexterity at his own particular trade, seems, in this manner, to be acquired at the expense of his intellectual, social, and martial virtues. But in every improved and civilised society this is the state into which the labouring poor, that is, the great body of the people must necessarily fall unless the government takes some pains to prevent it.[11]

While the division of labor may improve economic output and create unprecedented wealth, it also erodes, in the working classes, one of the most human qualities—the ability to think. Without the ability to think, Smith concludes, one's quality of life suffers. Therefore, he argues, it is essential for the state to provide quality public education in order to prevent the majority of society from succumbing to the divorce between mental and physical labor caused by the division of labor.

Folker Fröbel, (1939–) Otto Kreye, (1936–1999) and **Jürgen Heinrichs** set out to update Adam Smith for the late 20th century, during which time, the division of labor became unprecedentedly global. Fröbel, Kreye, and Heinrichs were colleagues at the Max Plank Institute for the Study of Living Conditions of the Scientific and Technical World in Starnberg, Germany. The Institute, founded in 1970 by Carl Friedrich von Weizsäcker, was known as a hub for left-leaning social science in Germany. Its faculty was strongly influenced by the left student movement.[12] From the beginning of the Institute, Kreye and Heinrichs headed a research group on "the economics of developing countries" and were soon joined by Fröbel. Together, this research team revolutionized the way social scientists thought of the global economy, though today, their legacy is not commensurate with their contributions. This is likely because of the office politics surrounding the demise of the Max Plank Institute for the Study of Living Conditions of the Scientific and Technical World.

When Carl Friedrich von Weizsäcker retired in 1980, Jürgen Habermas was then appointed director. The Institute was closed a year later after Habermas resigned amidst controversy. While Weizsäcker had hoped that Habermas would continue to support the left social critique that resulted from research groups at the Institute, Habermas took the directorship expecting to focus on empirical work divorced from contemporary political debates.[13] Habermas soon tried to dismiss Fröbel, Heinrichs, and Kreye, because, in

Habermas's view, they failed to support his new vision of the Institute and instead, tried to carry on Weizsäcker's legacy. Fröbel, Heinrichs, and Kreye took Habermas to labor court over their dismissal and before the case could come to verdict, Habermas resigned, telling Der Speigel that Fröbel, Heinrichs, and Kreye "represented their interests without consideration of the conditions of the research institute as a whole," and added that anyway, the Institute had a "failed history" and a staff without convincing professional qualifications.[14] While the Institute was known for its research in economic development, philosophy of science, and social policy, its legacy remains tied to Fröbel, Heinrichs, and Kreye's legacy of research on globalization years before globalization as a concept had gained traction in academia.

Before Theodore Levitt coined the term "globalization" in 1983, Fröbel, Heinrichs, and Kreye were investigating "unprecedented world economic and political cooperation."[15] Their thesis on the transformation of the global division of labor revolutionized debates in International Political Economy in the German-speaking academy of the late 1970s, and then, once translated into English, similarly influenced political economy of the English-speaking academy of the early 1980s. They remain best known for their book *Die neue internationale Arbeitsteilung: Strukturelle Arbeitslosigkeit in die Industrielandern und die Industrialisierung der Entwicklungslander* (1977), abridged and translated to English as *The New International Division of Labor* (1980). This work can be characterized as Adam Smith's *The Wealth of Nations*, updated for the 1970s and beyond. The book describes the "fundamental issues" confronting "corporate management in 1977," thereby providing "a blueprint for a new economic era" characterized by the end of the postwar economic order.[16] The changes in the global economy of the 1970s, Fröbel, Heinrichs, and Kreye contend, "could force companies into the most radical and painful reassessments of their plans and strategies in living memory," in an era in which "growth, translated into improved living conditions has become of the basic expectations of all the world's citizens, including the poorest."[17] The expectation of economic growth and linearly increasing standard of living, Fröbel, Heinrichs, and Kreye argue, will have to be rethought as structural changes in the global economy will soon no longer support such expectations.

For Fröbel, Heinrichs, and Kreye:

> the determining force, the prime mover, behind capitalist development is… the valorization and accumulation process of capital, and not, for example, any alleged tendency towards the extension and deepening of the wage labour/capital relation or of the 'unfolding' of productive forces.[18]

In other words, the ultimate goal of capitalism is the accumulation of capital; the exploitation of labor through production is simply one of several

198 *Theories of Labor and Capitalism*

means to this end. The exploitation of labor in the production process is preferable to capital, only if (1) constraints impeding the deepening of wage labor are overcome easily and (2) if greater profits can be made via the production process compared to other avenues of profit such as the financial sector and so on. As such, techniques for increasing the productivity of labor, and thereby the rate of exploitation of labor, is an essential tool for realizing profits in the context of the production process. Fröbel, Heinrichs, and Kreye list several techniques historically employed by capital to increase the rate of exploitation. They include the development of science and technology, improvements in transportation, communication, and management techniques, the production of goods for mass production, the creation of a reserve army of labor thereby devaluing wages, and a monopoly on knowledge of the production process so that "the machine employs the worker, and not the worker the machine."[19]

In the conjuncture of the 1970s, Fröbel, Heinrichs, and Kreye argue, the global economy shifted from one in which the production process is the ideal way to accumulate capital to a global economy in which manufacturing yield little profit margins. Evidence of this shift, they explain, includes the relocation of most manufacturing from core to the periphery, declining investment rates in manufacturing, and rising structural unemployment in manufacturing hubs within the core.[20] This shift has been made possible through three key advancements: (1) the development of a global labor market and a global reserve army of labor; (2) through the development of technology and management techniques that make it possible for unskilled labor to perform complex processes; (3) technologies of transportation that render the site of production and the site of management independent of geography.[21] By creating this international division of labor, capital has managed to stave off a potential crisis of profitability in manufacturing.[22]

However, this relocation of the site of production from the core to the periphery has created economic problems in the core, including rising unemployment and fiscal problems for states, even as it has allowed capital to maintain a certain level of profitability. And the new international division of labor is not likely to spur economic development in the Global South either, but instead, "manifest itself as continued underdevelopment" as the same "dependent and uneven development of plantation agriculture and mining, which as up until now typified the socio-economic development of the underdeveloped countries, is, in addition, being reproduced in the industrial sphere as well."[23] The future of the new international division of labor, Fröbel, Heinrichs, and Kreye contend, will be characterized by structural unemployment in the core and continued underdevelopment in the periphery.[24] Fröbel, Heinrichs, and Kreye caution that "it is of little use to attribute blame to the companies involved" in this global economic shift. "If the consequences of this development are considered unacceptable and if an alternative path of development is thought necessary," they write:

> the first step is to seek to understand the structure and the rationality within which companies can only act as they do. Alternative courses of development are therefore a question of an alternative mode of production or an alternative form of society.[25]

This alternative vision for society, Fröbel, Heinrichs, and Kreye argue, can only be realized if workers in the core discard their self-image as the global labor aristocracy and unite with workers in the periphery to realize their common goals. And furthermore, in creating a global labor market, the new international division of labor contains within it the possibility of a global workers movement. The only hope for a more just global economy, Fröbel, Heinrichs, and Kreye posit, is in a worker-led furthering of globalism.

In both *The Wealth of Nations* (1776) and *The New International Division of Labor* (1980), globalization is seen as an economic and social process that can potentially create unprecedented wealth, however unevenly distributed. But in both books, globalization's negatives are similarly described. The takeaway of these two great works of political economy is not to resist globalism, but instead, to push back against the human consequences of globalization which disproportionately fall on the working classes.

Notes

1 Adam Smith, *The Wealth of Nations* (New York: Alfred A. Knopf, 1776 [1991]), 5.
2 *Ibid.*, 6.
3 *Ibid.*, 7–9.
4 *Ibid.*, 58.
5 *Ibid.*, 59.
6 *Ibid.*, 60.
7 *Ibid.*, 60.
8 Adam Smith, *The Wealth of Nations*, Books IV–V (New York: Penguin, 1776 [1999]), 310.
9 *Ibid.*, 360–368.
10 *Ibid.*, 368–369.
11 *Ibid.*, 368–369.
12 M. Drieschner, "Die Verantwortung der Wissenschaft: Ein Rückblick auf das Max-Plank-Institut zur Erforschung der Lebensbedingungen der wissenschaftlich technischen Welt (1970–1980)," in *Wissenschaft und Öffentlichkeif*, eds. T. Fischer and R. Seising (Frankfurt: M. Lang 1996), 173–198.
13 Der Spiegel "Davor hatte ich Angst: Mit dem Rücktritt des Soziologen Jürgen Habermas als Institutsdirektor ist der Versuch gescheitert, das Starnberger Max-Planck-Institut weiterzuführen," *Der Spiegel* (5 May 1981).
14 *Ibid.*
15 Folker Fröbel, Jürgen Heinrichs, and Otto Kreye, *The New International Division of Labour* (Cambridge: Cambridge University Press, 1980), 1.

200   *Theories of Labor and Capitalism*

16 *Ibid.*, 1.
17 *Ibid.*
18 *Ibid.*, 25.
19 *Ibid.*, 30.
20 *Ibid.*, 33.
21 *Ibid.*, 35–36.
22 *Ibid.*, 45.
23 *Ibid.*, 403.
24 *Ibid.*, 405.
25 *Ibid.*

26 Radicalization through Difference

Jacques Rancière/Mohammed Ali El Hammi

Jacques Rancière (1940–) was born in Algiers in 1940. He did his PhD in philosophy under the guidance of Louis Althusser and was part of the group that put together *Lire le Capital* (1965). But he broke from Althusser because of Althusser's view that the dominated are dominated because they are ignorant of their domination and because of Althusser's loyalty to the *Parti Communiste Français* during May 1968. In 1969, Rancière joined the radical experimental university *Centre Universitaire Expérimental de Vincennes*, which became Paris VIII in 1971. After 1968, Rancière associated with left critics of the *Parti Communiste Français* who were inspired by Maoism and the Chinese Cultural Revolution. He retired from Paris VIII in 2000 and is now a professor emeritus at the European Graduate School in Switzerland.

While Rancière's work encompasses many themes and topics, and he is perhaps best known for his work on aesthetics, his 1981 book *La nuit des prolétaires* (1981) holds great sway among contemporary labor historians in continental Europe. The provocations in the book open up new ways of thinking about working-class formation and problematize many of the accepted ways of thinking about exploitation, vanguardism, and class consciousness. Rancière's narrative calls our attention to the interruptions and suspensions in the everyday life of the worker. When the worker is not at the workplace or asleep, they are temporarily liberated from the labor process. Leisure time is valuable because "for this brief interval the constraint is broken that wedges the labourer between the entrepreneur, master of work, and bourgeois man."[1] These few hours of "what we will" is the only moment of liberty that the worker experiences. But this interruption of the alienated life of the worker is only temporary. "The emancipation of the workers," is, for Rancière:

> an undivided time without off seasons entailing an activity in which service — without servitude— to others is rewarded with the pleasure of being one's own master instead of having to sell oneself. An individual adventure hung in the imagination of this strange collective destiny: a bourgeois civilization without exploiters, a chivalry without lords, a mastery without masters or servants.[2]

DOI: 10.4324/9781003198291-30

202   *Theories of Labor and Capitalism*

This "freedom" Rancière describes is not so much a freedom from work, but a freedom from the perpetual anxiety of having to get and keep a job. Rancière describes the unremitting anxiety associated with either seeking employment or trying to remain employed as "the leprosy of 'how to stay alive'; the erosion of being by nothingness,"[3] "dying, not of hunger, but of moral destitution,"[4] and "the malady is called boredom: the mutual numbness of body and soul."[5] The perpetual anxiety of having to get and keep a job is, in Rancière's view, where the crushing boredom, bodily hardship, and soullessness of work is derived, not from the fact of the exploitation of labor by capital. The alienation of work, claims Rancière, comes not from working conditions, but instead, from the never-ending need to assure reproduction and the exhaustion and anxiety that this never-ending need produces. Rancière writes, "The hazards of selling one's labour power day after day" is "the very source and wellspring of an unremitting anguish associated not with working conditions or pay but with the very necessity of working itself."[6] He elaborates:

> The quality or nature of work is not its crucial feature. The crucial feature is abstraction: that is, the obligation of time spent every day in order to procure the means of subsistence for oneself. ... No one had ever heard it said that the soul could find its full and complete essence in productive work. ... the skilled nature of labour, the enrichment of the task involving the human spirit as well as the body, cannot compensate for the pain of working for a living. Indeed, it intensifies that pain insofar as it means that the time of necessary servitude will eat into the time for possible liberty.[7]

The worker knows that they are exploited by the very act of selling their labor power. However, this awareness of the exploitation inherent in the labor process is not enough to provoke the worker to revolt against capitalism. "It is not awareness of exploitation that will halt the producing machine," writes Rancière, but "a dream of vegetative life that would annihilate sorrow."[8] The imaginary of a different way of living life, in which the worker is free from this anxiety of having to assure reproduction through selling labor power, is instead the seed of radical action.

The awareness of this other way of being comes from the so-called "classless" intellectual. But this is not Lenin's revolutionary vanguard nor Gramsci's organic intellectual. The role of the radical intellectual is reinterpreted by Rancière as a disrupting "other" who can reveal to workers that there is a possibility for something other than a life of exploitation, i.e. a life of freedom. But the radical intellectual cannot control how this intervention will be received by the working classes. For "the worker needs to define the meaning of his own life and struggle."[9] Through the example of the bourgeoisie—both the lazy bourgeoisie who lives a life of leisure, and the bourgeois intellectual who dedicates their lives to science, art, policy, or other related endeavors—the worker gains not scientific or scholarly knowledge of their exploitation, but through this awareness of another way of living, the worker maintains their "passions and desires for another world."[10] Without this imaginary of a life of freedom, the life of the worker is nothing but "survival and subsistence," "work and sleep."[11]

Rancière's provocations have great resonance in the contemporary context. In both academic and popular circles there is an idea that with neoliberal precarity and offshoring anxiety about job retention is a new social phenomenon, particularly for younger workers. However, *La nuit des prolétaires* (1981) shows us that this unrelenting anxiety of having to get and keep a job and the crushing boredom, bodily hardship, and soullessness that accompanies it is and has always been a fact of life under capitalism for those who sell their labor power for wages. And furthermore, his analysis reveals that it is through social inequality that the working classes see that it is possible to live a life without this anxiety and precarity, and thereby create a radical imaginary of a different, freer life, one in which there is more than simply "survival and subsistence," "work and sleep."[12]

Mohammad Ali El Hammi (1890–1928) was born in Hammet-Gabès, Tunisia, around 1890. He moved to Tunis at age eight after his mother died. He was sent to study at *Kuttab Sidi Nasr* by his Aunt and worked as a domestic in the home of the Austrian Consul, where he began to learn German, French, and Italian.[13] Soon, he worked his way to chauffeur and accompanied the Austrian Consul on trips to Europe.[14] In the medina of Tunis, he met Tahar Haddad, who would later be an important interlocutor and comrade in founding the Tunisian trade union movement. El Hammi left Tunisia in 1920 to study political economy at the Humboldt University of Berlin. In Berlin, he first encountered Marxist theory and gravitated to faculty who taught Marxist political economy. His favorite course in university was a course taught by August Muller on workers' cooperatives. Upon his return to Tunis in 1924, he began associating with other nationalists and began work on proposals about how to create a cooperative economy in Tunisia. But in working toward his goal of an economy based on cooperatives, he soon realized that the trade union and workers movement in Tunisia was not yet fully formed. During the 17th August strike, 1924, El Hammi founded Tunisia's first trade union, the *Confédération générale des travailleurs tunisiens*. It was important to El Hammi that this union be independent from the Communist Party, and he said, "mon travail cherche à organiser et défendre les intérêts du prolétariat tunisien exploité par le capitalisme mondial." In February 1925, Hammi was arrested by French colonial officials, convicted of being a threat to internal security for his communist affiliations and sentenced to ten years of banishment from the French Empire. His comrade Tahar Haddad recounts that during three days of intense interrogation by the French, El Hammi deftly laid out his vision for syndicalism in Tunisia.[15] El Hammi was deported from Tunisia to Italy, but was refused entry by Italian officials. El Hammi then went to Turkey, Egypt, and eventually

204　*Theories of Labor and Capitalism*

Saudi Arabia, where in 1928 he died in a suspicious car crash at the age of 37. His remains were repatriated to Tunisia in 1968.

While El Hammi's writings and speeches are believed to be lost to history, some excerpts of his speeches remain available in archives and secondary sources.[16] Most of El Hammi's thought is preserved through an account of his life and work written by his comrade, friend, and fellow trade unionist, Tahar Haddad. In *La naissance du movement syndical tunisien* (1927), Haddad recounts El Hammi's influence on his own prolific writings on class and gender, along with El Hammi's personality, biography, and quotes that reveal El Hammi's views on political economy. However, it is unclear in the text from where these quotes are drawn.

While Haddad is remembered as one of the greatest Tunisian intellectuals of his generation,[17] he credits his contemporary, El Hammi, with teaching him the general principles of political economy and colonialism through the many conversations they had in Tunis following El Hammi's return from Berlin.[18] These exchanges between El Hammi and Haddad led to a new school of radical thought in Tunisia, one that fused a European intellectual tradition with Maghrebi[19] and Ottoman traditions, thereby creating a hybrid Occident/Orient thinking about the political economy of Tunisia.[20]

While El Hammi had a unique vision for a more just Tunisia, Haddad observed, "Mais ses ides au départ étaient trop ambitieuses pour le pays... particulièrement les travailleurs, composante principale de l'enterprise, en ce qu'ils souffrent de la cherté de la vie, tandis que l'agriculture et l'industrie nécessitent de plus grands capitaux."[21] While El Hammi was keen to reorganize the Tunisian economy around worker cooperatives,[22] he soon realized that this was perhaps too ambitious a plan given the level of economic development in Tunisia. So, instead of his initial goal of creating a cooperative economy, El Hammi, with the aid of his comrades, founded the first anti-colonial independent trade union in a French colony.[23] Haddad provides several reasons for why Tunisia was able to foster this kind of innovation. He claims that first, the *kuttab* made education more widely accessible compared to other French colonies, and thereby created an intellectual avant-garde for the burgeoning labor movement. Second, Tunis has been an important trading center both for European countries, such as France and Italy, but also for the Ottoman Empire. The openness and religious and ethnic diversity that comes with being a trading entrepôt, claimed Haddad, fostered "la pénétration rapide des différentes ideologies et methods de lutte ouvrières."[24] And finally, the founding members of the trade union, El Hammi included, were communist, but critical (like Rancière) of the *Parti Communiste Français*.

While this first anti-imperialist trade union organization in the French Empire was only in existence for a few months before its founders were either imprisoned or exiled, El Hammi remained concerned with the question of class struggle and the national independence movement. He was particularly consumed with the question of whether anti-imperialist syndicalist organizations should postpone the class struggle for the goal of national independence and form a broad class coalition, or to fight for both at once and thereby exclude bourgeois sympathizers of the nationalist movement. El Hammi's surviving writings fail to provide an answer for this question, but he thought that French colonialism had transformed the consciousness of the Tunisian working class. In close contact with the French colonial official, he believed, ethnically and religiously diverse Tunisian workers became racialized colonial subjects. This transformation, El Hammi theorized, revealed to the Tunisian worker just how necessary the anti-colonial trade union movement was to bring about meaningful emancipation from colonial rule along with economic justice. But El Hammi was also leery of a return to an imagined social past after independence. Key to bringing about an independent communist Tunisia, he believed, was overcoming certain "traditions" as an obstacle to communism, particularly regressive gender norms, by way of example.

In the early 1920s, creating a labor movement as part of a nationalist movement was a radical idea. It was a step away from the European trade union model that was singularly focused on labor internationalism. And while the trade union organization that El Hammi and his comrades created was short lived, in this move to combine syndicalism with anti-colonial nationalism, El Hammi was a visionary. He thought that the working class in Tunisia was different from the European worker, in that Tunisian workers' sense of exploitation came not from their class position but from their colonial status and experience of racialization. In this case, El Hammi concluded, labor internationalism was not appropriate as not *all* the world's workers faced the triple threat of capitalism, colonialism, and racism.

El Hammi's way of thinking about capitalism, colonialism, race, and class was certainly before its time. And even though his writings may be lost, his legacy lives on. Several scholars credit the influences of El Hammi with shaping Tunisia's vibrant contemporary labor movement and with certain tactical successes of the left during the Tunisian Revolution of 2011 as compared to the Egyptian Revolution.[25]

Both Rancière and El Hammi's theoretical focus is on the ideological foundations of the experiences of labor. Exploitation is a central fact of labor in the capitalist world-economy, but so is the perpetual anxiety of having to get and keep jobs, as is the experience of racism and structural location in the world-system for the Global South worker. But it is through the encounter with the intellectual who has seen the lives of the idle bourgeoisie or with the European colonial official that these differences reveal the possibility of a freer way of existing. Both Rancière and El Hammi show us that the intellectual vanguard needs to be rethought. For Rancière, there is a disrupting "other" who can reveal to workers that there is a possibility for something other than exploitation, but the radical intellectual cannot control how their presence will be received by the working classes. El Hammi is like the worker-intellectual that Rancière depicts, as someone who was a domestic worker from a young age but then went to study in Europe. El Hammi's biography

206 Theories of Labor and Capitalism

upon his return to Tunis is yet another example of the process of translation of ideas from intellectual to worker, showing how revolutionary ideas are transformed through juxtaposition. For El Hammi similarly demonstrates that exploitation becomes articulable through comparison. He theorized that through the experience of colonial oppression, the Tunisian working classes would finally take up action against their exploitation and wage the dual struggle against colonialism and capitalism. For both Rancière and El Hammi, the potential for the kind of radical consciousness that will lead to revolutionary action comes through comparison. For Rancière, it is found by the French workers who compare themselves to the idle capitalist, and for Hammi it is found by the Tunisian workers in comparing themselves to the French colonial official.

Both theorists show that the worker is aware of their exploitation but that this awareness alone is insufficient to compel the worker to take up trade union politics. What added utility we get in contrasting El Hammi's thought with Rancière's is that El Hammi's theory of the Tunisian trade union movement of the 1920s can give us the tools to put Rancière's work in conversation with anti-racist and anti-imperialist scholarship. These theorists similarly show that awareness of the exploitation inherent in the labor process is not enough to provoke the worker to revolt against capitalism. From *La nuit des prolétaires* (1981), we see that workers' unrelenting anxiety of having to get and keep a job contrasted with the bourgeois who doesn't have to worry about securing a livelihood through work is what compels the worker to radical action against capital. El Hammi shows that in the colonial context, exploitation alone is similarly not enough to compel the worker to action, but in the encounter with the colonial official, the worker is compelled to radical action through their experience of imperial domination and racism.

Notes

1 Jacques Rancière, *Proletarian Nights: The Workers' Dream in Nineteenth-Century France* (London: Verso, 1981 [2012]), 79.
2 *Ibid.*, 48.
3 *Ibid.*, 72.
4 *Ibid.*, 75.
5 *Ibid.*, 76–77.
6 *Ibid.*, 54.
7 *Ibid.*, 58.
8 *Ibid.*, 63.
9 *Ibid.*, 20.
10 *Ibid.*
11 *Ibid.*
12 *Ibid.*
13 Eqbal Ahmad and Stuart Scharr, "M'hamed Ali and the Tunisian Labour Movement," *Race & Class* 19, no. 3 (1979): 255; Tahar Haddad, *La naissance du movement syndical tunisien* (Paris: L'Harmattan, 1927 [2013]), 149.

14 Tahar Haddad, *La naissance du movement syndical tunisien* (Paris: L'Harmattan, 1927 [2013]), 149.
15 Tahar Haddad, *La naissance du movement syndical tunisien* (Paris: L'Harmattan, 1927 [2013]), 211.
16 Ahmad and Scharr, "Tunisian Labour Movement," 254.
17 Haddad, *La naissance*, 15.
18 *Ibid.*, 21.
19 Haddad draws extensively from the work of Ibn Khaldun, for example. See Part II, Chapter 9 of this volume for more on Khaldun.
20 *Ibid.*, 23.
21 *Ibid.*, 57.
22 *Ibid.*, 151.
23 *Ibid.*, 66.
24 *Ibid.*, 67.
25 Mohamed-Salah Omri, "No Ordinary Union: UGTT and the Tunisian Path to Revolution and Transition," *Workers of the World* 1, no. 7 (2015): 14–29.

27 Resistance against the Market and Struggles of Newly Emerging Working Classes

Karl Polanyi/Beverly Silver

Karl Polanyi (1886–1964) was born Károly Pál Pollacsek in 1886 to a Jewish family in Vienna, Austria. He attended the University of Budapest where he was involved in left student politics. He then received his J.D. in 1913. After returning to Vienna, Polanyi founded a group of radical Jewish intellectuals who met to discuss and promote a scientific worldview. He also worked as a journalist, taught part time, and conducted private seminars on socialism.

He and his family fled Vienna in 1933 to London, where he became involved with the Christian Left and taught economic history at Oxford and the University of London. In 1940, he was stranded in America as a result of the War, and settled at Bennington College in Vermont, where he obtained a Rockefeller Foundation grant to write *The Great Transformation* (1944).

His immigration to the United States was complicated by his marriage. Though Polanyi was a Fabian Socialist, he married Ilona Duczynska, a revolutionary communist. After World War II, Polanyi was offered a teaching position at Columbia University, but because the couple was unable to obtain a United States visa for Duczynska given her political activity, Polanyi and Duczynska instead immigrated to Canada, living in a Toronto suburb from which he commuted to New York City.

The Great Transformation (1944) continues to be one of the most important works of political economy. Polanyi examines a long sweep of history to trace cycles of the world economy, linking civil society to the expansion and contraction of the world economy. Polanyi claimed that "what appeared primarily as an economic problem was essentially a social one," while the working class is exploited by the very fact of the extraction of surplus value, it may appear that an exploited worker is financially better off having been exploited. But his or her exploitation, while it may or may not be individually beneficial, "was wreaking havoc with his social environment, his neighborhood, his standing in the community, his craft; in a word, with those relationships to nature and man in which his economic existence was formerly embedded."[1] Polanyi viewed the cyclical movement of the capitalist world-economy from the perspective of civil society and likened it to a swinging pendulum that at times pushed toward the "free market," and before realizing the goals of a completely liberalized economy, civil society would push for more protection, swinging the pendulum toward protectionism until capital

DOI: 10.4324/9781003198291-31

again pushed back toward liberalism. For "the self-protection of society," Polanyi claimed, is "incompatible with the functioning of the economic system itself."[2] While *The Great Transformation* (1944) takes a macrostructural approach to describe the long run trajectory of the global economy, it also offers important insights into how these transformations affect labor and labor movements. Showing how, at the heart of the double movement, is a mobilization by labor to regulate and constrain the labor market through protective legislation, trade unions, social insurance, and so on.

Beverly Silver (1957–) grew up in Detroit during a period of working-class struggle. Before leaving Detroit for Barnard where she earned a BA in economics, she was involved in the United Farm Workers Union and solidarity campaigns for Chile. After completing her BA, she received her PhD from SUNY-Binghamton where she was a part of the World Labor Research Group at the Fernand Braudel Center. She is currently a professor of sociology at The Johns Hopkins University and the director of the Arrighi Center for Global Studies. Her work focuses on global labor struggles and the politico-economic structures of global capitalism. In a 2005 interview with *analyse & kritik*, Silver was asked to compare her intellectual standpoint to that of operaismo. She stated:

> But there are several differences between the operaismo as it developed in Italy and the influences that came to me, to this book. In 1971 Arrighi and others formed the Gruppo Gramsci. From the start, in their perspective there was a very strong Third Worldism and global perspective, which was something that was not really there in the early operaismo. A second difference is a much stronger combined theoretical and empirical approach, as opposed to the more philosophical tendencies within much of operaismo. One of the strong emphases in the Gruppo Gramsci was on the actual, concrete study of empirical conditions on the ground as they influenced the nature of workers' bargaining power. In this sense they were closer to Romano Alquati and Sergio Bologna than to Mario Tronti and Toni Negri.[3]

While some have mistaken Silver's work for workerism or autonomist Marxism, in her view, operaismo was Eurocentrist and too philosophical, neglecting workers' actual conditions. She sees her work, in contrast, as an empirically grounded Third Worldism.

In *Forces of Labor* (2003), her best-known book, she argues that where capital goes, labor unrest follows. Writing during a time of crisis for labor movements in North America and Europe, Silver shows that structural transformations in the global economy have shifted most industrial production from the Global North to the Global South, and that while labor struggles might be less visible to those of the Global North, in the places to which capital has relocated labor unrest has proliferated as a direct result.

210 *Theories of Labor and Capitalism*

To further flesh out this process, Silver identifies two types of labor unrest engendered by recent structural transformations of the capitalist world-economy: Marx-type unrest and Polanyi-type unrest.[4] Polanyian unrest, shows Silver, is the backlash against the unmaking of working classes by workers whose long-established social compacts are being unmade by global capital's relocation to the Global South. Marxian unrest in contrast is, according to Silver, the struggles of newly made working classes to establish certain fundamental rights, working conditions, and social protections.

Silver's analysis of working-class movements in the global longue durée points to a fundamental contradiction of global capitalism.[5] The expansion of capital to places where wages are low and working classes weaker tend to, in the long run, strengthen labor by engendering militant working-class movements. The concessions won by those movements make labor more expensive, thereby increasing costs of production and "tend to drive the system toward crises of profitability."[6] States, in Silver's view, tend to make the situation worse by breaking social compacts in order to increase profitability. This type of state intervention, generally referred to as neoliberalism, creates crises of legitimacy for both the state and capital, along with resistance movements.

Through her global and longue durée perspective, Silver is better able to describe the contradictory trajectory of global capitalism than those which focus on one geography and/or a specific period of time. While in the *Great Transformation* Polanyi provides a nonlinear perspective on England's politico-economic development that more accurately described how economic development proceeds in practice, by opening the analysis to a more global and longer historical timeframe, Silver is able to explain seemingly contradictory events in a holistic way, thereby not only providing an even better description of how capitalism functions in the current conjuncture, but in so doing, also aids labor struggles by providing a more empirically sustained description of global labor struggles; a foundation on which one can then create an actionable strategy toward a more just and equal world-economy.

Notes

1 Karl Polanyi, *The Great Transformation* (Boston: Beacon Press, 1944 [2001]), 134–135.
2 *Ibid.*, 135.
3 Beverly Silver, "Wo das Kapital hingeht, geht auch der Konflikt hin." Beverly Silver über Arbeiter Innenmacht, Operaismus und Globalisierung" interview by *analyse & kritik* (19 August 2005): 14.
4 Beverly Silver, *Forces of Labor: Workers' Movements and Globalization since 1870* (Cambridge: Cambridge University Press, 2003), 20.
5 *Ibid.*
6 *Ibid.*

28 Culture, Labor, and the Global South

E.P. Thompson/Rajnarayan Chandavarkar

E.P. Thompson (1924–1993) was born Edward Palmer Thompson in Oxford, England, in 1924. His parents were Methodist missionaries. Thompson left school to fight in World War II and was stationed on the Italian front. His older brother was killed during the War. When Thompson returned to England, he matriculated at Corpus Christi College at the University of Cambridge, where he became involved in the Communist Party of Great Britain. In 1946, Thompson started the Communist Party Historians Group along with Eric Hobsbawm and others. In 1952, Thompson and the Communist Party Historians Group founded the journal *Past and Present*, which remains one of the most reputable history journals. In 1965, Thompson began teaching history at Warwick University.

Thompson was instrumental in creating the New Left and participated in the founding of the *New Left Review*. However, he was soon pushed out of his editorial position by Perry Anderson, Tariq Ali, and other Trotskyists who wanted the journal to strike a very specific line and refrain from direct engagement in leftist politics. Thompson left *New Left Review* and found a greater affinity with the intellectual community of the journal *Socialist Register*. Thompson gravitated in particular to Raymond Williams and Stuart Hall with whom Thompson wrote the *May Day Manifesto* in 1967. By the 1970s, Thompson left his position at Warwick to engage in full-time activism. He was particularly involved in the anti-nuclear cause, and by some accounts, single-handedly responsible for Britain's Peace Movement. However, Thompson's legacy still remains tied to his best-known intellectual contribution: *The Making of the English Working Class* (1963).

E.P. Thompson's *The Making of the English Working Class* (1963) marked a dramatic substantive and methodological break with previous ways of doing historiography. Thompson analyzed working-class formation not as an emanation of social structure but as an active process in which workers exhibit a great deal of agency.[1] He also relaxed the category of "class" so that many diverse forms of social experience and political conflict were brought under the umbrellas of class struggle, class consciousness, and class formation. Thompson's innovative approach had far-reaching influence across the historical social sciences. *Making* (1963) was also a foundational text for the Birmingham School of Cultural Studies, an intellectual movement that,

DOI: 10.4324/9781003198291-32

212   *Theories of Labor and Capitalism*

through its Marxist exploration of the relationship between culture and political economy, contributed to bringing about the cultural turn in social theory that took hold from the late 1970s until the 2000s, and did a particularly good job of theorizing class and class struggle.[2]

But Thompson's work—and Thompson himself—had a very particular reading among Indian historians and historiography, an effect dramatized in the late 1970s when Thompson was elected president of the Indian History Congress and rode into the congress on the back of an elephant, eliciting cheers from the crowd of Indian historians.[3] Subaltern Studies historians, in particular, gravitated to Thompson because, through his study of English working-class formation, voice, experience, and narration of the marginalized came to the fore, but also because in Thompson's history, the past is the beginning of the political situation of the present. The past becomes, for Thompson, a long description of the present, and the only way to know about the past is to know the present. This way of thinking about the past is fitting for Subaltern Studies, given their goal of understanding current political developments in India through analysis of India's independence movement and postcolonial state formation.

While Subaltern Studies historians lauded Thompson, one of Thompson's staunchest critics was a labor historian of India, who innovated a new approach to Indian labor history. **Rajnarayan Chandavarkar (1953–2006)** was born in Mumbai, India, in 1953, and moved to England where he completed his undergraduate studies at Gonville and Caius College, Cambridge. A talented cricketer, he was invited to try out for Middlesex. He completed his PhD in history at Trinity College, Cambridge, under the supervision of Anil Seal. He then became a fellow at Trinity College, Cambridge, from 1979 until his sudden death in 2006. Far from the typical Cambridge lifer, Rajnarayan Chandavarkar was a committed Marxist and is among the greatest Indian labor historians. His undergraduate advisor, Gareth Stedman Jones, who served on the editorial board of the *New Left Review*, was a lasting influence on Chandavarkar's work. Chandavarkar is best known for his 1998 book *Imperial Power and Popular Politics: Class, Resistance and the State in India, c. 1850–1950* (1998), in which he analyzes the critical role that working-class movements played in India's capitalist development.

Imperial Power and Popular Politics (1998), Chandavarkar's major work, is important because it is one of the first Indian labor histories to articulate a world-historical perspective. In so doing, Chandavarkar urges the reader not to view India as a "defective variant of the West,"[4] but instead as a component of the global economy. While it is undeniable that the world-economy has adversely affected the development of the Indian economy, Chandavarkar shows how, as a result of working-class unrest, India has had some agency in how it received the impact of its incorporation into the European world-system[5] (Chandavarkar 1997, 327). In his conceptualization of the global economy, Chandavarkar's influences include Immanuel Wallerstein[6] and Giovanni Arrighi.[7] But Chandavarkar's work is important not only for its contributions toward a global analysis of Indian labor, but also for his fervent critical engagement with Subaltern Studies historian's treatment of labor histories of the Global South.[8]

Chandavarkar argues that problems of working-class unity in India stemmed not from communal issues and an enduring precapitalist culture, as Dipesh Chakrabarty would contend, but, instead, from colonial repression and a historical legacy of uneven development.[9] Chandavarkar was critical of Thompson as appropriated by Subaltern Studies, because, he claims, when Subaltern Studies historians borrowed an emphasis on culture from Thompson:

> "inheritance" turned, in Dipesh Chakrabarty's hands into a static, timeless, indeed Orientalist characterization of a "traditional" Indian, implicitly "Hindu" culture – in Bengal, a predominantly Muslim province. Whereas in India, Chakrabarty argues, "hierarchy and the violence that sustains it remain the dominant organizing principles of everyday life", Britain and the West is, by contrast, characterized by egalitarianism, individualism and democracy.[10]

In Chakrabarty's reliance on Thompson, Chandavarkar contends, Bengali society (which Chakrabarty conflates with *Indian* society) is made into England's proverbial other.

In Chandavarkar's later work, this debate between Chandavarkar and Chakrabarty over Thompson's legacy and relevance for Indian labor history continues. In *Imperial Power and Popular Politics* (1998), Chandavarkar claims that classical Marxist and Modernization theory teleologies do not easily fit outside of the advanced capitalist countries, and therefore Subaltern Studies historians drew on Thompson's concept of culture. "Culture," Chandavarkar writes, "especially 'popular culture' provided an alternative to 'class consciousness' and offered a looser category for the discussion of the ideologies and political actions of workers in the context of economic backwardness."[11] In his attempt to expose the Eurocentricity of Subaltern Studies historiography, which he traces to their particular reading of Thompson, Chandavarkar claims that Subaltern Studies historians have generated a new form of Eurocentrism in which the history of Indian society takes a backseat to the intellectual foundations of colonialism. In their concern with how colonial discourse and its hegemonic classes represented colonial subjects, Subaltern Studies historians "rather like colonial ideologues have increasingly assumed the mantle of representing the native."[12] Furthermore, this focus on colonial discourse makes India and Indian society appear as simply a product of colonization, that is, simply a construct and consequence of the hegemonic colonial discourse. Subaltern Studies scholars, he argues, discard human agency as "another delusion fostered by the enlightenment."[13] Chandavarkar is concerned then by the implications of discarding human agency, since one cannot change the world unless one acknowledges its materiality.

214 Theories of Labor and Capitalism

The consequence of eschewing agency is, according to Chandavarkar, that Subaltern Studies is "deeply conservative" because "If we refuse to acknowledge the materiality of the social world, we could not possibly change it."[14] Instead, historians must "create and enter the space between this level of 'brute reality' and the discourse which is generated by, and relates to it, whether in India or the West."[15]

E.P. Thompson's substantive and methodological break with previous ways of doing historiography revolutionized historiography in and of the Global North. But because of its emphasis on class culture, in its translation to the Global South by Dipesh Chakrabarty, the power of Thompson's method as social critique was lost. Rajnarayan Chandavarkar shows through both his critical essays and in his empirical work that critical labor histories of the Global South can be done, but that labor historians working outside of Europe and North America must borrow from different historiographical traditions that provincialize the European labor movement, and reject the European working class as the template to which all other working classes must conform.

Notes

1 E.P. Thompson, *The Making of the English Working Class* (New York: Vintage, 1963), 9.
2 Stuart Hall, "Cultural Studies: Two Paradigms," *Media, Culture and Society* 2 (1980): 57–72.
3 Rajnarayan Chandavarkar, "The Making of the Indian Working Classes: EP Thompson and Indian History," *History Workshop Journal* 43 (1997): 179.
4 *Ibid.*, 7.
5 Rajnarayan Chandavarkar, *Imperial Power and Popular Politics: Class, Resistance and the State in India, c. 1850–1950* (Cambridge: Cambridge University Press, (1998), 327.
6 See Part II, Chapter 1 of this volume.
7 See Part II, Chapter 6 of this volume.
8 Rajnarayan Chandavarkar, *The Origins of Industrial Capitalism: Business Strategies and the Working Classes in Bombay, 1900–1940* (Cambridge: Cambridge University Press, 1994), 240; Chandavarkar, *Imperial Power and Popular Politics,* 333–335.
9 *Ibid.*
10 Chandavarkar, "Indian Working Classes," 183.
11 Chandavarkar, *Imperial Power and Popular Politics,* 19.
12 *Ibid.*, 21.
13 *Ibid.*, 22.
14 *Ibid.*
15 *Ibid.*

Part V

Capitalism's Uncertain Future

These are uncertain times. From one rather too general point of view, the very nature of capitalism as we know it is to unsettle the worlds it intrudes upon. There is of course a question, for which Andre Gunder Frank is a *provocateur*, whether the modern world is inherently or necessarily capitalist. It is at least plausible to suggest conversely that the modern world, such as it is, is a world created by capitalism. To be modern, thereby, is to be currently or eventually under the sway of capitalism.

But to speak of capitalism's uncertain future is to finesse the generic question of the nature of the modern by taking for granted that capitalism exists to such a degree that what uncertainty it protrudes on the world at hand is sufficiently different to the world it pokes away at that it can be considered a thing in and off itself—that is, a something that can phase in and out of various degrees of uncertainty. Thus, to speak of the uncertainty of these times is, precisely, to stipulate a time at hand that in principle is a time shared by reader and writer. This of course is risky business because some writings endure long enough to address readers already or long since in a world different from the one presumed to be currently uncertain. Yet, once again, we fall back into the question of uncertainty itself as the primal feature of modern cultures (which is why, by the way, the nature of cultures—high and low—have been so preoccupying to modern thinkers after Kant and Hegel and Marx, then too of Matthew Arnold in 1867, Adorno and Horkheimer in 1945, Marcuse in 1964, and so on). One could go so far as to say that whenever a world must invent the idea of its culture as a salient feature of their global reality it is trying to ask a version of Durkheim's question, "Where and what is the moral glue that holds this mess together?"

This wordy introduction to a series of essays on Capitalism's Uncertain Future serves at least to complicate the issue for the casual reader who might suppose that the book itself and this section in particular is less about the empirical realities of our worlds than the ideologies and theories that portend a given state of global affairs. It is all too easy for moderns to neglect the fact that, like their cultures, their ideas (including pretentious theories and preposterous ideologies) have the indexical qualities of numeric and formulaic statements.

DOI: 10.4324/9781003198291-33

216 *Capitalism's Uncertain Future*

This section includes some of the more prominent thinkers who are themselves evidence of the uncertainties of their worlds that have been, for a long time now, worlds that owe their being to the hard hand of capitalism's distorting effects on the already indefinite and vulnerable realities with which we must live. For one rather oblique observation: any section of essays that begins with Michael Foucault and includes Noam Chomsky is necessarily stretching the normal boundaries of reason—unless of course the reason for the section is to represent the true state of the uncertain art of uncertainties. Foucault, oddly, was the author who complicated the prevailing theories of when and how the modern world began by making empirical claims for the notion that the modern arose amid ubiquitous and more or less simultaneous changes—not in the economies but—in a range of disciplines from the birth of the clinic, to surveillance as a method of criminal correction, to the very human sciences themselves, and so on. Whatever one thinks of Foucault's way of dealing with the modern, it turns out to be striking for being based on methods of thinking about the world as opposed to emergent cultures required by a political economy. Chomsky, by contrast, is himself two things at once—at the least, one of the inventor's of structural linguistics, while also being the most widely published radically left critic of the geopolitics of modern capitalism. His method, in both instances, is traditionally modern, linearly rational, and insistently systematic. Yet both Foucault and Chomsky also started the postmodern practice of making language and its practice the central factor in modernity. This is of course just an example of the array of thinkers who ought to be considered in order to present a fair picture of the uncertain world as it is.

Elsewhere in the between of Foucault and Chomsky we offer a cafeteria in which Aimé Césaire is one of the greats among decolonizing writers and Herbert Marcuse is the foremost early critique of modern televisual culture. Both were formed in Europe, yet neither thinks in the manner of anything like your standard European theoretical cultures. Then, too, some might be surprised to see Henry David Thoreau here in the company of critics like Giorgio Agamben and Achille Mbembe. Yet, Thoreau's *Walden Pond* was the first attack on the not yet modern scientific agribusiness, while it was Agamben who challenged the complicity of the modern state in death-dealing and Mbembe who applied Agamben's ideas to Israel's police state in the West Bank. In this, imagine the relation of Gayatri Spivak, the Brahmin Derridean who put the global subalterns on the map, with Zygmunt Bauman, the Polish freedom fighter who was among the first to describe the postmodern wasting of human lives.

And so on. The point is that, appearances aside, the superficial chaos of the topics and authors in this section are meant to represent the deep structural chaos that capitalism imposed on the modern world.

29 The Disciplinary Empire and the Resisting Multitude

Michel Foucault/Michael Hardt and Antonio Negri

Michel Foucault (1926–1984) was born in Poitiers and studied at the *École Normale Supérieure (ÉNS)*, where Louis Althusser was one of his teachers. He completed his state doctorate in 1960. Early in his career, Foucault lived and worked outside France—in Uppsala, Warsaw, and Hamburg—and in his later years, he was a frequent visitor to the United States (particularly Berkeley). From 1964 to 1968, he was head of the Department of Philosophy at the University of Clermont-Ferrand. He was on the faculty at Vincennes in Paris during the events of 1968. Foucault became professor of history and systems of thought at the Collège de France in 1970, and his first writings were on mental illness and madness in Western history. *Madness and Civilization* is the English version of his French work *Folie et deraison* (1961). Other books include *Birth of the Clinic* (1963), *The Order of Things* (1966), *The Archaeology of Knowledge* (1971), *Discipline and Punish* (1975), and the series of historical studies of sexuality begun in 1976 and finished in the last year of his life. His studies of sexuality are considered classical contributions to current social theories of sexuality. Foucault died of AIDS in 1984.

Still, in the decades since, the originality of his thinking is evident in a continuing series of edited books, most based on his lectures at the *Collège de France*, notably *Society Must Be Defended* (2003 [1997]). Had he survived he would have no doubt advanced those ideas even more than his posthumously published lectures allow. He remains a pivotal and still powerful voice altering how social theory must reconsider the modern age and the ubiquity of power/knowledge ever assaulting us and, by definite implication, the role of capitalism as an instrument of biopolitics.

Whenever Foucault was asked if he was a Marxist, he gave roughly the same reply: "It is as much impossible to be a historian without being a Marxist, as it would be to be a physicist without being Newtonian." Such a remark is clever in a Parisian sort of way—an affirmation wrapped in a wry sort of denial. Yet, in the Paris of his day, everyone, with rare exception, was compelled to assume some sort of an attitude toward Marx. The one Foucault took was definite if cryptic. Still it is possible to trace its origins and development by considering Foucault's important concept of the *biopolitical* Carceral Society that grew out of his concept of *power/knowledge*. In general terms, *power/knowledge* serves to suffuse power and knowledge into an

DOI: 10.4324/9781003198291-34

218 *Capitalism's Uncertain Future*

intimate conceptual relation, such that the one cannot be considered apart from the other. Foucault's joined binary concept would seem to remind of Marx's post-Hegelian theory of the cultural superstructure determined by the interests of the material infrastructure. But Foucault's thinking is not so much dialectical as dynamically totalizing. This is clear in *Discourse on Language*, his 1970 inaugural lecture at the *Collège de France*, which is published as an appendix to *The Archaeology of Knowledge* (1971). He begins the lecture with a statement on power's effect on discourse (a generic term for language in action):

> I am supposing that in every society the production of discourse is at once controlled, selected, organized, and redistributed according to a certain number of procedures, whose role is to avert its powers and its dangers to cope with chance events, to evade it ponderous, awesome materiality.[1]

It is clear that Marx is in the background of Foucault's critical assessment of knowledge but, as dire as this portrait is, there is little room for a concept of false consciousness that allows, in principal, for true revolutionary consciousness. The use of *archaeology* is the figure to describe the relation of power to knowledge suggests how *power/knowledge* operates in society, and why Foucault eventually supplanted *power/knowledge* with *biopower* and its political forces. Biopower operates archaeologically through and throughout the multiple layers of social and historical discourse all interpenetrating each other, or to use Gilles Deleuze and Felix Guattari's figure in *A Thousand Plateaux* (1980),[2] it works rhizomatically—every which way at once without a single explanatory tap root.

In a sense, all of Foucault's books deal with what he came to call the *carceral archipelago*, by which expression he put a poetic touch on the harsh states of exception political biopower imposes on those over whom the State exercises dominion. The topics of his historical studies all took as their subtext, biopolitical confinement—*Madness and Civilization: A History of Insanity in the Age of Reason* (1961),[3] *Birth of the Clinic: An Archaeology of Medical Perception* (1963),[4] *The Order of Things: An Archaeology of the Human Sciences* (1965), *Discipline and Punish* (1975), and *The History of Sexuality* (three volumes in his lifetime: 1976, 1984, 1984). Each is about modern institutions thought to be normal if not caring that turn on a principle of the State's right to confine individuals in mental hospitals, clinics, the human sciences with their rigid disciplinary barriers, prisons, and Victorian sexual repressive manners than confine sexual pleasure in a secretive underground where, ironically, it flourishes. In "The Carceral," the concluding chapter of *Discipline and Punish*, he writes:

> The carceral texture of society assures both the real capture of the body and its perpetual observation; it is, by its very nature, the apparatus of punishment that conforms most completely to the new economy of

power and the instrument for the formation of knowledge that this very economy needs. Its panoptic functioning enables it to play this double role. By virtue of its methods of fixing, dividing, recording, it has been one of the simplest, crudest, also most concrete, but perhaps most indispensable conditions for the development of this immense activity of examination that has objectified human behavior.[5]

Discipline and Punish where Foucault identifies Jeremy Bentham's Panopticon is the primary historical instance of surveillance punishment, whereby the incarcerated are subjected to constant observation meant to impose, if not encourage, moral rehabilitation. In fact, panoptical observation planted the terrible seed that grew into penitentiary surveillance by which the prisoner is confined in a rigid punitive institution. Foucault thus poses the rehabilitative prison as the foundational model for the Carceral Society writ large.

Foucault was not by any means a forthright theorist of capitalism, but somehow his comment about not being able to be an historian without being Marxist always lurked behind everything, especially in the totalizing nature of biopower throughout the economy. Then, too, unlike Marx, Foucault has little noteworthy to say about the recovery of freedom from the Carceral Society, except in the posthumously published *Collège de France* lectures *Society Must Be Defended*. The question posed by the title is: Against what must society be defended? The answer is the disciplinary control of a sovereign state that, Foucault observes, has a degree of multiplicity such that power can resist political incarceration:

> [I]t seems to me that the theory of sovereignty assumes from the outset the existence of a multiplicity of powers that are not powers in the political sense of the term; they are capabilities, possibilities, potentials, and it can constitute them as powers in the political sense of the term only if it has in the meantime established a moment of fundamental and foundational unity between possibilities and powers, namely the unity of power.[6]

To be sure, this is far from a definite theory of resistance, but then these were lectures only loosely formulated as lectures usually are (even at the *Collège de France*).

The *Society Must Be Defended* lectures were in 1976, just when Foucault was beginning the *History of Sexuality* series that, it happens, contains the most systematic exposition of biopower in all of its dispensations in its first volume of the series. Even more, and surprisingly, given the subject of the sexuality series, the same book offers the most explicit statement of theme that remains latent through most of the previous works:

> This bio-power was without question an indispensable element in the development of capitalism: the latter would not have been possible

220　*Capitalism's Uncertain Future*

without the controlled insertion of bodies into the machinery of production and the adjustment of the phenomena of population to economic process.[7]

This is not a full-blown theory of capitalism's development, to be sure, but this passage nails the point that Foucault steps well beyond Marx's crypto-Hegelian dialectic. Capitalism lurks always on the edge of the Carceral Society. That it does not—and cannot—come out as such is because biopower is about the disciplinary control of bodies and subjects for which, prior to the 1960s in France, Marx's 1868 *Capital I* was the among the important available serious exposition of early industrial capitalism. Foucault's latent theory of technocratic capitalism's biopower a century later is what, one could suggest, a deep critical and historical theory of capitalism looked like in Foucault's day and ours.

Michael Hardt (1960–) was born in Bethesda, Maryland, a suburb of Washington, DC, the proximity to which suggests that the politics of American global power was in his spiritual blood. At Swarthmore College, he studied engineering, which similarly suggests that by training he was well enough informed about technologies that early in life moved him to political action on climate change and alternative energy sources. At graduate school in comparative literature at the University of Washington, he translated Antonio Negri's book on Spinoza, which led, in time, to their working together on *Empire*.[8] Hardt's 1990 dissertation was on Gilles Deleuze, after which he began teaching at the University of Southern California before taking a position at Duke University as a professor of Italian and Comparative Literature. **Antonio Negri** (1933–) was born in Padua, in the northeast of Italy, to a family familiar with militant communist politics. Though his father died when the boy was but an infant, his father's politics seem to have had a lasting influence on Antonio. When he had but 17 years, Negri became active in political causes sympathetic to communist practices. Ultimately, he joined the Italian Socialist Party. Somehow, amid all this, his scholarly and academic career also flourished well enough for Negri to join the politics faculty of the University of Padua. In time, he also served as a visiting professor at the *École Normale Supérieure* where he became personally and intellectually known to Michel Foucault and Gilles Deleuze, among others of the French left literati who came to his defense when Negri was accused of complicity in the Red Brigade murders and terrorist activities. He spent time in prison after conviction for charges never proven. He was released at one point, whereupon he fled to France. Eventually, however, he returned to Italy to serve out his term. In 2003, he was released definitively, thus ending a 20-year ordeal. Antonio Negri is a personage of firm beliefs and honorable behavior in contrast to those who would ruin him.

Hardt and Negri's *Empire* was published in 2000 to much acclaim and no little disparagement. In one sense, it is confusing to many readers because it is somehow clearly Marxist, but in ways that are not familiar. The very use of "Empire" as the stand alone title conjures the long, mostly ancient tradition of empires like the Roman and the Ottoman. Yet, in truth, they mean to suggest that the world of the 21st century is an Empire of a very different sort. For one, their idea of Empire engulfs and supplants the *imperium* associated with dominant nation-states that continued, in many ways, the methods of the ancient imperia into the modern era—including the British and America global imperia as well as those of the manifestly vicious Nazi and Stalinist regimes. Empire dominates by another means:

> The arsenal of legitimate force for imperial intervention is indeed already vast and should include not only military intervention but also other forms such as moral intervention and juridical intervention. In fact, the Empire's powers of intervention might be best understood as beginning not directly with its weapons of lethal force but rather with its moral instruments.[9]

While the modern imperia, like the British and American ones, were mixed in their uses of violent and juridical or moral means, Empire deploys its powers more directly as moral tactics born of aggressive purposes. Among the primary influences evident in Hardt and Negri's thinking are, not surprisingly, Michel Foucault whose idea of biopower, as we've seen, "refers to a situation in which what is directly at stake in power is the production and reproduction of life itself."[10]

While *Empire* clearly affirms Foucault's idea, they do not consider it sufficiently refined to entertain today's global order as they see it:

> Saying that Empire is good in itself, however, does not mean that it is good for itself. Although Empire may have played a role in putting an end to colonialism and imperialism, it nonetheless constructs its own relationships of power based on exploitation that are in many respects more brutal than those it destroyed. The end of the dialectic of modernity has not resulted in the end of the dialectic of exploitation.[11]

Here is where Hardt and Negri, notwithstanding their relations with Foucault, take an important step beyond his of modern biopower. Notably, *Empire* transcends and leaves in the conceptual dust the modern imperia by fundamentally altering the capitalist mode of production. "Capital seems to be faced with a smooth world—or really, a world defined by new and complex regimes of differentiation and homogenization, deterritorialization and reterritorialization."[12] The notion of a "smooth world" is, one supposes, an instance of the authors reaching for a soft expression for a world order that is every bit as destructive and dangerous as the one it replaces, a literary mistake they quickly correct a few pages on:

> The Empire we are faced with wields enormous powers of oppression and destruction, but that fact should not make us nostalgic in any way for the old forms of domination. The passage to Empire and its processes

222 *Capitalism's Uncertain Future*

of globalization offer new possibilities to the forces of liberation. Globalization, of course, is not one thing, and the multiple processes that we recognize as globalization are not unified or univocal. Our political task ... is not simply to resist these processes but to reorganize them and redirect them toward new ends. The creative forces of the multitude that sustain Empire are also capable of autonomously constructing a counter-Empire, an alternative political organization of global flows and exchanges.[13]

This is a remarkably challenging proposition that not only goes beyond Foucault's biopower, but points to a way around Marx's rather clumsy thinking on class difference defined by a purportedly general, if not universal, capitalism.

Empire allows for the possibility of resistance to domination and exploitation made possible by an inherently countervailing feature of Empire, or, put crudely, by Empire's capacity to do good by resisting its own evil ways. At first one assumes that Hardt and Negri are headed toward using the other major influence on their thinking—Deleuze and Guattari, who do in fact advance Foucault's notion of biopower by introducing a positive theory of material economic forces and the social production of life as well as capital value. But, alas, even Deleuze and Guattari don't dig deep enough. Deleuze and Guattari, Hardt and Negri say, "discover the productivity of social reproduction (creative production, production of values, social relations, affects, becomings), but manage to articulate it only superficially and ephemerally, as a chaotic, indeterminate horizon marked by the ungraspable event."[14] Hardt and Negri aim to do what, in their opinion, Deleuze and Guattari failed to do—to provide the descriptive nuances of this strange global Empire. As a general rule, they succeed in describing to the nation-states the inability of the modern order to regulate, much less control, the shifts and movements of the global economy. "The primary factors of production and exchange— money, technology, people, and goods—move with increasing speed across national boundaries."[15] They put this forward as the main reason why the old imperial order has been superseded; in effect, killed.

They describe Empire as an order in which all of a society's spheres (as Max Weber called them) are comingled (as Weber believed they were not). "The political, the social, the economic, and the vital here all dwell together. They are entirely interrelated and completely interchangeable."[16] The key word that ties Hardt and Negri back to Foucault by way of Deleuze and Guattari is "vital," which is to say that here, life itself is released from the strict disciplining of biopower to join an almost happy family of commingled spheres moving in every which direction toward and away, up and down, in and out in respect to each other. Again, here, near the end of the book, the discussion circles back to where it began: "Biopower thus refers to a situation in which what is directly at stake in power is the production and reproduction of life itself."[17] This, of course, points simultaneously to the production of life pure-and-simple *and* to capitalism's mode of production which, it ought to be noted, is a notion that goes back to Marx's 1844 manuscript on the power of capitalism to alienate the worker from her product, thus from the value she produces, then from her fundamental human nature, and ultimately from herself.

But the problem Hardt and Negri solve less readily, if at all, is at play interior to the dynamic movements in Empire—that between its destructive force opposed to its democratic aspects propose an interior revolutionary force for constructive good. One element in this interplay between, if I may, evil and good is rather interestingly presented, if not fully developed. From one angle, the relation between the two is suggested with plausible if general evidence: "Moral intervention often serves as the first act that prepares the stage for military intervention. In such cases, military deployment is presented as an internationally sanctioned police action."[18] Here, for a change, Hardt and Negri are somewhat specific in illustrating what they mean. They point to nongovernmental organizations like Oxfam and the Red Cross, the media, international charitable organizations, and even the UN that are often on the ground in areas where the civil order is unstable because of large numbers of refugees, opposing tribes and parties on the verge of open hostilities, or authoritarian regimes in decline attacking their own citizens. In effect, Hardt and Negri seem to be arguing (all too abstractly) that the morally good (so to speak) agencies calm social misery and political tensions paving the way for national or international police or military interventions. Then, too, this merely accounts for the way violence of various kinds (such as civil strife that creates refugees, authoritarian threats that turn, in one notable case, to the bombing or poisoning of the weak) depend on moral agencies to organize, confine, and quiet the injured and provoked.

But from another angle, Hardt and Negri's two-way street between the evil and good sides of Empire is somewhat less clearly defined and described. Here, they revert to the working concept of the *multitude* (their own version of Deleuze and Guattari's multiplicities). Empire, as they conceive it, is open, loose, and dynamic ways thus consistent with their inclination to invent and deploy concepts that support their disposition to Empire as a welter of multiplicities:

> The ontological fabric of Empire is constructed by the activity beyond measure of the multitude and its virtual powers. These virtual, constituent powers conflict endlessly with the constituted power of Empire. They are completely positive since their "being against" is a "being-for," in other words, a resistance that becomes love and community. We are situated precisely at that hinge of infinite finitude that links together the virtual and the possible, engaged in the passage from desire to a coming future.[19]

224 *Capitalism's Uncertain Future*

And here one comes upon the most frustrating aspect of *Empire*—the book. Its claims and propositions are intriguingly suitable to the world one sees when looking honestly beyond local, regional, and national interests. Even when what one sees is a plague of antidemocratic authoritarian regimes that not only preoccupy those who worry about political process but have a most decisive and fluid effect on global markets—from stock markets to grocery shelves, from interest rates to the cost of housing, and more—then add in a global pandemic and the refusal of some to do anything about protecting those at risk and the uncertainties are all the more acute. And capitalism, writ large, is clearly at the epicenter of the flux and flow of it all:

> Production becomes indistinguishable from reproduction; productive forces merge with relations of production; constant capital tends to be constituted and represented within variable capital, in the brains, bodies, and cooperation of productive subjects. Social subjects are at the same time producers and products of this unitary machine. In this new historical formation, it is thus no longer possible to identify a sign, a subject, a value, or a practice that is "outside."[20]

Empire is a world order in which everyone and everything are on the inside—dangling, pushed and shoved, resisting the dominating forces. "The multitude is not formed simply by throwing together and mixing nations and peoples indifferently; it is the singular power of a new city."[21] One pauses—a new city? Is this a figurative move of some kind? City? Empire? Cities? Singular? Plural? What gives? Again, Hardt and Negri return to their key concept—multitudes:

> A new geography is established by the multitude as the productive flows of bodies define new rivers and ports. The cities of the earth will become at once great deposits of cooperating humanity and locomotives for circulation, temporary residents and networks of the mass distribution of living humanity.[22]

The reader is at times, as here, treated to an inspiring homily when she may prefer a down-to-earth explanation.

Yet, there is much here that invites serious reflection, of which the most striking is the long section in the concluding section of *Empire*, mysteriously titled *Endless Paths (The Right to Global Citizenship)*. *Empire* is a strange, if enticing, book about a world order viewed as a new city of endless paths that allow for the right of global citizenship. Abstract, yes. But still, there is genius here. Democratic citizenship is redefined in global terms where the push and pulls of the social, the economic, the political, and of life itself remain vital spheres that threaten human beings even as they promise new global cities.

Notes

1 *The Discourse on Language* in Michel Foucault, *Archeology of Knowledge* (Routledge, 2002 [1969]), 216.
2 Gilles Deleuze and Félix Guattari, *A Thousand Plateaus: Capitalism and Schizophrenia* (University of Minnesota Press, 1987).
3 Michel Foucault, *Madness and Civilization: A History of Insanity in the Age of Reason* (Routledge, 2006).
4 Michel Foucault, *Birth of the Clinic: An Archaeology of Medical Perceptions* (Tavistock, 1973 [1963]).
5 Michel Foucault, "The Carceral" in *Disciple and Punish: The Birth of the Prison* (Vintage: 1995 [1975]), 293–309.
6 Michel Foucault, *Society Must Be Defended* (Picador: 2003 [1997]), 43–44.
7 Michel Foucault, *History of Sexuality: An Introduction, Volume I* (Random House: 1978 [1976]), 140–141.
8 Michael Hardt and Antonio Negri, *Empire* (Harvard University Press, 2000).
9 *Ibid.*, 35.
10 *Ibid.*, 23.
11 *Ibid.*, 44.
12 *Ibid.*, xiii.
13 *Ibid.*, xv.
14 *Ibid.*, 28.
15 *Ibid.*, 11.
16 *Ibid.*, 406.
17 *Ibid.*, 24.
18 *Ibid.*, 37.
19 *Ibid.*, 361.
20 *Ibid.*, 385.
21 *Ibid.*, 395.
22 *Ibid.*, 397.

30 Mass Media and Cultural Violence

C.L.R. James/Herbert Marcuse

C.L.R. James (1901–1989), as we have seen, was born Cyril Lionel Richard James in Tunapuna, Trinidad, where he went to local schools, then to Queen's Royal College (QRC) in Port of Spain. There he flourished equally as a student and an athlete. James's youthful commitment to being a club cricketer was in many ways the beginning of his place in and attention to the role of media in public life. He was superior enough as a scholar to be invited upon graduation from QRC to teach English and History when he was but 18. These experiences of his youth were so intermingled that they would remain prominent throughout his life, especially in his famous book on cricket. *Beyond A Boundary* was simultaneously, yet not purely, a memoir of his days in the sport and a gentle social analysis of the class basis of the sport—thus, by inference, of life in a British colony. In 1932, when James moved to England, he quickly became a public intellectual with a book soon to be published and as the author of a regular column on cricket for the *Manchester Guardian.* Again, mass media were part of his emergence as a public figure in the United Kingdom.

In England, James began a prolific writing career spanning history, the arts, theater, and social criticism. His 1934 play on Tousssaint L'Ouverture and the slave revolt in Haiti opened in a London theater, starring Paul Robeson. Later, he wrote a social history of the Haitian revolution *The Black Jacobins* (1963), which became one of his best-known books among the 36 he wrote. Other of his best-known books are *The Case for West-Indian Independence* (1934); *World Revolution, 1917–1936: The Rise and Fall of the Communist International* (1937); *State Capitalism and World Revolution* (1950); *Beyond A Boundary* (1993 [1983]); *Nkrumah and the Ghana Revolution* (1977); *American Civilization* (1992 [1950]); and *Beyond A Boundary* (1993 [1983]). A quick look on this short list suggests the degree to which he remained a public literary figure, an unrelenting and discriminating theorist of Marxism, a theorist of revolutions, a student of sport and other topics in his countless essays and lectures.

Interestingly, even his more political writings anticipated later theories of the relation between Capitalism and media technology. For example, consider his 1950 book (a pamphlet really) *State Capitalism and World Revolution,*

DOI: 10.4324/9781003198291-35

Mass Media and Cultural Violence   227

a history of theories of State Capitalism from Stalin to Lenin. Trotsky statements like the following are typical:

> For the Stalinist bureaucracy, state-property converts labor "from the drab burden it was under capitalism into a matter of honor and glory, a matter of prowess and heroism." The intelligentsia tells the workers: You work. The workers, on the other hand, continue to resist speed up and the discipline of accumulated capital, stratified or otherwise. This is called by the Stalinists "the old outlook on labor," a "capitalist survival in the popular consciousness." This is no longer a question of Soviet youth and textbooks in political economy. It is now the workers counterposing to the bureaucracy another "ideology" which the Stalinists admit "may spread to alarming dimensions."[1]

James is able to examine the several sides of a theoretical practice in order to expose the differences among structural sectors in Stalin's State Capitalism—bureaucrats, workers, and public intelligentsia.

James's criticism of the Stalinist model is clear from the first: "State-capitalism is in itself *the* total contradiction, absolute antagonism. In it are concentrated all the contradictions of revolution and counter-revolution." But then he adds what was, in 1950, quite an astute anticipation of what Alvin Gouldner, in *The Dialectic of Ideology and Technology* (1978), called the role of a New Class of technological intellectuals. James: "The crisis of production today is the crisis of the antagonism between manual and intellectual labor." There could hardly have been in the day a more dramatic visual conflict that of the changing fate of labor after it turned more and more to the intellectual work a new class of technically sophisticated actors.

Important to add is the fact that James never repeats vacuous assumptions made out of ideological dogma. In "The Hegelian Logic: The Doctrine of Being" in *Notes on Dialectics, II* (1948), the subject sounds monotonously familiar, but James begins with a philosophically original line of thought based on an observation that grows into his own philosophical axiom while also calling appropriate attention to the fact that those who work are drawn from the larger mass population:

> Now we have men who work. That is the quality which distinguishes them. When something "becomes" out of the mass it has a "quality." The quality we take is work. But as you pile up the men who work, you catalogue them, work is not enough. Some are tailors, some shoemakers, some cowboys, some engineers. The list is endless. Some work well, some badly. Some work well but stay at home every morning. We soon find ourselves concerned with more than quality. We find that we must look not at quality but at *quantity* of work. Preoccupation with quality has led us to *quantity*. But quantity too is limited. The more you

228 *Capitalism's Uncertain Future*

contemplate it, deal with it, you find that it is impossible to keep tab of the quantity of work of tailors, cooks, deep-sea divers by measuring work in the abstract. You have to get some common *measure*. The three divisions of the Doctrine of Being are Quality, Quantity, and Measure.

If only the young Marx of 1844 had lowered the voltage in his own most philosophical manuscripts, he might have gotten over Hegel's methods and meanings. James set down his observation on workers and their products as the groundwork for his own dialectic of Being itself:

> Something immediately involves something else. Continue with something like quality, and its other, quantity, will take form. A completely abstract something is the same as nothing, that is its other. Something "Becomes" out of nothing. It always has its limit, its barrier. And this limit, barrier, is burst through, at a certain stage, to establish the other, its other. All this takes place in the sphere of determinate being, simple quality.

James's ventured into extremely difficult subjects with a clear eye, an independent mind, and graceful prose.

Needless to say, James, was acutely aware of the terrible violence the colonized system brought down on those it dominated. At the same time, when he addressed those crucial to the decolonizing movement, he spoke to the world itself. Nowhere was this more apparent than in a speech he delivered in Accra in July 1960, just when the decolonizing movement was well under way and the newly independent nations were finding their way in a capitalist world that wanted their resources and cared little about the welfare of their workers. The 1960 lecture appeared as a chapter in *Nkrumah and the Ghana Revolution* in 1977, well after Nkrumah had died leaving Ghana one of the more successful new nations, especially when compared to, at the extreme, Congo under Mobutu Sese Seko. Near the beginning of his lecture, James declares himself a proponent of Nkrumaism which, he said, "...claims that every vestige of colonialism must be wiped away from every corner of Africa."[2] The line was greeted with loud applause. He then goes on say that were the advanced capitalist nations to adopted Nkrumah's values, it would lead to the "emancipation of all oppressed peoples" the world over. More applause followed.

This is not an instance of James's elegant literary style, but it does suggest James's ability to adjust mode to purpose. In 1960, James had been back in Trinidad for two years. He was working precisely on his own version of Nkrumaism in Trinidad, which had won independence in 1958. So, in Ghana in 1960, he brought his reputation and experience back to Africa to stir and inform Ghana's and the world's oppressed people. Visiting lecturers, even famous ones, do not automatically excite their audiences who are, just as often, bored by a stranger's views on their society. Yet James found simple but direct words to excite those gathered in Accra to hear him. It was not just the words but the ideas that excited—in particular the idea that Nkrumaism could change the world. 1960 was well before the world revolution of 1968, when many in both the Global South and the North began to imagine a global revolution inspired by the oppressed people of the world. Near the end, echoing Marx's Mr. Moneybags, James addresses the leaders of the Capitalism world-system: "Mr. Capitalist, you will have to treat the workers in [your countries] as we are treating our workers."[3] Still more applause. This, just after he had given the most simple and honest definition of class capitalism. "Capitalism produces for profit. It produces where it likes, when it likes, how it likes, governed always by the necessity of profit."[4]

For James, the issue was not primarily democracy so much as liberation from oppression. This, in spite of the fact that Ghana and Trinidad, in the day, had already introduced democratic politics in their different ways. Was this an overly radical idea of revolutionary change, one that ignored state formation as so many African nations did? Not likely. Trinidad's independence from its democratic colonizers in Britain had come peacefully, in part because of its long history with colonizers—Spanish and French and English. As a result, Trinidadians had long lived with the French language and Spanish institutions before becoming a British Crown Colony. They were, in this sense, accustomed to dealing with political and social differences. It is not, of course, the case that independent Trinidad was without a burdensome legacy of its colonial past. With Trinidad in mind, Ghana in some ways was a model of the more radical resistance effort required to remake the world. If Trinidad enjoyed a degree of relatively benign colonial rule, this fact also gave him a vision unavailable in Ghana and Africa, generally an image of global prospects of racial and cultural integration. It was not incidental that his early life in so public a sport as cricket was one performed before an especially sophisticated public audience. This fact contributed to his ability to speak and write to and about the world by then foremost, if different, colonial power.

James accepted speaking engagements in the United States in 1938. He remained there off and on until he was deported in 1953—deported no doubt because of the radical Marxism for which he came to be known in an America paralyzed by the Red Scare fabricated by Senator Joseph McCarthy. In her introduction to *American Civilization*, Anna Grimshaw says that "James did for American Marxism what Lenin had done for Marxism in Russia."[5] She was not referring to the magnitude of Marxism in America (never great) but to the way he interpreted Marx's ideas in respect to American culture and history. James opens *American Civilization* with the following unsurprising statement: "The American civilization is identified in the consciousness of the world with two phases of the development of world history. The first is the Declaration of Independence. The second is mass production."[6] A draft of the book was begun early in his stay in the United States after 1938 and finished in 1950. It was, as one might suppose, a series of chapters written

230 *Capitalism's Uncertain Future*

in response to his travels and observations over those 12 years. *American Civilization* includes among its eight chapters studies of "Individuality 1776–1876," "The American Intellectuals of the Nineteenth Century," and "Popular Art and Modern Society,"—each probing and even shocking for the author's appreciation of the ways America's history and literature invented a largely, if not wholly unique, cultural and political disposition.

The first, on Individuality, touches on early Revolutionary America's debt to classic political philosophers like John Locke, but also comments on Alexis de Tocqueville's *Democracy in America*, which he uses to make a pungent point on the fate of American democracy. He thought that much of early American political thought was due to an older, more European version of democracy that was dominated by an upper class of wealthy merchants who profited from shipping, whaling, and fishing in general as well as cotton production. But this economic system led to a transformation of the economic and political system as labor became more prominent class along with the small farmers in the West. His conclusion on this historical sketch was that America had, like Europe, produced a class of intellectuals who created a distinctively American literature.

Then, in the chapter on American intellectuals in the 19th century, James follows with a formidable exposition of the writers who shaped their nation's literary imagination—Walt Whitman, Herman Melville, and the Abolitionists, in particular. "Popular Arts and Modern Society," written well into the 1940s, stands up very well to Theodore Adorno and Max Horkheimer's famous 1949 essay on mass culture, "Cultural Industry: The Enlightenment as Mass Deception." While James's essay is not nearly so tendentiously critical of American mass culture as Adorno and Horkheimer's, James does what they do not. He provides a detailed survey of the elements of mass culture: from Charlie Chaplin films to Dick Tracy and other comic book characters, then to Al Capp's cartoons, even Dashiell Hammet's *The Maltese Falcon* and *The Thin Man*.

What James accomplished in *American Civilization* is all the more impressive in light of the biographical fact, given his immediate experiences in the colonial world, his reading of severe Marxist writers, and his ingenuous idea that the First World (as once it was called) needs to learn lessons from the Third. But, again, he achieved what he achieved, not in spite being formed by living in the Global South but because of it. And nowhere is this better illustrated than in his book on cricket. *Beyond A Boundary* (1993 [1983]) was written after *American Civilization*, yet these two works have a common thread—both turned, to a large extent, on the importance of public spectacles as a curative element for a nation's divisions and troubles. In *American Civilization*, in the chapter on popular culture, James likens American mass culture to the Athenian tragedies[7] that moved audiences to feel—to weep and wonder—at the agonies portrayed, just as say the film *Casablanca* encouraged people, in the day, to hope for a way out of Nazi domination, even at the expense of losing a loved one. Similarly, *Beyond A Boundary* is purportedly part memoir and part introduction to cricket, the dominant sport in Trinidad. And at the heart of *Beyond A Boundary* is the chapter "What is Art?" where he returns to the relations between popular art and Greek theater. Cricket, he says "... is first and foremost a dramatic spectacle. It belongs to the theater, ballet, opera and the dance."[8] Here the spectacle is high culture, to be sure, thus seemingly at odds with the reference to the popular and healing appeal of Greek theater in *American Civilization* at the end of its chapter "Popular Art and Modern Society."[9] Both of these books were written before the heyday of cultural studies, even before Adorno and Horkheimer's disquisition on the cultural industry as deception. So, James can be forgiven for seeming to ignore the distinction between high and mass cultures. Still, he is saying that the Greek tragedies served a social purpose for all cultures, high and lower. Then, too, in the Greek tragedies, as in Shakespeare's early modern tragedies, perhaps even the drama of the Roman gladiators, and certainty of the Olympic Games for the Greeks, there was no difference between high and low spectacles and their effect on those who watched them. Whatever may be, it does seem that for James, cricket in Trinidad reached down below its apparent high culture and British nature to touch the masses. If football matches of all kinds are low and mass culture sports, then cricket is a high culture sport. But, when it comes to spectacles, the differences between the two are negligible.

In *Beyond A Boundary*, James makes two related points about cricket as a spectacle. First, the primary action is between the batsman and the bowler who are much more the dramatic focus of a match than baseball's pitcher and batter, where all the players on the diamond are considered part of the dramatic action. Cricket, as James puts it:

> ... is so organized that at all times it is compelled to reproduce the central action which characterizes all good drama since the day of the Greeks to our own: two individuals pitted against each other in a conflict that is strictly personal but no less strictly representative of a social group.[10]

Then, second, cricket shares "...with all dramatic spectacles ... the relation between event (or if you prefer, contingency) and design, episode and continuity, diversity in unity, the battle and the campaign, the part and the whole."[11] This second aspect of the spectacle extends the theme of the first, in the sense that the drama between batsman and bowler bears the story of the whole match, or more to the point, their personal interactions create the tension by which the drama of the social group is broadcast.

For most not familiar with the game, these points are likely to make limited sense. Yet, the evidence that James is addressing issues more global than cricket in Trinidad is that he begins the book with an explanatory note on this sport and its basic rules and descriptive terminology that itself begins with reference to the title *Beyond A Boundary*: "the themes of this

232 *Capitalism's Uncertain Future*

book... reach far beyond the boundaries of the cricket field." That James is using his experience with cricket to write for and to a wider world is most evident in the way he returns, again, to Greek drama to suggest how even an upper-class British sport can stimulate a sense of democratic possibilities. The final pages of "What is Art?" are a sophisticated theory of drama in human life that begins with the game and rises to the role of democratic values in economic life:

> The basic notions of cricket represent physical action which has been the basis not only of primitive but of civilization life for countless centuries. In work and play they were the motions by which men lived and without which they would perish. The Industrial Revolution transformed our existence. Our fundamental characteristics as human beings it did not and could not. The bushmen reproduced in one medium not merely animals but the line, the curve, the movement. It supplied in the form they needed a vision of the life they lived. The Hambledon men who made modern cricket did the same. ... One form was fixed the other had to be constantly re-created. The contrasts can be multiplied. ... Each fed the need to satisfy the visual artistic sense.[12]

Dramatic art is the ubiquitous and long enduring social fact of human being without which nations and tribes would die.

James was formed aesthetically not by the concert hall or the museum, but by his sport. He had been subjected in his cricket life to racial exclusions familiar to colonial peoples. The trajectory of his intellectual life was a sternly radical Marxist theory that he deployed to develop a global theory of economic and geopolitical oppression in Africa and the Caribbean, and by extension all of the Global South. Yet these labors did not keep him from learning and appreciating the cultural ways of America, the core state in a world economy that oppressed those with whom he was personally close.

C.L.R. James was not primarily concerned with capitalism. Just the same, he invented a remarkably, if qualifiedly, positive view of the culture of the capitalist world economy. For most born into a colony, such a system may not have the means and manners needed to study the evils of capitalism that are all too evident. But James chose not to dwell on these facts of colonial life in order to reach for the promises available even to the oppressed. That he used an upper-class colonizer's sport to convey popular art at the heart of social democracy is far more than a tribute to his far-ranging genius. It is a flag for the inherent ability of all people, whatever their status, to salute the promise made possible by a well-played spectacle.

Readers may wonder why C.L.R. James appears twice in our book. It is not because he was somehow more important than others. Rather, it is because he was one of the very few in his day who was both a disciplined and accomplished public intellectual *and* one who was attuned to the effects of mass culture and its technical apparatus on the masses.

Herbert Marcuse (1898–1979) was born in Berlin to an upper-middle class Jewish family, which at the time was safely integrated into the local society. In 1916, after Gymnasium, he entered military service where he first developed his critical attitude toward Germany that, in turn, sparked Marcuse's interest in Marxism. In 1919, after the War, he studied first at Humboldt University before beginning doctoral studies in literature, philosophy, and economics at Freiburg. Marcuse's thesis on literature and art was accepted in 1922—and there began his lifelong theoretical interest in aesthetics, always shaped by a strong but original Marxist theory. After graduate studies, he returned to Berlin and worked for a while in the book business while being supported by his father. This allowed him the relative freedom to read Martin Heidegger's *Being and Time*, which led to his mature knowledge of philosophy, after which he returned to Freiburg to study with Edmund Husserl and Heidegger (a relation that ended in 1932 due to political differences).

When the Nazis rose to power, an academic position in Germany was out of the question. So, Marcuse joined the Frankfurt Institute for Social Research which was itself at risk in the face of the ominous and ubiquitous Nazi threat to free critical thinking and research. The Institute, since its founding in 1923, had rapidly become Europe's most prominent center for critical theoretic research. Marcuse joined Max Horkheimer, Theodor Adorno, Walter Benjamin, Erich Fromm, and other of the great Critical Theorists, as they came to be called. In 1933 the Institute closed down and moved to New York City, where it remained until 1951 when most—excluding Marcuse and Fromm—returned to Frankfurt eventually to be joined by a new generation of theorists, chief among them Juergen Habermas.

In the United States, Marcuse's critical philosophy matured all the more, in some good part because of his service for US Office of War Information that after the War becomes the CIA. He taught thereafter at Columbia, Harvard, and Brandeis where he was embraced by its Left-Jewish Culture. It was at Brandeis that Marcuse wrote his most famous book, *One Dimensional Man* (1964), which became a companion piece of sorts to his nearly as famous *Eros and Civilization* (1955). *One Dimensional Man* turned out to be a political textbook for New Left student activists. Marcuse then taught at the University of California at San Diego from 1965 to 1970, where his fame as a radical left thinker caused Governor Ronald Reagan to terminate his employment. He lived another nine years as a citizen of the United States often visiting Germany. He died of a stroke in Germany while on the way to fulfill an invitation by Juergen Habermas to lecture at the Max Planck Institute. His ashes found their way to the United States but were returned for burial in Berlin.

It may seem odd to put Marcuse next to C.L.R. James because they came from and lived in such different worlds. Marcuse was from Berlin. He travelled with leading intellectuals of Europe and America. James was from a small Caribbean colony. He travelled mostly across the Global South, while

234 *Capitalism's Uncertain Future*

passing through London and cities in America. Marcuse was an inspiration to student rebels and intellectuals wherever he went, James was best
known mostly to those who shared his peripheral social status. Yet, both
were Marxists of different brands and both gave a good portion of their intellectual energies to developing a critical theory of aesthetics—that, in different ways, called attention to capitalism's investment in mass culture and
its effects on populations—debilitating (in Marcuse's case) or empowering
(in James's). Mass culture, thought James, had the ability to bring to life the
popular drama of democracy as Athens did for the Greek theater. For Marcuse, what may have been true to Greek and other premodern democracies,
was no longer the case when technology turned popular, even high culture,
into a repressive mechanism.

Marcuse, however, was by no means a critic of culture in general or even
of high culture. In one sense, he agreed with Adorno in this respect. But
he shared one foundational point with his Institute colleagues, as Martin
Jay describes it in *The Dialectical Imagination: A History of the Frankfurt and
the Institute for Social Research, 1925–1950*: "What distinguished the Frank-
fort's School's sociology of art from its more orthodox Marxist progenitors,
however, was its refusal to limit cultural phenomena to an ideological reflex
of class interests."[13] Adorno and Horkheimer were hardly orthodox, even
if their critique of mass culture was a seemingly orthodox attack on the
Culture Industry as a capitalist enterprise. Marcuse's general theory of art,
however, enjoys a degree of accord with Adorno's, but he went beyond them
in writing a systematic aesthetic theory. In *The Aesthetic Dimension: Toward a
Critique of Marxist Aesthetics* (1978 [1977]), Marcuse writes of the revolutionary possibilities of art: "Art's separation from the process of material production has enabled it to demystify the reality reproduced in this process."[14]
More generally, Marcuse provides a nuanced account of art critical of the
bourgeois status quo:

> I shall submit the following thesis: the radical qualities of art, that is
> to say, its indictment of the established reality and its invocation of the
> beautiful image (*schoener Schein*) of liberation are grounded precisely in
> the dimensions where art transcends its social determination and eman-
> cipates itself from the given universe of discourse and behavior while
> preserving its overwhelming presence. Thereby art creates the realm in
> which the subversion of experience proper to art becomes possible: the
> world formed by art is recognized as a reality which is suppressed and
> distorted in the given reality.[15]

Art can be, in certain forms, a means to portray the distortions of civil society's false claim to freedom and liberty.

It is evident thereby that Marcuse's Marxist aesthetics is theoretically able
to identify the refinement with which art *can* expose the duplicitous nature
of bourgeois art: "Deception and illusion have been qualities of established

reality throughout recorded history. And mystification is a feature not only of capitalist society. The work of art on the other hand does not conceal that which is. It reveals."[16] Later, he adds a boldly revolutionary idea: "Art breaks open a dimension inaccessible to other experience, a dimension in which human beings, nature, and things no longer stand under the law of the established reality principle."[17]

The argument in *The Aesthetic Dimension* would seem to be a carryover from the optimistic elements in his earlier book *Eros and Civilization* in 1955 and a break from the shatteringly negative theory of mass art in *One Dimensional Man* in 1964. Yet Marcuse corrects the false impression of the earlier book in a 1966 Political Preface to the 1955 version—this by granting the grounds supposing the more positive sense of culture and art: "Eros and Civilization: the title expressed an optimistic, euphemistic, even positive thought, namely, that the achievements of advanced industrial society." Then, Marcuse forthrightly corrects himself:

> This optimism was based on the assumption that the rationale for the continued acceptance of domination no longer prevailed, that scarcity and the need for toil were only "artificially" perpetuated — in the interest of preserving the system of domination I neglected or minimized the fact that this "obsolescent rationale had been vastly strengthened (if not replaced), by even more efficient forms of social control.

Eros and Civilization is Marcuse's most systematic contribution to one of the projects of the Frankfurt School—to fuse Freud and Marx into a critical social theory. To this end, he necessarily (as the words in Preface imply) turned to Freud's idea of the dual drive theory of the Unconscious psyche. This is to juxtapose the struggle between life and death in the psyche of an individual and by extension (as Freud argued in 1929 in *Civilization and Its Discontents*) in the modern world itself. At the least, Freud allowed Marcuse to introduce a dynamic notion of the struggle between social life and social death, that is, between those aspects of culture and art that encourage critical, even revolutionary, thinking and those aspects that undermine critical thinking:

> Mass democracy provides the political paraphernalia for effectuating this introjection of the Reality Principle; it not only permits the people (up to a point) to choose their own masters and to participate (up to a point) in the government which governs them — it also allows the masters to disappear behind the technological veil of the productive and destructive apparatus which they control, and it conceals the human (and material) costs of the benefits and comforts which it bestows upon those who collaborate. The people, efficiently manipulated and organized, are free; ignorance and impotence, introjected heteronomy is the price of their freedom.

236   *Capitalism's Uncertain Future*

Here, Marcuse is supremely clear about the dual drives of mass democracies. They can, on the one hand, give life to human freedom when the people choose freely their leaders, but on the other, they can be death dealing by introjecting them with attitudes of "ignorance and impotence." This, again, is from the Political Preface in 1966—two years after the publication of *One Dimensional Man* where Marcuse's aesthetic theory turns precisely to the debilitating effects of mass and even high cultures. But, in addition, here too is Marcuse's nod to the two sides of the modern world in respect to its technologies: on one side, "A comfortable, smooth, reasonable, democratic unfreedom prevails in advanced industrial civilization, a token of technical progress,"[18] while on the other side: "Freedom of enterprise was from the beginning not altogether a blessing."[19] The latter alternative he then immediately pounds home with a thoroughgoing critique of the modern:

> The distinguishing feature of advanced industrial society is its effective suffocation of those needs which demand liberation... Here, the social controls exact the over-whelming need for the production and consumption of waste; the need for stupefying work where it is no longer a real necessity; the need for modes of relaxation which soothe and prolong this stupefaction; the need for maintaining such deceptive liberties as free competition at administered prices, a free press which censors itself, free choice between brands and gadgets.

The very mention of "brands and gadgets" serves as a lead to the most important political concept associated with Marcuse: *repressive desublimation.*

Repressive desublimation is the malignancy Marcuse diagnoses as the cause of one-dimensional thought and behavior—which, to put it all-too-simply, is the condition whereby individuals lose the ability to think critically and act politically against the prevailing social order. Sublimation, by contrast, is the psychic (and social) process by which thoughts and feelings are repressed in the Unconscious mind (and in culture) by the semiconscious Superego (or the dominant cultural values). Here, the mind/culture distinction is partially collapsed. In Freudian theory, the Superego is the aspect of the psyche that imposes external cultural norms on the mind where the Ego does the work of repressing them into the Unconscious where they encounter the Unconscious libidinal drives—there to create a largely Unconscious struggle between the life and death drives and more generally between the repressed desires and the expectations of society. Sublimation is when repressed desires express themselves in a subliminal form different from their repressed form. A classic example of the process is the archetypical Puritan for whom sexual desire is impure; yet being unable completely to resist it, they act it out in not so obviously external action. In the case of the ideal typical Puritan, they work to create a pure community by expelling those who will not conform to their norms (or by hanging witches). Hanging Salem's witches was, in effect, an expression of forbidden sexual desire. It is, of course, hard to imagine the Puritan as a kind of critical theorist before the fact when in his reality he [*sic*] was acting to affirm and protect a community's values.

Unsurprisingly, Marcuse describes this in very different terms; for example, in respect to his aesthetic theory:

> Artistic alienation is sublimation. It creates the images of conditions which are irreconcilable with the established Reality Principle but which, as cultural images, become tolerable, even edifying and useful. Now this imagery is invalidated. Its incorporation into the kitchen, the office, the shop; its commercial release for business and fun is, in a sense, desublimation—replacing mediated by immediate gratification. But it is desublimation practiced from a "position of strength" on the part of society, which can afford to grant more than before because its interests have become the innermost drives of its citizens, and because the joys which it grants promote social cohesion and contentment.[20]

In this apparently bland statement, Marcuse packs all the explosiveness of his mind-jarring concept of repressive desublimation. It may not seem so, but the passage reflects the basic principle of his aesthetic theory in general. If art is alienated from reality—from, in Freudian language, the Reality Principle—art is thereby alienated from political and social realities themselves. In earlier modern times, art enjoyed a degree of distance that allows for the sublimation of an impulse toward criticism of the governing order. Then comes the distinguishing "Now"—artistic imagery which had a degree of critical efficacy is "invalidated." Art, such as it is, becomes, under the reign of techno-society, shopping, business, and entertainment that are considered "fun." This is the happiness society to which Marcuse refers to throughout the book. Happiness seals the dominant culture's authority to repress the established order's democratic impulse for political criticism. "...[T]here are many ways in which the unhappiness beneath the happy consciousness may be turned into a source of strength and cohesion for the social order," but chief among these ways is the power of mind-numbing but comfortable familiarity with the goods and services sold by the dominating capitalist social order. Hence, the single most telling paragraph in *One Dimensional Man*:

> The productive apparatus and the goods and services which it produces "sell" or impose the social system as a whole. The means of mass transportation and communication, the commodities of lodging, food, and clothing, the irresistible output of the entertainment and information industry carry with them prescribed attitudes and habits, certain intellectual and emotional reactions which bind the consumers more or less pleasantly to the producers and, through the latter, to the whole. The products indoctrinate and manipulate; they promote a false consciousness which is immune against its falsehood. And as these beneficial products become

238 *Capitalism's Uncertain Future*

available to more individuals in more social classes, the indoctrination they carry ceases to be publicity; it becomes a way of life. It is a good way of life – much better than before – and as a good way of life, it militates against qualitative change. Thus, emerges a pattern of *one-dimensional thought and behavior* in which ideas, aspirations, and objectives that, by their content, transcend the established universe of discourse and action are either repelled or reduced to terms of this universe.[21]

To which, Marcuse adds the basic assumption of his aesthetic theory of art in late modern times: "The absorbent power of society depletes the artistic dimension by assimilating its antagonistic contents."[22]

In such times as these, art is reduced to flashy cars, empty promises, nifty fashions, titillating television, sex in the backseat of cars, desire for the newest and best dishwashers, the purported joy of a tract home in a suburb named "Country Way."[23] For Americans old enough to remember, this was the collective dream of the 1950s. *One Dimensional Man*, published in 1964, was a book about this America projected onto the whole of the then still enveloping inert new social order where literary art, television melodramas, highway cigarette ads, and more stimulate desire for a vague, apolitical happiness:

> In contrast, desublimated sexuality is rampant in O'Neill's alcoholics and Faulkner's savages, in the *Streetcar Named Desire* and under the *Hot Tin Roof,* in *Lolita,* in all the stories of Hollywood and New York orgies, and the adventures of suburban housewives. This is infinitely more realistic, daring, uninhibited. It is part and parcel of the society in which it happens, but nowhere its negation. What happens is surely wild and obscene, virile and tasty, quite immoral-and, precisely because of that, perfectly harmless.[24]

Marcuse's aesthetic theory goes far beyond the mass culture industry that Horkheimer railed against. For Marcuse, everything is mass culture produced by a capitalist industry aiming to please the masses in order to castrate their political organs.

In the end, Marcuse did not give up hope. The global resistance movements of and around 1968 led him to publish *An Essay on Liberation* in 1969, which began: "Now, … this threatening homogeneity has been loosening up, and an alternative is beginning to break into the repressive continuum."[25]

Notes

1 C.L.R. James, Raya Dunayevskaya, and Grace Lee Boggs, *State Capitalism and World Revolution* (Oakland, CA: PM Press, 2013 [1950]).

2 C.L.R. James, *Nkrumah and the Ghana Revolution* (Chicago: Lawrence Hill Books, 1977), 162.

3 *Ibid.*, 173.

4 *Ibid.*, 171.

5 Anna Grimshaw, Introduction to *American Civilization*, C.L.R. James (London and New York: Routledge, 1993 [1950]), 11.
6 *Ibid.*, 27.
7 *Ibid.*, 149–159.
8 C.L.R. James, *Beyond A Boundary* (Durham, NC: Duke University Press, 1993 [1983]), 196.
9 James, *American Civilization*, 149–159.
10 James, *Boundary*, 196.
11 *Ibid.*, 197.
12 *Ibid.*, 209.
13 Martin Jay, *The Dialectical Imagination: A History of the Frankfurt School and the Institute of Social Research, 1923–1950* (Boston: Little, Brown, 1973), 178.
14 Herbert Marcuse, *The Aesthetic Dimension: Toward a Critique of Marxist Aesthetics* (Boston: Beacon Press, 2014 [1977]), 22.
15 *Ibid.*, 7.
16 *Ibid.*, 56.
17 *Ibid.*, 72.
18 Herbert Marcuse, *One Dimensional Man* (Boston: Beacon Press, 1964), 1.
19 *Ibid.*, 7.
20 *Ibid.*, 72.
21 *Ibid.*, 12.
22 *Ibid.*, 61.
23 *Ibid.*, 73.
24 *Ibid.*, 76.
25 Herbert Marcuse, *An Essay on Liberation* (Boston: Beacon, 1969), vii.

31 The Poverty of Development Economics

Abhijit V. Banerjee and Esther Duflo/Samir Amin

After the 2008 financial crisis, development policy was in a crisis of its own.[1] Then came along *Poor Economics* (2011). This book was field changing for development economics along with mainline development policy. It was greeted with great praise, given numerous awards, and quickly became the agenda-setting book for development economists across the globe. It appeals to the development expert who got into the field in order to help the world's poor, but also promises to eradicate poverty without upending the failing Washington Consensus.

Poor Economics (2011) offers to help economists aid the worlds' poor while keeping existing socioeconomic structures intact. It claims that changing the unit of analysis and methodology of development economics can deliver results without a major theoretical paradigm shift. It urges development economists to talk directly to the poor in order to learn about their poverty, to ask smaller questions, make smaller interventions; in other words, to commit to projects that would lend themselves well to the use of randomized controlled trials (RCTs). Abhijit V. Banerjee (1961–) and Esther Duflo (1972–) shy away from the big questions of "capitalism," "democracy," and "inequality" by implying that these topics are not for scholars with pragmatist concerns. They write:

> Instead of discussing how best to fight diarrhea or dengue, many of the most vocal experts tend to be fixated on the 'big questions': What is the ultimate cause of poverty? How much faith should we place in free markets? Is democracy good for the poor?[2]

In so doing, big questions are reframed by Banerjee and Duflo as indulgent navel-gazing, while RCTs that lend themselves to smaller interventions are seen as practical solutions to poverty. They make this argument because we cannot conduct a Randomized Controlled Trial to uncover the nature of capitalism, the causes of poverty, or whether democracy has any effect on social inequality, we should instead shift focus away from these unsolvable-by-RCTs questions and instead to smaller policy puzzles that *can* be solved through Randomized Controlled Trials. Throughout their book Banerjee and Duflo consistently dismiss "big questions" with vague statements such as, "In any case, it is not clear that answering some of these big

DOI: 10.4324/9781003198291-36

questions, like whether foreign aid works, is as important as we are sometimes led to believe."[3]

Banerjee and Duflo's book encourages economists to rethink development economics not as an endeavor to ask the macroeconomic questions about inequalities rife to our global economy, but instead, to see development economics as "a matter of choosing the right project to fund… and then figuring out how best to run it."[4] Through RCTs and in talking to the poor it is possible to understand exactly where the poor face hardships and how they think about economic decision-making. This approach makes it possible to design better policy. This approach is, however, not without its limitations. One of the fixations of development economists that is lost through this approach is the link between economic growth and poverty eradication. In their focus on the micro-processes of the poor, Banerjee and Duflo are not concerned with national-level economic growth. Even if poverty has nothing to do with economic growth, they claim, it is nonetheless important to combat systemic poverty.[5] This is a major breakthrough for mainline development economists, who have long argued that we should care about poverty eradication only so much as it is correlated with growth. Poverty should be combatted, Banerjee and Duflo contend, by "listen[ing] to poor people themselves and forc[ing] ourselves to understand the logic of their choices."[6]

There is more in this new agenda to be wary of. In their claim that eradicating poverty is simply a matter of enacting the right policies, they claim that history and historical analysis do not matter. One of their five key analytical takeaways is that "poor countries are not doomed to failure because they are poor, or because they had an unfortunate history."[7] Banerjee and Duflo claim that historical approaches to development tend to believe that there exists "some grand conspiracy of elites to maintain their hold on the economy," and that the "true" cause of poverty has "more to do with some avoidable flaw in the detailed design of policies."[8] It's unclear how they are able to make this claim since they don't consider historical development in their analyses, nor do they cite scholars who argue that poverty is a conspiracy of a cabal of elites, nor do they collect macro-level data that would allow them to make that claim. So, one would have to look to other research to assess whether or not history matters when it comes to development outcomes.

The utility of their approach, they claim, is that "it is possible to improve governance and policy without changing the existing political and social structures."[9] The crisis of development economics and policy stemmed from calls from below that claimed that development policy, specifically the neoliberal Washington Consensus, failed to improve the outcomes of the world's poor and instead advantaged the world's wealthiest. These critics claimed that only systemic change will address the needs of the world's poor. In this book, Banerjee and Duflo provide a new model for development policies that would similarly fail to offer the systemic change needed to improve the lives of the world's poor en masse.

242 *Capitalism's Uncertain Future*

In directing development scholarship away from big questions that help us better describe, understand, and critique global political economy, Banerjee and Duflo not only attempt to fix the ideological crisis that neoliberal development economics has faced in recent decades, but in so doing, they are also making development economics far less intellectually interesting. Historically, development economics was one of the subfields where scholars could ask big questions in order to better understand why the global economy is the way it is. Banerjee and Duflo's rethinking of the subfield transforms it into a technocratic exercise that shies away from any attempt to understand the underlying structures of global political economy. Although this approach certainly helps neoliberal development economists reinvent themselves after the crisis of the Washington Consensus, it does so without offering a macro-theory of capitalism. While one can certainly question the politics underlying this move, one also thinks of the neoliberal intellectuals of the 1990s, like Francis Fukuyama (see Plys' Introduction to this volume) for example, who never shied away from the big questions of global political economy. It remains to be seen how successful this approach will be in the long term if development economists increasingly bracket topics such as capitalism, democracy, and inequality. But for now, certainly, this turn in development economics is an abdication of the field's former intellectualism.

The subfield would be better served in revisiting the work of development economist Samir Amin, in order to animate contemporary scholarship.

Samir Amin (1931–2018) was born in Cairo, Egypt, in 1931 to two medical doctors—one Egyptian and one French. Amin attended a French school in Egypt and then left to study in Paris. Upon moving to Paris, he joined the *Parti Communiste Français* (French Communist Party), but later grew critical and associated instead with Maoists. After finishing his PhD in 1957, he returned to Cairo and worked in public sector administration during the wave of nationalization in Egypt. He also joined the Egyptian Communist Party, which was illegal at the time. In 1960, he returned to France, where he worked in the department of economic and financial studies for a few months before moving to Mali to work for the Malian Ministry of Planning. In 1963, he abandoned his policy career for academia becoming a professor at the University of Dakar and then *Paris VIII*. For some observers,[10] Samir Amin was the first development economist to question mainline development economics, instead viewing so-called "underdevelopment" and neo-imperialism as part of the structure of the capitalist world economy. This view, first developed in his PhD thesis, would later influence the Latin American Dependency school of economists along with World-Systems analysts.

In contrast to Banerjee and Duflo, Samir Amin takes a macro-historical approach to analyzing the causes of poverty in the Global South. For Amin, poverty is not only a result of the capitalism/imperialism nexus, but is also

Poverty of Development Economics   243

rooted in how capitalism and imperialism affect global class formation. Amin explains this dynamic as:

> ... the centre of gravity of the exploitation of labour by capital (and, in the first place, by monopoly capital which dominates the system as a whole) has been displaced from the centre of the system to its periphery. The mass of surplus value (in all its forms— absolute and relative, apparent and masked by price structures) extracted from labour in the periphery has been increasing steadily since the end of last century.[11]

Amin shows that the increasing immiseration of the Global South is a result of the capitalism and imperialism nexus. To put it in the language of contemporary development economists, poverty is a result of the structures of global political economy.

But to understand how capitalism and imperialism engender poverty in the peripheries of the capitalist world economy, Amin finds historical perspective essential. He writes:

> The history of the periphery shows two phases in quick succession: a first phase marked by a surplus in the balance of payments, corresponding to the opening up of a country as a colony, the establishment of the underdeveloped economy, the development of underdevelopment, followed by a phase of chronic tendency to deficit, corresponding to the crisis of the system, the blocking of growth based upon external demand. The foreign-exchange standard conceals for a time this tendency toward external deficit; sooner or later however, this obliges the underdeveloped countries to go in for monetary independence— an independence that cannot represent a real solution of the problem, but can only give rise to additional monetary disorders. Since the underdeveloped economies are extraverted, all their problems emerge in the balance of payments.[12]

In order to reveal the deeper structural mechanisms behind poverty and inequality, Amin takes a historical perspective to show how global capitalism and imperialism adversely affect economic outcomes for the Global South.

Capitalism and imperialism don't simply disadvantage the Global South—the structures of global political economy ensure prosperity for the Global North *because of* poverty in the Global South. Amin explains:

> The periphery plays a role which is far from negligible in the mechanism of international recovery.... During a depression in the advanced countries a considerable mass of labor is thrown out of employment. All incomes contract - profits first and foremost, but wages, too. During the preceding period of prosperity, new enterprises were set up, which are now working at a reduced rate. The burden of unutilized productive

244 *Capitalism's Uncertain Future*

capacity weighs heavily, making recovery all the more difficult. In the underdeveloped countries, on the other hand, while oscillations in the predominant form of income, ground rent, are very considerable, this is not true of the mixed incomes of the bulk of the population, and especially of income from subsistence economy. From a certain moment onward, the relative rigidity of the underdeveloped markets may thus constitute a factor of recovery. The existence of exchange relations between the periphery and the center of the system offers the latter the possibility of finding new external markets through the disintegration of the indigenous precapitalist economy. The further disintegration of primitive indigenous production at the end of the depression is reflected in a new wave of exports from the advanced countries. However, the money incomes distributed as a result of this imply a future increase in imports. This is why the opening of new external outlets does not constitute a final solution of the problem. In theory, this opening of a new field for the extension of capital is not needed in order that recovery may take place. This recovery is due very largely to a deepening of the internal market caused by the generalizing of a new, more capital intensive technique. Nevertheless, we observe, after each depression at the center, the opening of new outlets in the periphery, which thus play an active role in the mechanism of international recovery. The same thing happens during the cumulative process that is characteristic of the prosperity period. For the development of prosperity, marked by the growth of total income, is reflected in an increase in the share taken by profits, and consequently in an increase in the relative volume of saving that is accumulated. The relative share taken by wages decreases. Accordingly, capacity to consume falls farther and farther behind capacity to produce. The new equipment created by investment of the additional saving is not long in throwing on to the market a mass of consumer goods that cannot be absorbed. The working of the accelerator maintains for a time the illusion of the profitability of the new equipment made necessary by the increase in the absolute volume of consumption. There is thus overproduction of consumer goods, since the purchasing power distributed and destined for purchase of these goods (mainly wages) is less than the total value of this production. Trade between the advanced and underdeveloped countries continues, also, to conceal this imbalance, and so contributes to protracting the periods of prosperity. Exchange between advanced and underdeveloped countries in no way constitutes, of course, the solution to alleged general overproduction by the capitalist countries. Development of the capitalist countries is perfectly possible even when there are no precapitalist milieus to be disintegrated. But the advanced countries, which are always ahead of their backward partners in exchange, take the offensive by exporting to them. Only later does the structure of the underdeveloped countries become modified, adapting itself to the evolution of production in the advanced countries so as to make possible the export of primary products to them. Imbalance is therefore a permanent feature of trade relations between the center and the periphery of the system. This permanent imbalance is; however, always being corrected. It therefore plays, in the development of the most advanced countries, only the role of a catalyst, comparable to credit. It is the products that tend to be overproduced during the prosperity phase that are the first to seek an outlet in the economies of the periphery - namely, manufactured consumer goods. Contrariwise, the growing demand of the advanced countries, during the prosperity phase for those products that are relatively least plentiful leads to adjustment of the structure of the underdeveloped countries to the needs of the most advanced economies. The underdeveloped economies specialize in producing goods the supply of which tends to be less than the demand for them in the advanced countries during the prosperity phase: primary products that contribute to the equipment of the advanced countries - in the main, raw materials. Exchange of consumer goods, in respect of which supply is greater than demand, for intermediate goods, in respect of which, on the contrary, demand is greater than supply, thus facilitates the upward trend in the advanced countries. We can now appreciate better the real place occupied by the periphery in the world conjuncture. Although the extension of the capitalist mode of production to the periphery is not essential to the working of the mechanism of accumulation, this extension plays the role of a catalyst and an accelerator of growth at the center.[13]

In this extended quotation from *Unequal Development: An Essay on the Social Formations of Peripheral Capitalism* (1973), Amin describes the mechanism through which poverty in the peripheries sustains growth and prosperity in the centers of the capitalist world economy. Without the peripheries to absorb excess production and provide cheaper labor, there would be no growth in the center of the global economy.

His central question in *L'imperialisme et le développement inégal* (1976) is, "How, in the common struggle against capitalism, which is of necessity a struggle against imperialism, can concrete class struggles be articulated both in the centre and in the periphery?"[14] While this is undeniably a big question, it also strikes at the heart of the problem of "underdevelopment." In our effort to understand the working-class struggle in the peripheries, we must understand how uneven economic development across the global economy affects the working classes of the Global South. Because, as Amin puts it, "the chief characteristics of the capitalist system in its imperialist phase—the transfer of the contradictions of the capitalist mode of production from its dominant imperialist centres to its dominated periphery."[15] Poverty is a result of how contradictions of capitalism are transferred to the peripheries in order to stave off crisis in the center. For this reason, Amin concludes, "Comprendre la nature de l'impérialisme constitue la question centrale de notre époque."[16]

246 *Capitalism's Uncertain Future*

In this endeavor to better understand why poverty is concentrated in the Global South, Amin is critical of microeconomic methods used by development policymakers and mainline development economists. Analyses on a micro-level, demonstrates Amin, are simply "a technique," "a description of behaviour without explanation," "despite the sophisticated apparatus, it is no more than common-sense accounting; or, if it has some pretence at theory, it abandons this common sense accounting and becomes ideological trickery."[17] Instead, Amin calls for a global historical analysis, "by going back to the global plan of historical materialism, that of the class struggle, and placing this struggle once again in its true worldwide context."[18]

This global historical analysis leads Amin to very different prescriptions as compared to Banerjee and Duflo. "The peoples of the three continents (Africa, Asia, Latin America)..." he writes:

> ... are confronted today with a system that is, in many respects, analogous to the one in place at the end of the Second World War: a colonial system that does not recognize their sovereign rights, imposes them on the economic system that is convenient for the oligopolies of the imperialist center, even the appropriate political systems. The expansion of the neoliberal system over the last few decades is no less than the construction of apartheid on a world scale.[19]

The full human toll of unequal development cannot be understood without a world-historical perspective.

Amin calls for "a globalization based on negotiation, rather than submission to the exclusive interests of the imperialist monopolies. It also makes possible the reduction of international inequalities."[20] He adds:

> In conclusion: audacity, more audacity, always audacity. What I mean by audacity is therefore: (i) For the radical left in the societies of the imperialist triad, the need for an engagement in building an alternative anti-monopoly social bloc. (ii) For the radical left in the societies of the peripheries, to engage in building an alternative anti-comprador social bloc.[21]

Amin shows us that not only through asking the big questions can we understand poverty in the Global South, but also that thinking on a macroscale is the only way to combat the problem. The problem is world-historical, so the solution must necessarily be world-historical as well. Only by asking "big questions" can we understand the underlying causes of poverty. True, these questions do not allow development economists to showcase the latest techniques in econometrics and other quantitative methods, but if certain methods divert our attention away from the most important questions, then what good are they?

Notes

1 Nancy Birdsall and Francis Fukuyama, "The Post-Washington Consensus: Development After the Crisis," *Foreign Affairs* (March/April 2011); Jean Grugel, Pia Riggirozzi, and Ben Thirkell-White, "Beyond the Washington Consensus? Asia and Latin America in search of More Autonomous Development," *International Affairs* 84, no. 3 (2008): 499–517; Robert K. McCleery and Fernando De Paolis, "The Washington Consensus: A post-mortem," *Journal of Asian Economics* 19, no. 5–6 (2008): 438–446; Joseph E. Stiglitz, "Is there a Post-Washington Consensus Consensus?" in *The Washington Consensus Reconsidered*, eds. Serra Narcis and Joseph E. Stiglitz (Oxford: Oxford University Press, 2008), 41–56.
2 Abhijit V. Banerjee and Esther Duflo, *Poor Economics: A Radical Rethinking of the Way to Fight Global Poverty* (New York: Public Affairs, 2011), 3.
3 *Ibid.*, 5.
4 *Ibid.*
5 *Ibid.*, 267.
6 *Ibid.*, 272.
7 *Ibid.*, 270.
8 *Ibid.*, 270–271.
9 *Ibid.*, 271.
10 Samir Amin, *Samir Amin: Pioneer of the Rise of the South* (New York: Springer, 2014), 10.
11 Samir Amin, *L'Imperialisme et le développement inégal* (Paris: Éditions de minuit, 1976), 17.
12 Samir Amin, *Unequal Development: An Essay on the Social Formations of Peripheral Capitalism* (New York: Monthly Review Press, 1973 [1976]), 251–252.
13 *Ibid.*, 283–286.
14 Amin, *L'Imperialisme*, 19.
15 *Ibid.*, 22.
16 *Ibid.*, 15.
17 *Ibid.*, 44.
18 *Ibid.*, 112.
19 Samir Amin, *The World We Wish to See: Revolutionary Objectives in the Twenty-First Century* (New York: Monthly Review, 2008), 73.
20 Samir Amin, "Audacity, More Audacity," *Review of Radical Political Economics* 45, no. 3 (2013): 406.
21 *Ibid.*, 408.

32 Neo-Liberalism and the Madness of Economic Reason

Nancy Fraser/David Harvey

Nancy Fraser (1947–) was born in Baltimore, Maryland. She was educated at Bryn Mawr College outside Philadelphia, after which she earned a PhD at the CUNY Graduate Center in New York City. She then taught at Northwestern University for a good while, before joining the faculty of the New School for Social Research as Henry and Louise A. Loeb Professor of Political and Social Science and Professor of Philosophy. She remains there still.

Since its founding in 1919, the New School has been home to Left thinkers, including John Dewey, Thorstein Veblen, and Charles Beard in the early years. After 1933, the New School became known as the University in Exile because it served as a home for Europeans fleeing Italian and German Fascism. Even now, the New School offers a course devoted to the careful appreciation of Theodor Adorno and Max Horkheimer's 1947 book *The Dialectic of Enlightenment*, written during their exile in the United States. All this is to say that Nancy Fraser remains at the New School because it is for her the all-but-perfect intellectual home. She has devoted her writing life to her own version of critical theory and is recognized in Europe as one of the world's leading social theorists—this so much so that she was introduced for talk in Germany as one of North America's leading intellectuals. Such recognition is rare for any American, because even now (with some exceptions) the nation's philosophers resist taking deep consideration of the major German and French philosophies. The New School has long been an exception to this cultural silliness.

Nancy Fraser's first, and still important book, *Unruly Practices: Power, Discourse and Gender in Contemporary Social Theory* in 1989 is all the proof one needs of her early close reading of European social theories. She began the book with a statement of method that has guided her academic and political thinking over the years to come:

> I argue repeatedly that politics requires a genre of critical theorizing that blends normative argument and empirical sociocultural analysis in a "diagnosis of the times." In this, I am affirming a fairly classical left view found in Marx and in the Frankfort school of Critical Theory. At the same time, I am opposing a tendency in some sections of the academic Left to engage in what can only appear as esoteric forms of

DOI: 10.4324/9781003198291-37

discourse unless and until connections to practice are elaborated, indeed mediated, through sociopolitical analysis.[1]

Though the second sentence in this passage inclines toward an esoteric discourse of its own, her position is clear enough.

Fraser's book itself is a fair elaboration of these principles. In the book's three sections—roughly: Foucault and power; Derrida and deconstruction; and Habermas and gender—she respectfully interprets each tradition with an eye to important political issues, including the sexual body, technocracy, women and welfare, and more generally Late Capitalism. Given that, from the first, she made her theoretical and political preferences clear, Fraser is fair but predictably critical of the Foucauldian and Derridean lines (with Richard Rorty thrown in). A tribute to her broader sense of fairness is that she is also criticizes Habermas in respect to what, for her, is a crucial political issue, the needs of women in the late capitalist lifeworld. Habermas, she writes, "...fails to address the issue of how to restructure the relation of child rearing to paid work and citizenship."[2] In the same place, she continues:

> Habermas's categories tend to misrepresent the causes and underestimate the scope of the feminist challenge to welfare state capitalism. In short, the struggles and wishes of contemporary women are not adequately clarified by a theory that draws the battle line between system and lifeworld institutions.

Fraser obviously parts with Habermas and German critical theory general over more than a principle of theoretical feminism. Her feminism has always been, to varying degrees, concretely focused on practical problems of women living in a patriarchal world in which the feminine, in all its manifestations, is diminished, often eradicated from the dominant culture. Looking back from the 2020s to Fraser's 1989 book, some might suppose that this is an extreme statement. It is, but only in the sense that she did not write in such a stern manner of the realities for women then still so stark. Even today, when many women are prominent in public positions of power and authority, the starkness of patriarchy casts a cloud over women who still must struggle on meager, irregular government payments, while their children must go to inferior public schools, and their partners, if men, are all too often away in prison, to their graves, or to the wandering life; then too, women's political successes are met with scorn and in several notorious cases they are deprived of the victories they fairly won. In 1989, all was not bleak for women, but neither was it bright. Though a third-wave feminism moved out into its own in the 1970s, in 1974 Dorothy Smith's now classic article on feminist standpoint theory "Women's Experience as a Radical Critique of Sociology" challenged the masculinist aloofness of mainstream social theory. Also in the same year, Carol Stack's *All Our Kin* told the story of women getting by in public housing on slim pickings by cooperating with each other as if they

250 *Capitalism's Uncertain Future*

were kin. These and other feminist ventures began a slow but definite shift how those bold enough to care ought to think about women's experience. Yet it would be a good while until feminism's *annus miraballis* in 1990, when books like Judith Butler's *Gender Trouble*, Patricia Hill Collins' *Black Feminist Thought* as well as Fraser's *Unruly Practices* in 1989 brought forth a major advance beyond these earlier pioneering works. A plainspoken token of that was then advanced is Patricia Hill Collins' phrase (borrowed from bell hooks) the *matrix of domination*, which conveys the fact of life that all who live in capitalist societies are caught on one or another or several dominating vectors.

Yet, even these advances required time for readers to digest in order to nourish the will to work on the streets. Still now, more than three decades later, on the verge of a return of a version of sanity in 2021, the success of women's public efforts is good but not dazzling. Yet, when Nancy Fraser, in the subtitle to her 1989 book used the words "power, discourse, and gender," was in a sense teasing the reader to look down and deep at the practical problems of women who seek to live self-consciously as feminists. Many still are caring for children alone, paying ever higher rents, while participating, when they can, in political actions that might support both their sense of womanhood and the needs and wants of daily life. In other words (again, so far as I know, Fraser doesn't say it this way), she is writing about capitalisms, in all their several natures, as at least the most important, if not the sole, pillar of the patriarchal State since Marx began writing about the capitalism of his day.

Fraser made a series of theoretically political steps after *Unruly Practices* in 1989. *Justice Interruptus: Critical Reflections on the "Postsocialist"* (1997) is a collection of her articles published in the 1990s. By "postsocialist" she means to retain socialism as a critical ideal after the events 1989 when the collapse of Soviet Union and its East Bloc spelt an historical end to more than the Cold War. Second, but interestingly, she suggests that this event might be causally related to the rise on the cultural Left of identity politics, in respect to which she says that the events of "… 1989 led to a shift in "the political imaginary" with, to her, an important difference:

> More deeply, … we are witnessing an apparent shift in the political imaginary, especially in terms in which justice is imagined. Many actors appear to be moving away from a socialist imaginary, in which the central problem of justice is redistribution to a "postsocialist" imaginary, in which the central problem of justice is recognition. With this shift, the most salient social movements are no longer defined in terms of "classes" who are struggling to defend their "interests," end "exploitation," and win "redistribution." Instead, they are cultural defined "groups" and "communities of value" who are struggling to defend their "identities," end "cultural domination," and win "recognition." The result is

a decoupling of cultural politics from social politics, and the relative eclipse of the latter by the former.[3]

With this poignant statement as preface, Fraser begins the collection with an article previously published in 1995 in *New Left Review,* "From Redistribution to Recognition? Dilemmas in Justice is a Postsocialist Age," which is the first of a good many subsequent discussions of the dilemma framed in relation to economic issues such as "After the Family Wage: A Postindustrial Thought Experiment" interspersed with astute, even argumentative, comments on the views of other major feminist theorists such as "False Antitheses: A Response to Seyla Benhabib and Judith Butler." *Justice Interruptus,* thereby, is the first readily available book-length discussion of Fraser's contestation with those she considered "recognition" or identity theorists of social justice.

Fraser takes a mediating position between the two Left political extremes— redistribution and recognition—a position she argues is made possible from within the experience of a social movement, in particular, feminist politics: "Within social movements such as feminism, for example, activist tendencies that look to redistribution as the remedy for male domination are increasingly disassociated from tendencies that look instead to recognition of gender differences."[4] That social movements engaged in real on-the-ground politics might clarify relations that otherwise would remain philosophical is a telling point as to Fraser's underlying beliefs about the world as lived, and important to remind, this is the significant difference with Habermas. A lifeworld is an analytic category. Fraser, though not known for being a social activist, is clear enough about the importance of sociopolitical movements to understanding her philosophical principles. Important to add that when her topic changes, she knows to change her theoretical structure, as in her 2010 book *Scales of Justice: Reimagining Political Space in a Globalizing World,* where she writes of how globalizing require a reframing:

> I shall argue, first, that theories of justice must become three-dimensional, incorporating the political dimension of *representation* alongside the economic dimension of *distribution* and the cultural dimension of *recognition.* I shall also argue that the political dimension of representation as encompassing three levels. The combined effect of these two arguments will be to make visible a third question, beyond those of the "what" and the "who," which I shall call the "how." This question, in turn, inaugurates a paradigm shift: what the Keynesian-Westphalian frame cast as the theory of social justice must now become a theory of *postwestphalian democratic theory.*[5]

The literary genius of Nancy Fraser is her ability to express enormously complicated ideas in a kind of plain language that allows the reader to assume

252 *Capitalism's Uncertain Future*

she gets the drift of what is being said. There are occasionally notions that require unpacking. One of them is *post-Westphalian democratic theory*. The Treaty of Westphalia in 1648 demarcated the territorial limits of what thereafter came to be known as the modern nation-states. Hence the idea that a nation is defined first and foremost by its territorial borders. Once, centuries later, globalization took hold as the reality of late-modern States able to deploy late and all-but-post-modern technologies and their military and financial methods, the Westphalian norm fell when, as Fraser puts it (following Hardt and Negri's *Empire*), states were able "to govern at a distance through flexible fluctuating networks that transcend structured institutional sites."[6]

What Fraser is doing here is an important example to other social philosophers. Justice emerges, after *Unruly Practices* where it was the latent theme, to become the prevailing theme that guides her from "Gender and the Politics of Need Interpretation" in the 1989 book to a more focused theoretical gaze on the redistribution versus recognition controversy among feminists in and about 1995. Then, a decade later, in the essay "Mapping the feminist imagination: from redistribution to recognition to representation" (2005),[7] she refined the 1995 two-dimensional model (if that is the word) into three dimensions where political *representation* takes a coequal theoretical place alongside *redistribution* and *recognition*. Then, in 2007, a *NLR* essay "Reframing Justice in a Globalizing World"[8] resets the tripartite scheme in the salient, more general terms of justice and globalization—which then becomes, one must say, the literary frame for this reframing in *Fortunes of Feminism: From State-Managed Capitalism to Neoliberal Crisis* (2013). This is a book of essays organized in what she calls a "Drama in Three Acts."

Fraser thus returns to feminism after state-managed capital during the 2010s in the economic crisis of Neoliberalism. The three acts of the drama of feminism's relations to capitalism are instructively identified:

1   Feminism Insurgent: Radicalizing Critique in the Era of Social Democracy
2   Feminism Tamed: From Redistribution to Recognition in the Age of Identity
3   Feminism Resurgent? Confronting Capitalist Crisis in the Neoliberal Era

One might say that this is a little too much already with the titles. I think not for two reasons. Fraser's titles and headers are remarkably lucid as to which ideas are pursued at each turn. But also, when Fraser's literary oeuvre is followed from the beginning to the present, the reader learns a good lesson in just how central feminism is to a better understanding of capitalism as it has come to be.

In a tiny 2019 book (or pamphlet) with huge implications, *The Old is Dying and the New Cannot Be Born*, Fraser traces what she considers the dying of, yes, the old capitalist order but also of the moribund Neoliberal order down to the waning years of the Trump regime which, she argues, put an end the "hegemony of progressive Neoliberalism." As oxymoronic as this may sound, her original interpretation of the times makes sense: "The progressive-neoliberal bloc combined an expropriative, plutocratic economic program with a liberal-meritocratic politics of recognition. The distribution component of this amalgam was neoliberal."[9] Here she refers to the Reagan-Thatcher-Clinton era in which government support for the poor was cut in favor of direct and indirect benefits to the wealthy. Against which, so-called progressive "New Democrats" pursued policies of recognition that did little more that name and identify those excluded while subjecting them to policies of redistribution that kept them in place—hence the progressive-neoliberal hegemony that encouraged a reactionary Neoliberalism comprising "Christian evangelicals, south whites, small town Americans, and [the] disaffected working class"—in other words, the base that elected Donald Trump which he eventually lost control of as his four years passed by.

Against all this, Fraser proposes a "Strategy of Separation," arising from two basic splits:

> First, less privileged women, immigrants, and people of color have to be wooed away from the lean-in feminists, the meritocratic anti-racists and mainstream LGBTQ+ movement, the corporate diversity and green-capitalists who hijacked their concerns, inflecting them in terms consistent with neoliberalism …. Second, Rust Belt, southern, and rural working-class communities who have to be persuaded to desert their current crypto-neoliberal allies. The trick is to convince them that the forces promoting militarism, xenophobia, and ethnonationalism cannot and will not provide them with the essential material prerequisites for good lives, whereas a progressive populist bloc just might.[10]

Shades of the Occupy Wall Street Movement in 2011!

Fraser wants, however, to make something clear: "I am not suggesting that a progressive-populist bloc should mute pressing concerns about racism, sexism, homophobia, Islamophobia, and transphobia."[11] What she is against is "moralizing condescension, in the mode of progressive neoliberalism." What she helps us to be clear about is not, primarily, adopting the smug, commonplace, *neoliberal* attitudes that run though media. Rather, she insists that the paralyzing pseudo-progressive ideas are so much a presence in our times *because* of the global force of neoliberal capitalism. If, on this point, there is reason to pause before Fraser's theoretical acuity, it is because of her political locutions. When she writes of *hegemonic progressive neoliberalism*, the phrase suggests that progressive attitudes are somehow on an equal hegemonic footing with Neoliberalism (with a capital N). Neoliberal capitalism is the scam that plays with the stages of capitalist development to suggest that it was still somehow "liberal" in the classic sense of "free market" economies in which all would thrive by a simple devotion to their self-conceived

254 *Capitalism's Uncertain Future*

best interests, protected, of course, by a mysterious Invisible Hand. That—as now we who would think know—Adam Smith was a philosophical mythmaker does little more than give permission to the mythmakers of our time. Whatever the capitalisms that came to be after the 18th century were in point of economic reality: "capitalism" was, as still it is, a metaphor to suggest the way the world is. In actual historical fact, there have been any number of political, social, and economic experiments—none of them permanent; all of them ever changing.

What makes Nancy Fraser's writings so instructive is that since the 1980s, she has sought to calibrate these changes while using, as she and we must, a variant of the preexisting nomenclature. That one must do as has been done, does not demand that the names we give to the various stages of whatever we are commenting upon prevent us from making the fine, nonobvious discrimination of the deeper changes that exhaust the utility of preexisting vocabulary to name. Nancy Fraser does this about was well as it can be done. Yet, her resort to locutions like *hegemonic progressive neoliberalism* should be called into question, as one can assume she will in a forthcoming book. That *neoliberalism* pretends to be a new and better, if necessary, kind of capitalism is all but absurd. Fraser gets this. But still, she has not yet gotten the full force of the historical reality that, by whatever name, economic reason—practical and scientific—dooms the possibility that any political movement can fundamentally change the sordid nature of capitalism's now global economic reasoning. Her call for a "separation" of progressive from Neoliberal is a good beginning, one made good by her method of making the contentions among feminist thinkers a hard drive for reprogramming social and political theory.

No one, so far, has gotten this quite right. Fraser in many ways is a leading light, so to speak, of thinkers who have begun the process of not just "rethinking" economic reason but reworking it on the grounds of daily life. As a measure of what she has done against what needs to be done, it helps to turn now to a thinker, different in many ways from Fraser, yet just as clear about, in his phrase, "...capital and the madness of economic reason."

David Harvey (1935–) was born in Gillingham in Kent, UK. There, he attended a grammar school for boys before becoming a student at St. John's College, Cambridge, where, also, he took his PhD with an empirical historical study of hops production in the region. Hence, the irony that he did not stray all that far from home until he began a writing life of books that influenced thinking the world over. Harvey's first major book was a popular and well-regarded text, *Explanation in Geography*, after which he moved on intellectually. While at the University of Bristol in the 1960s, he began, as did others in the day, a turn toward Marxism, a step that played a role in his move to Johns Hopkins University, where Geography and other programs were similarly inclined toward radical left ideas.

In 1973, Harvey published *Social Justice and the City* in which his Marxist philosophy inspired a theory of urban spaces that was critical of capitalism's avaricious domination of social spaces. Ever since, his radical ideas grew more expansive and focused on a variety of subjects (even as Marxism grew less exotic among academics). He remained at Johns Hopkins with an interlude at Oxford (1987–1993), until leaving Baltimore for New York City and a distinguished professorship at the CUNY Graduate Center, where he remains today.

One of Harvey's most discussed books in the early New York period was *The Condition of Postmodernity* (1987), which began with the often ignored distinction between modernity and modernism—hence also: that between, as he puts it: POSTmodernISM and postMODERNism, a distinction that is a little too cute and not well explained. What he means becomes easier to understand in the book's two chapters in the last section where he distinguishes between "Postmodernity as an historical condition" and "Postmodernism as a hall of mirrors." In a stand-alone, half page preface to the book, Harvey's distinction and the main argument of the book are concisely summarized, so much so that one wonders why the similar has not been offered to readers by other authors:

> There has been a sea-change in cultural as well as in political-economic, practices since 1972. This sea-change is bound with the emergence of new dominant ways in which we experience space and time.
>
> While simultaneity in the shifting dimensions of time and space is no proof of necessary or causal connection, strong a priori grounds can be adduced for the proposition that there is some kind of necessary relation between the rise of postmodernist cultural forms, the emergence of more flexible modes of capital accumulation, and a new round of "time-space compression" in the organization of capitalism.
>
> But these changes, when set against the basic rules of capitalistic accumulation, appear more as shifts in surface appearance rather that as signs of the emergence of some entirely new postcapitalist or postindustrial society.[12]

The book itself thus follows the steps in this argument.

Part One of *The Condition of Postmodernity* examines the modernity to postmodernity issue in culture. Part Two outlines the stages of 20th-century capitalism from Fordism to what he calls flexible accumulation (roughly finance capitalism). Part Three concerns the compression of space and time, by which is meant the degree to which new technologies have changed how the spatial and temporal worlds are experienced as closer and faster-moving to the degree that time overwhelms space. Part Four, "Cracks in the mirrors, fusions at the edges," is the conclusion of the argument as to the condition of postmodernity, which ends with the entirely ambivalent statement:

> There are some who would have us return to classicism and others who seek to tread the paths of the moderns. From the standpoint of the

256 *Capitalism's Uncertain Future*

latter, every age is judged to attain 'the fullness of its time, not by being but by becoming.' I would not agree more.[13]

To call this "ambivalence" is not to disparage. Harvey, the urban geographer, aims to take cultural postmodernism seriously, while attending to the way the world is experienced as compressed down from its classically remote and fixed state. Harvey, the Marxist geographer, cannot leave modernism because capitalism is inherently so modern that even its post-Fordist flexibilities does not make something other and radically different.

That Harvey is not by any means a vulgar Marxist is apparent in his *Justice, Nature & the Geography of Difference* (1996), which is, in its way, a *tour de force*. Some might suppose that *The Condition of Postmodernity* suffers from being a bit too schematic as to structure and programmatic as to content. But *Justice, Nature & the Geography of Difference* serves the function of defining the troubling vectors that form an asymptote at some distant point toward which space, time, and nature rise without ever meeting—a point that is no place in particular. Harvey puts it this way: "I try to define a set of workable concepts for understanding space-time, place, and environment (nature)."[14]

For this book, the prefatory text is Adrienne Rich's poem, *An Atlas of the Difficult World*, in which the final lines are:

I promised to show you a map you say but this is a mural
then yes let it be these are small distinctions
where do we see it from is the difference.

This book is more down to earth, in some good part because Harvey's Marxism is wrapped around political issues of which those discussed in Part Four are pivotal: Justice, Difference, and Politics; or, as he defines the concepts in Chapter 12: "Class Relations, Social Justice, and the Political Geography of Difference." These convergent political problems are a result of a straightforward historical fact of capitalism's global expansion. Global capitalism has the effect of creating new places that become "permanences with the flux and flow of capital circulation," a fact central to the geography of capitalism that Harvey develops later on the same page:

New territorial divisions of labor and concentrations of people and labor power, new resource extraction activities and markets form. The geographical landscape which results is not evenly developed but strongly differentiated. "Difference" and "otherness" are *produced* in space through the simple logic of uneven capital investment, a proliferating geographical division of labor, an increasing segmentation of reproductive activities and the rise of spatially ordered (often segregated) social distinctions …[15]

These lines, coming as they do after, again, a careful explanation of facts and concepts necessary to a "political geography of difference," are brilliant, even poetic in an abstract sort of meter. They achieve the necessary ambivalence with which *The Condition of Postmodernity* ended. Harvey repairs the cracks in cultural postmodernism's mirror to reflect just how its high theory of "otherness" and "difference" can be brought down to earth. Marx's vocabulary can be reworked to speak the truth of justice, nature, and a geography of difference. Harvey doesn't go as far as Bruno Latour in collapsing the neoclassical dichotomy nature/culture. Instead, he leaves them as they were received after the 19th century in order to bring environment justice under a new sun (1966, 431): "The work of synthesis has to be on-going since the fields and terrains of struggle are perpetually changing as the capitalist socio-ecological dynamic changes."[16]

No wonder then that the title of his next book *Spaces of Hope* (2000), a collection of published essays and lectures of the 1990s, fills in gaps in his line of thought with topics such as "Uneven geographical developments and universal rights" and "Responsibilities toward nature and human nature." But also, Harvey opens up new topics that once, few, if any, would have expected a serious Marxist to entertain: "The body as an accumulation strategy," and "Body politics and the struggle for a living wage." What the entries in this compendium have in common is precisely, as he says at the first, "The difference a generation makes." This organizing theme owes to the biographical fact that 1998, when the book came together, was the 30th anniversary of 1968 from which he dates his own revolutionary generation, when, for him, "the streets of Baltimore burned" from rioting, as did the streets of Paris, Berlin, Mexico City, and other cities the world over. The hope of a new generation, and those of his who are still engaged, is that they and he will seize "the courage of our own minds and are prepared to take an equally speculative plunge into the unknown." After which, he concludes: "What Marx called 'the real movement' that will abolish 'the existing state of things' is always there for the taking. That is what gaining the courage of our minds is all about."[17]

The year after *Spaces of Hope*, Harvey published another collection of essays *Spaces of Capital: Towards a Critical Geography* (2001) that covers writings more or less in and of the saga of the generation of 1968, from 1974 to 1989, beginning with "Reinventing Geography"—an interview with the editors of the *New Left Review* (previously published by the same group of editors in 2000). The interview itself is instructive because there is no better place to follow Harvey's account of his thinking from *Explanation of Geography* in 1969 to his then present 2000, when, at 65 years, his Marxist geography had achieved a considerable maturity. For example:

> ...While the adaptability of capitalism is one of its prime weapons in class struggle, we should not underestimate the vast swathe of opposition it continues to generate. The opposition is fragmented, often highly localized, and endlessly diverse in terms of aims and methods. We have to think of ways to help mobilize and organize this opposition, both actual and latent, so that it becomes a global force and a global presence.[18]

258 *Capitalism's Uncertain Future*

It would be hard to imagine a more mature political assessment based on years of intellectual and empirical study of capitalism and the world it dominates. As all collections do, the book wanders quite a bit, even as it is packed with *aperçus* such as "Geography is too important to be left to geographers."[19] And, "Geographical knowledges occupy a central position in all forms of political action."[20] The latter crystallizes the former. Disciplines remove those who earn their daily bread from academic writing about the worlds they aim to study. But political actions are always and necessarily on the ground in given spaces.

Most poignant of all his memorable observations occurs in his discussion of the production of spatial organization in the 1985 essay "The Geopolitics of Capitalism," where he appropriates a line from Marx's *Grundrisse*: "Capitalism, Marx concludes, is necessarily characterized by a perpetual striving to overcome all spatial barriers and 'annihilate space with time.'"[21] Though *Spaces of Capital: Towards a Critical Geography*, as a whole, is a disappointment for its disjointed putting together of divergent essays, this one line and its chapter are worth the price of a heavy book. Here, Harvey points us to *Notebook V* in the *Grundrisse* where, more than any other place in Marx's many writings, the point of time–space compression comes sparklingly clear. Unfortunately, in my edition of the *Grundrisse*—which seems to be the same as the one Harvey's cites—I do not find the exact line he quotes, but I could find the longer passage from which the quote is drawn:

> *Circulation time thus appears as a barrier to the production of labour* = an increase in necessary labor time = a decrease in surplus labour time = a decrease in surplus value = an obstruction, a barrier to the self-realization process of capital. Thus, while capital must on the one side strive to tear down every spatial barrier to intercourse, i.e. to exchange, and conquer the whole earth for its market, it strives on the other side to annihilate this space with time, i.e. to reduce to a minimum the time spent in motion from one place to another. The more developed the capital, therefore, the more extensive the market over which it circulates, which forms the spatial orbit of its circulation, the more does it strive simultaneously for an even greater extension of the market and for greater annihilation of space by time.[22]

The passage is so wonderfully literary (even in translation) and, to the point of labor time's space, one wonders why Marx did not include it in Part Five of *Capital I*, where he discusses the working day and surplus value page after page of clumsy formulaic notions meant, one supposes, to make the facts of the matter plain to the common reader when, in fact, it bores the reader to tears. It is to Harvey's enduring credit that in getting to the key passage in Marx he used it to formulate capitalism's compression of time–space as central to its vulgar methods for accumulating capital.

The balance of this chapter in Harvey's *Spaces of Capital* is in effect an *explication de texte* in which he demonstrates, step by step, how the time–space problem works to destructive ends:

> The theoretical argument I have here set out is, I hold, as fundamental to the elucidation of our present plight as it is to the interpretation of the historical geography of capital. *If I am correct, and I hasten to add that I hope I am grossly in error and that history or others will quickly prove me so to be, then the perpetuation of capitalism in the twentieth century has been purchased at the cost of death, havoc and destruction wreaked in two world wars.*[23]

In the two decades since he wrote these lines, Harvey, who turned 85 in 2020, has published a good many books, none of which—so far as I can tell (it is all too much for me to read in the finite time available to an 84-year-old)—gives evidence that he has *not* been proven wrong about capitalism's deadly havoc. Still, in 2005, for example, *A Brief History of Neoliberalism* provides the best history of Neoliberalism from its beginnings early in the 1970s to early in the 2000s begins with a devastating portrayal of what it has wrought (the quote is from Paul Treanor):

> The process of neoliberalization has, however, entailed much 'creative destruction', not only of prior institutional frameworks and powers (even challenging traditional forms of state sovereignty but also of division of labour, social relations, welfare provisions, technological mixes, ways of life and thought, reproductive activities, attachments to the land and habits of the heart. Insofar as neoliberalism values market exchange as 'an ethic in itself, capable of acting as a guide to all human action, and substitution for all previous ethical beliefs', it emphasizes the significance of contractual relations in the marketplace. It holds that the social good will be maximized by maximizing the reach and frequency of market transactions, and it seeks to bring all human into the domain of the market.[24]

It would be hard to say worse about any form of capitalism.

In *Seventeen Contradictions and the End of Capitalism* (2014), Harvey is empirically explicit, as always he is, in describing the then current crises of capitalism. Then, too, as usually he does, Harvey states his purpose, which turns out to be intriguing:

> So what I am seeking here is a better understanding of the contradictions of *capital*, not of *capitalism*. I want to know how the economic engine of *capitalism* works the way it does, and why it might suffer and stall and sometimes appear to be on the verge of collapse. I also want to show why this economic engine should be replaced and with what.[25]

260 *Capitalism's Uncertain Future*

Overlooking the first line which requires the thinking reader to wonder how the contradictions of capital would not entail the same in capitalism, the final sentence is, if not new to him, extraordinarily inviting. Readers may therefore be motivated to immediately skip the book's main chapters on the 17 contradictions and turn to its conclusion "Prospects for a Happy but Contested Future: The Promise of Revolutionary Humanism." Here the reader is, as often before, treated to a wide-ranging discussion of religion and the world religions, of the Renaissance, and much more, before coming to Frantz Fanon to whom he returns often in previous writings—but never quite so warmly as:

> ...[W]hat is so stunning about *The Wretched of the Earth*, and what indeed brings tears to the eyes on a close reading and makes it so searingly human, is the second half of the book, which is taken up by devastating descriptions of the psychic traumas of those on both sides who found themselves forced by circumstances to participate in the violence of the liberation struggle.[26]

The liberation struggle in Africa and wherever it takes place is a struggle (if I may say it this way) not so much about capital as about capitalism's avaricious greed, yes, to extract surplus value, hence capital, wherever it can be had. But where historically it was first had and remains to be had is on the backs of colonized people beginning with the first waves of conquest and colonization in the 16th century, which were unarguably the first seeds of a global capitalism. Of course, Harvey is not naïve on this point even if he surprises by his primary distinction as to where the contradiction resides.

His last line in this book is telling: "There are, as we have seen, enough compelling contradictions within capital's domain to foster many grounds for hope," that is, the hope of those able to cry openly at the suffering caused by capitalism's greed for endless capital accumulation. Those tears may be where a revolutionary humanism begins and ends. Harvey makes the point less succinctly and more fully in *Marx, Capital, and the Madness of Economic Reason*:

> To be sure, capital is not the only possible subject for any thorough and complete reckoning of current ills. But to pretend that it has nothing to do with our current ailments and that we do not need a cogent, as opposed to fetishistic and apologetic representation of how it works, how it circulates and accumulates among us, is an offence that human history, if it manages to survive that long, will judge severely.[27]

Notes

1 Nancy Fraser, *Unruly Practices: Power, Discourse and Gender in Contemporary Social Theory* (Minneapolis: University of Minnesota Press, 1989), 6.

2 *Ibid.*, 137.

Neo-Liberalism 261

3 Nancy Fraser, *Justice Interruptus: Critical Reflections on the "Postsocialist"* (New York and London: Routledge, 1997), 2.

4 Nancy Fraser, "Recognition without Ethics?" *Theory, Culture & Society* 18 (2001): 21.

5 Nancy Fraser, *Scales of Justice: Reimagining Political Space in a Globalizing World* (New York: Columbia University Press, 2010), 15.

6 *Ibid.*, 126.

7 Nancy Fraser, "Mapping the Feminist Imagination: From Redistribution to Recognition to Representation," *Constellations: An International Journal of Critical and Democratic Theory* 12 (2005): 295–307.

8 Nancy Fraser, "Reframing Justice in a Globalizing World," in *Global Inequality: Patterns and Explanations*, eds. David Held and Ayse Kaya (Cambridge: Polity Press, 2007) 252–271.

9 Nancy Fraser, *The Old Is Dying and the New Cannot Be Born* (London: Verso, 2019), 11–16.

10 *Ibid.*, 31–40.

11 *Ibid.*, 33.

12 David Harvey, *The Condition of Postmodernity* (Oxford: Basil Blackwell, 1987), vii.

13 *Ibid.*, 359.

14 David Harvey, *Justice, Nature & the Geography of Difference* (Oxford: Basil Blackwell, 1996), 2.

15 *Ibid.*, 295.

16 *Ibid.*, 431.

17 David Harvey, *Spaces of Hope* (Berkeley: University of California Press, 2000), 255.

18 David Harvey, *Spaces of Capital: Towards a Critical Geography* (New York: Routledge, 2001), 24.

19 *Ibid.*, 116.

20 *Ibid.*, 233.

21 *Ibid.*, 327.

22 Karl Marx, *Grundrisse* (Harmondsworth, Middlesex: Penguin Books [with *New Left Review*] (1973 [1857–58]), 539.

23 *Ibid.*, 343; emphasis added.

24 David Harvey, *Brief History of Neoliberalism* (Oxford: Oxford University Press, 2005), 3.

25 David Harvey, *Seventeen Contradictions and the End of Capitalism* (Oxford: Oxford University Press, 2014), 11.

26 *Ibid.*, 290.

27 David Harvey, *Marx, Capital, and the Madness of Economic Reason* (Oxford: Oxford University Press, 2018), 209–210.

33 The Great Economic Divide and Globalization

Joseph Stiglitz/Jürgen Osterhammel

Joseph Stiglitz (1943–) was born in 1943 in Gary, Indiana. His mother was a schoolteacher and his father an insurance salesman. Stiglitz received his BA from Amherst College in 1964, and then his PhD in Economics from MIT in 1967. After completing his PhD, he held positions at Cambridge, Yale, Oxford, Stanford, Princeton, and Columbia. In 2001, Stiglitz won the Nobel Prize just a year before his best-known book *Globalization and its Discontents* (2002) became a worldwide bestseller.

Globalization and Its Discontents (2002) was published at a time when mainline academic, social policy, and to some extent, popular readers had a seemingly insatiable appetite for books on globalization. Thomas Friedman's popular book *The Lexus and the Olive Tree* (1999) extolled the virtues of globalization in its drive for prosperity and development, while expressing reservations about the ability of individual regions to retain their cultural identity given globalization's tendency to homogenize. This "clash of cultures" thesis presented in Thomas Friedman's book was very much a rehashing of earlier academic arguments presented, for example, in Benjamin Barber's *Jihad vs. McWorld* (1995)[1] and Samuel Huntington's *Clash of Civilizations* (1996). Friedman's optimism about economic globalization was borrowed from scholars and policymakers like Francis Fukuyama (1992),[2] Paul Streeten (1987),[3] John Williamson (1993),[4] who had previously celebrated the unprecedented economic opportunities associated with increased global economic connectedness. *The Lexus and the Olive Tree* (1999) was one of the more popular of many books that saw globalization as a positive development that could potentially eradicate poverty and help people across the globe to improve their lives.

Soon after this "globalization as panacea" discourse reached its peak in the mid-1990s, criticism of the social consequences of so-called "economic globalization" increasingly gained traction. For example, Naomi Klein's *No Logo* (2000)[5]; Dani Rodrik's *Has Globalization Gone Too Far?* (1997)[6]; much of Robert Wade's writings; Noam Chomsky's *Profits Over People* (2011)[7]; and other high-profile public intellectuals began to chime in with their own critiques of globalization and its attendant policies—structural adjustment, deregulation, privatization, and so on. But *Globalization and Its Discontents* (2002) was particularly important as it reached beyond an academic and

DOI: 10.4324/9781003198291-38

left-leaning popular audience, thereby initiating a broad popular conversation on the contradictions of globalization. This book showed more people than ever that, while globalization brought enormous benefits to some, others had been made worse off as a result.[8] Stiglitz's book cut through political partisanship to show people from a range of viewpoints and persuasions that the social consequences of globalization could no longer be ignored if it is truly to bring the benefits its adherents promise.

Stiglitz wrote the book because he was intrigued by how, in the 1990s, not only did people in the developing world protest against austerity programs that were "too harsh," but so did teenagers in the developed world.[9] While perhaps it was a positive development that young people across the globe had strong opinions about free trade agreements, Stiglitz was surprised that the protests young people had "provoked an enormous amount of soul-searching" in the West, and therefore, he believed, a scholarly analysis of the social dislocations associated with globalization was warranted. From 1990 to 2000, Stiglitz notes, the number of people living in poverty increased by 100 million while world income increased by 2.5% annually.[10] These figures indicate that globalization had led to increased inequality. In other words, while profits for mostly Western companies grew, the poor of the developing world were subject to price increases, austerity, and further personal and national indebtedness.

To better understand the process that engendered such inequality, Stiglitz examines the policies of the International Monetary Fund (IMF) and World Bank because, he argues, they had been the primary institutions charged with major global economic issues in the 1980s and the 1990s. Through these two institutions, Stiglitz argues, the richest countries in the world, that largely control and finance international financial institutions, act not in the best interest of the country to which they are providing loans, but in the interest of global capital with which they have strong ties. IMF's austerity measures cut health expenditures, leading to an AIDS crisis in Thailand, for example. They also cut education funding in many countries which increased costs for local families, leading many households in the developing world to choose not to send their daughters to school. These cuts benefited investors financially, but had negative social and economic consequences for the poorest citizens of countries receiving IMF and World Bank loans.

Globalization, defined as increased interconnectedness, Stiglitz rightly points out, is inherently neither "good" nor "bad," but the power relations of who decides how it is put into practice leads to concerns about the "environment, democracy, human rights, and social justice."[11] Rather than focusing on relieving those outcomes, the institutions charged with promoting economic development actually encouraged globalization through privatization, liberalization, and fiscal austerity as ends in and of themselves.[12] The philosophy of these institutions seems to be, in the words of Stiglitz, "what the financial community views as good for the global economy *is* good for the global economy, and should be done."[13] What's missing from the

264 *Capitalism's Uncertain Future*

standard IMF or World Bank policy program is, seemingly, any awareness that further enriching the already wealthy does not translate to an improvement in living conditions for all.

What Stiglitz believes would help to improve economic conditions in the developing world is through a change in governance at international financial institutions like the IMF and World Bank. The United States, and the interests of Wall Street in particular, Stigliz argues, should be diminished and representatives of the developing world should be given a voice in the practices, procedures, and policies of those lending institutions that, in Stiglitz's view, are critical resources for developing countries. Votes at the World Bank are allocated on the basis of economic power. As a result, the countries whose fate is affected by the decisions made by the World Bank have little say in the process.

Toward the end of *Globalization and Its Discontents*, Stiglitz lists the "key reforms required" in order to make the international financial system more just and equal. Many of these concerns still have not been addressed, almost 15 years after Stiglitz first proposed them. They include: (1) awareness that market liberalization and short-term capital flows have externalities and costs beyond the immediate lender and borrower; (2) bankruptcy reform so that the creditor is not also the bankruptcy judge; (3) fewer bailouts; (4) improved banking regulations; (5) improved risk management to mitigate consequences of exchange rate volatility; (6) improved safety nets; and (7) improved response to crisis.[14] Stiglitz also urges the IMF in particular to think more about possible systemic problems with its models along with a plea to direct attention to the "expected poverty and unemployment impact of its programs."[15] Development, proposes Stiglitz, should not be about helping the interests of finance capital in the developing world, nor should it be about creating or further enriching an elite class in cities of the developing world. Development, in Stiglitz's view, "is about transforming societies, improving the lives of the poor, and enabling everyone to have a chance at success and access to health care and education."[16] In other words, development should be about improving social outcomes, not about increasing wealth.

Since 2003, when the United States launched the "War on Terror," academia and policymakers began to lose interest in globalization as a topic. By the 2008 financial crisis, even fewer scholars and policymakers were interested in the study of globalization. Given the increasing chaos and global conflict, the economic exuberance of those who thought that globalization would be a panacea for the global political economy were rendered silent by new events. The IMF and World Bank, as a result, began to rethink development policy. As a result, there was a general sense that the globalization conjuncture had come to a close; that is, until recently, when historians resurrected academic discourse on globalization by thinking of it in historical perspective. Some important scholarly works in this relatively new field include A.G. Hopkins' edited volume *Globalization in World History* (2002),[17]

Barry Eichengreen's *Globalizing Capital* (2008),[18] and Sven Beckert's *Empire of Cotton* (2016).[19]

However, the globalization scholar today who has come closest to making a popular impact akin to Joseph Stiglitz with *Globalization and its Discontents* (2003) is Jürgen Osterhammel. In December 2016, the sales of Osterhammel's *The Transformation of the World: A Global History of the Nineteenth Century* (2014) spiked after English language newspapers picked up the story of how German Chancellor Angela Merkel, when recovering from a ski accident in 2013, decided to read the 1,167-page book from cover to cover. And, as she said in an interview, Merkel's assessment of the book's implications for the present came to exert significant influence on how she views the world and Germany's role in it. The German Chancellor further told the press that she had invited Osterhammel to Berlin to give a private lecture so that she could have the opportunity to learn more from his research.

Jürgen Osterhammel (1952–) was born in 1952 in Wipperfürth, Germany. His father was a physicist and his family emphasized the importance of science. When he was at *gymnasium* in Hanau in the late 1960s, politics became an important question for the young Osterhammel. Both then and today, he said in an interview in *Itinerario*, that history, for him, was rooted in contemporary concerns.[20] As a young student, Osterhammel was influenced by Hegel, Nietzsche, Bertolt Brecht, Heidegger, Sartre, Ernst Bloch, Hannah Arendt, and much of the Frankfurt school. Osterhammel had wanted to study philosophy with Theodor Adorno, but Adorno died in 1969, a year before Osterhammel took his Abitur. Instead, he decided to study in Marburg. His opposition to the War in Vietnam led Osterhammel to take an interest in the Third World, even though the history curriculum at Marburg was German-centric. To broaden his understanding of global history, he read Paul Baran and Immanuel Wallerstein and became influenced by dependency theory.[21] After finishing at Marburg, he went to study at the London School of Economics as a *Studienstiftung des Deutchen Volkes* scholarship holder, where he had more opportunities to explore global history and non-Western history. He received his PhD in modern history in 1980 from the University of Kassel. Currently, Osterhammel is a professor of modern history at the University of Konstanz.

In an interview with *The Guardian* about Merkel's interest in his work, Osterhammel explained how, as an historian, he thinks about globalization:

> I rather prefer to talk of globalisations in the plural, meaning that different spheres of life undergo processes of extension at varying speeds, and with specific reach and intensity. If we cling to the concept of 'globalisation', we should not see it as a continuous and uninterrupted march toward an imaginary 'global modernity'. Globalisation is not a smooth and benign master process such as 'modernisation' used to be construed 50 years ago. It is always uneven, discontinuous, reversible, contradictory, producing winners and losers, no force of nature but manmade.[22]

266 *Capitalism's Uncertain Future*

What Osterhammel and other global historians argue is that the global-ization of the 1990s is just one of several historical periods in which there is increasing global interconnectedness. For a more academic audience, Osterhammel explained that the book "includes all kinds of concepts and theorems without committing itself to any grand theory be it Marxism, or world-system theory, or post-colonialism. My approach is deliberately eclectic."[23]

In the less than a decade from when Stiglitz published *Discontents* (2003) to when Osterhammel published *Die Verwandlung der Welt. Eine Geschichte des 19. Jahrhunderts* (2009), scholarship on globalization underwent a dramatic shift. From debating the positive and negative aspects of unprecedented interconnectedness, the historical turn in globalization studies provided new insights not just into the processes of globalization, but globalization's relationship to the longer history of capitalism. While this historical turn was not led by Osterhammel,[24] his book is perhaps the most popular work that historicizes globalization. Through this historical turn, the globalization debate is no longer an attempt to describe the current conjuncture, but instead it has become a debate on the meaning of capitalism both past and present. By historicizing globalization, Osterhammel and others show that what is really being described by those examining globalization is, in fact, global capitalism. However, Osterhammel finds that "a new synthesis is still lacking," as too many scholars of globalization think only of global capitalism today and not about capitalism in the past.[25] In failing to do so, Osterhammel argues, the globalization literature fails to distinguish between what is new about the current global economy and what is a standard feature of capitalism from its origins. Osterhammel then, based on his study of globalization in the 19th century, provides the reader with eight generalizations about 19th-century capitalism that can help put contemporary capitalism in perspective. He contends that: (1) capitalism is not simply exchange and circulation but also a special organization of production; (2) the goal of capitalism is the accumulation of capital; (3) capitalism leads to the commodification of most, if not all, things and relations; (4) capitalism has the flexibility to use the most productive technologies and organizational forms; (5) states create markets and lead the transition to capitalism; (6) capitalism is closely tied to the state; (7) reshaping the physical environment has been linked to the ability to accumulate capital; and (8) the development of capitalism led to great mobility.[26]

While Stiglitz provided a groundbreaking analysis of the social consequences of global economic policies in the 1990s, by reading Stiglitz as Osterhammel might have us do—that is, from a historical perspective in order to better understand the historical development of global capitalism—would be to see that what Stiglitz is describing is not just social policy for a specific historical moment, but a study that, if historicized, can provide insights into the nature of capitalism by comparing current politico-economic developments to previous parallel moments in history.

Notes

1 Benjamin Barber, *Jihad vs. McWorld* (New York: Times Books, 1995).
2 Francis Fukuyama, *The End of History and the Last Man* (New York: Free Press, 1992).
3 Paul Streeten, "Structural Adjustment: A Survey of the Issues and Options," in *Development Studies: A Reader*, ed. Stuart Corbridge (Oxford: Oxford University Press, 1987).
4 John Williamson, "Democracy and the Washington Consensus," *World Development* 21 (1993): 1329–1336.
5 Naomi Klein, *No Logo* (Toronto: Vintage Canada, 2000).
6 Dani Rodrik, *Has Globalization Gone Too Far?* (Washington: Institute for International Economics, 1997).
7 Noam Chomsky, *Profit over People* (New York: Seven Stories Press, 2011).
8 Joseph E. Stiglitz, *Globalization and its Discontents* (New York: WW Norton and Company, 2002), 253.
9 *Ibid.*, 3–4.
10 *Ibid.*, 5.
11 *Ibid.*, 20.
12 *Ibid.*, 53.
13 *Ibid.*, 195.
14 *Ibid.*, 236–240.
15 *Ibid.*, 240.
16 *Ibid.*, 252.
17 A.G Hopkins, ed., *Globalization in World History* (New York: WW Norton & Co, 2002).
18 Barry Eichengreen, *Globalizing Capital* (Princeton: Princeton University Press, 2008).
19 Sven Beckert, *Empire of Cotton* (New York: Alfred A. Knopf, 2014).
20 Andreas Weber and Jos Gommans, "'You Turn a Page and Then There Is Suddenly Something on a Turtle': An Interview with Jürgen Osterhammel," *Itinerario* 35, no. 3 (2011): 8.
21 *Ibid.*, 10.
22 Osterhammel in Philip Oltermann, "Angela Merkel and the History Book That Helped Her Worldview," *The Guardian* (29 December2016).
23 Osterhammel in Weber and Gommans, "An Interview with Jürgen Osterhammel," 15.
24 One of the earliest attempts to historicize the globalization debate is the 1995 special issue of the journal *International Labor and Working Class History*, in which Charles Tilly, Immanuel Wallerstein, Aristide Zolberg, Eric Hobsbawm, and Lourdes Benería debate the relationship between global capital flows and labor rights.
25 Jürgen Osterhammel, *The Transformation of the World: A Global History of the Nineteenth Century* (Princeton: Princeton University Press, 2014), 669.
26 *Ibid.*, 669–672.

34 The Structural Nature of Capitalism

Joseph Schumpeter/Thomas Piketty

Joseph Schumpeter (1883–1950) was born in Třešť, a small town that was a part of the Austro-Hungarian Empire and today is in the Czech Republic. As a child, his father having died, he and his mother moved to Vienna. Thereafter, he considered himself ethnic German. In time, he earned the PhD at the University of Vienna, after which he became professor of Economics and Politics at the University of Graz. After the Great War, he moved to Germany where he took an initial interest in economic policy in the form of proposing programs for eliminating Germany's war debt. His public presence led him to become president of two different banks, but both ventures ended badly. After teaching at the University of Bonn, he taught at Harvard for a while. In this period, his strong—perhaps even extreme—opposition to anything smacking of socialism inspired him to oppose Franklin Delano Roosevelt's New Deal. Just the same, he rose prominently in the ranks of global economists.

Schumpeter's early economic formation was earned by his affiliation with the German Historical School of Economics, among whom Max Weber and Werner Sombart were younger associates. He worked closely with Weber on editorial projects and wrote an encyclopedia article on him. Sombart was particularly notable for his contribution to the concept of capitalism's *creative destruction*—a concept that Schumpeter deployed in his deep structural idea that capitalism, being an ever-evolving economic system, necessarily destroyed much in order to develop. His very use of such an expression points to the fact that he was, if not a trickster, at least conceptually devilish. Time and again, he wrote of capitalism in terms that those unfamiliar with his larger literary corpus might suppose he was a Marxist of an uncertain kind. Anything but.

In *Capitalism, Socialism and Democracy* (1942), he spent a good portion of the early section analyzing and criticizing Marxism. Where Marx saw the destruction of capitalism as issuing from a worker's revolution from below, Schumpeter saw its destructive force as inherent to capitalism's constant search for new means and modes of growth—to which end the bourgeoisie were a dynamic and positive factor in the economic sphere's relation to the State. As he asserts in *State Imperialism and Capitalism,* his substantial 1919 essay:

> It is in the *state* that the bourgeoisie with its interests seeks refuge, protection against external and even domestic enemies. The bourgeoisie

DOI: 10.4324/9781003198291-39

The Structural Nature of Capitalism   269

seeks to win over the state for itself, and in return serves the state and state interests that are different from its own.[1]

In the same essay, he begins with the remarkable idea that where there is free trade in resources and "foodstuffs," they are traded on a global marketplace even when they serve the needs of a given nature. Then, he adds, without embarrassment: "Where the cultural backwardness of a region makes normal economic intercourse dependent on colonization, it does not matter, assuming free trade, which of the 'civilized' nations undertakes the task of colonization." Then again, this was in 1919. Still, in respect to a fact of capitalism's history:

> Although the relation between capitalists and entrepreneurs is one of the typical and fundamental conflicts of the capitalist economy, monopoly capitalism has virtually fused the big banks and cartels into one. Leading bankers are often leaders of the national economy.

Even here, where Schumpeter is analyzing the place of entrepreneurs in capitalism, he introduces the role of conflict as the nature of beast.

But in the relation between capitalists and entrepreneurs, the conflict is, one might say, remotely connected to Marx's idea of a revolution from below. More to the point, it is a feature that identifies the distinctive role of the entrepreneur. His 1912 book *Theory of Economic Development* is one of the two most enduringly valuable of his many works. Here is where, among much else, Schumpeter identifies the dynamic role of the entrepreneur in economic development: "By 'development,' [therefore], we shall understand only such changes in economic life as are not forced upon it from without but arise by its own initiative, from within."[2] He goes on to clarify that while the producer drives change and the consumer's "wants" are the energic force for change, while the banker is a crucial *tertium quid* in financing the changes, the motive force that brings these together is enterprise. Thus, he adds in the next section of Chapter 2:

> We now come to the third of the elements with which our analysis works, namely the new combination of means of production and credit. Although all three elements form a whole, the third may be described as *the fundamental phenomenon of development*. The carrying out of new combinations we call "enterprise"; the individuals whose function it is to carry them out we call "entrepreneurs."

As a mark of Schumpeter's intellectual originality (and of his relations with Weber), he adds a pungent description of the personal qualities necessary to the entrepreneur, who must have a dream, an impulse to fight to win, and "joy at getting things done," thus: "Our type seeks out difficulties, changes in order to change, delights in ventures. This group of motives is the most distinctly anti-hedonist of the three."

270 *Capitalism's Uncertain Future*

In our day, one might say, we already know this do we not? In a sense we do, and we are likely to assume that the idea is an elaboration of Weber's spirit of capitalism. Yet, it turns out not. In his other most important book, the posthumous *magnum opus*, *History of Economic Analysis* (1954),[3] Schumpeter quibbles with this all-too-easy assumption. Amid some 1,200 pages of deep history and analysis of economic reasoning since the Greeks (completed by his widow Elizabeth Boody, also an economic historian), the patient reader comes upon a surprising passage in a section on the role of the relationship between Feudal economies and the bourgeois class in modern capitalism:

> There was no such thing as a New Spirit of Capitalism in the sense that people would have had to acquire a new way of thinking in order to be able to transform a feudal economic world into a wholly different capitalist one. So soon as we realize that pure Feudalism and pure Capitalism are equally unrealistic creations of our own mind, the problem of what it was that turned the one into the other vanishes completely.

There could not be a sharper disagreement with Weber's *Protestant Ethic and the Spirit of Capitalism.* In a note on this remark, Schumpeter carries on:

> This problem is a typical instance of what may be termed Spurious Problems, that is to say, of those problems that the analyst himself creates by his own method of procedure. For purposes of abbreviated description, we construct abstract pictures of social 'systems' that we endow with a number of well-defined characteristics in order to contrast them sharply. This method of (logically) Ideal Types has, of course, its uses, though it inevitably involves distortion of the facts. But if, forgetting the methodological nature of these constructions, we put the 'ideal' Feudal Man face to face with the 'ideal' Capitalist Man, transition from the one to the other will present a problem that has, however, no counterpart in the sphere of historical fact. Unfortunately, Max Weber lent the weight of his great authority to a way of thinking that has no other basis than a misuse of the method of Ideal Types.

Though this is perhaps too much detail for present purposes, but it serves to illustrate Schumpeter's scrupulous comparative method where, here, he was able to part ways from a fellow associate of the Historical School of the day in order to ferret out fine points of the history and nature of capitalism. The entrepreneur was not a generic new social form of human being in the modern era, but a particular actor among the others—producer, consumer, and banker.

The entrepreneur, Schumpeter instructs us, is in fact an artifact of sociocultural change over the centuries so much as the agent who prods with pleasure the others toward change.

The Structural Nature of Capitalism   271

Schumpeter's general theory of economic change under capitalism is that it arises from within a socioeconomic system, not from outside and not (in his line) a bomb exploding to dismantle a prior stage-making development of a new necessary.

Thomas Piketty (1971–) was born in Clichy, a suburb of Paris on the Seine. His parents were, before his birth, quite leftist and involved in the 'Mai 68 protests. Thomas, however, was not tempted by actual Marxism as practiced in the Soviet Union, though the example of his parents may have inspired his general interest in Marx and Socialism. After an elite education in Paris at the *École Normale Supérieure* (ÉNS), Piketty earned his PhD in wealth distribution and inequality at the London School of Economics, after which he became a professor at MIT, then at the *École des hautes études en sciences* back in Paris. He teaches here now, with a joint position at the Paris School of Economics which he founded in 2006.

Piketty then left academic teaching for a while to advise the French Socialist Party. His own brand of democratic socialism was evident in his writing for the left journal *Libération* (which had been founded by Jean Paul Sartre). Piketty quickly rose to international fame as an economist. He advised the British Labour Party, among such positions. In 2015, he returned as professor to the London School of Economics while renewing his academic positions in Paris, where he published the first of two magisterial books.

Piketty's *Capital in the Twenty-First Century* (2014 [2013]) shook more than a few academic worlds, in some part because of its title. Marxists and others on the left assumed wrongly that *Capital* in the title meant to announce a book about Marx's economic theory. Mainline economic readers and thinkers more accurately assumed it was about the fate of capital growth in *Capital in the Twenty-First Century*. It was; but more, much more.

Piketty's second just as important book *Capital and Ideology* (2020 [2019]) was, if anything, more controversial—a fact weirdly indicated by an early (as of November 2020) *Wikipedia* entry on Piketty's book that says nothing original about the book itself but lists and comments on what must have been all its major or available reviews. This in itself says something about *Capital and Ideology*. It is very long, 1,100 pages or so, and as Idrees Kahloon wrote in the *New Yorker* in March 2, 2020 in "Thomas Piketty Goes Global," the book "broke an (admittedly unsteady) card table and later caused a carry-on to exceed the weight limit on an (admittedly stingy) European airline." Kahloon quickly followed: "There is a reason for the heft." His review is spiced with witty remarks, yet it is favorable and, it seems to me, reliable. This, in contrast to Paul Krugman's "Piketty Turns Marx on His Head" in the *New York Times* (March 8, 2020) that denounced *Capital and Ideology* as way too long while lacking in focus, therefore unreadable, unclear as to the meaning of ideology, and otherwise mistaken or beside the point; this from the almost always reliable Nobel Prize winner Krugman (who had praised Piketty's earlier work on taxation). I bother with these random remarks only

272 *Capitalism's Uncertain Future*

to suggest that Piketty's second book inspires a considerable interest even among ordinary readers who might not have not wanted to take on the task of reading a book close to twice as long as *Capital in the Twenty-First Century's* 600+ pages. Not all will read all.

Both books exhibit the signs of a leading French intellectual who began serious education at the hyper-elite *ÉNS*, where students learn to do and say everything on their subject in the most elegant way possible, while being able and willing upon examination to qualify or correct themselves. Thus, in a response to criticism of *Capital in the Twenty-First Century*, Piketty promptly demonstrated in a nuanced, short 2,015-word article in a prestigious professional journal that he realized there were flaws, but that he did what he could with the data he had:

> My first objective in this book is to present this body of historical evidence, and to try to analyze the many economic, social, and political processes that can account for the various evolutions that we observe in the different countries since the Industrial Revolution. I stress from the beginning that we have too little historical data at our disposal to be able to draw definitive judgments. On the other hand, at least we have substantially more evidence than we used to. Imperfect as it is, I hope this work can contribute to put the study of distribution and of the long run back at the center of economic thinking.[4]

After which, he goes on to defend his notable formula for the point he argues[5]: "That said, the way in which I perceive the relationship between $r > g$ and inequality is often not well captured in the discussion that has surrounded my book." For example, "I do not view $r > g$ as the only or even the primary tool for considering changes in income and wealth in the twentieth century, or for forecasting the path of inequality in the twenty-first century."

Back to *Capital in the Twenty-First Century* itself, what is $r > g$? Piketty defines it right from the start[6] as the divergence in wealth that occurs when r or the rate of growth in investments and dividends, interest and rents, and other aspects of capital itself and g or growth that increases at a *lesser* rate than capital because growth of the economy as a whole is measured by income and productivity. As it turns out, in spite of the algebraic notations, the theory is generally easy to grasp because of the historical details Piketty (a proponent of economics as part of the human sciences, including history) advances. The bulk of the book's 600+ pages is a presentation of that history from, in his words, Old Europe to the New World, then to the Capital-Labor Split in the Twentieth Century. The latter is, evidently, central to his argument. If labor grew at the *same* rate as capital, then $r > g$ does not hold. Piketty then provides graphic displays of evidence, as often he does.[7] In the later 19th century, financial and economic records show that in France and Britain, labor grew at a greater rate than capital. But rather early in the 20th century, especially before, because of, and after the Great War, capital

The Structural Nature of Capitalism 273

investments in industry took off and making the labor sector efficient, thus, in time, reducing the effect of labor as the cause of capital investment. This labor-capital nexus reached its peak between the 1970s and 2010 after beginning earlier with the post-World War II reconstruction in Europe and Asia. Piketty's research allowed him to project[8] the already extreme income inequality between the upper classes (in the United States) of 75% and the lower class of 15%. This range is less than the Occupy Wall Street Movement of 2011 because its 99%–1% figures were about wealth, of which the lower classes have almost none (except for the relatively few who own homes) and the higher classes have a seemingly ever-increasing share.[9]

From so simple a summary, it might be hard to say, as commentators like Kahloon and Krugman have, why so many pages? The answer, for better or worse, is that the narrative line of the book is replete with discussions of the data *and* the economic literature on his subject, not to mention his references to just how a reading of Jane Austen and Honoré de Balzac novels get capital wrong because they tell stories only of rent and land wealth.

In the end, Piketty provides a balanced judgment of the contradiction in $r > g$:

> The overall conclusion of this study is that a market economy based on private property, if left to itself, contains powerful forces of convergence, associated in particular with the diffusion of knowledge and skills; but it also contains powerful forces of divergence, which are potentially threatening to democratic societies and to the values of social justice on which they are based. ... The principal destabilizing force has to do with the fact that the private rate of return on capital r, can be significantly higher for long periods of time that the rate of growth of income and output, g.[10]

These high-minded and sincerely expressed ideals of liberal and humanist hope for democratic societies led him in the same concluding section to propose a solution, namely "a progressive annual tax on capital." Piketty recognizes the extreme difficulty here, that: "the progressive tax on capital, requires a high level of international cooperation and regional political integration." So bold and broad a proposal requires a second book that diagnoses and explains how such a radical solution can be had. For those who fail to appreciate all the numeric and other sorts of economic science, they should keep well in mind Piketty's oft-repeated insistence that economics, if a science, is a human science.

Capital and Ideology starts right off with the clearest possible statement of his purpose based on underlying social justice principles:

> From this historical analysis one important conclusion emerges: what made economic development and human progress possible was the struggle for equality and education and not the sanctification of property,

274 *Capitalism's Uncertain Future*

stability, or in equality. The hyperinegalitarian narrative that took hold after 1980 was in part a product of history, most notably the failure of communism. But it was also the fruit of ignorance and of disciplinary division in the academy. The excesses of identity politics and fatalist resignation that plague us today are in large part consequences of that narrative's success. By turning to history from a multi disciplinary perspective, we can construct a more balanced narrative and sketch the outlines of a new participatory socialism for the twenty-first century. By this I mean a new universalistic egalitarian narrative, a new ideology of equality, social ownership, education, and knowledge and power sharing. This new narrative presents a more optimistic picture of human nature than did its predecessors—and not only more optimistic but also more precise and convincing because it is more firmly rooted in the lessons of global history.[11]

It would be hard to imagine opening lines that so succinctly précis the need, its reason, and what is to be done in respect to *a new participatory socialism*. He could not be more emphatic as to the degree to which his economics is a human science; in addition, being persistently historical is also political and philosophical. In the end, Piketty turns to John Rawls *Theory of Justice* (1971) for the outline of his theory of social justice:

A just society is one that allows all of its members access to the widest possible range of fundamental goods. Fundamental goods include education, health, the right to vote, and more generally to participate as fully as possible in the various forms of social, cultural, economic, civic, and political life. A just society organizes socioeconomic relations, property rights, and the distribution of income and wealth in such a way as to allow its least advantaged members to enjoy the highest possible life conditions. A just society in no way requires absolute uniformity or equality.[12]

But he quickly turns to the help he received "...from hundreds of citizens, researchers and journalism in many countries... [who gave him] access to previously closed sources in Brazil, India, South African, Tunisia, Lebanon, Ivory Coast, Korea, Taiwan, Poland, and Hungary and, to a lesser extent, China and Russia.

Piketty means to get beyond the Euro-American bias of his first book and to make good on a truly global theory that might justify his idea of a participatory social justice again to inequality. The 1,000+ pages following are filled with those data and the analyses that are too many to summarize here. But his conclusions, in their coherence, suggest just how well they have informed his thinking.

The substance of his argument and the majority of *Capital and Ideology*'s many pages begins with a well-documented history of "The Inequality

The Structural Nature of Capitalism   275

Regimes of History" (Parts 1 and 2), from ternary societies (clerical and religious, noble and warrior, and common laboring classes) to slave and colonial societies (including mixed and persistent cases like India), up to (in Part 3) "The Great Transformation of the Twentieth Century" that gave rise to the global inequalities of our times.

In *Capital and Ideology*, Piketty makes up for the necessary sketchiness of the conclusion to *Capital in the Twenty-First Century* with ample discussions of his several proposals,[13] each of which is stated with an historical example or a probable historical outcome. The first proposal is the experiment of sharing power in firms that began in Germanic and Nordic Europe early in the 1950s, where workers who owned no capital served in government or on corporate boards. He admits[14] however that progressive wealth taxes, as the first-order method for increasing the circulating of capital, are a challenge due to the difficulty of preventing "unlimited concentration of ownership which does not serve the general interest." Then, he points to the history that early in the late modern era of progressive wealth, an inheritance tax had a leveling effect, especially in Europe, but one insufficient to level the differences in Europe between 2010 and 2020 but not in the United States. Still, the ideal is to create a "universal endowment" by international taxes on property, inheritance as well as income. After careful presentation of the actual and projected evidence, Piketty admits that this is a hard row to how, but possible. He offers[15] in table 17.1 a suggestion of how the endowment derived, at least, from capital taxation might lead to the just society he seeks.

As still another sign of his realistic politics, he admits that the first-order challenge will be writing "fiscal justice into the Constitution," especially in America and even in Europe. Here again, he returns to a theory of *political* economy:

> All the historical trajectories we have looked at in this book show how intimately the structure of inequality is related to the nature of the political regime. Whether we were looking at premodern trifunctional societies or nineteenth century proprietarian societies or slave societies or colonial societies, it was the way political power was organized that allowed a certain type of inequality regime to persist. People sometimes think that the political institutions of Western society achieved a kind of unsurpassable perfection in the parliamentary democracy of the mid twentieth century. In fact, one can certainly improve on the parliamentary democratic model, which is increasingly contested.[16]

Again he qualifies by admitting that this will require what he calls "just democracy" with "just borders," or "Rethinking Social Federalism on a Global Scale." Piketty realizes that this may be the biggest hurdle of all because of the ability of the global economy to reshape the classical political models of democracy from a nation-state ideology to a global one. Yet, as he said at the beginning: "Every society, every inequality regime, is characterized by a set

276 *Capitalism's Uncertain Future*

of more or less coherent and persistent answers to these questions about its political and property regimes." This may well be one of the points where Krugman has doubts about the accuracy of his definitions and merit of all his ideas. Still, Piketty, the *ÉNS* student, does not give up on his disposition to look to the possible post-empirical social values that can make the world a better place. In the end, he writes of history itself:

> The history of inequality cannot be reduced to an eternal clash between oppressors of the people and proud de fenders [*sic*]. On both sides one finds sophisticated intellectual and institutional constructs. To be sure, on the side of the dominant groups, these constructs are not always devoid of hypocrisy and reflect a determination to remain in power, but they still need to be studied closely. Unlike the class struggle, the struggle of ideologies involves shared knowledge and experiences, respect for others, deliberation, and democracy. No one will ever possess the absolute truth about just ownership, just borders, just democracy, just taxes and education. The history of human societies can be seen as a quest for justice. Progress is possible only through detailed comparison of personal and historical experiences and the widest possible deliberation.[17]

Some in this age, where humanistic philosophy is so lost to the common mind, may reject such a broadly noble if not completely scientific judgment. But, if there is progress of any good kind, it must look to a future that is not yet.

Whatever the uncertain future of capitalism may be, thinkers like Schumpeter and Piketty have recommended where its dynamic and enduring elements can be found. In Schumpeter's case, well after his death, the entrepreneur who became more than he could have imagined, as Piketty and others would—entrepreneurs of excellent education, technical skills, and access to cybernetic tools. Piketty, later by a generation, knew all this and more. Being French rather than Austro-German, he gave in to the philosophical possibilities that realistically *could be* beyond what is known in political, economic, and historical fact.

Notes

1 Joseph Schumpeter, "State Imperialism and Capitalism," reprinted in *Imperialism and Social Classes*, Paul Sweezy (Fairfield: August M. Kelley, 1954 [1919]).
2 Joseph Schumpeter, *The Theory of Economic Development* (Cambridge: Harvard University Press, 1934 [1912]), Chapter 2.
3 Joseph Schumpeter, *History of Economic Analysis* (Oxford: Oxford University Press, 1954).
4 Thomas Piketty, "About *Capital in the Twenty-First Century*," *American Economic Review: Papers & Proceedings* 105, no. 5 (2015): 48.
5 Thomas Piketty, *Capital in the Twenty-First Century* (Cambridge: Harvard University Press, 2014 [2013]), 25.
6 *Ibid.*, 25.

7 *Ibid.*, 200–201.
8 *Ibid.*, 246–250.
9 *Ibid.*, 375–376.
10 *Ibid.*, 571.
11 Thomas Piketty, *Capital and Ideology* (Cambridge: Harvard University Press, 2020 [2019]), 3.
12 *Ibid.*, 967–968.
13 Beginning at *Ibid.*, 972.
14 *Ibid.*, 975.
15 *Ibid.*, 982.
16 *Ibid.*, 1022–1023.
17 *Ibid.*, 1035.

35 Capitalism and the Environmental Crisis

Henry David Thoreau/William Nordhaus

Henry David Thoreau (1817–1862) was born in Concord, Massachusetts, where he died in his 42nd year. Save for a few years infancy when his family lived in Chelmsford, then Boston and his years at Harvard College, Thoreau lived in Concord his whole life. Concord was home even when he was away on his well-known trips—to the Maine Woods and Mt Katahdin; Mt Monadnock and Mt Washington; a trip in 1850 to Canada and the St. Lawrence River; North on the Concord and Merrimack Rivers with his brother; Fire Island to search for the remains of Margaret Fuller who drowned offshore with her Italian husband and their child; up and down the River between Wayland and Billerica for a commissioned survey of all the bridges on the Concord River; and of course for his many lyceum lectures throughout the Northeast.

It hardly need be said that Thoreau is famous the world over for *Walden*, which began with his declaration of independence from the world as it was becoming:

> When I wrote the following pages, or rather the bulk of them, I lived alone in the woods, a mile from any neighbor, in a house which I built myself, on the shore of Walden Pond, in Concord, Massachusetts, and earned my living by the labor of my hands only.

Though indeed he returned to civilization—and regularly visited town while living on the Pond, once to get arrested for failure to pay taxes—life at Walden Pond from 1845 to 1847 stood for him as the measuring rod for life as it ought to be lived, as distinct from lives as they were lived in town and beyond. One of his better-known lines from the book is a sharp criticism of civilized life: "The mass of men lead lives of quiet desperation."

Walden was anything but a personal memoir. In fact, Thoreau used his two years, two months, and two days in the woods by a pond as a token of everything in the world that should be avoided. In 1847, he returned to live in town where he solidified his friendships with Ralph Waldo Emerson, Margaret Fuller, and the remarkable group of writers and intellectuals, including Louisa May Alcott and Nathaniel Hawthorne, that made Concord the town that gave Susan Cheever the title to her book *American Bloomsbury*.

DOI: 10.4324/9781003198291-40

Thoreau was in the thick of all this, even while attending, as best he could, to a degree of solitary life.

Walden is a work of critical social theory. But critical of what? There is no single answer. Among his targets were slavery, especially the Fugitive Slave Law; mundane life that was preoccupied with news of the wider world; the infusion of the modern-thinking people who thought nothing of the Tahatawan people who had farmed the land for hundreds of years; and of the first English settlers who brought with them premodern farming methods. Then, too, Concord was already becoming what it is now—a suburb of Boston, linked to the city by train and trails. Laura Dassow Walls puts this range of critical topics clearly in her *Thoreau: A Life*:

> ...[T]horeau witnessed the final collapse of this two-hundred-year old system. When he went to Walden Pond in 1845 change was visible everywhere: the new railroad cut right across Walden's prettiest cove; the subsistence farms failing, eroded away by the global marketplace. Few of his neighbors still ate "rye 'n' Injun" bread, or wore homespun "linsey-woolsey." Now they cooked on stoves, heated with coal, built with Maine white pine, cut their woodlots to fuel the railroads, planting them in English hay to feed new breeds of cattle they slaughtered for the Boston market and packed for the West Indies. They filled their pantries with China tea, slave-grown sugar, prairie wheat flour, tropical oranges and pineapples; they wore Georgia cotton, China silks, Canada furs, British woolens.[1]

So, in one sense, Thoreau was a critic of the modern world as it was invading Concord and, by implication, the simpler life in small towns and country villages.

In *Walden*, Thoreau is clear as to his purpose by the Pond:

> I went to the woods because I wished to live deliberately, to front only the essential facts of life, and see if I could not learn what it had to teach, and not, when I came to die, discover that I had not lived.

This is the familiar declaration from the second chapter *Where I Lived, and What I Lived For. Walden* that began with an introduction, *Economy*, in which he described in precise detail how cheaply he could live in a cabin made by his own hands. *Economy* must be read as a stern critique of capitalism's dangerous excesses: "Most of the luxuries, and many of the so-called comforts of life, are not only not indispensable, but positive hindrances to the elevation of mankind." Comments like this are one reason that Thoreau is rightly respected for speaking out on important public issues in his day in shorter essays: *Slavery in Massachusetts, A Plea for Captain John Brown,* and *Civil Disobedience* (an attack on taxation policies).

280 *Capitalism's Uncertain Future*

But the most systematic of his critical theories is buried in a controversial chapter in *Walden, The Bean-Field*. Thoreau was clear about his narrative strategy. *Walden* was composed so as to condense his more than two years at the Pond into a single year of seasons. A first glance at the table of contents can disguise this story line under all the other of its narrative lines: a series of random topics: *Reading, Sounds, Solitude, Visitors*; an apparent series on local geography: *The Bean-Field, The Village, The Ponds, Baker Farm*; then, oddly: *Higher Laws*, which turns out to be a low-key transcendentalist exposition; after which *Brute Neighbors* is an unusual sequel to *Higher Laws* because it is a most particular commentary on his observations of the vicissitudes of animal life surrounding the Pond. Then, finally, amid all this the careful reader discerns the seasonal line with chapters on *Housewarming, Winter Visitors, Winter Animals, The Pond in Winter, Spring. Housewarming* is the autumnal essay in which the focus is on the chimney he built and the wood gathered for heat for the coming winter. Then, in time, the story of this year passed on to spring, unqualifiedly *Spring*. But, if the underlying scheme of the book is the four seasons, where is summer?

In this story of many twists and turns, summer is covered by the book's most controversial chapter *The Bean-Field*, which is the hook on which hangs the fictional frame of *Walden* as an annual cycle of events in his story of his life apart from civil society. *The Bean-Field* begins, however, in a strange way: "Meanwhile my beans, the length of whose rows, added together, was seven miles already planted...." Seven miles of beans in two and a half acres? Obviously far beyond what anyone could eat even in a year. Plus which, his bean field by the side of the road exposed him to rebuke for the time of the planting: "Beans too late! Peas so late!"—comments that were pointedly more than passing observations. The field side complaints are at the center of the controversy.

Thoreau wrote *The Bean-Field* chapter as a response to Henry Colman, a one-time Unitarian minister who turned to the surveying of crop lands in Massachusetts, whereupon he became an authority on agriculture in the East. Colman meant to justify farming in Massachusetts by a method Thoreau strenuously opposed. Colman argued that farmers, even in the East, could be more productive if they would learn to apply scientific methods of cultivation. Thoreau would have nothing of it. His bean field was, he wrote, "one field not in Mr. Colman's report." In a journal entry of March 7, 1847, Thoreau explains that his attitude toward the field was also a response to actual scientific farmers who in the winter swooped down "on our pond—with many car-loads of ungainly-looking farming tools, sleds, ploughs, drill-barrows, turf-knives, spades, saws, rakes, and each man was armed with a double-pointed pike-staff... as if they were bent on making this a model farm." *The Bean-Field* chapter is only apparently a simple story of farming in the summer of 1846, when in fact it is a political manifesto of the extent to which then modernizing science is ruining local well-being.

Thus it is that *The Bean-Field* appears in *Walden* as the summer anchor in its annual cycle of life on the pond. *The Bean-Field* turns out be a running critical assault not just on Henry Colman's model farm but even more on the coming of scientific agribusiness. The chapter ends:

> The true husbandman will cease from anxiety, as the squirrels manifest no concern whether the woods will bear chestnuts this year or not and finish his labor with every day and sacrificing in his mind not only his first but his last fruits.

No one would blame those who read this as hopelessly naive. But then again, this could be radical anti-Anthropocene politics.

Walden was published in 1854 when the Kansas-Nebraska Act fixed the nation's destiny on a civil war of four bloody years in which the industrial capitalism on the American North defeated and all but ended the feudal system of the enslaved South that, in its way, was a form of industrial agribusiness when the cotton gin mechanized cotton production. The nation had long before been headed toward this conjuncture wherein modern industrial capitalism changed everything—not just in America but the world over. It was then that the Anthropocene, which, though it had to wait more than a century for its name, thrust itself on a human world, a world that, as Thoreau understood, would be less human than it had been. The Anthropocene is a world in which man takes over and dominates the earth, its plant and vegetable life, its animal husbandry, its forests—all of which and more are depleted to the end of their coming destruction. The Anthropocene is post-geological and post-human because it is domination not by free and critical human beings but by an avaricious capitalism that cares about nothing but surplus values that abolish living and breathing human values.

William D. Nordhaus (1947–) was born in Albuquerque, New Mexico. He went to Phillips Andover Academy in Andover, Massachusetts, after which he studied at Yale for BA and MA degrees. There too, Nordhaus was a member of the hyper-prestigious but secretive Skull and Bones Society. In 1967, he completed the PhD in Economics at MIT, and later joined the faculty at Yale. Here, apart from being a world-class scholar, Nordhaus served as a regular participant in collegial seminars, as Provost and Vice President for Finance and Administration, and many other ways. He has been a visiting associate at the *Instituts d'études politiques* in France and a fellow of Clare Hall, Cambridge University, and numerous similar positions the world over. All this in addition to service to the United States government as a member of The Council of Economic Advisors to President Jimmy Carter as well as a member of the board of the Boston Federal Reserve Bank—not to mention election to academically highly regarded positions, such as President of the American Economic Association and Member of the National Academy of Sciences.

282 *Capitalism's Uncertain Future*

One might ask how anyone could do all this while remaining a very nice person and still doing the kind and degree of scholarly work that caused him to be awarded the Nobel Prize in Economic Science in 2018 for, in the words of the announcement, "integrating climate change into long-run macroeconomic analysis." On the day of the announcement, Professor Nordhaus was cheered by his students who admire him, but even more, he turned his honor back to Yale for the way, from his student days to the years of work with colleagues and students, his 20 books and more articles than one can imagine, Yale nurtured him and provided an environment in which his creative scholarship could thrive.

For many, the scholarship culminated in more-or-less accessible books like *The Climate Casino: Risk, Uncertainty, and Economics for a Warming World* (2013), which begins:

> I will use the metaphor that we are entering the Climate Casino. But this I mean economic growth is producing unintended but perilous changes in the climate and earth systems. These changes will lead to unforeseen but probably dangerous consequences. We are rolling the climatic dice the outcome will produce surprises, and some of them are likely to be perilous. But we have just entered The Climatic Casino, and there is still time to turn around and walk back out.[2]

These lines were written in 2013. In the 2020s, it may be too late to walk back the game that, beyond Nordhaus's metaphor, some would say is the risk of capitalism's bet that the world will produce economic growth more or less forever. Nordhaus would not put it this way; he is far too much the economic scientist who attends to the quantitative evidence. Still, in 2013 he knew we were playing a dangerous game.

The analysis in *The Climate Casino* is true to the book's subtitle *Risk, Uncertainty, and Economics for a Warming World*. Early in the first chapter, Nordhaus introduces his model for the risks, possible solutions, and economics of climate change. The reader soon comes upon a diagnostic model that sketches the basic steps from the economic causes of climate change to its specific impacts, and how these impacts lead to natural and economic consequences which, in turn, lead to *possible* policies that *might*, in turn, ameliorate the original climate crisis. More specifically, cyclical model present four causal and possibly effective factors. They are, first, "economic growth leads to CO_2 emissions (driving, heating and cooling, air travel, …)." Then, second, "rising CO_2 concentrations and other forces lead to climate change (temperature, precipitation, sea-level rise, …)" that, third, cause a degree of climate change "[that] imposes ecological and economic impacts (lower corn yields, coastal flooding, ocean acidification, …)." But here, with the fourth turn of the vicious circle, Nordhaus begins to make the best possible case for climate change: "Climate change policies reduce emissions (cap-and-trade, carbon taxes, regulations, …)." Of course, Nordhaus is not naïve, and certainly he does not suppose that between the third turn on causes and fourth on policies—and by implication, the fourth on the expectation that policy *might* change the economy of carbon emissions. A Casio model necessarily entails a gamble with no sure outcomes. These are *possibilities*.

Nordhaus still today bets on his Casino model, *The circular flow of global warming, science, and policy*, which is also at the heart of his 2018 acceptance speech at the Nobel Prize ceremonies in Sweden and central to a 2020 lecture in Zurich, "The Economics of Climate Change." He is humble about the Casino Model. In respect to its simplicity, Nordhaus acknowledges that there are other models that integrate many more variables. This, in itself, is symptomatic of his desire to make his essential points available to the general public. But this should not be taken as simplicity of mind or method.

One example of the elevated empirical and mathematical language behind his thinking is Nordhaus's 2000 book with Joseph Boyer *Warming the World: Economic Models of Global Warming*, which concludes with a plain spoken and optimistic statement:

> The slower pace of future climate change is a hopeful but cautionary note to end on. Perhaps the reader can rest more soundly with the current evidence that climate change in the coming century is unlikely to enter the catastrophic range, particularly if effective steps are taken to slow climate change. The size of the revisions in the projections in the last decade and the fact that they come from so many different sources, however, are reminders of the enormous uncertainties that society faces in understanding and coping with the climate-change problem. So while we may sleep more soundly at night, we must be vigilant by day for changes that might lead our globe.[3]

Yet, Nordhaus does not pull his punches. Even the genial Nobel Prize lecture turns on the serious problems noted by the question marks in his Casino model.

First and foremost is the challenge of the climate reduction. Though Nordhaus, quite understandably, does not get into the role of capitalism in thwarting climate control, the leftish reader will have no trouble making the connection. Since, as he says, "climate change imposes ecological *and economic* impacts," the environmental crisis is necessarily tied to the global capitalist world economy. Floods, rising sea levels, fires, acidification of the oceans, crop failures are among the more newsworthy indices of the extent to which carbon fuels and carbon derivatives like plastic are warming the world. In a rare slip into technical language when speaking to the general public, he says in the Nobel Lecture: "Global warming is the colossus of all externalities." He further dramatizes the assertion with a Goya painting in the Prado of an enormous monster looming over frightened villagers fleeing for their lives. The point is that such a looming threat to the global environment runs up against the economic and social cost of reducing carbon emissions.

284 *Capitalism's Uncertain Future*

The economic costs of a total shift from carbon to renewable fuels are expensive (to say the least) because they are driven by capital-seeking corporations and their political allies that will not readily give up their investments of fossil fuels. Then, too, there are social costs, including the wrenching undermining of established practices, of which job loss is perhaps the most dramatic. Then, too, the economic and the social costs verge into one when floods and fires destroy homes along the coasts and their inland forests. Costs of this magnitude affect capital markets, not to mention markets for capital goods, homes, cars, travel.

The ideal global accord for CO_2 reduction is a maximum increase of CO_2 of not more than 2°C, which is all-but-impossible in anything like a short run. At one point, he suggests that the target must be measured against a timeline of a century or more. Then, too, also in the Nobel Lecture, another barrier to CO_2 reduction is the free-rider problem. Some nations will meet the goal in time, others won't; but those who refuse to join in will still gain the benefit of global reduction in emissions. Even if all but one of the just less than 200 nations participate (as in the Paris Accords), the withholding of a single large nation (such as the United States after 2017 can negatively affect the global situation. For which Nordhaus offers the idea of a Climate Club of nations that bear the cost of global reduction from which nonmembers enjoy the benefits. This Club can bill the free dues covering the benefits of the Club. These are primary cap-and-trade that has been resisted, but also tariffs that, he says, work in the following way:

> Non-members are penalized through tariffs. • Proposal here involves a regime with two features: – Target carbon price, say \$50 per ton CO_2 – Penalty tariff on non-participants, say 3% uniform • So the "dues" to the club are expensive abatement, while the "penalties" for non-membership are tariffs on exports to the club region.

In a 2020 lecture "The Economics of Climate Change," Nordhaus offers much the same argument with a striking clarification. To reach the 2°C goal, the world would have to reach zero admissions around 2040. To meet anything like this goal the world would have to settle for a 4°C change. Nordhaus is realistic in the way a rigorous scientist can be—by following the facts and the mathematics by which they can make interpretable sense to the public. When the facts are foreboding, they must be faced for what they are.

In one sense, Henry David Thoreau and William Nordhaus could not be farther apart—not just in time but also in method. Thoreau wrote stories. Nordhaus wrote equations. Just the same, differences aside, each took on what was for them, in their different times, a looming crisis of the Anthropocene Age. For Thoreau it was the awful disruption of local life by the merciless rise of capitalism—its consumption of agricultural practices and market cultures of all kinds. For Nordhaus the crisis is the asymptote of a carbon-dependent global economy.

Notes

1 Laura Dassow Walls, *Thoreau: A Life* (Chicago: University of Chicago Press, 2017), 8.
2 William D. Nordhaus, *The Climate Casino: Risk, Uncertainty and Economics for a Warming World* (New Haven: Yale University Press, 2013), 1.
3 William D. Nordhaus and Joseph Boyer, *Warming the World: Economic Models of Global Warming* (Cambridge: MIT Press, 2000), 178.

36 Silenced and Wasted Lives in the Capitalism Order

Gayatri Chakravorty Spivak/Zygmunt Bauman

Gayatri Chakravorty Spivak (1942–) was born in Kolkata, India, to a middle-class family. Her father, a physician; mother, a social and charity activist. To Gayatri's chagrin, they were Brahmin but, as she says, at least their standing was of a lesser rank in the caste. In her early years, she was educated at the British missionary school, St John's Diocesan Girls' Higher Secondary School, before studying at Presidency College, a public Hindu university, then at the University of Calcutta before graduate studies at Cornell University—from a colonizer's primary school to a Hindu higher education to an Ivy League graduate school. In a sense these facts of her family's status and education typifies a life lived, to date, always in transition, always going somewhere. While doing extraordinarily complicated academic work, Spivak somehow also maintained her allegiance to Marxist thought and practice. In "Always Creating a Stir Wherever She Goes," a 2002 *New York Times* feature on Spivak, her mother, an avid reader of her daughter's work, is reported to have said, after finishing her long preface to and translation of Jacques Derrida's Of Grammatology, "But dear, how are you going to reconcile your communism with this?"

Spivak's preface to Derrida's *Of Grammatology* won her the early acclaim that in time became all but universal in the academic world. Yet, her work was also greeted with skepticism, even consternation, for the shockingly obscure ideas that confused the faint of heart. *Of Grammatology* was the book where Derrida detailed his famous concept of deconstruction, which is often wrongly used to mean "take apart." In fact, it means something far more subtle—roughly, as Derrida put it, deconstruction is meant to put all concepts "under erasure." By this he means to say that the apparent meaning of concepts is a mash up of conflicting, often opposing, meanings; as a result, they can only make honest sense when the received and assumed meanings are erased in order that their many and deeper meanings can be used with respect for their different, often unavailable, meanings. One example would be capitalism (a term that Spivak herself would deconstruct in later writings). Capitalism is normally used by those faithful to its ideological promises to refer to a singularly coherent and progressively good modern economic system in which free markets are its driving force. In fact, actual capitalisms never were anything like this absurdly simple concept, as Marx

DOI: 10.4324/9781003198291-41

was the first to demonstrate in *Capital I*. In a fashion, it is not far wrong to say that capitalisms are anything but what they are commonly thought to be. To deconstruct any such macro-concept, one must erase its given meaning so it can be used to describe a much more complex state of historical affairs.

Gayatri Spivak's 91-page Translator's Preface to Of Grammatology is, in a sense, a deconstruction of Derrida's concept of writing, another key concept. Writing, however, is not limited to written texts. Rather, writing also refers to all the ways the face of the earth is disfigured or decorated—by roadways, monuments, buildings, farms, tunnels, and more, almost endlessly. Hence, grammatology is a sort of science of all human inscriptions. Writing thus is quite the opposite of speaking. Speech assumes, even requires, a presence—the one who speaks. Writing, by contrast, works on the fact that the source of writing is always necessarily absent. Whether the texts are letters found in historical archives or hiking trails in the woods or anything of the like, who may have first inscribed them is lost to those who read or follow them. They are, strange to say, present even as they are removed from the scene of the writing.

Spivak, in one of her more accessible passages in her Preface, describes Derrida's ironic notion of writing as a present/absence for which she refers to his deployment of Freud's theory of the dream as a trace:

> [Derrida] emphasizes the presence of Freud in what comes close to becoming Derrida's master concept — "differance" spelled with an "a." Let us fasten on three moments in [in his use of the term] — "differing," deferring," and "detour." I have spoken of the radically other, which is always different, nonidentical. Add to this the structure of perennial postponement of that which is constituted only through postponement. The two together — "difference" and "deferment"— both senses present in the French verb "différer," and both "properties" of the sign under erasure — Derrida calls "differance." This difference—being the structure (a structure never being quite there, never by us perceived, itself deferred and different) of our psyche — is also the structure of "presence," a term itself under erasure. For difference, producing the differential structure of our hold on "presence," never produces presence as such.[1]

Even the faithful reader might well be put-off as much by Spivak's commentary as by Derrida's original. They are "put-off" in the sense that the language of deconstruction can never be clear because the meanings can never be present "as such."

Think about it this way: Is not capitalism one of the structures with and in which we must live? Yet where is it? Is capitalism—the thing itself—ever present to us any more than any other social structure is? No. It is always different from us and comes to us deferred. We may work for a capitalist enterprise, but those we work with are not capitalism any more than are the

288 *Capitalism's Uncertain Future*

corporations or markets or schools that serve the capitalist system without being present in its structural nature. Capitalism is always absent to its workers and even to its bosses. On this central feature of all structures, Spivak is able to be somewhat less opaque in her book *An Aesthetic Education in the Era of Globalization*:

> Capital is a writing, which we must not read merely in terms of producing objects for use, a few for ourselves and many more for others, and not being given enough money to get more for ourselves. Reading the archives of capitalism, Marx produces a critique, not of cultural, but of economic politics—hence a critique of political economy, of political economism. In the current global postcolonial context, our model must be a critique of political culture, political culturalism, whose vehicle is the writing of readable histories, mainstream or alternative. I think it might be useful to write power in Marx this way: "power is the name one attributes to a complex strategical situation—the social relations of production—forming a particular society, where society is shorthand for the dominance of [a] political mode of production.[2]

Here is the answer to Gayatri Spivak's mother's question about her Derrida book. Her own deconstruction of Derrida's main concepts entails a number of different methods (if that is the word). For one, she in effect tries to enter into Derrida's own conceptual system. For another, as in the quoted passages here on Freud and Marx, she "read" out these two figures and others, notably Nietzsche, Heidegger, Saussure, Husserl, Jakobson, Lacan, Lévi-Strauss, Hegel, Rousseau. Yet, her "reading" was not, as you would expect, reading in the common sense of the activity, so much as an insertion of her text into the body of Derrida's text which, in turn, is not linearly present; not an argument; nor an exegesis. Reading, in this sense, allows the primary source (here, Derrida's French text) to stand on its own, available for a reading that itself cannot be page by page as if following a plot. In the day, many of Derrida's followers popularized reading as a way of coming to terms with a structured set of events, as in: How do you read what they did? Not: What do you think of what they did?

Gayatri Spivak has a good many intellectual and political projects. She may not, as her mother wondered, even be Derridean, however much she may have benefitted from the early work on his ideas. About a decade after the Derrida translation, she wrote about her feminism in *In Other Words* in relatively plain language:

> I cannot speak of feminism in general. I speak of what I do as a woman within literary criticism. My own definition of a woman is very simple: it rests on the word "man" as used in texts that provide the foundation for the corner of the literary criticism establishment that I inhabit. You

might say at this point, defining the word "woman" as resting on the word "man" is a reactionary position. Should I not carve out an independent definition for myself as a woman? Here I must repeat some deconstructive lessons I have learned over the past decade that I often repeat. One, no rigorous definition of anything is ultimately possible, so if one wants to, one could go on deconstructing the opposition between man and woman, and finally show that it is a binary opposition that displaces itself. Therefore, as a "deconstructivist," I cannot recommend that kind of dichotomy at all, yet, I feel that definitions are necessary in order to keep us going, to allow us to take a stand. The only way that I can see myself making definitions is in a provisional and polemical one: I construct my definition as a woman not in terms of a woman's putative essence but in terms of words currently in use. "Man" is such a word in common usage. Not a word, but the word. I therefore fix my glance upon this word even as I question the enterprise of redefining the premises of any theory.[3]

Here, it is obvious she is deconstructing—without being slavish about—the approach's more obtuse terminology, while remaining faithful to its central ideas that everything must be put under erasure because everything is different and always at a distance from any theory of it or, important to add, in life lived as or in relation to such basic undefinable concepts as woman.

This theoretical method or approach is abundantly evident in Spivak's famous 1988 essay, "Can the Subaltern Speak?,"[4] which is reprinted and uploaded countless times. The concept "subaltern" originally referred to military personnel of lower ranks. But Spivak and Ranajit Guha (the Indian historian who more than anyone served to establish subaltern studies as a field of study) redirected the term to refer to all those pressed into social basements and excluded from what benefits there may be for the rest of society. "Can the Subaltern Speak?" presents subaltern studies in a difficult but readable essay that, like the Preface to Of Grammatology, deconstructs the sources that demonstrate the complicated meanings of subaltern—from Marx and Freud to Foucault and Derrida (among many others), all woven around a dramatic story that perfectly well illustrates the silence and exclusion of those relegated to the global colonial world's dark social and economic basement. Here the colonizing of global capitalism is assailed for its violence. "The clearest available example," she writes, "of epistemic violence is the remotely orchestrated, far-flung, and heterogenous project to constitute the colonial subject as Other." The subalterns are not in their excluded positions because they have failed. They are created as subjects other to the dominating capitalist world-system.

In Part II of the essay, Spivak, following Ranajit Guha, locates the subaltern among, but at the bottom of, the four strata of socioeconomic positions the colonial world imposed on India. The elite comprise, first, the dominant

290 *Capitalism's Uncertain Future*

all-India foreign groups and, second, the dominant all-India indigenous groups that derive their status through service to and identification with the interests of the foreign groups that before 1947 were the British colonizers and after independence are the NGOs and the corporations and agencies of international capitalism. The third structural level comprises groups that are regional and local as opposed to national. Their status is that of being an in-between group of indigenous people at state and local level who have no voice other than when they speak in voices acceptable to the interests of the two all-India elite groups. Then, fourth, are the masses (of which, millions in India), including the subaltern who have no social importance in the sense of being of direct value to the three dominant groups. About the subaltern, Spivak makes the nuanced point that they are a doubled-over group:

> If, in the context of colonial, production the subaltern has no history and cannot speak, the subaltern as female is even more deeply in the shadow. ... The contemporary division of labor is a displacement of the divided field of nineteenth-century territorial imperialism.

The subaltern group is twice-displaced—without voice before dominant groups and heterogenized—split up and dispersed among the regions and villages.

In Part IV of "Can the Subaltern Speak?" Spivak dwells on the traditional Vedic practice of Sati, by which a widow on the occasion of a husband's death would sacrifice herself on his funeral pyre. Under the British colonial regime, sati was prohibited, which led to the assumption that the prohibition was an instance of the white colonizer saving brown women from brown men. In the records of British missionaries, the East India Company, and of white women, there is no record that these women wanted to die. In particular, Spivak adds, no one, not even contemporary white feminists, gave these women credit for wanting to die. None even considered the possibility that Hindu women had a voice in the matter. Of which, Spivak remarks: "Imperialism's image as the establisher of the good society is marked by the espousal of the woman as an object of protection from her own kind." In other words, subaltern women are so completely Other as to be incapable of speaking on behalf of their own wishes.

This historical crumb would seem today to be lost in the sea of ancient habits too shocking and remote to merit a closer reading. Spivak has much more to say of course about the oddity of sati and the failures to appreciate it for what it may well have been. In the end of the essay, however, she makes it clear that Sati is much more than what it seems. For one thing, in modern India sati is a common name for females. It is meant to bestow on the infant the promise of being a good wife. The ancient practice is reclaimed from its Hindu past in order to define a woman as (or no more than) a good wife who would sacrifice herself in another way. In other words, the silence of the subaltern woman survives in different form in later times. This, Spivak makes clear in the last lines of the essay, is the challenge for the feminist:

> The subaltern cannot speak. There is no virtue in laundry lists with 'woman' as a pious term. Representation has not withered away. The female intellectual as intellectual has a circumscribed task which she must not disown with a flourish.

At the broader reaches of this difficult and important essay, there is a subtext (or one might even say a hypertext).

Capitalism silences. The colonizing of the globe by Europeans that began around 1500 was not an innocent search for new worlds. It was the beginning of the capitalist world economy that could not have grown into what it is today had it not silenced millions of people by murder and slavery but also by casting them into a global subaltern class.

Zygmunt Bauman (1925–2017) was born in Poznan, Poland, from where, during World War II, his family emigrated to the Soviet Union. Later, as a young man of 18 years, Bauman fought with the Free Polish Army against the Nazi occupiers of Poland. He rose to the rank of captain, but in 1953 he was purged from the army by the Communists. Just the same, he remained in Poland through graduate studies and began his academic career as a lecturer in the social sciences at the University of Warsaw. In 1971, he emigrated to England for a professorship at the University of Leeds, a position he held until retirement in 2001. Thereafter, he actually increased the range of topics considered in the 91 books he published—25 of his 66 books in English came after retirement (as did 4 of the 25 published in Polish). This was more than all but a few sociologists. Bauman wrote with an authentic literary voice and trustworthy political convictions that were dispositions shaped, one assumes, by his early experiences in Eastern Europe.

Bauman's earliest books (in Polish) examined such subjects as Lenin's theory of democracy (in 1957) and British socialism (1959). After his migration to Leeds in 1971, he began a series of reinterpretations of basic sociological subjects, including *Culture as Praxis* (1973), *Toward a Critical Sociology* (1976), *Hermeneutics and Social Science* (1978). It is a bit futile, however, to attempt to codify his bibliography along a linear trajectory. Not only are there too many books to fathom in a short review, but when fresh topics came to the fore, Bauman seldom left behind those that came earlier. *Modernity and the Holocaust* (1989)[5] is one of the later sociological writings that brought up to date his thinking on the experience of his European generation, who in their youth saw Poland and nearly everything else melt before the Nazi onslaught. In fact, Europeans like Bauman who, though young, were old enough to be engaged in World War II and its aftermath lived with the melting away of the cultural world into which they were born. Their vocation, for those who would accept it, was to try to rebuild what could be rebuilt of the passing order.

292 *Capitalism's Uncertain Future*

Bauman's writings were as voluminous, if not as complicated, as Gayatri Spivak's. Both are giants in their contributions to thinking and rethinking the world in the half century from the 1970s to the 2020s. But the key difference in their contributions is expressed best by the key words of their social theories: silence and waste. Spivak, daughter of a once-colonized nation, grew up with the convoluted silence she sought to explain as best one could to the world globalized by empty talk. Bauman, son of a crumbling European civilization, grew up with the terrible waste of human lives and cultural norms he sought to rebuild by a colossal, almost frenetic, oeuvre of nearly 100 books and countless talks and short writings for over 60 years from 1957 to 2017.

Bauman was not pretentious enough to think that he, or anyone else, could rebuild a culture in ruins after World War II. As a person, he was a generous and kind man. As a public figure and personage, he was a member of a European postwar generation that could do no other than rebuild on the ashes—or, to use his figure of speech, to come to terms with the new world he saw, liquid modernity. At the opening of *Liquid Modernity* (2000),[6] first of a series of books on the liquidity theme, he wrote:

> The extraordinary mobility of fluids is what associates them with the idea of "lightness" There are liquids which, cubic inch for cubic inch, are heavier than many solids, but we are inclined nonetheless to visualize them all as lighter, less "weighty" than everything solid. We associate "lightness" or "weightlessness" with mobility and inconstancy: we know from practice that the lighter we travel the easier and faster we move.

Zygmunt Bauman did not cut the notion of liquid modernity out of thin air. He took it from what may be the most lyrical of the stinging lines in *The Communist Manifesto* (1848):

> All that is solid melts into air, all that is holy is profaned, and man is at last compelled to face with sober senses his real conditions of life, and his relations with his kind. The need of a constantly expanding market for its products chases the bourgeoisie over the entire surface of the globe.

These four lines of prose poetry were meant to lay waste to the idea that capitalism arose from free markets that ignored the deep secret of capitalism's cruel oppression of its labor force. Zygmunt Bauman deploys the words as the text for which *Liquid Modernity* is the exegesis.

The book itself turns on the difference between heavy and light capitalisms. Heavy capitalism was the early industrial system Marx laid out and then dissected in *Capital*. Bauman, however, uses Fordism early in the 20th century as his main example of heavy capitalism, which he describes in the following way:

Silenced/Wasted Lives in Capitalism Order   293

Fordism was the self-consciousness of modern society in its "heavy," "bulky," or "immobile" and "rooted," "solid" phase. At that stage in their joint history, capital, management and labour were all, for better or worse, doomed to stay in one another's company for a long time to come, perhaps forever–tied down by the combination of huge factory buildings, heavy machinery and massive labour forces. ... Heavy capitalism was obsessed with bulk and size, and, for that reason, also with boundaries, with making them tight and impenetrable.[7]

Henry Ford's assembly line factories were based on Frederick Winslow's late 19th century principles of scientific management by which labor was subjected to the rule of industrial efficiency. Right away, Bauman turns to the comparison with light capitalism. "In its heavy stage, capital was as much fixed to the ground as were the laborers it engaged." Then:

Nowadays capital travels light - with cabin luggage only, which includes no more than a briefcase, a cellular telephone and a portable computer. It can stop-over almost anywhere, and nowhere needs to stay longer than the satisfaction lasts. Labour, on the other hand, remains as immobilized as it was in the past - but the place which it once anticipated being fixed to once and for all has lost its past solidity; searching in vain for boulders, anchors fall on friable sands. Some of the world's residents are on the move; for the rest it is the world itself that refuses to stand still.

Against the "Heavy/Light Capitalism" contrast, Bauman posits "Heavy/Light Modernity" in which both sides of the historical differences turn out to have several dispensations:

Heavy modernity kept capital and labour in an iron cage which none of them could escape. Light modernity let one partner out of the cage. "Solid" modernity was an era of mutual engagement. "Fluid" modernity is the epoch of disengagement, elusiveness, facile escape and hopeless chase. In "liquid" modernity, it is the most elusive, those free to move without notice, who rule.[8]

Passages like this one are not Bauman at his literary best. Yet as clumsy as the terminology is, he is headed somewhere, drawn, it seems, by the force of the key text from *The Communist Manifesto* (1848): "All that is solid melts into air. ..."

Liquid Modernity serves primarily to outline the social forms of liquidity that are embellished in five subsequent books in the series: *Liquid Love: On the Frailty of Human Bonds* (2003), *Liquid Life* (2005), *Liquid Fear* (2006), *Liquid Times* (2006), and *Culture in a Liquid Modern World* (2006). This library embellishes the primal concept, but it also exaggerates it to breaking point. Each of the books seeks to apply the liquidity theme to the several human

294   *Capitalism's Uncertain Future*

spheres mentioned in their titles. Yet each is unfailingly provocative. And each, soon enough, lands on the question of waste, for example, on desire in *Liquid Love*: "Consumables attract, waste repels. After desire comes waste disposal."[9] Inscrutable perhaps, until Bauman later on in the same book raises the register to the structural level:

> In our liquid modern times, the powers-that-be no longer seem interested in drawing the boundary between "right" and "perverse" sex. The reason perhaps is the fast fading demand for the employment of spare sexual energy in the service of "civilizing causes" [read: the production of discipline over the patters of routine behavior functional in a society of producers].[10]

Then, in *Liquid Fear*[11] (pp. 45–46), a similar idea in respect to what he calls the dread of death: "Death has been incorporated in the flow of life; no longer being the irrevocable end of life, it has become the integral (and possibly indispensable) part." Here, Bauman quietly invokes capitalism's endless accumulation of capital that requires always an industrial reserve of useable souls that cannot hope for an otherworldly eternity, a point magnified in *Culture in a Liquid Modern World*: "Progress, in short, has moved from a discourse of the shared improvement of life to a discourse of personal survival."[12] Then, he again raises the idea to its structural effect:

> Modern migration—currently in full flow and gathering momentum despite frenetic attempts to hold it back—introduces the age of diasporas: an infinite archipelago of ethnic, religious and linguistic settlements, heedless of the pathways marked out and paved by the imperial/colonial episode, and steered instead by the logic of the global redistribution of living resources and the chances of survival peculiar to the current stadium of globalization.[13]

Or, as he puts it in *Liquid Modernity*: "Refugees, the displaced, asylum seekers, migrants, the sans papiers, they are the waste of globalization."[14]

Bauman's theory of capitalisms, heavy and light, is dark and especially so because light capitalism—so commonly thought of as free floating and inherently better than what came before—is much the worse by half, which is the main point of his *Wasted Lives*:

> The production of "human waste," or more correctly wasted humans (the "excessive" and "redundant," that is the population of those who either could not or were not wished to be recognized or allowed to stay), is an inevitable outcome of modernization, and an inseparable side-effect of order-building (each order casts some parts of the population as "out of place," "unfit," or "undesirable") and of economic progress (that cannot proceed without degrading and devaluing the previously effect modes

of "making a living" and therefore cannot but deprive their practitioners of their livelihood).[15]

Thus, it is that the world Bauman, from his youth on, sought to rebuild, was already too far gone.

Spivak's silence was in many ways more hopeful, at least to extent that in "Can the Subaltern Speak" and elsewhere, she means to teach academic feminists to give voice to the subalterns. Hers is a more optimistic world than Bauman's. Yet, neither views capitalism as anything less than the bitter pill that cuts deep into the tenons of hope one can have in the worlds to come.

Notes

1 Gayatri Chakravorty Spivak, translator's preface to *Of Grammatology*, by Jacques Derrida, trans. Gayatri Spivak (Baltimore: The Johns Hopkins University Press, 1997), xliii.
2 Gayatri Chakravorty Spivak, *An Aesthetic Education in the Era of Globalization* (Cambridge: Harvard University Press, 2013), 59.
3 Gayatri Chakravorty Spivak, *In Other Words: Essays in Cultural Politics* (New York: Routledge, 1998 [1987]), 102–103.
4 Gayatri Chakravorty Spivak, "Can the Subaltern Speak?" in *Marxism and the Interpretation of Culture*, eds. Cary Nelson and Lawrence Grossberg (New York: Macmillan, 1988), 271–313.
5 Zygmunt Bauman, *Modernity and the Holocaust* (Ithaca: Cornell University Press, 1989).
6 Zygmunt Bauman, *Liquid Modernity* (Cambridge: Polity, 2000).
7 *Ibid.*, 57–58.
8 *Ibid.*, 120.
9 Zygmunt Bauman, *Liquid Love: On the Frailty of Human Bonds* (Cambridge: Polity, 2003), 9.
10 *Ibid.*, 57.
11 ///ztgmunt Bauman, Liquid Fear.
12 Zygmunt Bauman, *Culture in a Liquid Modern World* (Cambridge: Polity, 2011), 24.
13 *Ibid.*, 34.
14 Bauman, *Liquid Modernity*, 58.
15 Zygmunt Bauman, *Wasted Lives. Modernity and its Outcasts* (Oxford: Polity, 2004), 6.

37 Left Extremes: Authoritarians v. Libertines

Slavoj Žižek/Noam Chomsky

Slavoj Žižek (1949–) was born in Ljubljana in former Yugoslavia (current-day Slovenia) in 1949. He completed his PhD in 1981 at the University of Ljubljana on the topic of German Idealism, after which he went to Paris to study with Jaques Alain Miller, Jaques Lacan's son-in-law. In Paris, Žižek wrote a second dissertation, a Lacanian reading of Hegel. Žižek is currently a faculty member at the European Graduate School and founder and president of the Society for Theoretical Psychoanalysis in Ljubljana.

Less than a week before the 2016 United States presidential elections, Žižek endorsed then candidate Donald Trump in an interview with BBC's Channel 4 News. "I'm horrified at him," Žižek said of Trump:

> I'm just thinking that Hillary is the true danger. Why. She built an impossible all-inclusive coalition. The one point when I fully agreed with Trump was, you remember, when Bernie Sanders endorsed Hillary? He said, Trump, it simply wasn't true. He said it's like somebody from Occupy Wall Street endorsing Lehman Brothers. In every society there is a whole network of unwritten rules, how politics works and how you build consensus. Trump disturbed this. And if Trump wins, both big parties, Republicans and Democrats, would have to return to basics, rethink themselves, and maybe some things can happen there. That's my desperate, very desperate hope that if Trump wins, listen. America is still not a dictatorial state, he will not introduce fascism. But it will be a kind of big awakening. New political processes will be set in motion, will be triggered. But I am well aware that things are very dangerous here, not only all these white supremacy groups, but listen, Trump openly said, and there's a report saying that he'll probably do it, you know how important in the United States the Supreme Court is? He's already said he will nominate right wingers. So there are dangers but I'm just afraid that Hillary stands for this absolute inertia, the most dangerous one, because she is a Cold Warrior and so on, connected with banks, pretending to be socially progressive.

Žižek's support for Trump over Clinton in the 2016 presidential elections was rooted in a desire to disrupt politics as usual, which is an increasingly

DOI: 10.4324/9781003198291-42

popular idea on both the extreme right and left. But Žižek's views on current politics while framed as Marxisant have implications that are traditionally associated with the right, such as his support for Donald Trump.

In an article Žižek wrote for *The Statesman,* he commented on the mass assault of women by refugees near the train station in Cologne, Germany, on New Year's Eve 2016. Wrote Žižek:

So what if we conceive of the Cologne incident as a contemporary version of *faire le chat*? As a carnivalesque rebellion of the underdogs? It wasn't the simple urge for satisfaction of sexually starved young men – this could be done in a more discreet, hidden way – it was foremost a public spectacle of installing fear and humiliation, of exposing the "pussies" of the privileged Germans to painful helplessness. There is, of course, nothing redemptive or emancipatory, nothing effectively liberating, in such a carnival – but this is how actual carnivals work. This is why the naive attempts to enlighten immigrants (explaining to them that our sexual mores are different, that a woman who walks in public in a mini skirt and smiles does not thereby signal sexual invitation, etc.) are examples of breath-taking stupidity – they know this and that's why they are doing it. They are well aware that what they are doing is foreign to our predominant culture, but they are doing it precisely to wound our sensitivities. The task is to change this stance of envy and revengeful aggressiveness, not to teach them what they already know very well.

The Eurocentricity of this line of argumentation is obvious, along with its alignment with what is typically thought of as right-wing politics. Žižek assumes that refugees are envious of the West, and therefore are intentionally lashing out against it by assaulting "our women": Western women. But the underlying rightist current in much of Žižek's writings and comments on current events that is most troubling is his seeming endorsement of authoritarianism.

In an essay comparing Foucault's support for the Iranian Revolution and Heidegger's support for the Nazi Party, Žižek writes, "Foucault's Iranian engagement, like Heidegger's Nazi engagement, was in itself (in its form) an appropriate gesture, the best thing he ever did, the only problem being that it was (as to its content) a commitment in the wrong direction."[1] Žižek provocatively claims that these theorists' commitments to authoritarian right-wing movements that led to many deaths at the hands of the state was appropriate in form, just misguided in content. Žižek elaborates:

Why was Iran, then, for Foucault the object of 'interpassive authenticity', the mythical Other Place where the authentic happens- Cuba, Nicaragua, Bolivia today... - and for which Western intellectuals have an inexhaustible need? And, incidentally, one could redeem in the same

298 *Capitalism's Uncertain Future*

way not only the enthusiasm evoked by Stalinist Russia in many Western intellectuals and artists in the 1930s and 1940s, but even the enthusiasm stoked in those who were otherwise bitter critics of Stalinism by the Maoist Cultural Revolution: what matters was not the brutal violence and terror in China, but the enthusiasm fired up by this spectacle amongst Western observers... (And— why not?- one could claim the same for the fascination of Nazi Germany for some Western observers in the first four years of Hitler's rule when unemployment fell rapidly, and so on!)[2]

This reading of Foucault's interest in Iran has several possible interpretations: (1) Žižek is endorsing fascism and engaging in Eurocentrism, (2) he is condemning Western intellectuals for their ongoing eroticization of the "Orient" and flirtations with fascism, and (3) because these two diametrically opposed interpretations of this passage are equally valid, perhaps neither or both meanings are intended. Later in this same essay though, Žižek writes:

What Heidegger was looking for in Nazism (to avoid a misunderstanding: not only due to an accidental error in his personal judgement but due to a flaw in his theoretical edifice itself) was a revolutionary Event, so that even some measures he imposed on the Freiburg University during his brief tenure as its rector bear witness to his intention to enact there a kind of 'cultural revolution' (bringing students together with workers and soldiers— which, in itself, is not a fascist measure, but something Maoists tried to do in the Cultural Revolution).[3]

Here we see that, for Žižek, the form of revolution matters more than the left or right content—just as Trump's election would shake things up, so too does Heidegger's Nazism. The content of the shake-up is less of a concern for Žižek than its actual happening, because in the shake-up there is the potential for a turn leftward. Žižek therefore urges us to celebrate the revolutionary Event without regard for its content. Of course, historically, these shake-ups could and often did result in authoritarianism.

Perhaps Žižek's essay "Stalinism Revisited: Or, How Stalin Saved the Humanity of Man" offers more insights into Žižek's flirtations with fascism. In analyzing Bukharin's last speech to the Central Committee in 1937, Žižek compares the crowd's laughter at Bukharin's threat of suicide to the crowd's laughter at Joseph K. in Frantz Kafka's *The Trial*. "In such a universe," Žižek claims, "there is no place for even the most formal and empty right of subjectivity, on which Bukharin continues to insist."[4] In the Stalinist moment, demonstrates Žižek, there is only "objective meaning," and therefore "disagreement with the official party line can only be the result of direct hypocrisy and deceit. What is more surprising," Žižek writes, "is the readiness of Western Communist observers to perceive this hypocrisy as a true psychological fact about the accused."[5] In other words, Žižek argues that it is one thing that Stalinist should usher in a literalist meaning to all political discourse, but it is another thing for Communist sympathizers outside of the USSR, especially in the West, to similarly contend that to disagree with the official party line is to be knowingly deceitful and hypocritical. The elimination of subjective meaning, for Žižek, is the essential fact about authoritarian communism. We might interpret this argument as against fascism in all forms—both left and right—but Žižek pulls us in another direction:

> It is here that one has to make the choice: the 'pure' liberal stance of equidistance towards leftist and rightist 'totalitarianism' (they are both based on the intolerance of political and other differences, the rejection of democratic and humanist values, and so on) is *a priori* false, one *has* to take sides and proclaim one fundamentally 'worse' that the other— for this reason, the ongoing 'relativization' of fascism, the notion that one should rationally compare the two totalitarianisms, etc., always involves the— explicit or implicit— thesis that fascism was 'better' than Communism, an understandable reaction to the Communist threat.[6]

Thereby, Žižek closes off the possibility of condemning fascism *tout court* and urges the reader to take sides.

He then juxtaposes Stalinist discourse with the letters written between Heidegger and Marcuse on Nazism, claiming that:

> Marcuse was justified in replying that the thin difference between brutally expatriating people and burning them in a concentration camp is the line that, at the moment, separated civilization from barbarism. One should not shrink from going a step further

Žižek urges:

> The thin difference between the Stalinist gulag and the Nazi annihilation camp was also, at that historical moment, the difference between civilization and barbarism. Let us take Stalinism at its most brutal: the dekulakization of the early 1930s. Stalin's slogan was that 'kulaks as a class should be liquidated'— what does this mean? It can mean many things... but it did *not* simply mean to kill them all. The goal was to liquidate them *as a class*, not as individuals. Even when the rural population was deliberately starved (millions of dead in Ukraine, again) the goal was not to kill them all, but to break their backbone, to brutally crush their resistance, to show them who was the master. The difference— minimal, but crucial— persists here with regard to the Nazi de-Judaization, where the ultimate goal effectively was to annihilate them as individuals, to make them disappear as a race. In this sense, then, Ernest Nolte is right: Nazism *was* a repetition, a copy of Bolshevism— in Nietzsche's terms, it was a profoundly *re-active* phenomenon.[7]

300 *Capitalism's Uncertain Future*

After urging the taking of sides, Žižek then reveals that whether choosing right or left during that earlier passage, Stalinism and Nazism are inextricably linked and both morally reprehensible.

Žižek's writing is at the same time repulsive and compelling. When writing for an academic audience he excites the Hegelian in all of us, but in so doing, he leads his reader into a logic that usually brings that reader to a morally uncomfortable conclusion, often about one's own political views, made even more reprehensible given that the journey to that unsettling end was riveting and convincing. In so doing, he could be interpreted as: (1) exposing the Western intellectual tradition for its moral failures, (2) simply acting as provocateur by providing fodder for intellectual masturbation in privileging style and flourish over political content, or (3) perhaps he really is what his critics say, a fascist in Marxist clothing. Regardless of how we interpret him, his work reflects the current conjuncture in which Western intellectuals strive to be non-Eurocentric leftist radicals while still reifying all the mainline markers of career prestige along with its attendant inequalities, in which social theory is more about how things are said rather than what is said, in which neo-Nazis dress like hipsters and lead a political movement from their bedrooms through internet memes on Reddit. Žižek holds up the mirror and shows us the current conjuncture in all of its beauty, discomfort, and contradiction. In so doing, it's difficult to discern whether he is the fascist or whether we are the fascists.

In contrast to Žižek's interview with BBC Channel 4 News, Noam Chomsky, when interviewed by *The Guardian* on the 2016 on the American presidential election, said that "If I were in a swing state, a state that matters, and the choice were Clinton or Trump, I would vote against Trump. And by arithmetic that means hold your nose and vote for Clinton." In explaining what he found most troubling about Trump, Chomsky said:

> We don't really know what he thinks. And I'm not sure he knows what he thinks. He's perfectly capable of saying contradictory things at the same time. But there are some pretty stable elements of his ideology, if you can even grant him that concept. One of them is: 'Climate change is not taking place.' As he puts it: 'Forget it.' And that's almost a death knell for the species – not tomorrow, but the decisions we take now are going to affect things in a couple of decades, and in a couple of generations it could be catastrophic.[8]

Neither Chomsky nor Žižek can muster much excitement about the prospect of a Clinton presidency, but Chomsky's endorsement of Clinton, while similarly rooted in radical left politics, requested the opposite action of voters in the United States.

Noam Chomsky (1928–) was born in 1928 in Philadelphia, USA. Chomsky's mother was involved in radical politics, while his father was a professor of Hebrew who was born in Ukraine. Chomsky received his PhD in linguistics from the University of Pennsylvania, and since 1955 has been a professor of linguistics at Massachusetts Institute of Technology. While interested in anti-authoritarian left politics ever since he was a teenager, Chomsky first became active in political protest in 1962 when he began to speak out against the Vietnam War. His involvement in political protest led him to write essays and books on politics in addition to his scholarly writings in linguistics.

In *Chomsky on Anarchism* (2005), a series of essays that lay out Chomsky's political philosophy, he candidly describes his view on political praxis. For Chomsky, "the essence of anarchism... [is] the conviction that the burden of proof has to be placed on authority and that it should be dismantled if that burden cannot be met."[9] He believes that anarchism helps to identify structures of authority, hierarchy, and domination in all aspects of social life and in identifying them, it helps us to challenge them. "Unless a justification can be given" for any given power structure, Chomsky contends "they are illegitimate and should be dismantled, to increase the scope of human freedom."[10] As such, Chomsky urges the left to be libertarian and democratic in direct contrast to Bolshevism and Leninism, on which Chomsky writes, "If the left is understood to include Bolshevism then I would flatly dissociate myself from the left. Lenin was one of the greatest enemies of socialism, in my opinion."[11] The aim of the left, in the short term especially, claims Chomsky, should be to "extend democracy and human rights."[12] The obvious targets, posits Chomsky, are "state power and private tyranny," but issues of democracy and human rights arise in many other human relationships as well, including those between, for example, "parents and children, teachers and students, men and women," and so on.[13] Chomsky believes that "more than ever libertarian socialist ideas are relevant," and that the general public overwhelmingly regards the current economic system as "inherently unfair" and the political system as serving "special interests."[14] Deepening democracy, therefore, would only advance causes of social and economic justice.

In the week leading up to the 2016 US presidential election, Žižek and Chomsky were among the most prominent public intellectuals to comment on how left-leaning US voters could best contribute to a more just and equal future. While the two views might seem diametrically opposed—and they are when it comes to their epistemic position—their views on the election, and their theoretical writings were similarly rooted in challenges to an authoritarian, Soviet-style Marxism. Chomsky and Žižek typify the two strands of politics that have captivated a significant portion of the Western left—poststructuralist and psychoanalytic Marxism on the one hand, and anarchist political economy on the other. What's most interesting about the fact that these two viewpoints have captivated the majority of young leftists is that they both reject the authoritarian left politics of the majority of the 20th century. This contemporary radical left in both its poststructural and political economy oriented variants agrees, in contrast to Leninism and Bolshevism, that both Soviet-style communism and right-wing fascism were

302 *Capitalism's Uncertain Future*

authoritarian. Thereby, the political future envisioned by these different epistemes of the radical left is more democratic and anti-authoritarian than ever before.

Notes

1 Slavoj Žižek, *In Defense of Lost Causes* (London: Verso, 2008), 108.
2 *Ibid.*, 108.
3 *Ibid.*, 142.
4 *Ibid.*, 235.
5 *Ibid.*
6 *Ibid.*, 262.
7 *Ibid.*, 262–263.
8 Leo Benedictus, "Noam Chomsky on Donald Trump," *The Guardian* (20 May 2016).
9 Noam Chomsky, *Chomsky on Anarchism* (Oakland: AK Press, 2005), 178.
10 *Ibid.*, 178.
11 *Ibid.*, 182.
12 *Ibid.*, 193.
13 *Ibid.*, 192.
14 *Ibid.*, 188.

38 Assemblage Theory

The New Necessary Analytics of Capitalism

Gilles Deleuze and Félix Guattari/Manuel Delanda

Gilles Deleuze (1925–1995) began his academic career as a philosopher and author of works so original that Michel Foucault once wrote, "perhaps one day this century will be called Deleuzian." Like many of the philosophers of the 1960s in Paris, Foucault included, Deleuze's writing went far beyond philosophy to embrace politics, literature, and psychoanalysis as well as social theory. Suffering a debilitating terminal disease, he committed suicide in 1995. In the revolutionary 1960s, Deleuze met Félix Guattari (1930–1992) who was of much the same formation and trajectory. They met at the University of Vincennes, a hotbed of revolutionary activity in Paris during the events of *Mai '68*. Then began their collaboration that issued, first, in *Anti-Oedipus* in 1972, followed by *A Thousand Plateaus* in 1980. Though both contributed to the philosophical originality of these two, now classic works, Guattari was more the psychoanalyst—hence the subtitle to the two-volume books: *Capitalism and Schizophrenia*.

Guattari also published *The Machinic Unconscious: Essays in Schizoanalysis* in 1979 (the year before *A Thousand Plateaus* appeared). Deleuze, however, was unrelentingly the philosopher who wrote books of analytic interpretation that caused some (notably Manuel DeLanda) to conclude that Deleuze was the lead author of their two books and thereby the one chiefly responsible of their philosophical attitude. *Anti-Oedipus* and *A Thousand Plateaus* have been slow to gain recognition in the Anglophone world, in large part due to their extreme difficulty and perverse originality when measured by the ruler of traditional, modern linear (or, as Deleuze and Guattari would say, arboreal) philosophy. Their most famous concept is the *rhizome*—a literary figure in service of a profound rethinking of culture and politics rooted in obscure, underground connections without beginning or end. Their rhizomatic method is distinct from arboreal philosophy.

Whether or not Deleuze was the primary philosopher of the two (as some suppose), it is indisputable that he produced a long list of philosophical works written in his uncommon literary style. Foremost among these were his *doctorat d'État* thesis *Difference and Repetition* (1968), then *Logic of Sense* (1969), and his secondary thesis *Expressionism in Philosophy: Spinoza* that was not published until 1990. In these and other works written across his literary life, Deleuze critically examined the major philosophers of the modern era,

DOI: 10.4324/9781003198291-43

304 *Capitalism's Uncertain Future*

especially Leibniz, Spinoza, Kant, and Nietzsche. Yet, his expositions were always executed with a twist. As the authors of the Deleuze entry in *The Stanford Encyclopedia of Philosophy* put it in respect to concepts like *multiplicity*:

> Tying together the themes of difference, multiplicity, virtuality and intensity, at the heart of *Difference and Repetition* we find a theory of Ideas (dialectics) based neither on an essential model of identity (Plato), nor a regulative model of unity (Kant), nor a dialectical model of contradiction (Hegel), but rather on a problematic and genetic model of difference.

Difference was the bridge concept that spanned the waters to *assemblage theory*.

Deleuze and Guattari were not alone in rethinking *and* rephrasing the analytic vocabulary by which it now seems necessary to think and speak about the world as it is. Michel Foucault in *Discipline and Punish* (1977 [1975]) transformed his concept of *biopower* into a more poetic concept: *carceral archipelago*, which is meant to signify the way a sovereign state deploys biopower to discipline its population into a virtual prison in which citizens are, in effect, incarcerated in a string of islands. Put somewhat too simply, Foucault had in mind the ways modern democratic societies contradict their own false claims to be promoting the liberty of individuals.

While Foucault's *biopower* tends to retain a touch of the liberal democratic assumption that allows the political subject retain some possibility of resisting the objective force of political biopower, Deleuze and Guattari insist (to put it crudely) that a subject's desires enjoy no particular freedom from the capitalist war machine. At the extreme, they view the modern social order as subject to a "barbaric despotic machine" that eliminates altogether distinctions between interior and exterior, between the new and the old—which is to say, between the modern and the traditional: "The founding of this despotic machine or the barbarian socius can be summarized in the following way: a new alliance and a direct filiation. The despot challenges the lateral alliances and the extended filiations of the old community."[1] Others do the similar, notably Giorgio Agamben who in *The Coming Community*, which is dire to the extreme: "This means that the planetary petty bourgeoisie is probably the form in which humanity is moving toward its own destruction."[2]

That *Anti-Oedipus* as much as *A Thousand Plateaus* also engage the doomsday of modern society is evident in the first lines of the earlier work (1977 [1972]) where the machinic organ looms:

> It is at work everywhere, functioning smoothly at times, at other times in fits and starts. It breathes, it heats, it eats. It shits and fucks. What a mistake to have ever said the id. Everywhere it is machines—real ones, not figurative ones: machines driving other machines, machines being driven by other machines, with all the necessary couplings and

The New Necessary Analytics of Capitalism   305

connections. An organ-machine is plugged into an energy-source-machine: the one produces a flow that the other interrupts. The breast is a machine that produces milk, and the mouth is a machine coupled to it. The mouth of the anorexic wavers between several functions: its possessor is uncertain as to whether it is an eating-machine, an anal machine, a talking-machine, or a breathing machine (asthma attacks). Hence, we are all handymen: each with his little machines.

Thus begins a book that, by its title and content, would appear to be primarily the work of Guattari, the psychoanalyst. But here, *Anti-Oedipus* announces itself as a work in which the hidden murk of the Unconscious Id is a machine for the primary functions of the body of the human person in her primary social relations.

Guattari's *The Machinic Unconscious* begins by posing the question: "Would the unconscious definitively speak an untranslatable language?" He answers by citing Jacques Lacan's notion that the language of the unconscious is not at all like ordinary language. It is instead a *matheme*, which has the quality of *abstract machines* able to "traverse various levels and establish and demolish stratifications." *The Machinic Unconscious* then continues with what could well be an introduction to the book with Deleuze of the next year:

> The coordinates of existence function like so many space-time and subjective coordinates and are established on the basis of *assemblages which are in constant interaction and incessantly engaged in a process of deterritorialization and singularization causing them to be decentralized in comparison to one another*, while assigning them "territories of replacement" in spaces of coding. This is why I shall oppose territories and lands to machinic territorialities. By distinguishing them from set logic, a "mechanism" of the assemblage will only recognize relative identities and trajectories.[3]

Then, unsurprisingly, Deleuze and Guattari began *A Thousand Plateaus* precisely with a statement that assemblage theory applies to virtually all social things, beginning with books like theirs:

> A book has neither object nor subject: it is made of variously formed matters and very different dates and speeds. To attribute the book to a subject is to overlook this working of matters, and the exteriority of their relations. ... In a book, *as in all things, there are lines of articulation or segmentarity, strata and territories; but also, lines of flight, movements of deterritorialization, and destratification.* Comparative rates of flow on those lines produce phenomena of relative slowness and viscosity, or, on the contrary, of acceleration and rupture. All this, lines and measurable speeds, constitutes [*sic*] an assemblage. A book is an assemblage of this kind, and as such unattributable.[4]

306 *Capitalism's Uncertain Future*

The book begins with a chapter that deploys their famous literary idea: *Rhizome*. A reader new to this kind of thing might see through the glass darkly that the book means to untangle the rhizomatic roots moving in every which direction. Yet, anyone who has written anything of a certain kind—whether term paper, a resume, a business report, much less a book—realizes that writing is just as Deleuze and Guattari say it is. One begins with a thought, a wish, or an assignment, then imagines a welter of themes and ideas through which one must find a way forward. But, Deleuze and Guattari differ from those who try to impose their own sense of order on the unruly roots. They are honest about the thousand plateaus that constitute an assemblage as opposed to a plot—which is to say, a composition in which the lines and flows comprise a series of nonhierarchical equivalences that cannot be reduced to a singular organizing level of meaning and power. Hence, they say, in reference to the tangle of concepts and neologisms they used to explain an assemblage: "We just used words that in turn function for us as plateaus. RHIZOMATICS = STRATOANALYSIS = SCHIZOANALYSIS = STRATOANALYSIS = PRAGMATICS = MICROPOLITICS. These words are concepts, but concepts are lines..."[5] Still, one might note the last concept in this line. MICROPOLITICS, in an assemblage, could well be a line that points to some other part of their book, in particular the penultimate chapter where their theory of the state and implicitly of capitalism is found. Chapter 13: "7000 B.C.: Apparatus of Capture," turns out to be where they begin to unpack their all-too-nuanced theory of the State, followed by an abbreviated but pungent analytic history of capitalism.

As often they do, Deleuze and Guattari begin with an unusual reference, in this case, to George Dumézil's description of the ancient mythologies of political sovereignty:

> The State apparatus is ... animated by a curious rhythm, which is first of all a great mystery: that of the Binder-Gods or magic emperors, *One-Eyed* men emitting from their single eye signs that capture, tie knots at a distance. The jurist-kings, on the other hand, are *One-Armed* men who raise their single arm as an element of right and technology, the law and the tool.[6]

Even readers unacquainted with Dumézil's reference to the distinction between the "fearsome magician-emperor" and the "jurist-priest-king" can sense the unraveling of the knotty lines of a theory. First, the date 7000 B.C. assigned to Chapter 13 exposes a startling axiom as to political sovereignty. The difference between Dumézil's two types does *not* derive from a modern dichotomy between ancient magic and modern judicial reason. *Both* are ancient which implicitly challenges the linear notion that the very concept of a state apparatus is a thoroughly modern idea, often associated with the Peace of Westphalia in 1648. Then, second, the alert reader might be shocked to read two-pages on that the war machine is the dynamic energy between the magical and juridical states: "Thus, there is a tempting three-part hypothesis: the war machine is 'between' the two poles of political sovereignty, and assure the passage from one pole to another." Deleuze and Guattari only seem to be untying a tangle when in fact they are insisting on the ever-growing lateral rhizome as a direct dismissal of the traditional arboreal tap root of linear history. Where progressive history of the modern rational state as issuing over time from the collapse of the traditional imperium, they argue that there is no temporal discontinuity between—in Max Weber's vocabulary—the traditional and the rational. By contrast, Deleuze and Guattari insist that each pursues its own course against the other energized by the ever in the offing of the external war machine.

Important to say here that just before *The Apparatus of Capture* is Chapter 12: "1227: Treatise on Nomadology—the War Machine" which begins much as the successor chapter did—with a reference to Dumézil's myths of the magician-king of fear and jurist-priest of apparent reason. It begins also with of the Norman wooden chariot dated to the Fifth to Fourth Centuries B.C. The image is significant because, when all is said and done, this chariot is a primitive instance of the War Machine, which itself, as they say, is "exterior to the State apparatus." To make it all too simple but accurate enough, the reference to Nomadology alludes to the fact that everything is moving from here to there, which is to say that territories are themselves fluid, subject to deterritorialization as the lines of an assemblage move hither and yon; hence the force of a the war machine: "[Hence the distinction] ...we would like to propose between the *machine* and the *assemblage*: a machine is like a set of cutting edges that insert themselves into the assemblage undergoing deterritorialization, and draw variations and mutations of it."[7]

Specifically, the war machine is both exterior to the State apparatus and is not war itself but the technologies that war uses in attempts to defeat threats to itself—a normal state of affairs. Of course, as time went by, capitalism figured mightily in the production of these technologies. Still, the important question behind all this is: How, more generally, does capitalism play its cards in respect to a political economy that can be conceived as rhizomatic plateaus moving in a matrix of lines of difference and conflict?

One supposes that in accordance with their assemblage theory, Deleuze and Guattari might be taking sides against the political corollary to progressive time, the stratified hierarchy to which they oppose, as their book's title suggests, *n-number of plateaus.* But just when the troubled reader settles into an appreciation (if not an understanding) of their theoretical method, they revert to Marx, who was nothing if not the pure-perfect dialectician in which the capitalist mode of production can only be explained by the conviction that the material always and everywhere dominates the ideal. So when Deleuze and Guattari introduce Marx, they remain well within the dogma of vulgar Marxism: "We shall call the first pole of capture imperial

308   *Capitalism's Uncertain Future*

or despotic. It corresponds to Marx's Asiatic modern of production."[8] And just after:

> Following the Marxist description: a State apparatus is erected upon the primitive agricultural communities is erected upon the primitive agricultural communities, which already have lineal-territorial codes; *but it overcodes them* submitting them to the power of a despotic emperor, the sole and transcendent public-property owner, the master of the surplus or the stock, the organizer of large scale works (surplus labor), the source of public functions and bureaucracy. This is the of the bond, the knot.

Then on the following page: "It is not the State that presupposes a mode of production; quite the opposite, it is the State that makes production a 'mode.'"[9]

It is hard to tell if Deleuze and Guattari suddenly realized that they have tied themselves in a knot that holds them to a position they did not intend. Or whether—as thinkers formed by revolutionary Paris in *'Mai 68* where Vincennes was the epicenter of radical Marxist culture—they may have drifted back into a mode of thought that contradicts to some degree what they were writing in 1980, more than a decade later, when they were well into late-middle age, an age when radical ideas soften into a kind of poetic quagmire. Often those thus adrift must relax into the familiar because the new is so hard to figure. Even when they try to reconfigure the old ways, they seem to reveal the extent to which Marx influenced their theory of the State: "It operates by stratification; in other words, it forms a vertical, hierarchized aggregate that spans the horizontal lines in a dimension of depth."[10]

Where Deleuze and Guattari catch their breath is, important to note, when they outline a theory of capitalism represented by a good many crosscutting plateaus that, to mix their metaphors, is also rhizomatic—so much so that it is difficult to represent the horizontal lines, even in a rhizomatic book. Yet, they daringly introduce a very un-rhizomatic chart to account for capitalism.[11] Here they insist that they are still extending (if not translating) Marx's theory of capital: "A three-headed apparatus of capture, a 'trinity formula' derived from that of Marx (although it distributes things differently) ..." This line is associated with a footnote that serves only to justify their parenthetical admission that in distributing things differently, their scheme is not true to Marx. To make their defensiveness all the more embarrassing, they cite "On the Trinity," Chapter 48 of *Capital III*—where in a book that itself had run its course after the systematic brilliance of *Capital I*, almost accidently introduces a trinitarian afterthought to the three enormous volumes on capital. Yet, Marx's offhanded trinity is true enough to the discussion in *A Thousand Plateaus* where they describe the dynamic quality of the assemblage of political sovereignty. To repeat, their line is not the least bit Marxist: "Thus, there is a tempting three-part hypothesis: the war machine is 'between' the two poles of political sovereignty and assure the passage from one pole to another"—where, remember, the two poles, mythologically put, are the fearsome emperor and the wise king.

The section in which Deleuze and Guattari outline their surprisingly clear and concise economic theory is titled simply *Proposition XII. Capture*, which raises the question of what they mean by *capture* about which they have little to say. As it happens, the English word is taken ultimately from the Latin *capere* meaning "to seize or take." The word is the same in both French and English. Here, then, is another link to their theory of sovereignty—both the fearsome emperor and the judicial king capture or "seize" their rights by different means, both of which act in relation to the dynamic bipolar war machine creates in any political assemblage. There is no reason to doubt that Deleuze and Guattari think of political sovereignty and capital as means taken by force—a force not reluctant to engage in violence. Hence, their atypically graphic presentation of capital and capitalism entails three modes of capture—land, work, and money— each of which further entails quite a few vectors representing the rhizomatic plateaus of capital.

Not surprisingly, if they are true to their idea of political economy as capturing rights and capital being accumulated in and around a rhizomatic assemblage, then they are up against literary odds that will not yield to two-dimensional diagrams like those they offer on pages 443–444 of *A Thousand Plateaus*.

Graphically put, LAND, WORK, MONEY (capitalized as they are in the book) might appear to be the main axis (as in the X axis in a formal graph). Yet, each of its titular terms is set with an opposing factor: LAND (as opposed to territory), WORK (as opposed to activity), MONEY (as opposed to exchange). The oppositions thus break the very notion of an X/Y graph. One soon sees that there is no principal axis—no axis indeed. Why didn't Deleuze and Guattari use at least a three-dimensional illustration (as they did on page 487 in the following chapter)? It is possible that they meant to retain an element of Marx's vertical theory by which the material subjugates the ideal. More likely, they must have just plain understood that a visual diagram might help a reader even when it is woefully inadequate to their assemblage theory. If so, this is to their credit.

Where they succeed, however, is in displaying what would seem to be the degrees of difference in the three modes of capture—this by introducing another line of nuance to the extreme right of the three captures. In respect to LAND, the right-hand line seems to comprise both a medium and an actor, as in:

LAND
(as opposed to territory)

Rent
The Landowner

310   *Capitalism's Uncertain Future*

But, then, in addition, they introduce another set of qualifiers as to the method of capture which in themselves suggest a line of force between direct and monopolistic:

LAND
(as opposed to territory)

Rent
The Landowner

a) Direct comparison of land,
   differential rent
b) Monopolistic appropriation
   of land, absolute rent

They do the same with different contents for the other two captures:

WORK
(as opposed to activity)

Profit
The Entrepreneur

a) Direct comparison of activities, labor
b) Monopolistic appropriation of labor, surplus labor

MONEY
(as opposed to exchange)

Taxation
The Banker

a) Direct comparison of the object exchanged, the commodity
b) Monopolistic appropriation of the means of comparison, the issuance of currency

Again, a wink at Marx, but not an eyes wide-open portrayal of Marx.

So, at long last, it is time to ask: Why bother with these diagrammatic nuances that, it would seem, don't quite make the whole thing clear? The answer may well be that the authors do not think it is possible or desirable to make the world as it is clear. The graphic presentation on pages 443–444 may have been meant to call attention to the inscrutability of this world as it has come to be since the last few decades of the 20th century. But, even here, the somewhat too neatly triangulated elements are themselves qualified and, in the case of WORK, they are qualified by a flush left qualification: Stock, which it would seem is misplaced. They say, just below the graphic exercise: "The three simultaneous aspects: land and seeds, money. Land is stockpiled territory, the tool is stockpiled activity, and money is stockpiled exchange." Upon reading this, some will say, simply: WHAT?

Here, I must confess that I, Charles Lemert, am the author of this chapter. No one else should be implicated in the way I present these ideas (and least

The New Necessary Analytics of Capitalism 311

of all my coauthor, Kristin Plys). I realize that at times when I try to conceal my own confusion as to what is going on here, it may appear that I am making a bit of academic fun of the book. Not so—at least, not intentionally so. Then again, they may be making fun of the world as it presents to the naked eye, which may or may not be a laughing matter. What I really need to confess is serious enough that I want to clear the decks for it. I believe that Deleuze and Guattari were doing something very important here. Social theory has been all too willing to attempt to make the complicated clear. We tend to call this kind of practice "explanation"—a practice Deleuze and Guattari may have succumbed to in their graphic attempt to make the unclear clear. What is important about *A Thousand Plateaus*, in particular, is that Deleuze and Guattari are writing and thinking in terms that mirror the utterly, perhaps impossibly, complicated nature of the world as it has come to be. If we continue trying to explain it by reducing such a world to plain language, then we will be lost.

The world today is complicated because, among other reasons, capitalism has passed into a still another inexplicable iteration similar to the way that neoliberalism has shown itself to be the fraudulent gimmick it always was. Yet, if neoliberalism was meant to reimagine market capitalism on a global plane, then too social democracies that were originally imagined as the political sovereignty of nation states find themselves unable to do much more than huff and puff about "the people" in a world where there is no singular "people." By consequence, authoritarian anxiety steals its way into the global sphere where the uptight upright are trying it figure it all out. Whatever else Deleuze and Guattari have accomplished, they have left us with two mind-changing figures of speech: the *rhizome* and the *assemblage*, both of which are fluid enough to begin to help those willing to try to understand this world, a world that, it turns out, is so far beyond postmodern as to require a nomenclature only a few have only begun to imagine.

As for the ideas of Deleuze and Guattari, there may be an interpreter who makes passable sense not just of what they wrote but of what they saw in the world as it is now, a good quarter century after they passed from the scene. Such a one may well be Manuel DeLanda.

Manuel DeLanda (1952–) was born in Mexico City. Since 1975, he has lived mostly in New York City and identifies as of joint US-Mexican citizenship. It would be hard to name anyone whose work could be called social theory who has passed through as many different professional accomplishments. After arriving in New York City in 1975, he began as a student and then a producer of films such as *Raw Nerves: A Lacanian Thriller* in 1980. As the title of this one suggests, his films were influenced by European social thought. In 1979, early in DeLanda's time in New York City, he earned an MFA at the School of Visual Arts. Then, years later, in 2010, he earned a PhD from the European Graduate School in Switzerland where he now teaches a globally popular course on assemblage theory. Unsurprisingly, at the European Graduate School, he holds the Gilles Deleuze Chair

312   *Capitalism's Uncertain Future*

in Philosophy. DeLanda also teaches architecture at Princeton's School of Architecture and at the University of Pennsylvania School of Design. He has held similar positions at Columbia University and the University of Southern California.

DeLanda's books are, in one aspect, similar to the joint writings of Deleuze and Guattari in that they are peppered with numerous references to a seemingly impossible variety of sources. (Then too, some readers will be taken aback by the extent to which DeLanda authoritatively refers to a good many works of contemporary American social theory and sociology.)

Of particular note relative to Deleuze and Guattari's assemblage theory is DeLanda's *Intensive Science and Virtual Philosophy* (2002) which begins with an introductory essay, "Deleuze's World." The book itself is largely an analytic interpretation of Deleuze's philosophy. This is the book where the implication is drawn that DeLanda seems to consider Deleuze the principal author of the joint books with Guattari. In his defense, here he is writing a straightforwardly philosophical study in which he refers widely to Deleuze's other major works written without Guattari. In a sense, the complaint (if that is what it is) is of little merit, except for the fact that it tends to suggest unfairly that Guattari was a lesser, even minor, figure in their joint books— both of which are better known outside Deleuzian circles where the concern is with general aspects of assemblage theory as a way of thinking about a *well-after-postmodern* political economy.

The key book for understanding DeLanda's understanding of Deleuze is *A New Philosophy of Society: Assemblage Theory and Social Complexity* in 2006. As the subtitle suggests, this is social philosophy by another name—social theory.[12] This is the book in which DeLanda offers a relatively straightforward interpretation of his view of assemblage theory. It is especially valuable to those puzzled (as most are) by the rhizomatic nature of Deleuze and Guattari's idea of a book. DeLanda does not write rhizomatically, which is not to say that he is engaged in analytically reductive "explanation."

A New Philosophy of Society begins right off with DeLanda's declaration of his underlying philosophical position in relation to what he calls social ontology. If philosophical realism considers reality to be independent of the mind, as he says,[13] then a social philosophy (or social ontology as he calls it) can*not* realistically do this, "...because most social entities, from small communities to large nation-states, would disappear altogether if human minds ceased to exist." The distinction is important to DeLanda's assemblage theory, because "... unlike organic totalities, the parts of an assemblage do not form a seamless whole."[14] An ecosystem is normally conceived as an organic whole, hence a totality. But in DeLanda's view, social systems are a different matter. As a result, he is obliged to dismiss organic theories of society, namely the "young Durkheim, the older Marx, and functionalists such as Talcott Parsons."[15] By contrast, among sociologists, he favors Max Weber's social ontology because of Weber's famous idea of the separation of social spheres, as between the religious and the economic in his *Protestant Ethic and* *the Spirit of Capitalism* where a religious idea detached itself from Protestant Christianity to attach itself in time to the economic sphere where it provided the entrepreneurial ethic so essential to Capitalism.

Without bothering about the all-too-many philosophical and artistic variations of philosophical realism, we can say that DeLanda's assemblage theory is about real social worlds that are real not just because we think them but because we live in and with them, and as they change and move about they move us with them. But here arises an important variant in DeLanda's assemblage theory as opposed to Deleuze's. One of the most important accomplishments drawn from DeLanda's theory of assemblages as opposed to totalities is, in my view, the effective dismissal of micro-macro dilemma that has haunted social and economic thought since their modern beginnings (about which more later). To see how DeLanda got to this point, it is helpful, first, to study his most systematic summary of his theory:

> First of all, unlike wholes in which parts are linked by relations of interiority (that is, relations which constitute the very identity of the parts) assemblages are made up of parts which are self-subsistent and articulated by relations of exteriority, so that *a part may be detached and made a component of another assemblage*. Assemblages are characterized along two dimensions: along the *first dimension* are specified the variable roles which *component parts may play*, from *a purely material role to a purely expressive one, as well as mixtures of the two*. A second dimension characterizes processes in which these components are involved: processes which *stabilize or destabilize the identity of the assemblage*.[16]

Obviously, this is a mouthful. But at least it labels the parts and dimensions of an assemblage.

DeLanda, unfortunately, offers very few extended examples. But it is possible to draw a plausible example from an author he discusses at considerable length.[17]

At some risk of confusing the matter, I propose to introduce Tilly's basic factors necessary for collective action as a way of introducing DeLanda's categories. Charles Tilly's resource-mobilization theory—originally in *Mobilization to Revolution* (1978)—provides a plain enough model for the elements at play when collective action can be mobilized for social change, even revolution.[18] One of the basic features of Tilly's resource mobilization model is that, like DeLanda, he assumes that collective action requires, at the least, an existing organization (one of the essential features of DeLanda's assemblage). While DeLanda argues that there are many different kinds of assemblages ranging from the smaller to the larger, his main point is that an assemblage can play a part in an initial state of affairs only to depart later for another relation. Similarly (and empirically) in respect to social movements, it is a given that a collective action may arise in one set of social relations, then under certain conditions move to join another. But

314   *Capitalism's Uncertain Future*

organizations in and of themselves lead nowhere, unless they encourage and help people in need formulate a shared issue expressive of their interests around which collective action can be mobilized. In many movements—for example, the American Civil Rights Movement where the parallel of Tilly's resource-mobilization theory with Delanda's assemblage theory begins with the fact that, in the 1950s and early 1960s, the Black Church served as the originating organization.

The earliest notable instance when a new assemblage in the Civil Rights Movement began to form for the purpose of direct action protests against segregation was the 1955–56 Montgomery, Alabama year long bus boycott. The Montgomery movement began December 5, 1955, shortly after Rosa Parks refused to move to the back of a city bus. This was the organizing moment when the lesser and dispersed assemblages started to break away from their rural and hidden past. And, in Tilly's terms, when resources were mobilized well enough to begin to change, in DeLanda's language, into an assemblage more visible. The emerging site, now nationally known, of the Montgomery Movement was Dexter Avenue Baptist Church located in the shadow of the Alabama State Capitol. The Church was prominent in the City. Its prestige owed in some good part to its important pastors, one of whom was Martin Luther King, Jr. who, in 1954 became Dexter's pastor at an age of but 26 years. All but immediately, the nation's and the world's attention were focused on King and the Movement he led. The televised images of blacks walking miles to work while refusing to use the bus system not only put the City's commercial interests at risk, but, when they appeared in Europe with its many corporate customers for Alabama steel, the threat arose that both city and state would suffer serious economic loss. When, a year later, the 1956 Christmas shopping season had begun, the City gave up. Blacks rode the buses from then on.

It is important here to remember the two dimensions of DeLanda's assemblage theory: that, first, the "component parts may play [... variable roles] from a purely material role to a purely expressive role, as well as mixtures of the two"; then the second dimension has to do with the way the components can "stabilize the identity of the assemblage." The Montgomery Movement was expressive but also the beginning of its material modality in that money and on-the-ground activists from the North and across the South began to join in to support local blacks walking to work or driving to work. In respect to Tilly's resource-mobilization theory, this was the conjuncture when the embryonic movement began to become a collective action contender, first against local government, in time against the state and national governments. It is not inconsequential that in 1954 the United States Supreme Court handed-down its Brown v. Education decision that outlawed separate but equal school segregation which brought the federal government into conflict with the South's racist social structures. The historical confluence of local events in Montgomery with changes in the nation's legal structure, opened what DeLanda called a transformation in the expressive and material aspects the original assemblage of the Black churches such that Dexter Avenue Baptist in Montgomery became an early, if not exclusive, beginning of the emergence of a distinctly new and more potent assemblage. Briefly put, Tilly's point on this stage is that "Collective action costs something" but it brings benefits even if "...costs and benefits are uncertain" all contenders for greater power have imperfect knowledge of the system while also competing with each other. This pretty much characterizes the beginning story of the American Civil Rights Movement from 1955 in Montgomery until 1965 when, after a decade during which people were killed while others joined the movement, the Selma, Alabama movement crossed the Edmund Pettis Bridge and marched the 50 miles to the State Capitol in Montgomery to close the circle that began there. That march and the events from which it grew inspired a new national Voting Rights Act later in 1965. Then a radically movement assemblage was formed only to itself be changed into still another, radically different, Black Power movement in November 1966 formed around the Black Panther Party from which still another assemblage came to be—one that drew up the global decolonizing movements in Africa.

For DeLanda, the local and the structural are not oppositive elements of social process but part and parcel of a societal assemblage (which is not a totality). Social assemblages, thus defined, are, as DeLanda says, "...made up of parts which are self-subsistent and articulated by relations of exteriority." The rural Black churches in the South, for example, were a classic example of the smaller, local social units that were self-subsistent parts and perfectly able to stand on their own even as they were caught up in some other national global assemblage. As the changed and become part of something more grand they were units but not building blocks that were functionality necessary. As they grow and change an assemblage can find other ways of doing what it does.

The problem here, for those not yet attuned to assemblage theory, could be said to be the cultural habit of thinking of nations, institutions, and other social elements in functionalist terms, that is, as necessary organic aspects of the whole without which all will die. Another of DeLanda's corollary critiques is a sharp rejection of the nature-culture divide. There are natural assemblages (beehives, ant colonies, bat bedrooms, for examples) that can be detached from their exterior spheres, just as there are social ones. In a sense (though he doesn't say this), ecosystem is the wrong word for social and natural systems. That societies (and ecosystems) are too often narrowly thought of in functionalist terms is not a practice limited to academic thinkers. Ordinary members (who may or may not be citizens) too often think of their social entities in functional terms. Nations in particular are thought of has having a strictly defined membership assigned to various neighborhoods and places where they "belong" in order to pursue to possibilities or endure the inferior statuses to which they are assigned. That, even in the most severe applications of this scheme (slavery for example), some move out and up is the evidence that arrangements of this sort are not necessary.

316 *Capitalism's Uncertain Future*

So, here are two important advances that DeLanda's assemblage theory contributes to social theory by casting serious doubt on two of the most treasured but unproductive dichotomies. In his view, neither the *micro/macro* dichotomy nor the *nature/culture* distinction is good enough to understand modern societies in all their complexities as they have come to be. Plus which, the two follow logically from each other: if micro is not opposed to macro, then also nature is not distinct from culture. Or put more discursively, if nature doesn't think, least of all in terms of scale and nature and culture are of the same order of things, then whatever cultures think of themselves, if they are assemblages, then we are mistaken to ignore the fact that, like nature, they are not organized according to micro-macro scales.

Of course, to say this *might* be so, does not make it so. Assemblage theory is a theory, but it is a theory that begins to push us toward a better understanding on the world as it has become, and especially so when it comes to the relations between capitalism and democracy. Here DeLanda makes a particularly helpful contribution. If we can go way back to Deleuze and Guattari's claim that their assemblage theory is true to Karl Marx, DeLanda offers a better way. He breaks with them and Marx by turning to Fernand Braudel. In *Assemblage Theory*,[19] DeLanda makes the strong declaration that capitalism is no longer the dominating structural aspect of the Western world or the pervasive force in modern social life. This clearly is primarily an indictment of Marx's theory capitalism but also, by implication, of classic and contemporary liberal theories. The book itself begins with a frontal attack on Deleuze and Guattari's attachment to Marxism and a strong attachment of his own to Braudel's theory of the modern world and capitalism. Graham Harmon, the series editor of *Assemblage* Theory, aptly says of DeLanda's understanding of Braudel that he views capitalism as "a set of sets...intertwined assemblages of all different sizes ... no longer able to reify Capitalism in the manner of 'State,' 'Society,' 'Market'..."[20] This of course refers to DeLanda's interpretation of Braudel, but it rings true even in reference to Braudel's classic work, *The Mediterranean World in the Age of Philip II*,[21] which is early if not pre-capitalist in its historical reference. Yet, even in that book's theory of three historical times—*long enduring, conjunctural, event histories*—Braudel is framing the vast Mediterranean World of the day as an assemblage without differences between nature and culture, nor between small and grand. Enduring time is not *bigger* than event time. It is, in effect, another element in a temporary assemblage. In fact, enduring historical time actually accounts for the place of land, mountains, seas, climates, and the like in the nature of local events and certainly conjunctures. Napoleon was defeated at Waterloo—a place on the ground in a storm that washed away his normal tactical method. Early in *A New Philosophy of Society: Assemblage Theory and Social Complexity*, DeLanda makes just this point: "Markets ... should be viewed as concrete organizations (that is, concrete market places or bazaars) and this fact makes them assemblages made out of people and

The New Necessary Analytics of Capitalism   317

the material and expressive goods people exchange."[22] Then, a few lines on, DeLanda quotes Braudel at length, beginning in his words:

In these terms, the smallest economic assemblage has always been, as Braudel says: ...a complex consisting of a small market town, perhaps the site of a fair, with a cluster of dependent villages around it. Each village had to be close enough to the town for it to be possible to go to the market and back in a day. But the actual dimensions of the unit would equally depend on the available means of transport, the density of settlement and the fertility of the area in question.

The reference to Braudel is from his *The Perspective of the World*.[23] Especially in this work, Braudel systematically laid out the theoretical principles entailed in his general concept of a world economy (that, in turn, influenced Immanuel Wallerstein's world-system analysis). The important foundational fact of Braudel's concept is that "world" in *world economy* is not an adjective alluding to an economy that spans the globe. *World economy* is in and of itself a compound noun defining an economy that has, what today we would call, a global reach. In Braudel's words, in *Perspective of the World*:

A *world-economy* (an expression I have used in the past as a particular meaning of the German term *Weltwirtschaft*) only concerns a fragment of the world, an economically autonomous section of the planet able to provide for most of its own needs, a section to which its own internal links and exchanges give a certain organic unity.[24]

Except for the locution "organic unity," this is as close to being assemblage theory before the fact as can be. Actually, in *A Thousand Plateau* in 1980, Deleuze and Guattari quote Braudel precisely on this general point just after the longish allusion to Marx for their graph of the three captures, where they quote Braudel himself: "There can only be a world-economy when the mesh of the network is sufficiently fine, and when exchange is regular and voluminous enough to give rise to a central zone."

In the 2006 book, DeLanda cites Braudel even more often than he does Charles Tilly (and remarkably, more even than Deleuze). But it is not just citations that make the point as to DeLanda's assemblage theory being Braudelian, not Marxian. DeLanda, by not getting tangled up in Deleuze's rhizomatic literary effect, is at least able to sort out the features of an assemblage that are otherwise that too often are beclouded by foggy words and concepts. It is not that DeLanda is reverting to logical explanation - he is describing in an abstract sort of way. Hence a kind of puzzle exists between the theories of Deleuze and Delanda. For one, Deleuze and Guattari in making their book rhizomatic are entering the world as it was then and is now, since, at least, the world revolution of 1968 that fractured the half-millennium modern world-system, from 1500 to 1990. Thereafter, the capitalist world-system has lapsed into a now many decades-long period of uncertainty. No one was been able to come to terms with the uncertainty

318 *Capitalism's Uncertain Future*

of both Wallerstein's world-system and Braudel's world-economy. Just the same, DeLanda deploys Braudel to lend theoretical flesh to Deleuze and Guattari's skeletal assemblage theory.

In following while amplifying Braudel's world-economy, DeLanda's assemblage theory, allows us to see at the least that capitalism as it has become in our time as a series of world economies that detach and reattach as time goes by. It is no longer enough to say that the world-system, such as it is, is multipolar. It is that, but much more. Consider then examples of how DeLanda's assemblage theory allows us to think of capitalisms around the world since, say, 1990. At the end of the Cold War, many thought of American capitalism as the true and only world economy. But that turns out to have been far from the case. Already in the 1990s, Deng Xiaoping's economic reforms led to a new kind of mixed economy in which capitalist markets operate well enough within a still authoritarian State. There could hardly be a better example of a capitalist assemblage than China today as it moves about the world in Africa, the Caribbean, even Australia where China once mined Australia's Outback.

Meanwhile, in 1987 the World Economic Forum grew out of the European Management Forum to become what it is today, when its late January meetings in Davos gather thousands of the world's corporate leaders and economic policymakers in order to advance what came to be called neoliberal capitalism. Such a capitalism had little but legend to do with classically liberal free markets and invisible hands. The World Economic Forum encourages a capitalism in which Braudel's local markets and bazaars are an afterthought at best. It is a world economy of corporate interests. Then, too, among the most assemblage-like of various capitalist world economies were the BRIC economies (Brazil, Russia, India, and China) that early in the 21st century were widely thought to be the future of capitalism. Yet Brazil reverted to an authoritarian regime in 2018 when a regressively authoritarian, Jair Bolsonaro, won control of Brazil's political system and led the way to its economic stagnation. Meanwhile, India by contrast emerged as a robust export economy able to challenge China for dominance in the region, while China continued in its way eventually to undermine Hong Kong as one of the world's most important capital stock markets, while Russia drifted along its. Then, too, there is South Korea's economy built around chaebols—large corporate conglomerations with family ties. And on it goes. There are many more instances of mixed economies, some more or less capitalist, others but a shadow of capitalism. Neither classic liberal or neoliberal market theory, nor any of the Marxisms, not even European Social Democratic economies can put forth a coherent model for these many and proliferating instances of capitalist assemblages.

Yet, of the several ideas and their tangents associated with assemblage theories, there is sufficient congruence to encourage a radical rethinking of received notions as to what capitalism has become. Whatever else it is, there are few good reasons remaining to consider capitalism either a singular or a meta-macro structure of the worlds it inhabits. It is possible to say that there are as many capitalisms as there are democracies. And why should it be otherwise? From the first, capitalisms have always sneaked into cultural and political nooks and crannies to infuse the altogether nasty notion that potential workers are, if not truly free, free enough to subject themselves to any mode of production that promises a meager reward for their labor power. This terrible fact of modern life is true—whether the laborers work on the few factory floors that remain, or in the every growing fast-food industry flipping greasy burgers for the poor, or in call centers in Mumbai or South Dakota selling stuff only the lonely buy, and on and on. Wherever workers work in any capitalist system they are ground down in no time for the inhuman end of producing surplus value, whether material or expressive.

Whatever else assemblage theories offer, they evoke the possibility of a world in which, in principle, the assembled parts of the many capitalisms can detach, remove themselves, to find another—perhaps better—place to do what they do. In fact, that may be what the mixing and matching of capitalisms the world over are doing without regard to the inherited rules of economic rights and wrongs that, over more than a half-millennium, have not much made the world a better place for most and certainly for all human societies.

Notes

1 Gilles Deleuze and Felix Guattari, *Anti-Oedipus: Capitalism and Schizophrenia*, trans. Robert Hurley, Mark Seem, and Helen R. Lane (New York: Viking Press, 1977 [1972]), 182.
2 Giorgio Agamben, *The Coming Community*, trans. Michael Hardt (Minneapolis: University of Minnesota, 1993 [1990]), 64.
3 Félix Guattari, *The Machinic Unconscious: Essays in Schizoanalysis* (Semiotext(e), 2011 [1979]), 11; emphasis added.
4 Gilles Deleuze and Félix Guattari, *A Thousand Plateaus: Capitalism and Schizophrenia* (Minneapolis: University of Minnesota Press (1987 [1980]), 3–4; emphasis added.
5 *Ibid.*, 22.
6 *Ibid.*, 424.
7 *Ibid.*, 333.
8 *Ibid.*, 427.
9 *Ibid.*, 429.
10 *Ibid.*, 433.
11 *Ibid.*, 443–444.
12 In addition, there is a 2016 book, *Assemblage Theory*, which is a collection of essays on and around the general theme of titular subject where, here and there, DeLanda clarifies several of his exceptions with Deleuze.
13 Manuel DeLanda, *A New Philosophy of Society: Assemblage Theory and Social Complexity* (London: Continuum Books, 2006), 1.
14 *Ibid.*, 4.
15 *Ibid.*, 5.
16 *Ibid.*, 18–19; emphasis added.
17 *Ibid.*, 59–63, 66, 87, 92.
18 Charles Tilly, *From Mobilization to Revolution* (New York: Random House, 1978), 98–99. More generally this book by Tilly was arguably the foundation text of resource

320   *Capitalism's Uncertain Future*

mobilization theories, of which since there have been many subsequent books and experts. DeLanda does not refer to this book by Tilly in *A New Philosophy of Society* but he does quote and refer to Tilly as many times as he cites Deleuze. See Charles Tilly, *Stories, Identities, and Political Change* (Lanham, Maryland: Rowman & Littlefield, 2002). In contrast to both DeLanda and Deleuze, Tilly's theory over many years was deeply and broadly based on empirical social history.

19 Manuel DeLanda, *Assemblage Theory* (Edinburgh: Edinburgh University Press, 2016), 40–41.

20 *Ibid.*, ix.

21 Fernand Braudel, *The Mediterranean and the Mediterranean World in the Age of Philip II* (New York: Harper & Row, 1972 [1949]).

22 DeLanda, *Philosophy of Society*, 17.

23 Fernand Braudel, *The Perspective of the World* (New York: Harper & Row (1984 [1979]), 280–282.

24 *Ibid.*, 22.

Part VI

Exploitation and Exclusion

39 Exploitative Capitalism in the Global South

The Dar es Salaam School

The Invisible Committee said it best: "Everyone agrees. It's about to explode." That the current conjuncture is marked by crisis is hardly a bold or surprising claim. From the top-down, the crisis—a result of the contradictions of neoliberal capitalism—can be richly and accurately described using existing theories of political economy. So why bother devising a theory of capitalism from the Global South? Because these top-down theories of capitalism either describe the terminal crisis of capitalism within the Global North[1] or describe the crisis of the entire world economy from a Global North perspective,[2] few theories of political economy describe and explain the crisis from the perspective of the working classes of the Global South. As a result, many of the popular theories of capitalism are inadequate in describing key structural processes in and of the Global South. However, more importantly, because they are inaccurate descriptors, they are not useful for designing a praxis that would dismantle structures of capitalism and imperialism.

What must a theory of capitalism then do in order to be a "theory of the Global South?" The idea of "the Third World writing its own history" seems only to reaffirm the opposition of Orient and Occident in privileging some narratives over others based solely on the ascriptive characteristics of who writes them.[3] Some have argued theories of the Global South must accurately describe the lived social realities of the Global South.[4] But really, is it the case that the best we can do is create theory with the experiences of the Global South in mind rather than the mainline model of forcing Global South case studies into Eurocentric theories? Others contend that theories of the Global South must be distinct from the epistemology of the European Enlightenment.[5] It is, however, unclear given how all-encompassing and contradictory the European Enlightenment is in producing structures of knowledge, whether it would be possible to work fully outside of European modes of thought, which are themselves hybrid, barring some radical restructuring of the academy and of knowledge production. While many theorists are claiming to do non-Eurocentrist theory or theory of the Global South, the reality is, it's difficult to craft one when there's no consensus as to what a "theory of (or for) the Global South" really is, nor what it is meant to do.

DOI: 10.4324/9781003198291-45

324   *Exploitation and Exclusion*

Can Marxist political economy offer a solution? In the introductory essay to this book, I closed with an analysis of Marx's essays on India, concluding that he reproduced the common imperialist views of his time in his analysis of global capitalism from the perspective of India's economic development. Now, I return to the question of whether classical Marxism can accurately describe capitalism as seen from the Global South.

Left Challenges to Marxism-Leninism

The First International/Biennio Rosso/Global Maoism

To begin such an endeavor, my launching point is to evaluate previous examples of theoretical debates where left critics questioned the ability of Marxism to adequately describe and explain the political economy of capitalism from the perspective of the peripheries of the capitalist world-system. In the theoretical cleavages resulting from the First International, along with the debates between Maoism and Marxism-Leninism in the second half of the 20th century, left critiques of Marxism that endeavor to better explain and describe economic and political conditions from the peripheries of the capitalist world-system emerge. In this section of the essay, I'll detail the debates between Marxists and anarchists in the First International through the Biennio Rosso, and then examine the debates between Maoists and Marxist-Leninists in the second half of the 20th century. Through these debates between anarchists and Marxists and then later between Maoists and Marxists, I contend, one can better craft a political economy of capitalism as seen from working-class movements of the Global South.

The First International

From 1864 to 1972, the goal of the International Workingmen's Association, now referred to as the First International, was to unite the anti-capitalist (socialist, communist, anarchist, and trade unionist) left. In the context of this endeavor, Marx and Bakunin engaged in vociferous debates, as a result of which "Marx's theory acquired certain of its defining accents and rigidities and developed its character."[6] Even though "these early political battles ended in 1872 with Bakunin's expulsion from the IWA, the war of which they were a part continued and indeed, continues still."[7] In other words, the Marx/Bakunin debate still continues to this day among left theorists and strategists.

In characterizing the First International, Alvin Gouldner contends that it is well not to overemphasize Marx and Bakunin's differences, but instead, to begin any assessment of the debates of the First International by citing commonalities. Both Marx and Bakunin posited that the economic foundations of society were more significant in determining social outcomes compared to political and ideological superstructures; both asserted the overthrow of capitalism as the ultimate goal of the left; both were opposed to so-called "bourgeois individualism" and instead believed in the ideals of cooperation and communal life; both were avowed atheists; both saw themselves as natural scientists of the social world; and both began their scholarly endeavors as staunch Hegelians.

One of the most significant cleavages between Marx and Bakunin is with respect to the role of the state. While Marx believed that a centralized state in which workers owned the means of production was the ideal outcome of revolutionary struggle,[8] Bakunin went further in wanting to dismantle structures of power and class privilege wherever he observed them. Said Bakunin, even "sincere socialists and revolutionaries" are potentially corrupted by power. With a centralized state that controls the means of production, decried Bakunin:

> a new privileged class of bureaucrats and educated would arise, the state would grow more powerful than ever, and the mass of society would simply have exchanged one master for another. Thus Bakunin could only think that Engel's formulation — "Do away with capital... and the state will fall of itself" was a fairytale of which German intellectuals were mindlessly fond.[9]

While Marx focused on how the dominant class rules through the state,[10] Bakunin theorized that the state rules through the dominant class. This distinction is important, as it not only lends itself to a different understanding of the key locus of state power, but also implicates a distinct set of tactics and strategies for dismantling the capitalist world-system.

Gouldner analyzes Bakunin's differences from Marx when it comes to theorizing the state:

> Bakunin thus regarded Marx's socialism a bourgeois socialism— not because Marxism sought to secure the future of the bourgeois economy or its bourgeois proprietors, but because Bakunin felt Marxism was imbued with bourgeois *sentiments* and *culture* and expressed the elite ambitions of a New Class of intellectuals that had grown out of the old moneyed capitalists.[11]

But I contend that Gouldner doesn't go far enough in his analysis of this difference; this cleavage is not *only* from the fact that Marx came from an elite background in a more developed country, but because Bakunin was theorizing the capitalist world-system from the peripheries of his era. From this perspective, Bakunin more readily intuited the exploitation, exclusion, power, and hierarchies inherent in the capitalist world-system, particularly as articulated outside of the core.

The differences between Marx and Bakunin are not simply those of theory and praxis but a much more profound division. Gouldner contends that

326   *Exploitation and Exclusion*

Marx being German and Bakunin being Russian in this debate, "each was steeped in his own different culture and ethnocentrism that were an abiding source of mutual irritation and suspicion."[12] Furthermore, claims Gouldner, this was also the source of Bakunin's conviction of the revolutionary power and potential of the peasant classes, while Marx saw peasants as a petty bourgeoisie with no revolutionary promise.[13] I would take Gouldner's argument a step further and propose that this division between Marx and Bakunin is not simply one of tensions between a German perspective focused on the agency of the working class and a Russian perspective concerned with the agency of the peasants, but instead, the perspective of someone analyzing capitalism from its core versus an analysis of capitalism as seen from its peripheries. "Bakunin knew both Western and Eastern Europe first-hand and he understood at once that Marx's theory had been limited by the special conditions of its origin and development."[14] As such, Bakunin is among the first theorists of capitalism from the perspective of the Global South.

Revisiting the debate of the First International is important because it demonstrates that "the forms and institutions of the old society will not simply fall away: they will become entrenched, denying the possibility of genuine liberation. They must therefore be removed straight away—their destruction must be the first revolutionary act."[15] The anarchist perspective that emerged from the debates of the First International showed that Marx's idea of a dictatorship of the proletariat was, in effect, a dictatorship *over* the proletariat. According to Gouldner:

> Bakunin thought that the whole idea of the proletariat as itself a ruling class was ludicrous, and he believed that what Marxism implied was the culmination of power in the hands of a new state dominated by a new class of bureaucrats and technocrats.[16]

Bakunin's revolution, however, was "to be an act of thoroughgoing destruction; going well beyond a political or even economic change, it would level the ground for a new beginning."[17]

This anarchist perspective is consistent with some of the Marxisant theory we've detailed in this book, particularly those who contend that the state is a precondition for capital accumulation like Braudel and the Annales School or the German Historical School. What makes these approaches more accurate descriptions of the capitalist system is that they understand that it doesn't matter which class controls the state, the state will always perpetuate some form of hierarchy, inequality, and exploitation that benefits the class that controls the state.

Biennio Rosso

Several decades after the First International, the *Biennio Rosso* provided yet another context for debating Marxism and its left alternatives. The *Biennio*

Rosso was a period of revolutionary insurrection in Italy from 1919 to 1921, during which workers occupied and self-managed their factories and other workplaces. Worker self-management was a strategy that was generally advocated by Anarcho-Syndicalists during the *Biennio Rosso*, but there were active debates, mainly in Antonio Gramsci's journal *L'Ordine Nuovo* and the Anarchist newspaper *Umanità Nova*, on how to build an enduring workers' revolution on the basis of the factory councils.

Errico Malatesta principally articulated the anarchist perspective while Antonio Gramsci put forth the Marxist strategy. These debates between Gramsci and Malatesta stem from the legacy of the First International. Bakunin moved to Italy in the 1860s and was an integral part of the development of Anarchism in Italy.[18] Italian anarchists had a significant presence at the First International, including Errico Malatesta and Carlo Caifero. Bakunin, Malatesta, and Caifero then attempted anarchist insurrections in Florence in 1869 and in Bologna in 1874. Italian anarchism flourished throughout the later part of the 19th century, and in 1912, the *Unione Sindacale Italiana* was founded in Modena as an attempt to institutionalize the Italian anarchist legacy of the First International.

During the *Biennio Rosso* (1919–1921), Marxists and Anarcho-Syndicalists famously debated how workers' revolutions could succeed. Antonio Gramsci argued that the workers' struggle would succeed only if workers were to take over the state, thus creating a workerist state favorable to the factory councils, along with other ideals and goals of the revolution. In the journal *L'Ordine Nuovo*, Antonio Gramsci (1919) writes:

> It consists in an effort aimed at shattering the bourgeois state machine and forming a new type of state in whose framework the liberated productive forces find an adequate form for their further development and expansion; in whose organization they find strong defences and the necessary and sufficient arms to suppress their adversaries.[19]

Following Bakunin, Anarcho-Syndicalists, such as Errico Malatesta, theorized that the state would crumble as a result of worker ownership of the means of production. Malatesta hypothesized that the state would be powerless to suppress the factory councils if the syndicalist movement were to remain strong. Malatesta (1965) writes:

> workers thought that the moment was ripe to take possession once [and] for all the means of production. They armed for self-defence. . . and began to organise production on their own. . . And the government stood by because it felt impotent to offer opposition.[20]

Malatesta was confident that through a strong union movement and control of the means of production, the state would be powerless to suppress the factories. Most Italian collectives chose this anarchist route, only to see the

328 *Exploitation and Exclusion*

state repress their workplaces after a successful Fascist takeover led by Benito Mussolini's Blackshirts. Malatesta's strategy to keep the state in a state of crisis did not work, since Fascists were able to seize that opening to establish an authoritarian state.

The "chaos and violence" of this experiment with worker-occupied and -managed firms in Northern Italy, the debates between Left parties and trade unions and those between Marxists and Anarcho-Syndicalists were used by Fascists in propaganda campaigns to justify Mussolini's rule.[21] The defeated Anarcho-Syndicalist faction of the Biennio Rosso went on to not only form a revolutionary anti-fascist alliance,[22] but also linked the anti-fascist struggle to that of opposing the colonization of Ethiopia. The autonomous workers' anti-fascist alliance contended that the autonomist workers movement must demonstrate a consistent position against authoritarianism in all forms, and even outside of Europe.[23] This position necessitated anti-fascists to take an anti-colonial position on Italy's aggression in Eastern Africa. While admittedly this position seems an obvious one, other leftist groups in Fascist Europe failed to link the anti-fascist struggle with the anti-colonial struggle in the fight against global authoritarianism.

Global Maoism

Over time, this Marx/Bakunin division would come to be characterized as the distinction between a Scientific and a Critical Marxism. The legacy of Bakunin's Critical Marxism was foundational to "Third Worldist" thought.[24] While anarchism and Anarcho-Syndicalism may be the more popular left critique of Marxism in the Global North today, Maoism, since the 1960s, has been and remains far more popular in the Global South (albeit with key exceptions during the World Revolution of 1968).[25] But this disjoint between which left critiques resonate in different structural locations of the world-system is surprising, given that "Mao's antecedents reach back through Bakunin to Weitling."[26] Both Anarchist and Maoist critiques of Marxism are rooted in a similar concern of dismantling the many hierarchies of capitalist power as seen from the peripheries of the system.

Just as Bakunin critiqued Marxism from the perspective of the peripheries of the capitalist world economy of his day, central to Mao's thought was not just the dependent development stemming from the expansion of capitalism from Europe to the rest of the world through colonialism and other processes, but a more encompassing concept of uneven development. Writes Althusser: "For as Mao puts it in a phrase as clear as the dawn, 'Nothing in this world develops absolutely evenly'... it does not concern imperialism alone, but absolutely 'everything in this world.'"[27] Capitalism, as seen from the world regions where the uneven development of capitalism could be best intuited, led anti-capitalist theorists to more accurately describe the historical development of global capitalism. Furthermore, these regions were

Exploitative Capitalism in Global South 329

also more likely to put those theories to use in forming more successful anti-capitalist praxis. As Althusser identifies:

> The revolution, governed by capitalism's basic contradiction, did not succeed until Imperialism, and succeeded in the 'favourable' conditions that were precisely points of historical rupture, the 'weakest links': not England, France or Germany, but 'backward' Russia (Lenin), China and Cuba (ex-colonies, lands exploited by Imperialism).[28]

Maoism was particularly well suited to not only describe capitalism as seen from the Global South in the mid-20th century, but also to animate movements of resistance against the capitalist world-system. Or as Frederic Jameson put it, "Maoism," was the "richest of all the great new ideologies of the 60s."[29] For Mao, the revolution must occur not just by "the revolutionary conquest of the bourgeois state, its destruction," but as a result of a long-term class war.[30] Just as Bakunin had earlier pointed out the flaws of Marx's revolution as a dictatorship *over* the proletariat rather than a dictatorship *of* the proletariat, so too did Mao observe that workers' revolution entailed the destruction of the state entirely along with a long-term class struggle.

But unlike Bakuninism, which was popular in Eastern and Southern Europe and among diaspora communities across the Americas, Maoism became an animating ideology for much of the globe. Maoism was central to mid-20th-century Third Worldism. In Mao's conceptualization of the Third World, he sought solidarity with Asia, Africa, and Latin America against the "capitalist imperialism" of the First World and the "social imperialism" of the Second World.[31] Third Worldism, then, was "an alternative that promised national liberation from capitalist hegemony, and the possibility of entering global history not as its object but as an independent subject."[32] As such, Maoism was not just suited to critique European imperialism and uneven capitalist development, but could also elucidate "The paradoxical, or dialectical, combination of decolonization and neocolonialism."[33] Maoism showed:

> that the graceful, grudging or violent end of old fashioned imperialism certainly meant the end of one kind of domination but evidently also the invention and construction of a new kind— symbolically, something like the replacement of the British Empire by the International Monetary Fund.[34]

Through its complex understanding of capitalism, imperialism, and class struggle, Maoism was well equipped to explain the transition from uneven development as a result of imperialism to uneven development as a result of new international financial institutions such as the IMF and World Bank.

In the contemporary context, Maoism continues to be relevant for Global South movements against capitalism and imperialism. Intellectual leaders of

330   *Exploitation and Exclusion*

Third Worldist movements across the Global South had Maoist influences, including Subcomandante Marcos of the Zapatista Movement, Jose Maria Sison of the New People's Army in the Philippines, Abimael Guzman of the Shining Path in Peru, Abdullah Ocalan of the Kurdish Communist Party, Black Panthers in Oakland, California, and Charu Mazumdar of the Naxalite Movement in India.[35,36] "Their insistence on revolutionary authenticity represented a criticism of conventional communist politics."[37] Maoism, in these contexts:

> pertained primarily to issues of class struggle under conditions of imperialism, and the role of the peasantry in the revolution... In Maoist movements in the Third World, as in the Chinese Revolution, class struggle was linked inextricably to issues of national independence and development.[38]

In other words:

> the Maoist strategy of self-reliant development — the promise to end the economic dependency the legacy of colonialism has left to the developed world — was another source of attraction to Third World radicals... the Maoist strategy of development promised to 'delink' national economies from globalizing capitalism and reconstruct them to serve local needs rather than the demands of global capital.[39]

To summarize the debates between Marxism and left alternatives in dialectal terms: for Marx, synthesis, thesis, and antithesis are transcended and the old remains in the new in a transformed way that allows for liberation; but for Bakunin and Mao, the antithesis obliterates the thesis and therefore synthesis is something fundamentally new. Old hierarchies of the thesis and antithesis are destroyed, thereby making way for liberation. The major difference between these two approaches hinges on the transformation versus the destruction of the state. As Alain Badiou writes, "we cannot be content with seizing state power as such and must destroy the machine of the bourgeois state."[40] The broader problem is that Marxist theory is "trapped within an authoritarian bind"[41] in its insistence on state transformation rather than destruction. Theories grounded in anarchism and Maoism escape the authoritarian bind because they analyze capitalism from the perspective of the Global South. In so doing, they are able to offer insights and strategies of resistance that Marxism cannot.

As we have demonstrated in this book, particularly in the theories of Mustafa Khayati, Nestor Makhno, Ulrike Meinhoff, Bhagat Singh, Joseph Edwards, Lucia Sanchez Saornil, Noam Chomsky, and other antiauthoritarians, the larger problem with Marxist theory is that it inhibits theories of capitalism from accurately describing capitalism as seen from the Global South. In its statism, Marxism retains an authoritarian current that

Exploitative Capitalism in Global South   331

reproduces the authority and power of the capitalist state, and therefore the capitalist system. This makes classical Marxism a good descriptor of capitalism as seen from the dominant perspective, i.e. the capitalist class and the states of the Global North, but in its ability to craft a praxis towards a more just and democratic future for *all* of the world's inhabitants, it falls short.

Radical Political Economy and the Dar es Salaam School

Can we devise a political economy of capitalism as seen from the Global South that internalizes the Anarchist and Maoist critiques of Marxism-Leninism? Yes, I believe that the class analysis developed by the anti-imperialist Marxist tradition, particularly Frantz Fanon and Walter Rodney, can provide the foundations of a political economy that better describes and analyzes capitalism as seen from the Global South.

In the late 1960s, the University of Dar es Salaam, attracted radical political economists from across the globe, including Immanuel Wallerstein, Walter Rodney, Issa Shivji, and Giovanni Arrighi (who joined the University of Dar es Salaam in 1966 after being deported from Rhodesia for his participation in Rhodesia's movement for national liberation).[42] This group of political economists working in Dar es Salaam in the 1960s has been termed by some as the "Dar es Salaam School of History." Indian labor historian Sabyasachi Bhattacharya claims that the Dar es Salaam School, like the critical Latin American historians of the 1970s, solved the Global South's problem of "historylessness," i.e. that the history of the Global South was not the history of the people who forged society, but a history of "great" men. The Dar es Salaam School, claims Bhattacharya, paved the way for postcolonial social science to take up "intellectual decolonization" by practicing "history from below."[43]

However, the concept of "history from below" comes not from the "Third World," but from English historians of the early 20th century.[44] Therefore, "history from below" is not inherently "Third Worldist" nor even necessarily Left,[45] but through the historiographical methods of the Dar es Salaam School, claims Bhattacharya,[46] "history from below" can be *made* Left and "Third Worldist." To tell a critical history of workers and peasants in the Global South, Bhattacharya contends, historical analysis must go beyond simply broadening the scope of history or adding new subjects for analysis.[47] First, one must break with nationalist historiography. Second (and more importantly), one must view decolonization as not a struggle against colonialism for all people, but instead, "one must not 'render the colonial epoch in the history of the colonial people without class struggles.'"[48] In other words, historical analysis must not view decolonization as affecting all colonial subjects equally, but through the lens of class struggle in order to analyze how decolonization differentially affects different social classes.

In contrast to a scientific Marxist strategy of formal class analysis,[49] class analysis has the greatest explanatory power when situated in the global

332 *Exploitation and Exclusion*

context and seen dialectically.[50] A dialectical approach allows for a class analysis in which the class structure is seen as an ever-evolving and changing structure. Changes in the global class structure then are best seen from the peripheries of the capitalist world-system, as changes to the organization of global commodity chains alters the class structure.[51] While some scholars argue that this expansion derives from a search for new markets, colonialism and neo-imperialism are the key mechanism through which the capitalist system expands[52] and the global class structure thereby changes.

Frantz Fanon (1963) shows that the historical relations of production of the Global South that began with imperialism created a class structure with four main class categories: the bourgeoisie, the proletariat, the semi-proletariat, and the peasant classes.

While the proletariat of Europe and North America is the main antagonist of capital, the same does not hold for the postcolonial world. Fanon writes that:

> in colonial territories the proletariat is the kernel of the colonized people most pampered by the colonial regime. The embryonic urban proletariat is relatively privileged. In the capitalist countries, the proletariat has nothing to lose and possibly everything to gain. In the colonized countries, the proletariat has everything to lose.[53]

In the colonial context, the proletariat is among the few who have formal employment. As such, the working classes occupy a relatively privileged position in the class structure. As such, demonstrates Fanon, "This element makes up the most loyal clientele of the nationalist parties and by the privileged position that they occupy in the colonial system represent the 'bourgeois' fraction of the colonized population."[54] The postcolonial working class, given its relative privilege vis-à-vis semi-proletarian and agrarian classes, comprises the most loyal constituents of nationalist parties and continue to uphold the colonial class structure from which they continue to benefit.

The semi-proletariat, in contrast, is the revolutionary vanguard of the postcolonial class structure. Writes Fanon: "The lumpenproletariat, this cohort of starving men, divorced from the tribe and clan, constitutes one of the most spontaneously and radically revolutionary forces of a colonized people."[55] Because it is one of the most radical of the class forces in the postcolonial context, Fanon argues that:

> any national liberation movement should give this lumpenproletariat maximum attention. It will always respond to the call to revolt, but if the insurrection thinks it can afford to ignore it, then this famished underclass will pitch itself into the armed struggle and take part in the conflict, this time on the side of the oppressor.[56]

It is essential for any movement that endeavors to radical social change that it appeals to and harness the insurrectionary potential of the postcolonial semi-proletariat.

The semi-proletariat's radical potential is only rivaled by the peasant classes, of whom Fanon claims:

> it is obvious that in colonial countries only the peasantry is revolutionary. It has nothing to lose and everything to gain. The underprivileged and starving peasant is the exploited who very soon discovers that only violence pays. For him there is no compromise, no possibility of concession. Colonization or decolonization: it is simply a power struggle.[57]

While the semi-proletariat has a propensity for insurrection, for Fanon, the peasant classes are the true revolutionary class within the postcolonial class structure, for it is the peasant who bears the brunt of colonialism and has only violence by way of resistance.

The national bourgeoisie is the villain of Fanon's postcolonial class analysis. "The national bourgeoisie," he writes:

> which takes over power at the end of the colonial regime, is an underdeveloped bourgeoisie. Its economic clout is practically zero, and in any case, no way commensurate with that of its metropolitan counterpart which it intends replacing. In its wilful narcissism, that national bourgeoisie has lulled itself into thinking that it can supplant the metropolitan bourgeoisie to its own advantage. But independence, which literally forces it back against the wall, triggers catastrophic reactions and obliges it to send out distress signals in the direction of the former metropolis... This national bourgeoisie possesses neither industrialists nor financiers. The national bourgeoisie in underdeveloped countries is not geared to production, invention, creation, or work. All its energy is channelled into intermediary activities. Networking and scheming seem to be its underlying vocation. The national bourgeoisie has the psychology of a businessman, not that of a captain of industry. And it should go without saying that the rapacity of the colonists and the embargo system installed by colonialism hardly left it any choice.[58]

The national bourgeoisie, who are often the very class that leads the movement for national independence, keep the colonial system in place and supplant the class rule of the colonial regime with their own class rule. Unlike the colonial rulers, however, who are representatives of global capital, the national bourgeoisie are mere middlemen and women, who by virtue of the node they occupy in global value chains, cannot hope to supplant the global capitalist class, and therefore, cannot get out from under the yoke of the former colonial regime.

334 *Exploitation and Exclusion*

Walter Rodney provides us with a richer description of this postcolonial class structure by way of his analysis of the class structure of British Guiana. Slavery and Indentured labor, claims Rodney, played an important role in constituting the labor regime of the capitalist world-system across the Global South.[59] While the fact of forced and coerced labor is not the constitutive fact of the Global South, it does continue to structure capitalist relations of production. Because the types of production that take place in the peripheries of the capitalist system are the least profitable for capital,[60] workers in the Global South are subject to more exploitative relations of production compared to workers in the Global North where more lucrative profit-making activities are located.

In colonial British Guiana, "First and foremost, the class struggle was waged between free workers and plantation managers around the question of how much could be extracted from the labourer in any given work situation."[61] The national bourgeoisie and the semi-proletarian working classes comprised the key class antagonism. Plantation owners strategized to prevent potential labor unrest through several mechanisms. While during the economic crisis of the 1890s wage cuts were common, plantation managers "devised techniques to punish resistance and reward self-effacing behaviour."[62] New indentured labor was regularly brought from India's Gangetic Plains because newly arrived laborers were less militant than workers who had been living in Guyana for a while.[63] Plantation owners also restricted the political participation of the racialized colonial working class. They "controlled registration and pre-election procedures, and they had the backing of the courts. In October 1891, it was reported that the planters were withholding registration forms and preventing their distribution."[64]

The role that colonial capital and the local working classes played in the class structure of Guyana fits well with Fanon's class analysis. British colonial capital controlled both state institutions and the plantation economy and used this politico-economic power in order to keep workers alienated:

> The most sharply defined of the existing classes in British Guiana comprised the capitalists, who owned most of the means of production controlled the institutions of the colonial state, and secured most of the surplus alienated through wage labour or market mechanisms. The remarkable extent of planter political power meant that steps were taken to keep other classes underdeveloped, and the boundaries between them were very fluid. The working class was particularly restricted because of the peripheral nature of the economy and because sociopolitical relations favoured the persistence of indentureship.[65]

The persistence of indentureship, especially after the abolition of slavery, allowed British colonial capital to keep other classes from realizing their class interests by pitting emancipated Afro-Guyanese workers against indentured Indo-Guyanese workers.

The use of brown and black forced labor was central to the introduction of capitalism to the Americas. Imperialism furthered the interests of European capital through the exploitation of labor.[66] In British Guiana, for example, British colonial rulers stoked class and racial tension in order to divide and rule. British strategy of reinforcing racial divisions between Brown and Black working classes "held back the development of a plantation workers' movement."[67] "The tragedy of... Guyana and Trinidad," claims Walter Rodney, "is the fact that both [black and brown workers] are held captive by the European ways of thinking."[68] Both brown and black workers internalized the racial tensions that the British stoked to prevent working classes from uniting across racial lines.

While Imperialism made racism global in order to divide and ultimately exploit a global racialized working class,[69] systems of slavery and indenture were similarly foundational in creating globalized capitalist relations of production which provided a basis for workers across the Global South to realize labor solidarity. Writes Rodney: "Guiana had long been a part of the international division of labour—ever since slavery—and the working class of the nineteenth century was in a position to recognize its affinities with labour elsewhere."[70] C.L.R. James's astute observation on the theoretical relationship between race and class was that:

> The race question is subsidiary to the class question in politics, and to think of imperialism in terms of race is disastrous. But to neglect the racial factor as merely incidental is an error only less grave than to make it fundamental[71]

shows how these questions of race and class are central to understanding postcolonial political economy. Because of the global reach of the European colonial empires, but more importantly, their underlying capitalist logic, despite the racial and class divides in British Guiana and elsewhere, labor solidarity locally and globally, claims Rodney, is possible.

"Capitalism," more broadly, Rodney posits:

> has created its own irrationalities such as a vicious white racism... the irrationality of incredible poverty in the midst of wealth and wastage even inside the biggest capitalist economies, such as that of the United States of America. Above all, capitalism has intensified its own political contradictions in trying to subjugate nations and continents outside of Europe, so that workers and peasants in every part of the globe have become self-conscious and are determined to take their destiny into their own hands.[72]

When analyzing and describing capitalism from the perspective of the Global South, as Rodney so deftly elucidates in the passage above, the labor question is central. One cannot view capitalism from the Global South,

336   *Exploitation and Exclusion*

therefore, without centering the analysis in class struggle. This is even more salient today than in Fanon and Rodney's time, as most of the world's production now takes places in the Global South. The exploitation of a racialized postcolonial labor force continues to structure capitalist relations of production to this day.

Exploitation and Capitalism in the Global South

The Dar es Salaam school of historiography called for a break with nationalist historiography, and in so doing, urged researchers to view colonial history and the post-independence histories through the lens of class struggle. Thereby, the Dar es Salaam School instructs us on how to create a theory of capitalist political economy from the Global South perspective. That is, to craft a theory of political economy of the Global South, one must center historical and theoretical narratives in the context of postcolonial class struggles.

Narratives of postcolonial class struggle are central to understanding and describing capitalism from the perspective of the bottom-up. However, it would be fallacious to assume that the fundamental fact of capitalism is the exploitation of labor by capital. Capitalism is a system in which capital is a means to power. Therefore, the fundamental fact of capitalism is the endless accumulation of capital. The exploitation of labor is one of several means to that end.

"Capitalist rulers," explains Giovanni Arrighi, "tend to increase their power by piling up wealth in a small container and increase the size of their container only if it is justified by the requirements of the accumulation of capital."[73] Capitalists are limited by the states in which they are located, expanding to other territories when capital accumulation so requires. Because expansion—what neoliberals might call "opening new markets"—is central to the endless accumulation of capital, capitalists employ territorial expansion as a means to augment profit. Even though power is accrued through the endless accumulation of capital in the context of a capitalist world-system, capitalists often "identify power with the extent of their command over scarce resources and consider territorial acquisitions as a means and a by-product of the accumulation of capital."[74]

Imperialism and capital accumulation, therefore, go hand in hand in the context of the capitalist world system. The historic peripheries were incorporated into the capitalist world economy in such a way that benefitted capital in the core of the capitalist world economy. The exploitation of Global South labor is just one of several strategies Europe employed in order to profit from imperialist territorial expansion. As Dan Nabudere has shown:

> although the time scale, participants, and immediate aims differed, this expansionism, particularly in the 18th and 19th centuries, had one common objective: the accumulation of surplus products (including

'surplus' human products known as slaves) as well as surplus value created in these countries.[75]

Europe's initial reason for establishing imperial outposts in Africa and Asia was related to its objective to better place itself within trade routes to and from Asia. Over time, this imperial expansion was not solely about securing access to trade routes but also in creating pools of cheap or free labor, along with raw materials for manufacturing inputs and other means of accumulating surplus value.

While from the top-down we can see imperialism as fundamentally about finance capital,[76] from the perspective of the working classes of the Global South for whom the world of finance capital remains elusive, imperialism is experienced as the exploitation of labor. The rate of exploitation of labor is much higher in the peripheries of the capitalist world-system compared to in its core. "la soumission croissante du travail au capital à l'échelle du système dans son ensemble," Samir Amin elucidates, "ce qui traduit par one extension de l'aire de la soumission formelle à la périphérie."[77] Therefore, "il faut replacer la contradiction pays développés-pays sous-développés dans l'ensemble des contradictions qui caractérisent la lutte des classes à l'échelle mondiale."[78] The overexploitation of labor in the postcolonial world is the underlying cause of limited opportunities for capital accumulation and ultimately financialization led by and for the Global South. "La lutte des classes, dans toute sa complexité, reste au centre de tous les problèmes," [79] claims Samir Amin, "et une périodisation corrects du système ne peut reposer que sur l'analyse des modifications dans les conditions de celles-ci."[80] In other words, because the fundamental fact of capitalism from the perspective of the working classes of the Global South is the hyper-exploitation of labor by imperial and neo-imperial capital, one cannot analyze capitalism from a Global South perspective without grounding that description and analysis in a class struggle paradigm.

While in the heyday of the Dar es Salaam School, analysis of class struggle in the Global South as a way to better understand and describe the capitalist world economy was relatively common practice, this mode of analysis has fallen out of fashion. Instead, the concept of exclusion as a way to describe the condition of the working classes of the Global South has become increasingly popular.[81] But, I contend, there cannot be exclusion without exploitation for there is a dialectal relationship between exploitation and exclusion. Global South workers are hyper-exploited because of their historical exclusion from the comparatively less exploitative labor arrangement found in the core. They are coerced into free labor or compelled to sell their labor power cheaply because they are part of a reserve army of labor. They are a part of this reserve army of labor because they only have opportunities to sell labor power extremely cheaply and/or infrequently, which can only but provide a life on the margins. The state and capital, both in the colonial period and postindependence, remain complicit with this arrangement as the

Exploitation and Exclusion

national capitalist class (as middlemen) and international capital are the ultimate beneficiaries. As such, exploitation, I contend, remains the preferable lens with which to analyze capitalism from the perspective of the working classes of the Global South.

Those who are excluded from the capitalist world economy, Harry Braverman terms, following Marx, "the stagnant relative surplus population." These members of the global working class are irregularly, marginally, or casually employed and live precarious lives earning barely enough to survive. "The stagnant relative surplus population," Braverman explains, "irregularly and casually employed, furnishes to capital," in Marx's words, "an inexhaustible reservoir of disposable labour-power. Its conditions of life sink below the average normal level of the working-class; this makes it at once the broad basis of special branches of capitalist exploitation."[82] This so-called excluded class increases with the relative power of capital and is fundamental to the successful extraction of surplus value by capital. Writes Marx:

> the relative mass of the industrial reserve army increases therefore with the potential energy of wealth. But the greater this reserve army in proportion to the active labour-army, the greater is the mass of a consolidated surplus-population, whose misery is in an inverse ratio to its torment of labour. The more extensive, finally, the lazarus-layers of the working-class, and the industrial reserve army, the great is official pauperism. This is the absolute general law of capitalist accumulation. Like all other laws it is modified in its working by many circumstances, the analysis of which does not concern us here.[83]

In other words, the more workers who are kept in precarious conditions relative to those exploited in formal employment, the greater the capital's ability to accumulate capital from the production process. Through increasingly locating production in the Global South and in using unfree and/or racialized labor forces, the historical processes of imperialism, neo-imperialism, slavery, indenture, offshoring, and export processing zones, all allow for capital to realize ever-larger profit margins, furthering capitalist growth and the endless accumulation of capital. The Dar es Salaam School's call for grounding analyses of capitalism in a class struggle-based approach,[84] therefore remain just as salient today as they were in the 1960s and the 1970s, if not more so, as now most of the production process is located in the Global South under conditions of hyper-exploitation. Or as Walter Rodney put it, "Now the 'have nots', who are the mass of the black people, know that things have been getting worse."[85]

Conclusions

While the current crisis of the capitalist world-system can be adequately described and analyzed from the perspective of finance capital based in the

Global North, one can't fully understand social conditions in the Global South without also taking a class struggle-based approach. In order to fully take up this class struggle approach, we need to move beyond the classical Marxist framework to fully incorporate imperial expansion and the hyper-exploitation of labor that it engenders as one of the essential facts about capitalism. While left critics of Marx, from Bakunin to Malatesta to Mao, rightfully pointed out some of the flaws of Marxist political economy in describing and analyzing capitalism from the perspective of the Global South, the best theoretical tools for doing so are found in the Dar es Salaam School. Anti-imperialist political economists such as Walter Rodney, Giovanni Arrighi, Issa Shivji, Immanuel Wallerstein, Dan Nabudere, John Saul, Yashpal Tandon, and others crafted a theory of global capitalism in which imperialism and class struggle were at the fore of the analysis. In so doing, the insights of the Dar es Salaam School must be recovered in order to craft a better political economy of global capitalism.

Notes

1 Robert Brenner, *The Boom and the Bubble: The US in the World Economy* (London: Verso, 2002); Robert Brenner, *The Economics of Global Turbulence* (London: Verso, 2006); Klaus Dörre Stephan Lessinich, and Hartmut Rosa, *Sociology, Capitalism, Critique* (London: Verso, 2015); Gretta Krippner, *Capitalizing on Crisis* (Cambridge: Harvard University Press, 2011); Richard D. Wolff, *Capitalism's Crisis Deepens* (Chicago: Haymarket Books, 2016); Nick Srnicek and Alex Williams, *Inventing the Future: Postcapitalism and a World Without Work* (London: Verso, 2015); Wolfgang Streek, *How Will Capitalism End?* (London: Verso, 2016).

2 Craig Calhoun and Georgi Derlugian, eds. *Business as Usual: The Roots of the Global Financial Meltdown* (New York: New York University Press, 2011); Ha-Joon Chang, *23 Things They Don't Tell You about Capitalism* (New York: Bloomsbury Press, 2010); David Harvey, *The Limits to Capital* (London: Verso, 2006); David Harvey, *The Enigma of Capital And The Crises of Capitalism* (Oxford: Oxford University Press, 2010); Paul Mason, *Postcapitalism: A Guide to Our Future* (New York: Farrar, Straus and Giroux, 2015).

3 Gyan Prakash, "Writing Post-Orientalist Histories of the Third World: Perspectives from Indian Historiography," *Comparative Studies in Society and History* 32, no. 2 (2009): 383.

4 Samir Amin, *Eurocentrism* (New York: Monthly Review Press, 2009); Samir Amin, *Global History: A View from the South* (Cape Town: Pambazuka Press, 2011); Raewyn Connell, *Southern Theory* (Cambridge: Polity Press, 2007).

5 Andre Gunder Frank, *ReOrient* (Berkeley: University of California Press, 1998); Julian Go, *Postcolonial Thought and Social Theory* (Oxford: Oxford University Press, 2016); Walter D. Mignolo, *Local Histories/Global Designs: Coloniality, Subaltern Knowledges, and Border Thinking* (Princeton: Princeton University Press, 2000).

6 Alvin W. Gouldner, "Marx's Last Battle: Bakunin and the First International," *Theory and Society* (1982): 853.

7 *Ibid.*, 853.

8 Marx in Robert Tucker, ed. *The Marx-Engels Reader* (New York: W.W. Norton and Company, 1972), 490.

9 Gouldner, "Marx's Last Battle," 865.

10 Marx in Tucker, *Marx-Engels Reader*, 490–491. See also, Saul Newman, *From Bakunin to Lacan: Anti-Authoritarianism and the Dislocation of Power* (Lanham: Lexington Books, 2007), 23.

11 Gouldner, "Marx's Last Battle," 872; emphasis original.

340 *Exploitation and Exclusion*

12 *Ibid.*, 857.

13 *Ibid.*, 858.

14 *Ibid.*, 873.

15 Newman, *Bakunin to Lacan*, 28.

16 Gouldner, "Marx's Last Battle," 876.

17 *Ibid.*, 874.

18 T.R. Ravindranathan, *Bakunin and the Italians* (Montreal: McGill University Press, 1988), 18.

19 Antonio Gramsci, "Sindacati e Consigli" *L'Ordine Nuovo* (11 October 1919): 159–160.

20 Errico Malatesta, *Malatesta: Life and Times*, ed. V Richards (London: Freedom House, 1964), 134.

21 Paolo Spriano, *L'Occupazione delle fabbriche* (Torino: Giulio Einaudi Editore Spa, 1964), 137.

22 Luigi Di Lembo, *Guerra di classe e lotta umana: L'anarchismo in Italia dal Bienno rosso alla Guerra di Spagna (1919–1939)* (Pisa: BFS Edizioni, 2001), 190.

23 *Ibid.*, 192.

24 Gouldner, "Marx's Last Battle," 881.

25 See Julian Bourg, "The Red Guards of Paris: French Student Maoism of the 1960s," *History of European Ideas* 31 (2005): 472–490; Camille Robcis, "'China in Our Heads': Althusser, Maoism, and Structuralism," *SocialText* 30, no. 1 (2012): 51–69; Daniel Singer, *Prelude to Revolution: France in May 1968* (Chicago: Haymarket Books, 2013); Quinn Slobodian, *Foreign Front: Third World Politics in Sixties West Germany* (Durham: Duke University Press, 2012).

26 Gouldner, "Marx's Last Battle," 853–854.

27 Louis Althusser, *For Marx* (London: Verso, 2005 [1965]), 166.

28 *Ibid.*, 172–173.

29 Frederic Jameson, "Periodizing the 60s," *SocialText* 9/10 (1984): 188.

30 Louis Althusser, *On the Reproduction of Capitalism: Ideology and Ideological State Apparatuses* (London: Verso, 2014), 151.

31 Arif Dirlik, "Mao Zedong Thought and the Third World/Global South," *Interventions: International Journal of Postcolonial Studies* 16, no. 2 (2014): 235.

32 *Ibid.*, 236.

33 Jameson, "Periodizing the 60s," 184.

34 *Ibid.*, 184.

35 See Chapter 7 of this volume.

36 Dirlik, "Mao Zedong Thought," 247.

37 *Ibid.*, 248.

38 *Ibid.*, 249.

39 *Ibid.*, 254.

40 Alain Badiou, *The Communist Hypothesis* (London: Verso, 2010), 274.

41 Newman, *From Bakunin to Lacan*, 29.

42 Giovanni Arrighi and David Harvey, "The Winding Paths of Capital," *New Left Review* 56 (2009): 61–94.

43 Sabyasachi Bhattacharya, "History from Below," *Social Scientist* 11, no. 4 (1983): 3.

44 See Iles and Roberts 2012 for an excellent overview and anti-authoritarian critique of the European origins of 'history from below'.

45 See also Vinay Bahl, "What Went Wrong with 'History from Below'," *Economic and Political Weekly* 38, no. 2 (2003): 135–146.

46 Bhattacharya, "History from Below," 5.

47 *Ibid.*, 6.

48 Shivji quoted in Bhattacharya, "History from Below," 8.

49 Erik Olin Wright, *Class Counts: Comparative Studies in Class Analysis* (Cambridge: Cambridge University Press, 1997); Erik Olin Wright, ed. *Approaches to Class Analysis* (Cambridge: Cambridge University Press, 2005).

Exploitative Capitalism in Global South 341

50 Immanuel Wallerstein, *The Capitalist World-Economy* (Cambridge: Cambridge University Press, 1979), 222.
51 Immanuel Wallerstein, *Historical Capitalism with Capitalist Civilization,* (London: Verso, 1983), 36.
52 *Ibid.*, 39.
53 Frantz Fanon, *Wretched of the Earth* (New York: Grove Press, 1963 [2004]), 64.
54 *Ibid.*
55 *Ibid.*, 81.
56 *Ibid.*, 87.
57 *Ibid.*, 23.
58 *Ibid.*, 98.
59 Walter Rodney, *How Europe Underdeveloped Africa* (Washington: Howard University Press, 1974); Walter Rodney, *A History of the Guyanese Working People, 1881–1905* (Baltimore: The Johns Hopkins University Press, 1980).
60 Giovanni Arrighi and Jessica Drangel, "The Stratification of the World-Economy: An Exploration of the Semi-peripheral Zone," *Review* 10, no. 1 (1986): 9–74.
61 Walter Rodney, *A History of the Guyanese Working People, 1881–1905* (Baltimore: Johns Hopkins University Press, 1980), 160.
62 *Ibid.*, 154–155.
63 *Ibid.*, 155.
64 *Ibid.*, 168.
65 *Ibid.*, 218.
66 Walter Rodney, *The Groundings with My Brothers* (London: Bogle L'Overture Publications Ltd, 1969), 25.
67 Rodney, *Guyanese Working People*, 219.
68 Rodney, *Groundings with My Brothers*, 33.
69 See Howard Winant, "Is Racism Global?" *Journal of World-Systems Research* 23, no. 2 (2017): 505–510.
70 Rodney, *Guyanese Working People*, 165.
71 C.L.R. James, *The Black Jacobins* (New York: Vintage, 1963), 283.
72 Rodney, *How Europe Underdeveloped Africa*, 10.
73 Giovanni Arrighi, *The Long Twentieth Century* (London: Verso, 1994), 33.
74 *Ibid.*, 33.
75 Dan Wadada Nabudere, *Imperialism in East Africa Vol.1: Imperialism & Exploitation* (London: Zed Books, 1981), 5; Dan Wadada Nabudere, *The Political Economy of Imperialism* (London: Zed Books, 1977), 31, 35; See also Rodney, *How Europe Underdeveloped Africa*, 50.
76 Nabudere, *Imperialism in East Africa*, 14; Giovanni Arrighi, *The Geometry of Imperialism* (London: New Left Books, 1978), 116; Emmanuel Arghiri, *Unequal Exchange: A Study of the Imperialism of Trade* (New York: Monthly Review Press, 1972), 44;
77 Author's translation: The growing subordination of labor to capital on the level of the system as a whole results in the extension of the sphere of formal subordination in the periphery. Samir Amin, *L'impérialisme et le développement inégal* (Paris: éditions de Minuit, 1976), 142.
78 Author's translation: We must view the contradiction between developed and underdeveloped countries in relation to the totality of contradictions that characterize the global class struggle. Amin, *L'impérialisme et le développement inégal*, 142–143.
79 Author's translation: The class struggle in all of its complexity is at the core of these problems. *Ibid.*, 144.
80 Authors' translation: And it is only by analyzing its changing conditions that we can arrive at a correct periodization of the system. Samir Amin, *L'impérialisme et le développement inégal* (Paris: éditions de Minuit, 1976), 144.
81 Asef Bayat, "From Dangerous Classes to Quiet Rebels: Politics of the Urban Subaltern in the Global South" *International Sociology* 15, no. 3 (2000): 533–557; Nancy Fraser,

342 *Exploitation and Exclusion*

"Injustice at Intersecting Scales: On 'Social Exclusion' and the 'Global Poor'," *European Journal of Social Theory* 13, no. 3 (2010): 363–371; AbdouMailq Simone, *For the City Yet to Come: Changing African Life in Four Cities* (Durham: Duke University Press, 2004).

82 Harry Braverman, *Labor and Monopoly Capital: The Degradation of Work in the Twentieth Century* (Monthly Review Press, 1998), 268.

83 Marx in *Ibid.*, 269.

84 Bhattacharya, "History from Below," 8; Nabudere, *Political Economy of Imperialism*, 270, 279; Issa Shivji, Class *Struggles in Tanzania* (New York: Monthly Review, 1977), 55–56; Yashpal Tandon, ed. *University of Dar es Salaam Debate on Class, State & Imperialism* (Dar es Salaam: Tanzania Publishing House, 1982).

85 Rodney, *Groundings with My Brothers*, 13.

40 Capitalism's Zones of Exclusion and Necropolitics

Giorgio Agamben and Achille Mbembe

Foucault's Carceral Archipelago

The best-known reference to a zone of exclusion is the Ukrainian city Pripyat, which was evacuated days after the melt down of the nearby Chernobyl nuclear plant on April 26, 1986. This zone still cannot support human life. Today, vegetative and resilient animal life occupy the ruins of the otherwise dead city. Social theoretical versions of *zones of exclusion* define dead zones as the inevitable consequence of necropolitics—not as evacuated but populated; not made by explosive disasters but by the subtle exclusionary force of institutional confinement.

It was Michel Foucault who sowed the seeds that grew into a full-blown social theory of zones of exclusion. Early in his writing life, Foucault began working on the history of socially modern institutions that functioned duplicitly to liberate moderns while also excluding them into a network of confinements. The confining institutions in these histories were (listed here by the dates of their appearances in France): the asylum (*The History of Madness*, 1961), the hospital (*The Birth of the Clinic*, 1963), the human sciences (*The Order of Things*, 1966), the political culture of modern knowledge (*The Archaeology of Knowledge*, 1969), the penal system (*Discipline and Punish*, 1975), and ultimately, the repressive idea of sexuality that actually encourages sex (*The History of Sexuality* [three volumes 1976, 1984, 1984; the last two published in the year of his death]).

What these books have in common is an epistemic tension between liberty and confinement, a tension that vibrates in the power field that electrifies the modern state's equivocal relation to the social relations of individuals. For example, from *The History of Madness*: "Confinement was reserved in a definitive manner for limited confinement of people answerable to the law, and for the mad."[1] In other words, as the modern world created institutions for the care of the mentally ill, admission to an asylum is governed by law. The mad are thereby locked up in a zone of exclusion on the authority of State power.

As we have seen, Foucault said much the same in his other historical books, each of which developed, step-by-step, into what became his authoritative theory of *biopower*:

- In an historical study of the birth of modern hospitals that depends not only on State power's control of the health care system but even more on

DOI: 10.4324/9781003198291-46

344 *Exploitation and Exclusion*

a system of education that defines the patient's human nature in respect to her body as a socially governed object of informed medical attention: "... medicine is not defined as clinical unless it is also defined as an encyclopaedic knowledge of nature and knowledge of man in society"[2];

- In a society's system of knowledge and education, "... what we discover ... is a group of *rules* that are immanent in a practice, and defined it in its specificity ..."[3]; in other words, institutions defining areas of legitimate thought—the academic disciplines that have trapped thinking in little boxes;

- In his history of the birth of the modern prison: "We have seen that, penal justice, the prison transformed primitive procedure into a penitentiary technique; the carceral archipelago transported this technique from the penal institution to the entire social body"[4]; and don't fail to note the expression *the carceral archipelago*—a forerunner of *zone of exclusion*; and

- In respect to sexuality in the modern era, Foucault outlines the notion of *biopower* "...as an indispensable element in the development of capitalism; the latter would not have been possible without the controlled insertion bodies into the machinery of production and adjustment of the phenomenon of population to economic processes."[5]

All of this is well expressed in *Society Must Be Defended*, the book version of one of Foucault's *Collège de France* lecture series presented ten years before the Chernobyl disaster on March 17, 1976:

> ... [I]n terms of his relationship with the sovereign, *the subject is, by rights, neither dead nor alive*. From the point of view of life and death, the subject is neutral, and it is thanks to the sovereign that the subject has the right to be alive or, possibly, the right to be dead. In any case, *the lives and deaths of subjects become human rights only as a result of the will of the sovereign*. That is, if you like, the theoretical paradox. And it *is a theoretical paradox that must have as its corollary a sort of practical disequilibrium*. ... The right of life and death is always exercised in an unbalanced way; the balance is always tipped in favour of death. *Sovereign power's effect on life is exercised only when the sovereign can kill.*[6]

The first question one could ask of such a remarkable statement is: Why must *society* be defended? The short answer is because society is the open, dynamic, even (one hesitates to say) free sphere of social activity not under the authority of the Sovereign, of the State.

Then, too, one might wonder, doesn't the Sovereign refer to medieval *ancien régimes* governed by a royal personage and a strict vertical hierarchy in which the masses have no rights other than those the throne might decree? *Society Must Be Defended* is, like all of Foucault's books and lectures, a complex social history from Roman and biblical times to the modern revolutions and

Zones of Exclusion and Necropolitics   345

the Nazi and Stalinist regimes—of which the invention of the 19th-century modern historical thinking is the model of a societal order wherein "the subject is, by rights, neither dead nor alive." Foucault has in mind, in effect, the modern purportedly democratic social orders in Europe for which *The Declaration of the Rights of Man and the Citizen* of 1789 was meant to free the citizen and the social subject from traditionalist, authoritarian sovereign regimes. Hence:

> ... [the] *theoretical paradox that must have as its corollary a sort of practical disequilibrium* ... [because] disciplinary constraints had to both function as mechanisms of domination and be concealed to the extent that they were the mode in which power was actually exercised, the theory of sovereignty had to find expression in the juridical apparatus...[7]

The paradox unbalances practical social life. The social order, in the modern era, creates a new historical subject:

> ...that speaks in a history and a subject of which history speaks... and must also have the appearance of a new domain of objects, a new frame of reference, a whole field of processes that had previously been not just obscure but totally neglected.[8]

Society therefore is binary—divided into races opposed to each other, groups at war: "...[B]eneath the lies that would have us believe that the social body is governed by either nature resources or functional demands, we must rediscover the war that is still going on, war with all its accidents and incidents."[9]

Society Must Be Defended, being a transcript of eleven lectures at the *Collège de France* that are not well tied together. At times, they are almost conversational. Foucault in 1976 was outlining a book like other of his books in which the narrative flow is easy to follow. Just the same, in other of his *Collège de France* lectures he began to develop details of what might have been the book that never was. Still, *Society Must Be Defended* makes two important contributions. The first is that Foucault opens the door to the possibility of viewing the necropolitical system of the modern Sovereign as opposed in a war between binaries in which proto democratic social forces resist the necropolitical sovereign institutions. The second contribution *Society Must Be Defended* is that it puts historical meat on the bones of *the carceral archipelago (that) transported this technique from the penal institution to the entire social body*—a zone of exclusion that pervades the modern social order.

Gilles Deleuze and Félix Guattari: Capitalism and Schizophrenia

In 1972 Gilles Deleuze, a philosopher, and Félix Guattari, a psychoanalyst, published *Anti-Oedipus: Capitalism and Schizophrenia* (1977 [1972]). It was the

346 *Exploitation and Exclusion*

first in a two-book series, the second of which was the magnum opus of their collaboration, *A Thousand Plateaus: Capitalism and Schizophrenia* (1987 [1980]). These two books combined are 1,010 pages of intentionally tangled and multidimensional ideas.

Yet, expanding on my earlier discussions of these books, far from explaining capitalism and schizophrenia or Marx and Freud, the authors are entirely indifferent to their own often inscrutable manner of thinking. The truth is they believe that truth itself is inscrutable. *Anti-Oedipus: Capitalism and Schizophrenia*, for example, begins:

> It is everywhere, functioning smoothly at times, at other times in fits and starts. It breathes, it heats, it eats. It shits and fucks. What a mistake to have ever said *the* id. Everywhere *it* is machines—real ones, not figurative ones: machines driving other machines, machines being driven by other machines, with all the necessary couplings and connections. The organ-machine is plugged into an energy-source-machine: the one produces a flow that the other interrupts. The breast is a machine that produces milk, and the mouth a machine coupled to it.[10]

Where Foucault (who wrote a preface to this book) spoke of a theoretical paradox, Deleuze and Guattari write of (and in) strange couplings of sources and concepts—and mean every word of it all. Their model (if the word applies at all) is of modern society as a *desiring machine*. "Everywhere *it* is machines—real ones ..." Here, the *it* is a play on the psychoanalytic *id*—that deep, unconscious source of desires that is, in effect, the primordial "organ-machine ... plugged into an energy-source-machine"—of which capitalism is the machine that, as Foucault would put it in his 1976 lecture: "Capitalism ... would not have been possible without the controlled insertion of bodies into the machinery of production and adjustment of the phenomenon of population to economic processes."[11] While Foucault's biopower tends to retain a binary element in the sense of the subject being subjugated by objective social forces, Deleuze and Guattari insist that (to put it crudely) a subject's desires enjoy no particular freedom from the capitalist machine. They would never put it so straightforwardly as did Foucault. Instead, they invent the notion of "the barbaric despotic machine" that eliminates altogether distinctions between interior and exterior between the new and the old, which is say the modern and the traditional: "The founding of this despotic machine or the barbarian socius can be summarized in the following way: a new alliance and a direct filiation. The despot challenges the lateral alliances and the extended filiations of the old community."[12]

Deleuze and Guattari's *A Thousand Plateaus: Capitalism and Schizophrenia* (1980) is at once vastly more several sided and complex, yet surprisingly easy to summarize. They "... suggest an entirely different schema, one favouring rhizomatic, rather than arborified, functioning and no longer operating on these dualisms."[13] After all this, it may not be necessary to detail their dualisms as inside/outside, subject/object, lateral/linear. Their figure of speech, the *rhizome*, aims to suggest their intentionally unstable sense of how social things operated. A rhizome, unlike a tree, has no roots. Social relations (one cannot really use a term like social order) are not organized around a core, a center, a Sovereign, a constitution, a legal order, or anything of the kind. Rather, social relations are rhizomic—plants that do not have a tap root as do trees. There are plants that grow under the water or the earth's surface. They grow horizontally in every which direction like water lilies, ginger root, bamboo trees that can spring up some distance from their source. Those who have seen bamboo plantings near a building realize that in due course, the bamboo is also destructive of sidewalks, foundations, anything in its way. Everyone, thus, is a nomad in a body of things they define as a War Machine. Unlike *Anti-Oedipus*, *A Thousand Plateaux* is a book about everything. Social things are caught up in the same countless plateaux as are physical, chemical, and organic things, all of which are stratified: "The strata are phenomena of thickening on the Body of the earth, simultaneously molecular and molar: accumulations, coagulations, sedimentations, foldings."[14]

Here, a theory of zones of exclusion folds back on itself. Since everything is excluded, then also everything is included. The Body of the earth is a universal zone of exclusion that includes all things. To the hopeful, this may sound weird. It is, at least, metaphorically, like Noah's Ark or, prosaically, like Marx's failed political theory. Marx could not inspire a worker's revolution because his theory of production demonstrated the basic fact of economic life—that if the bodies of workers are alienated from themselves, then capitalists are necessarily alien to themselves. If this, then capitalism itself is alienated from itself as it proves by its ultimately absurd doctrine of the necessary pursuit of ever more accumulating capital. Such an idea is the political economic equivalent to Noah's flood. A War Machine, like religious fiction, is another figurative way of describing the odds that defy the possibility that there could ever have been sufficient natural and human resources to ward off the final entropic moment were the Machine itself grinds to a halt. Or as Giorgio Agamben puts it in *The Coming Community*: "This means that the planetary petty bourgeoisie is probably the form in which humanity is moving toward its own destruction."[15]

Giorgio Agamben's Bare Life

Giorgio Agamben's best-known book is *Homo Sacer: Sovereign Power and Bare Life* (1998 [1995]). Right off, it is plain to see, first, that the title's mention of sovereign power indicates that Foucault is important to Agamben's thinking. But, however, the mention of *Homo Sacer* indicates something different from Foucault's concept of the state of exception is in play. Agamben both uses Foucault as a point of departure while providing his own history of the classical origins and modern history of Foucault's theory of biopower under the banner of his concept of *bare life*.

348 *Exploitation and Exclusion*

The similarities and differences can be nicely illustrated by comparing their differences as to what is at stake. Here, first, is Foucault's description of biopower and modern war, followed by his previously quoted line on capitalism—at the end of *History of Sexuality, I*:

> Wars are no longer waged in the name of a sovereign who must be defended; they are waged on behalf of the existence of everyone; entire populations are mobilized for the purpose of wholesale slaughter in the name of life necessity: massacres have become vital. It is as managers of life and survival, of bodies and the race, that so many regimes have been able to wage so many wars, causing so many men to be killed. ... One might say that the ancient right to take life or let live was replaced by a power to foster life or disallow it to the point of death. ...[16]

This biopower was without question an indispensable element in the development of capitalism; the latter would not have been possible without the controlled insertion of bodies into the machinery of production and the adjustment of the phenomena of population to economic processes.

Agamben, by contrast, in *Homo Sacer: Sovereign Power and Bare Life*,[17] makes the Nazi death camps the defining historical moment of the modern state of exception:

> *The camp is the space that is opened when the state of exception begins to become the rule.* In the camp, the state of exception, which was essentially a temporary suspension of the rule of law on the basis of a factual state of danger, is now given a permanent spatial arrangement, which as such nevertheless remains outside the normal order. ...

In this light, the birth of the camp in our time appears as an event that decisively signals the political space of modernity itself. It is produced at the point at which the political system of the modern nation-state, which was founded on the functional nexus between a determinate localization (land) and a determinate order (the State) and mediated by automatic rules for the inscription of life (birth or the nation), enters into a lasting crisis. The State, thereby, decides to assume directly the care of the nation's biological life as one of its proper tasks. If this, then the structure of the nation-state is, in other words, defined by the three elements: land, order, birth.

Today, it is not the city but rather the camp that is the fundamental bio-political paradigm of the West.

The camps of which Agamben wrote were primarily those of the Nazi regime. Even though the Soviet Gulag camps also come to mind, Agamben (unlike Foucault) has little to say about them. The Nazi regime is primary because unlike even Stalin's Great Purge of expelled party members, Hitler's death camps were more completely at the heart of his political power.

The conclusion to Agamben's book is, in a sense, less an empirical conclusion than an empirically informed deduction from Agamben's logical premise that entails the unusual relation of *bare life* to *homo sacer*: "The protagonist of this book is bare life, that is, the life of homo sacer (sacred man), who may be killed and yet not sacrificed, and whose essential function in modern politics we intend to assert." This is the proposition with which his book begins. *Homo Sacer* is an historical figure owing originally to Greek and Roman sources, mixed, of course, with aspects of religious (most pointedly Christian) cultures. Though Agamben does not say it in so many words, it would seem that Christ is the pure perfect *homo sacer*. According to Christian legend, the Christ was killed but his crucifixion was not a religious sacrifice. He was considered to have been the Son of God, which means that he could not have been a lamb slaughtered to appease God. *Homo Sacer* is a putative form of bare life—or the ambivalent form of life in community that is, at once, subject to being killed but also defiled, even dirty, such that he cannot be sacrificed.

Reading Agamben can make your head hurt. Every chapter is replete with Greco-Roman references and terms. Even readers familiar with some of the histories and languages are forced outside whatever Agamben is saying, even while he seems to know what he is talking about. It may be stretching a somewhat dubious interpretation to say that his book puts the reader both inside and out of its meanings—which is precisely to the state of bare life, both inside and out of the regime of the political Sovereign:

> At once excluding bare life from and capturing it within the political order, the state of exception actually constituted, in its very separateness, the hidden foundation on which the entire political system rested. When its borders begin to be blurred, the bare life that dwelt there frees itself in the city and becomes both subject and object of the conflicts of the political order, the one place for both the organization of State power and emancipation from it.[18]

Bare life, thus defined, is where Agamben both embraces Foucault's state of exception while leaving it behind in order to offer his own nuanced but off-putting theory of modern democracy.

Agamben's state of exception is found first in the political form of the Greek polis—and, by extension, the Roman Empire—where:

> [H]omo sacer presents the originary figure of life taken into the sovereign ban and preserves the memory of the originary exclusion through which the political dimension was first constituted. The political sphere of sovereignty was thus constituted through a double exclusion, as an excrescence of the profane in the religious and of the religious in the profane, which takes the form of a zone of indistinction between sacrifice and homicide.[19]

350   *Exploitation and Exclusion*

Put somewhat plainly, modern democracies allow rights for the individual oxymoronically. The individual is at once "elevated" and "subjected" or, one could say, suspended both inside and outside sovereign power of the State. The citizen is, in effect, meant to serve as the source of State power to which she willingly subjects herself; and this, citizens do in respect to their bodies: "Corpus is a two-faced being, the bearer both of subjection to sovereign power and of individual liberties."[20]

Here, one returns to the line quoted earlier: "...[T]he structure of the nation-state is, in other words, defined by the three elements land, order, birth ..." Hence, the basic line from both the American *Declaration of Independence* in 1776 and the French *Declaration of Human Rights* in 1789. In the American version (that served as a model for the French): "All men are created equal [and] endowed by their Creator with certain inalienable rights ... among these are life, liberty, and the pursuit of happiness." Agamben: "The nation—the term derives etymologically from *nascere* (to be born)—thus closes the open circle of man's birth."[21] Hence, biopower is where the modern State begins and from which all human rights such as they are derived:

> It goes without saying, especially in recent times, that democratic nations bare life is ever and always at risk of being killed. From this fact of modern political life, Agamben comes to the zenith of the trajectory of *homo sacer*: from the Roman empire to the modern democratic state to the death camps.

In this light, the birth of the camp in our time appears as an event that decisively signals the political space of modernity itself. It is produced at the point at which the political system of the modern nation-state, which was founded on the functional nexus between a determinate localization (land) and a determinate order (the State) and mediated by automatic rules for the inscription of life (birth or the nation), enters into a lasting crisis, and the State decides to assume directly the care of the nation's biological life as one of its proper tasks.[22]

Here, according to Agamben, the democratic State is a state of exception in which its sacred values cannot help but lead to death—to death camps as a definitive political order in which all life is bare and all are sacrificed.

It is easy to suppose that this is all too much. For those who so suppose, the challenge would be to try to suggest where in history, and especially in the history of these times, democratic politics have NOT become bio-political and, pointedly, death-dealing.

Achille Mbembe: Necropolitics

Achille Mbembe draws on all the sources discussed here, in particular Foucault and Agamben. As Agamben advanced Foucault's state of exception, Mbembe pushed beyond Agamben's bare life, to a theory of *necropolitics*.

Mbembe's famous 2003 essay *Necropolitics* in *Public Culture*[23] adds to the litany of gloomy terms about modern democracy. In particular, he extends the empirical range of previous notions of the modern War Machine to include slavery, colonization, the Rwandan genocides. But also (controversially) he presents Palestine as, if not a paradigm, at least a primal example of necropolitics by which Palestinians are imprisoned with strong borders, guard towers, and gates that lock them off from Israel to be sure, but also from free access to what rights the global order may offer. Then too, Mbembe retells Frederick Douglass's account of the cruelty of planation masters who beat and otherwise brutalized slaves:

> Violence, here, becomes an element in manners, like whipping or taking of the slave's life itself: an act of caprice and pure destruction aimed at instilling terror. Slave life, in many ways, is a form of death-in-life.[24]

Then, more generally, in respect to the zone of exception upon which modern global capitalism was established, Mbembe turns to the West's global colonies—among which the slave system in the antebellum American South must be included as an internal colony alongside, by implication, all internal economic colonies the world over. "Global colonies," he says, "are the zone where the violence of the state of exception is deemed to operate in the service of 'civilization' … The colonies are not organized in a state form and have not created a human world."[25] The colonial system abandons all pretense of rights and rules, deemed beside the point because the colonized are subhuman "savages."

Hence, the original and still pertinent fact of colonies of all kinds. They are zones of exception deprived of rights to life, liberty, and order that are essential to capitalism's avaricious exploitation of the peripheral region's natural resources and cheap but deadly labor. Necropolitics, thereby, is a good enough term for the final, ultimate state of exception whereby democracy is, at least, bare life but, even more, dead to its own rights.

AbduMalique Simone: Cityness in the Global South

AbduMalique Simone, as I have said in the preface to his *City Life from Jakarta to Dakar* (2010), is an urbanist unlike all but a few. Simone breaks the mold of traditional thought by the utterly straightforward method of working and living in real cities and, with particular vigilance, cities of the Global South, that are inconvenient to academic thinking about a city as an instance of *the* City. Simone thereby knows of what he speaks because, apart from being a careful observer, he has lived seriously among the cities of which he writes. Simone, like Mbembe, grew up in Africa. The Global South for him is not a geographic category but a living reality. He thus is able both to tolerate and appreciate cities in the Global South that are characterized by contradictions and absurdities.

352   *Exploitation and Exclusion*

Those who allow themselves to remain distant observers of urban life in the Global South can only peer from afar without understanding them. Simone's expression for this fact of these cities is *cityness*—an assemblage of people and things always coming and going:

> Buildings, layouts, provisioning systems try to hold together and stabilize relationships between materials, environments, bodies, and institutions. ... Urban infrastructure attempts to bring these elements into circuits of association that constitute both bodies and territories in ways that must be continuously calibrated and readjusted. ... As a result, things and people come and go, intensify and withdraw their engagements, and, in the end, every arrangement is temporary. Connections break down, collectivities generate unanticipated outcomes, penetrate across territories and associations for which they are unprepared.[26]

Today in the Global North only a tourist newly landed in one of these so-called modern cities would describe Chicago, New York, Paris, Munich, Tokyo and Beijing in such terms might think of them in this way. In truth, Simone, himself a professor of Urban Studies, means to defy all forms of city planning and urban sociology that attempt to impose an enduring order on such places. His idea of *cityness* refers to life in assemblages of people migrating from zones dead from civil wars, crop failure, fire, free cutting, and much else of the kind.

What is particularly important about Simone's writing on cityness is that his reports are not entirely accounts of utter hopelessness. He means what he says about the sudden and surprising adjustments, comings and goings of people who from Jakarta to Dakar learn to live with somehow. In effect, Simone makes a case for the possibility that in the most peripheral regions of city life, where there is neither clean water nor sewage, it is the people themselves who are the infrastructure. Such conditions as these may not be ideal, but neither are they as deadly like Agamben in his worst moments or even Foucault and Deleuze and Guattari in their better moments of concrete theory suggest. Zones of exception are real, but if we are to trust Simone, even Mbembe, they can be escaped and lived in.

Whatever we are to say today about capitalism's relation to social democracy must be said in the full and honest acknowledgment that from the beginning of the modern world-system, capitalism at home and in its global colonies has perpetuated zones of exclusion in which bare life is the order of the day.

Notes

1   Michel Foucault, *The History of Madness* (London: Routledge, 2006 [1961]), 422.
2   Michel Foucault, *Birth of the Clinic: An Archaeology of Medical Perception* (New York: Vintage Books, 1975 [1963]), 72.

3 Michel Foucault, *Archaeology of Knowledge* (New York: Pantheon Books, 1972 [1969]), 46.

4 Michel Foucault, *Discipline and Punish* (New York: Vintage Books, 1979 [1975]), 298.

5 Michel Foucault, *History of Sexuality: An Introduction* (New York: Pantheon Books, 1978 [1976]), 140–141.

6 Michel Foucault, *Society Must Be Defended* (New York: Picador, 1997 [1976]) 240; emphasis added.

7 *Ibid.*, 37.

8 *Ibid.*, 134.

9 *Ibid.*, 57.

10 Gilles Deleuze and Félix Guattari, *Anti-Oedipus: Capitalism and Schizophrenia* (New York: Viking Press, 1977 [1972]), 1.

11 Foucault, *History of Sexuality*, 141.

12 Deleuze and Guattari. *Anti-Oedipus*, 182.

13 Gilles Deleuze and Félix Guattari, *A Thousand Plateaus: Capitalism and Schizophrenia* (Minneapolis, London: University of Minnesota Press, 1987 [1980]), 328.

14 *Ibid.*, 502.

15 Giorgio Agamben, *The Coming Community* (Minneapolis: University of Minnesota Press, 1993 [1990]), 64.

16 Foucault, *History of Sexuality*, 138, 140.

17 Giorgio Agamben, *Homo Sacer: Sovereign Power and Bare Life* (Stanford: Stanford University Press, 1998), 168, 174, 181.

18 Agamben, *Homo Sacer*, 10.

19 *Ibid.*, 83.

20 *Ibid.*, 125.

21 *Ibid.*, 128.

22 *Ibid.*, 174–175.

23 Achille Mbembé and Libby Meintjes, "Necropolitics," *Public Culture* 15, no. 1 (2003): 11–40.

24 *Ibid.*, 21.

25 *Ibid.*, 24.

26 AbduMalique Simone, *City life from Jakarta to Dakar: Movements at the Crossroads* (New York: Routledge, 2010), 7–8.

Bibliography

1 Karl Mark, Capital I (1867)

Agamben, Giorgio. *Means without End: Notes on Politics*. Minneapolis: University of Minnesota Press, 1996 (2000).

Aglietta, Michel. *A Theory of Capitalist Regulation*. London: New Left Books, 1976 (1979).

Arrighi, Giovanni. *The Long Twentieth. Century* London: Verso, 1994.

Baran, Paul A. and Paul M. Sweezy. *Monopoly Capital: An Essay on the American Economic and Social Order*. New York: Monthly Review, 1966.

Braudel, Fernand. *Civilization and Capitalism 15th–18th Century, Volume 3, The Perspective of the World*. New York: Harper and Row, 1979 (1984).

Brenner, Robert. "The Agrarian Roots of European Capitalism" in *The Brenner Debate: Agrarian Class Structure and Economic Development in Pre-Industrial Europe*, pp. 213–328 edited by T.H. Aston and C.H.E. Philpin. Cambridge: Cambridge University Press, 1985.

Brenner, Robert. "The Origins of Capitalist Development: A Critique of Neo-Smithian Marxism." *New Left Review* 104 (July–August 1977): 25–92.

Chibber, Vivek. *Postcolonial Theory and the Specter of Capital*. New Delhi: Navayana, 2013.

Deleuze, Gilles and Félix Guattari. *Anti-Oedipus*. New York: Penguin Classics, 1972 (2009).

Derrida, Jaques. *Specters of Marx: The State of the Debt, the Work of Mourning and the New International*. New York: Routledge, 1993 (1994).

Friedman, Milton. *Capitalism and Freedom*. Chicago: University of Chicago Press, 1962 (2002).

Fukuyama, Francis. *The End of History and the Last Man*. New York: The Free Press, 1992.

Grief, Avner. *Institutions and the Path to the Modern Economy: Lessons from Medieval Trade*. Cambridge: Cambridge University Press, 2006.

Harvey, David. *The Condition of Postmodernity*. London: Blackwell, 1990.

Hilferding, Rudolf. *Finance Capital: A Study of the Latest Phase of Capitalist Development*. London: Routledge, 1910 (2006).

Hobson, John A. *Imperialism: A Study*. New York: Cosimo Classics, 1902 (2005).

Jameson, Frederic. *Postmodernism: Or, the Cultural Logic of Late Capitalism*. Durham: Duke University Press, 1991.

Kocka, Jurgen. *Geschichte des Kapitalismus*. München: Verlag CH Beck oHG, 2014.

Kondratieff, Nikolaï Dimitrievitch. *Les Grands Cycles de la Conjoncture*. Paris: Economica, 1992.

Lenin, VI. *Imperialism the Highest Stage of Capitalism*. New York: International Publishers, 1939.

Lipietz, Alain. "New Tendencies in the International Division of Labor: Regimes of Accumulation and Modes of Regulation" in *Production, Work, Territory: The Geographical*

356   *Bibliography*

Anatomy of Industrial Capitalism, edited by Allen J. Scott and Michael Storper, 16–40. Boston: Allen & Unwin, 1986.

Luxembourg, Rosa. *The Accumulation of Capital*. London: Routledge, 1913 (2003).

Mandel, Ernest. *Late Capitalism*. London: New Left Books, 1972 (1975).

Marx, Karl. "On Imperialism in India" in *The Marx-Engels Reader*, edited by Robert C. Tucker, 653–664. New York: WW Norton and Company, 1853 (1978).

Marx, Karl. *Capital Vol. 1*. New York: Penguin, 1867 (1990).

Marx, Karl. *The German Ideology*. New York: International Publishers, 1846 (1976).

Mokyr, Joel. *A Culture of Growth: The Origins of the Modern Economy*. Princeton: Princeton University Press, 2017.

North, Douglass C. *Understanding the Process of Economic Change*. Princeton: Princeton University Press, 2005.

North, Douglass C. and Robert Paul Thomas. *The Rise of the Western World: A New Economic History*. Cambridge: Cambridge University Press, 1973.

Polanyi, Karl. *The Great Transformation: The Political and Economic Origins of Our Time*. Boston: Beacon Press, 1944 (2001).

Pomerantz, Kenneth. *The Great Divergence: China, Europe, and the Making of the Modern World Economy*. Princeton: Princeton University Press, 2000.

Ricardo, David. *Principles of Political Economy and Taxation*. Amherst: Prometheus Books, 1817 (1996).

Rosenthal, Jean-Laurent and R. Bin Wong. *Before and Beyond Divergence*. Cambridge: Harvard University Press, 2011.

Schumpeter, Joseph A. *Capitalism, Socialism and Democracy*. New York: Harper and Row, 1942 (1976).

Smith, Adam. *Inquiry into the Nature and Causes of the Wealth of Nations*. New York: Alfred A. Knopf, 1776 (1991).

Streek, Wolfgang. *How Will Capitalism End?* London: Verso, 2016.

Sweezy, Paul M. *The Theory of Capitalist Development*. New York: Monthly Review, 1942 (1970).

Von Hayek, Friedrich. *The Road to Serfdom*. Chicago: University of Chicago Press, 1944 (1994).

Wallerstein, Immanuel. *Historical Capitalism with Capitalist Civilization*. London: Verso, 1983 (1996).

2   Karl Mark, Estranged Labor (1844)

Abamben, Giorgio. *Homo Sacer: Sovereign Power and Bare Life*. Stanford University Press, 1998.

Althusser, Louis. "On the Young Marx: Theoretical Questions [1961]" in *For Marx*. Vintage/Random House, 1970.

Althusser, Louis. *Lenin and Philosophy*. Monthly Review Press, 1971.

Anzaldúa, Gloria. *Borderlands/La Frontera: The New Mestiza*. Spinsters/Aunt Lute, 1987.

Beckert, Sven. *Empire of Cotton: A Global History*. Knopf, 2015.

Engels, Friedrich. *The Conditions of the Working Class in England*. Moscow: Foreign Languages Publishing House, 1962 (1845).

Girard, René. *Things since the Foundation of the World*. Stanford University Press, 1987.

Gouldner, Alvin W. *The Coming Crisis of Western Sociology*. Basic Books, 1970.

Gouldner, Alvin W. *The Dialectic of Ideology and Technology: The Origins, Grammar, and Future of Ideology*. The Seabury Press, 1976.

Bibliography   357

Gouldner, Alvin W. *For Sociology: Renewal and Critique in Sociology Today.* Basic Books, 1973.
Gouldner, Alvin W. *The Future of Intellectuals and the Rise of the New Class.* The Seabury Press, 1979.
Gouldner, Alvin W. *The Two Marxisms: Contradictions and Anomalies in the Development of a Theory.* New York: The Seabury Press, 1980.
Hobsbawm, Eric. *The Age of Capital.* Random House, 1975.
Hobsbawm, Eric. *The Age of Extremes: A History of the World, 194–1991.* Random House, 1994.
Hochschild, Adam. *King Leopold's Ghost: A Story of Greed, Terror, and Heroism in Colonial Africa.* Mariner/Houghton-Mifflin, 1998.
Hofstadter, Richard. *The American Political Tradition.* Knopf, 1948.
Keynes, Maynard. *The Economic Consequences of the Peace.* Harcourt, Brace, and Howe, 1920 (1919).
Lemert, Charles. "Changing Global Structures in the Short Twentieth Century, 1914–1991," *Globalization: An Introduction to the End of the Known World,* 93–121. Routledge/Paradigm, 2015.
Lemert, Charles (with Paul Piccone), "Cruelty and Murder in the Academy: Alvin W. Gouldner and Post-Marxist Critical Theory" in *The Structural Lie: Small Clues to Global Things,* 49–75. Routledge/Paradigm, 2011.
Marx, Karl. *The Economic and Philosophical Manuscripts of 1844,* 20–35. Moscow: Progress Press, 1959.
Marx, Karl. *Capital: A Critique of Political Economy, Volume 1.* International Publishers, 1967.
Mbembe, Achille. "Necropolitics." *Public Culture* 15, no. 1 (2003): 11–40.
Robinson, Harriet H. "Early Factory Labor in New England." *Arthur and Elizabeth Schlesinger Library on the History of Women in America, Radcliffe Institute for Advanced Study, Harvard University* [archived MS of original, 1883].
Simone, Abdou Maliq. *For the City Yet to Come: Urban Life in Four African Cities.* Duke University Press, 2004.
Simone, Abdou Maliq. *City Life from Jakarta to Dakar: Movements at the Crossroads.* Routledge, 2010.
Taylor, Frederick Winslow. *The Principles of Scientific Management.* Harper and Brothers, 1911.
Wallerstein, Immanuel. *World-Systems Analysis.* Duke University Press, 2004.

3 Frantz Fanon/Immanuel Wallerstein

"Faculty Committee Submits Proposals." *Columbia Daily Spectator,* Sunday, April 28, 1968.
Fanon, Frantz. *Black Skin, White Masks* (1952), translated by Charles Lam Markmann. New York: Grove Press, 1967.
Frantz Fanon. *The Wretched of the Earth,* translated by Constance Farrington. New York: Grove Weidenfeld, 1961 (1963).
Wallerstein, Immanuel. *Geopolitics and Geoculture: Essays on the Changing World-system.* Cambridge University Press, 1991.
Wallerstein, Immanuel. *After Liberalism.* The New Press, 1995.
Wallerstein, Immanuel. *The End of the World as We Know It: Social Science in the Twenty-first Century.* University of Minnesota Press, 1999.
Wallerstein, Immanuel. *The Essential Wallerstein.* The New Press, 2000.
Wallerstein, Immanuel. *The Decline of American Power.* The New Press, 2003.
Wallerstein, Immanuel. *Uncertainties of Knowledge.* Philadelphia: Temple University Press, 2004.
Wallerstein, Immanuel. *World Systems Analysis: An Introduction.* Duke University Press, 2004.

358 *Bibliography*

Wallerstein, Immanuel. *The Modern World System IV: Centrist Liberalism Triumphant.* Berkeley: University of California Press, 2011.

Wallerstein, Immanuel. "Immanuel Wallerstein." Accessed November 25, 2020. https://www.iwallerstein.com.

4 Fernand Braudel/Andre Gunder Frank

Braudel, Fernand. *The Mediterranean and the Mediterranean World in the Age of Philip II,* 2 volumes. Harper & Row, 1973 (1963).

Braudel, Fernand. *Civilization and Capitalism: 15th–18th Century, Vol 1: Structures of Everyday Life.* Harper & Row, 1981 (1979).

Braudel, Fernand. *Civilization and Capitalism: 15th–18th Century, Vol 2: The Wheels of Commerce.* Harper & Row 1982 (1979).

Braudel, Fernand. *Civilization and Capitalism: 15th–18th Century, Vol 3: The Perspective of the World.* Harper & Row 1988 (1979).

Gunder Frank, Andre. "The Development of Underdevelopment," *Monthly Review* 18 (September 1966): 17–31.

Gunder Frank, Andre. *Capitalism and Underdevelopment in Latin America.* Monthly Review Press, 1967.

Gunder Frank, Andre. *ReOrient: Global Economy in the Asian Age.* University of California Press, 1998.

5 David Ricardo/Janet Abu Lughod

Abu-Lughod, Janet. *Before European Hegemony: The World-System A.D. 1250–1350.* New York: Oxford University Press, 1989.

Ricardo, David. *Principles of Political Economy and Taxation.* Amherst: Prometheus Books, 1817 (1996).

6 Friedrich Engels/Silvia Federici

Engels, Friedrich. "The Origin of the Family, Private Property, and the State" in *The Marx-Engels Reader,* edited by Robert C. Tucker, 734–759. New York: WW Norton and Company, 1884 (1978).

Engels, Friedrich. *The Condition of the Working Class in England.* Oxford: Oxford University Press, 1845 (2009).

Federici, Silvia. *Caliban and the Witch: Women, the Body, and Primitive Accumulation.* Brooklyn: Autonomedia, 2004 (2014).

Federici, Silvia. *Revolution at Point Zero: Housework, Reproduction, and Feminist Struggle.* Oakland: PM Press, 2012.

Green, John. *A Revolutionary Life: Biography of Frederick Engels.* London: Artery Publications, 2008.

7 Robert Brenner/Ellen Meiksins Wood

Aston, T.H. and C.H.E. Philpin, eds. *The Brenner Debate: Agrarian Class Structure and Economic Development in Pre-Industrial Europe.* Cambridge: Cambridge University Press, 1985.

Brenner, Robert "The Origins of Capitalist Development: A Critique of Neo-Smithian Marxism." *New Left Review* 104, pp. 25–92 (1977).

Wood, Ellen Meiksins. *The Origin of Capitalism: A Longer View.* London: Verso, 1999 (2002).

Bibliography 359

8 Antonia Gramsci/Giovanni Arrighi

Arrighi, Giovanni. *The Long Twentieth Century*. London: Verso, 1994.

Arrighi, Giovanni. *Adam Smith in Beijing*. London: Verso, 2007.

Arrighi, Giovanni and Beverly J. Silver. "Capitalism and World (Dis)order." *Review of International Studies* 27 (2001): 257–279.

Arrighi, Giovanni and Beverly J. Silver. *Chaos and Governance in the Modern World System*. Minneapolis: University of Minnesota Press, 1999.

Arrighi, Giovanni and David Harvey. "The Winding Paths of Capital." *New Left Review* 56 (2009): 61–94.

Gramsci, Antonio. *The Prison Notebooks*. New York: International Publishers, 1971.

9 Henri Pirenne/Oliver C. Cox

Cox, Oliver C. *The Foundations of Capitalism*. London: Peter Owen Limited, 1959.

D'Eramo, Marco. "Dock Life." *New Left Review* 96, pp. 85–99 (2015).

Graf, Arndt and Chua Beng Huat. *Port Cities in Asia and Europe*. London: Routledge, 2009.

Gramsci, Antonio. *Prison Notebooks*, 3 Vols. New York: Columbia University Press, 2007.

Hein, Carola. *Port Cities: Dynamic Landscapes and Global Networks*. London: Routledge, 2011.

Mah, Alice. *Port Cities and Global Legacies*. Palgrave MacMillan, 2014.

Meier, Sandy Prita. *Swahili Port Cities*. Bloomington: University of Indiana Press, 2016.

O'Flanagan, Patrick. *Port Cities of Atlantic Iberia, c. 1500–1900*. London: Routledge, 2016.

Pirenne, Henri. *Medieval Cities: Their Origins and the Revival of Trade*. Princeton: Princeton University Press, 1925 (1980).

Sassen, Saskia. *Cities in a World-Economy*. New York: Sage, 2011.

Simone, AbdouMaliq. *For the City Yet to Come: Changing African Life in Four Cities*. Durham: Duke University Press, 2004.

10 Nikolai Kondratieff/Ibn Khaldun

Durkheim, Emile. *The Division of Labor in Society*. New York: The Free Press, 1893 (1997).

Gramsci, Antonio. *The Prison Notebooks*. New York: International Publishers, 1971.

Khaldûn, Ibn. *The Muqaddimah: An Introduction to History*. Princeton: Princeton University Press, 1377 (2005).

Kondratieff, N.D. "Long Waves in Economic Life." *The Review of Economic Statistics* 17, no. 6 (1935): 106–115.

Plys, Kristin. "World-Systemic and Kondratieff Cycles." *Yale Journal of Sociology* (Fall 2012): 130–160.

11 Barrington Moore/Claudia Jones

Davies, Carole Boyce. *Left of Karl Marx: The Political Life of Black Communist Claudia Jones*. Durham: Duke University Press, 2008.

Jones, Claudia. *Claudia Jones: Beyond Containment*, edited by Carole Boyce Davies. Banbury: Ayebia Clarke Publishing Limited, 2011.

Moore, Barrington. *Social Origins of Dictatorship and Democracy: Lord and Peasant in the Making of the Modern World*. Boston: Beacon Press, 1966.

360 *Bibliography*

12 C.L.R. James/Walter Rodney

Grimshaw, Anna, introduction to *C.L.R. James: A Revolutionary Vision for the 20th Century.* The C.L.R. James Institute and Cultural Correspondence, New York, in co-operation with Smyrna Press, April 1991.

James, C.L.R. *Dialectic Materialism and the Fate of Humanity.* The C.L.R. James Archive (on-line), 1947.

James, C.L.R. *A History of Pan-African Revolt.* Oakland: PM Press, 2012 (1938; revised 1969).

James, C.L.R. *American Civilization,* edited by Anna Grimshaw and Keith Hart. Blackwell Publishers, 1993 (1950).

James, C.L.R. *Beyond a Boundary.* Duke University Press, 1993 (1963).

Rodney, Walter. *The Groundings with My Brothers.* London: Bogle-L'Ouverture Publications, 1969.

Rodney, Walter. *How Europe Underdeveloped Africa.* London: Bogle-L'Ouverture Publicationsand Dar es Salaam: Tanzanian Publishing House, 1973.

13 Mohandas Karamchand Ghandi/Bhagat Singh

Chandra, Ram. *History of the Naujawan Bharat Sabha.* Ludhiana: Unistar Books, 2007.

Habib, S Irfan. *To Make the Deaf Hear: Ideology and Programme of Bhagat Singh and His Comrades.* New Delhi: Three Essays Collective, 2007.

Javed, Ajeet. *Left Politics in Punjab, 1935–47.* Delhi: Durga Publications, 1988.

Josh, Bhagwan. *Communist Movement in Punjab.* Delhi: Anupama Publications, 1979.

Sharma, Shalini. *Radical Politics in Colonial Punjab.* London: Routledge, 2010.

Singh, Bhagat. *On the Path of Liberation,* edited by Shiv Verma. Chennai: Indian Universities Press, 2007.

Singh, Bhagat. *The Jail Notebook and Other Writings,* edited by Chaman Lal. Delhi: Leftword Books, 2007.

Skaria, Ajay. *Unconditional Equality: Gandhi's Religion of Resistance.* Minneapolis: University of Minnesota Press, 2016.

14 Vladimir Lenin/Nestor Makhno

Arshinov, Peter. *History of the Makhnovist Movement, 1918–1921.* London: Freedom Press, 2005.

Christman, Henry M., ed. *Essential Works of Lenin.* New York: Dover Publications, 1966.

Lenin, VI. *Imperialism: The Highest Stage of Capitalism.* New York: International Publishers, 1917 (1979).

Makhno, Nestor. "The Struggle against the State." *Dyelo Truda* 17 (1926): 5–6.

Makhno, Nestor. "A Few Words on the National Question in Ukraine." *Dyelo Truda* 19 (1928).

Makhno, Nestor. *The Russian Revolution in Ukraine.* Edmonton: Black Cat Press, 1936a (2007).

Makhno, Nestor. *Under the Blows of the Counterrevolution.* Edmonton: Black Cat Press, 1936b (2009).

Rodney, Walter. *The Russian Revolution: A View from the Third World.* London: Verso, 2018.

Skirda, Alexandre. *Nestor Makhno Anarchy's Cossack: The Struggle for Free Soviets in the Ukraine, 1917–1921.* Oakland: AK Press, 2004.

Tucker, Robert C., ed. *The Lenin Anthology.* New York: WW Norton and Co, 1975.

Bibliography 361

15 Albert Camus/Mustapha Khayati

Camus, Albert. *The Myth of Sisyphus*. 1942 (most popular on-line version: @https://www2.hawaii.edu/~freeman/courses/phil360/16.%20Myth%20of%20Sisyphus.pdf)

Khayati, Mustapha. "Class Struggles in Algeria." *Internationale Situationniste* 10 (March 1966).

Khayati, Mustapha. "Address to the Revolutionaries of Algeria and of All Countries." *Internationale Situationniste* 11 (October 1967).

Khayati, Mustapha. "Setting Straight Some Popular Misconceptions about Revolutions in the Underdeveloped Countries" in *Situationist International Anthology*, edited by Ken Knabb, 281–284. Berkeley: Bureau of Public Secrets, 2006.

Ross, Kristin and Henri Lefebvre. "Lefebvre on the Situationists: An Interview." *October* 79 (1997): 69–83.

Trespeuch-Berthelot, Anna "Mustapha Khayati" in *Dictionnaire biographique Mouvement ouvrier, mouvement social de 1940 à mai 1968* t.7, dir. C. Pennetier. Paris: Les Éditions de l'Atelier/Les Éditions Ouvrières, 2011.

16 Kwame Ture/W. E. B Du Bois/ Amílcar Cabral

Cabral, Amílcar. (1969). *The PAIGC Programme*. In Amílcar Cabral, *Revolution in Guinea*. London, 1974. Downloaded July 21, 2019. https://www.marxists.org/subject/africa/cabral/paigcpgm.htm

Cabral, Amílcar. *Return to the Source: Selected Speeches*. New York: Monthly Review Press with Africa Information Service, 1973.

Cabral, Amílcar. *The Weapon of Theory*. Havana: Address delivered to the first Tricontinental Conference of the Peoples of Asia, Africa, and Latin American in Havana in January 1966. Downloaded July 21, 2019 from https://www.marxists.org/subject/africa/cabral/1966/weapon-theory.htm

Carmichael, Stokely. *Black Power*. Speech at the University of California Berkeley: October 29, 1966. Downloaded from *Voices of Democracy* @ https://voicesofdemocracy.umd.edu/carmichael-black-power-speech-text/

Carmichael, Stokely. [Kwame Ture in 1992 edition] & Charles V. Hamilton. *Black Power: The Politics of Liberation in America*. New York: Random House, 1967/1992.

Du Bois, W.E.B. "The Study of the Negro Problems" in *The Annals of the American Academy of Political and Social Sciences*, 11 (January 1898a): 1–23. [Reprinted in Du Bois, W.E.B. *On Sociology and the Black Community*, edited by Dan S. Green and Edwin D. Driver. Chicago: University of Chicago Press, 1978.]

Du Bois, W.E.B. *The Negroes of Farmville, Virginia: A Social Study*. Washington: Government Printing Office; Department of Labor, 14 (January 1898b).

Du Bois, W.E.B. *The Souls of Black Folk*. New York: Bantam Books, 1903.

Du Bois, W.E.B. *The Autobiography of W.E.B. DuBois: A Soliloquy on Viewing My Life from the Last Decade of Its First Century*. Posthumously in New York: International Publishers, 1968.

Du Bois, W.E.B. *Black Reconstruction in America: 1860–1880*. New York: Harcourt Brace (New York: Free Press), 1935 (1992).

Lemert, Charles. "The Race of Time: Deconstruction, Du Bois, and Reconstruction, 1935–1873" in *The Race of Time: The Charles Lemert Reader*, 118–136. Routledge/Paradigm, 2009.

Lewis, David Levering. *W.E.B. Du Bois, 1868–1919: Biography of a Race*. New York: Henry Holt, 1994.

Lewis, David Levering. *W.E.B. Du Bois, 1919–1963: The Fight for Equality and the American Century*. New York: Henry Holt, 2001.

362   *Bibliography*

17 Mao Zedong/Charu Mazumdar

Ahmad, Nadeem. "Charu Mazumdar—the Father of Naxalism" *Hindustan Times*, last modified December 15, 2005.

Dasgupta, Biplab. *The Naxalite Movement*. Bombay: Allied Publishers, 1974.

Liu, Lydia, Rebecca E. Karl, and Dorothy Ko, eds. *The Birth of Chinese Feminism: Essential Texts in Transnational Theory*. New York: Columbia University Press, 2013.

Mazumdar, Charu. "March Onward by Summing up the Experience of the Peasant Revolutionary Struggle of India." *Liberation* 3, no. 2 (1969).

Meisner, Maurice. *Mao Zedong: A Political and Intellectual Portrait*. Cambridge: Polity Press, 2007.

Mukerjee, Arun Prosad. *Maoist 'Spring Thunder': The Naxalite Movement (1967–1972)*. Kolkata: KP Bagchi & Co, 2002.

Ray, Rabindra. *The Naxalites and Their Ideology*. New Delhi: Oxford University Press, 1988.

Zedong, Mao. *Selected Works of Mao Tse-Tung*, Vol. 1, Peking: Foreign Languages Press, 1965.

18 Muhammad Ali/Ulrike Meinhof

Ali, Muhammad and Richard Durham. *The Greatest: My Own Story*. New York: Random House, 1975.

Early, Gerald, ed. *The Muhammad Ali Reader*. New York: William Morrow, 1998.

Gast, Leon. *When We Were Kings*. New York: Polygram Film Productions USA Video, 1996.

Hauser, Thomas. *Muhammad Ali and the Spirit of the Sixties*. New York: Random House, 1991.

Hyde, Lewis. *Trickster Makes This World*. New York: Farrar, Strauss, and Giroux, 1998.

Kramer, David. "Ulrike Meinhof: An Emancipated Terrorist?" in *European Women on the Left: Socialism, Feminism, and the Problems Faced by Political Women, 1880 to the Present*, edited by Jane Slaughter and Robert Kern, 195–220. Westport: Greenwood Press, 1981.

Lemert, Charles. *Trickster in the Culture of Irony*. Cambridge: Polity Press, 2003.

Mailer, Norman. *The Fight*. Boston: Little, Brown, 1977.

Meinhof, Ulrike Marie. *Everybody Talks about the Weather—We Don't: The Writings of Ulrike Meinhof*, edited by Karin Bauer. New York: Seven Stories Press, 2008.

Remnick, David. *King of the World*. New York: Vintage/Random House, 1989.

19 Martin Luther King Jr./Ho Chi Minh

King, Jr., Martin Luther. *The Essential Writings and Speeches of Martin Luther King, Jr*, edited by James M. Washington. San Francisco: Harper Collins, 1986.

Minh, Ho Chi. *Down with Colonialism!* edited by Walden Bello. London: Verso, 2007.

Therborn, Göran. "From Petrograd to Saigon." *New Left Review* 48 (1968): 1–11.

20 Dipesh Chakrabarty/Eric Wolf

Chakrabarty, Dipesh. *Provincializing Europe*. Princeton: Princeton University Press, 2000 (2008).

Wolf, Eric R. *Europe and the People without History*. Berkeley: University of California Press, 1984 (1997).

Bibliography 363

21 Edward Said/Fredrick Jameson/ Aijaz Ahmad

Ahmad, Aijaz. "Jameson's Rhetoric of Otherness and 'National Allegory'." *Social Text* 17 (Autumn, 1987): 3–25.

Ahmad, Aijaz. *In Theory: Nations, Classes, Literatures.* London: Verso, 1992.

Ahmad, Aijaz. *In the Mirror of Urdu: Recompositions of Nation and Community, 1947–1965.* Shimla: Indian Institute of Advanced Studies, 1993.

Ahmad, Aijaz. "The Politics of Literary Postcoloniality." *Race & Class* 36, no. 3 (1995): 1–20.

Horkheimer, Max and Theodor Adorno. *Dialectic of Enlightenment.* Palo Alto: Stanford University Press, 1944.

Jameson, Fredric. *Sartre: The Origins of a Style.* New Haven: Yale University Press, 1961.

Jameson, Fredric. *The Prison-House of Language: A Critical Account of Structuralism and Russian Formalism.* Princeton: Princeton University Press, 1972.

Jameson, Fredric. "Postmodernism, or the Cultural Logic of Late Capitalism." *New Left Review* I, no. 146 (July–August 1984).

Jameson, Fredric. *Postmodernism, or the Cultural Logical of Late Capitalism.* Durham: Duke University Press, 1991.

Jameson, Fredric. *The Cultural Turn: Selected Writings on Postmodernism, 1983–1998.* London: Verso, 1998.

Meiskins Wood, Ellen. "Issues of Class and Culture: An Interview with Aijaz Ahmad." *Monthly Review* (October 1996): 10–28.

Said, Edward. *Culture and Imperialism.* New York: Knopf, 1993.

Said, Edward. *Joseph Conrad and the Fiction of Autobiography.* Cambridge: Harvard University Press, 1966.

Said, Edward. *Orientalism.* New York: Random House, 1978.

Said, Edward. *Out of Place.* New York: Random House, 1999.

Said, Edward. *The Politics of Dispossession: The Struggle for Palestinian Self-Determination, 1969–1994.* New York: Random House, 1994.

22 Frederick Winslow Taylor/Harry Braverman

Braverman, Harry. *Labor and Monopoly Capital.* New York: Monthly Review Press, 1998.

Edwards, Richard. *Contested Terrain: The Transformation of the Workplace in the Twentieth Century.* New York: Basic Books, 1979.

23 Edna Bonacich/Lucía Sánchez Saornil

Ackelsberg, Martha A. *Free Women of Spain: Anarchism and the Struggle for the Emancipation of Women.* Bloomington: Indiana University Press, 1991.

Bonacich, Edna. "A Theory of Ethnic Antagonism: The Split Labor Market." *American Sociological Review* 37, no. 5 (1972).

Bonacich, Edna. "Abolition, the Extension of Slavery, and the Position of Free Blacks: A Study of Split Labor Markets in the United States, 1830–1863." *American Journal of Sociology* 81, no. 3 (1975).

Bonacich, Edna. "Advanced Capitalism and Black White Race Relations in the US: A Split Labor Market Interpretation." *American Sociological Review* 41, no. 1 (1976).

Bonacich, Edna. "Working With the Labor Movement: A Personal Journey in Organic Public Sociology." *The American Sociologist* 36 (2005): 105–120.

364   *Bibliography*

Goutte, Guillaume. *Lucía Sánchez Saornil: Poetesse, Anarchiste, et Feministe.* Paris: Les Editions du Monde Libertaire, 2011.

Saornil, Lucía Sánchez. "The Question of Feminism" in *Anarchism: A Documentary History of Libertarian Ideas, Vol. 1: From Anarchy to Anarchism, 300 CE-1939*, edited by Robert Graham. Montreal: Black Rose Books, 1935, pp. 460–465 (2005).

24 Mikhail Bakunin/Joseph Edwards

Bakunin, Mikhail. *Bakunin on Anarchism*, edited by Sam Dolgoff. Montreal: Black Rose Books, 2002.

Edwards, Joseph. Matthew Quest Ed. *Workers' Self-Management in the Caribbean.* Atlanta: On Our Own Authority! Publishers, 2014.

Ravindranathan, T.R. *Bakunin and the Italians.* Montreal: McGill University Press, 1988.

25 Adam Smith/Folfer Frobel, Otto Kreye, Jürgen Heinrichs

Der Spiegel. "Davor hatte ich Angst: Mit dem Rücktritt des Soziologen Jürgen Habermas als Institutsdirektor ist der Versuch gescheitert, das Starnberger Max-Planck-Institut weiterzuführen." *Der Spiegel* (05 May 1981).

Drieschner, M. "Die Verantwortung der Wissenschaft: Ein Rückblick auf das Max-Plank-Institut zur Erforschung der Lebensbedingungen der wissenschaftlich technischen Welt (1970–1980)" in *Wissenschaft und Öffentlichkeif*, edited by T. Fischer and R. Seising, 173–198. Frankfurt: M. Lang, 1996.

Fröbel, Folker, Jürgen Heinrichs, and Otto Kreye. *The New International Division of Labour.* Cambridge: Cambridge University Press, 1980.

Smith, Adam. *The Wealth of Nations.* New York: Alfred A. Knopf, 1776 (1991).

Smith, Adam. *The Wealth of Nations*, Books IV–V. New York: Penguin, 1776 (1999).

26 Jacques Rancière/Mohammed Ali El Hammi

Ahmad, Eqbal and Stuart Scharr. "M'hamed Ali and the Tunisian Labour Movement." *Race & Class* 19, no. 3 (1979): 253–276.

Haddad, Tahar. *La naissance du movement syndical tunisien.* Paris: L'Harmattan, 1927 (2013).

Omri, Mohamed-Salah. "No Ordinary Union: UGTT and the Tunisian Path to Revolution and Transition." *Workers of the World* 1, no. 7 (2015): 14–29.

Rancière, Jacques. *Proletarian Nights: The Workers' Dream in Nineteenth-Century France* London: Verso, 1981 (2012).

Slama, Kaïs. "Mohammed Ali El Hammi Zwischen Berlin und Tunis (1919–1924): Zur Geschichte der Tunesischen Gewerkschaftsbewegung" in *Revolte und Tradition: Perspektiven deutsch-tunesischer Germanistik*, edited by Michael Hofmann, Chaouki Kacem, Brahim Moussa. Dresden: Thelem Universitätsverlag & Buchhandel, 2018, pp. 97–106.

27 Karl Polanyi/Beverly Silver

Polanyi, Karl. *The Great Transformation.* Boston: Beacon Press, 1944 (2001).

Silver, Beverly. *Forces of Labor: Workers' Movements and Globalization since 1870.* Cambridge: Cambridge University Press, 2003.

Silver, Beverly. "'Wo das Kapital hingeht, geht auch der Konflikt hin.' Beverly Silver über ArbeiterInnenmacht, Operaismus und Globalisierung" *analyse & kritik* 19 (14 August 2005).

Bibliography 365

28 EP Thomson/Rajnarayan Chandavarkar

Chandavarkar, Rajnarayan. *The Origins of Industrial Capitalism: Business Strategies and the Working Classes in Bombay, 1900–1940.* Cambridge: Cambridge University Press, 1994.

Chandavarkar, Rajnarayan. *Imperial Power and Popular Politics: Class, Resistance and the State in India, c. 1850–1950.* Cambridge: Cambridge University Press, 1998.

Chandavarkar, Rajnarayan. "The Making of the Indian Working Classes: EP Thompson and Indian History." *History Workshop Journal* 43 (1997): 177–196.

Hall, Stuart. "Cultural Studies: Two Paradigms." *Media, Culture and Society* 2 (1980): 57–72.

Thompson, E.P. *The Making of the English Working Class.* New York: Vintage, 1963.

29 Michel Foucault/Michael Hardt & Antonio Negri

Deleuze, Gilles and Félix Guattari, *A Thousand Plateaus: Capitalism and Schizophrenia.* University of Minnesota Press, 1987.

Foucault, Michel. *Birth of the Clinic: An Archaeology of Medical Perceptions.* Tavistock, 1973 (1963).

Foucault, Michel. *History of Sexuality: An Introduction, Volume I.* Random House, 1978 (1976).

Foucault, Michel. *Disciple and Punish: The Birth of the Prison.* Vintage, 1995 (1975).

Foucault, Michel. *Archeology of Knowledge.* Routledge, 2002 (1969).

Foucault, Michel. *Society Must Be Defended.* Picador, 2003 (1997).

Foucault, Michel. *Madness and Civilization: A History of Insanity in the Age of Reason.* Routledge, 2006.

Hardt, Michael and Antonio Negri. *Empire.* Harvard University Press, 2000.

Hardt, Michael and Antonio Negri. *Multitude: War and Democracy in the Age of Empire.* Penguin Books, 2004.

30 C.L.R. James/Herbert Marcuse

James, C.L.R. *Nkrumah and the Ghana Revolution.* Lawrence Hill and Company, 1977.

James, C.L.R. *The Black Jacobins.* Allison and Busby, 1980 (1963).

James, C.L.R. *American Civilization.* Routledge, 1993 (1950).

James, C.L.R. *Beyond A Boundary.* Duke University Press, 1993 (1983).

James, C.L.R. *World Revolution, 1917–1936: The Rise and Fall of the Communist International.* Duke University Press, 2017 (1937).

James, C.L.R., Raya Dunayevskaya, and Grace Lee Boggs. *State Capitalism and World Revolution.* PM Press, 2013 (1950).

Marcuse, Herbert. *Eros and Civilization.* Beacon Press, 1955.

Marcuse, Herbert. *One Dimensional Man.* Beacon Press, 1964.

Marcuse, Herbert. *Soviet Marxism: A Critical Analysis.* Columbia University Press, 1968.

Marcuse, Herbert. *An Essay on Liberation.* Beacon Press, 1969.

Marcuse, Herbert. *The Aesthetic Dimension: Toward a Critique of Marxist Aesthetics.* Beacon Press, 2014 (1977).

31 Abhijit V. Banerjee & Esther Duflo/Samir Amin

Amin, Samir. *Unequal Development: An Essay on the Social Formations of Peripheral Capitalism.* New York: Monthly Review Press, 1973 (1976).

Amin, Samir. *L'Imperialisme et le développement inégal.* Paris: Éditions de minuit, 1976.

Amin, Samir. *The World We Wish to See: Revolutionary Objectives in the Twenty-First Century.* New York: Monthly Review, 2008.

366 *Bibliography*

Amin, Samir. "Audacity, More Audacity." *Review of Radical Political Economics* 45, no. 3 (2013): 400–409.

Amin, Samir. *Samir Amin: Pioneer of the Rise of the South*. New York: Springer, 2014.

xBanerjee, Abhijit V. and Esther Duflo. *Poor Economics: A Radical Rethinking of the Way to Fight Global Poverty*. New York: Public Affairs, 2011.

Birdsall, Nancy and Francis Fukuyama. "The Post-Washington Consensus: Development after the Crisis." *Foreign Affairs* (March/April 2011).

Grugel, Jean, Pia Riggirozzi, and Ben Thirkell-White. "Beyond the Washington Consensus? Asia and Latin America in Search of More Autonomous Development." *International Affairs* 84, no. 3 (2008): 499–517.

McCleery, Robert K. and Fernando De Paolis. "The Washington Consensus: A Post-mortem." *Journal of Asian Economics* 19, no. 5–6 (2008): 438–446.

Stiglitz, Joseph E. "Is there a Post-Washington Consensus Consensus?" in *The Washington Consensus Reconsidered*, edited by Narcis Serra and Joseph E. Stiglitz. Oxford: Oxford University Press, 2008.

32 Nancy Fraser/David Harvey

Benhabib, Seyla, Judith Butler, Drucilla Cornell, and Nancy Fraser. *Feminist Contentions: A Philosophical Exchange*. New York and London: Routledge, 1995.

Fraser, Nancy. *Unruly Practices: Power, Discourse and Gender in Contemporary Social Theory*. Minneapolis: University of Minnesota Press, 1989.

Fraser, Nancy. *Justice Interruptus: Critical Reflections on the "Postsocialist."* New York and London: Routledge, 1997.

Fraser, Nancy. Recognition without Ethics? *Theory, Culture & Society* 18 (2001): 21–42.

Fraser, Nancy. "Mapping the Feminist Imagination: From Redistribution to Recognition to Representation." *Constellations: An International Journal of Critical and Democratic Theory* 12 (2005): 295–307.

Fraser, Nancy. "Reframing Justice in a Globalizing World," *New Left Review* 56 (2009).

Fraser, Nancy. *Scales of Justice: Reimagining Political Space in a Globalizing World*. New York: Columbia University Press, 2009.

Fraser, Nancy. *Fortunes of Feminism: From State-Managed Capitalism to Neoliberal Crisis*. London: Verso, 2013.

Fraser, Nancy. *The Old is Dying and the New Cannot Be Born*. London: Verso, 2019.

Harvey David. *The Condition of Postmodernity*. Oxford: Basil Blackwell, 1987.

Harvey, David. *Justice, Nature & the Geography of Difference*. Oxford: Basil Blackwell, 1996.

Harvey, David. *Spaces of Hope*. Berkeley: University of California Press, 2000.

Harvey, David. *Spaces of Capital: Towards a Critical Geography*. New York: Routledge, 2001.

Harvey, David. *Brief History of Neoliberalism*. Oxford: Oxford University Press, 2005.

Harvey, David. *Social Justice and the City*. Athens: University of Georgia Press, 2009 (1973).

Harvey, David. *Seventeen Contradictions and the End of Capitalism*. Oxford: Oxford University Press, 2014.

Harvey, David. *Marx, Capital, and the Madness of Economic Reason*. Oxford: Oxford University Press, 2018.

Held, David and Ayse Kaya, eds. *Global Inequality: Patterns and Explanations*. Cambridge: Polity Press, 2007.

Marx, Karl. *Grundrisse*. Harmondsworth, Middlesex: Penguin Books (with *New Left Review*), 1973 (1857–58).

Bibliography   367

33 Joseph Stiglitz/ Jürgen Osterhammel

Barber, Benjamin. *Jihad vs. McWorld*. New York: Times Books, 1995.

Beckert, Sven. *Empire of Cotton*. New York: Alfred A. Knopf, 2014.

Chomsky, Noam. *Profit over People*. New York: Seven Stories Press, 2011.

Eichengreen, Barry. *Globalizing Capital*. Princeton: Princeton University Press, 2008.

Fukuyama, Francis. *The End of History and the Last Man*. New York: Free Press, 1992.

Hopkins, A.G., ed. *Globalization in World History*. New York: WW Norton & Co, 2002.

Klein, Naomi. *No Logo*. Toronto: Vintage Canada, 2000.

Oltermann, Philip. "Angela Merkel and the History Book That Helped Her Worldview." *The Guardian*, 29 December, 2016.

Osterhammel, Jürgen. *The Transformation of the World: A Global History of the Nineteenth Century*. Princeton: Princeton University Press, 2014.

Rodrik, Dani. *Has Globalization Gone Too Far?* Washington: Institute for International Economics, 1997.

Stiglitz, Joseph E. *Globalization and its Discontents*. New York: WW Norton and Company, 2002.

Streeten, Paul. "Structural Adjustment: A Survey of the Issues and Options" in *Development Studies: A Reader*, edited by Stuart Corbridge. Oxford: Oxford University Press, 1987.

Weber, Andreas and Jos Gommans. "'You Turn a Page and Then There Is Suddenly Something on a Turtle': An Interview with Jürgen Osterhammel." *Itinerario* 35, no. 3 (2011): 7–16.

Williamson, John. "Democracy and the Washington Consensus." *World Development* 21 (1993): 1329–1336.

34 Joseph Schumpeter/Thomas Piketty

Piketty, Thomas. *Capital in the Twenty-First Century*. Cambridge: Harvard University Press, 2014 (2013).

Piketty, Thomas. "About *Capital in the Twenty-First Century*." *American Economic Review: Papers & Proceedings* 105 (2015): 48–53.

Piketty, Thomas. *Capital and Ideology*. Cambridge: Harvard University Press, 2020 (2019).

Schumpeter, Joseph. *The Theory of Economic Development*. Cambridge: Harvard University Press, 1934 (1912).

Schumpeter, Joseph. *Capitalism, Socialism and Democracy*. New York: Harper and Brothers, 1942.

Schumpeter, Joseph. *History of Economic Analysis*. Oxford: Oxford University Press, 1954.

Schumpeter, Joseph. "State Imperialism and Capitalism," reprinted in Paul Sweezy, *Imperialism and Social Classes*. Fairfield: August M. Kelley, 1954 (1919).

35 Henry David Thoreau/William Nordhaus

Nordhaus, William D. and Paul Samuelson. *Economics*. McGraw-Hill, 1985–2009; 12th edition through 18th edition.

Nordhaus, William D. and Joseph Boyer. *Warming the World: Economic Models of Global Warming*. MIT Press, 2000.

Nordhaus, William D. *The Climate Casino: Risk, Uncertainty and Economics for a Warming World*. Yale University Press, 2013.

Nordhaus, William D. "Projections and Uncertainties about Climate Change in an Era of Minimal Climate Policies." Working Paper 22933, National Bureau of Economic Research (http://www. nber.org/papers/w22933 (December 2016).

368   Bibliography

Nordhaus, William D. Climate Change: The Ultimate Challenge for Economics, Nobel Prize Acceptance Lecture at the Aula Magna, Stockholm (December 8, 2018).

Nordhaus, William D. "The Economics of Climate Change" a lecture given at The UBS Center of the University of Zurich (January 28, 2020).

Richardson, Robert D. *Henry Thoreau: A Life of the Mind.* University of California Press, 1986.

Thoreau, Henry David. *Walden and Other Writings,* edited by Brooks Atkinson. Random House/Modern Library Edition, 1992.

Thoreau, Henry David. *Wild Fruits: Thoreau's Rediscovered Last Manuscript.* W.W. Norton 2000.

Walls, Laura Dassow. *Thoreau: A Life.* University of Chicago Press, 2017.

36   Gayatri Chakravorty Spivak/Zygmunt Bauman

Bauman, Zygmunt. *Modernity and the Holocaust.* Cornell University Press, 1989.

Bauman, Zygmunt. *Postmodern Ethics.* Basil Blackwell, 1993.

Bauman, Zygmunt. *Liquid Modernity.* Polity, 2000.

Bauman, Zygmunt. *Society Under Siege.* Polity, 2002.

Bauman, Zygmunt. *Liquid Love: On the Frailty of Human Bonds.* Polity, 2003.

Bauman, Zygmunt. *Wasted Lives. Modernity and its Outcasts.* Polity, 2004.

Bauman, Zygmunt. *Liquid Life.* Polity, 2005.

Bauman, Zygmunt. *Liquid Fear.* Polity, 2006.

Bauman, Zygmunt. *Liquid Times: Living in an Age of Uncertainty.* Polity, 2006.

Bauman, Zygmunt. *Culture in a Liquid Modern World.* Polity, 2011.

Spivak, Gayatri Chakravorty. "Can the Subaltern Speak?" in *Marxism and the Interpretation of Culture,* edited by Nelson, Cary; Grossberg, Lawrence, 271–313. Macmillan, 1988.

Spivak, Gayatri Chakravorty. *In Other Words: Essays in Cultural Politics.* Routledge, 1998 (1987).

Spivak, Gayatri Chakravorty. *Selected Subaltern Studies,* edited with Ranajit Guha. Oxford University Press, 1988.

Spivak, Gayatri Chakravorty. *An Aesthetic Education in the Era of Globalization.* Harvard University Press, 2013.

37   Slavoj Žižek/Noam Chomsky

Benedictus, Leo. "Noam Chomsky on Donald Trump." *The Guardian* 20 May 2016.

Chomsky, Noam. *Chomsky on Anarchism.* Oakland: AK Press, 2005.

Žižek, Slavoj. *In Defense of Lost Causes.* London: Verso, 2008.

Žižek, Slavoj. "Slavoj Žižek: The Cologne Attacks Were an Obscene Version of Carnival." *The New Statesman,* 13 January, 2016.

38   Gilles Deleuze/Félix Guattari/Manuel Delanda

Braudel, Fernand. *The Mediterranean and the Mediterranean World in the Age of Philip II.* Harper & Row, 1972 (1949).

Braudel, Fernand. *Perspective of the World.* Harper & Row, 1984 (1979).

DeLanda, Manuel. *War in the Age of Intelligent Machines.* Zone Books, 1991.

DeLanda, Manuel. *Intensive Science and Virtual Philosophy.* Continuum Books, 2002.

DeLanda, Manuel. *A New Philosophy of Society: Assemblage Theory and Social Complexity.* Continuum Books, 2006.

Bibliography 369

DeLanda, Manuel. *Assemblage Theory.* Edinburgh University Press, 2016.

Deleuze, Gilles. *Expressionism in Philosophy: Spinoza.* Zone Books, 1990 (1968).

Deleuze, Gilles. *Logic of Sense.* Columbia University Press, 1990 (1969).

Deleuze, Gilles. *Difference and Repetition.* Columbia University Press, 1994 (1968).

Deleuze, Gilles and Félix Guattari. *Anti-Oedipus: Capitalism and Schizophrenia.* Viking Press, 1977 (1972).

Deleuze, Gilles and Félix Guattari, *A Thousand Plateaus: Capitalism and Schizophrenia.* University of Minnesota Press, 1987 (1980).

Guattari, Félix. *The Machinic Unconscious: Essays in Schizoanalysis.* Semiotext(e), 2011 (1979).

Tilly, Charles. *From Mobilization to Revolution.* Addison-Wesley Publishing, 1978.

39 The Dar Es Salaam School

Althusser, Louis. *For Marx.* London: Verso, 2005 (1965).

Althusser, Louis. *On the Reproduction of Capitalism: Ideology and Ideological State Apparatuses.* London: Verso, 2014.

Amin, Samir. *Imperialism and Unequal Development.* New York: Monthly Review, 1977.

Amin, Samir. *Eurocentrism.* New York: Monthly Review Press, 2009.

Amin, Samir. *Global History: A View from the South.* Cape Town: Pambazuka Press, 2011.

Arghiri, Emmanuel. *Unequal Exchange: A Study of the Imperialism of Trade.* New York: Monthly Review Press, 1972.

Arrighi, Giovanni. *The Geometry of Imperialism.* London: New Left Books, 1978.

Arrighi, Giovanni. *The Long Twentieth Century.* London: Verso, 1994.

Arrighi, Giovanni and Jessica Drangel. "The Stratification of the World-Economy: An Exploration of the Semi-peripheral Zone." *Review* 10, no. 1 (1986): 9–74.

Arrighi, Giovanni and David Harvey. "The Winding Paths of Capital." *New Left Review* 56 (2009): 61–94.

Badiou, Alain. *The Communist Hypothesis.* London: Verso, 2010.

Bahl, Vinay. "What Went Wrong with 'History from Below'." *Economic and Political Weekly* 38, no. 2 (2003): 135–146.

Bayat, Asef. "From Dangerous Classes to Quiet Rebels: Politics of the Urban Subaltern in the Global South." *International Sociology* 15, no. 3 (2000): 533–557.

Bhattacharya, Sabyasachi. "History from Below." *Social Scientist* 11, no. 4 (1983): 3–20.

Bourg, Julian. "The Red Guards of Paris: French Student Maoism of the 1960s." *History of European Ideas* 31 (2005): 472–490.

Calhoun, Craig and Georgi Derlugian, eds. *Business as Usual: The Roots of the Global Financial Meltdown.* New York: New York University Press, 2011.

Chang, Ha-Joon. *23 Things They Don't Tell You about Capitalism.* New York: Bloomsbury Press, 2011.

Connell, Raewyn. *Southern Theory.* Cambridge: Polity Press, 2007.

Di Lembo, Luigi. *Guerra di classe e lotta umana: L'anarchismo in Italia dal Bienno rosso alla Guerra di Spagna (1919–1939).* Pisa: BFS Edizioni, 2001.

Dirlik, Arif. "Mao Zedong Thought and the Third World/Global South." *Interventions: International Journal of Postcolonial Studies* 16, no. 2 (2014): 233–256.

Dörre, Klaus, Stephan Lessinich, and Hartmut Rosa. *Sociology, Capitalism, Critique.* London: Verso, 2015.

Fanon, Frantz. *Wretched of the Earth.* New York: Grove Press, 1963 (2004).

Frank, Andre Gunder. *ReOrient.* Berkeley: University of California Press, 1998.

370 *Bibliography*

Fraser, Nancy. "Injustice at Intersecting Scales: On 'Social Exclusion' and the 'Global Poor.'" *European Journal of Social Theory* 13, no. 3 (2010): 363–371.

Go, Julian. *Postcolonial Thought and Social Theory.* Oxford: Oxford University Press, 2016.

Gouldner, Alvin W. "Marx's Last Battle: Bakunin and the First International." *Theory and Society* Vol.11 (6) (1982), pp. 853–884.

Gramsci, Antonio. "Sindacati e Consigli." *L'Ordine Nuovo* (11 October 1919): 159–160.

Harvey, David. *The Limits to Capital.* London: Verso, 2006.

Harvey, David. *The Enigma of Capital and the Crises of Capitalism.* Oxford: Oxford University Press, 2010.

Iles, Anthony and Tom Roberts. *All Knees and Elbows of Susceptibility and Refusal: Reading History from Below.* London: The Strickland Distribution, 2012.

The Invisible Committee. *The Coming Insurrection.* Los Angeles: Semiotext(e), 2009.

James, C.L.R. *The Black Jacobins.* New York: Vintage, 1963.

Jameson, Frederic. "Periodizing the 60s." *SocialText* 9/10 (1984): 178–209.

Jones, Claudia. *Beyond Containment,* edited by Carole Boyce Davies. London: Ayebia Clarke Publishing Limited, 2011.

Malatesta, Errico. *Malatesta: Life and Times,* edited by V Richards. London: Freedom House, 1964.

Mason, Paul. *Postcapitalism: A Guide to Our Future.* New York: Farrar, Straus and Giroux, 2015.

Mignolo, Walter D. *Local Histories/Global Designs: Coloniality, Subaltern Knowledges, and Border Thinking.* Princeton: Princeton University Press, 2000.

Nabudere, Dan Wadada. *Imperialism in East Africa Vol.1: Imperialism & Exploitation.* London: Zed Books, 1981.

Nabudere, Dan Wadada. *The Political Economy of Imperialism.* London: Zed Books, 1977.

Newman, Saul. *From Bakunin to Lacan: Anti-Authoritarianism and the Dislocation of Power.* Lanham: Lexington Books, 2007.

Newman, Saul. *Postanarchism.* Cambridge: Polity, 2016.

Prakash, Gyan. "Writing Post-Orientalist Histories of the Third World: Perspectives from Indian Historiography." *Comparative Studies in Society and History* 32, no. 2 (2009): 383–408.

Rancière, Jacques. *Proletarian Nights.* London: Verso, 2012.

Ravindranathan, T.R. *Bakunin and the Italians.* Montreal: McGill University Press, 1988.

Robcis, Camille. "'China in Our Heads': Althusser, Maoism, and Structuralism." *SocialText* 30, no. 1 (2012): 51–69.

Rodney, Walter. *The Groundings with My Brothers.* London: Bogle L'Ouverture Publications Ltd, 1969.

Rodney, Walter. *How Europe Underdeveloped Africa.* Washington: Howard University Press, 1974.

Rodney, Walter. *A History of the Guyanese Working People, 1881–1905.* Baltimore: The Johns Hopkins University Press, 1981.

Shivji, Issa. *Class Struggles in Tanzania.* New York: Monthly Review, 1977.

Simone, AbdouMailq. *For the City Yet to Come: Changing African Life in Four Cities.* Durham: Duke University Press, 2004.

Singer, Daniel. *Prelude to Revolution: France in May 1968.* Chicago: Haymarket Books, 2013.

Slobodian, Quinn. *Foreign Front: Third World Politics in Sixties West Germany.* Durham: Duke University Press, 2012.

Spriano, Paolo. *L'Occupazione delle fabbriche.* Torino: Giulio Einaudi Editore Spa, 1964.

Srnicek, Nick and Alex Williams. *Inventing the Future: Postcapitalism and a World without Work.* London: Verso, 2015.

Streek, Wolfgang. *How Will Capitalism End?* London: Verso, 2016.

Tandon, Yashpal, ed. *University of Dar es Salaam Debate on Class, State & Imperialism.* Dar es Salaam: Tanzania Publishing House, 1982.

Tucker, Robert, ed. *The Marx-Engels Reader.* New York: W.W. Norton and Company, 1972.

Wallerstein, Immanuel. "Braudel on Capitalism, or Everything Upside Down." *The Journal of Modern History* 63, no. 2 (1991): 354–361.

Wallerstein, Immanuel. *The Capitalist World-Economy.* Cambridge: Cambridge University Press, 1979.

Wallerstein, Immanuel. *Historical Capitalism with Capitalist Civilization.* London: Verso, 1983.

Winant, Howard. "Is Racism Global?" *Journal of World-Systems Research* 23, no. 2 (2017): 505–510.

Wright, Erik Olin. *Class Counts: Comparative Studies in Class Analysis.* Cambridge: Cambridge University Press, 1997.

Wright, Erik Olin, ed. *Approaches to Class Analysis.* Cambridge: Cambridge University Press, 2005.

Wolff, Richard D. *Capitalism's Crisis Deepens.* Chicago: Haymarket Books, 2016.

40 Giorgio Agamben and Achille Mbembe

Agamben, Giorgio. *The Coming Community.* Minneapolis: University of Minnesota Press, 1993 (1990).

Agamben, Giorgio. *Homo Sacer: Sovereign Power and Bare Life.* Stanford: Stanford University Press, 1998.

Deleuze, Gilles and Félix Guattari. *Anti-Oedipus: capitalism and schizophrenia.* New York: Viking Press, 1977 (1972).

Deleuze, Gilles and Félix Guattari. *A Thousand Plateaus: Capitalism and Schizophrenia.* Minneapolis, London: University of Minnesota Press, 1987 (1980).

Foucault, Michel. *Archaeology of Knowledge.* New York: Pantheon Books, 1972 (1969).

Foucault, Michel. *Birth of the Clinic: An Archaeology of Medical Perception.* New York: Vintage Books, 1975 (1963).

Foucault, Michel. *The History of Madness.* London: Routledge, 2006 (1961).

Foucault, Michel. *History of Sexuality: An Introduction.* New York: Pantheon Books, 1978 (1976).

Foucault, Michel. *Discipline and Punish.* New York: Vintage Books, 1979 (1975).

Foucault, Michel. *Society Must Be Defended.* New York: Picador, 1997 (1976).

Mbembé, Achille and Libby Meintjes. "Necropolitics." *Public Culture* 15, no. 1 (2003): 11–40.

Simone, AbduMalique. *City Life from Jakarta to Dakar: Movements at the Crossroads.* New York: Routledge, 2010.

Index

Note: Page numbers followed by "n" denote endnotes.

Abbasid Empire 63, 64
Abernathy, R. 160
abortion 70
Absurdist Cycle 125
Abu-Lughod, J. 62–65; *Before European Hegemony: The World-System A.D. 1250–1350* 62
accumulation of capital 3, 5, 8, 11–16, 18, 25, 40, 71, 72, 75, 82, 83, 89, 92, 97, 119, 120, 167, 168, 197, 255, 258, 260, 266, 294, 326, 336–338
Adorno, T. 230, 231, 233, 234, 265; *The Dialectic of Enlightenment* 248
African Party for the Independence of Guinea and Cape Verde (PAIGC) 140, 141
Agamben, G. 17, 34, 216, 343; bare life 347–350; *The Coming Community* 304, 347; *Homo Sacer: Sovereign Power and Bare Life* 347–349
Age of Capital 24
Aglietta, M.: *A Theory of Capitalist Regulation* 13
agricultural sabotage 91
agricultural surplus 87
ahimsa 112
Ahmad, A. 98, 175–176; *In Theory* 176
Alcott, L. M. 278
Algerian Communist Party 125
Ali, M. 42, 98, 108, 151–153, 156, 157
Ali, T. 211
All-African People's Revolutionary Party 133
Althusser, L. 29, 31, 32, 37n6, 201, 328, 329; abandonment of Catholicism 33; *The Coming Crisis of Western Sociology* 28; *For Sociology: Renewal and Critique in Sociology Today* 28; "On the Young Marx: Theoretical Questions" 26

American Civil Rights Movement 27, 314–315
Amin, S. 242–246, 337; *L'imperialisme et le développement inégal* 245; *Unequal Development: An Essay on the Social Formations of Peripheral Capitalism* 245
anarchism 122, 189, 192, 301, 327, 328, 330
Anarcho-Syndicalism 328
Anarcho-Syndicalists 327, 328
Anderson, P. 211
Annales School 326
annihilation 148, 149, 186
annus miraballis 250
Anthropocene 281
anti-authoritarian communism 189
Apollinaire, G. 186
Arab-Islamic Empires 86
archaeology 218
Arditi del Popolo 80
Arnold, M. 215
Arrighi, G. 12, 39, 40, 81–84, 212, 331, 336, 339; *The Long Twentieth Century* 82
asabiyya 93–95
Asian mode of production 59, 60, 97, 308
assemblage 311; theory 304, 305, 307, 309
Auerbach, E.: *Mimesis: The Representation of Reality in Western Literature* 173
Austro-German Empire 121
authoritarian communism 189, 299
authoritarianism 14, 99, 297, 298, 328
autonomia 82
autonomy 112–113

Bachelard, G. 26
Badiou, A. 330
Bakunin, M. 93, 146, 189–190, 192, 324–330

374   *Index*

Bakuninism 329
Ball, H. 186
Bambule 154
Banerjee, A. V. 240–242, 246; *Poor Economics* 240
Baran, P. 9–11, 265
Barber, B.: *Jihad vs. McWorld* 262
bare life 347–350
Barthes, R.: *Writing Degree Zero* 172, 173
Bauman, Z. 291–295; *The Communist Manifesto* 292, 293; *Culture as Praxis* 291; *Culture in a Liquid Modern World* 293, 294; *Culture of Fear* 294; "Heavy/Light Modernity" 293; *Hermeneutics and Social Science* 291; *Liquid Fear* 293; *Liquid Life* 293; *Liquid Love: On the Frailty of Human Bonds* 293; *Liquid Modernity* 292–294; *Liquid Times* 293; *Modernity and the Holocaust* 284; *Toward a Critical Sociology* 291; *Wasted Lives* 294–295
Beard, C. 248
Beckert, S.: *Empire of Cotton* 265
Benhabib, S. 251
Benjamin, W. 233
Bentham, J. 219
Bhaba, H. 176
Bhattacharya, S. 331
Biennio Rosso 80, 326–328
Biko, S. 42
biopower 218, 219, 222–223, 304, 343–344, 346, 348, 350
Black Bourgeoisie School 88
Black Death 69
black nationalism 88
Black Panther Party 42, 132, 154
Black Power Movement 82, 107, 315
black working class consciousness 189–192
Blank, M. 119
Bloch, M. 52
Bolshevism 301
Bolsonaro, J. 318
Bonacich, E. 185–187
Boody, E. 270
Boyer, J.: *Warming the World: Economic Models of Global Warming* 283
Braudel, F. 11, 39, 47, 50, 52–58, 82, 318, 326; *Civilization and Capitalism: 15th–18th Century* 53–56; *The Perspective of the World* 55, 317; *The Structures of Everyday Life* 53–54; *Wheels of Commerce* 54–55; *The Mediterranean and the Mediterranean World in the Age of Philip II*

52–53, 55, 137, 316; *The Modern World-System, Vol I: Capitalism Agriculture and the Origins of the European World-Economy in the Sixteenth Century* 48
Braverman, H. 182–184, 338; *The Autobiography of Malcolm X* 182; *Labor and Monopoly Capital* 182
Brenner, R. 12–13, 39, 74–78; Agrarian Class Structure and Economic Development in Pre-Industrial Europe" 74
Brenner Debate 74, 78, 100
Brenner hypothesis 12
Brennerite Marxists 14, 18, 39
Brigate Rosse 154
Britain's Peace Movement 211
British Industrial Revolution 12, 13, 18, 39, 74, 89
British Labour Party 271
Bukharin, N. 92–93, 298
Butler, J. 251; *Gender Trouble* 250

Cabral, A. 140–144; *The Weapon of Theory* 143
Cahen, C. 129
Caifero, C. 327
California School of Economic History 15, 16, 18, 39
Camus, A. 125–128, 130–131, 133; *Caligula* 125, 126; *The Fall* 98, 125; *The First-Man* 125; *The Myth of Sisyphus* 125–128; *The Plague* 125; *The Stranger* 98, 125, 126
Canguilhem, G. 26
capital: accumulation 3, 5, 8, 11–16, 18, 25, 40, 71, 72, 75, 82, 83, 89, 92, 97, 119, 120, 167, 168, 197, 255, 258, 260, 266, 294, 326, 336–338; finance 6, 7, 74, 83, 120, 264, 337, 338; imperialist 176; industrial 120; monopoly of 5; *see also individual entries*
capitalism 4–5, 144; agrarian origins of 74–78; analyzing 17–19; city and foundations of 86–89; critiquing 19–20; definition of 76, 167; environmental crisis and 278–285; exploitative, in Global South 323–339; finance 7, 255; finance and 80–84; fiscal 24, 29; global 18, 20, 25, 39, 50, 63, 75, 88, 95, 98, 104, 107, 167, 168, 172, 176, 192, 209, 210, 243, 256, 260, 266, 289, 324, 328, 339, 351; late 10, 174, 249; monopoly 6, 9, 13, 269; order,

silenced and wasted lives in 286–295; postcolonial theories of 97–98; and precapitalist modes of production, distinction between 77; structural nature of 268–276; as a system 5, 12, 14, 16, 18, 39, 163; theory of 5–17, 20, 26, 30, 33, 46, 49, 89, 177, 179–180, 220, 242, 294, 308, 323; transition to 39, 61–65, 68, 69, 72, 74–76, 78, 87, 89, 266; truth of 11; uncertain future of 215–216; *see also individual entries*

capitalism/imperialism nexus 242–243

capitalist development 4, 5, 11, 13, 15, 20, 84, 89, 92, 95, 149, 167, 212, 253, 329

capitalist mode of production 4, 10, 68–69, 72, 97, 167, 168, 183, 221, 245, 307

capitalist theories, critique of 3–20

Capp, A. 230

carceral archipelago 218, 304, 343–345

Cardoso, F. H. 56

Carmichael, S. *see* Ture, K.

Carter, J. 281

Casablanca 230

Catholicism 89

Center for African Studies 140

Centre d'Études et de Documentation Économiques, Juridiques et Sociales 129

Césaire, A. 43, 45, 216; *Discourse on Colonialism* 41

Chakrabarty, D. 165, 167, 168, 213, 214; *Provincializing Europe* 165

Chandavarkar, R. 180, 212–214; *Imperial Power and Popular Politics: Class, Resistance and the State in India, c.:1850–1950* 212, 213

chaos 48

Chauri Chaura Incident 113

Cheever, S.: *American Bloomsbury* 278

Che Guevara, E. 42, 154

Chiang Kai-shek 161

Chibber, V.: *Postcolonial Theory and the Specter of Capital* 12

Chinese Communist Party 146

Chomsky, N. 216, 300–301, 330; *Chomsky on Anarchism* 301; *Profits Over People* 262

CHS *see* Comparative Historical Sociology (CHS)

cityness 351–352

Civil Rights Movement 159

Civil War 135, 137

class: consciousness 81, 189–192, 201, 211, 213; postcolonial analysis 99–103; rule 80–81; struggle 8, 11, 18, 102, 103, 115, 129, 149, 177, 184, 191, 204, 209, 211, 212, 245, 246, 329, 331, 334, 336–339

Classical Political Economy 7

Clay, C. M. 108, 151

Climate Club 284

CNT *see Confederación International de Trabajo* (CNT)

Cold War 49, 50, 161, 250, 318

collectivism 189

Collins, P, H.: *Black Feminist Thought* 250

Colman, H. 280, 281

colonialism 20, 88, 176, 177

Comaposada, M. 186

commercialization model 75

commodification 174–176, 266

commodity production 6, 10, 168

communication 19, 53, 87, 198

communism 130, 163; anti-authoritarian 189; authoritarian 189, 299

Communist Party Historians Group 211

Communist Party of Great Britain 211

Communist Party of India (CPI) 114, 148

Communist Party of Jamaica 190

Communist Party of Pakistan 114

Communist Party of Vietnam 161

Comparative Historical Sociology (CHS) 100, 102

Confederación International de Trabajo (CNT) 186

Confédération générale des travailleurs tunisiens 203

Congress of Racial Equality (CORE) 132

conjunctural history 53

Conrad, J.: *Heart of Darkness* 170

conservatism 49

contraception 69, 70

CORE *see* Congress of Racial Equality (CORE)

Cox, O. C. 39, 40, 87–89; *Caste, Class, and Race* 88; *The Foundations of Capitalism* 88, 89

CPI *see* Communist Party of India (CPI)

creative destruction 8, 10, 16, 259, 268

Crow, J. 138

cultural chauvinism 77–78

cultural violence 226–238

culture 211–214

cyclical theory of empire 91–95

376   *Index*

Damas, L. 43
Dar es Salaam School 331–339
Davies, C. B. 101
DDR *see* Deutsche Demokratische
    Republik (DDR)
Debord, G. 128
Declaration of Human Rights 350
Declaration of Independence 229, 350
decolonization 44–45, 102
deconstruction 286, 287
DeLanda, M. 303, 311–318; *Intensive
    Science and Virtual Philosophy* 312; *A New
    Philosophy of Society: Assemblage Theory
    and Social Complexity* 312, 316–317
Deleuze, G. 16, 220, 222, 223, 303–313,
    316–318; *Anti-Oedipus: Capitalism
    and Schizophrenia* 303–305, 345–346;
    Difference and Repetition 303, 304;
    Expressionism in Philosophy: Spinoza 303;
    Logic of Sense 303; *A Thousand Plateaus:
    Capitalism and Schizophrenia* 218,
    303–305, 308, 309, 311, 346, 347
democracy 114, 229, 230, 232, 234, 240,
    242, 263, 291, 311, 316, 349, 351,
    352; bourgeois 101; just 275; liberal 14,
    112, 113; parliamentary 99, 101–102
democratic citizenship 224
demographic model 75
dependency theory 56, 57
Derrida, J. 17, 249, 286–288; *Of
    Grammatology* 286, 287
Deutsche Demokratische Republic
    (DDR) 153
Deutsche Archer 189
development economics, poverty of
    240–246
Dewey, J. 248
Dick, M. 105
difference 304
diversity 123, 204, 231
Dostoyevsky, F.: *The Possessed* 125
Du Bios, W. E. B. 134–140, 161; *Black
    Reconstruction in America* 105, 137–139;
    The Crisis 136–137; *The Philadelphia
    Negro* 135, 136; *The Souls of Black Folk*
    134–136, 160; *The Suppression of the
    African Slave Trade to the United States of
    America 1638–1871* 134
Duplo, E. 240–242, 246; *Poor
    Economics* 240
Dumez, G. 306
Dundee, A. 151
Durkheim, E. 94

École Normal Supérieure (ÉNS) 31, 32, 271,
    272, 276
economic development 19
economic freedom 14, 29
economic justice 14, 159, 160, 205, 301
Edwards, J. 190–192, 330
Edwards, Z. 100
Exchanged, B.: *Globalizing Capital* 265
El Moudjahid 41
embeddedness 9
Emergency Laws 80
Emerson, R. W. 278
Engels, F. 72; *The Condition of the Working
    Class in England* 67; *The Origin of the
    Family, Private Property, and the State* 67
ÉNS see École Normale Supérieure (ÉNS)
Eurocentricity/Eurocentrism 297, 298
Eurocentrism 12, 15, 18, 19, 76–78,
    213, 298
European Enlightenment 15
European Management Forum 318
exclusion 337
existentialism 127
exploitation of labor 11, 120, 179,
    197–198, 202, 335–339

Fanon, F. 39, 41–47, 105, 117, 133, 141,
    154, 162, 260, 332–333; *Black Skin,
    White Masks* 41–44; *A Dying Colonialism*
    46; *The Wretched of the Earth* 42, 44–46
Faulkner, W.: *Requiem for a Nun* 125
Federici, S. 39, 68–69; *Caliban and the
    Witch* 68; *Revolution at Point Zero* 71–72
feminism 252
Ferrer, F. 123
feudalism 18, 109, 147, 270
feudal-patriarchal system 147
finance capital 6, 7, 74, 80–84, 120, 264,
    337, 338
First International 189, 324–327
Ford, H. 293
Fordism 29, 292–293
Foreman, G. 152
Foucault, M. 34, 216–222, 249, 298,
    303, 347; *The Archaeology of Knowledge*
    217, 218, 343; *Birth of the Clinic:
    An Archaeology of Medical Perception*
    217, 218; *The Birth of the Clini* 343;
    carceral archipelago 218, 343–345;
    *The Declaration of the Rights of Man and
    the Citizen* 345; *Discipline and Punish*
    217–219, 304; *Discourse on Language*
    218; *Folie et deraison* 217; *The History of*

Madness 343; *History of Sexuality, I* 348;
The History of Sexuality 218–220, 343;
*Madness and Civilization: A History of
Insanity in the Age of Reason* 217, 218;
*The Order of Things: An Archaeology of the
Human Sciences* 217, 218, 343
Fraser, N. 248–254; *Fortunes of Feminism:
From State-Managed Capitalism to
Neoliberal Crisis* 252; *Justice Interruptus:
Critical Reflections on the "Postsocialist"*
250–251; *The Old is Dying and the New
Cannot Be Born* 252–253; "Reframing
Justice in a Globalizing World" 252;
*Scales of Justice: Reimagining Political Space
in a Globalizing World* 251; "Strategy of
Separation" 253; *Unruly Practices: Power,
Discourse and Gender in Contemporary
Social Theory* 248–250, 252
Frazier, E. F. 88, 152
Freedmen's Saving and Trust Company 138
free market 9, 18, 24, 25, 29, 30, 208,
253, 286, 292, 318
French Communist Party 31, 33
Freud, S. 288; *Civilization and Its
Discontents* 235
Friedman, M. 14
Friedman, T.: *The Lexus and the Olive Tree*
262
Frisch, R. 91
Fröbel, F. 196–199; *Die neue internationale
Arbeitsteilung: Strukturelle Arbeitslosigkeit in
die Industrielandern und die Industrialisierung
der Entwicklungslander* 197
Fromm, E. 233
Fugitive Slave Law 279
Fukuyama, F. 14, 17, 242, 262
Fuller, M. 278

Gandhi, M. K. 98, 112–117
gender inequality 72
Genghis Khan 63
George, G. 152
German Historical School 7, 9, 11, 16, 18,
268, 326
G.I. Bill 166
Girard, R. 36
global capitalism 18, 20, 25, 39, 50, 63,
75, 88, 95, 98, 104, 107, 167, 168,
172, 176, 192, 209, 210, 243, 256,
260, 266, 289, 324, 328, 339, 351
global division of labor 194–199
globalization 71, 76, 78, 89, 179, 197, 199,
222, 246, 252, 262–266, 267n24, 294

Global North 12, 20, 120, 209, 229, 243,
328, 331, 334, 339, 352
Global South 12, 19, 20, 39, 117, 130,
151, 157, 163, 167, 174, 192, 198,
205, 209–214, 229, 232, 233, 242,
243, 245, 246; cityness in 351–352;
exploitative capitalism in 323–339
goals 17, 19, 81, 93, 115, 123, 139,
147–149, 168, 177, 182, 186, 190,
191, 195, 197, 199, 266, 284, 324,
325, 327
Gouldner, A. W. 32–34, 325–326; *The
Dialectic of Ideology and Technology* 227;
The Eleventh Thesis 28; *The Future of
Intellectuals and the Rise of the New Class*
33; *Theory and Society* 27; *The Two
Marxisms: Contradictions and Anomalies in
the Development of a Theory* 27, 28
Gramsci, A. 39, 80–82, 84, 327; *Prison
Notebooks* 80–81
Great Depression 24, 139
Great War of 1914 23, 24
Grief, A. 15
Grimshaw, A. 105–106, 229; *Dialectic
Materialism and the Fate of Humanity* 106
Gruppo Gramsci 82, 209
Guattari, F. 16, 222, 223, 303–312,
316–318; *Anti-Oedipus: Capitalism
and Schizophrenia* 303–305, 345–346;
Capitalism and Schizophrenia 303;
*The Machinic Unconscious: Essays in
Schizoanalysis* 303; *The Machinic
Unconscious* 305; *A Thousand Plateaus:
Capitalism and Schizophrenia* 218,
303–305, 308, 309, 311, 346, 347; *A
Thousand Plateaux* 218
Guha, R. 289
Gunder Frank, A. 39, 55–60, 75, 77, 215;
*Capitalism and Underdevelopment in Latin
America: Historical Studies of Chile and
Brazil* 57, 108; "The Development of
Underdevelopment" 57; *ReORIENT:
Global Economy in the Asian Age* 57–59
Gurudwara Nankana Sahib killings 113
Guru Granth Sahib 116
Guzman, A. 330

Habermas, J. 196–197, 233, 249
Habib, I. 117
Haddad, T. 203; *La naissance du movement
syndical tunisien* 204
Haitian Revolution 100
Hall, S. 211

378   *Index*

Hamilton, C. V.: *Black Power: The Politics of Liberation in America* 132, 134
Hammer, F. L. 132
Hammet, D.: *The Maltese Falcon* 230; *The Thin Man* 230
El Hammi, M. A. 180, 203–206
Hardt, M. 220–223; *Empire* 220–222, 224, 252
Harlem Renaissance 137
Harvey, D. 10–11, 254–260; *A Brief History of Neoliberalism* 259; *The Condition of Postmodernity* 255–257; *Explanation in Geography* 254; *Explanation of Geography* 257; *Justice, Nature & the Geography of Difference* 256; *Marx, Capital, and the Madness of Economic Reason* 260; *Seventeen Contradictions and the End of Capitalism* 259–260; *Social Justice and the City* 254–255; *Spaces of Capital: Towards a Critical Geography* 258; *Spaces of Hope* 256, 259
haute finance 83
Hawthorne, N. 278
Hayek, F. Von 13–14
"Heavy/Light Capitalism" 293
hegemonic progressive neoliberalism 253, 254
hegemony 9–10, 50, 81, 83, 163
Heidegger, M. 299; *Being and Time* 233
Heinrichs, J. 196–199; *Die neue internationale Arbeitsteilung: Strukturelle Arbeitslosigkeit in die Industrielandern und die Industrialisierung der Entwicklungslander* 197
Henry Ford's Motor Company 29
Hilferding, R. 6
"history from below" 331
Hobsbawm, E. 24, 29, 211
Hobson, J. 6, 10
Ho Chi Minh 98, 154, 161–163
Hofstadter, R. 25
Hopkins, A. G.: *Globalization in World History* 264
Horkheimer, M. 230, 231, 233, 234; *The Dialectic of Enlightenment* 248
Hughes, L. 43
Huntington, S.: *Clash of Civilizations* 262
Husserl, E. 233

Ideological State Apparatus 32
IMF *see* International Monetary Fund (IMF)
imperialism 78, 88, 100, 103, 119, 120, 124, 163, 176, 179, 192, 335, 337; capitalist 329; definition of 6–7; disciplinary 166; Hobson's critique of 6, 10; neo-imperialism 332; social 329; social process of 7; soft 104–110; Western, critique of 151–157
industrial capital 120
infanticide 70
International Monetary Fund (IMF) 263, 264
International Workingmen's Association (IWA) *see* First International
Invisible Committee 323
Iskra(The Spark) 119
issues 133, 134, 158, 159, 166, 177, 192, 197, 213, 249, 251, 263, 279, 301
Italian Socialist Party 220
IWA *see* International Workingmen's Association (IWA)

Jallianwala Bagh Massacre 113
James, C. L. R. 98, 104–107, 190, 226–234, 335; *American Civilization* 105, 226, 229–231; *Beyond a Boundary* 104, 226, 230–232; *The Black Jacobins* 100, 104, 226; *The Case for West-Indian Independence* 226; *The History of the Pan-African Revolt* 104–105; *La Divinia Pastora* 104; "Negroes, Women, and Intellectuals" 105; *Nkrumah and the Ghana Revolution* 226, 228; *Notes on Dialectics, II* 227–228; *State Capitalism and World Revolution* 226–227; *Triumph* 104; "World Revolution 1968" 106; *World Revolution 1917–1936: The Rise and Fall of the Communist International* 226
Jameson, F. 16, 98, 172–177, 329; *The Cultural Turn: Selected Writings on Postmodernism* 173; *Postmodernism, or, the Cultural Logic of Late Capitalism* 173; "Postmodernism, or, the Cultural Logic of Late Capitalism" 173–174
Jay, M.: *The Dialectical Imagination: A History of the Frankfurt and the Institute for Social Research 1925–1950* 234
Jinnah, M. A. 114
Jones, C. 100–103
Jones, G. S. 212
justice: economic 14, 159, 160, 205, 301; social 14, 301

Kafka, F.: *The Trial* 298
Kahloon, I. 271, 273
Kansas-Nebraska Act 281

Index 379

Keynes, J. M. 23–25
Khaldun, I. 39, 40, 93–95; *The Muqaddimah* 93
Khayati, M. 128–131, 330; *Groupe d'Étude et d'Action Socialistes Tunisien* 128; "l'Histoire des Perses d'ath-Tha'âlibî" ("Ath-Tha'âlibî's History of the Persians") 128–129; "On the Poverty of Student Life" 129; Setting Straight Some Popular Misconceptions about Revolutions in the Underdeveloped Countries" 129
King, M. L., Jr. 98, 116–117, 132, 158–164, 314; *I Have a Dream* 159, 160; *Letter from the Birmingham Jail* 159; *Stride Toward Freedom* 159; *Where Do We Go From Here?: Chaos or Community?* 160–161
Klein, N.: *No Logo* 262
Kondratieff cycle 8, 58
Kondratieff, N. D. 8, 9, 39, 40, 91–93, 95
Kreye, O. 196–199; *Die neue internationale Arbeitsteilung: Strukturelle Arbeitslosigkeit in die Industrielandern und die Industrialisierung der Entwicklungslander* 197
Kropokin, P.: *Mutual Aid* 121
Kropotkin, P. 146
Krugman, P. 271, 273, 276
Krupskaya, N. 119
Kuznets, S. 91

labor internationalism 191
labor process 181–184
labor theory of value 61; relationship with eonomic crisis 10
labor unrest 210
Lacan, J. 43, 305
Ladurie, E. L. R. 75, 77
Lahore Conspiracy Case of 1929–1930 114
late capitalism 10, 174, 249
Lazarsfeld, P. 46
League of Struggle for the Emancipation of the Working Class 119
Lee, A. 52
Lefebvre, H. 129
Lenin, V. I. 6–7, 98, 114, 119–122, 124, 154; "April Theses" 119; *Imperialism: The Highest Stage of Capitalism* 120
Leninism 301
Leninist Communist Party 80
Lévi-Strauss, C. 172
Levitt, T. 197
Lewis, J. 132

liberal democracy 14, 112, 113
liberalism 11, 14, 25, 30, 49; neoliberalism 252–254, 259
l'Institut d'Études politiques d'Aix-en-Provence 129
Lipietz, A. 13
liquidity 292–294
Liston, S. 152
long-distance trade 61–65
longue durée 12, 48, 53, 176, 177
L'Ordine Nuovo 80, 327
Lotta Continua 82
Lughod, J. A. 39
Luxemburg, R. 7, 154, 155

Madera, R. 82
Makeba, M. 133
Makhno, N. 98, 121–124, 330
Malatesta, E. 327–328
Malcolm X 42, 159
Malthusian models 75
management 198; corporate 197; risk 264; scientific 29, 181–183, 293; self-management 123, 130, 179, 189–192, 327
Mandel, E. 10; *Late Capitalism* 174
Maoism 148
Maoism, global 328–331
Mao Zedong 98, 146–149, 328; "Report on an Investigation of the Peasant Movement in Hunan" 147
March on Washington (1963) 159
Marco Polo 63
Marcos, S. 46
Marcuse, H. 154, 216, 233–238, 299; *The Aesthetic Dimension: Toward a Critique of Marxist Aesthetics* 234, 235; *Eros and Civilization* 233, 235; *An Essay on Liberation* 238; *One Dimensional Man* 233, 235–238
Margiella, C. 154
Marinetti, F. T. 186
market freedom 29
Marx, K. 3, 7, 8, 17, 19–20, 23, 25–28, 46, 59, 61, 67, 92, 137, 154, 189, 257, 307, 316, 324–326, 329, 338; *Capital* 4–6, 12, 19, 28, 35; *Capital I* 26, 28, 49, 137, 220, 258, 286–287, 308; *Capital III* 308; "Economic and Philosophical Manuscripts of 1844" 26; *Estranged Labour* 35; foundational theory of capitalism 30–31; *The German Ideology* 4, 26; *Grundrisse* 258; *Manuscripts* 31, 184, 223; theory of social things 172; *Theses on Feuerbach* 27

380 *Index*

Marxism 10, 11, 18–19, 26, 33, 88, 117, 154, 189, 190, 307; Critical 328; neo-Smithian 75; Third World 12, 100
Marxism-Leninism, challenges to: Biennio Rosso 326–328; First International 324–326; global Maoism 328–331
mass production 229
May Fourth Movement 146, 149n7
Mazumdar, C. 98, 148–149, 339
Mbembe, A. 30, 34, 35, 216; *Necropolitics* 350–351
McCarthy, J. 33, 229
McCarthy Era 101
McNeill, W.: *Pursuit of Power: Technology, Armed Force, and Society since AD 1000* 59
media 226–238
Meinhof, U. 153–157, 330
Meiskins Woods, E. 76–78; *The Origin of Capitalism* 76
Melville, H. 105, 230
Merkel, A. 265
Merton, R. K. 32, 33, 46
Mill, J. S. 61
Miller, J. A. 296
Mitchell, W. 91
modernity and modernism, distinction between 255
Mokyr, J. 15, 16
Mongol Empire 63, 64
monopoly capitalism 6, 9, 13, 269
Montgomery Movement 314
Moore, B., Jr. 99–103; *Social Origins of Dictatorship and Democracy: Lord and Peasant in the Making of the Modern World* 99, 100, 103
Moses, B. 132
Mujeres Libres 186
Muller, A. 203
multiplicity 314
municipality 87
Mussolini, B. 80

NAACP *see* National Association of Colored People (NAACP)
Nabudere, D. 336–337, 339
National Association of Colored People (NAACP) 136, 137, 139
National Liberation Front (Algeria) 43, 46
National Socialist German Worker's Party (German Workers Party) 24
Nation of Islam 42, 108, 151
Naujawan Bharat Sabha 113–114
Naxalite movement 148

Nazism 166
necropolitics 30, 31, 35, 350–351
Negri, A. 82, 220–223; *Empire* 220–222, 224, 252
Négritude movement 43, 44
Nehru, J. 114
neo-imperialism 242, 332, 338
neoliberalism 252–254, 259; hegemonic progressive 253, 254; "plagues" of 17; theory of 14
neoliberal theory 13
Neo-Marxists 10, 15, 18
neo-Smithian Marxism 75
New Deal 185, 268
New Institutional Economics 14, 15
New Institutionalism 14
New Institutionalists 15, 16, 18
New Left Review 211, 212, 257
Newton, H. 42
New York Daily Tribune 19
Niebuhr, R. 158–160
Nkrumah, K. 42, 133, 136, 143, 228
Nkrumaism 229
Nordhaus, W. 281–285; *The Climate Casino: Risk, Uncertainty, and Economics for a Warming World* 282–283
North, D. 14
North Atlantic slave trade triangle 98, 168
Norton, K. 152
Nygren, A. 158–159

objectives 83, 337, 346
Ocalan, A. 339
Occupy Wall Street Movement 273
oeuvre 3, 292
Office of War Information (US) 233
one-menism 191, 192
Operation Rolling Thunder 161–162
orientalism 171–172
Osterhammel, J. 265–266; *Die Verwandlung der Welt. Eine Geschichte des 19. Jahrhunderts* 266; *The Transformation of the World: A Global History of the Nineteenth Century* 265
overproduction 83

PAIGC *see* African Party for the Independence of Guinea and Cape Verde (PAIGC)
Palestinian Crisis 169
Palestinian National Council 169
Pan-Africanism 108
Pan-African Movement 137

Index 381

Panopticon 219
Paris Accords 284
Parsons, T. 32, 312
partial production 181
Parti Communiste Français 201, 204
Partito Comunista d'Italia 80
Passerini, L. 82
patriarchy 67, 147, 249; trade unionist theory of 185–187
Peace of Westphalia (1648) 24
Peasant's Labor Party 91
Piketty, T. 271–276; *Capital and Ideology* 271–275; *Capital in the Twenty-First Century* 271, 272, 275
Pirenne, H. 39, 40, 52, 86–87, 89; *Medieval Cities: Their Origins and the Revival of Trade* 87; Pirenne Thesis 86
Plys, K. 311
Poch y Gascón, A. 186
Polanyi, K. 48, 208–210; *The Great Transformation* 9, 208–210
political freedom 14, 29
political ideology 81
Pomerantz, K. 15
Postan, M. M. 75, 77
postcolonial class analysis 99–103, 333
postcolonialism 98, 155
postmodern era, definition of 173–174
postmodernism 98, 173, 177, 255–257
postmodernity 255–256
post-Westphalian democratic theory 252
power/knowledge 217–218
prajasatta 112
Prebisch, R. 56
Prigogine, I. 47–49; *The End of Certainty: Time, Chaos, and the New Laws of Nature* 48
primitive accumulation 69, 78, 137
protectionism 208
Proudhon, P.-J. 189
psychoanalysis: cultural 44; social 44
psychopathology 44

Quit India Movement 112

racism 77–78, 98, 185, 335; global 104–110, 161
radicalism 49
radicalization 201–206
radical political economy 331–336
RAF *see Rote Armee Fraktion* (Red Army Faction, RAF)
Rajguru, S. H. 114

Rancière, J. 201–206; *La nuit des prolétaires* 201, 203, 206; *Lire le Capital* 201
randomized controlled trials (RCTs) 240, 241
rape 69, 70
Rawls, J.: *Theory of Justice* 274
Raw Nerves: A Lacanian Thriller 311
RCTs *see* randomized controlled trials (RCTs)
Red Army 121, 122, 146
Regulation School 13, 15
rent 3–4
repressive desublimation 236, 237
Resistance Movement 128
resource-mobilization theory 313, 314
revolution 115–116
rhizome 303, 306, 311, 347
Ricardo, D. 5, 39, 61–65; *Principles of Political Economy and Taxation* 3–4, 61
Rich, A.: *An Atlas of the Difficult World* 256
Riemeck, R. 153
Rijal Hawa Rijal 93
Robeson, P. 226
Rockefeller Foundation 208
Rodney, W. 97–98, 107–110, 124, 331, 334–336, 339; *The Groundings with My Brothers* 107, 110; *A History of the Upper Guinea* 107–110; *How Europe Underdeveloped Africa* 108
Rodrik, D.: *Has Globalization Gone Too Far?* 262
Röhl, R. 153–154
Roosevelt, F. D. 268
Rorty, R. 249
Rosenthal, J.-L. 16
Rote Armee Fraktion (Red Army Faction, RAF) 154
Ruge, A. 189
Russian Revolution 129
Rytman, H. 37n6

Said, E. 169–174, 176, 177; *Culture and Imperialism* 170; *Joseph Conrad and the Fiction of Autobiography* 170; *Orientalism* 171–172, 177; *Out of Place* 169–170; *The Politics of Dispossession: The Struggle for Palestinian Self-Determination* 169
Saornil, L. S. 186–187, 330
Sartre, J.-P. 42, 43, 127, 133, 271; *Being and Nothingness* 127; *Sartre: The Origin of Style* 173
satyagraha 112, 113
Saul, J. 339

382   *Index*

Schmidt-Nielsen, K. 173
Schmitt, C. 34, 38n29
Schumpeter, J. 8–11, 91, 268–271, 276;
  Capitalism, Socialism and Democracy 268;
  History of Economic Analysis 270; *State
  Imperialism and Capitalism* 268–269;
  Theory of Economic Development 269
scientific management 29, 181–183, 293
SCLC *see* Southern Christian Leadership
  Committee (SCLC)
Scott, C. 158
SDS *see* Students for a Democratic Society
  (SDS)
Seale, B. 42
Seko, M. S. 228
Senghor, L. S. 43
sex-love 68
Shakespeare, W. 231
Shivji, I. 331, 339
SIA *see Solidaridad Internacional Antifascista*
  (SIA)
Silver, B. 83, 84, 209–210; *Forces of
  Labor* 209
Simone, A.: *City Life from Jakarta to Dakar*
  351–352
Singh, B. 113–116, 330
Sison, J. M. 330
Situationist International 128, 191
situationist theory of underdevelopment
  125–131
Skaria, A. 112
Skocpol, T. 100
Smith, A. 5, 7, 17, 75, 194–197, 254;
  *An Inquiry into the Nature and Causes
  of the Wealth of Nations* 3, 4; *The New
  International Division of Labor* 199; *Theory
  of Moral Sentiments* 194; *The Wealth of
  Nations* 58, 61, 194, 197, 199
Smith, D.: "Women's Experience as a
  Radical Critique of Sociology" 250
SNCC *see* Student Nonviolence
  Coordinating Committee (SNCC)
social inequality 121, 240
social justice 14, 301
social solidarity 94
society 55
Society Must Be Defended 217, 219, 344, 345
Solidaridad Internacional Antifascista
  (SIA) 186
Sombart, W. 88, 268
Southern Christian Leadership Committee
  (SCLC) 159
Sozializtische Deutche Studentenbund 153

Spivak, G. C. 216, 286–292, 295;
  *An Aesthetic Education in the Era of
  Globalization* 288; "Can the Subaltern
  Speak?" 289, 290, 295; *In Other Words*
  288–289; Translator's Preface to *Of
  Grammatology* 286, 287, 289
Stack, C.: *All Our Kin* 250–251
The Stanford Encyclopedia of Philosophy 304
state of exception 347, 349
Stiglitz, J. 262–266; *Discontents* 266;
  Globalization and its Discontents 262–265
strategy 63, 78, 80, 82, 89, 112, 113, 119,
  149, 182, 189, 253, 280, 327, 328,
  331, 335, 357
Streeten, P. 262
structural inequalities 55
structural nature of capitalism 268–276
Student Nonviolence Coordinating
  Committee (SNCC) 42, 132, 159
Students for a Democratic Society (SDS)
  27, 154
Studienstiftung des Deutchen Volkes 265
subaltern 289, 290
Subaltern Studies 212–214
Sumner, W. G. 99
Superego 236
Sweezy, P. 9–11, 88

Taft-Hartley Act 105
Tandon, Y. 339
tax code 87
Taylor, F. W. 29, 181–182
Taylorism 181–183
Thapar, S. 114
Therborn, G. 163
Third Worldism 329
"Third World" Marxism 12, 100
Thirty Years War 24
Thomas, R. P. 14
Thompson, E. P. 180, 211–214; *The
  Making of the English Working* 211–212;
  May Day Manifesto 211
Thoreau, H. D. 278–281, 285; *Slavery
  in Massachusetts, A Plea for Captain
  John Brown, and Civil Disobedience* 279;
  Walden 278–281; *Walden Pond* 216
Tilly, C. 314, 315, 317, 319–320n18; *The
  Mobilization to Revolution* 313
TimeSpace 48, 137, 139, 143
Tocqueville, A. de: *Democracy in
  America* 230
Touré, S. 133
Tousssaint L'Ouverture 226

trade unionist theory of patriarchy 185–187
Treanor, P. 259
Trotskyist Socialist Workers Party 104
Trotsky, L. 92
Tunisian Revolution of 2011 205
Tupacamaros 154
Ture, K. 42, 108, 132–134, 143, 144, 153; *Black Power: The Politics of Liberation in America* 132, 134

Umanità Nova 80, 327
uncertainty 48
Unione Sindacale Italiana 327
United Farm Workers Union 209

Veblen, T. 248
Versailles Peace Conference (1919) 23
Versailles Treaty 23, 24
violence: of the colonial world 44–45; cultural 226–238; of global colonization 163–164; working class, in national liberation 112–117
Voting Rights Act of 1965 159, 315

Wade, R. 262
Wages for Housework Movement 68, 71
Wallerstein, I. 11, 25, 39, 42, 46–50, 57, 75, 79, 106, 212, 317, 331, 339; *Capitalist Agriculture and the Origins of the European World-Economy in the Sixteenth Century* 49; *Centrist Liberalism Triumphant 1789–1914* 49; *Mercantilism and the Consolidation of the European World-Economy 1600–1750* 49; *The Modern World-System I: Capitalist Agriculture and the Origins of the European World-Economy in the Sixteenth Century* 108; *The Modern World-System* 55; *The Second Great Expansion of the Capitalism World-Economy 1730s–1840s* 49; *World-Systems Analysis: An Introduction* 48, 50
Wallersteinian World-Systems Analysts 39

Walls, L. D.: *Thoreau: A Life* 279
Walter Rodney Riots of 1968 190
War on Terror 264
Washington, B. T. 136
Washington Consensus 241, 242
Weather Underground 154
Weber, M. 59, 222, 268, 269, 307; *The Protestant Ethic and the Spirit of Capitalism* 36, 270, 312–313
Weizsäcker, C. F. von 196, 197
Western Imperialism, critique of 151–157
West Indian Forum and Committee on Racism and International Affairs 101
West Indian Gazette 101
When We Were Kings 153
Whitman, W. 230
Williams, A. D. 158
Williams, R. 211
Williamson, J. 262
witch trials 70–71
Wolf, E. 165–168; *Europe and the People Without History* 166–167
women: exploitation 68–69; oppression 68–69; unpaid labor 67–72
Wong, R. B. 16
Wood, E. M. 39, 175
worker self-management 189–192
working class violence, in national liberation 112–117
World Bank 263, 264
World Economic Forum (1987) 318
world-economy *versus* world-economies 55–56
world revolution of 1968 47, 50, 158–164, 328
World War I 8, 86, 91, 95
World War II 41, 50, 166, 211, 292
writing 287

Zionism 185
Žižek, S. 296–301; "Stalinism Revisited: Or, How Stalin Saved the Humanity of Man" 298; support for Trump 296–297

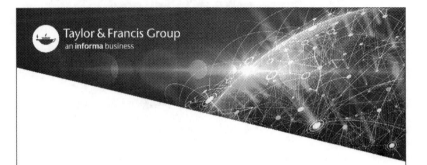